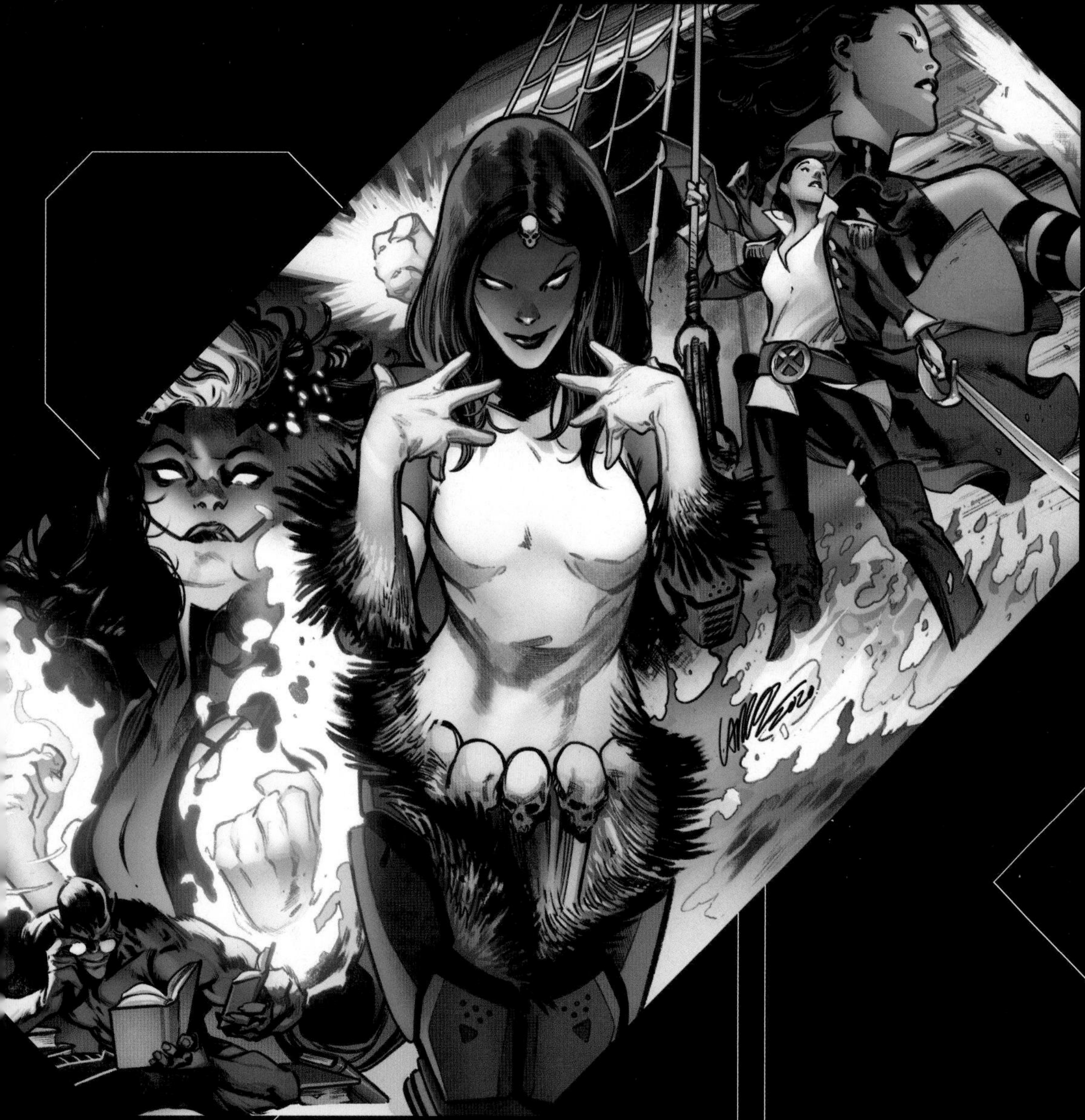

DAWN OF X VOL. 6. Contains material originally published in magazine form as X-MEN (2019) #6, X-FORCE (2019) #6, MARAUDERS (2019) #6, EXCALIBUR (2019) #6, FALLEN ANGELS (2019) #6 and NEW MUTANTS (2019) #6. First printing 2020. ISBN 978-1-302-92161-3. Published by MARVEL WORLDWIDE, INC., a subsidiary of MARVEL ENTERTAINMENT, LLC. OFFICE OF PUBLICATION: 1290 Avenue of the Americas, New York, NY 10104. © 2020 MARVEL. No similarity between any of the names, characters, persons, and/or institutions in this magazine with those of any living or dead person or institution is intended, and any such similarity which may exist is purely coincidental. **Printed in the U.S.A.** KEVIN FEIGE, Chief Creative Officer; DAN BUCKLEY, President, Marvel Entertainment; JOHN NEE, Publisher; JOE QUESADA, EVP & Creative Director; TOM BREVOORT, SVP of Publishing; DAVID BOGART, Associate Publisher & SVP of Talent Affairs; Publishing & Partnership; DAVID GABRIEL, VP of Print & Digital Publishing; JEFF YOUNGQUIST, VP of Production & Special Projects; DAN CARR, Executive Director of Publishing Technology; ALEX MORALES, Director of Publishing Operations; DAN EDINGTON, Managing Editor; SUSAN CRESPI, Production Manager; STAN LEE, Chairman, Emeritus. For information regarding advertising in Marvel Comics or on Marvel.com, please contact Vit DeBellis, Custom Solutions & Integrated Advertising Manager, at vdebellis@marvel.com. For Marvel subscription inquiries, please call 888-511-5480. **Manufactured between 2/28/2020 and 3/31/2020 by LSC COMMUNICATIONS INC., KENDALLVILLE, IN, USA.**

10 9 8 7 6 5 4 3 2 1

OF X

Volume
06

Writers:

Artists:

Color Artists:

Letterer

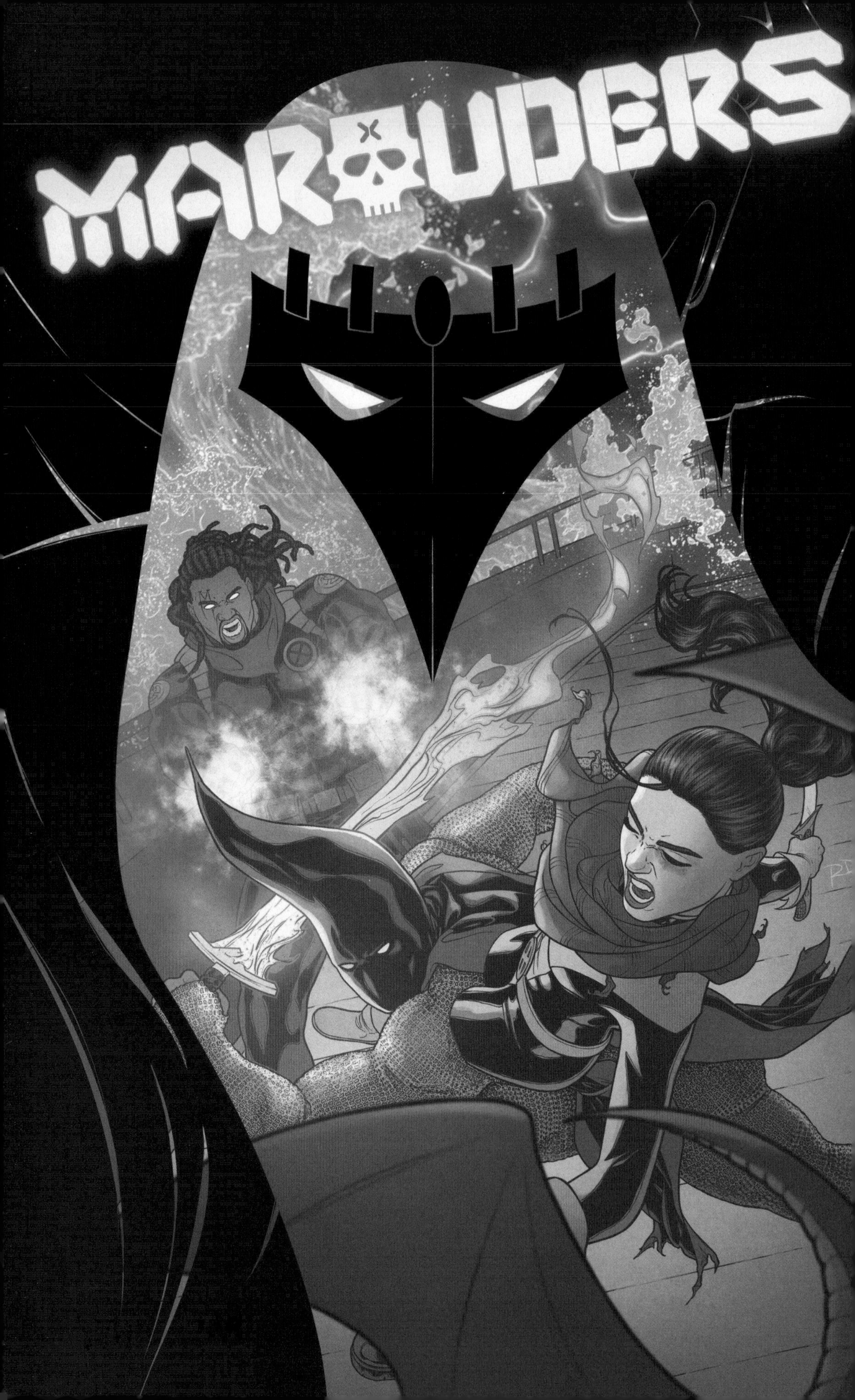
MARAUDERS

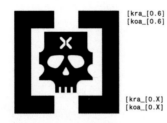

[kra_[0.6]
[koa_[0.6]

[kra_[0.X]
[koa_[0.X]

PAY YOUR DUES

Mayday! Shinobi Shaw's ship, the *Upstart*, sent out a distress signal from Madripoor Bay after coming under fire from the agents of *Homines Verendi*, a mysterious new organization that means to tear down the new age of mutantkind. Captain Kate Pryde and her crew sailed the *Marauder* to Madripoor hoping to rescue Shinobi and the refugee mutants in his care, but were intercepted by Hate-Monger and X-Cutioner in the name of Homines Verendi!

Pyro

Iceman

Kate Pryde

Lockheed

Bishop

Shinobi Shaw

Storm

Sebastian Shaw

[kra_[0.6]...]
[koa_[0.6]...]

[A._Shore_Thing]

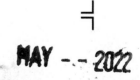

MAY -.- 2022

[00_mutant_piracy]
[00_sea_shores_X_]

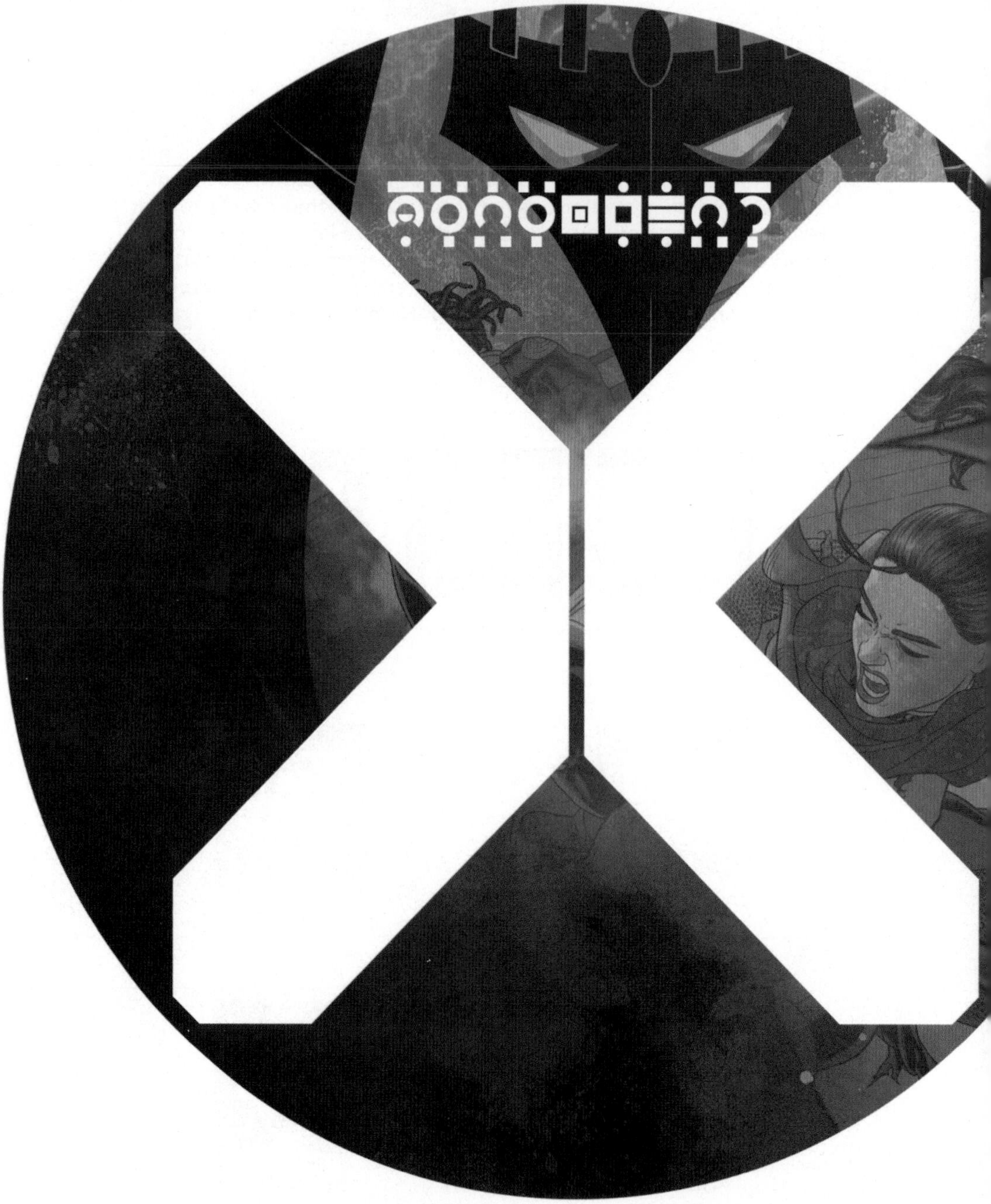

[00_mutant_piracy]
[00_sea_shores_X_]

GERRY DUGGAN..................................[WRITER]
MATTEO LOLLI & MARIO DEL PENNINO..............[ARTISTS]
ERICK ARCINIEGA & FEDERICO BLEE..........[COLOR ARTIST]
VC's CORY PETIT.............................[LETTERER]
TOM MULLER....................................[DESIGN]

RUSSELL DAUTERMAN & MATTHEW WILSON......[COVER ARTISTS]

ALAN DAVIS & CHRIS SOTOMAYOR....[VARIANT COVER ARTISTS]

NICK RUSSELL..............................[PRODUCTION]

JONATHAN HICKMAN...........................[HEAD OF X]
CHRIS ROBINSON.......................[ASSISTANT EDITOR]
JORDAN D. WHITE...............................[EDITOR]
C.B. CEBULSKI.........................[EDITOR IN CHIEF]

[06] MARAUDERS

[ISSUE SIX]..................A TIME TO REAP

[00_mutant_piracy]
[00_sea_shores_X_]

[00_00...0]
[00_00...5]

[00_boat__]
[00______]

[00______]

MAY -- 2022 [00______X]

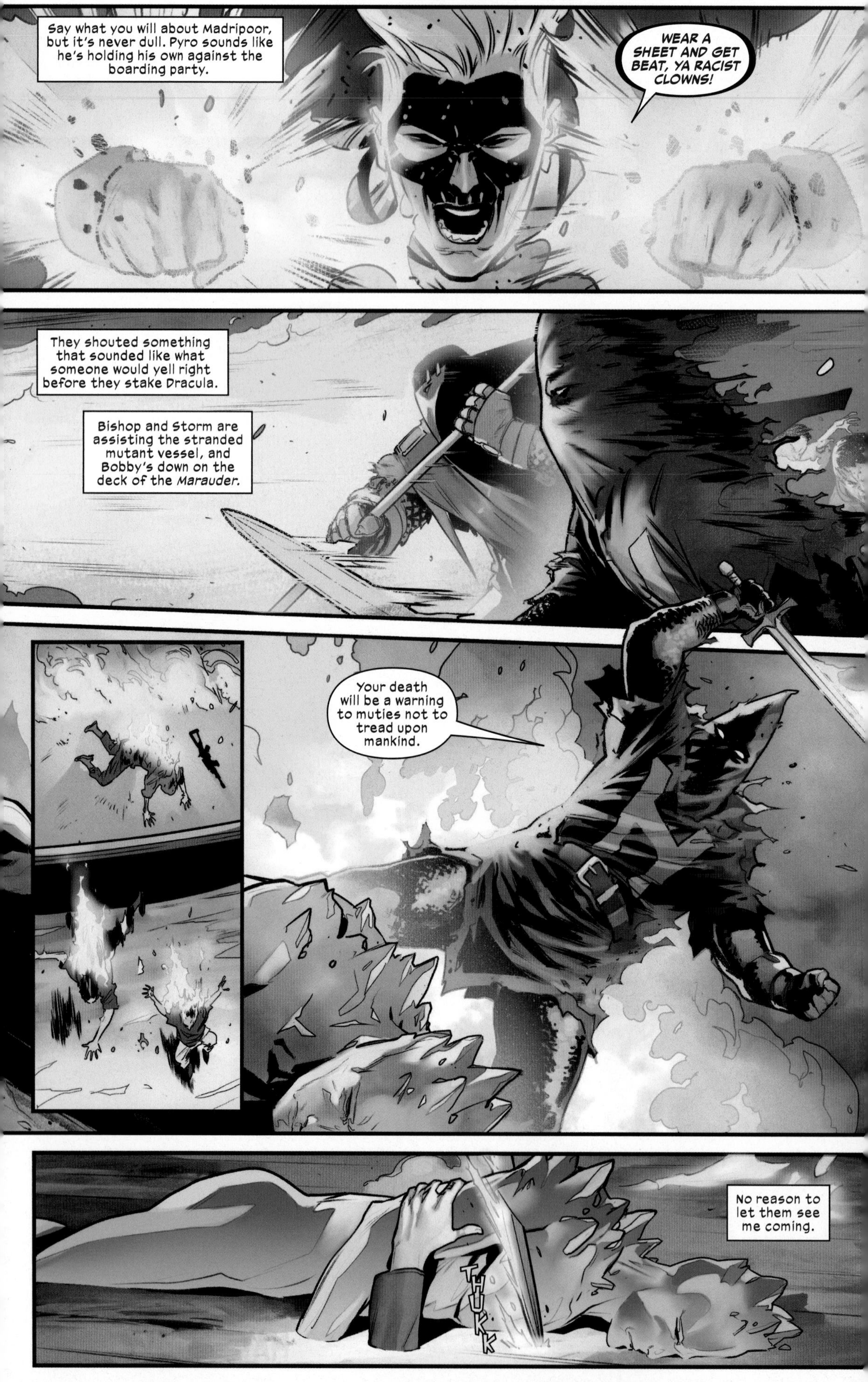

Say what you will about Madripoor, but it's never dull. Pyro sounds like he's holding his own against the boarding party.
WEAR A SHEET AND GET BEAT, YA RACIST CLOWNS!
They shouted something that sounded like what someone would yell right before they stake Dracula.
Bishop and Storm are assisting the stranded mutant vessel, and Bobby's down on the deck of the *Marauder.*
Your death will be a warning to muties not to tread upon mankind.
No reason to let them see me coming.
THUKK

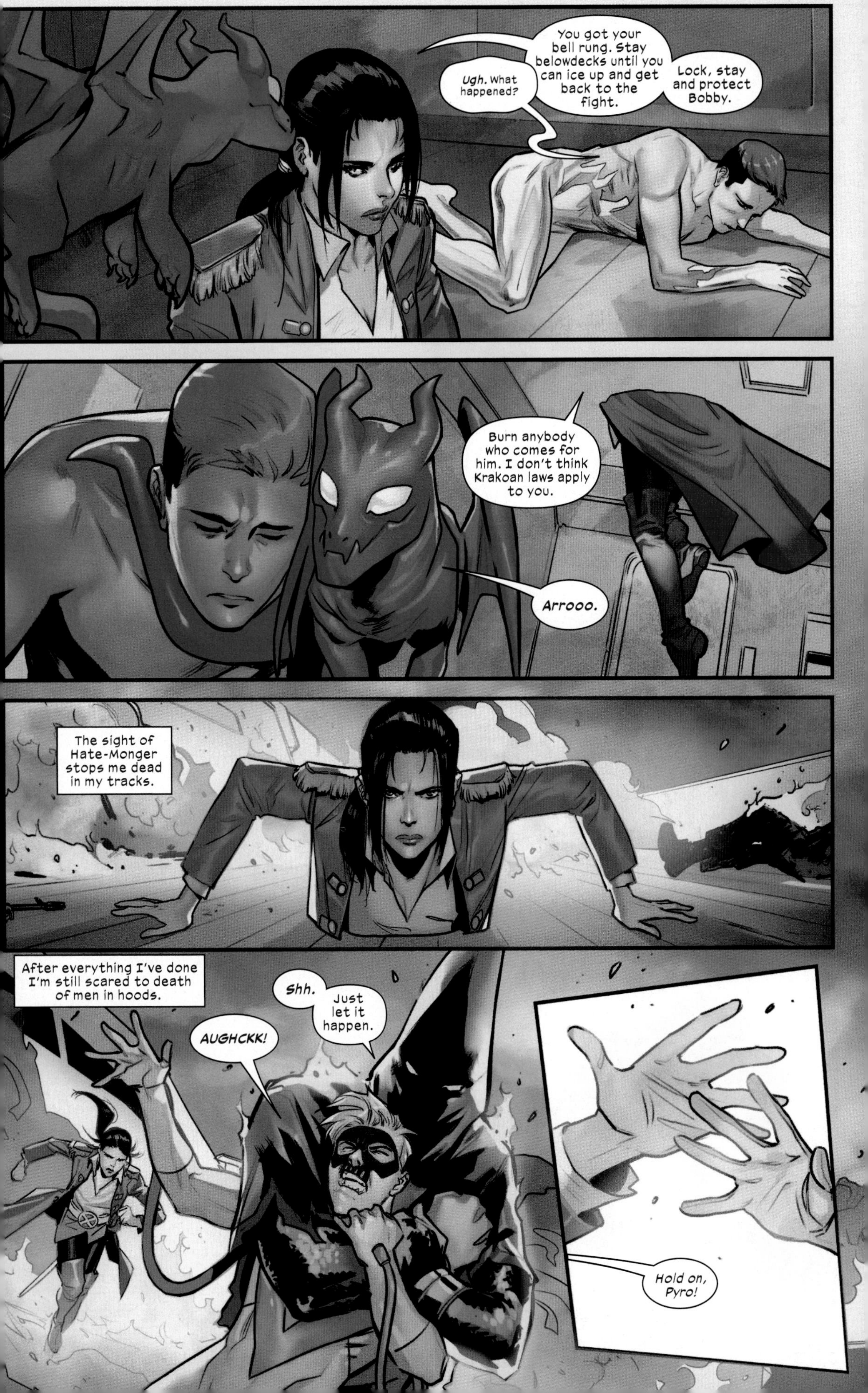
Ugh. What happened?
You got your bell rung. Stay belowdecks until you can ice up and get back to the fight.
Lock, stay and protect Bobby.
Burn anybody who comes for him. I don't think Krakoan laws apply to you.
Arrooo.
The sight of Hate-Monger stops me dead in my tracks.
After everything I've done I'm still scared to death of men in hoods.
Shh.
Just let it happen.
AUGHCKK!
Hold on, Pyro!

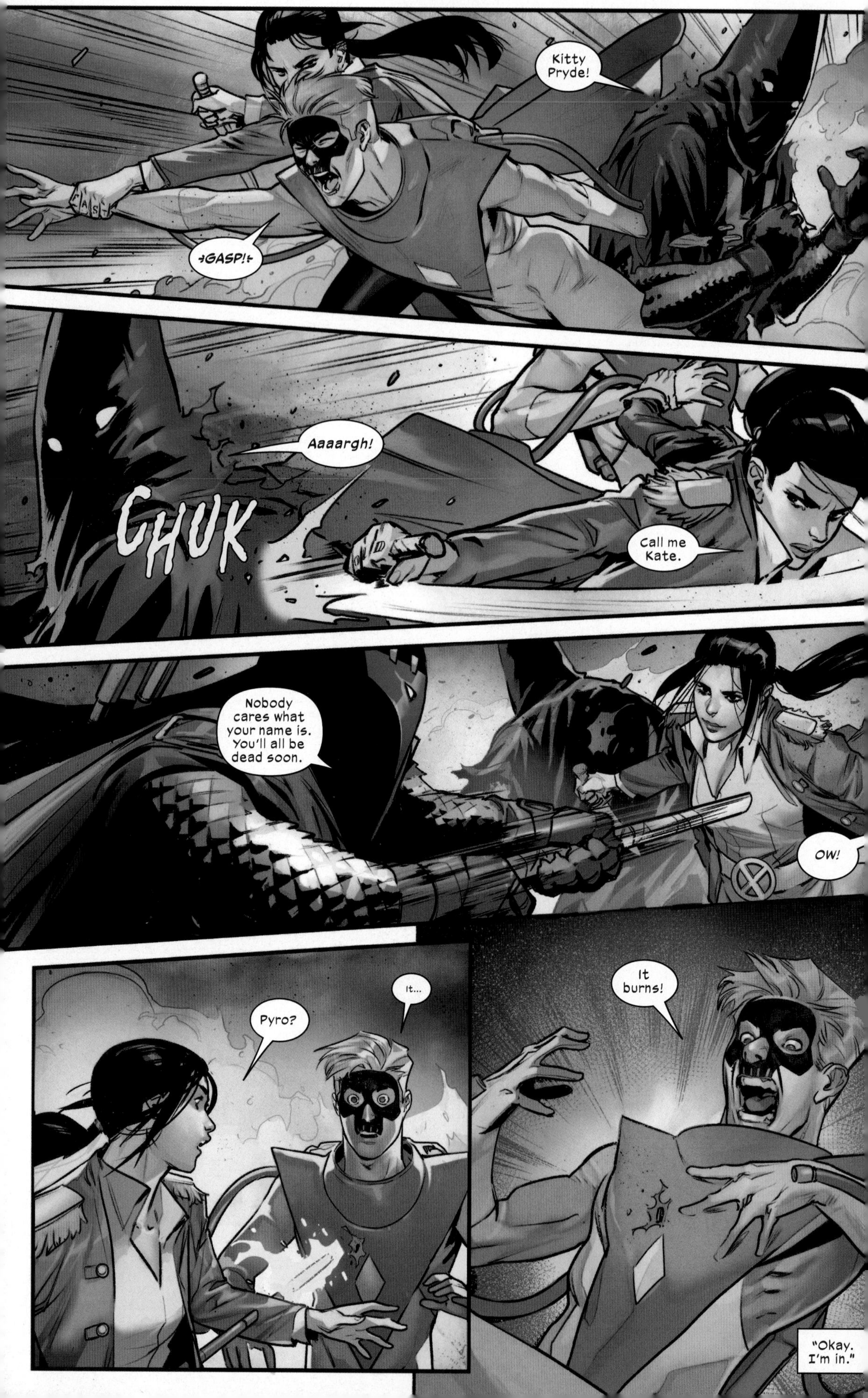
Kitty Pryde!
-GASP!-
Aaaargh!
CHUK
Call me Kate.
Nobody cares what your name is. You'll all be dead soon.
OW!
Pyro?
It...
It burns!
"Okay. I'm in."

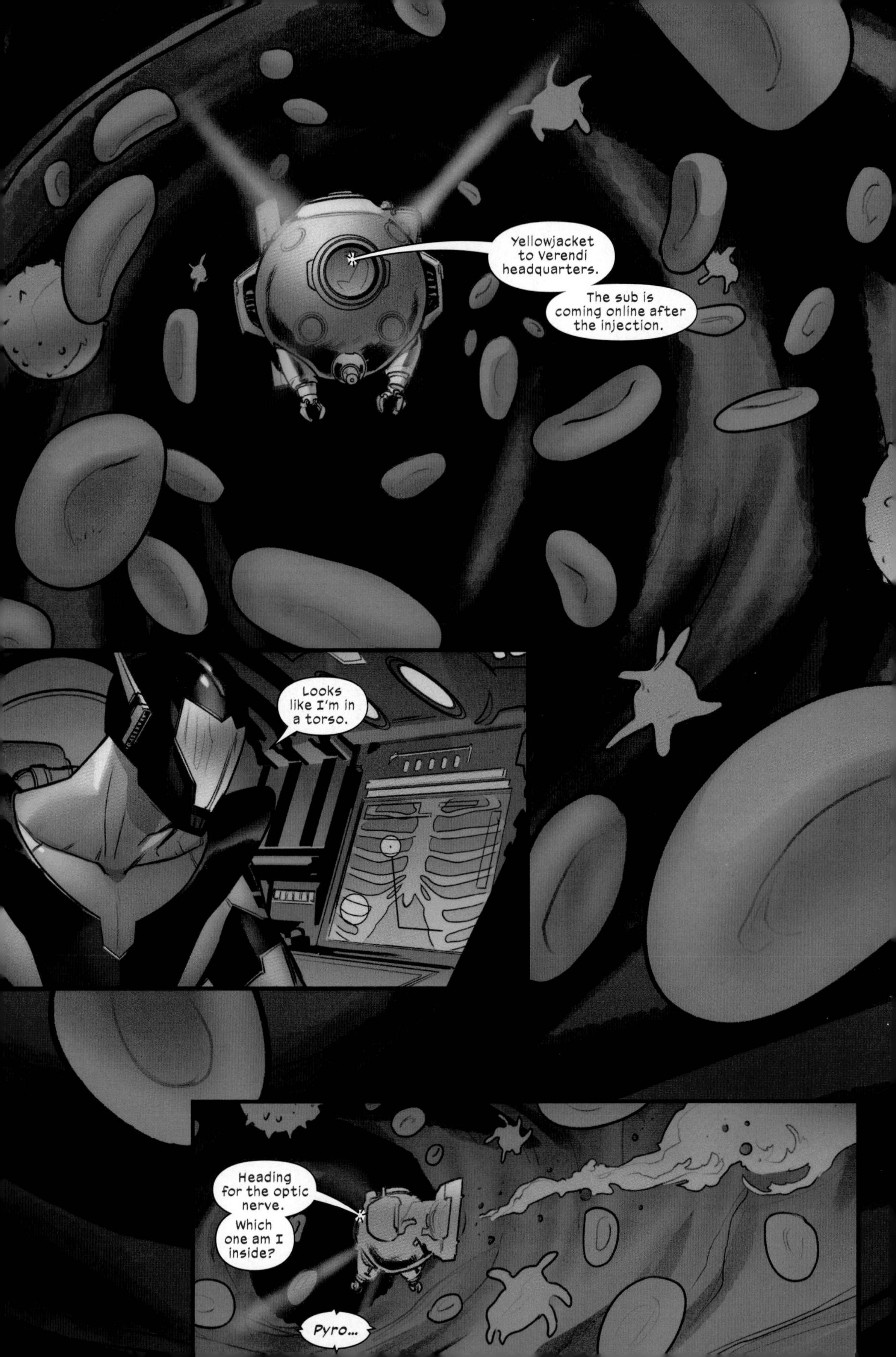
Yellowjacket to Verendi headquarters.
The sub is coming online after the injection.
Looks like I'm in a torso.
Heading for the optic nerve.
Which one am I inside?
Pyro...

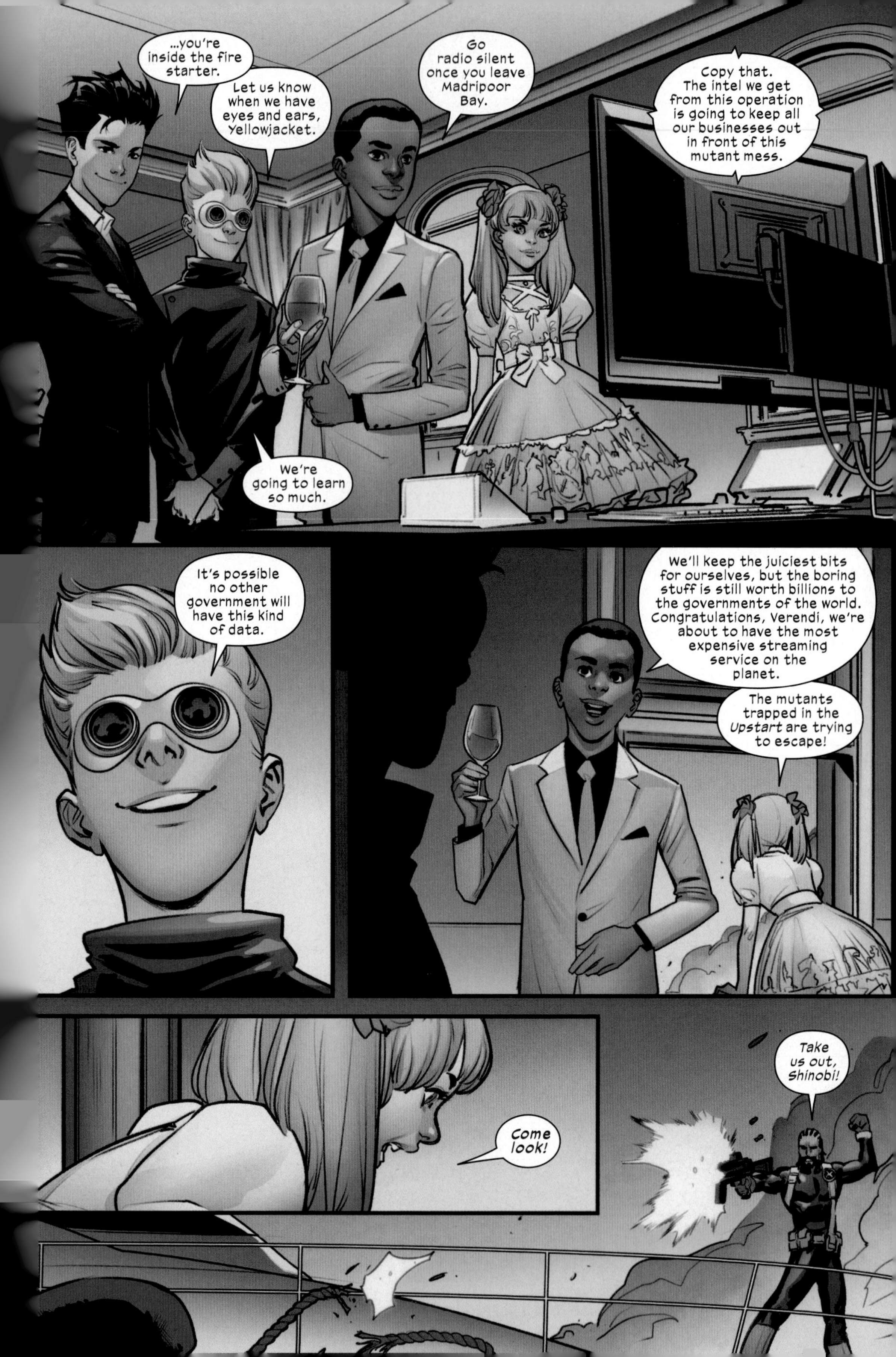
...you're inside the fire starter.
Let us know when we have eyes and ears, Yellowjacket.
Go radio silent once you leave Madripoor Bay.
Copy that. The intel we get from this operation is going to keep all our businesses out in front of this mutant mess.
We're going to learn so much.
It's possible no other government will have this kind of data.
We'll keep the juiciest bits for ourselves, but the boring stuff is still worth billions to the governments of the world. Congratulations, Verendi, we're about to have the most expensive streaming service on the planet.
The mutants trapped in the *Upstart* are trying to escape!
Come look!
Take us out, Shinobi!

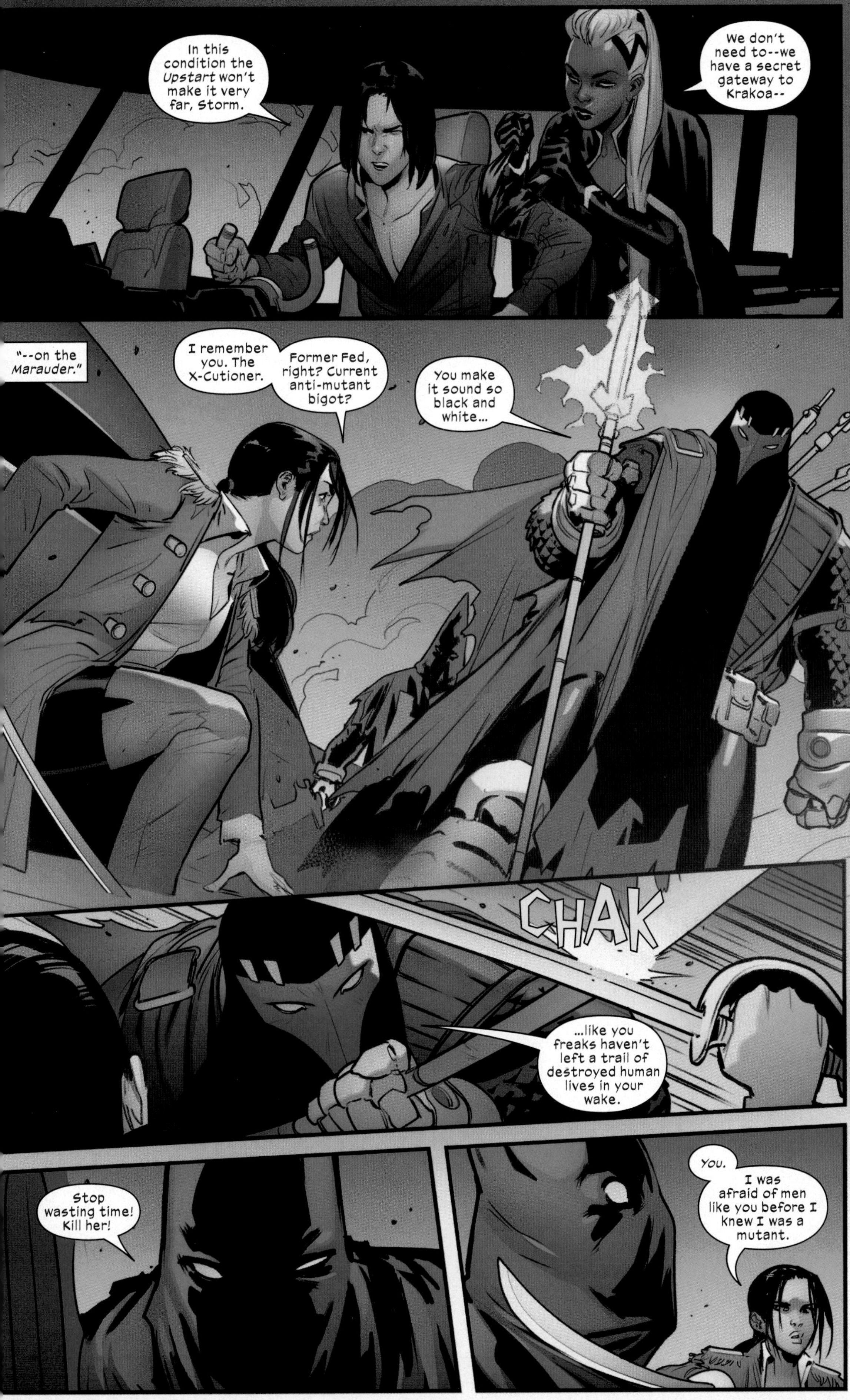

In this condition the *Upstart* won't make it very far, Storm.
We don't need to--we have a secret gateway to Krakoa--
"--on the *Marauder.*"
I remember you. The X-Cutioner.
Former Fed, right? Current anti-mutant bigot?
You make it sound so black and white...
CHAK
...like you freaks haven't left a trail of destroyed human lives in your wake.
Stop wasting time! Kill her!
You.
I was afraid of men like you before I knew I was a mutant.

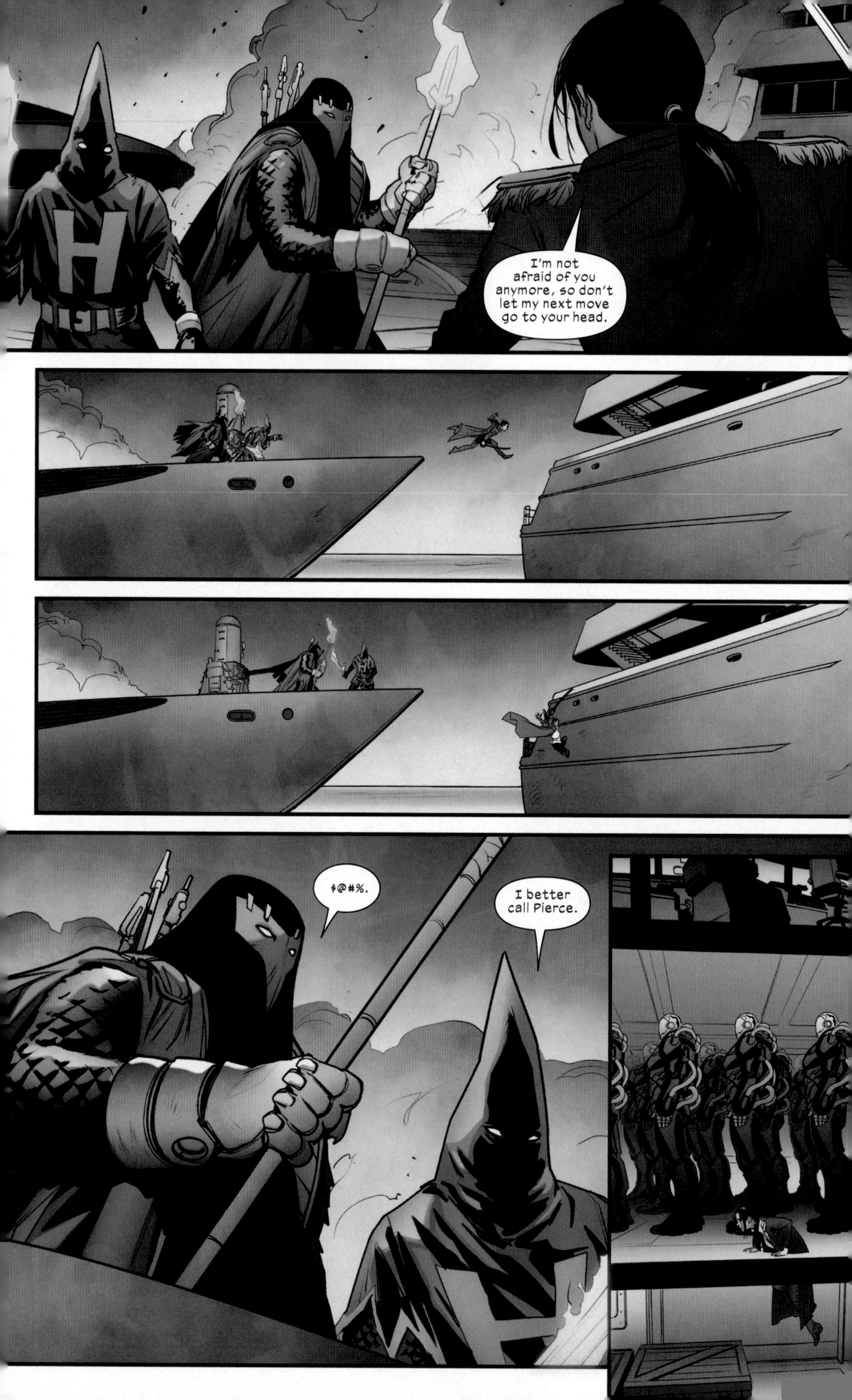
I'm not afraid of you anymore, so don't let my next move go to your head.
$@#%.
I better call Pierce.

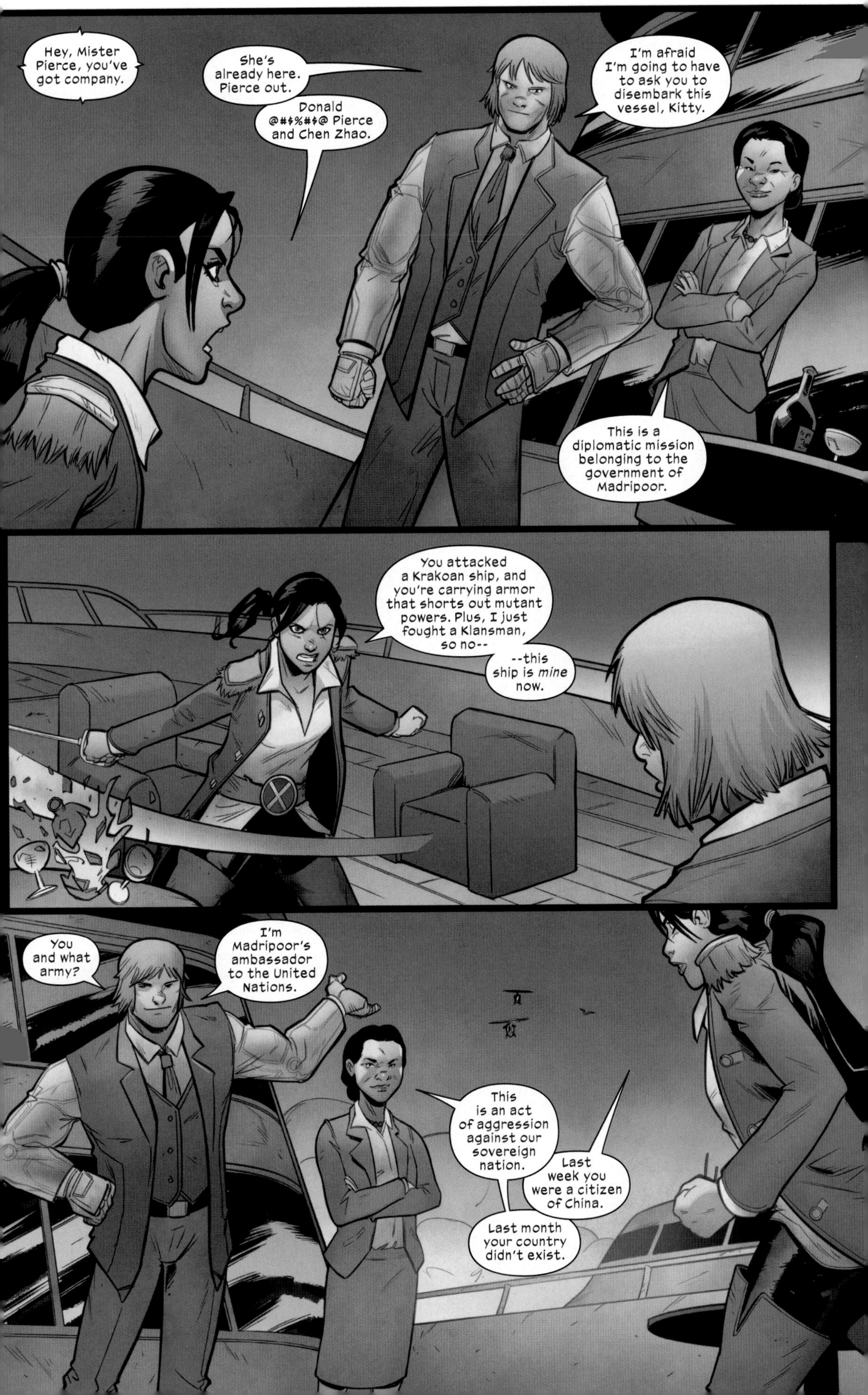
Hey, Mister Pierce, you've got company.
She's already here. Pierce out.
Donald @#$%#$@ Pierce and Chen Zhao.
I'm afraid I'm going to have to ask you to disembark this vessel, Kitty.
This is a diplomatic mission belonging to the government of Madripoor.
You attacked a Krakoan ship, and you're carrying armor that shorts out mutant powers. Plus, I just fought a Klansman, so no--
--this ship is *mine* now.
You and what army?
I'm Madripoor's ambassador to the United Nations.
This is an act of aggression against our sovereign nation.
Last week you were a citizen of China.
Last month your country didn't exist.

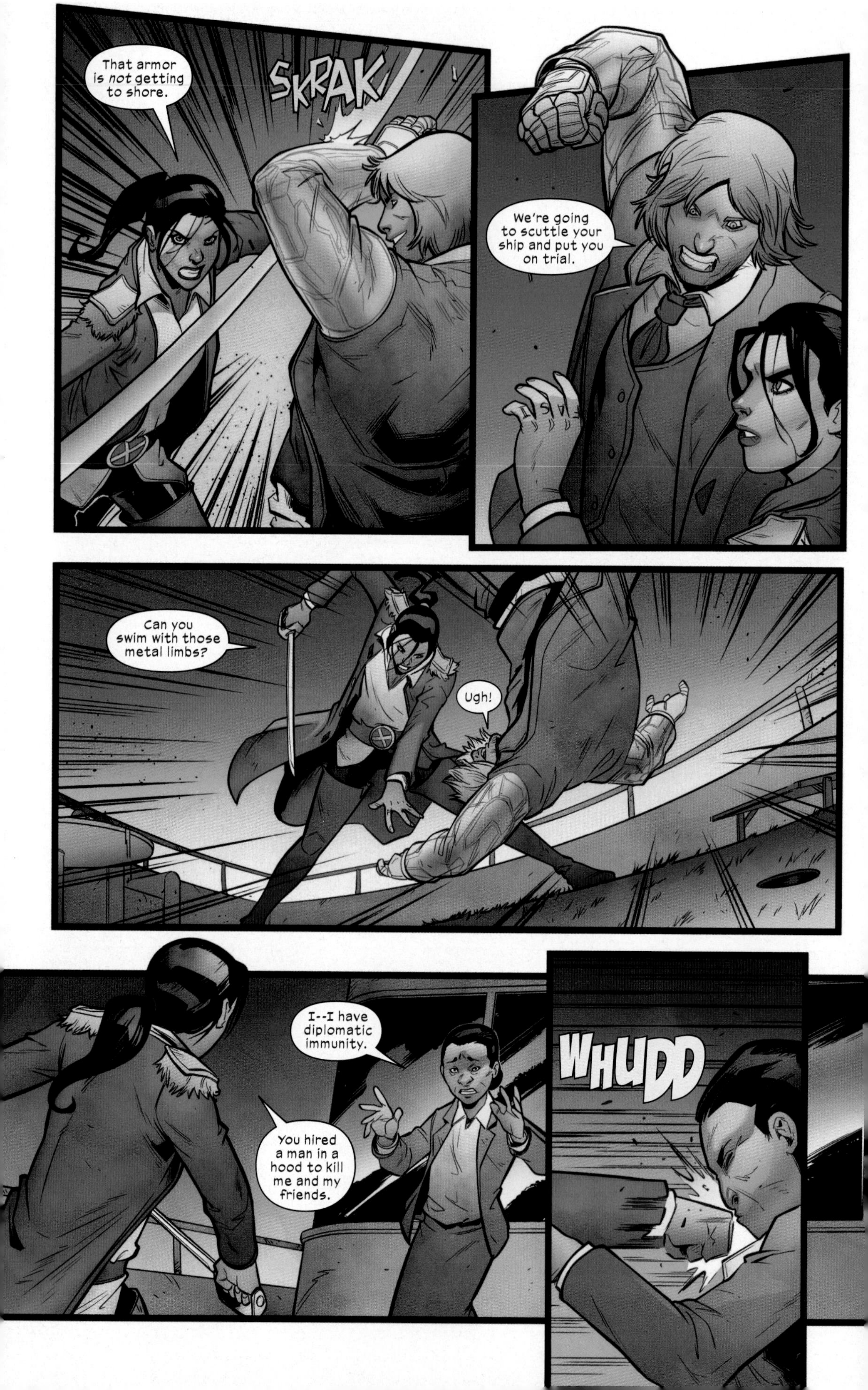
That armor is *not* getting to shore.
SKRAK
We're going to scuttle your ship and put you on trial.
Can you swim with those metal limbs?
Ugh!
I--I have diplomatic immunity.
You hired a man in a hood to kill me and my friends.
WHUDD

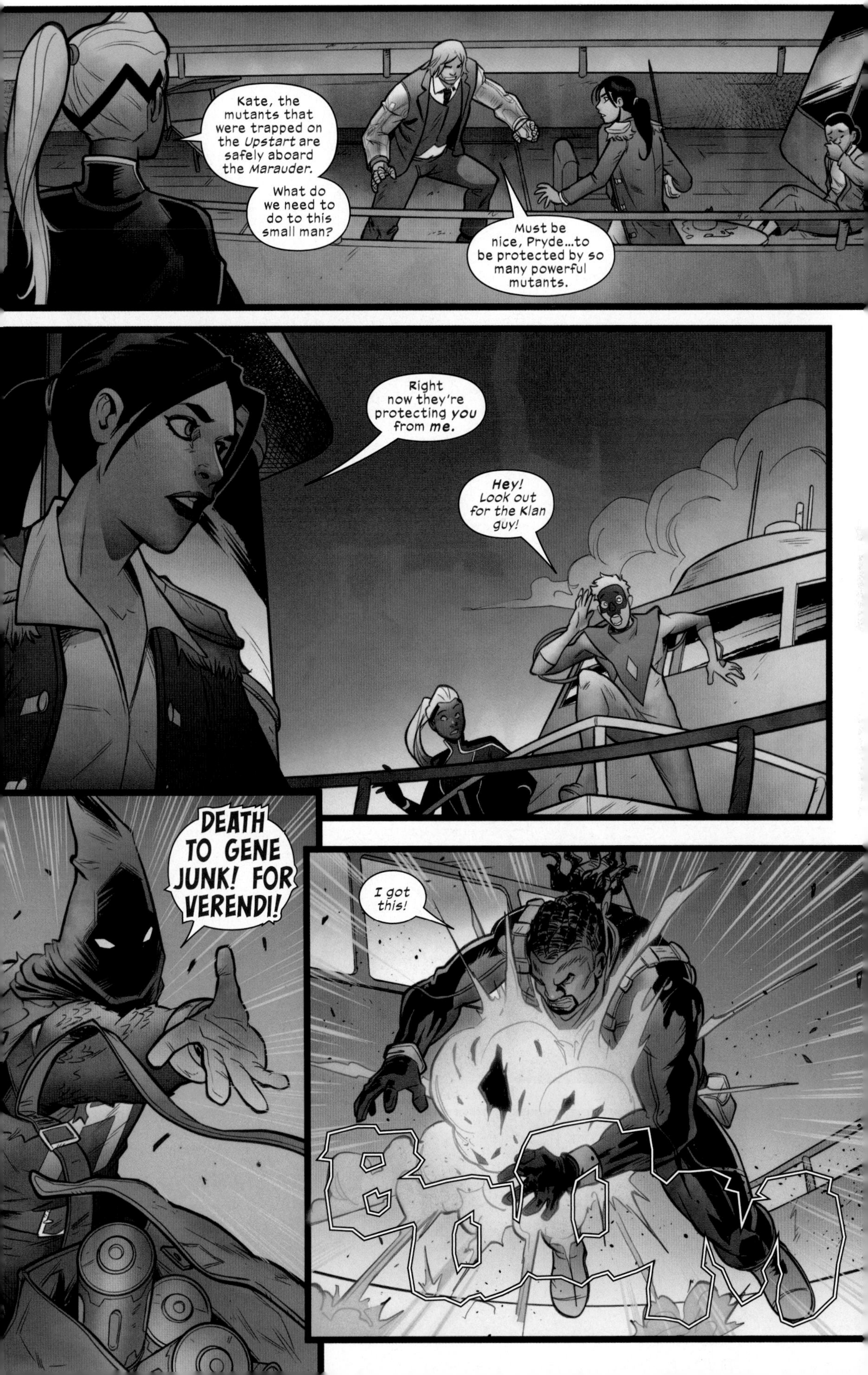
Kate, the mutants that were trapped on the *Upstart* are safely aboard the *Marauder.*
What do we need to do to this small man?
Must be nice, Pryde...to be protected by so many powerful mutants.
Right now they're protecting *you* from *me.*
Hey! Look out for the Klan guy!
DEATH TO GENE JUNK! FOR VERENDI!
I got this!

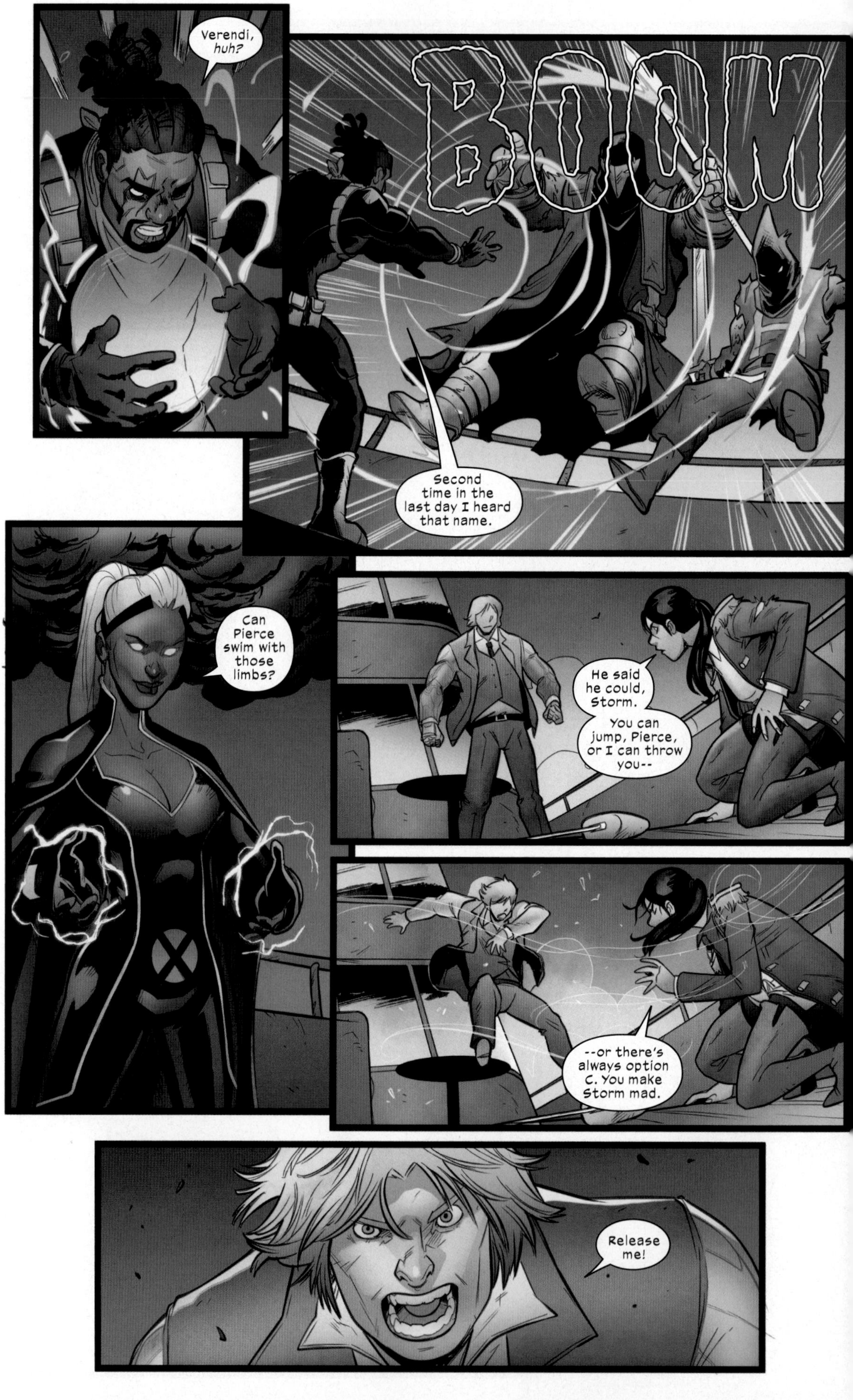
Verendi, *huh?*
BOOM
Second time in the last day I heard that name.
Can Pierce swim with those limbs?
He said he could, Storm.
You can jump, Pierce, or I can throw you--
--or there's always option C. You make Storm mad.
Release me!

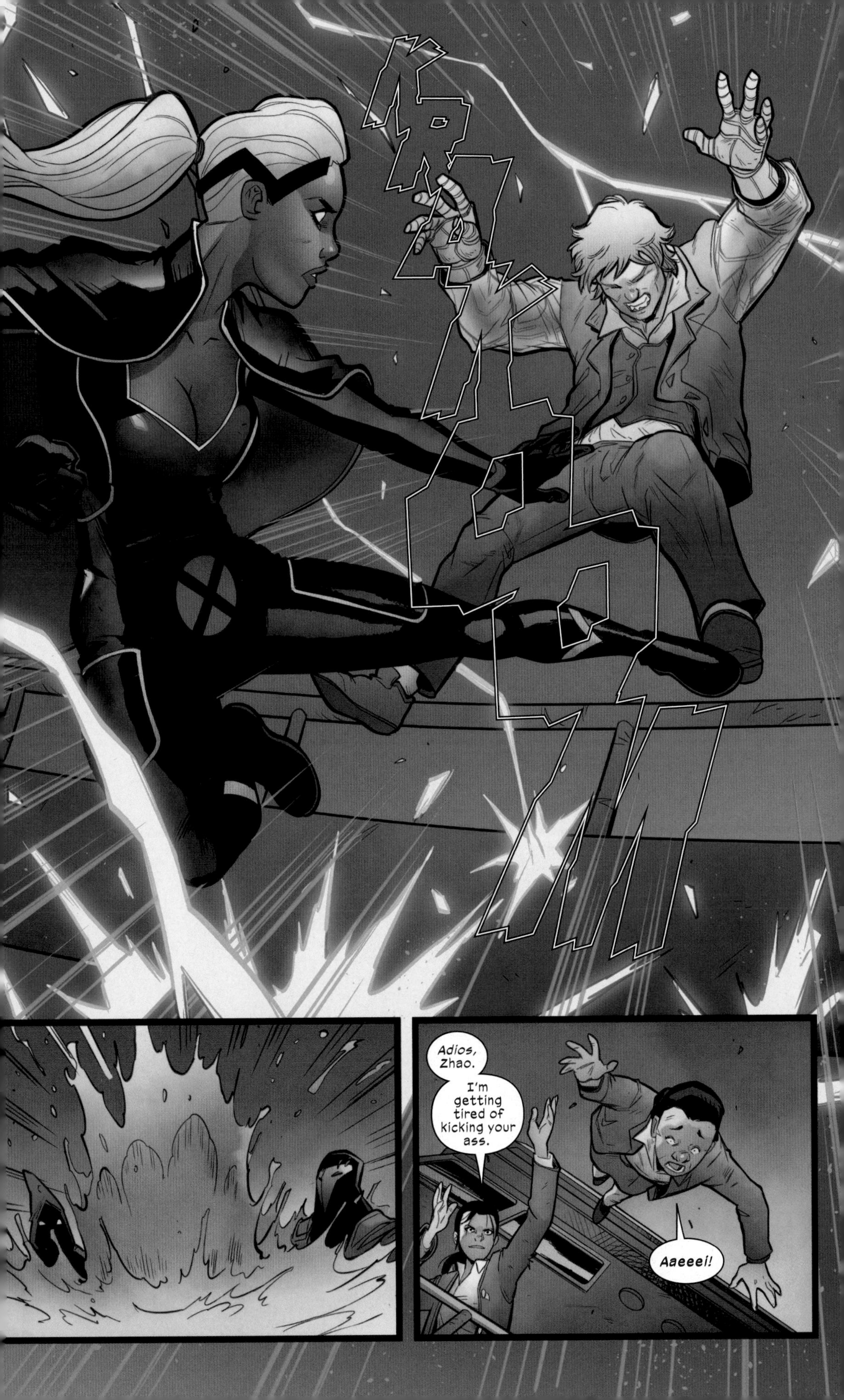

Adios, Zhao.
I'm getting tired of kicking your ass.
Aaeeei!

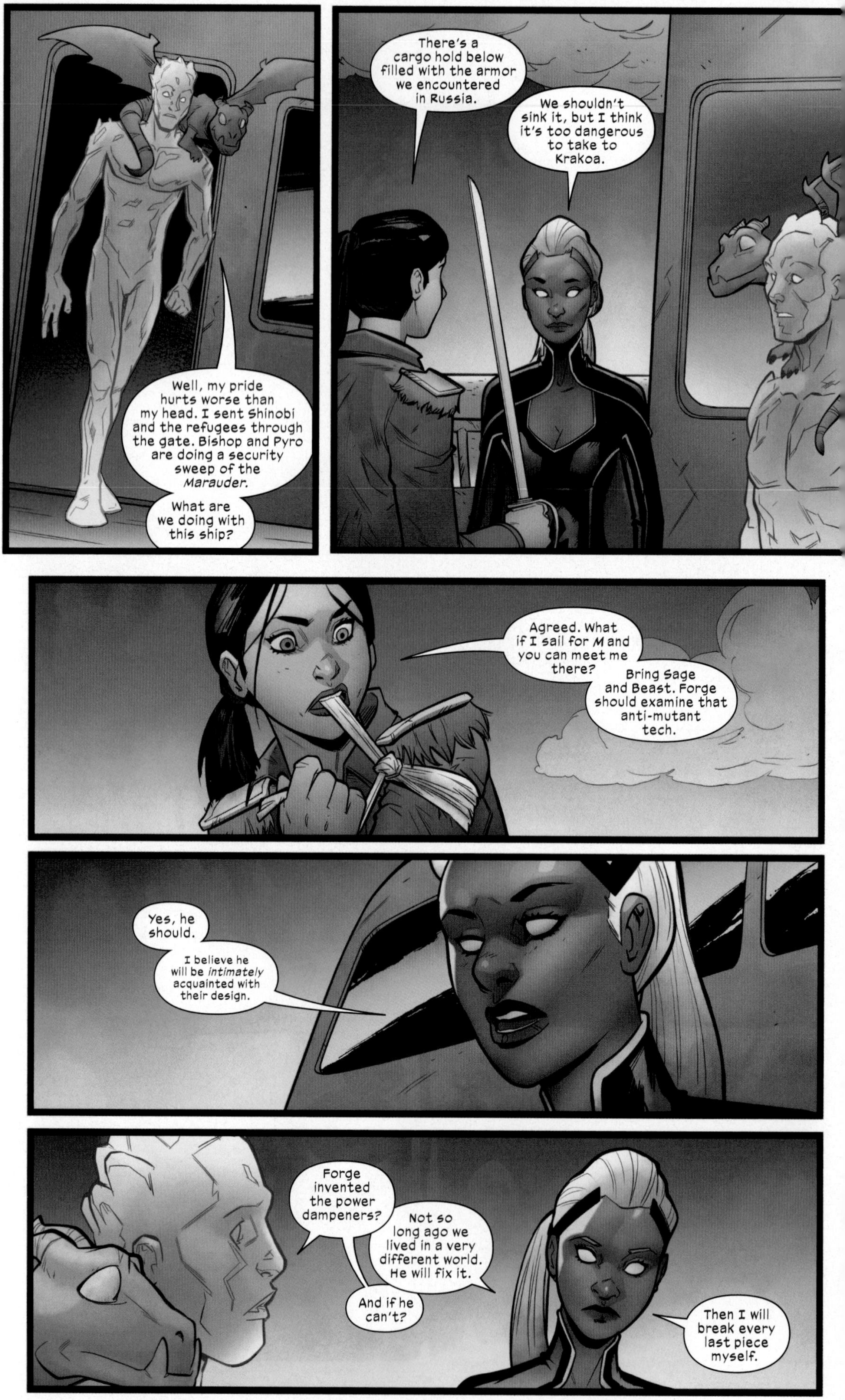

Well, my pride hurts worse than my head. I sent Shinobi and the refugees through the gate. Bishop and Pyro are doing a security sweep of the *Marauder*.
What are we doing with this ship?
There's a cargo hold below filled with the armor we encountered in Russia.
We shouldn't sink it, but I think it's too dangerous to take to Krakoa.
Agreed. What if I sail for *M* and you can meet me there?
Bring Sage and Beast. Forge should examine that anti-mutant tech.
Yes, he should.
I believe he will be *intimately* acquainted with their design.
Forge invented the power dampeners?
Not so long ago we lived in a very different world. He will fix it.
And if he can't?
Then I will break every last piece myself.

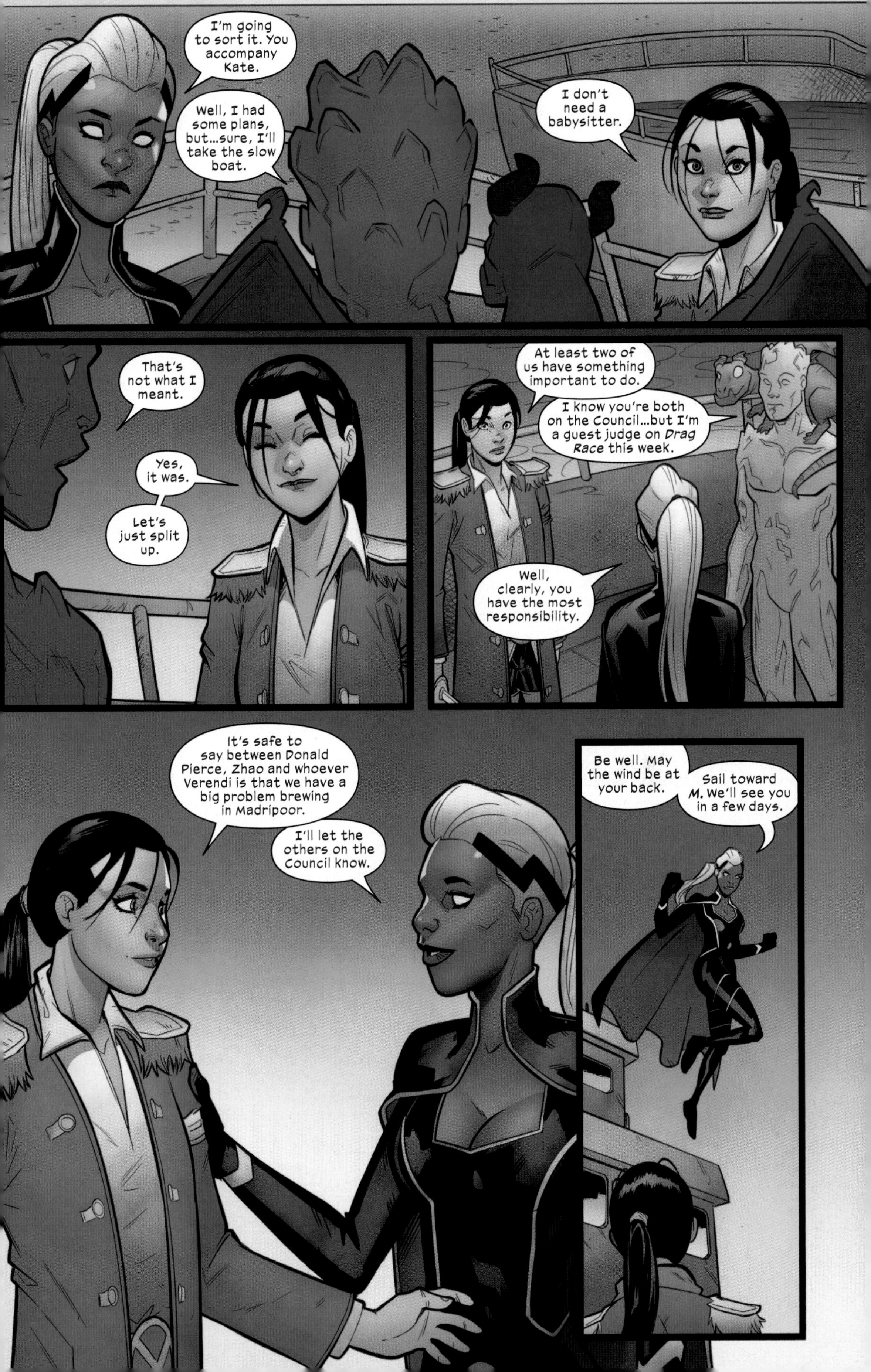
I'm going to sort it. You accompany Kate.
Well, I had some plans, but...sure, I'll take the slow boat.
I don't need a babysitter.
That's not what I meant.
Yes, it was.
Let's just split up.
At least two of us have something important to do.
I know you're both on the Council...but I'm a guest judge on *Drag Race* this week.
Well, clearly, you have the most responsibility.
It's safe to say between Donald Pierce, Zhao and whoever Verendi is that we have a big problem brewing in Madripoor.
I'll let the others on the Council know.
Be well. May the wind be at your back.
Sail toward M. We'll see you in a few days.

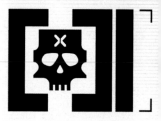

VERENDI SUB LOG

AUTHOR: Yellowjacket

—

I'm running silent.

Systems are running normal. I am no longer broadcasting live in case the mutants have a way to detect us.

However, I'm getting a clear image in black and white from Pyro's optic nerves. I can actually hear his voice booming through his bones, even though I haven't deployed the sound buoy.

At the moment, Pyro has the shakes from the adrenaline crash after the fight.

Shinobi Shaw and the Madripoorian mutants are walking through those magic gates. That is really cool!

No sign of Iceman, Pryde or Storm.

Right now Pyro has joined Bishop on a security sweep of the Marauder. This will be great: I'll learn all the ship's secrets.

Pyro has found an all-white wardrobe. It goes on FOREVER. There are white business suits, and uh, well -- more casual clothes. I guess Frost has a cabin on the ship?

Now he's calling in Bishop to see.

Bishop can't believe it either. Pyro's holding up some lingerie. You know what? He could rock that.

I can't believe this. You could probably wear a new outfit every day. This is some real Imelda Marcos ███████.

Okay, I think we're getting to some good stuff. We're out of the wardrobe and Pyro's opening a heavily fortified door.

It's a hair and nail salon.

What the hell kind of warship is this?

Well, Pyro made himself a couple of Long Island iced teas and now he's in the yacht's movie theater watching Rick and Morty.

I gotta say, we thought that these guys wanted to exterminate humanity, but I dunno -- they seem pretty chill.

The ship's turning toward Krakoa. I guess that's where I'll get to the good stuff.

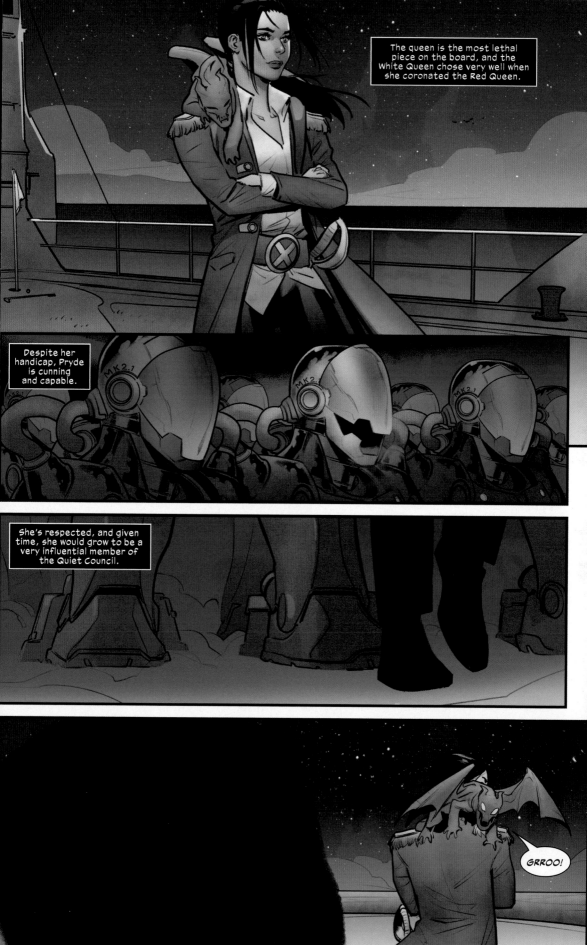

The queen is the most lethal piece on the board, and the White Queen chose very well when she coronated the Red Queen.

Despite her handicap, Pryde is cunning and capable.

She's respected, and given time, she would grow to be a very influential member of the Quiet Council.

GRROO!

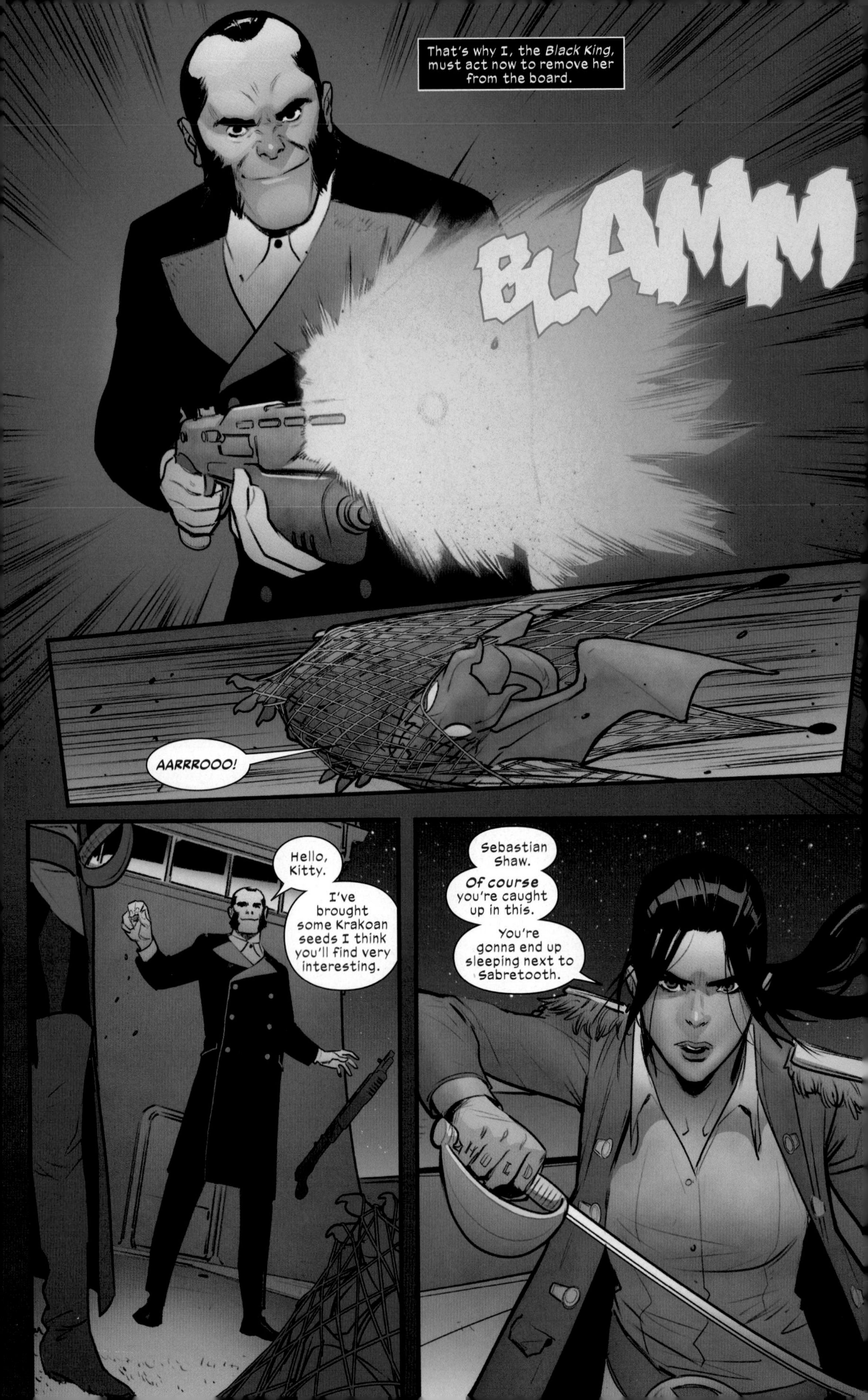
That's why I, the *Black King*, must act now to remove her from the board.
BLAMM
AARRROOO!
Hello, Kitty.
I've brought some Krakoan seeds I think you'll find very interesting.
Sebastian Shaw.
Of course you're caught up in this.
You're gonna end up sleeping next to Sabretooth.

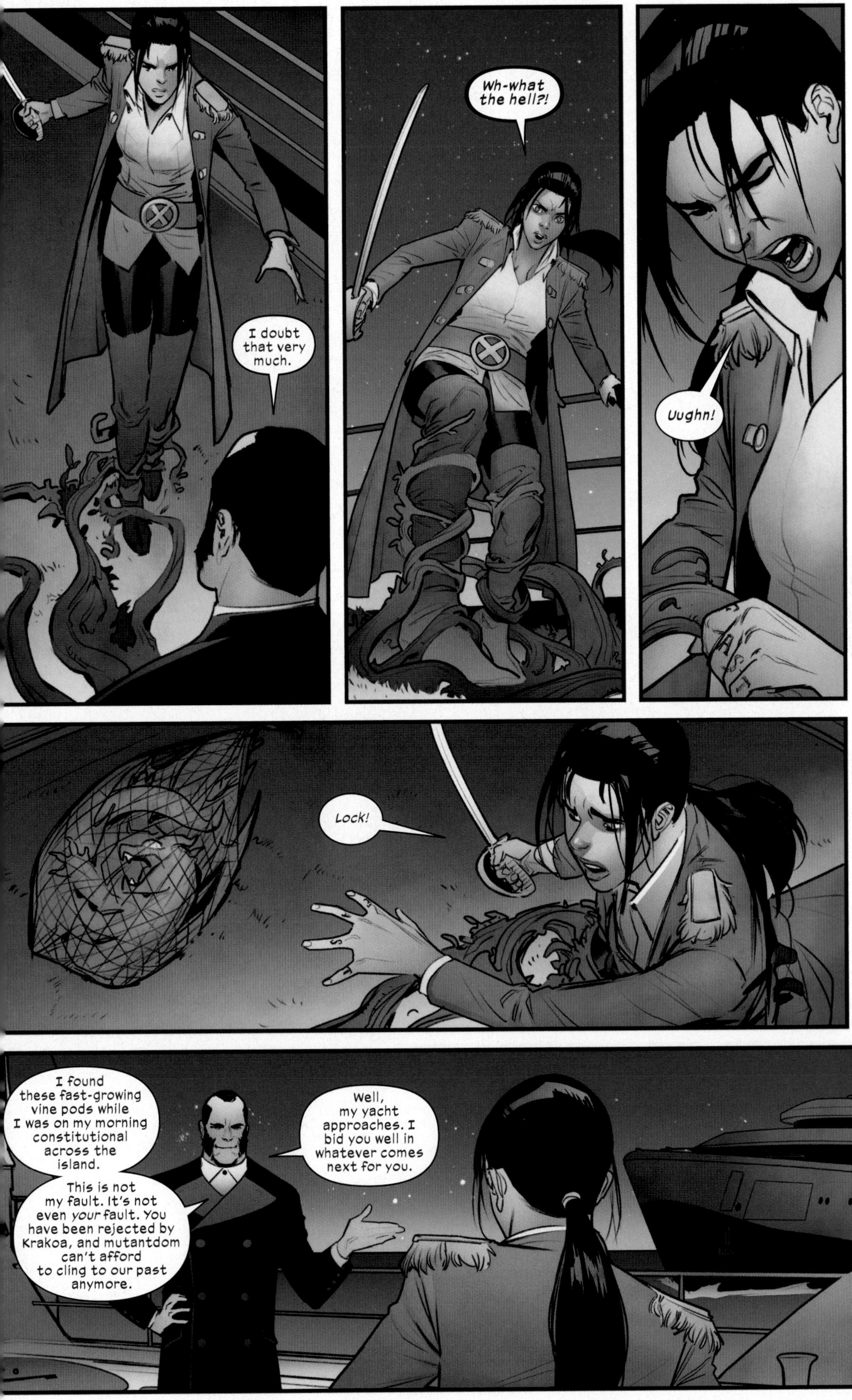
I doubt that very much.
Wh-what the hell?!
Uughn!
Lock!
I found these fast-growing vine pods while I was on my morning constitutional across the island.
This is not my fault. It's not even *your* fault. You have been rejected by Krakoa, and mutantdom can't afford to cling to our past anymore.
Well, my yacht approaches. I bid you well in whatever comes next for you.

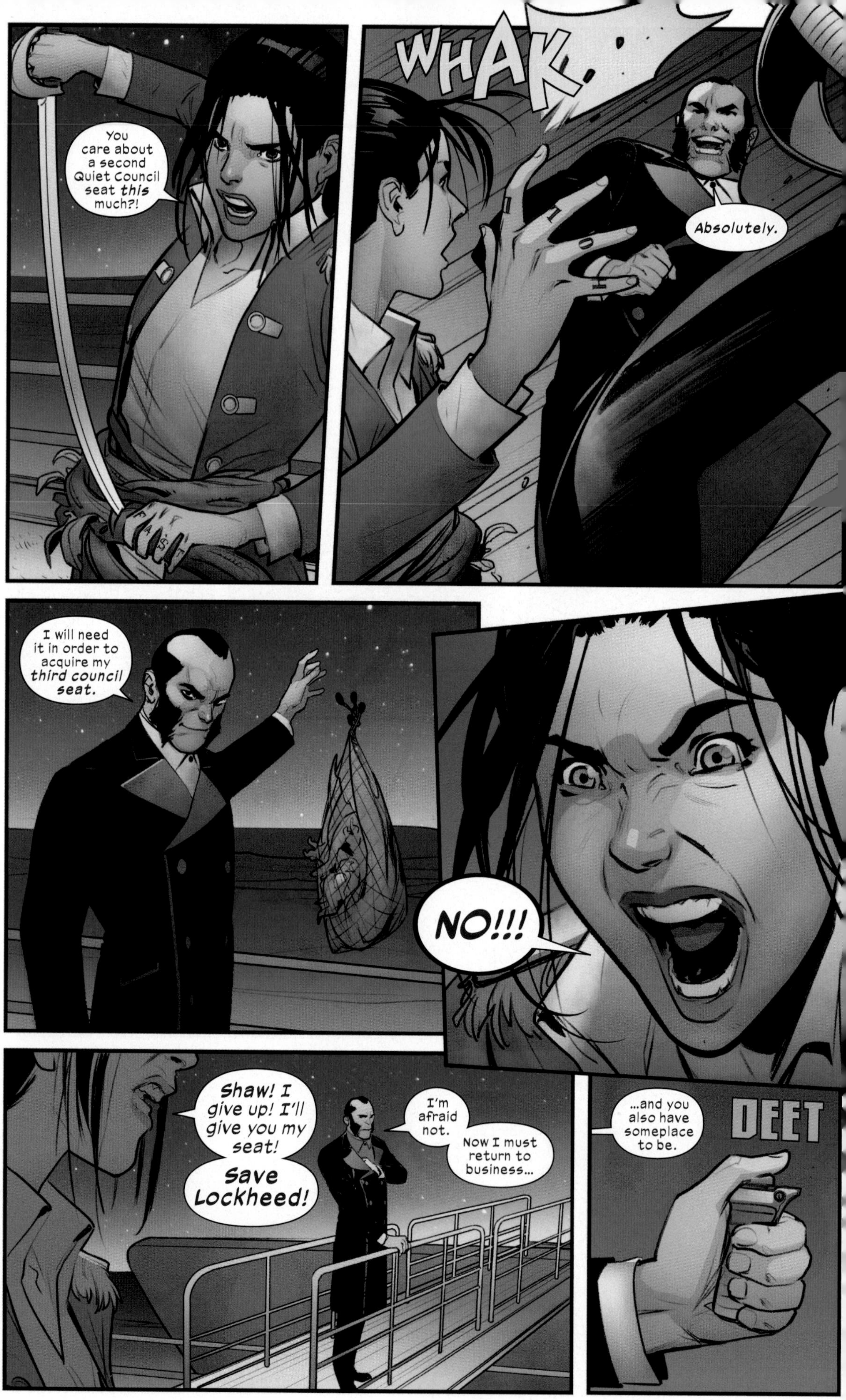
You care about a second Quiet Council seat *this* much?!
WHAK
Absolutely.
I will need it in order to acquire my *third council seat.*
NO!!!
Shaw! I give up! I'll give you my seat!
Save Lockheed!
I'm afraid not.
Now I must return to business...
...and you also have someplace to be.
DEET

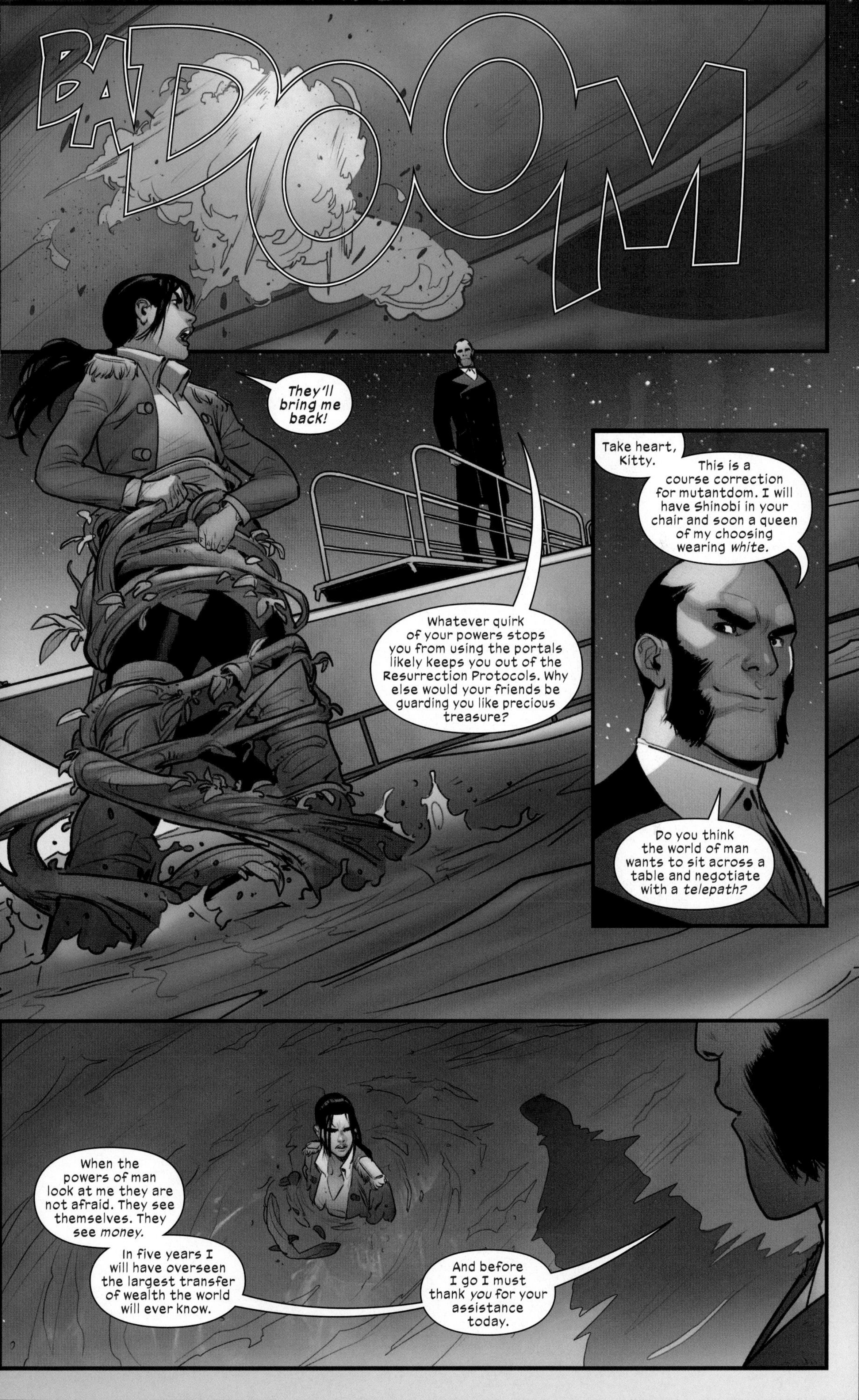
BADOOM
They'll bring me back!
Whatever quirk of your powers stops you from using the portals likely keeps you out of the Resurrection Protocols. Why else would your friends be guarding you like precious treasure?
Take heart, Kitty.
This is a course correction for mutantdom. I will have Shinobi in your chair and soon a queen of my choosing wearing *white*.
Do you think the world of man wants to sit across a table and negotiate with a *telepath?*
When the powers of man look at me they are not afraid. They see themselves. They see *money.*
In five years I will have overseen the largest transfer of wealth the world will ever know.
And before I go I must thank *you* for your assistance today.

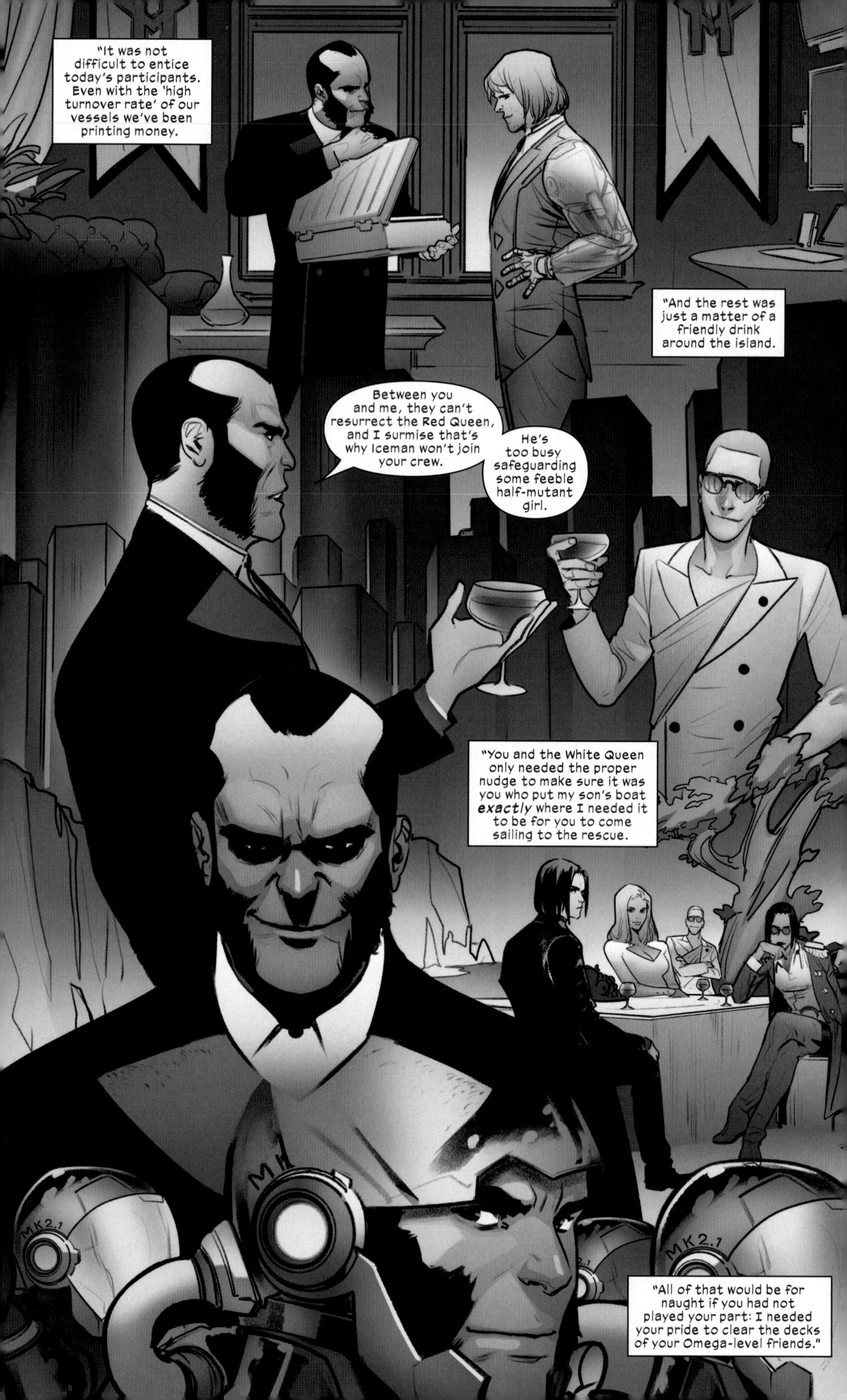
"It was not difficult to entice today's participants. Even with the 'high turnover rate' of our vessels we've been printing money.
"And the rest was just a matter of a friendly drink around the island.
Between you and me, they can't resurrect the Red Queen, and I surmise that's why Iceman won't join your crew.
He's too busy safeguarding some feeble half-mutant girl.
"You and the White Queen only needed the proper nudge to make sure it was you who put my son's boat *exactly* where I needed it to be for you to come sailing to the rescue.
"All of that would be for naught if you had not played your part: I needed your pride to clear the decks of your Omega-level friends."

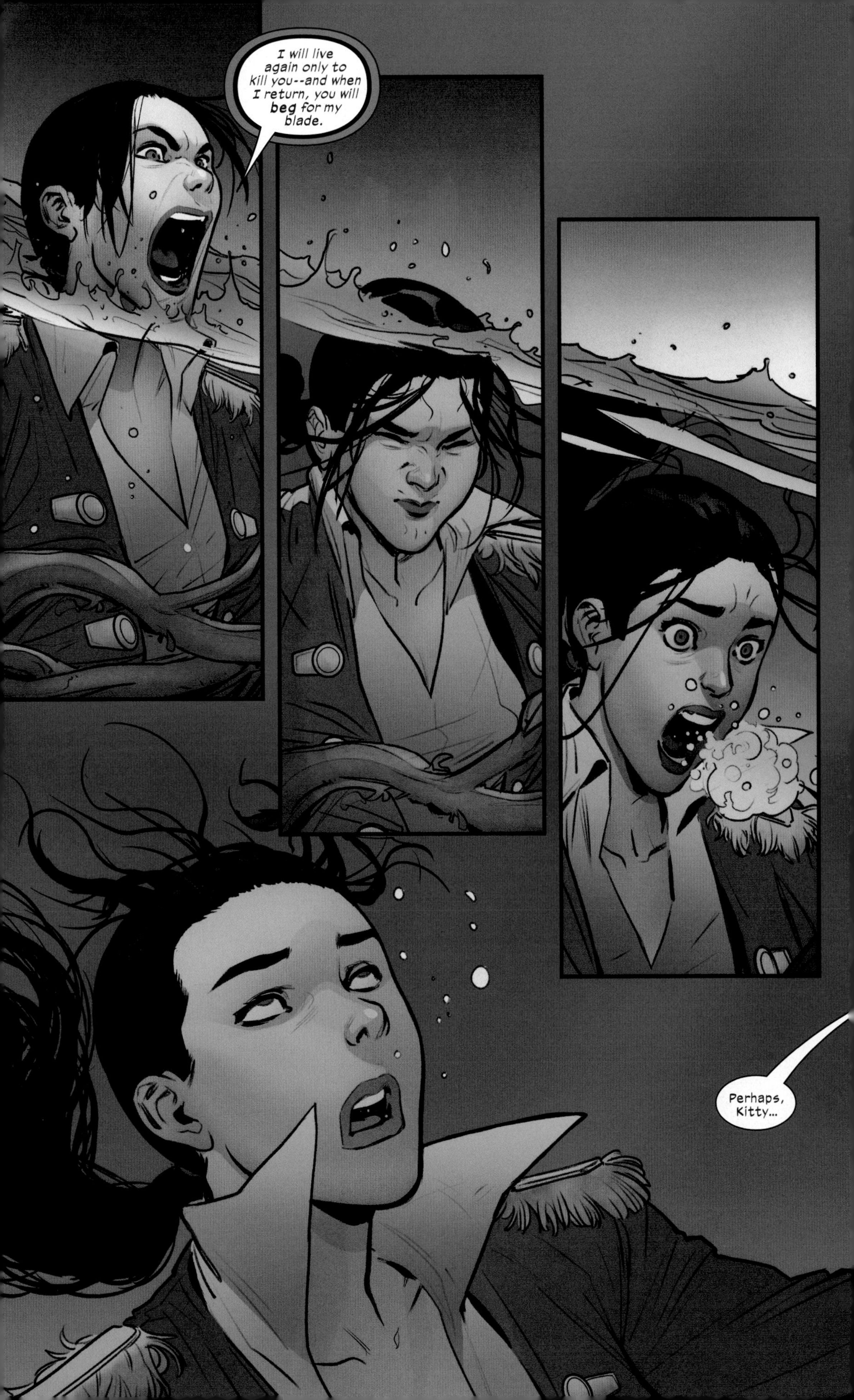
I will live again only to kill you--and when I return, you will beg for my blade.
Perhaps, Kitty...

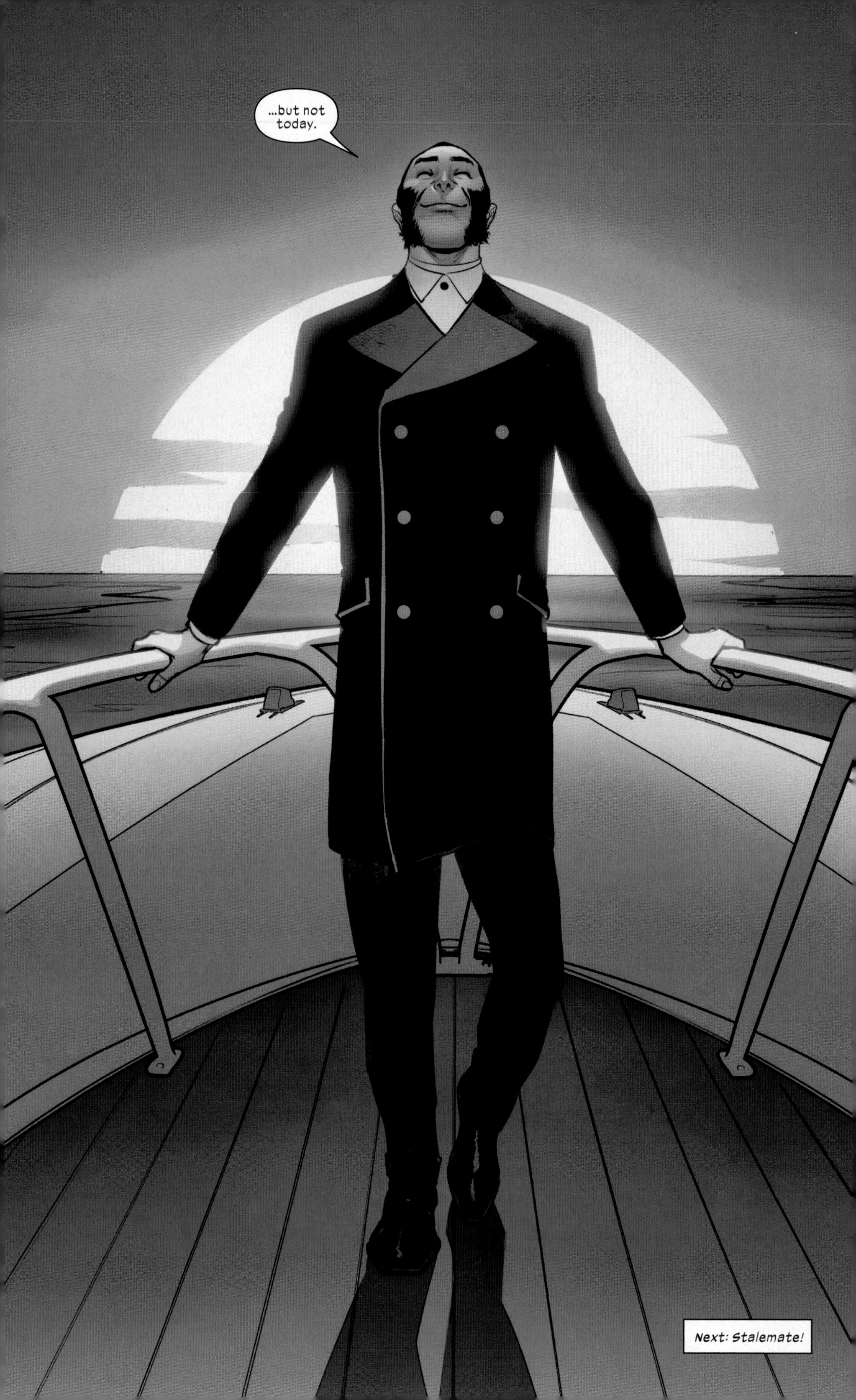
...but not today.
Next: Stalemate!

[dawn_of_x]

[kra_]
[koa_]

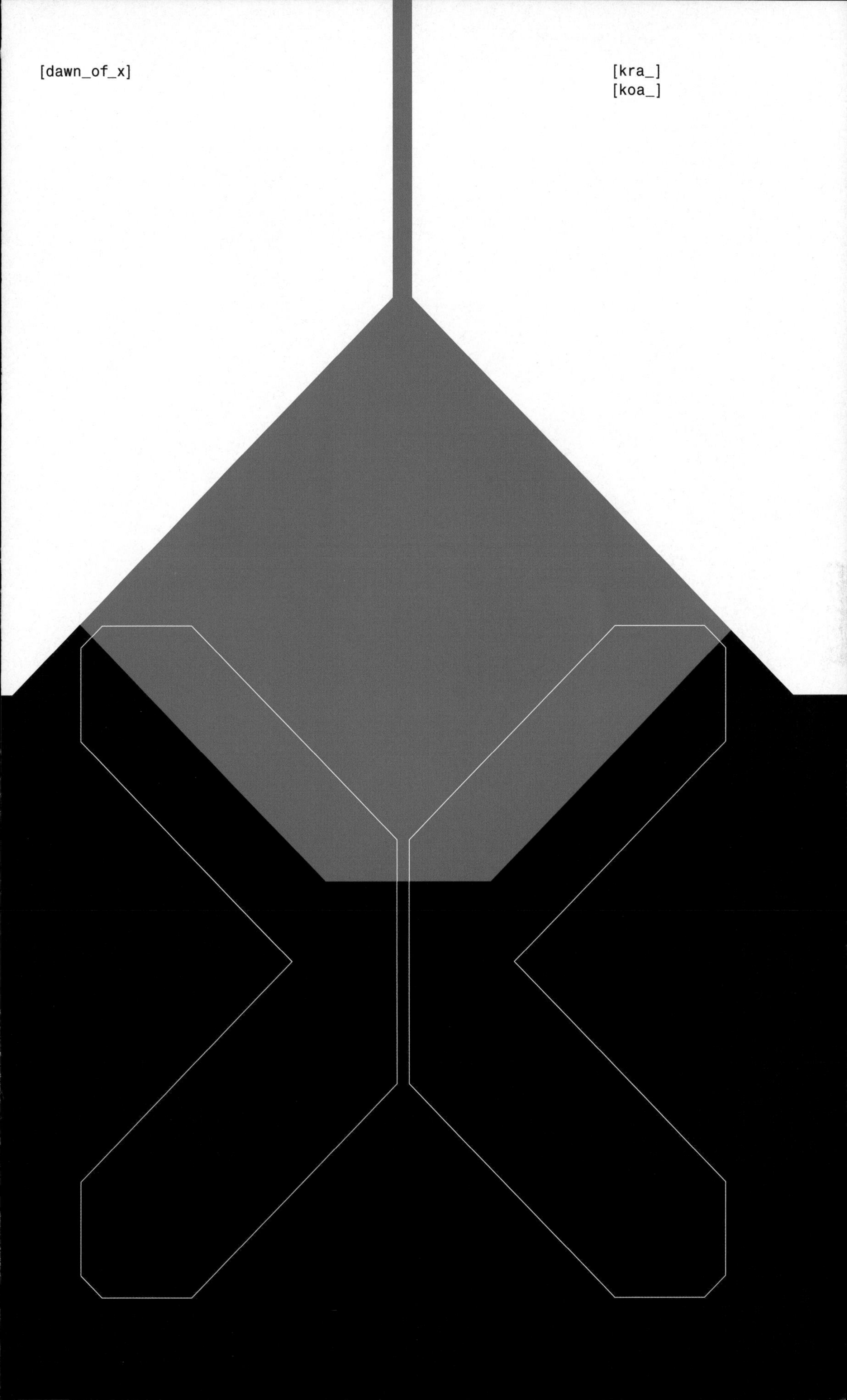

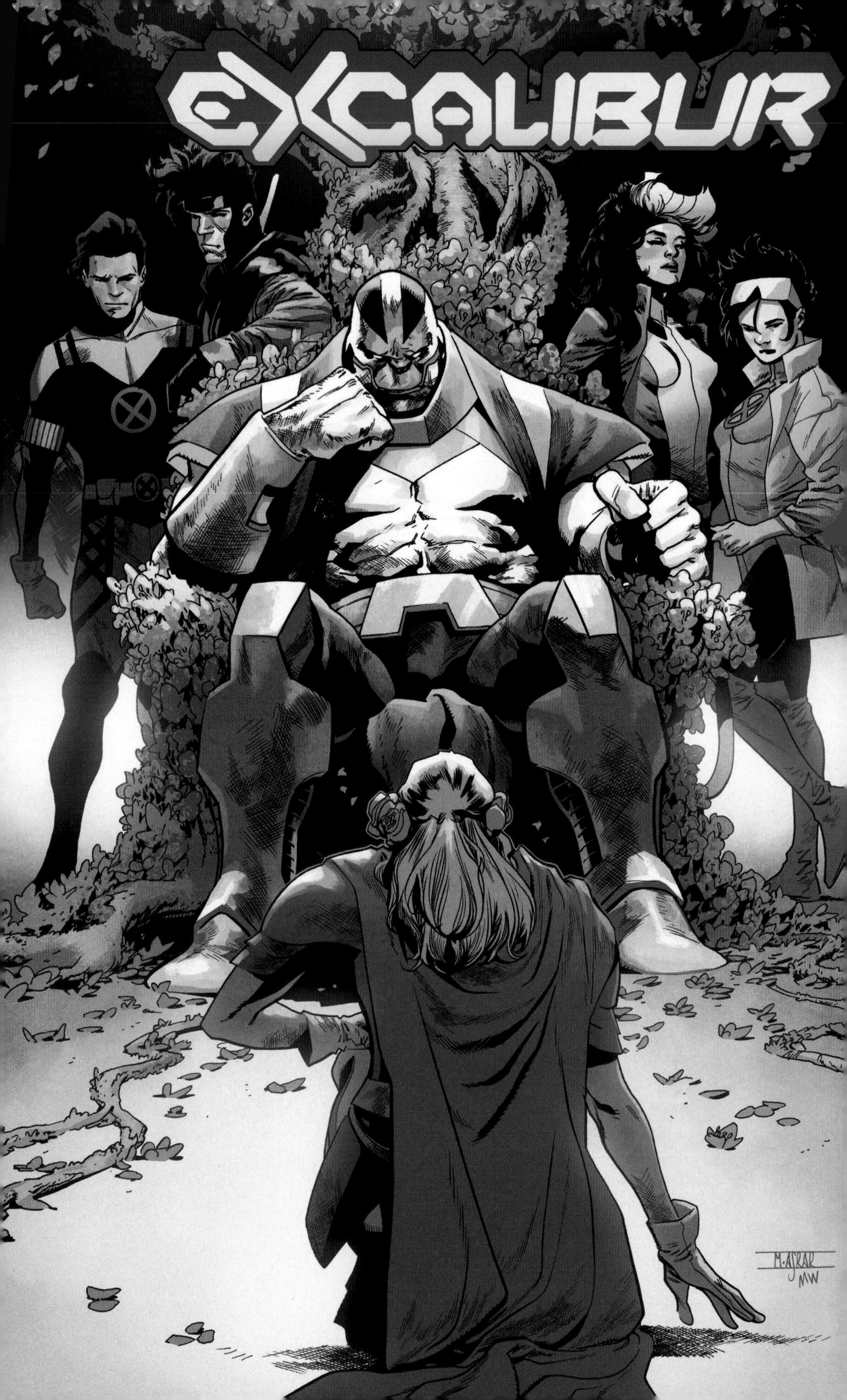
EXCALIBUR
M.ASRAR
MW

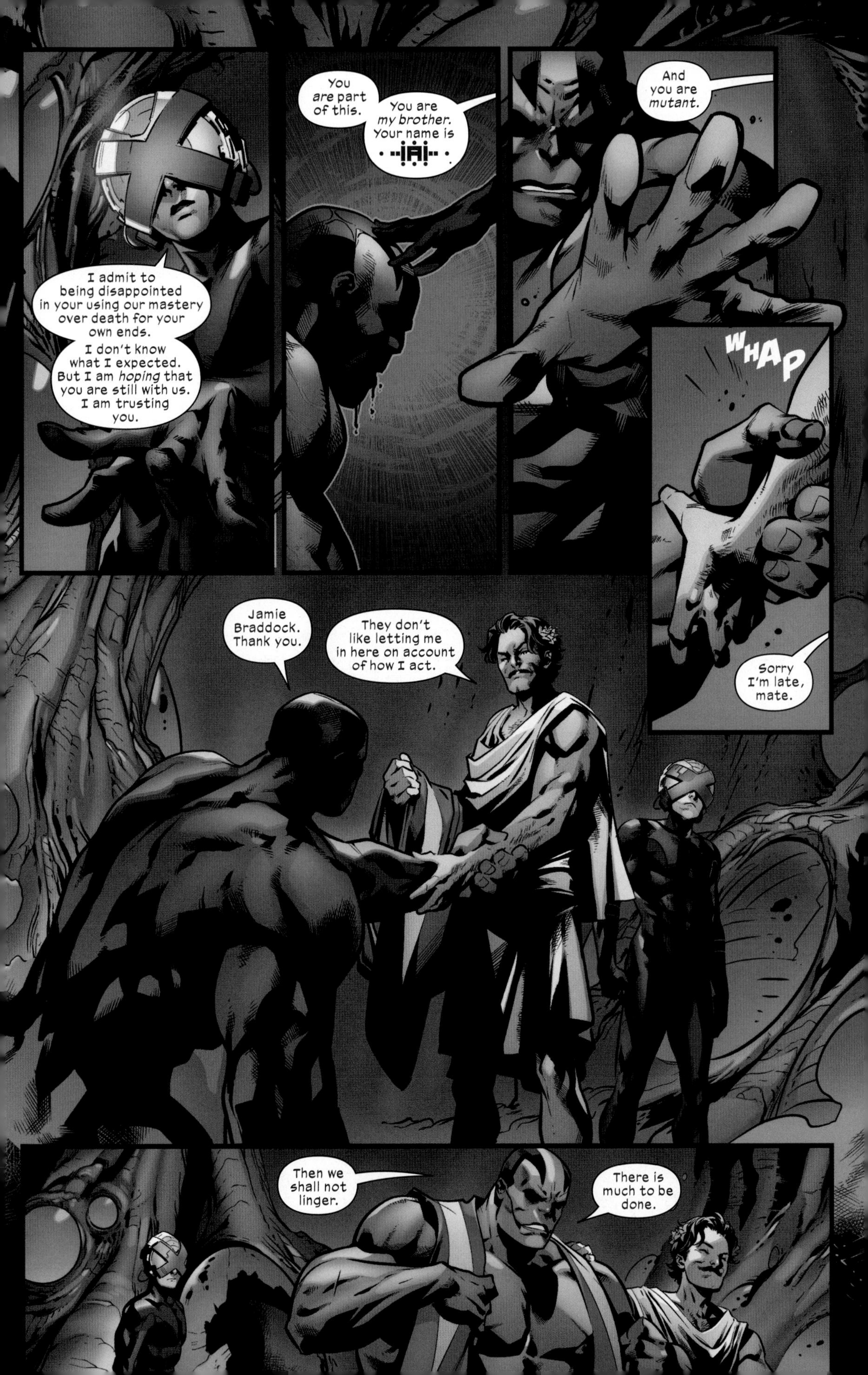
I admit to being disappointed in your using our mastery over death for your own ends.
I don't know what I expected. But I am *hoping* that you are still with us. I am trusting you.
You *are* part of this.
You are *my brother.* Your name is
And you are *mutant.*
WHAP
Sorry I'm late, mate.
Jamie Braddock. Thank you.
They don't like letting me in here on account of how I act.
Then we shall not linger.
There is much to be done.

CONQUERED AVALON

STARLIGHT CITADEL
WHITE WITCH FORCES
CONTESTED TERRITORY
KOBOLD BATTALION
CONQUERED AVALON
CASTLE CAMELOT

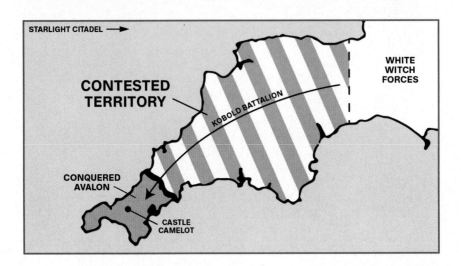

– 'Conquered Avalon' represents areas formerly under the rule of Morgan Le Fay, now held by King Jamie ("the Mad"). Some areas formerly under the rule of Queen Regent Le Fay are not currently under witchbreed control.

– While Kobold Battalion made it far enough forward to strike at Castle Camelot, the forces as a whole have not made it beyond the indicated line. For more on the geographical choke point marking the end of the White Witch's push forward and the official and brutal losses suffered there, see "The Battle of Imbolc Eve."

– While this map shows movement and placement of forces, Otherworld is a place of constant flux due to the thoughts and ideas that form it. Consider, then, the strength of a reality-warping Omega level mutant such as our Monarch.

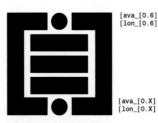

[ava_[0.6]
[lon_[0.6]

[ava_[0.X]
[lon_[0.X]

THE BEGINNING OF THE END

Betsy Braddock holds the title of Captain Britain! She and her team must defend Britain -- and all of Earth -- from mystical threats, like evil sorceress Morgan Le Fay, who is laying siege to Otherworld, attempting to claim it for her own... having already possessed Betsy's twin brother Brian. While the EXCALIBUR team managed to hold off a wave of monsters and complete the ritual to access Otherworld, it came at great cost -- a recently-awakened Rogue draining Apocalypse of his life force!

Apocalypse

Jamie
Braddock

Morgan
Le Fay

Captain
Britain

Shogo

Jubilee

Gambit

Rogue

Rictor

Brian
Braddock

[ava_[0.6]...]
[lon_[0.6]...]

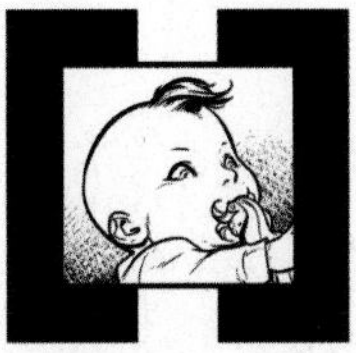

[All....HAIL.]

[00_so_below_X]
[00_as_above_X]

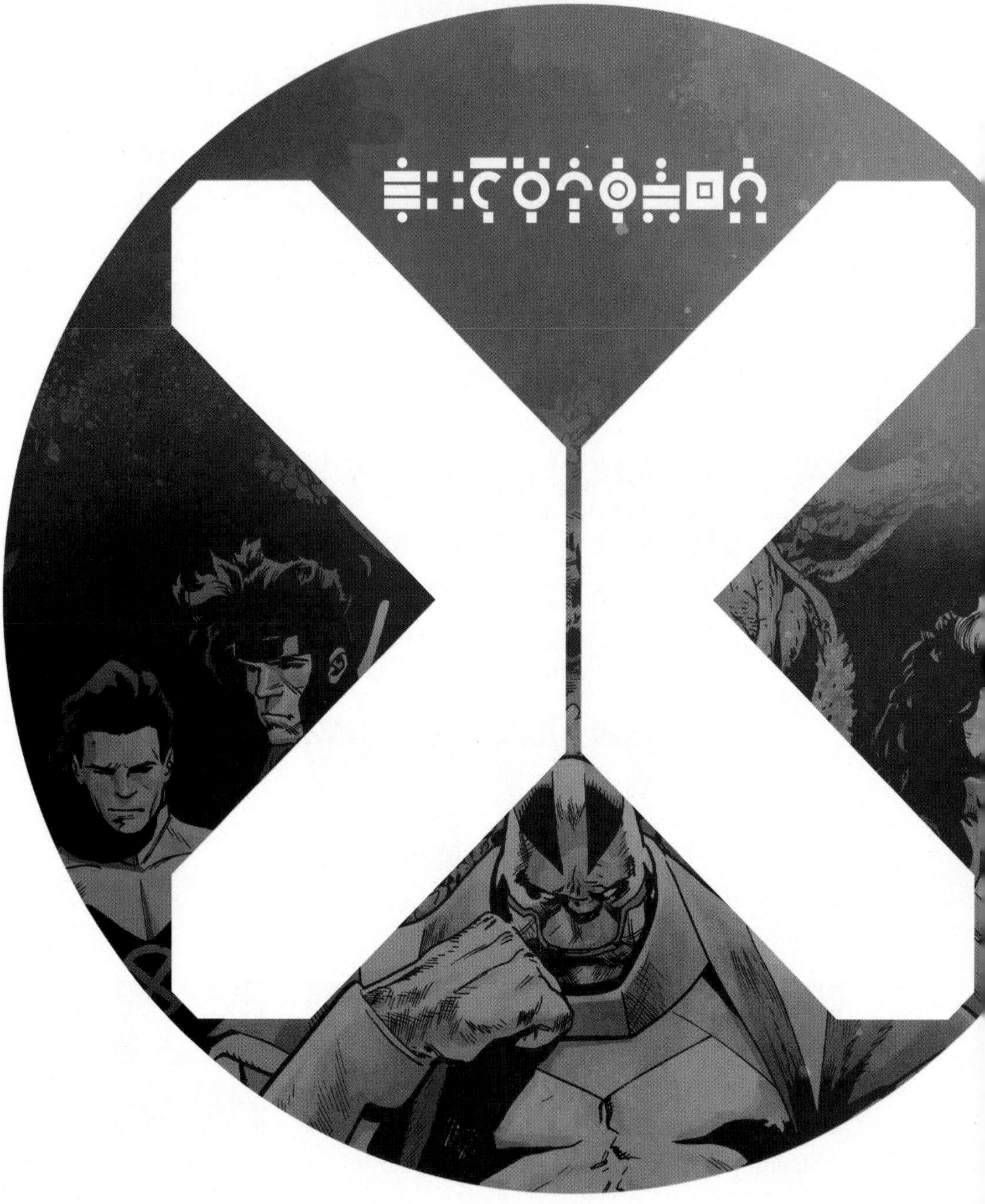

[00_so_below_X]
[00_as_above_X]

TINI HOWARD....................................[WRITER]
MARCUS TO......................................[ARTIST]
ERICK ARCINIEGA.........................[COLOR ARTIST]
VC's CORY PETIT.............................[LETTERER]
TOM MULLER.....................................[DESIGN]

MAHMUD ASRAR & MATTHEW WILSON...........[COVER ARTISTS]

TOMM COKER & MICHAEL GARLAND; MIKE MCKONE & MORRY HOLLOWELL.......................[VARIANT COVER ARTISTS]

NICK RUSSELL..............................[PRODUCTION]

JONATHAN HICKMAN............................[HEAD OF X]
ANNALISE BISSA......................[ASSISTANT EDITOR]
JORDAN D. WHITE...............................[EDITOR]
C.B. CEBULSKI.........................[EDITOR IN CHIEF]

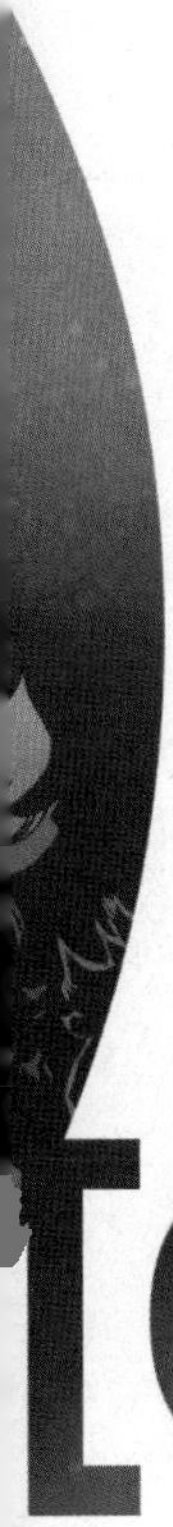

[06] EXCALIBUR

[ISSUE SIX]....VERSE VI: WATCH THE THRONE

[00_so_below_X]
[00_as_above_X]

[00_00.....0]
[00_00.....6]

[00_greater_]
[00_secrets_]

[00________]

[00_exist___]

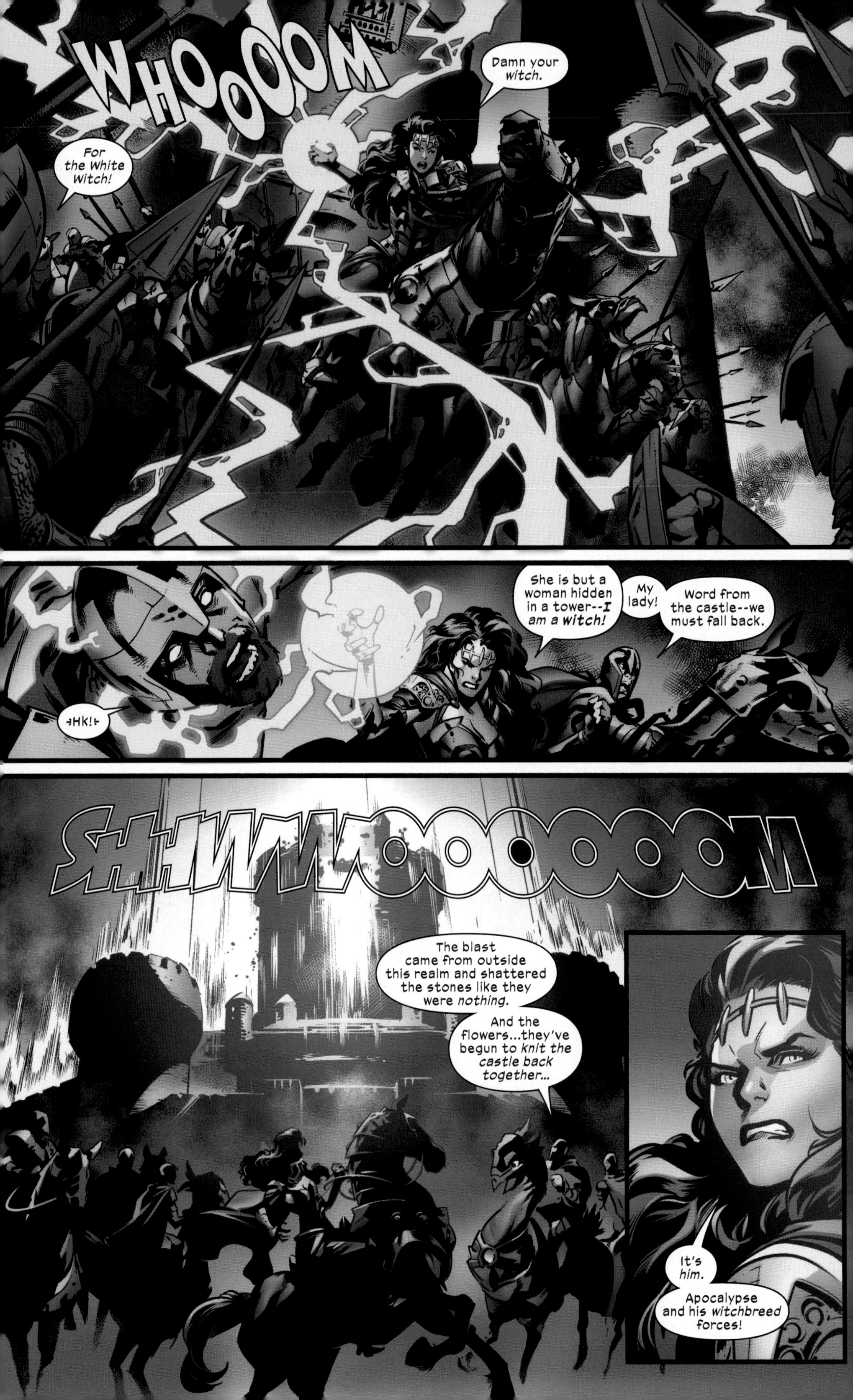
WHOOOOM
Damn your witch.
For the White Witch!
She is but a woman hidden in a tower--I am a witch!
My lady!
Word from the castle--we must fall back.
HK!
SHHWWOOOOOOOM
The blast came from outside this realm and shattered the stones like they were nothing.
And the flowers...they've begun to knit the castle back together...
It's him.
Apocalypse and his witchbreed forces!

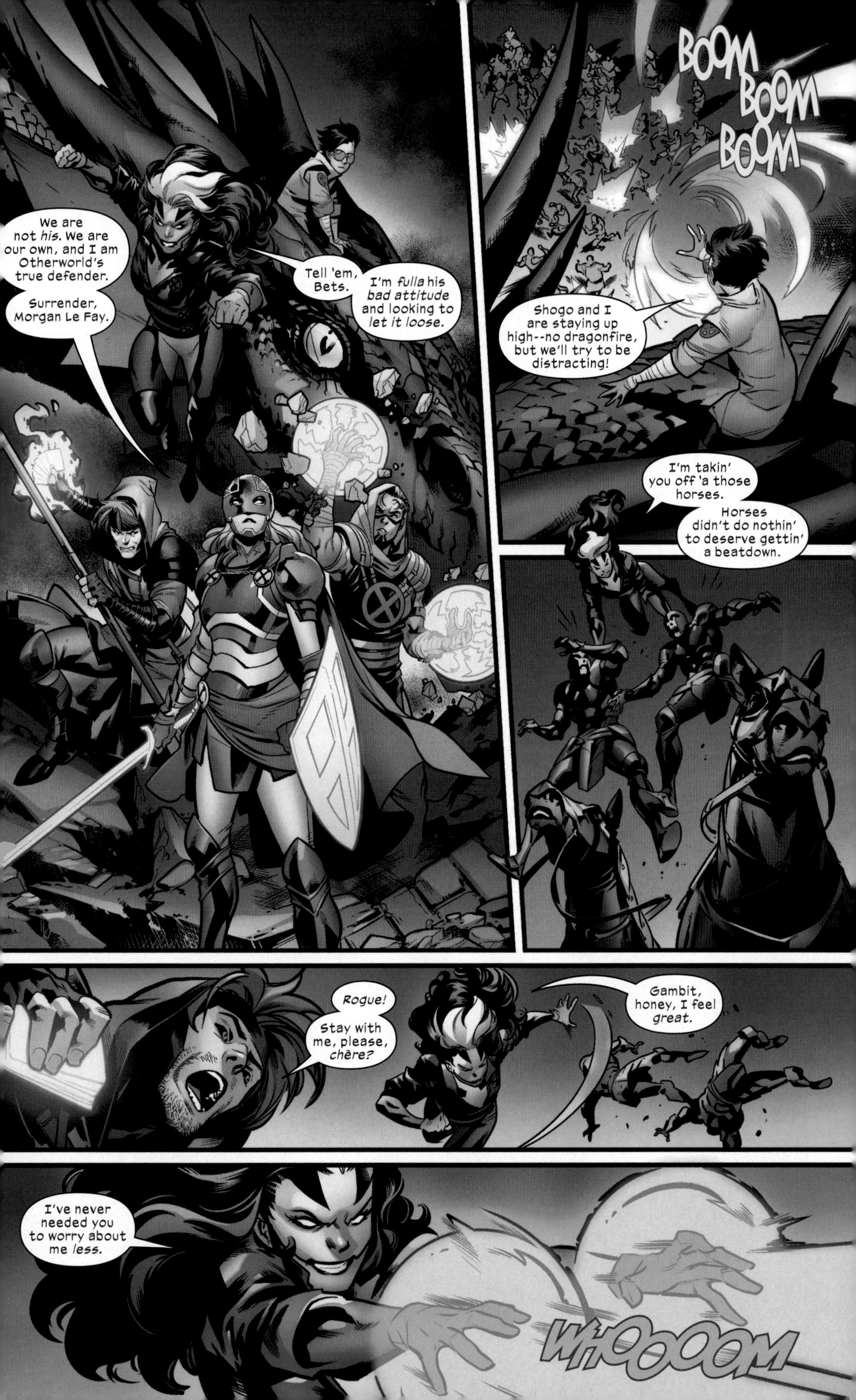
We are not *his*. We are our own, and I am Otherworld's true defender.
Surrender, Morgan Le Fay.
Tell 'em, Bets.
I'm *fulla* his *bad attitude* and looking to *let it loose*.
BOOM BOOM BOOM
Shogo and I are staying up high--no dragonfire, but we'll try to be distracting!
I'm takin' you off 'a those horses.
Horses didn't do nothin' to deserve gettin' a beatdown.
Rogue!
Stay with me, please, *chère?*
Gambit, honey, I feel *great*.
I've never needed you to worry about me *less*.
WHOOOOM

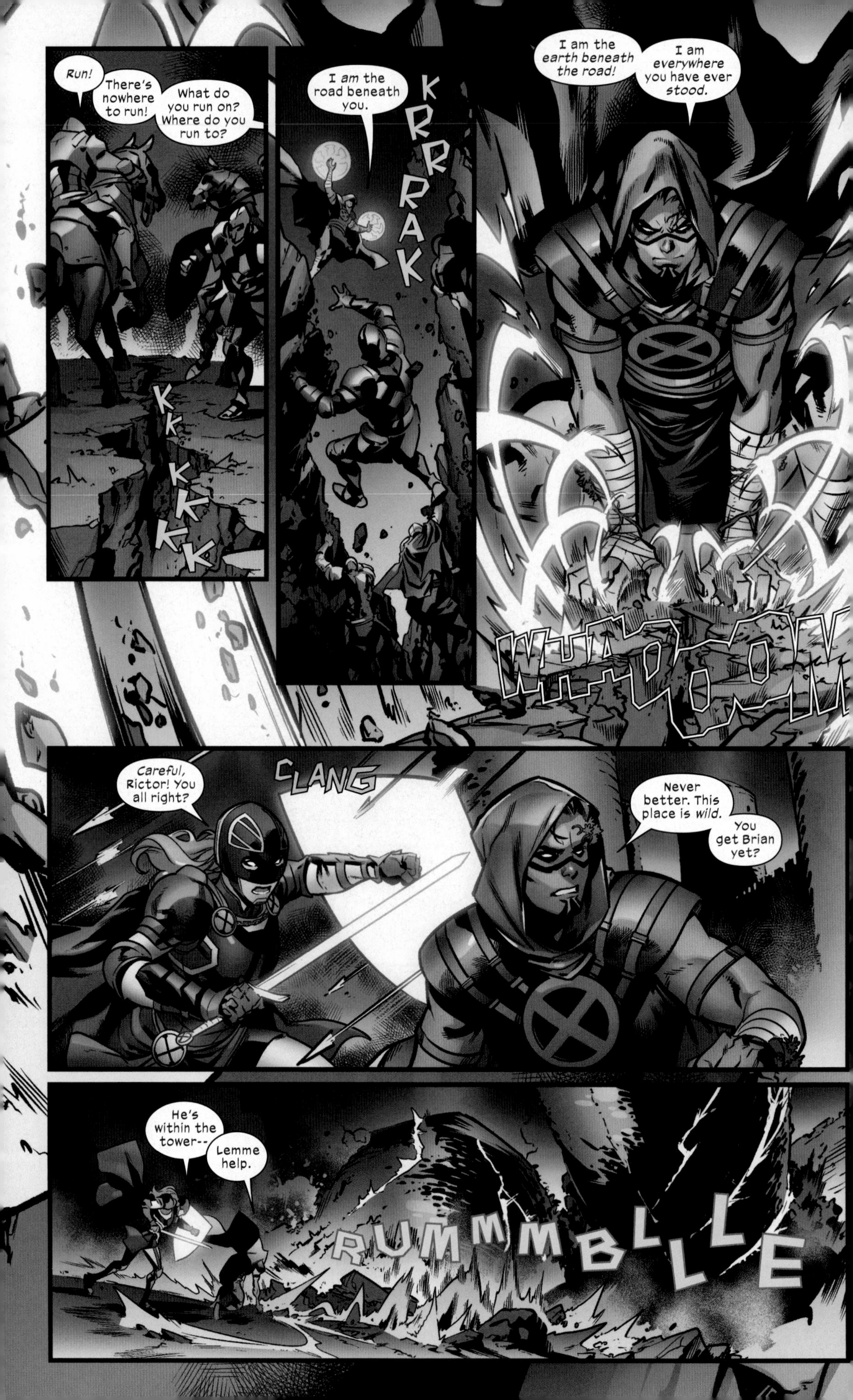
Run!
There's nowhere to run!
What do you run on? Where do you run to?
KKKKKKK
I *am* the road beneath you.
KRRRAK
I am the *earth beneath the road!*
I am *everywhere* you have ever *stood.*
WHOOOOM
Careful, Rictor! You all right?
CLANG
Never better. This place is *wild.*
You get Brian yet?
He's within the tower--
Lemme help.
RUMMMMBLLLE

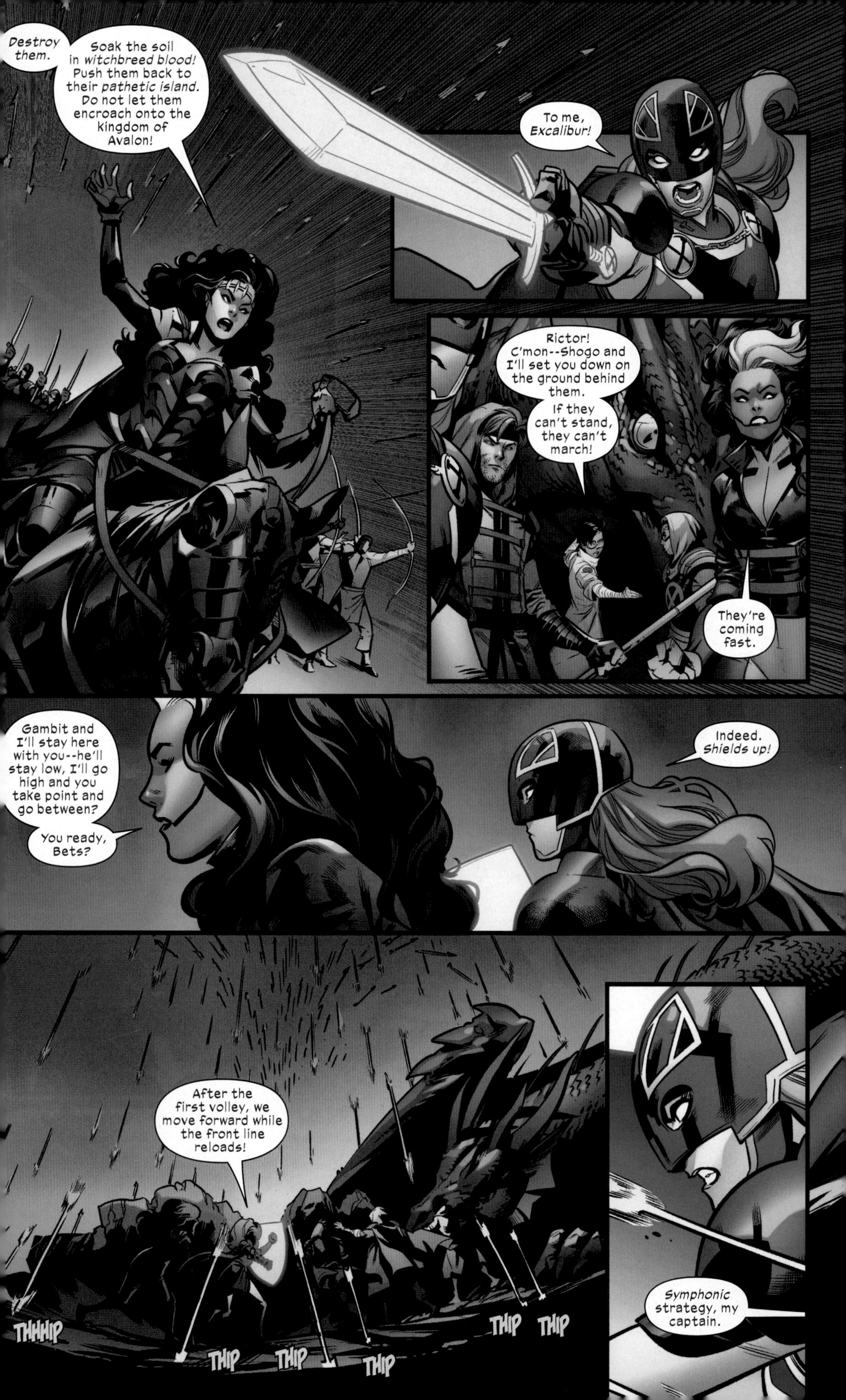

Destroy them.
Soak the soil in *witchbreed blood!* Push them back to their *pathetic island.* Do not let them encroach onto the kingdom of Avalon!
To me, *Excalibur!*
Rictor! C'mon--Shogo and I'll set you down on the ground behind them.
If they can't stand, they can't march!
They're coming fast.
Gambit and I'll stay here with you--he'll stay low, I'll go high and you take point and go between?
You ready, Bets?
Indeed. *Shields up!*
After the first volley, we move forward while the front line reloads!
THHHIP
THIP
THIP
THIP
THIP
THIP
Symphonic strategy, my captain.

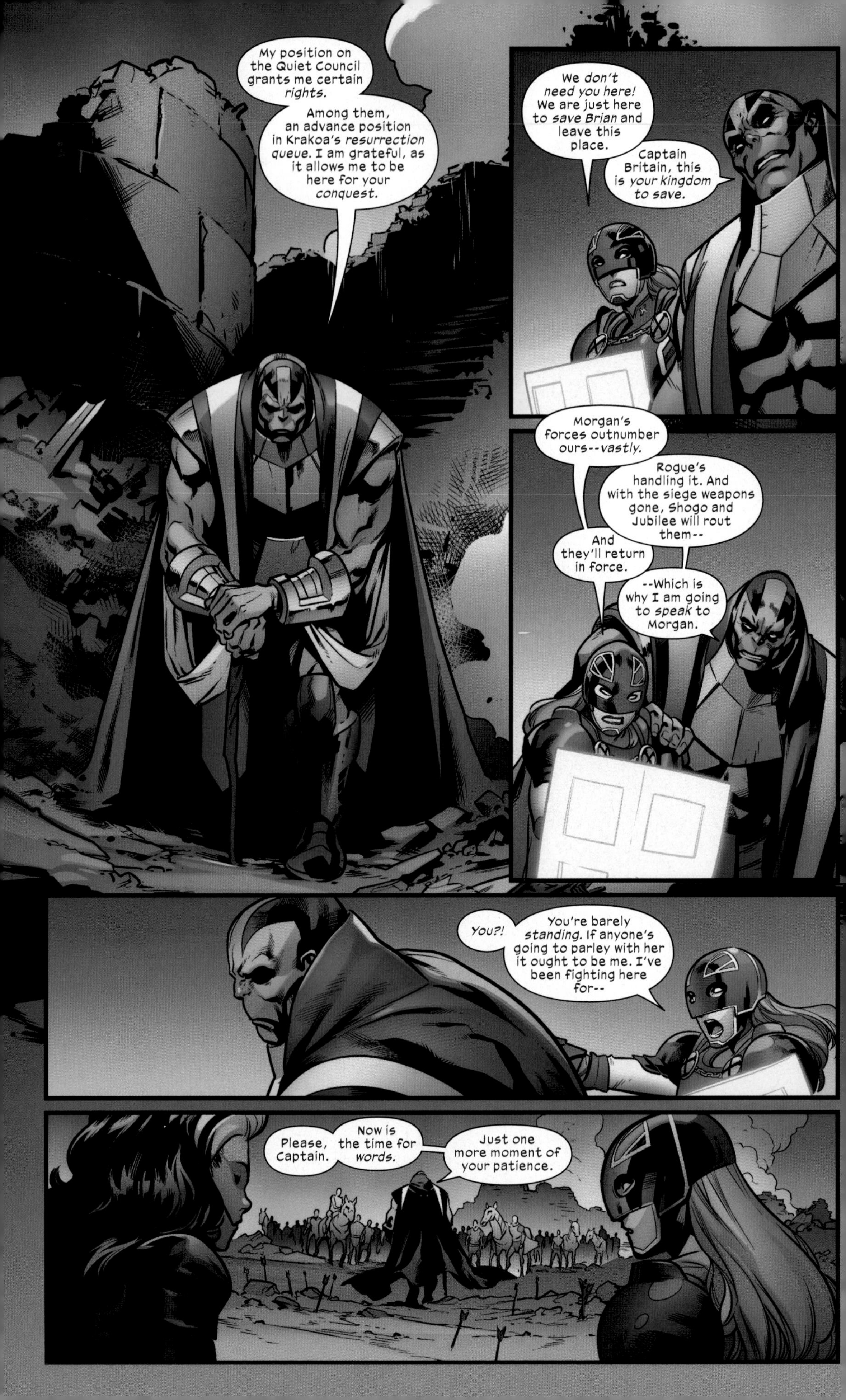
My position on the Quiet Council grants me certain *rights.*
Among them, an advance position in Krakoa's *resurrection queue.* I am grateful, as it allows me to be here for your *conquest.*
We *don't need you here!* We are just here to *save Brian* and leave this place.
Captain Britain, this is *your kingdom to save.*
Morgan's forces outnumber ours--*vastly.*
Rogue's handling it. And with the siege weapons gone, Shogo and Jubilee will rout them--
And they'll return in force.
--Which is why I am going to *speak* to Morgan.
You?!
You're barely *standing.* If anyone's going to parley with her it ought to be me. I've been fighting here for--
Please, Captain.
Now is the time for *words.*
Just one more moment of your patience.

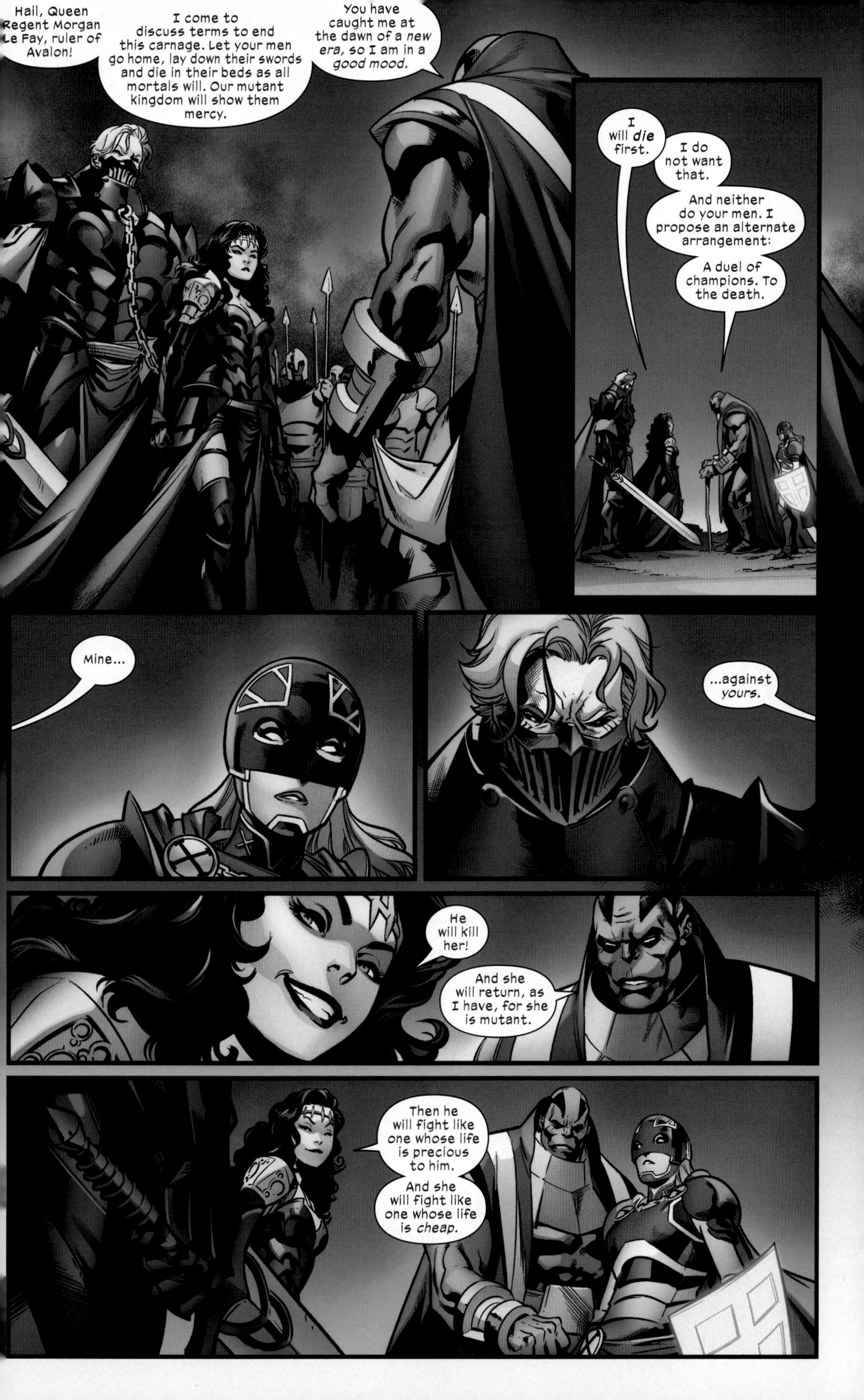
Hail, Queen Regent Morgan Le Fay, ruler of Avalon!
I come to discuss terms to end this carnage. Let your men go home, lay down their swords and die in their beds as all mortals will. Our mutant kingdom will show them mercy.
You have caught me at the dawn of a *new era,* so I am in a *good mood.*
I will *die* first.
I do not want that.
And neither do your men. I propose an alternate arrangement:
A duel of champions. To the death.
Mine...
...against *yours.*
He will kill her!
And she will return, as I have, for she is mutant.
Then he will fight like one whose life is precious to him.
And she will fight like one whose life is *cheap.*

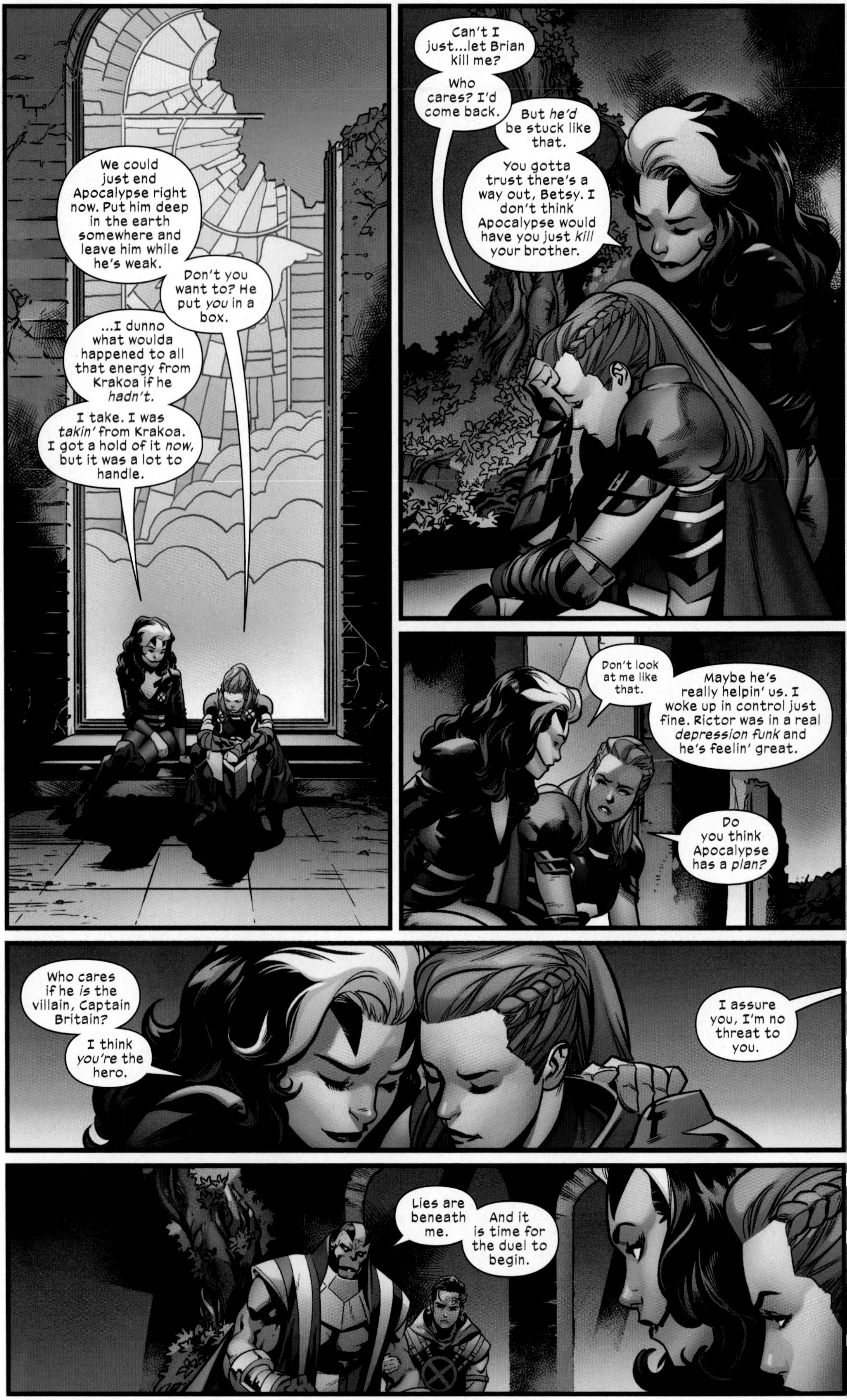
We could just end Apocalypse right now. Put him deep in the earth somewhere and leave him while he's weak.
Don't you want to? He put *you* in a box.
...I dunno what woulda happened to all that energy from Krakoa if he *hadn't.*
I take. I was *takin'* from Krakoa. I got a hold of it *now,* but it was a lot to handle.
Can't I just...let Brian kill me?
Who cares? I'd come back.
But *he'd* be stuck like that.
You gotta trust there's a way out, Betsy. I don't think Apocalypse would have you just *kill* your brother.
Don't look at me like that.
Maybe he's really helpin' us. I woke up in control just fine. Rictor was in a real *depression funk* and he's feelin' great.
Do you think Apocalypse has a *plan?*
Who cares if he *is* the villain, Captain Britain?
I think *you're* the hero.
I assure you, I'm no threat to you.
Lies are beneath me.
And it is time for the duel to begin.

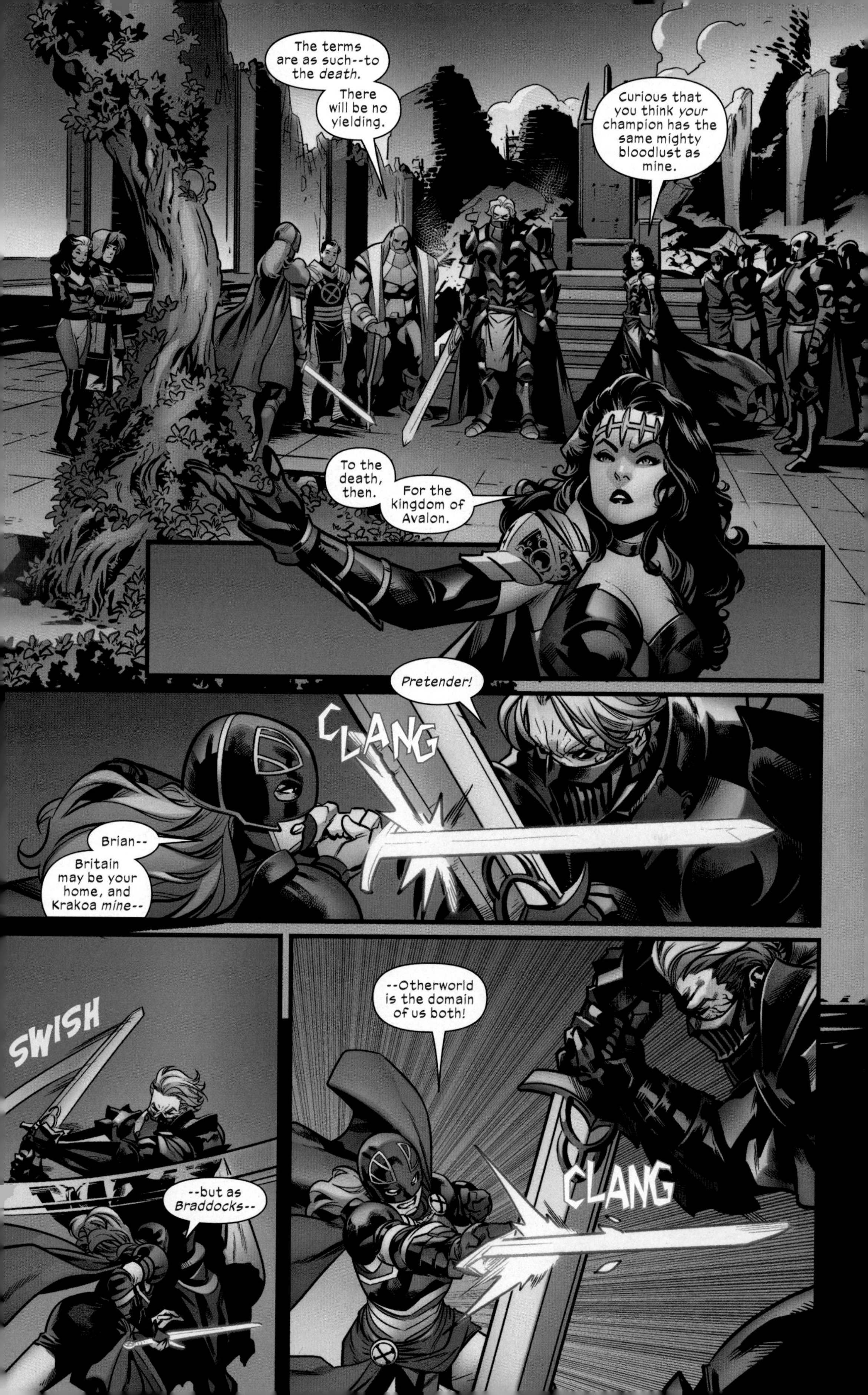
The terms are as such--to the *death*.
There will be no yielding.
Curious that you think *your* champion has the same mighty bloodlust as mine.
To the death, then.
For the kingdom of Avalon.
Pretender!
CLANG
Brian--
Britain may be your home, and Krakoa *mine*--
SWISH
--but as *Braddocks*--
--Otherworld is the domain of us both!
CLANG

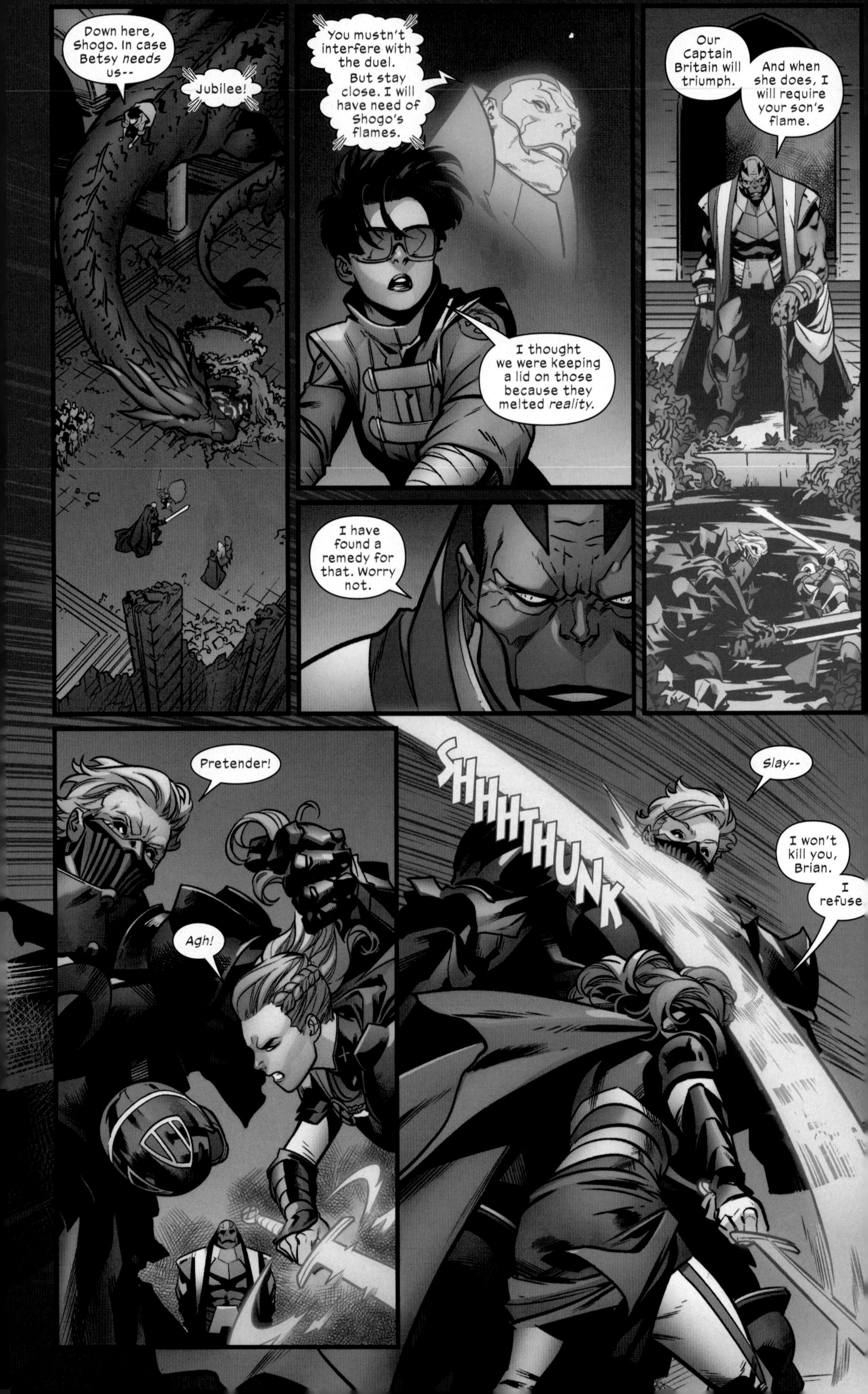

Down here, Shogo. In case Betsy *needs* us--
Jubilee!
You mustn't interfere with the duel. But stay close. I will have need of Shogo's flames.
I thought we were keeping a lid on those because they melted *reality*.
I have found a remedy for that. Worry not.
Our Captain Britain will triumph.
And when she does, I will require your son's flame.
Pretender!
Agh!
SHHHTHUNK
Slay--
I won't kill you, Brian.
I refuse

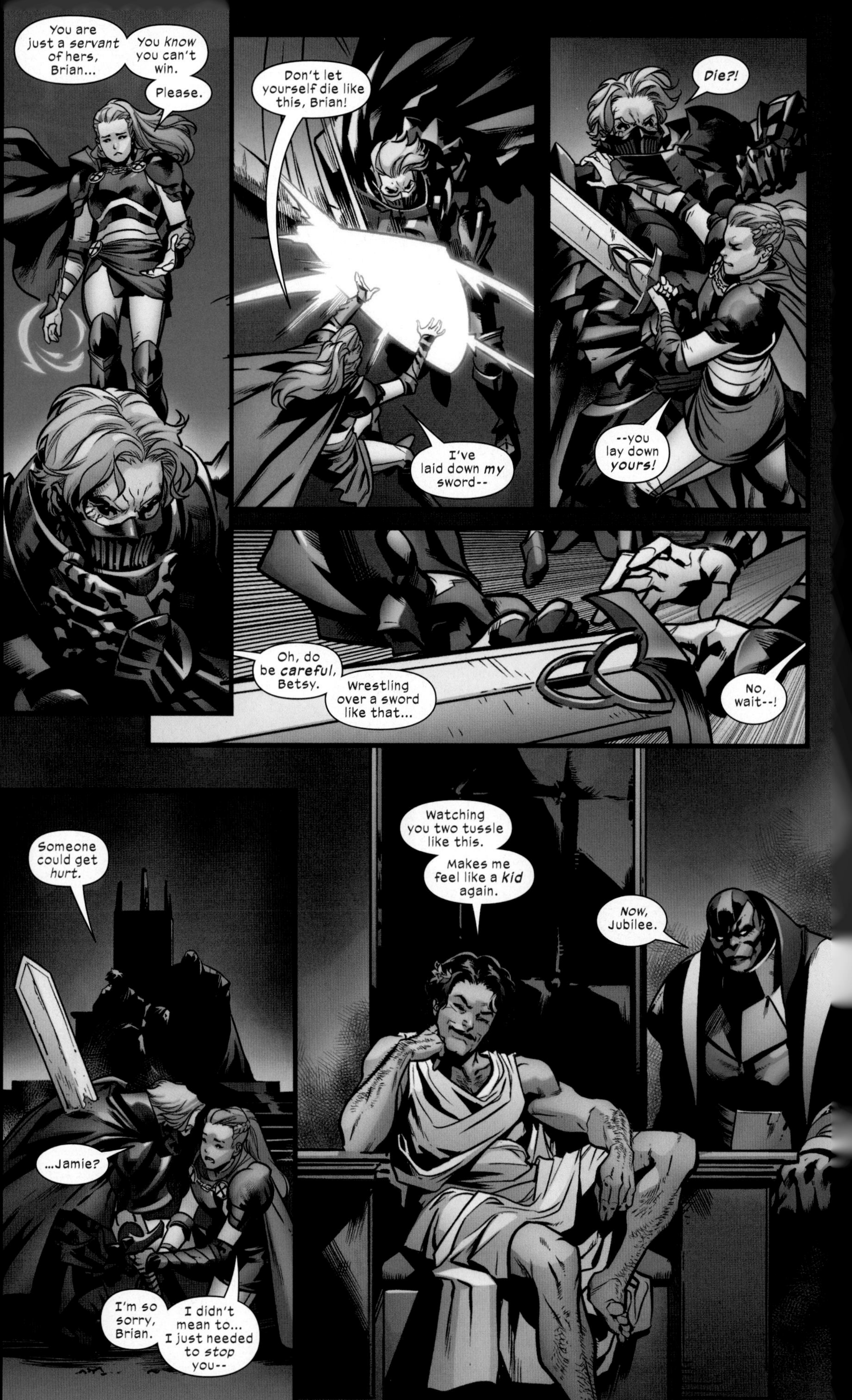

You are just a servant of hers, Brian...
You know you can't win.
Please.
Don't let yourself die like this, Brian!
I've laid down my sword--
Die?!
--you lay down yours!
Oh, do be careful, Betsy.
Wrestling over a sword like that...
No, wait--!
Someone could get hurt.
...Jamie?
I'm so sorry, Brian.
I didn't mean to... I just needed to stop you--
Watching you two tussle like this.
Makes me feel like a kid again.
Now, Jubilee.

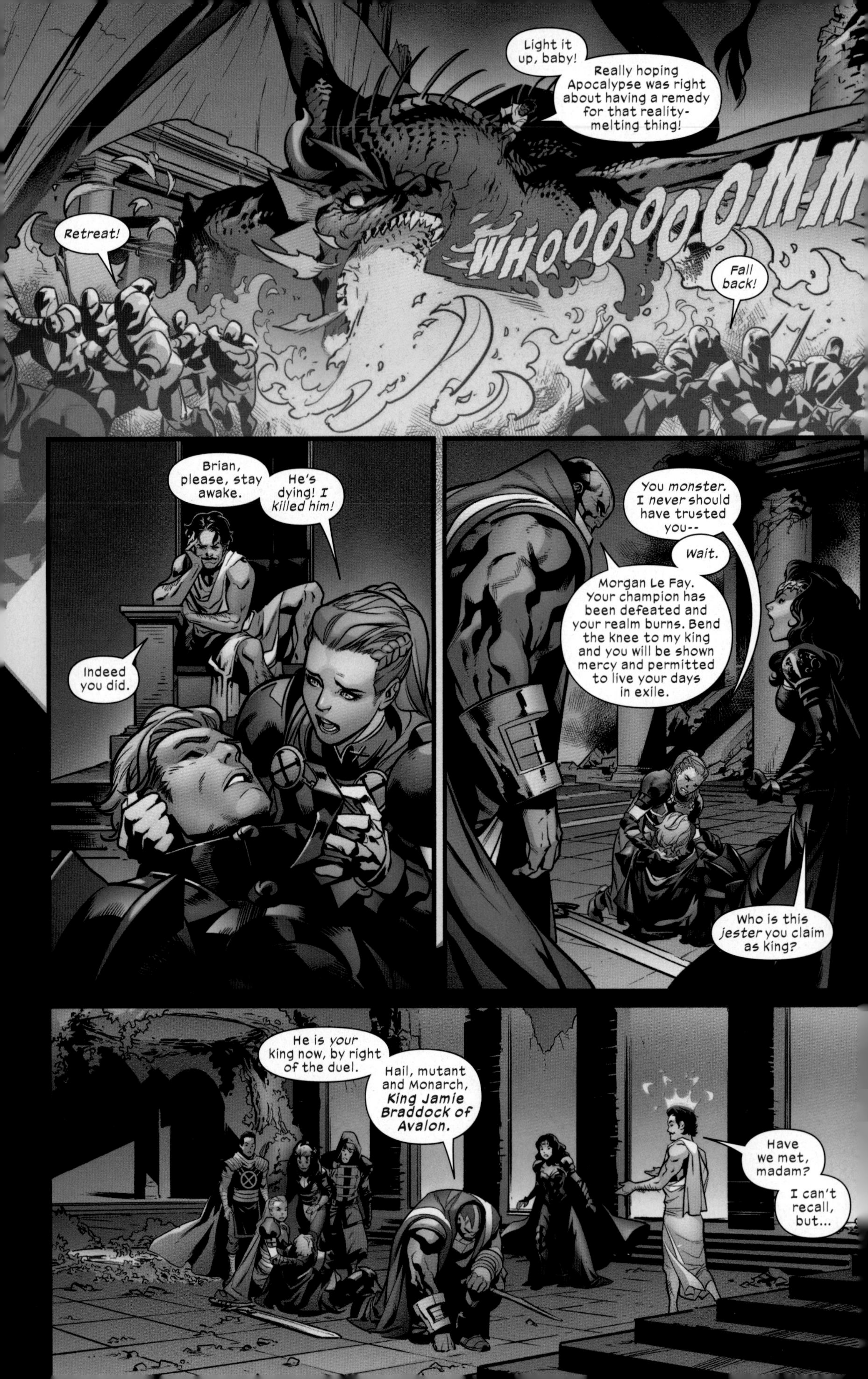
Light it up, baby!
Really hoping Apocalypse was right about having a remedy for that reality-melting thing!
Retreat!
WHOOOOOOOMM
Fall back!
Brian, please, stay awake.
He's dying! I killed him!
Indeed you did.
You monster. I never should have trusted you--
Wait.
Morgan Le Fay. Your champion has been defeated and your realm burns. Bend the knee to my king and you will be shown mercy and permitted to live your days in exile.
Who is this jester you claim as king?
He is your king now, by right of the duel.
Hail, mutant and Monarch, King Jamie Braddock of Avalon.
Have we met, madam?
I can't recall, but...

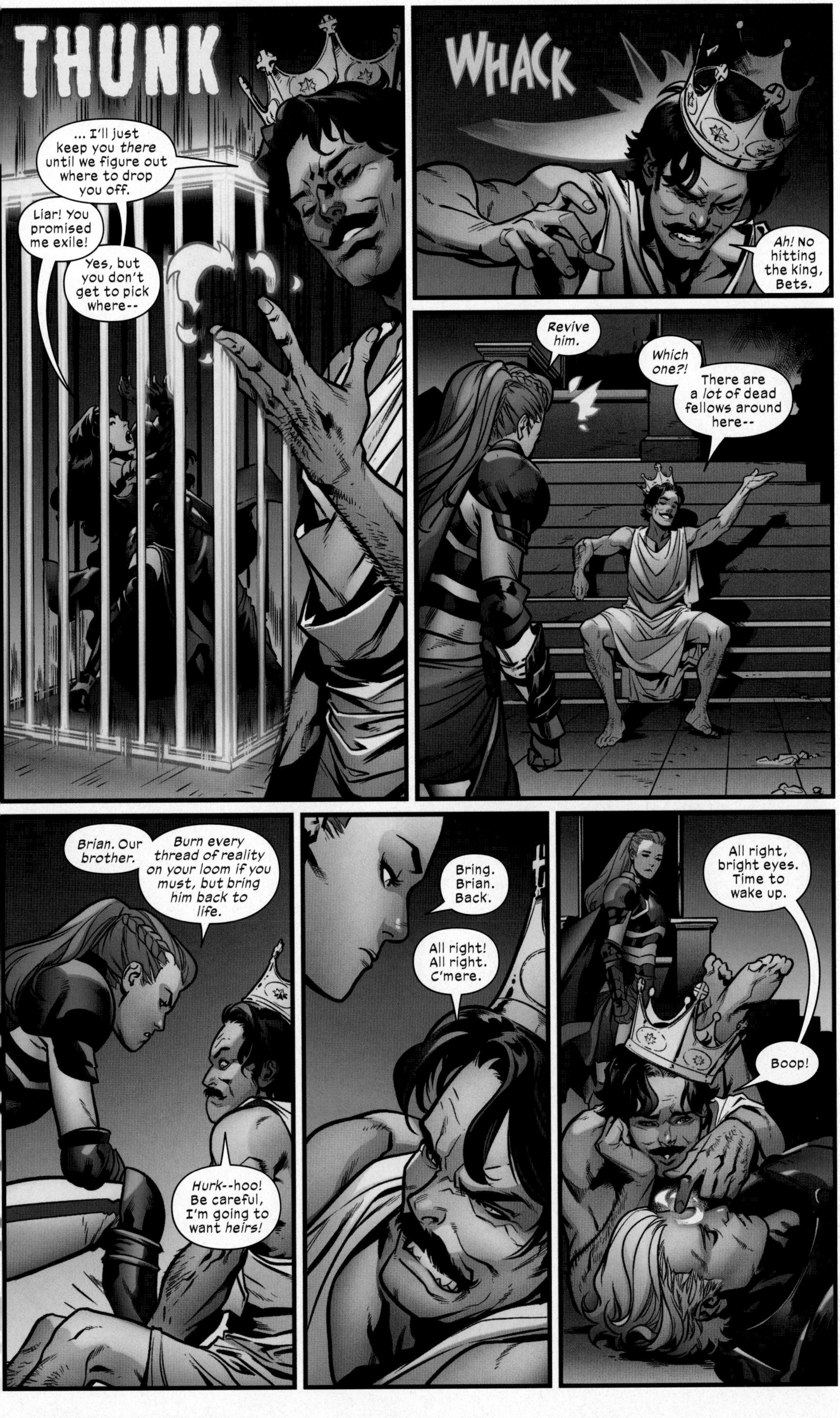
THUNK
... I'll just keep you *there* until we figure out where to drop you off.
Liar! You promised me exile!
Yes, but you don't get to pick where--
WHACK
Ah! No hitting the king, Bets.
Revive him.
Which one?!
There are a *lot* of dead fellows around here--
Brian. Our brother.
Burn every thread of reality on your loom if you must, but bring him back to life.
Hurk--hoo! Be careful, I'm going to want *heirs!*
Bring. Brian. Back.
All right! All right. C'mere.
All right, bright eyes. Time to wake up.
Boop!

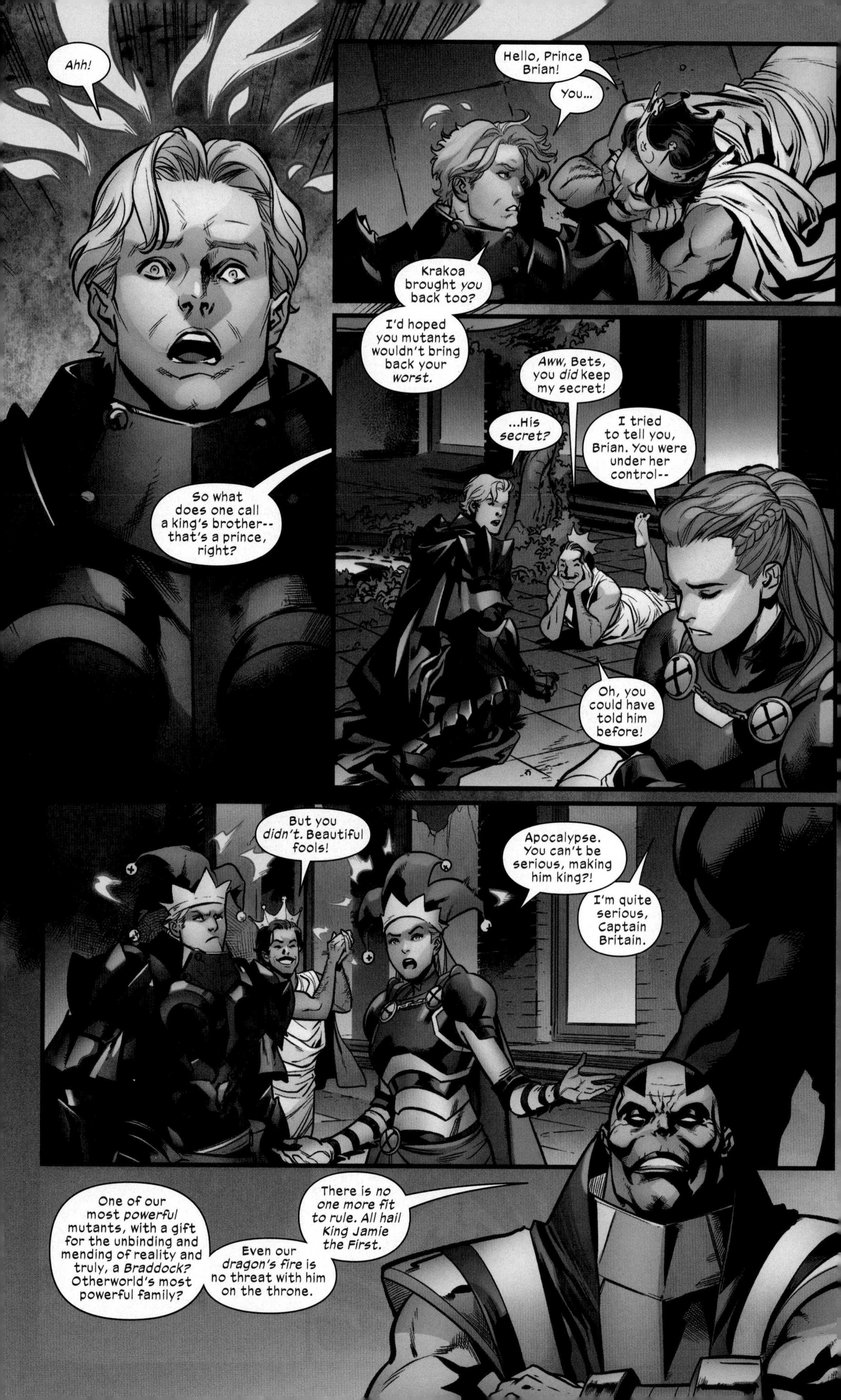
Ahh!
Hello, Prince Brian!
You...
Krakoa brought *you* back too?
So what does one call a king's brother--that's a prince, right?
I'd hoped you mutants wouldn't bring back your *worst*.
Aww, Bets, you *did* keep my secret!
...His *secret?*
I tried to tell you, Brian. You were under her control--
Oh, you could have told him before!
But you *didn't*. Beautiful fools!
Apocalypse. You can't be serious, making him king?!
I'm quite serious, Captain Britain.
One of our most *powerful* mutants, with a gift for the unbinding and mending of reality and truly, a *Braddock?* Otherworld's most powerful family?
Even our *dragon's fire* is no threat with him on the throne.
There is no one more fit to rule. All hail King Jamie the First.

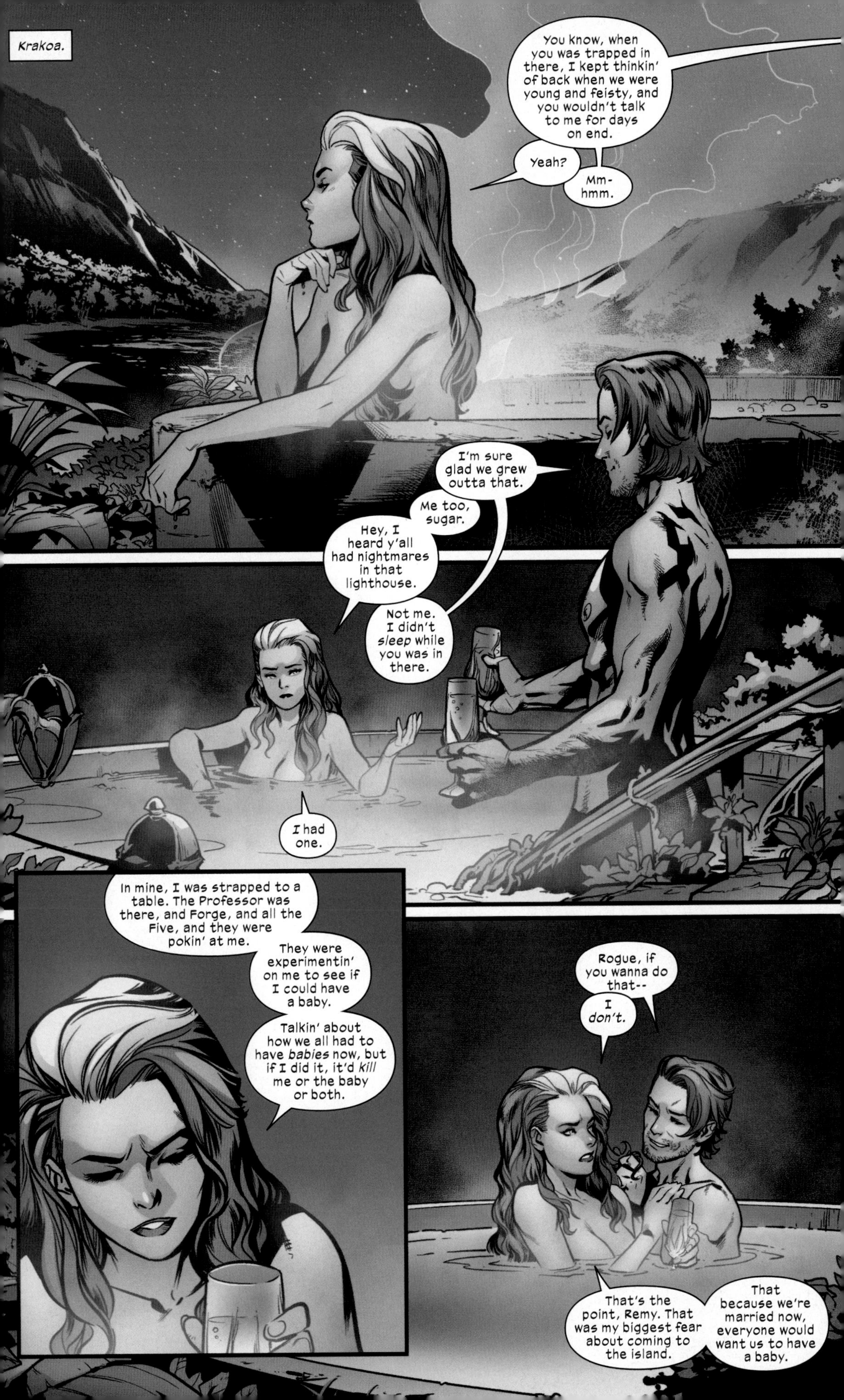
Krakoa.
You know, when you was trapped in there, I kept thinkin' of back when we were young and feisty, and you wouldn't talk to me for days on end.
Yeah?
Mm-hmm.
I'm sure glad we grew outta that.
Me too, sugar.
Hey, I heard y'all had nightmares in that lighthouse.
Not me. I didn't sleep while you was in there.
I had one.
In mine, I was strapped to a table. The Professor was there, and Forge, and all the Five, and they were pokin' at me.
They were experimentin' on me to see if I could have a baby.
Talkin' about how we all had to have babies now, but if I did it, it'd kill me or the baby or both.
Rogue, if you wanna do that--
I don't.
That's the point, Remy. That was my biggest fear about coming to the island.
That because we're married now, everyone would want us to have a baby.

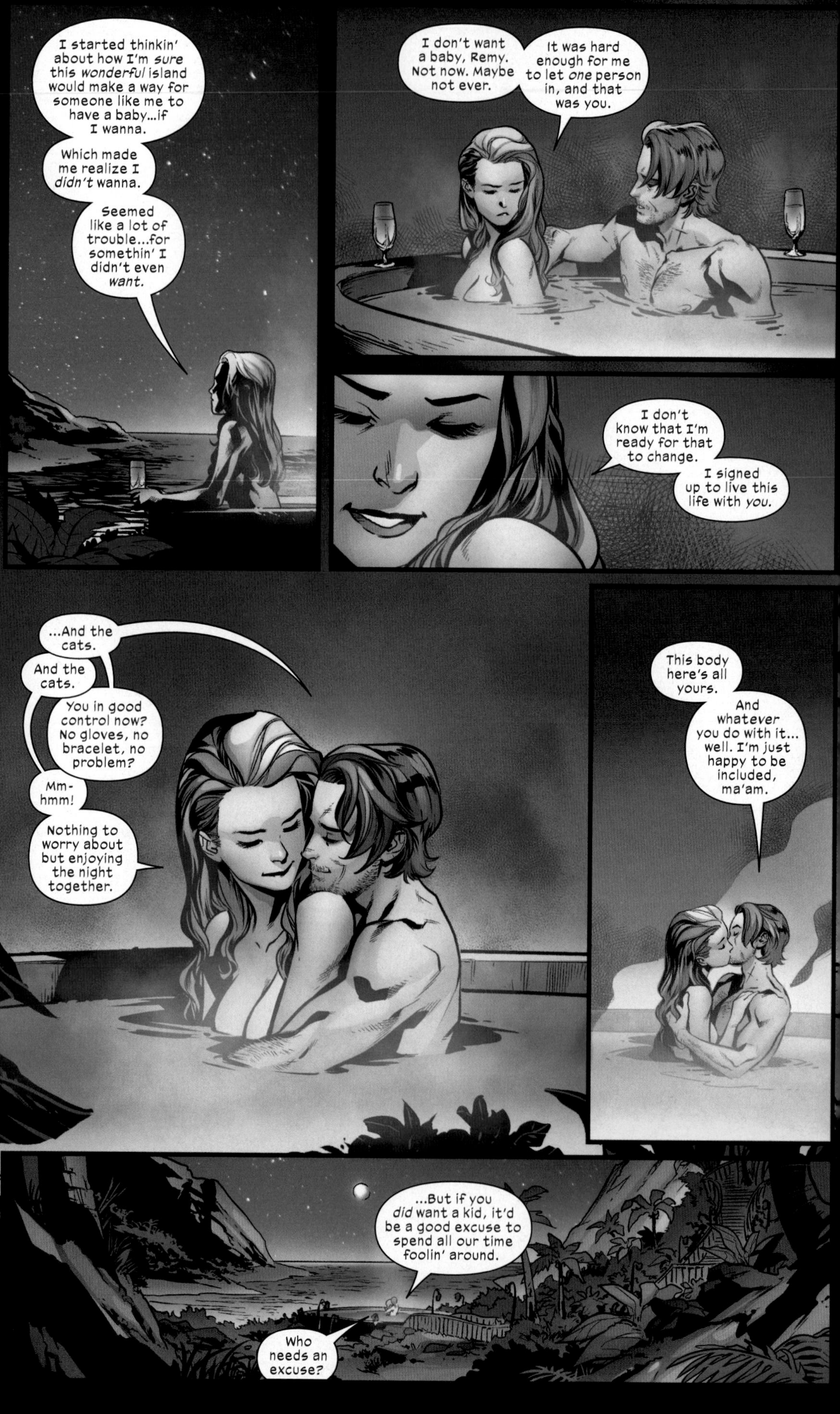
I started thinkin' about how I'm *sure* this *wonderful* island would make a way for someone like me to have a baby...if I wanna.
Which made me realize I *didn't* wanna.
Seemed like a lot of trouble...for somethin' I didn't even *want.*
I don't want a baby, Remy. Not now. Maybe not ever.
It was hard enough for me to let *one* person in, and that was you.
I don't know that I'm ready for that to change.
I signed up to live this life with *you.*
...And the cats.
And the cats.
You in good control now? No gloves, no bracelet, no problem?
Mm-hmm!
Nothing to worry about but enjoying the night together.
This body here's all yours.
And what*ever* you do with it... well. I'm just happy to be included, ma'am.
...But if you *did* want a kid, it'd be a good excuse to spend all our time foolin' around.
Who needs an excuse?

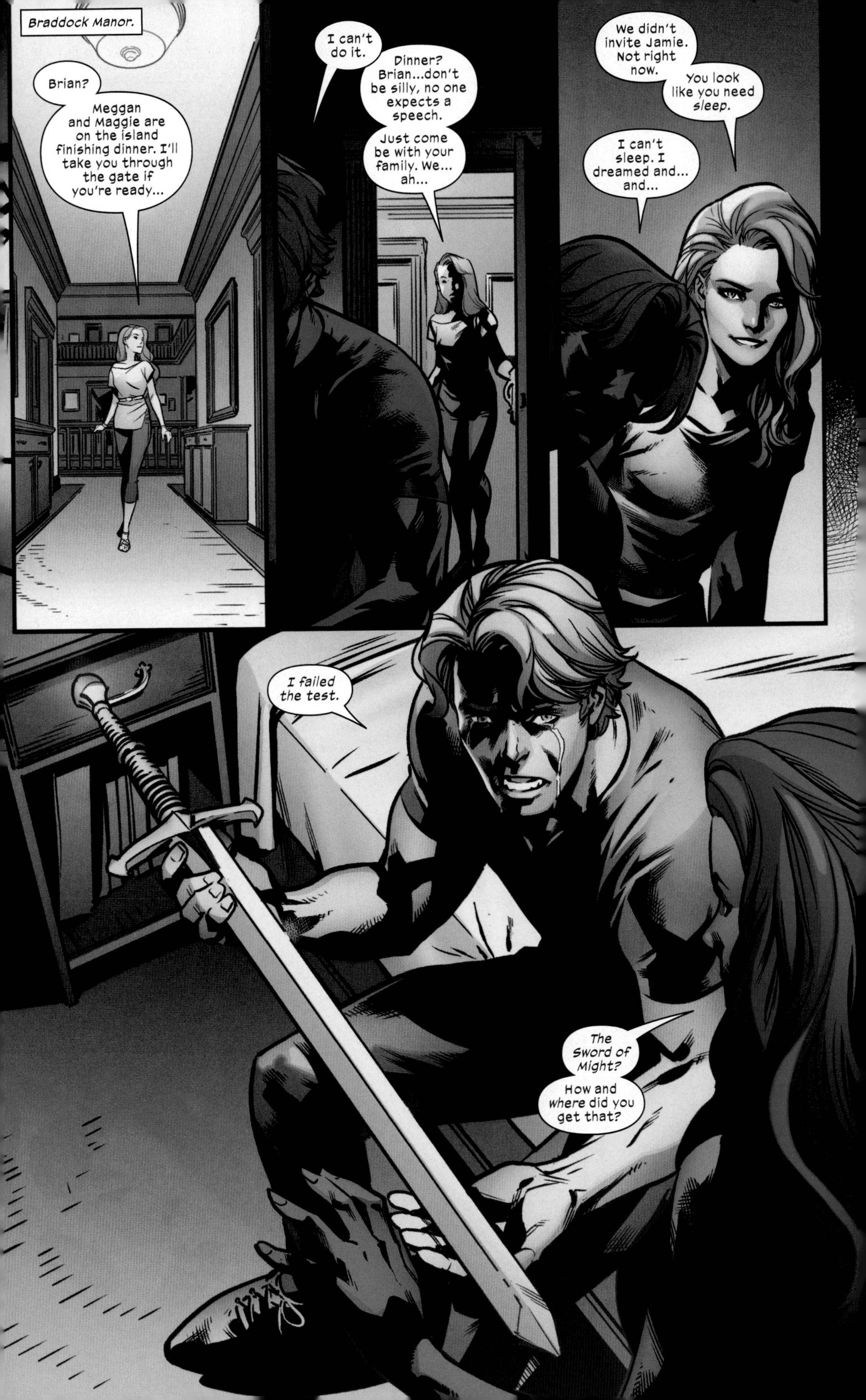
Braddock Manor.
Brian?
Meggan and Maggie are on the island finishing dinner. I'll take you through the gate if you're ready...
I can't do it.
Dinner? Brian...don't be silly, no one expects a speech.
Just come be with your family. We... ah...
We didn't invite Jamie. Not right now.
You look like you need *sleep.*
I can't sleep. I dreamed and... and...
I failed the test.
The Sword of Might?
How and where did you get that?

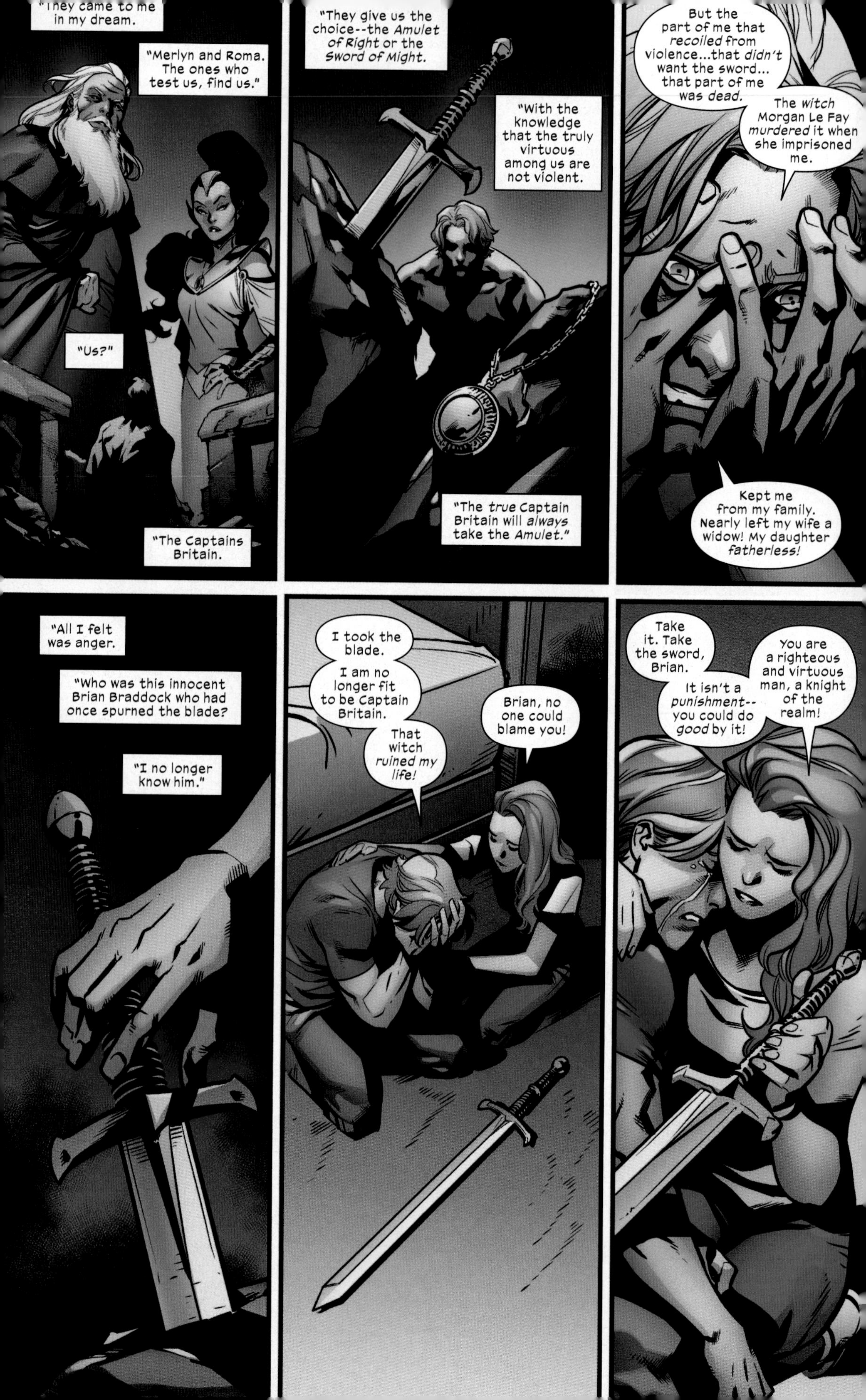
"They came to me in my dream.
"Merlyn and Roma. The ones who test us, find us."
"Us?"
"The Captains Britain.
"They give us the choice--the *Amulet of Right* or the *Sword of Might*.
"With the knowledge that the truly virtuous among us are not violent.
"The *true* Captain Britain will *always* take the *Amulet*."
But the part of me that *recoiled* from violence...that *didn't* want the sword... that part of me was *dead*.
The *witch* Morgan Le Fay *murdered* it when she imprisoned me.
Kept me from my family. Nearly left my wife a widow! My daughter *fatherless!*
"All I felt was anger.
"Who was this innocent Brian Braddock who had once spurned the blade?
"I no longer know him."
I took the blade.
I am no longer fit to be Captain Britain.
That witch *ruined my life!*
Brian, no one could blame you!
Take it. Take the sword, Brian.
It isn't a *punishment*--you could do *good* by it!
You are a righteous and virtuous man, a knight of the realm!

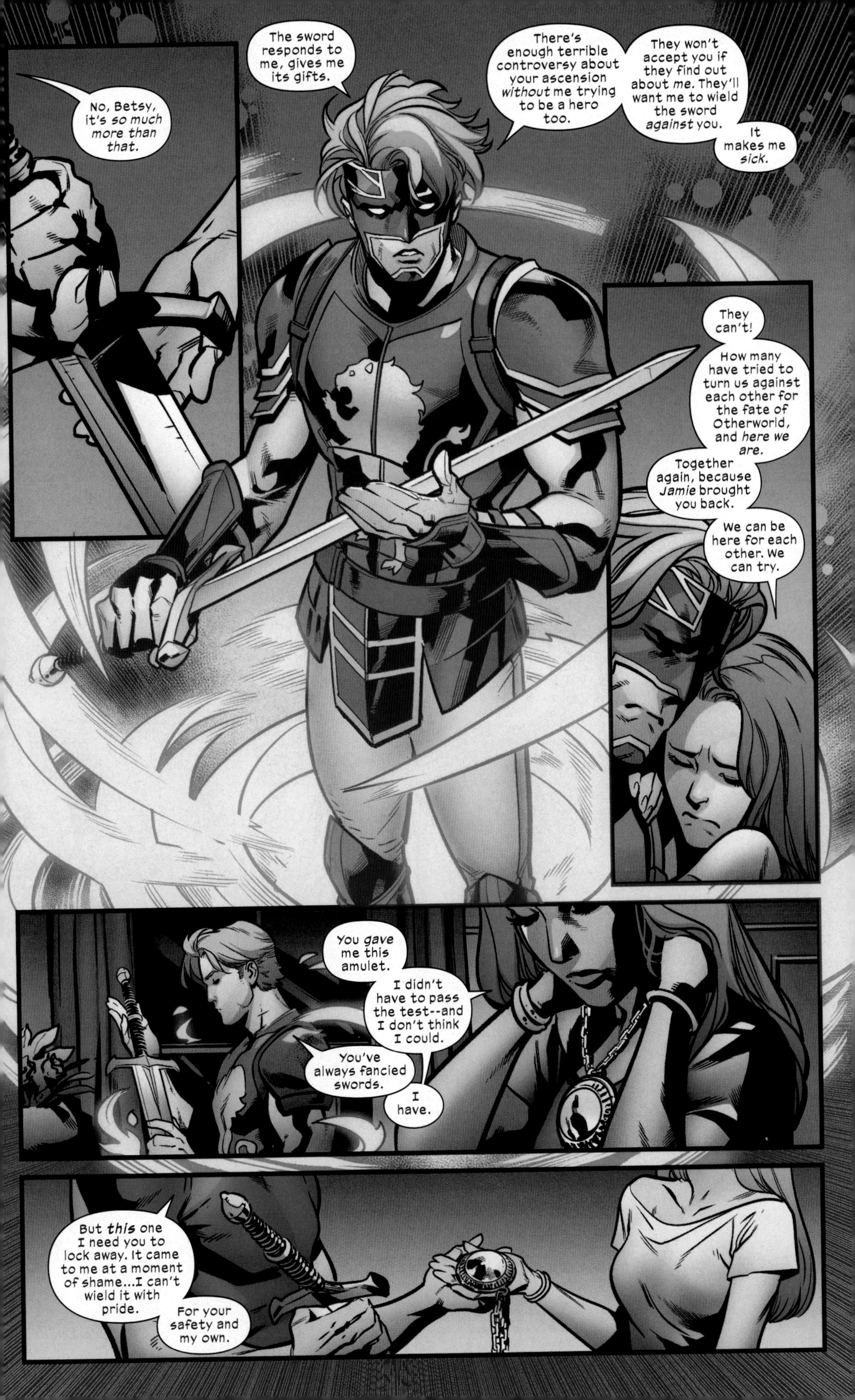

No, Betsy, it's so much more than that.
The sword responds to me, gives me its gifts.
There's enough terrible controversy about your ascension without me trying to be a hero too.
They won't accept you if they find out about me. They'll want me to wield the sword against you.
It makes me sick.
They can't!
How many have tried to turn us against each other for the fate of Otherworld, and here we are.
Together again, because Jamie brought you back.
We can be here for each other. We can try.
You gave me this amulet.
I didn't have to pass the test--and I don't think I could.
You've always fancied swords.
I have.
But this one I need you to lock away. It came to me at a moment of shame...I can't wield it with pride.
For your safety and my own.

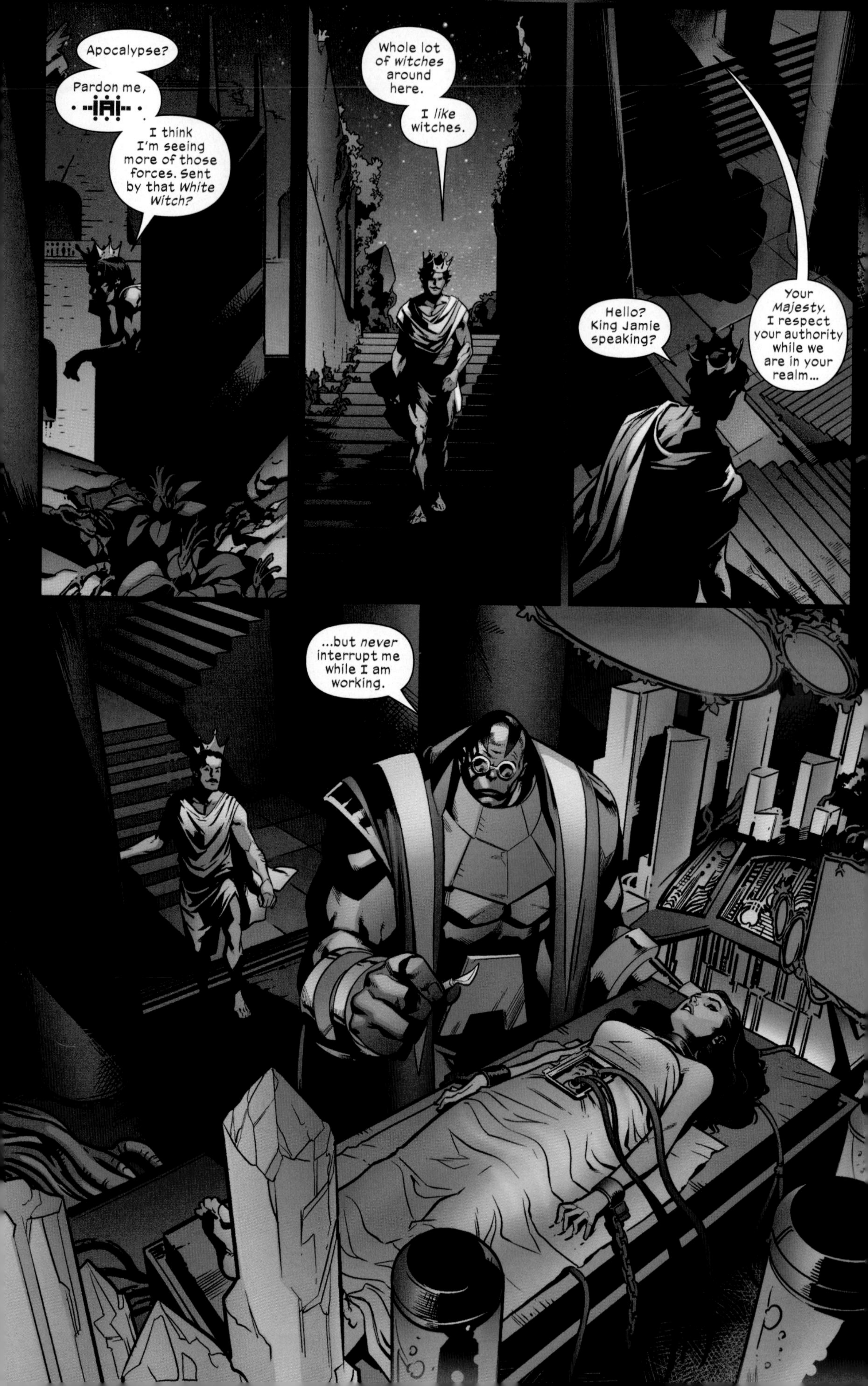
Apocalypse?
Pardon me,
I think I'm seeing more of those forces. Sent by that *White Witch?*
Whole lot of *witches* around here.
I *like* witches.
Hello? King Jamie speaking?
Your *Majesty.* I respect your authority while we are in your realm...
...but *never* interrupt me while I am working.

FROM THE GRIMOIRE OF

SAMPLE 1:

Recent experiments involving the dissection* of Morgan Le Fay resulted in the identification of one unidentified malignant component, heretofore referred to as Component Y.**

UPDATES TO PREVIOUS METHODOLOGY:

- *Include at least one Omega Level Mutate* ⬚⬚⬚⬚⬚⬚
- *Include mutate assistant of advanced age* ⬚⬚⬚⬚⬚
- *Include components of* ⬚⬚⬚⬚⬚⬚ *to protect and sanctify Magica Superior*

RESULTS: *Further notes pending.*

CONCLUSION:

- The magic of the Superior relies on strength of community, not exercise of power.
- Three is an insufficient number to form a coven.
- **Component Y is an active threat to Otherworld*** and will require containment both here and at the source.**

---

* Autopsy would be the incorrect word, as she remains very much alive.

** For more on Component Y's potential source, see my own *Notes upon an Ancient Darkness*, c. 1200 CE.

*** And perhaps elsewhere.

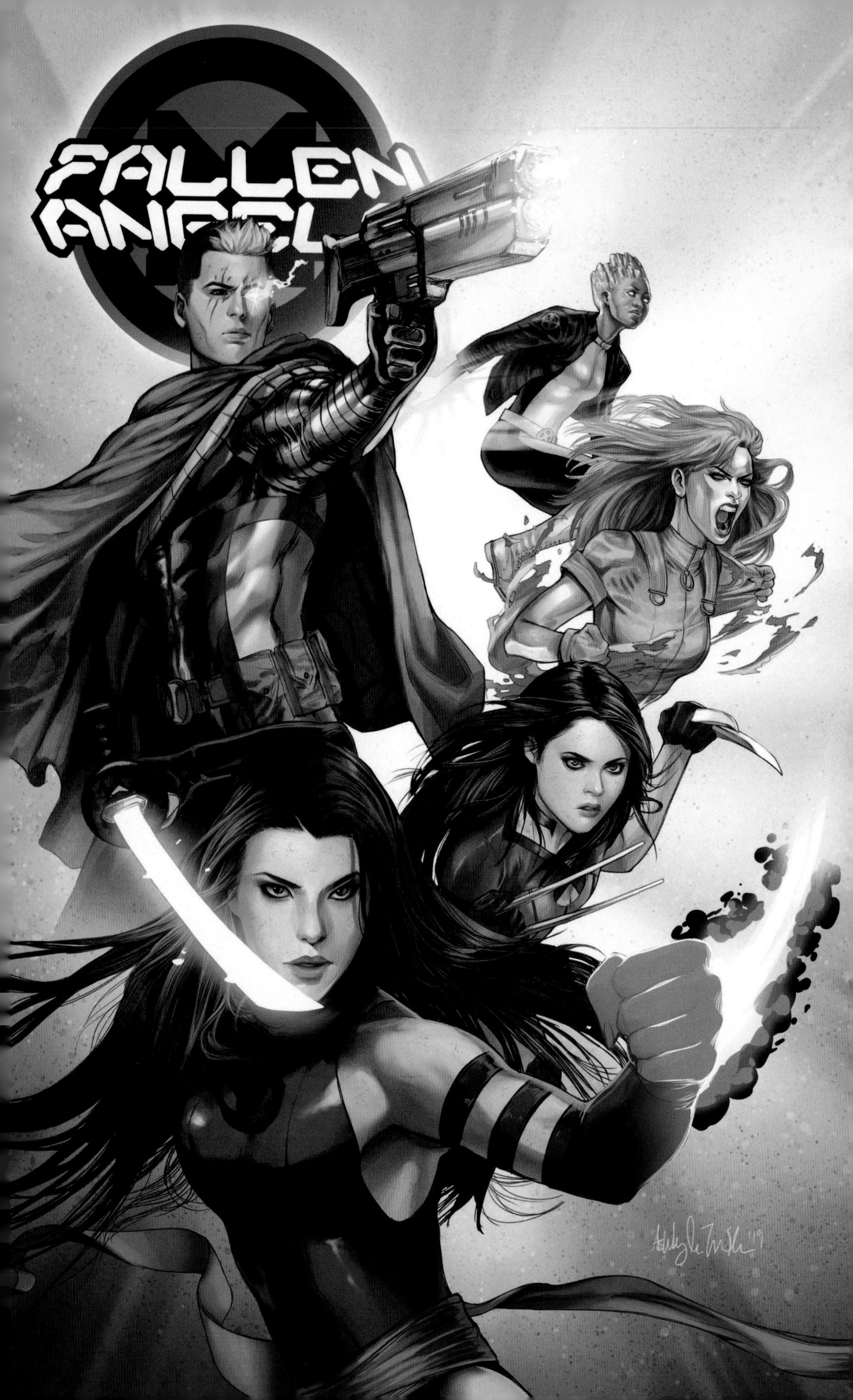
FALLEN

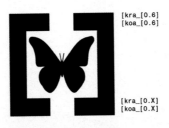

[kra_[0.6]
[koa_[0.6]

[kra_[0.X]
[koa_[0.X]

ALL IN TOGETHER NOW

Mutants around the world are flocking to the island-nation of Krakoa for safety, for security and to be part of the first mutant society.

Through a prophetic vision, Psylocke was made aware of a mysterious new enemy called Apoth, who was responsible for the creation of a dangerous new cyberdrug called Overclock and the children employed in its production. Psylocke, X-23, Cable, Bling! and Husk banded together to take the fight to Apoth in Dubai.

Psylocke

Cable

Husk

Bling!

X-23

Mister
Sinister

[kra_[0.6]...]
[koa_[0.6]...]

[A._ssa_ssin_]

[00_warrior_X__]
[00_lim_ited___]

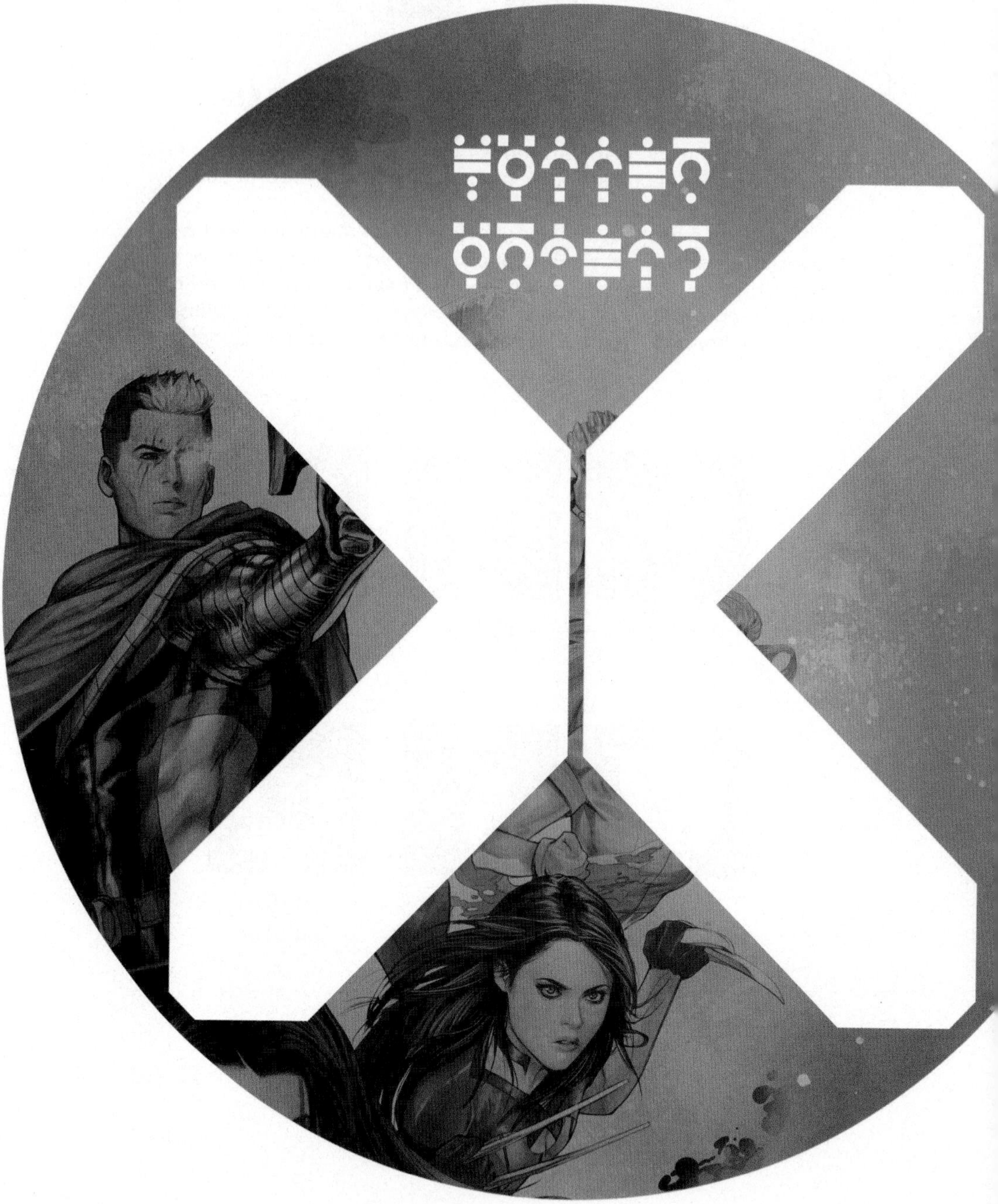

[00_warrior_X__]
[00_lim_ited___]

?φ::

BRYAN HILL.......................................[WRITER]
SZYMON KUDRANSKI..............................[ARTIST]
FRANK D'ARMATA..........................[COLOR ARTIST]
VC's JOE SABINO...............................[LETTERER]
TOM MULLER......................................[DESIGN]

ASHLEY WITTER............................[COVER ARTIST]

JUNGGEUN YOON....................[VARIANT COVER ARTIST]

NICK RUSSELL..............................[PRODUCTION]

JONATHAN HICKMAN...........................[HEAD OF X]
CHRIS ROBINSON......................[ASSISTANT EDITOR]
JORDAN D. WHITE...............................[EDITOR]
C.B. CEBULSKI.......................[EDITOR IN CHIEF]

[06] FALLEN ANGELS

[ISSUE SIX]..................CONCLUSION

[00_warrior_X__]
[00_lim_ited___]

[00_00...0]
[00_00...6]

[00_sword_]
[00_____]

[00_____]

[00_____X]

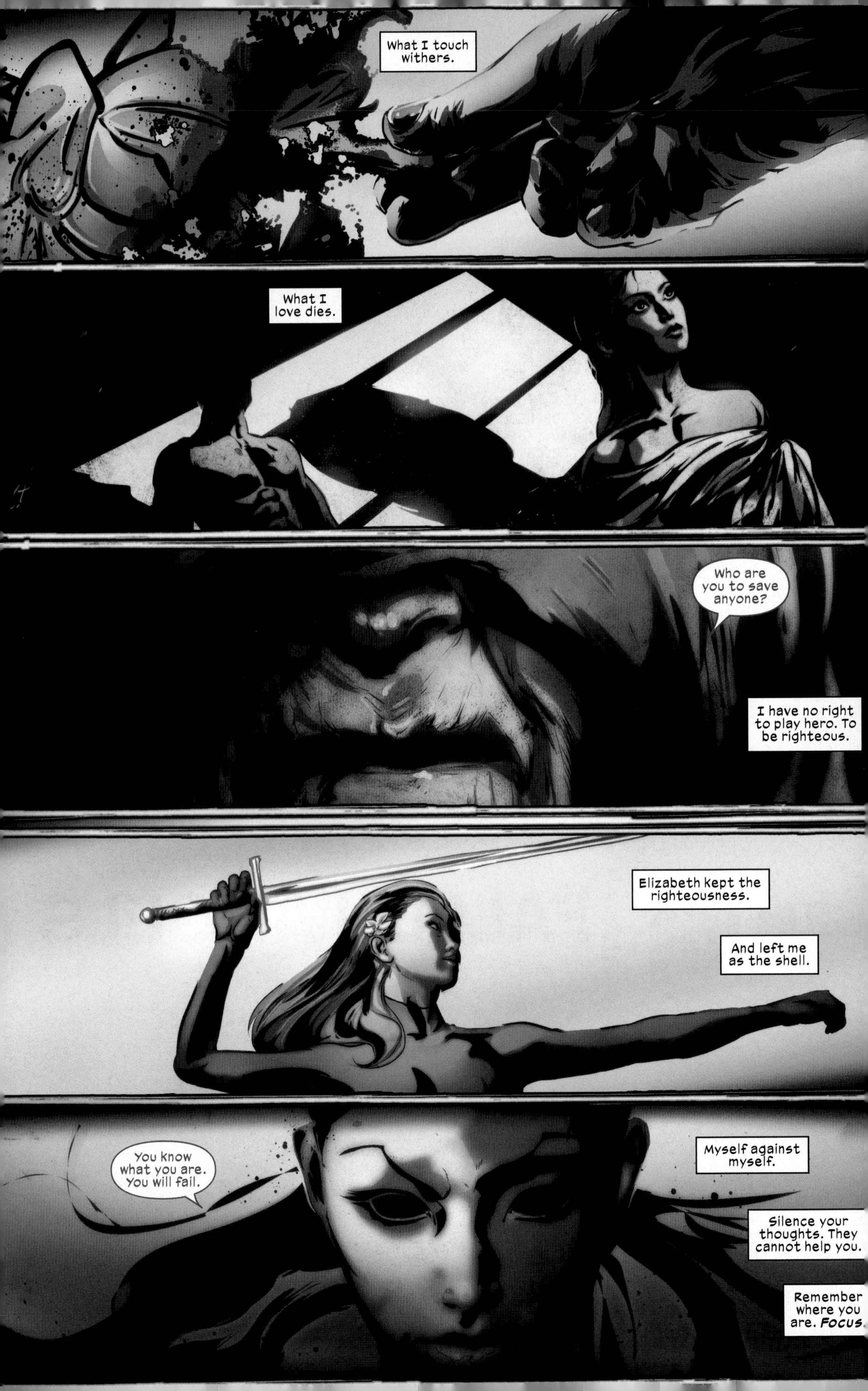
What I touch withers.
What I love dies.
Who are you to save anyone?
I have no right to play hero. To be righteous.
Elizabeth kept the righteousness.
And left me as the shell.
You know what you are. You will fail.
Myself against myself.
Silence your thoughts. They cannot help you.
Remember where you are. *FOCUS*.

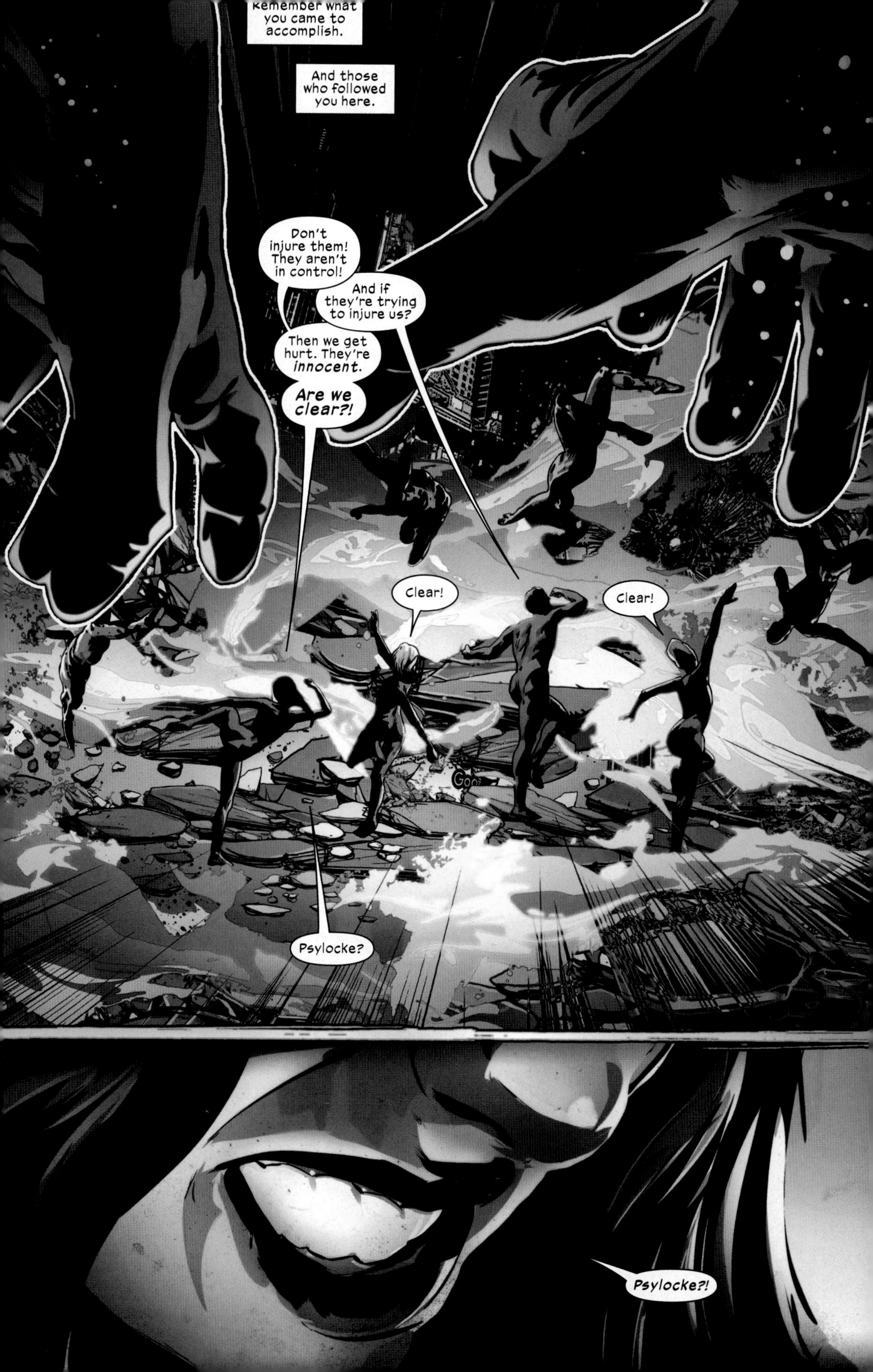
Remember what you came to accomplish.
And those who followed you here.
Don't injure them! They aren't in control!
And if they're trying to injure us?
Then we get hurt. They're *innocent*.
Are we clear?!
Clear!
Clear!
Psylocke?
Psylocke?!

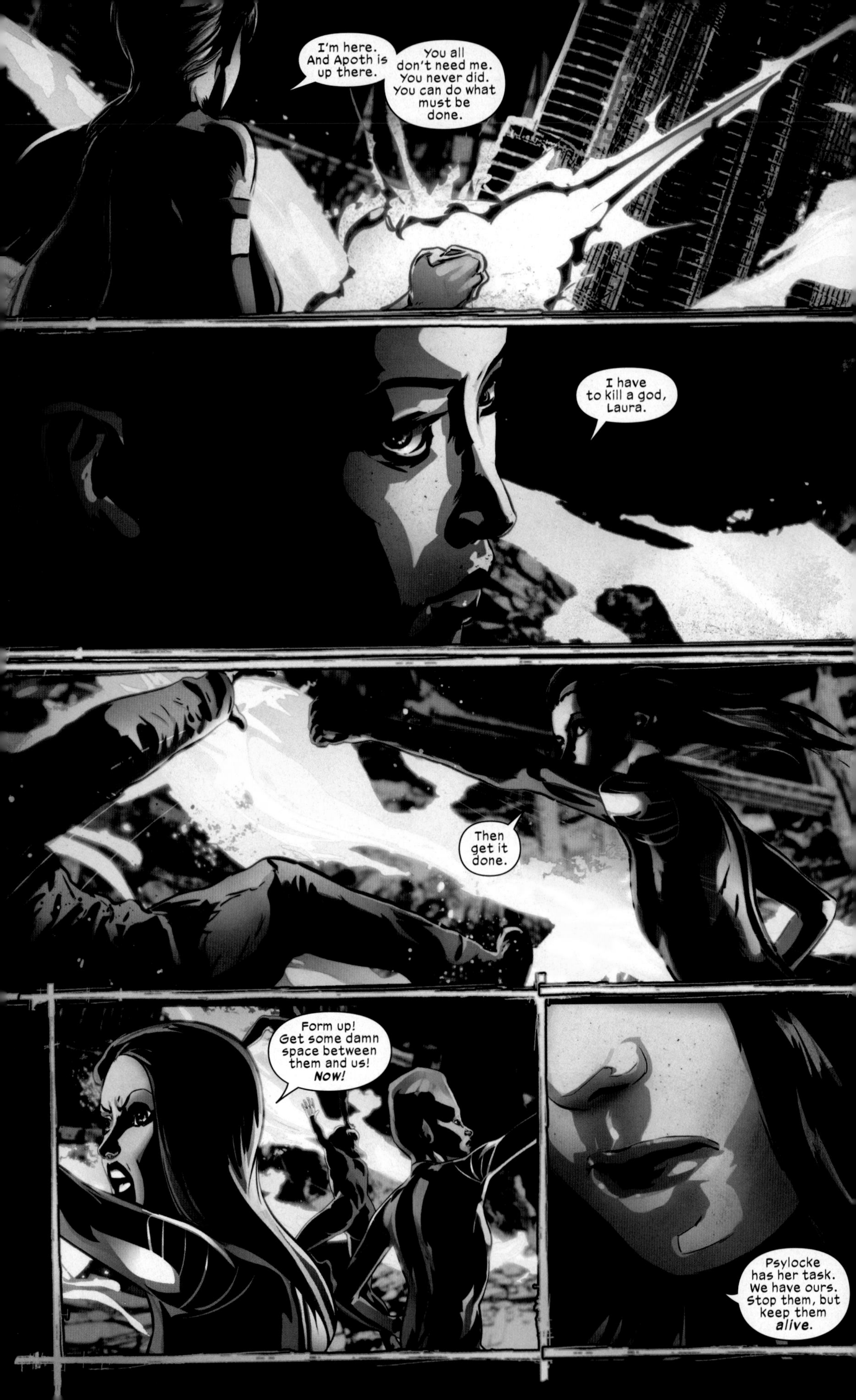
I'm here. And Apoth is up there.
You all don't need me. You never did. You can do what must be done.
I have to kill a god, Laura.
Then get it done.
Form up! Get some damn space between them and us! *NOW!*
Psylocke has her task. We have ours. Stop them, but keep them *alive*.

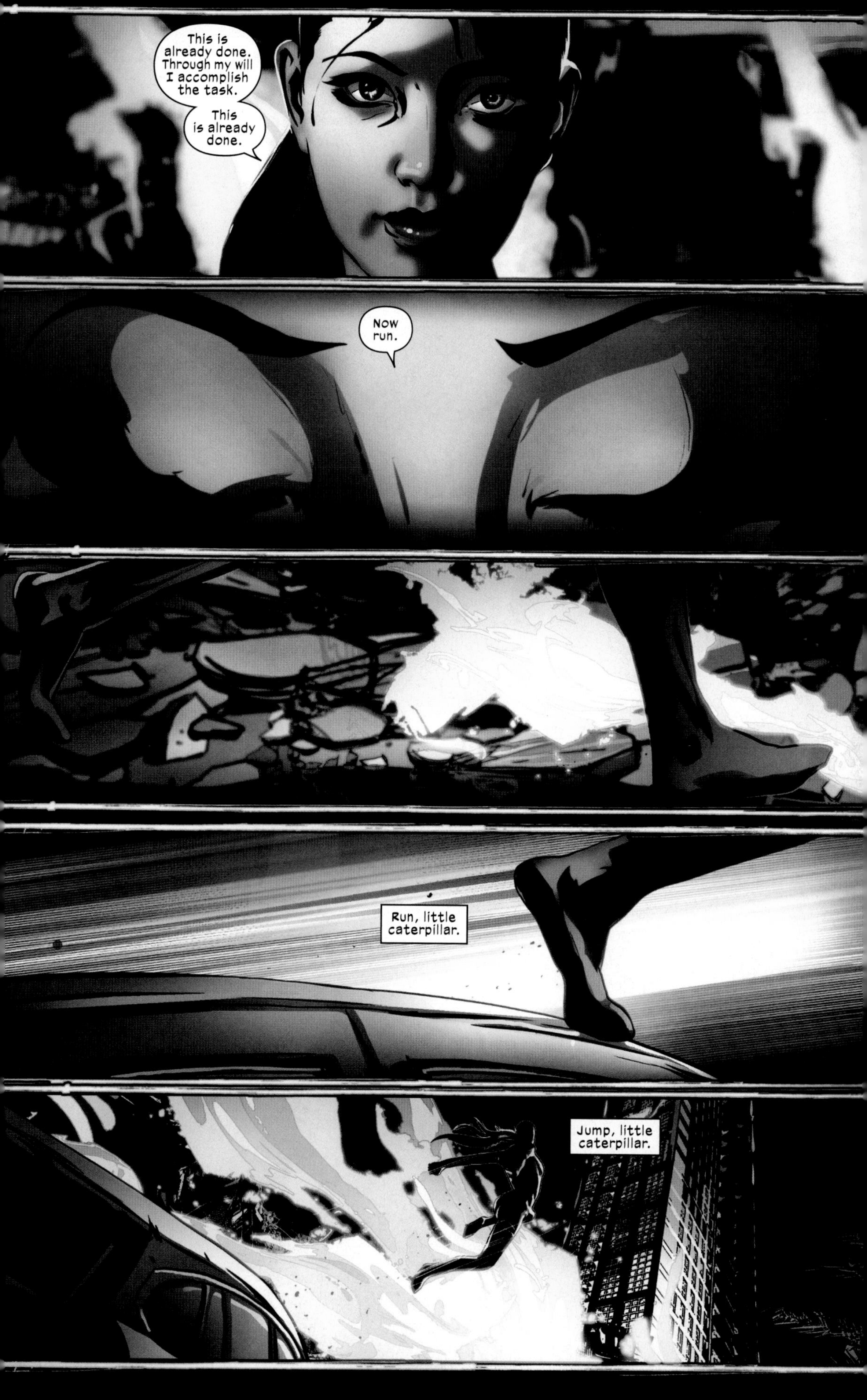
This is already done. Through my will I accomplish the task.
This is already done.
Now run.
Run, little caterpillar.
Jump, little caterpillar.

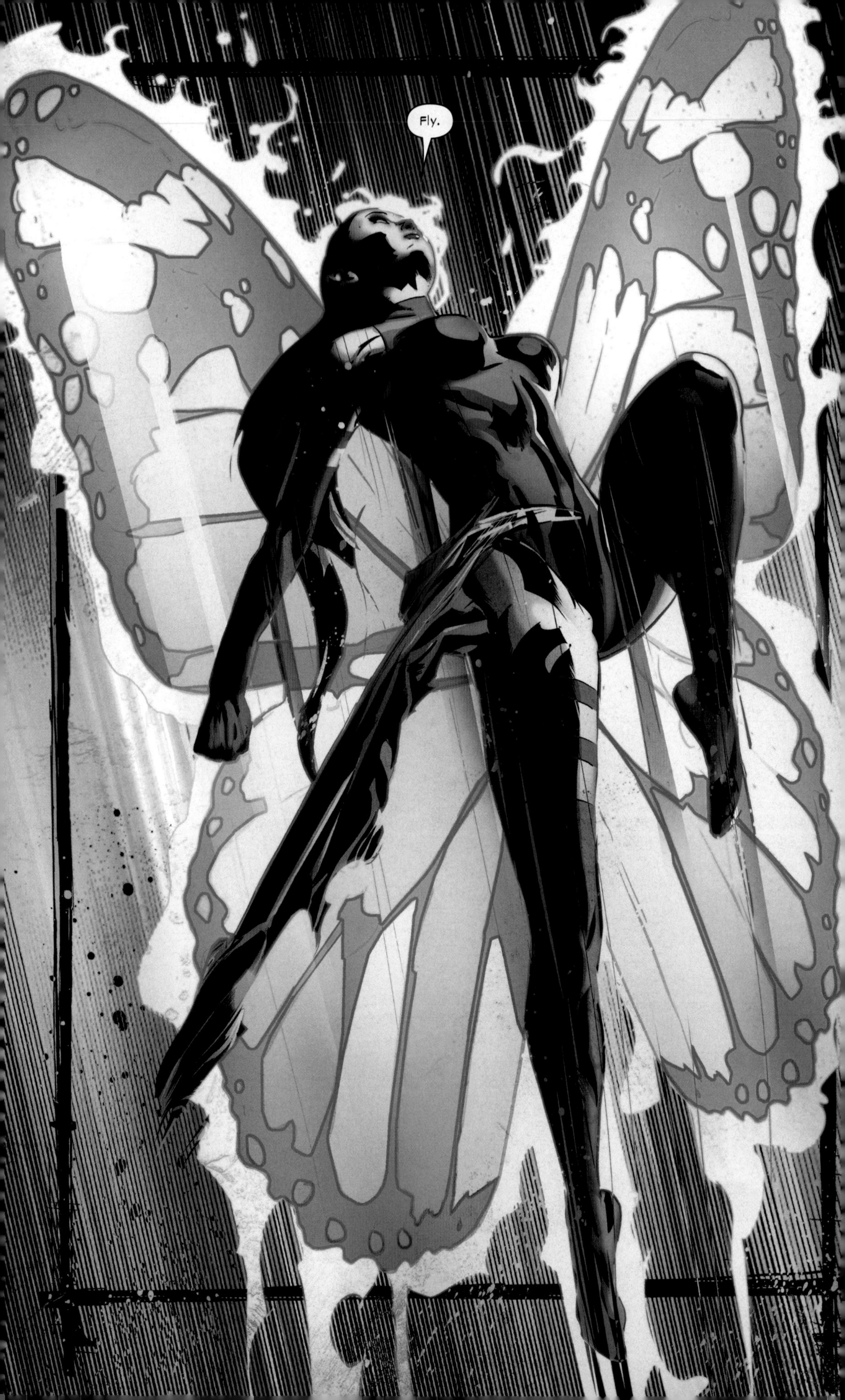
Fly.

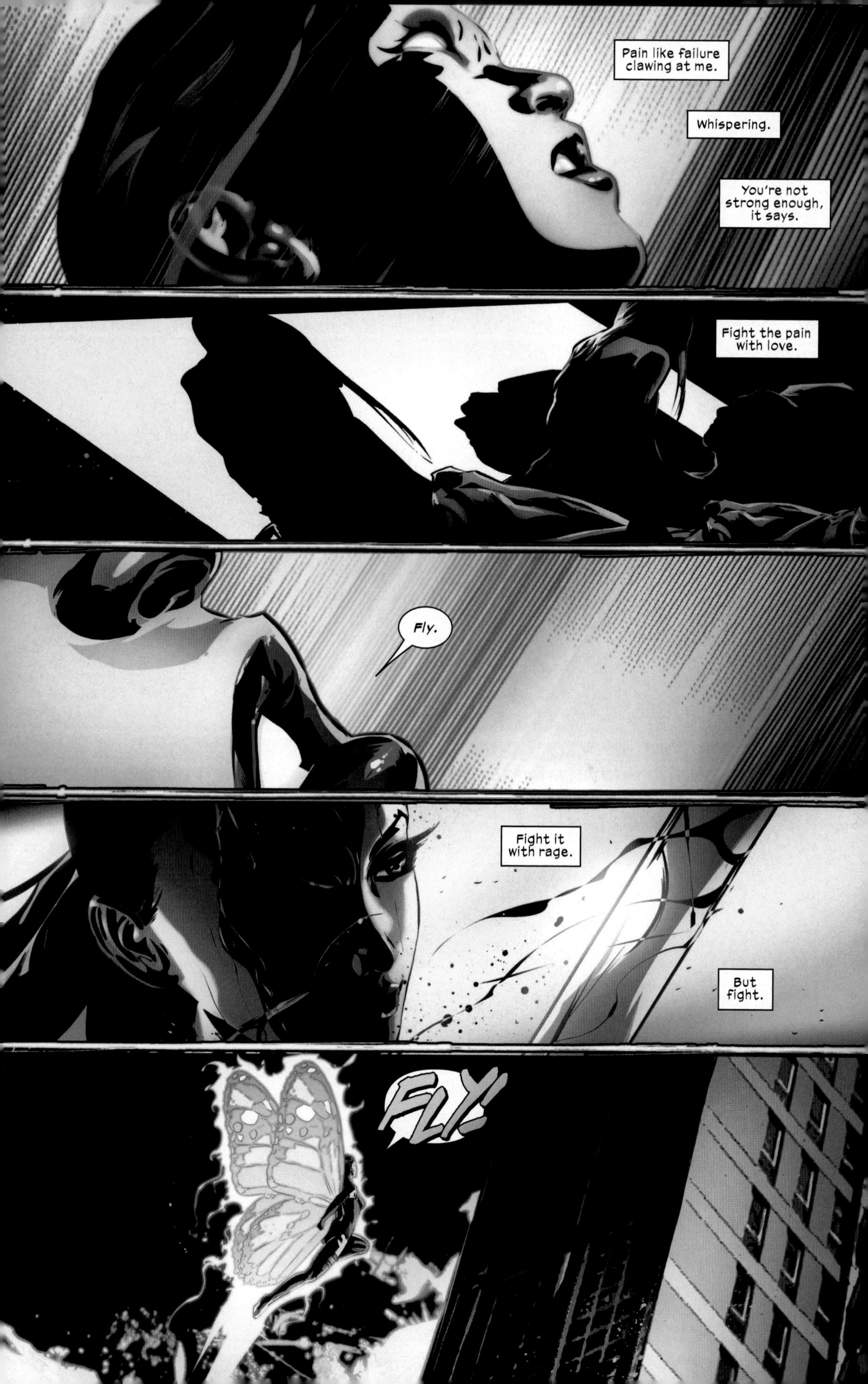
Pain like failure clawing at me.
Whispering.
You're not strong enough, it says.
Fight the pain with love.
Fly.
Fight it with rage.
But fight.
FLY!

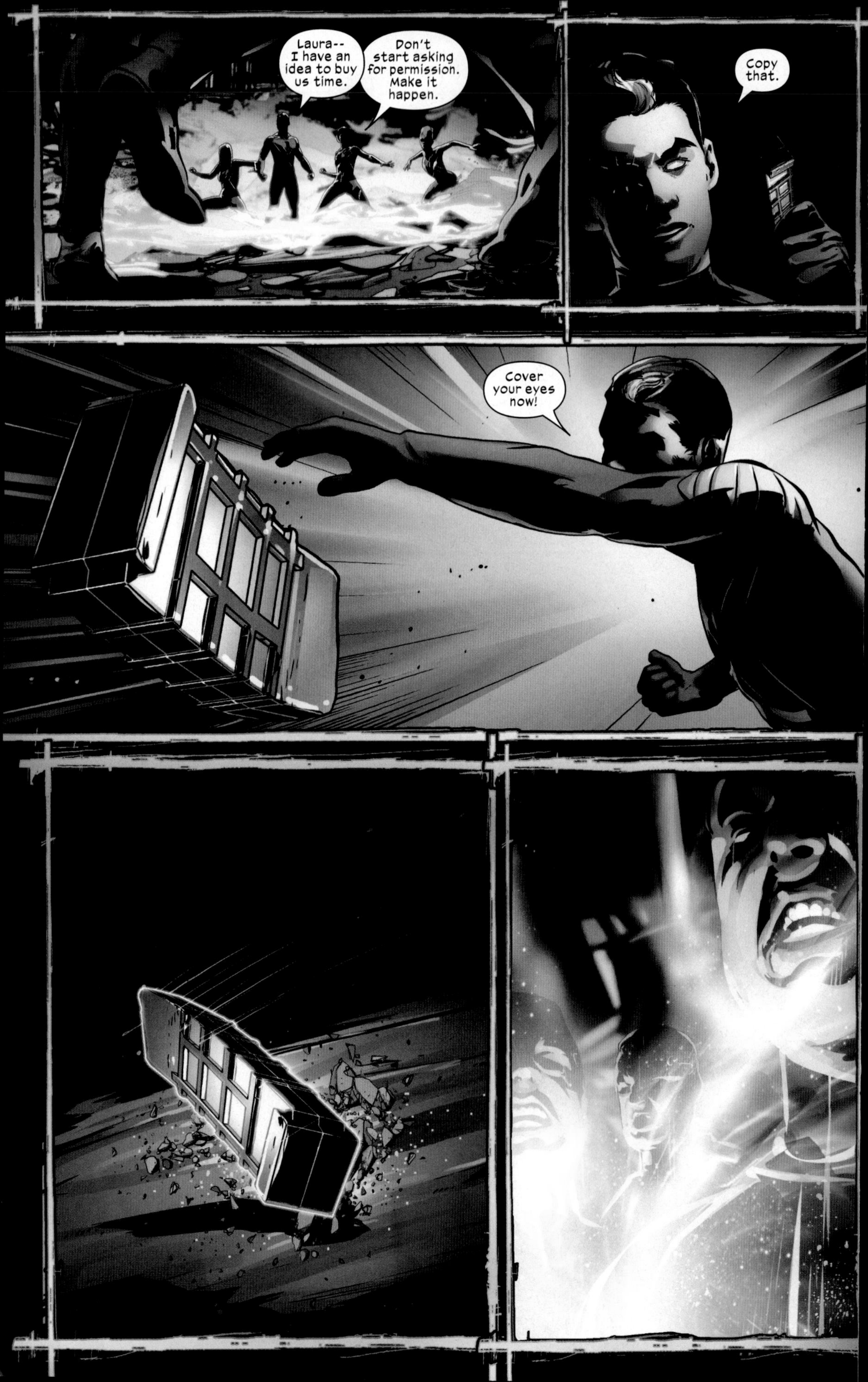
Laura-- I have an idea to buy us time.
Don't start asking for permission. Make it happen.
Copy that.
Cover your eyes now!

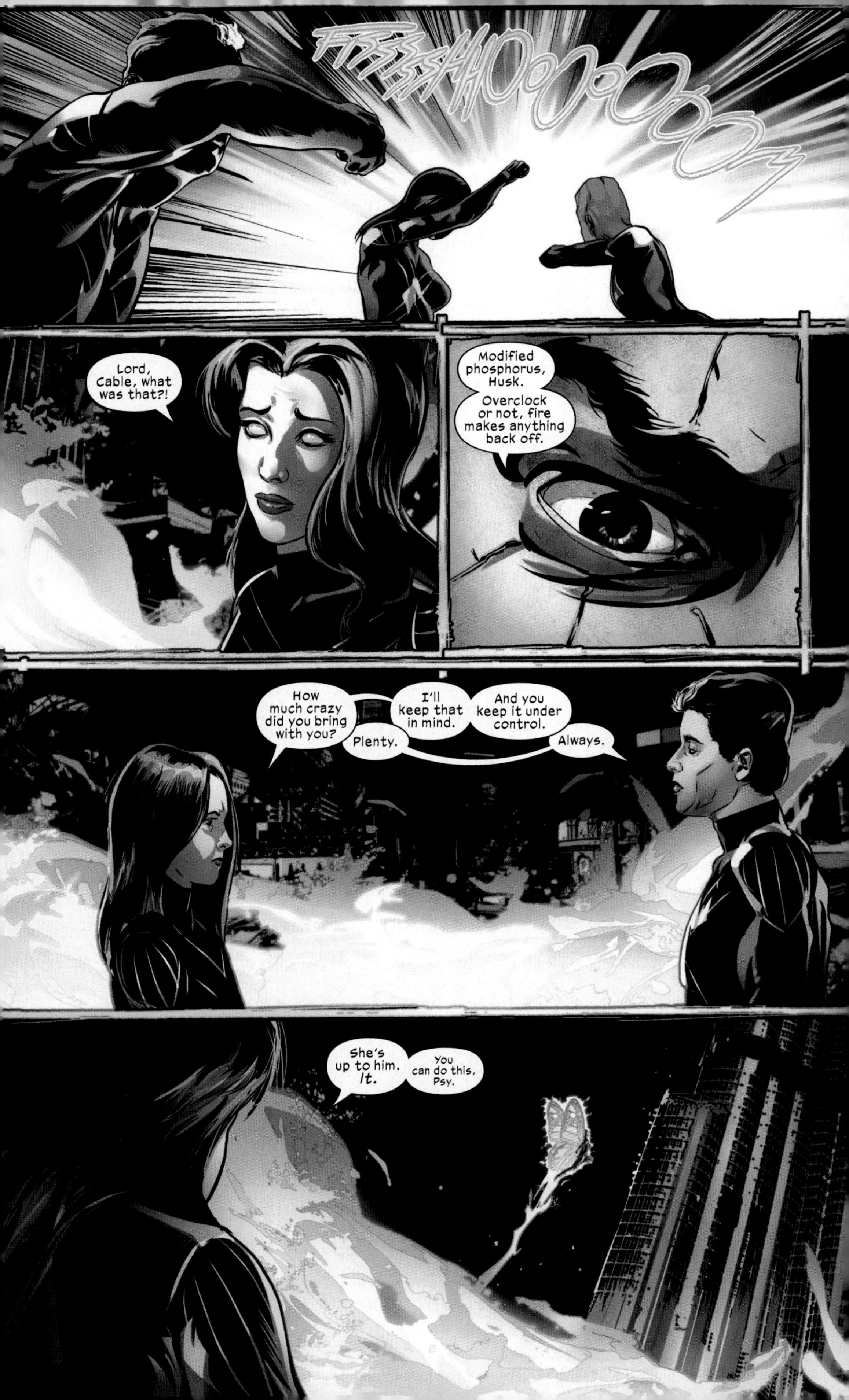
FSSSSHOOOOOOOM
Lord, Cable, what was that?!
Modified phosphorus, Husk.
Overclock or not, fire makes anything back off.
How much crazy did you bring with you?
Plenty.
I'll keep that in mind.
And you keep it under control.
Always.
She's up to him. *It.*
You can do this, Psy.

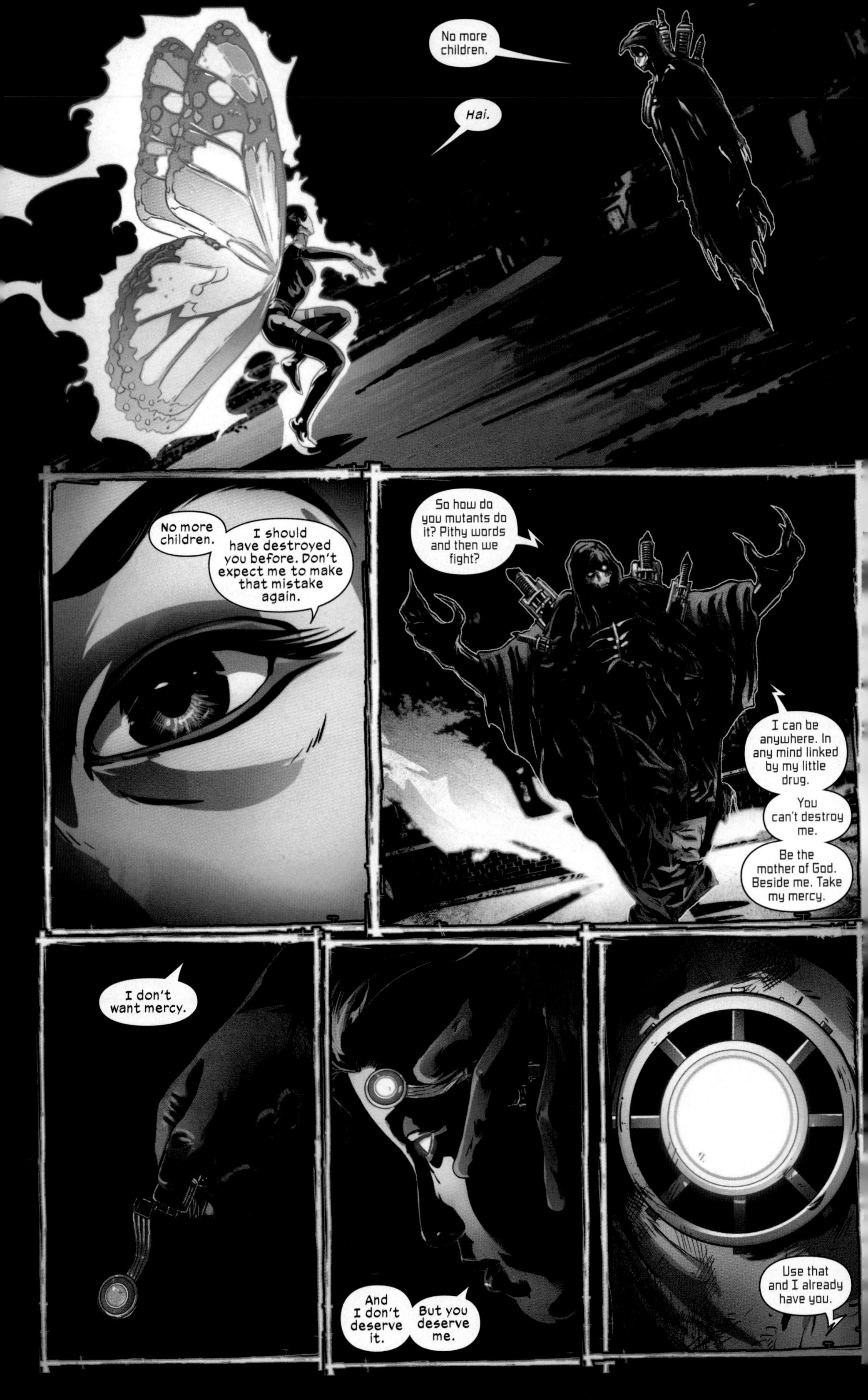

No more children.
Hai.
No more children.
I should have destroyed you before. Don't expect me to make that mistake again.
So how do you mutants do it? Pithy words and then we fight?
I can be anywhere. In any mind linked by my little drug.
You can't destroy me.
Be the mother of God. Beside me. Take my mercy.
I don't want mercy.
And I don't deserve it.
But you deserve me.
Use that and I already have you.

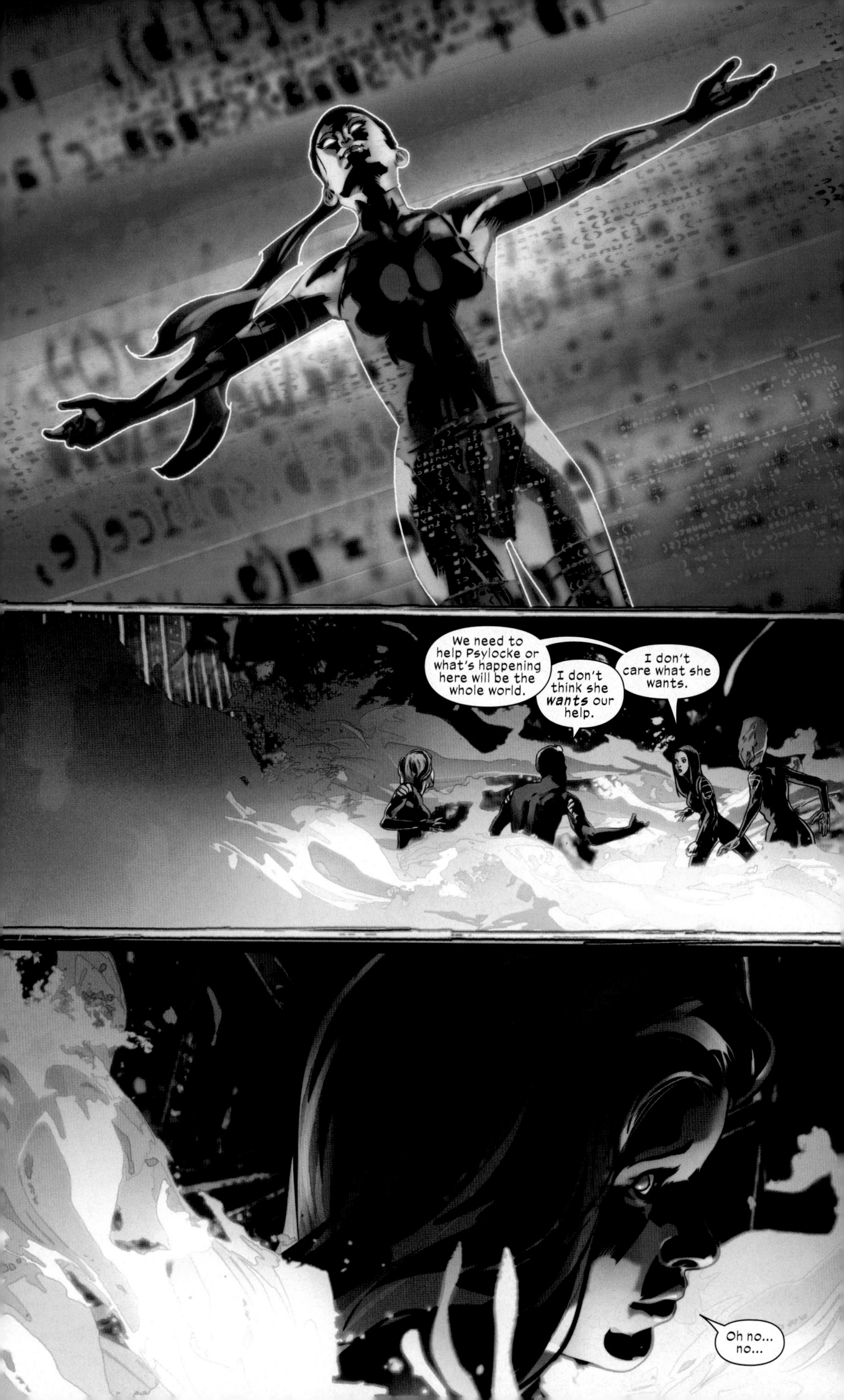
We need to help Psylocke or what's happening here will be the whole world.
I don't think she *wants* our help.
I don't care what she wants.
Oh no... no...

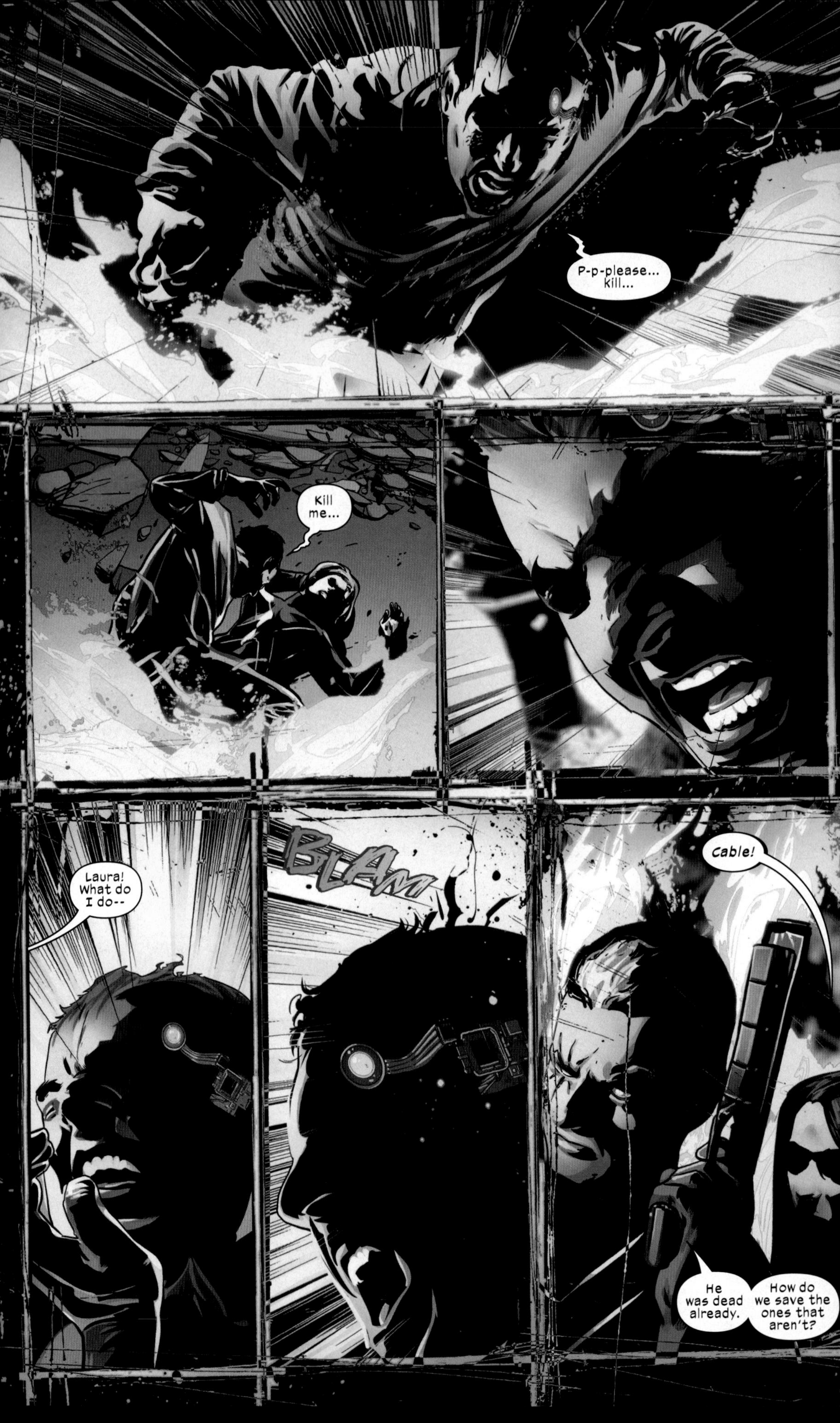
P-p-please... kill...
Kill me...
Laura! What do I do--
BLAM
Cable!
He was dead already.
How do we save the ones that aren't?

Fascinating. Your mutation of mind keeps you independent of me.

But not for long.

Do you think you have more power here? How are you so foolish?

Here, possibilities are infinite. My *power* is infinite.

Kneel. And I will spare you so much pain.

Kneel and I won't end you.

End me?

You can't even touch me. Try.

Walk to me and try.

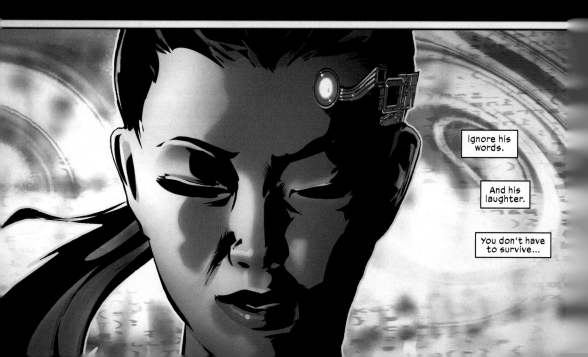

Ignore his words.

And his laughter.

You don't have to survive...

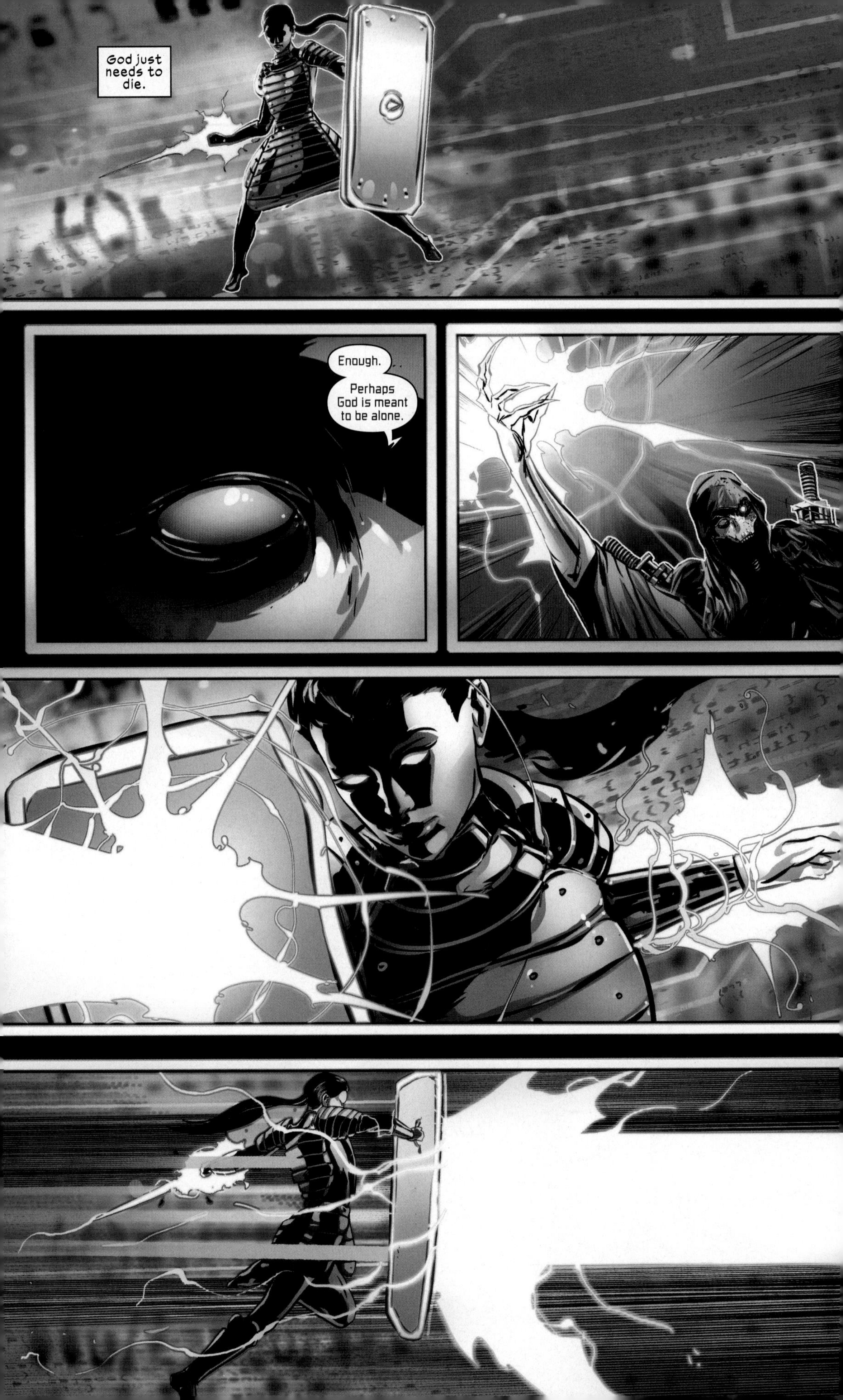

God just needs to die.
Enough.
Perhaps God is meant to be alone.

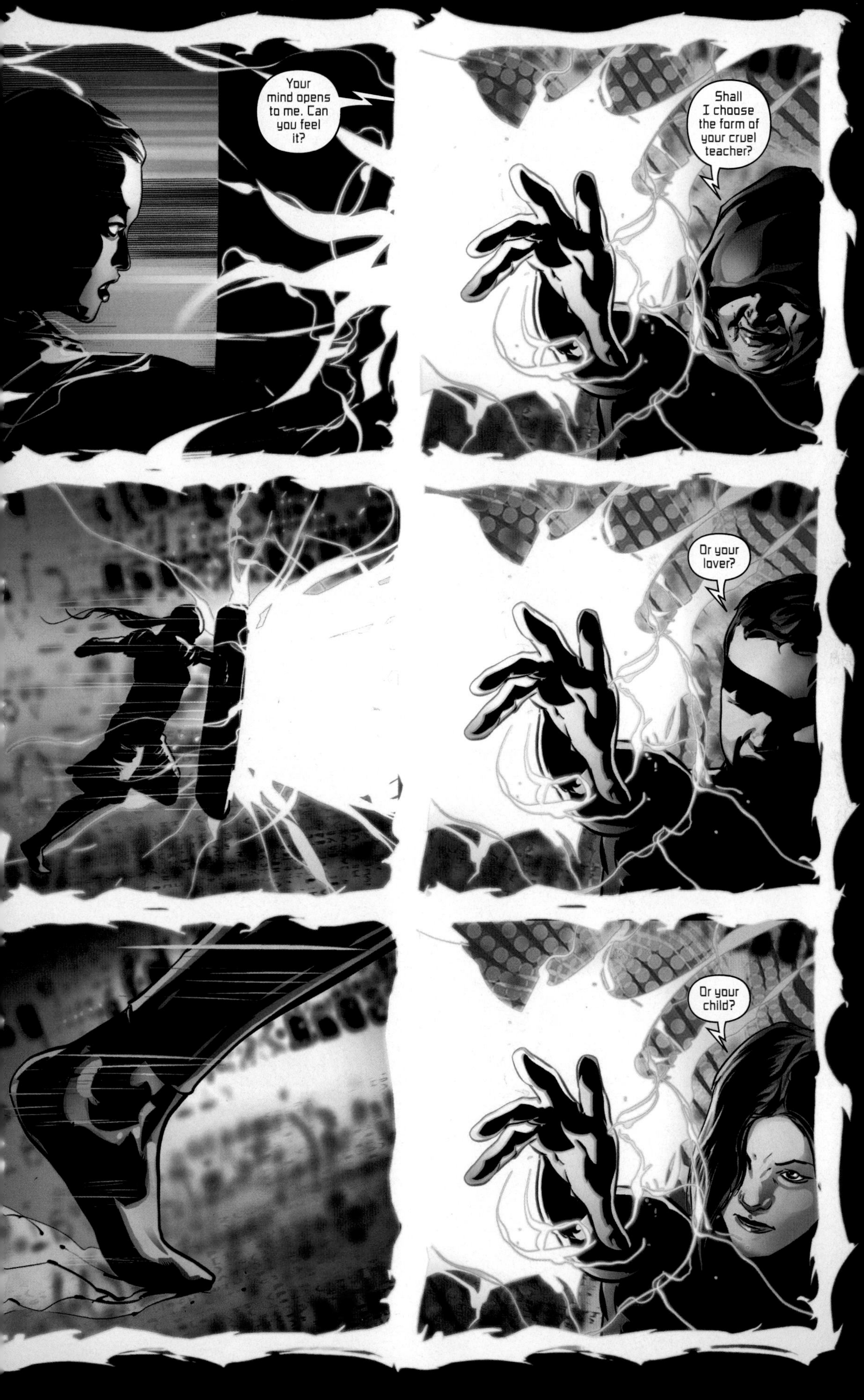

Your mind opens to me. Can you feel it?
Shall I choose the form of your cruel teacher?
Or your lover?
Or your child?

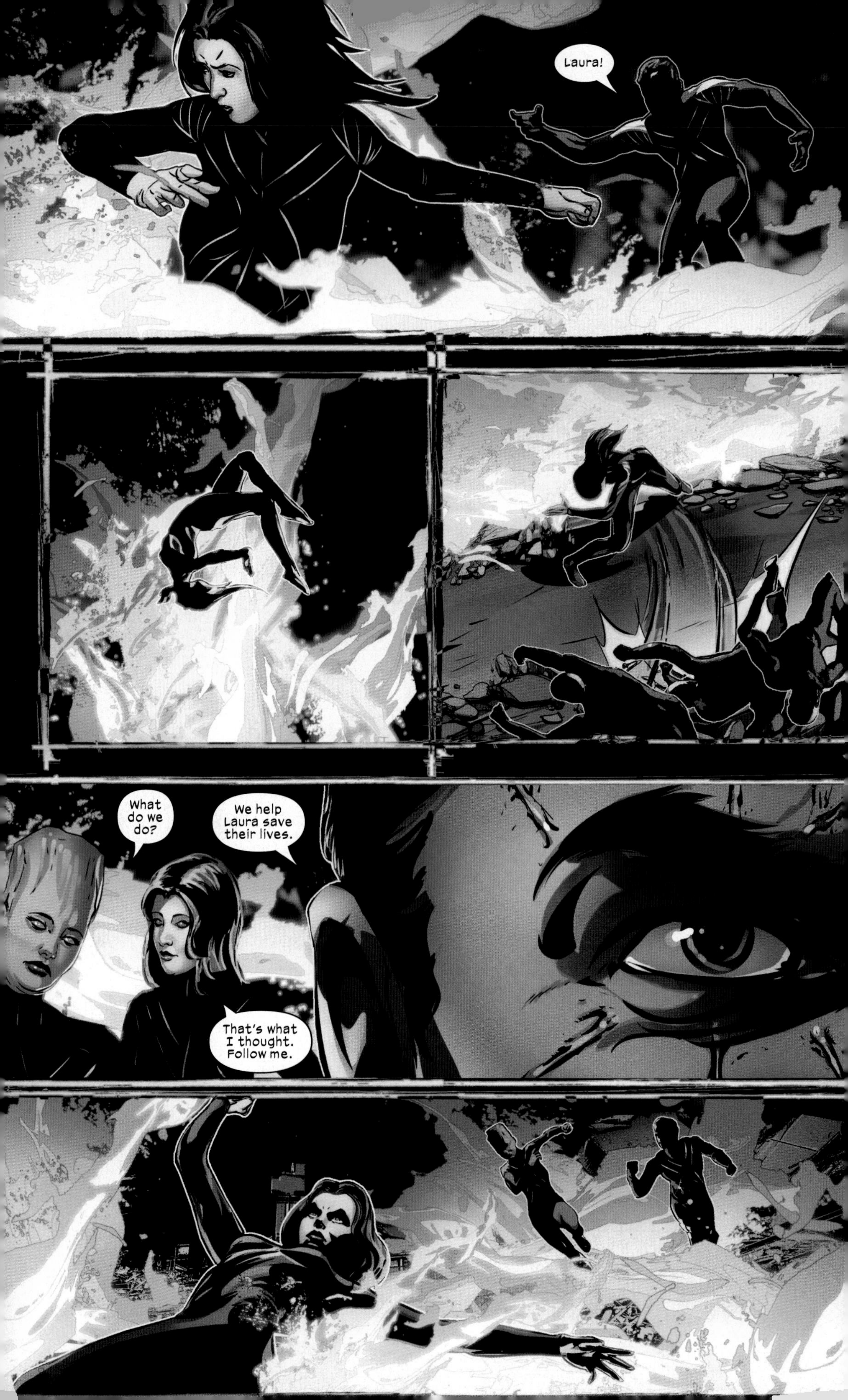
Laura!
What do we do?
We help Laura save their lives.
That's what I thought. Follow me.

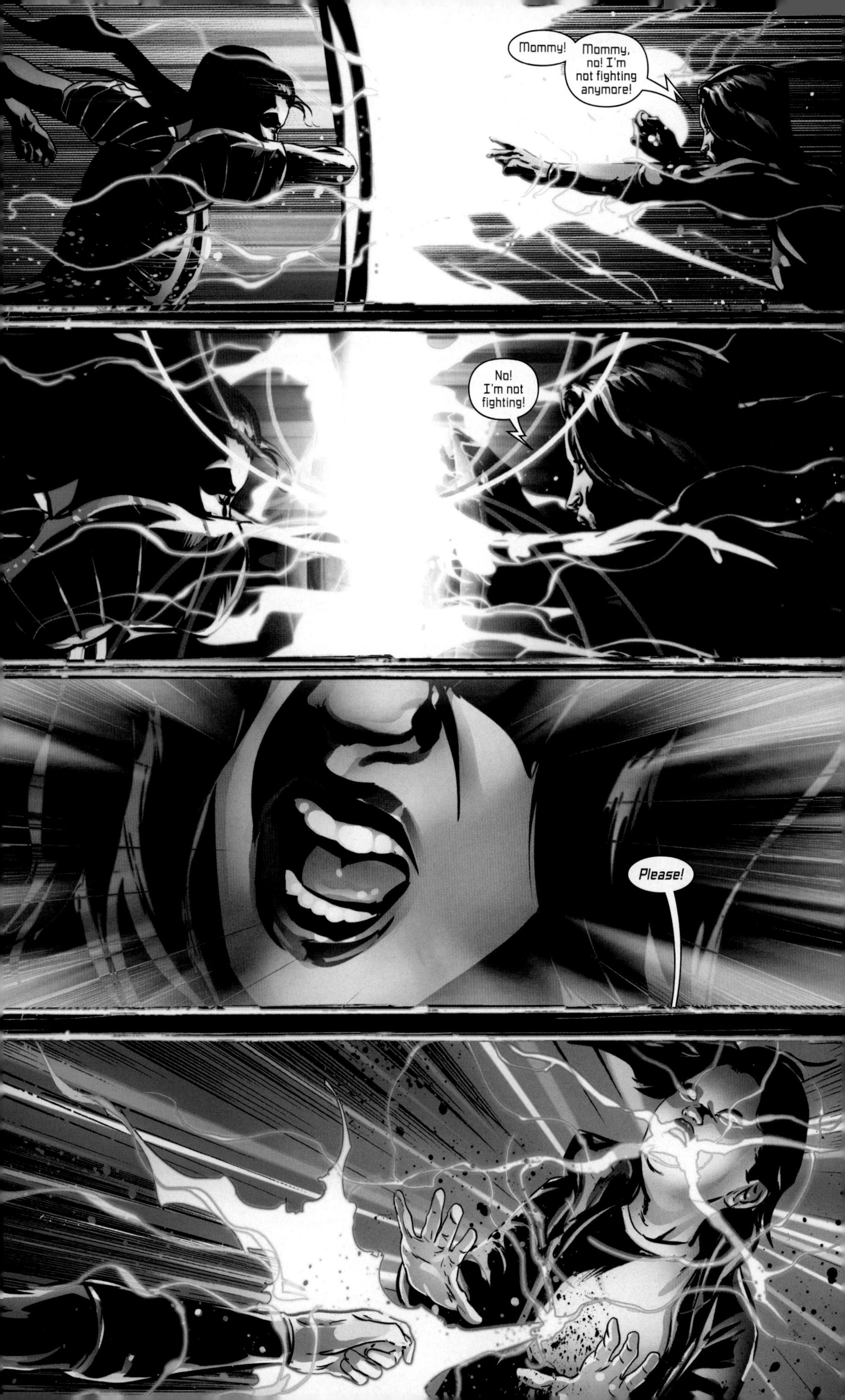
Mommy!
Mommy, no! I'm not fighting anymore!
No! I'm not fighting!
Please!

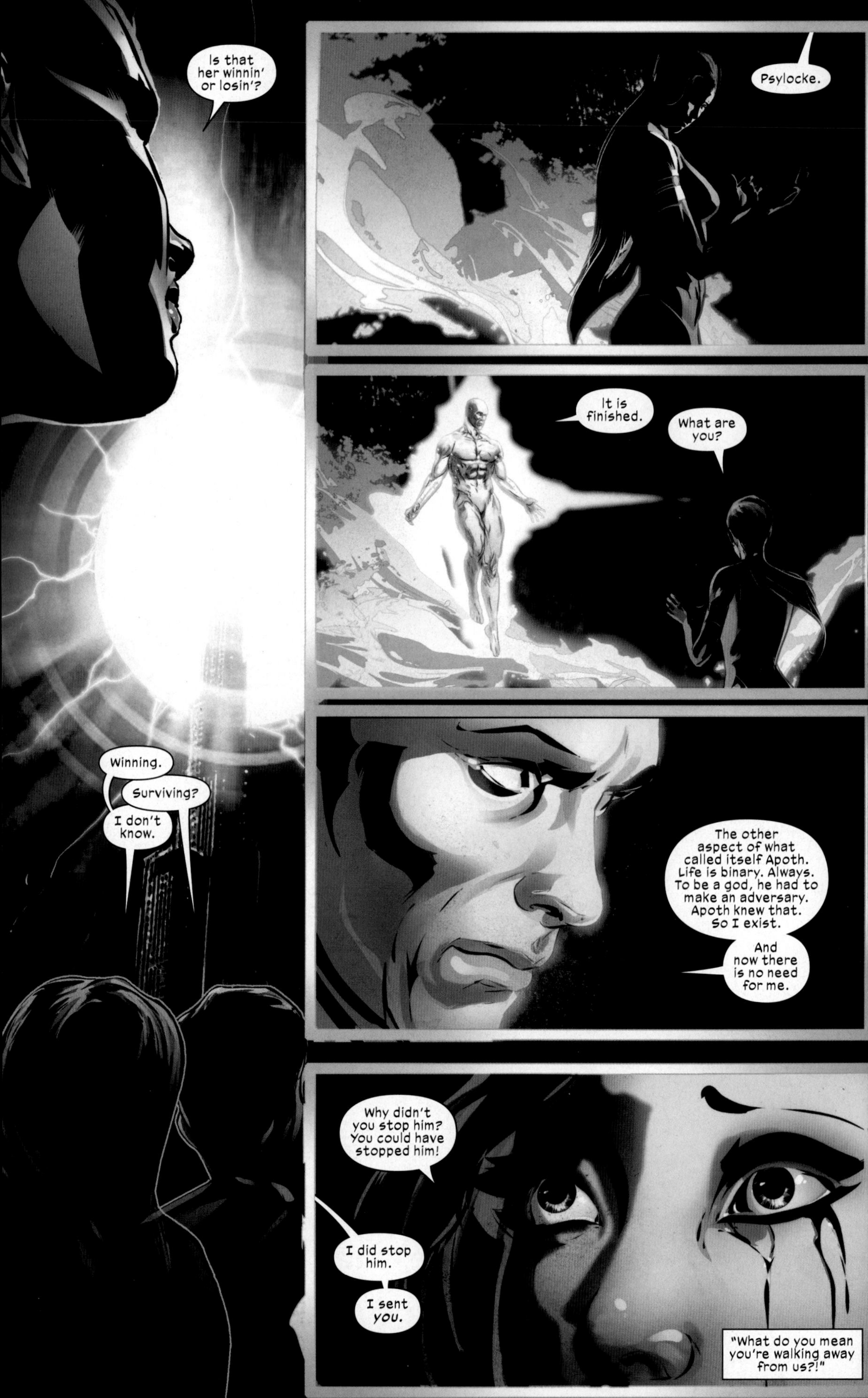
Is that her winnin' or losin'?
Psylocke.
Winning.
Surviving?
I don't know.
It is finished.
What are you?
The other aspect of what called itself Apoth. Life is binary. Always. To be a god, he had to make an adversary. Apoth knew that. So I exist.
And now there is no need for me.
Why didn't you stop him? You could have stopped him!
I did stop him.
I sent *you.*
"What do you mean you're walking away from us?!"

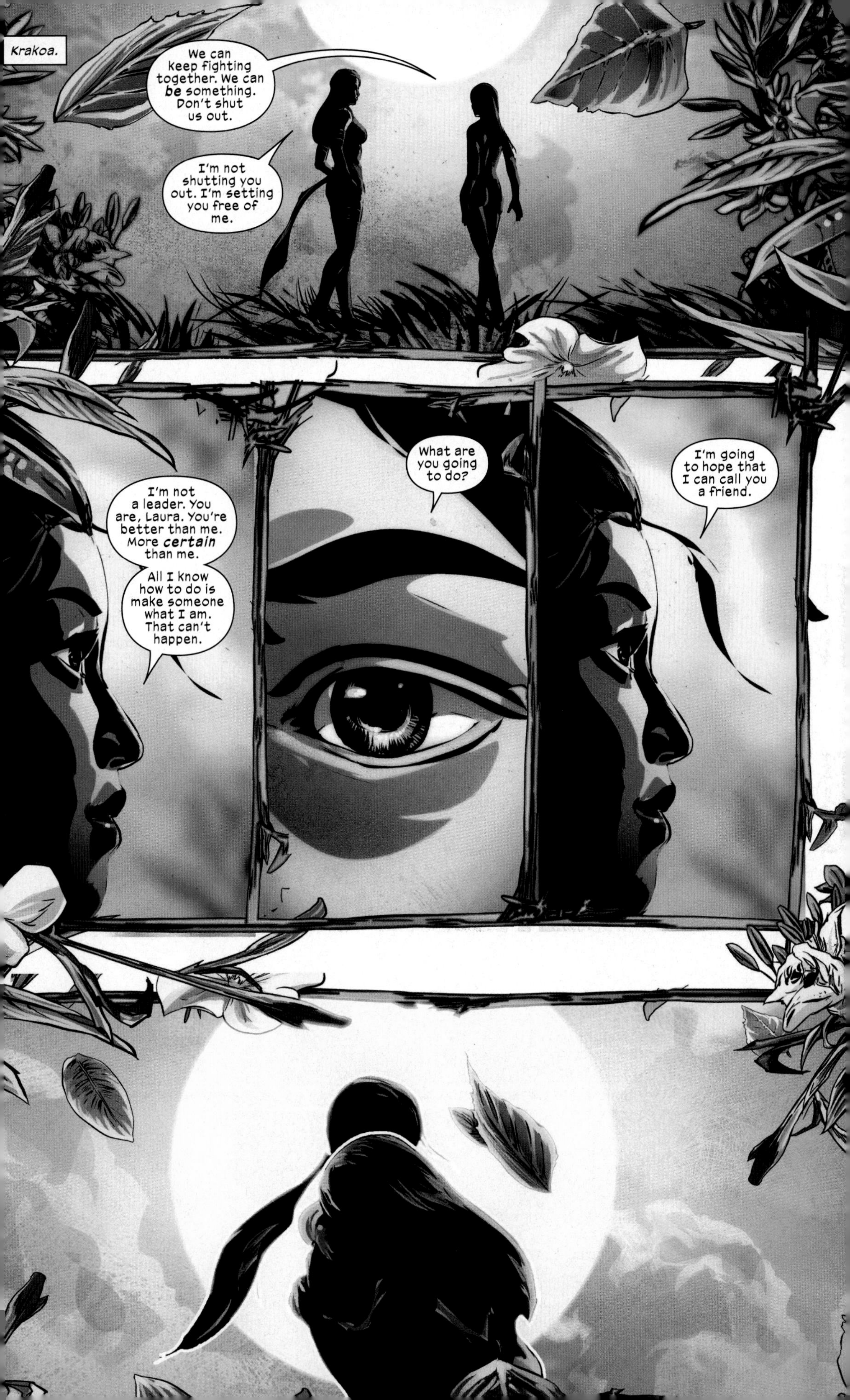
Krakoa.
We can keep fighting together. We can *be* something. Don't shut us out.
I'm not shutting you out. I'm setting you free of me.
I'm not a leader. You are, Laura. You're better than me. More *certain* than me.
All I know how to do is make someone what I am. That can't happen.
What are you going to do?
I'm going to hope that I can call you a friend.

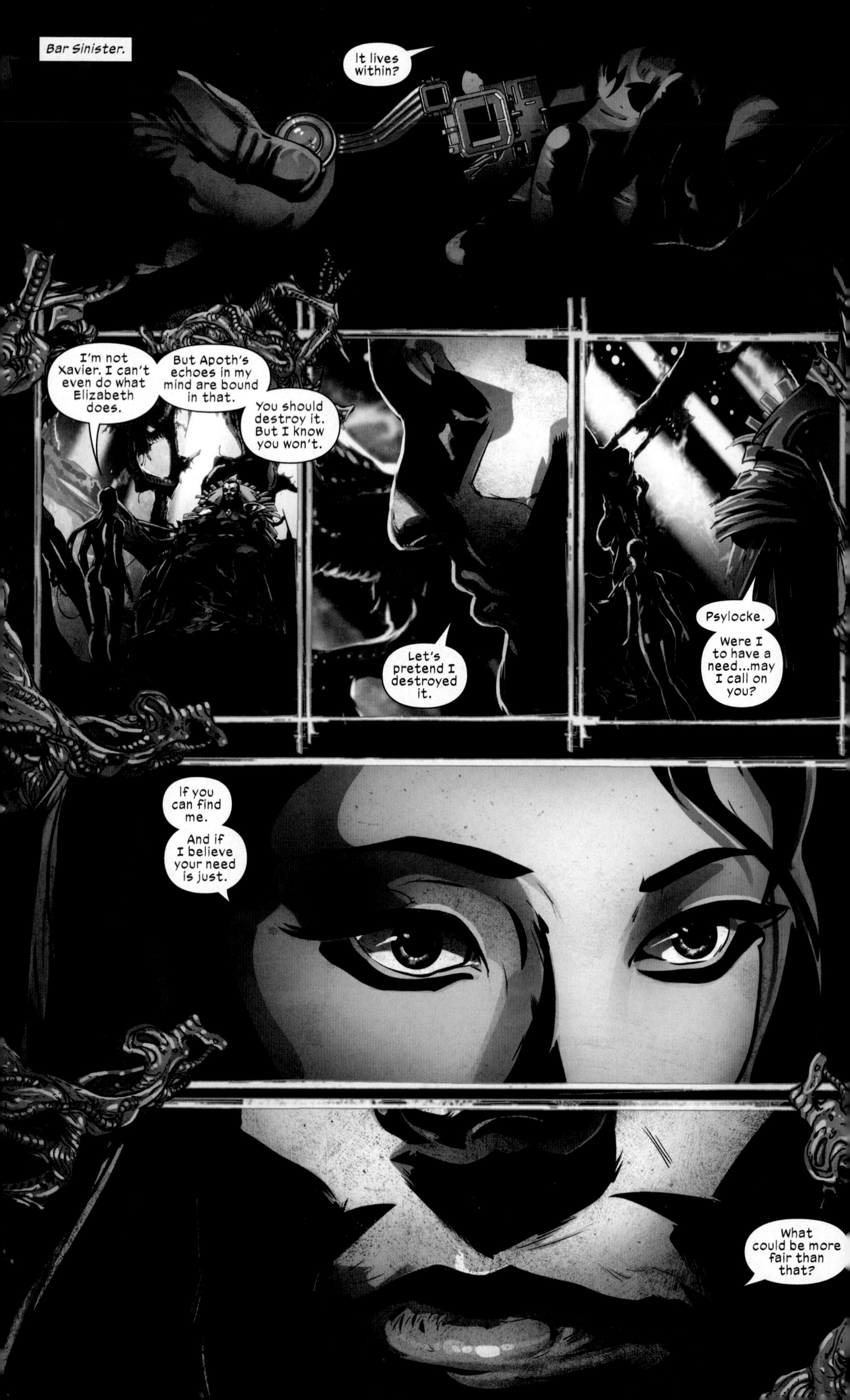
Bar Sinister.
It lives within?
I'm not Xavier. I can't even do what Elizabeth does.
But Apoth's echoes in my mind are bound in that.
You should destroy it. But I know you won't.
Let's pretend I destroyed it.
Psylocke.
Were I to have a need...may I call on you?
If you can find me.
And if I believe your need is just.
What could be more fair than that?

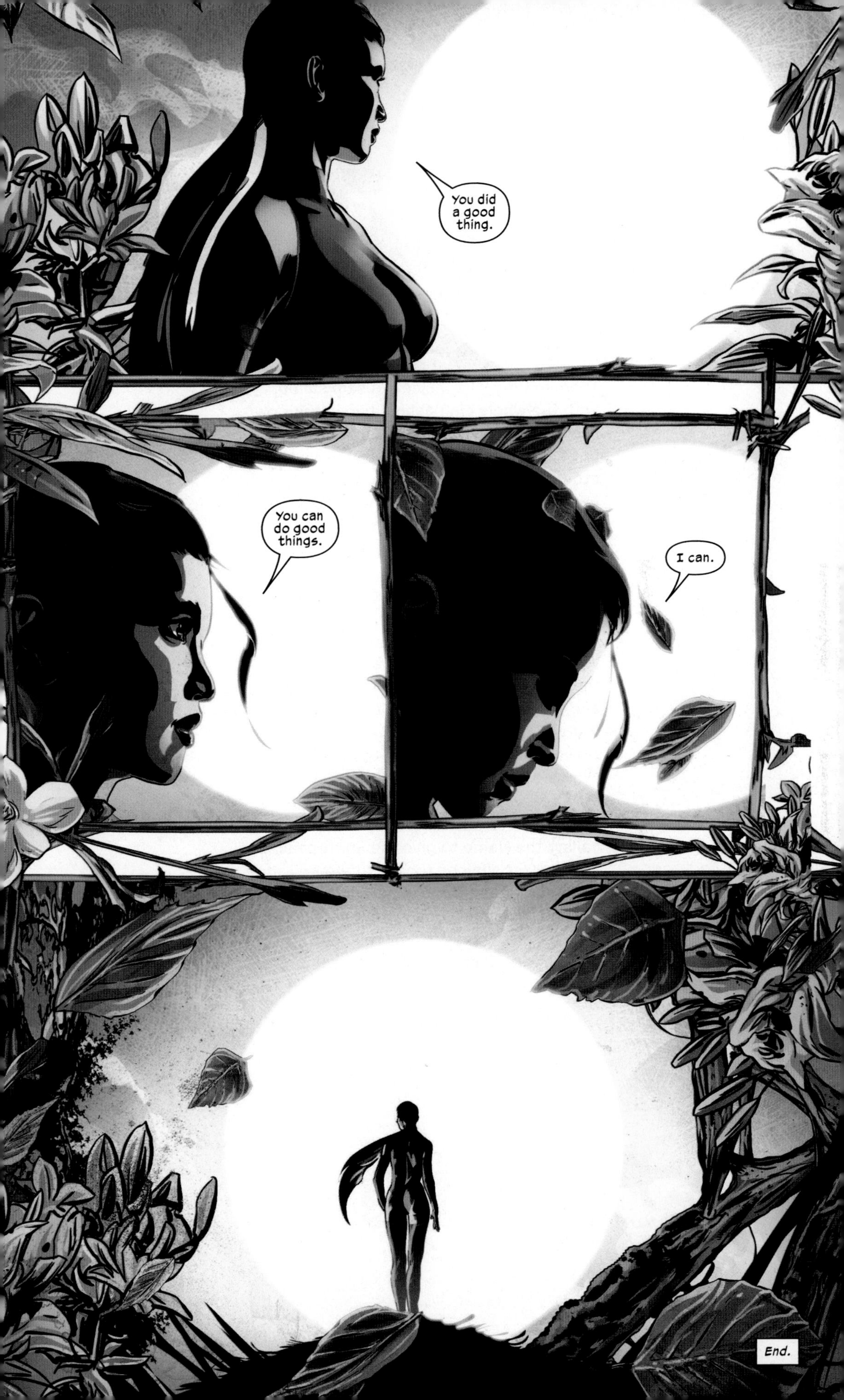
You did a good thing.
You can do good things.
I can.
End.

Then, in time, His Majesty's ship sailed,
with the whole clan behind him in their own.
Anxious to be aboard, I sought the shore,
but all the warships and the imperial barge
stood already far, far out to sea.
I was stranded. Reining in my horse,
I halted, at a loss for what to do.
There came then, galloping behind me,
Kumagai no Jirō Naozane,
shouting, "You will not escape my arm!"
At this Atsumori wheeled his mount
and swiftly, all undaunted, drew his sword.
We first exchanged a few rapid blows,
then, still on horseback, closed to grapple, fell
and wrestled on, upon the wave-washed strand.
But you bested me, and I was slain.
Now karma brings us face-to-face again.
"You are my foe!" Atsumori shouts,
lifting his sword to strike; but Kumagai
with kindness has repaid old enmity,
calling the Name to give the spirit peace.
They at last shall be reborn together
upon one lotus throne in paradise.
Renshō (Kumagai), you were no enemy of mine.
Pray for me, O pray for my release!
Pray for me, O pray for my release!

--From **"Atsumori"** by Zeami Motokiyo
(c. 1363 - c. 1443)

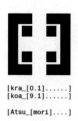

[kra_[0.1]......]
[koa_[9.1]......]

[Atsu_[mori]....]

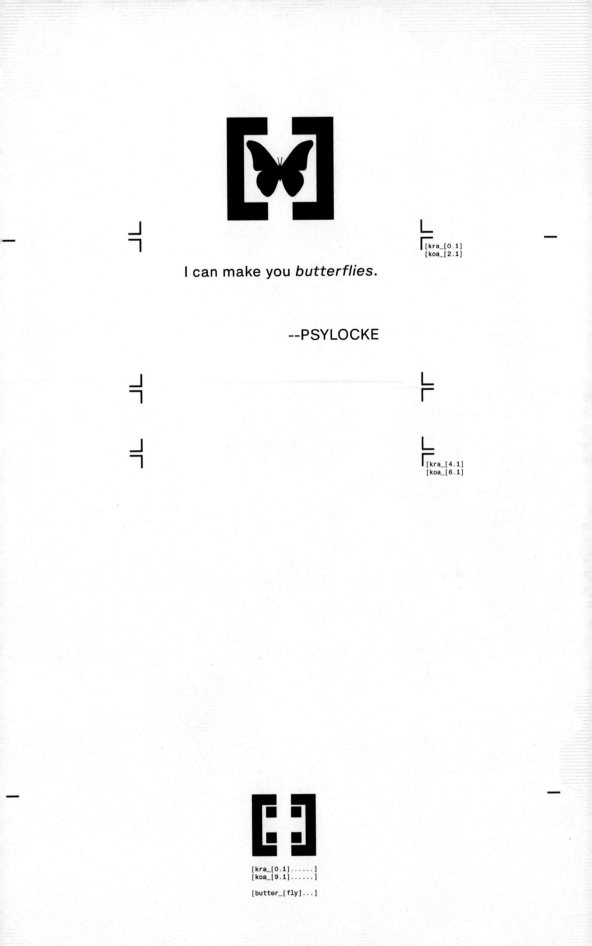

I can make you *butterflies*.

--PSYLOCKE

[kra_[0.1]
[koa_[2.1]

[kra_[4.1]
[koa_[6.1]

[kra_[0.1]......]
[koa_[9.1]......]

[butter_[fly]...]

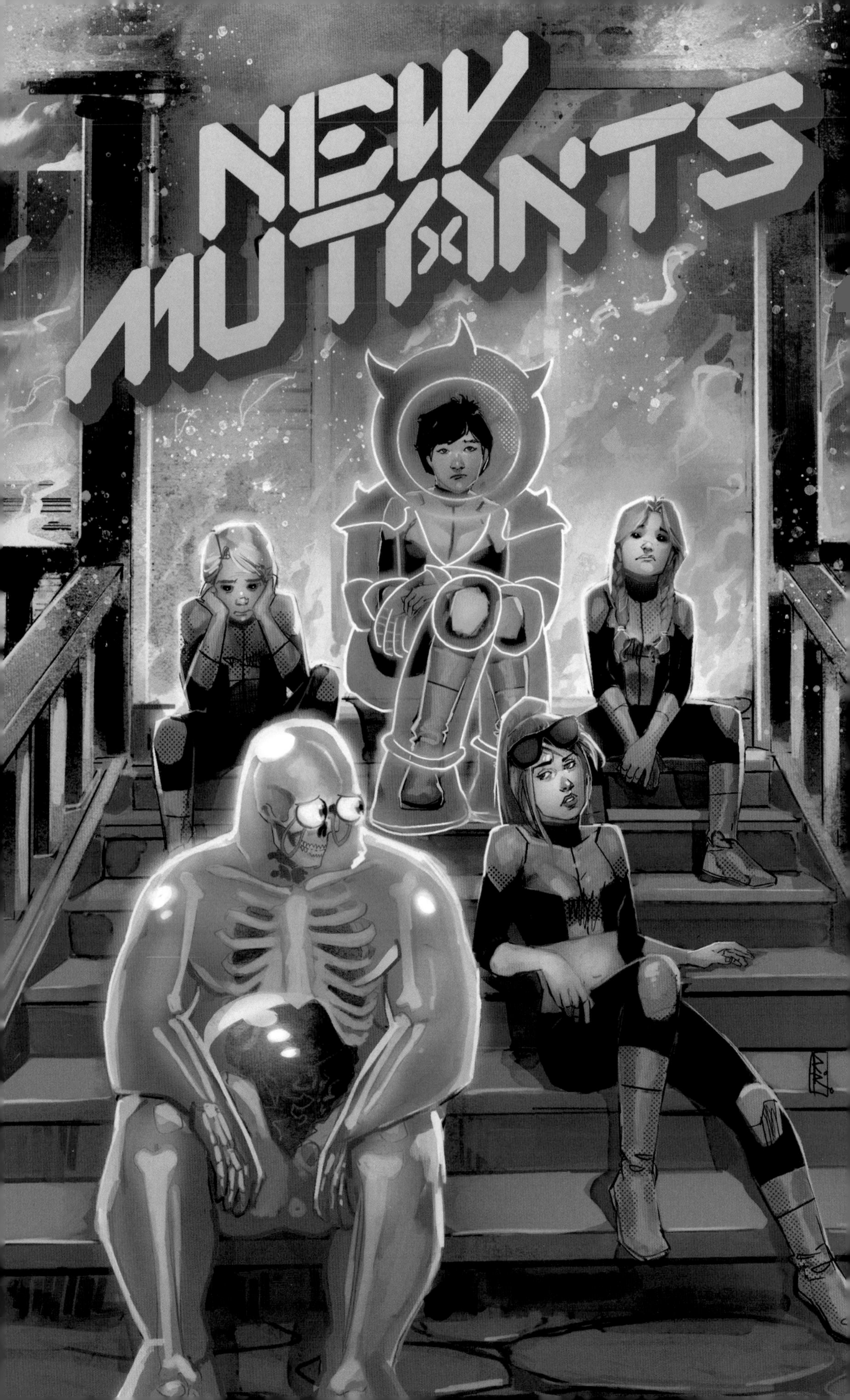
NEW MUTANTS

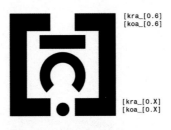

[kra_[0.6]
[koa_[0.6]

[kra_[0.X]
[koa_[0.X]

TICK, TICK...

Discovering that old friends Beak and Angel were missing from Krakoa due to Beak's ailing father, Armor, Glob, Maxime and Manon traveled to Nebraska. Their Krakoan medicine brought Beak's father back from the brink of death -- but before they could celebrate, armed gunmen burst onto the farm. Led by Túmulo, the gunmen demanded access to Krakoan drugs... and were willing to do anything to get them. Held hostage, the situation looked dire for the NEW MUTANTS -- then Boom-Boom arrived to even the score.

Armor

Boom-Boom

Glob

Maxime

Manon

Beak

Angel

[00_search___X]
[00_find_____X]

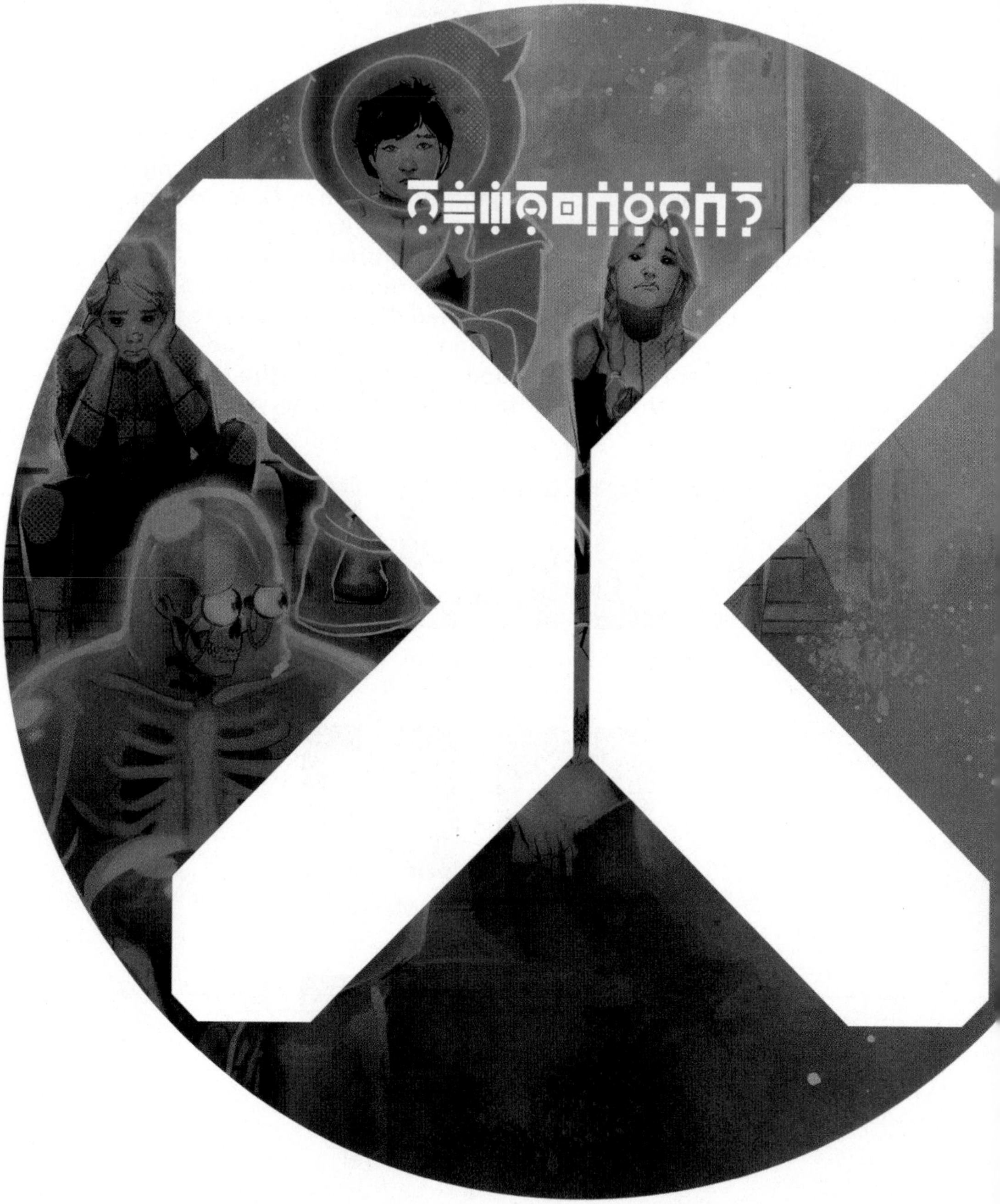

ED BRISSON...................................[WRITER]
FLAVIANO......................................[ARTIST]
CARLOS LOPEZ............................[COLOR ARTIST]
VC's TRAVIS LANHAM.........................[LETTERER]
TOM MULLER...................................[DESIGN]

ROD REIS................................[COVER ARTIST]

ADI GRANOV....................[VARIANT COVER ARTIST]

NICK RUSSELL.............................[PRODUCTION]

JONATHAN HICKMAN..........................[HEAD OF X]
ANNALISE BISSA...............................[EDITOR]
JORDAN D. WHITE.......................[SENIOR EDITOR]
C.B. CEBULSKI........................[EDITOR IN CHIEF]

[06]NEW MUTANTS

[ISSUE SIX]................NOT AS HOPED

[00_search___X]
[00_find_____X]

[00_00.....0]
[00_00.....6]

[00___krakoa]
[00_is_____]

[00_calling_]

[00_answer?_]

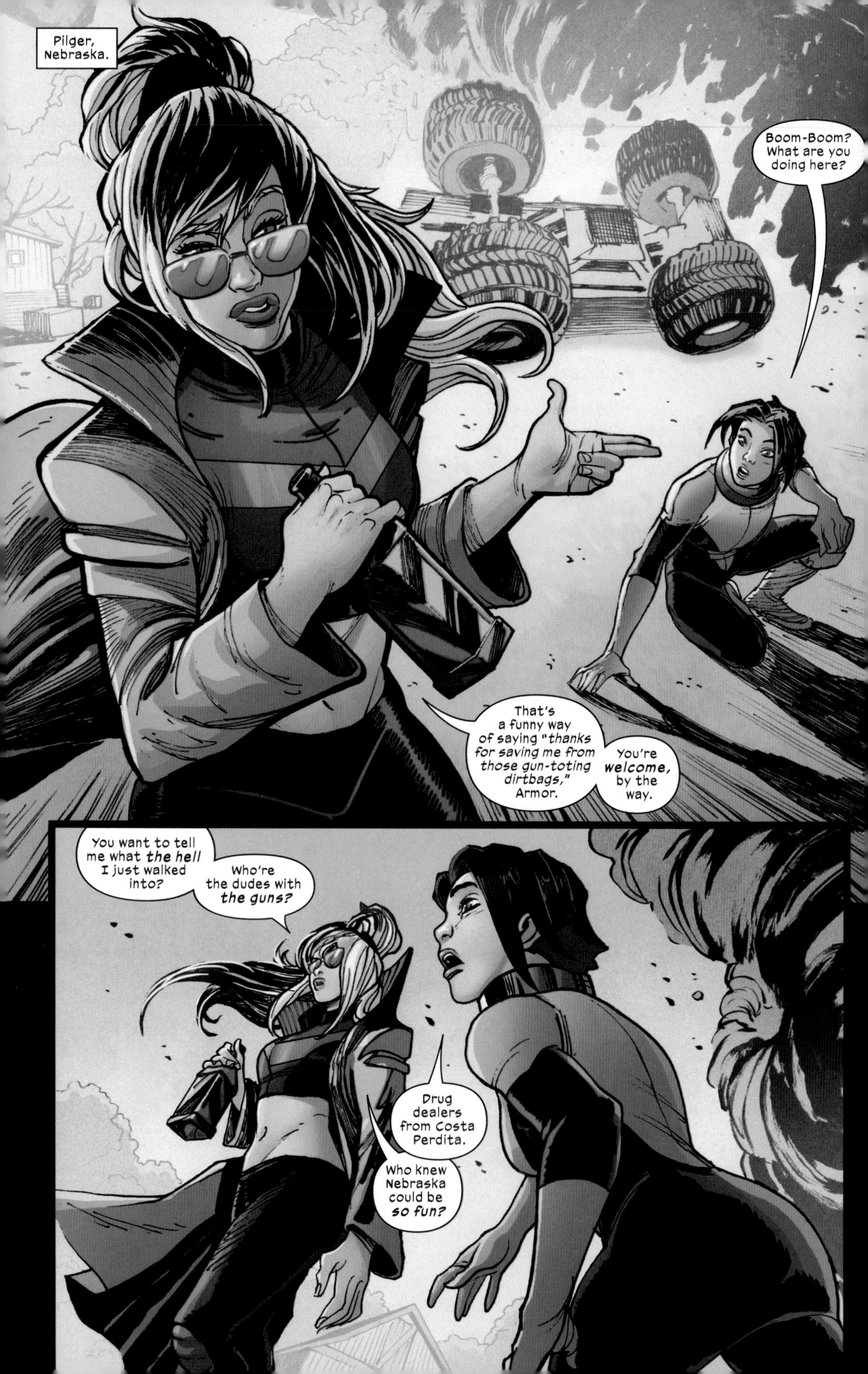
Pilger, Nebraska.
Boom-Boom? What are you doing here?
That's a funny way of saying "thanks for saving me from those gun-toting dirtbags," Armor.
You're welcome, by the way.
You want to tell me what the hell I just walked into?
Who're the dudes with the guns?
Drug dealers from Costa Perdita.
Who knew Nebraska could be so fun?

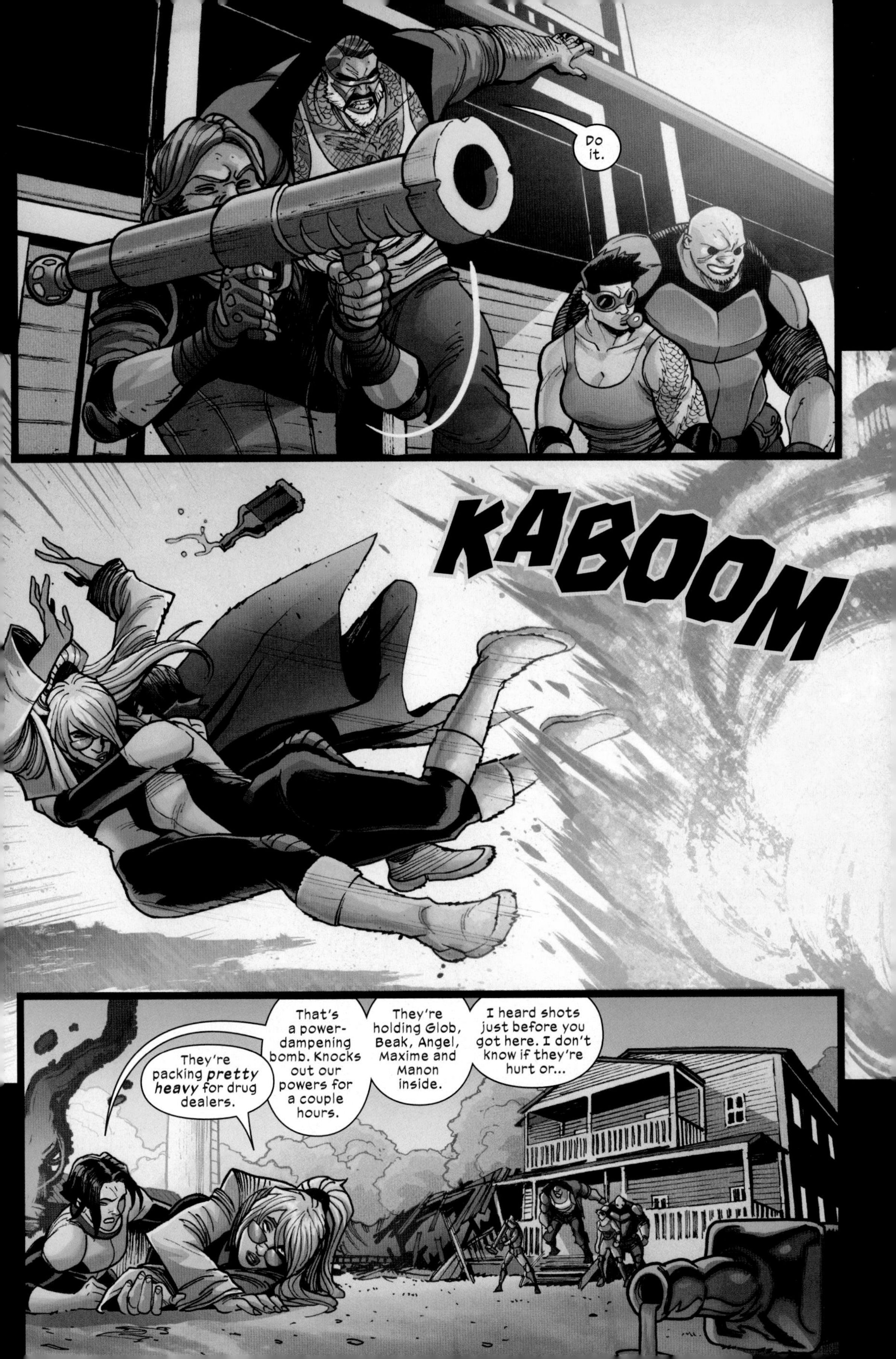
Do it.
KABOOM
They're packing *pretty heavy* for drug dealers.
That's a power-dampening bomb. Knocks out our powers for a couple hours.
They're holding Glob, Beak, Angel, Maxime and Manon inside.
I heard shots just before you got here. I don't know if they're hurt or...

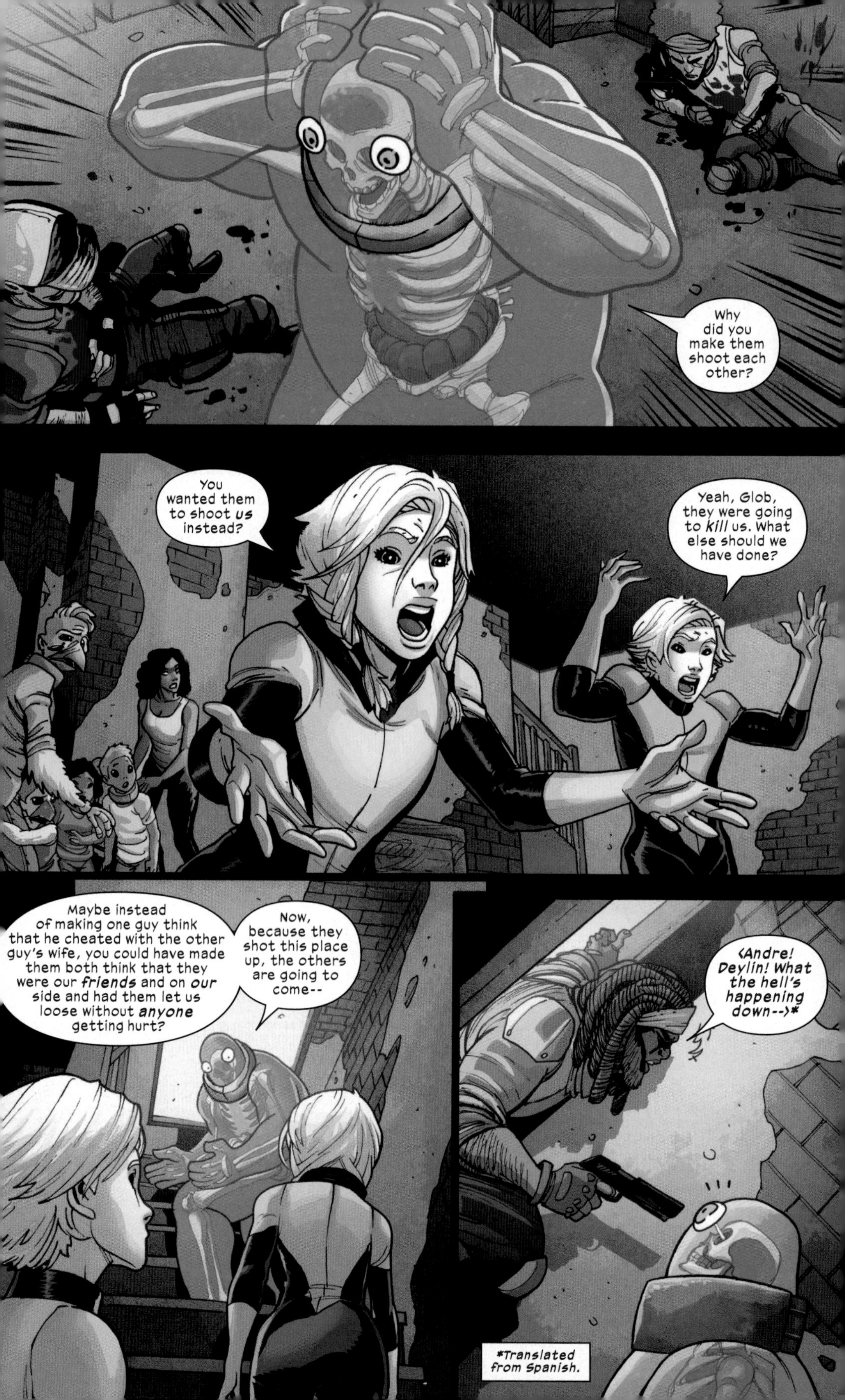
Why did you make them shoot each other?
You wanted them to shoot us instead?
Yeah, Glob, they were going to kill us. What else should we have done?
Maybe instead of making one guy think that he cheated with the other guy's wife, you could have made them both think that they were our friends and on our side and had them let us loose without anyone getting hurt?
Now, because they shot this place up, the others are going to come--
‹Andre! Deylin! What the hell's happening down--›*
*Translated from Spanish.

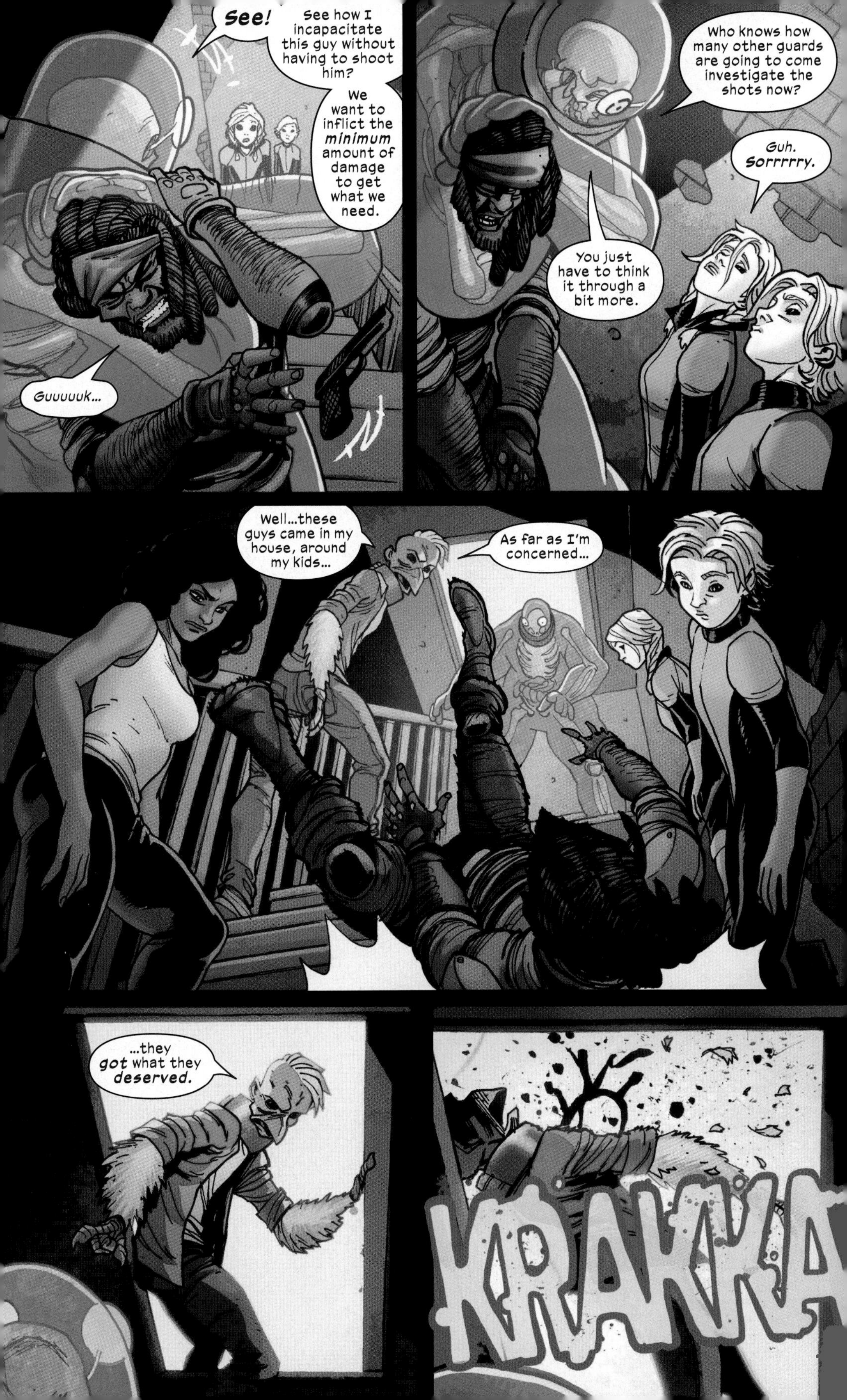
See!
See how I incapacitate this guy without having to shoot him?
We want to inflict the *minimum* amount of damage to get what we need.
Guuuuuk...
Who knows how many other guards are going to come investigate the shots now?
Guh. Sorrrrry.
You just have to think it through a bit more.
Well...these guys came in my house, around my kids...
As far as I'm concerned...
...they *got* what they *deserved.*
KRAKKA

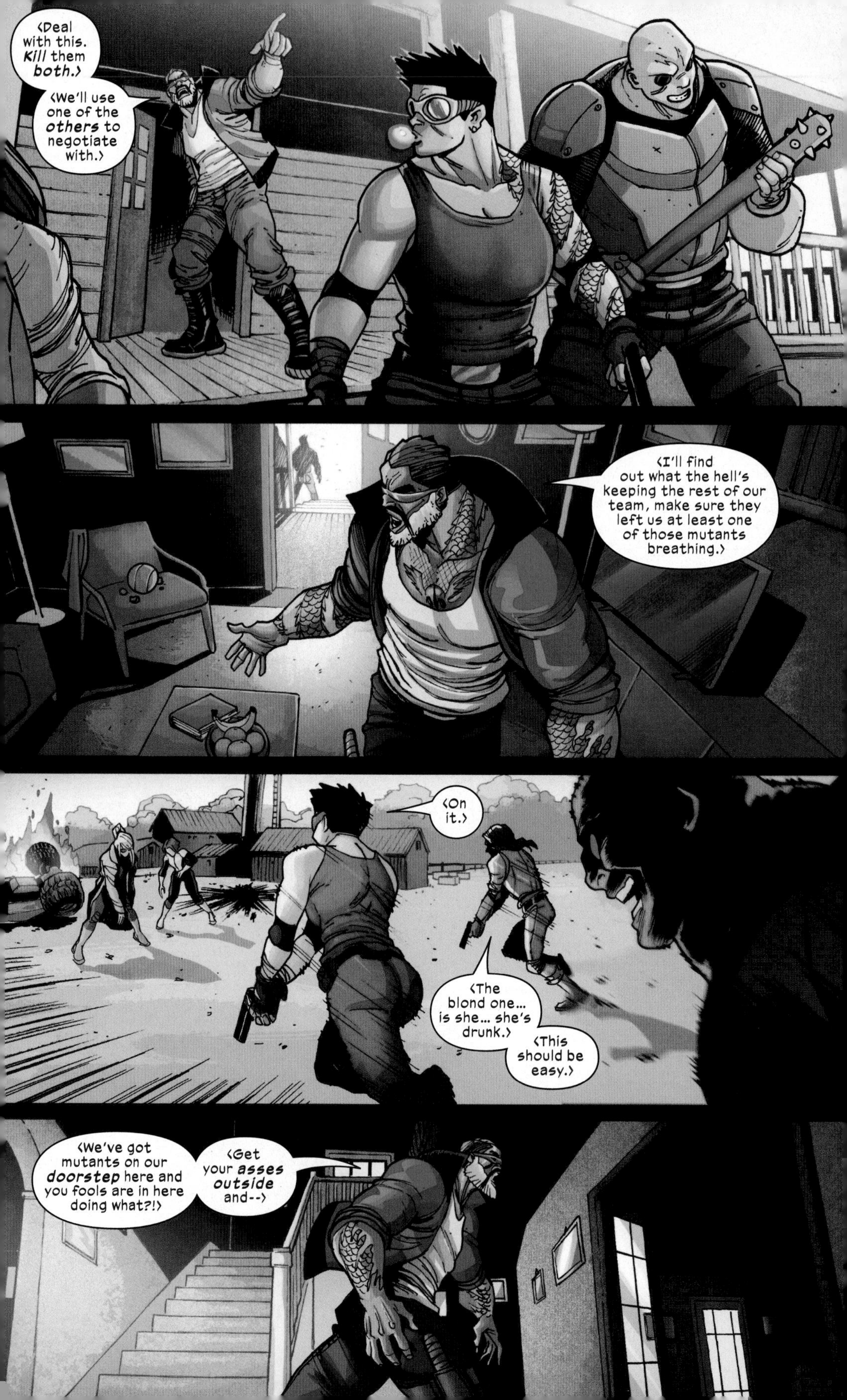
‹Deal with this. *Kill* them *both.*›
‹We'll use one of the *others* to negotiate with.›
‹I'll find out what the hell's keeping the rest of our team, make sure they left us at least one of those mutants breathing.›
‹On it.›
‹The blond one... is she... she's drunk.›
‹This should be easy.›
‹We've got mutants on our *doorstep* here and you fools are in here doing what?!›
‹Get your *asses outside* and--›

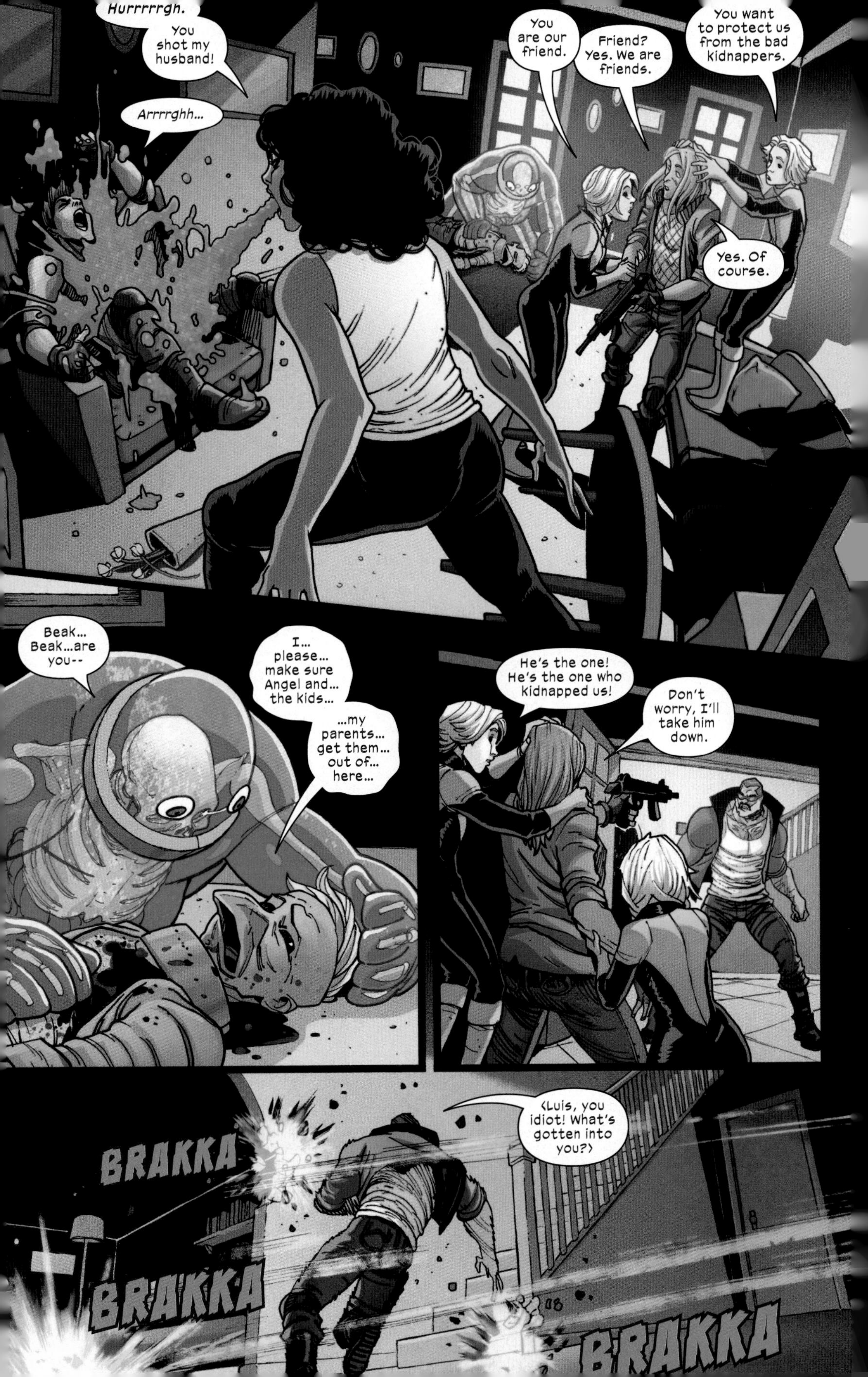
Hurrrrrgh.
You shot my husband!
Arrrrghh...
You are our friend.
Friend? Yes. We are friends.
You want to protect us from the bad kidnappers.
Yes. Of course.
Beak... Beak...are you--
I... please... make sure Angel and... the kids...
...my parents... get them... out of... here...
He's the one! He's the one who kidnapped us!
Don't worry, I'll take him down.
BRAKKA
‹Luis, you idiot! What's gotten into you?›
BRAKKA
BRAKKA

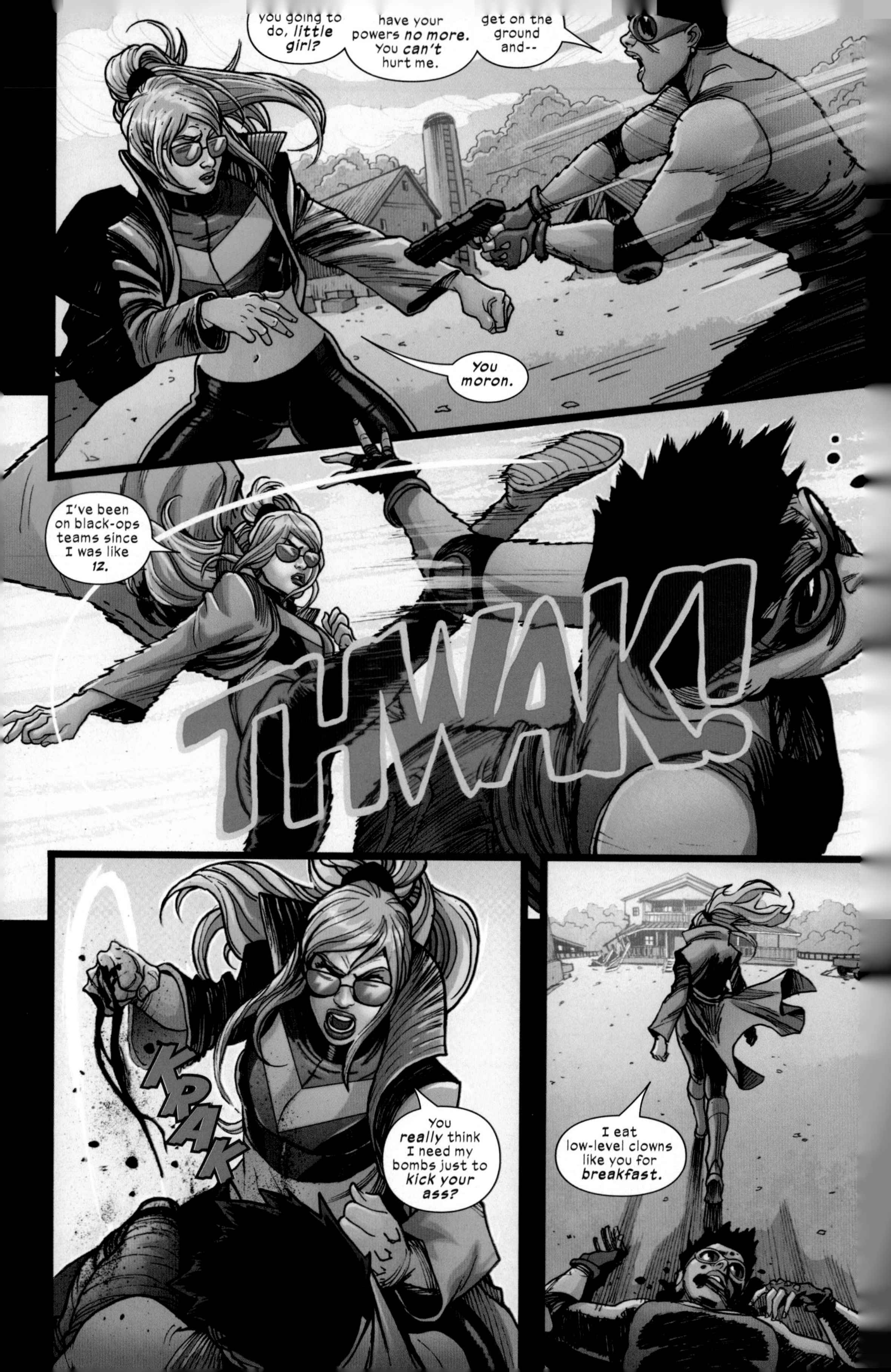
you going to do, little girl?
have your powers no more. You can't hurt me.
get on the ground and--
You moron.
I've been on black-ops teams since I was like 12.
THWAK!
KRAK
You really think I need my bombs just to kick your ass?
I eat low-level clowns like you for breakfast.

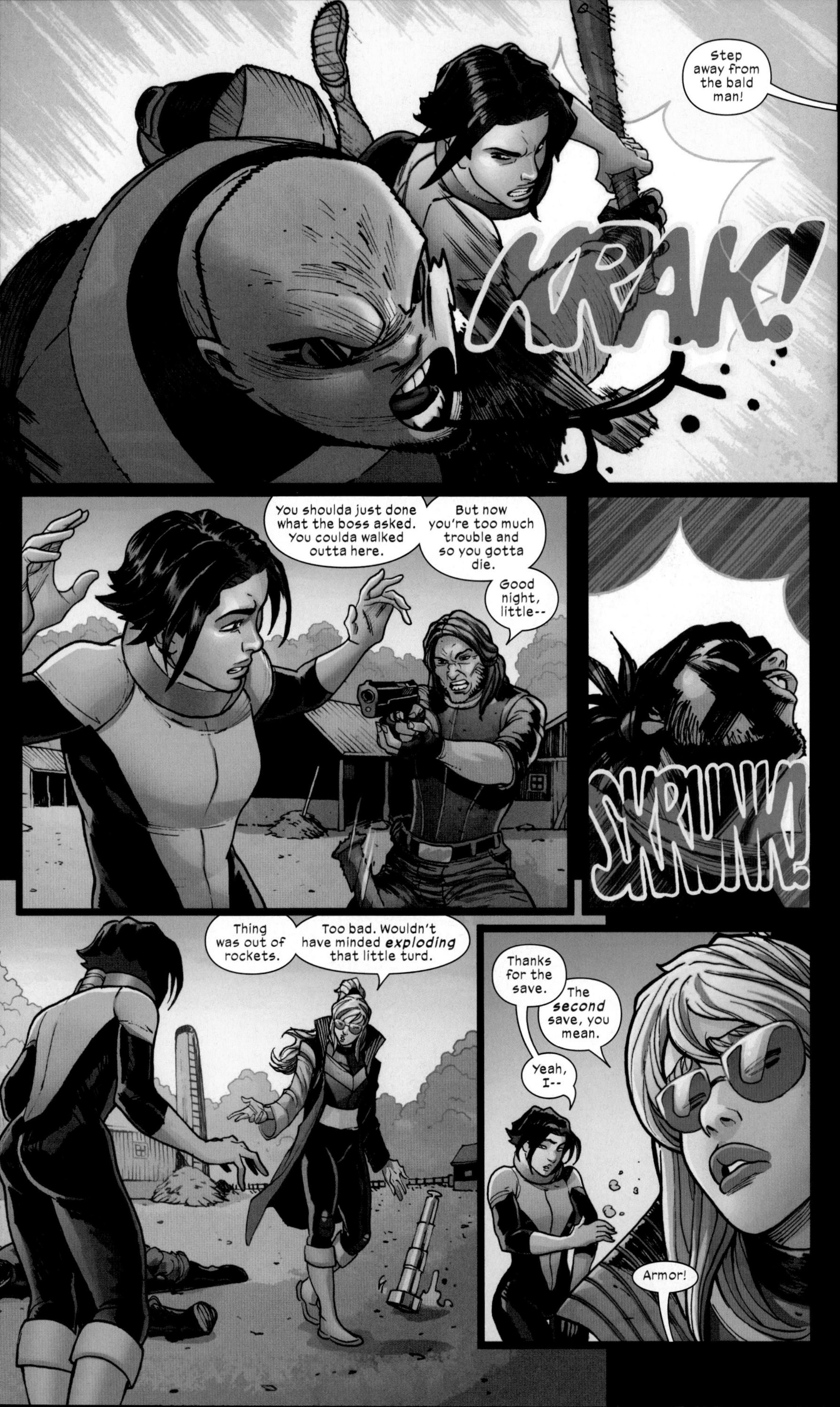

Step away from the bald man!
KRAK!
You shoulda just done what the boss asked. You coulda walked outta here.
But now you're too much trouble and so you gotta die.
Good night, little--
SKRUNK!
Thing was out of rockets.
Too bad. Wouldn't have minded *exploding* that little turd.
Thanks for the save.
The *second* save, you mean.
Yeah, I--
Armor!

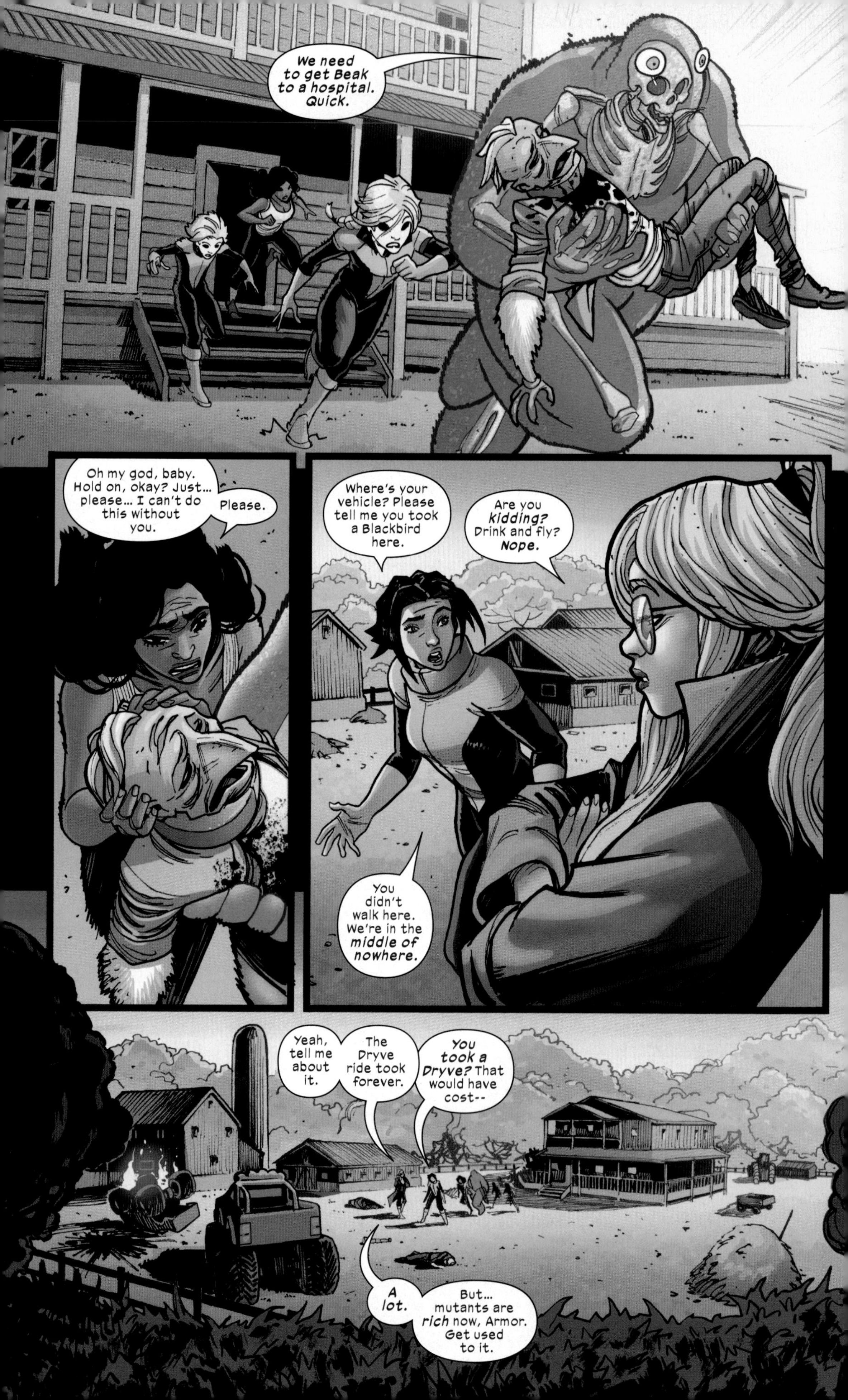

We need to get Beak to a hospital. Quick.
Oh my god, baby. Hold on, okay? Just... please... I can't do this without you.
Please.
Where's your vehicle? Please tell me you took a Blackbird here.
Are you kidding? Drink and fly? Nope.
You didn't walk here. We're in the middle of nowhere.
Yeah, tell me about it.
The Dryve ride took forever.
You took a Dryve? That would have cost--
A lot.
But... mutants are rich now, Armor. Get used to it.

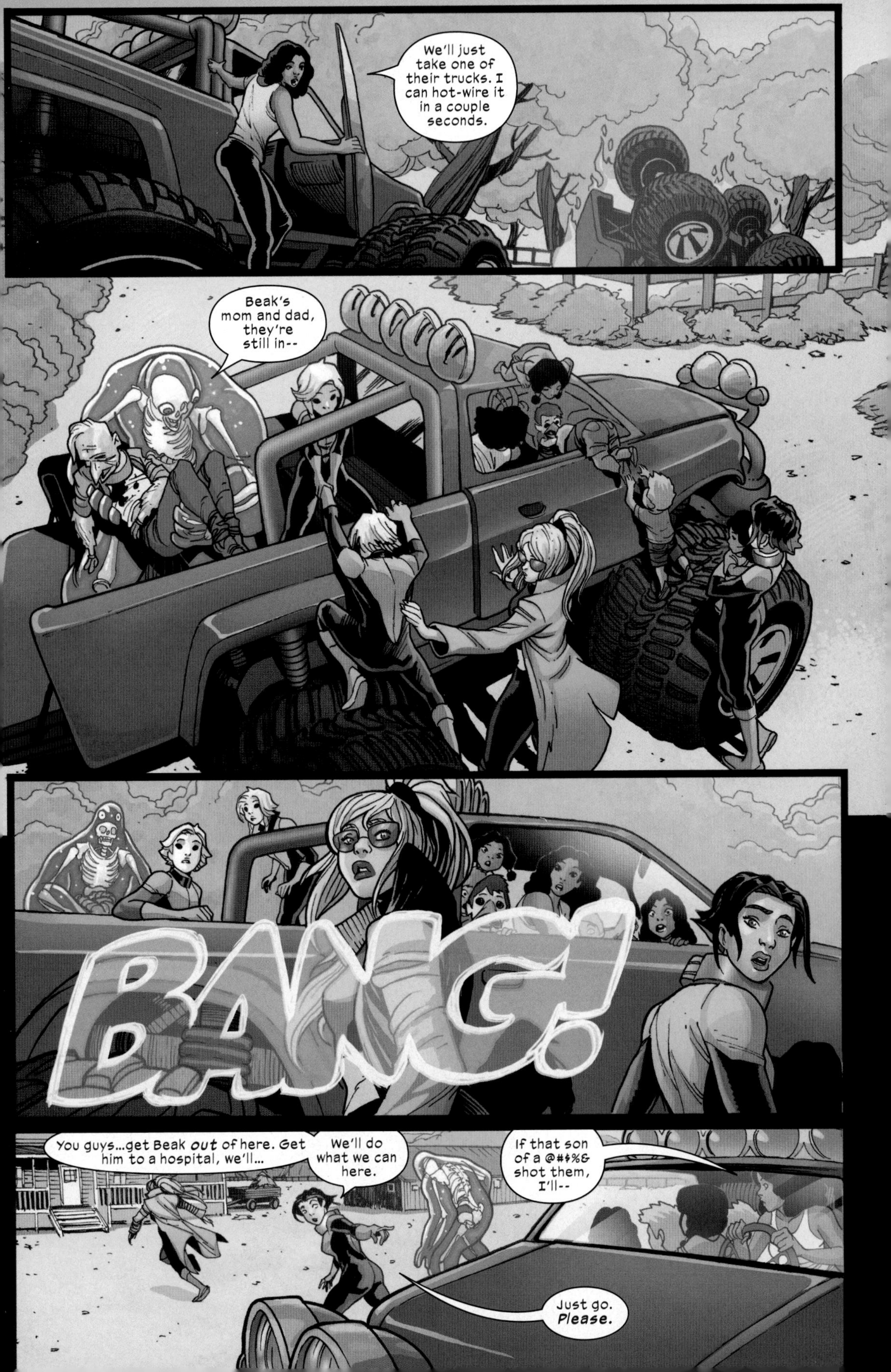
We'll just take one of their trucks. I can hot-wire it in a couple seconds.
Beak's mom and dad, they're still in--
BANG!
You guys...get Beak *out* of here. Get him to a hospital, we'll...
We'll do what we can here.
If that son of a @#$%& shot them, I'll--
Just go. *Please.*

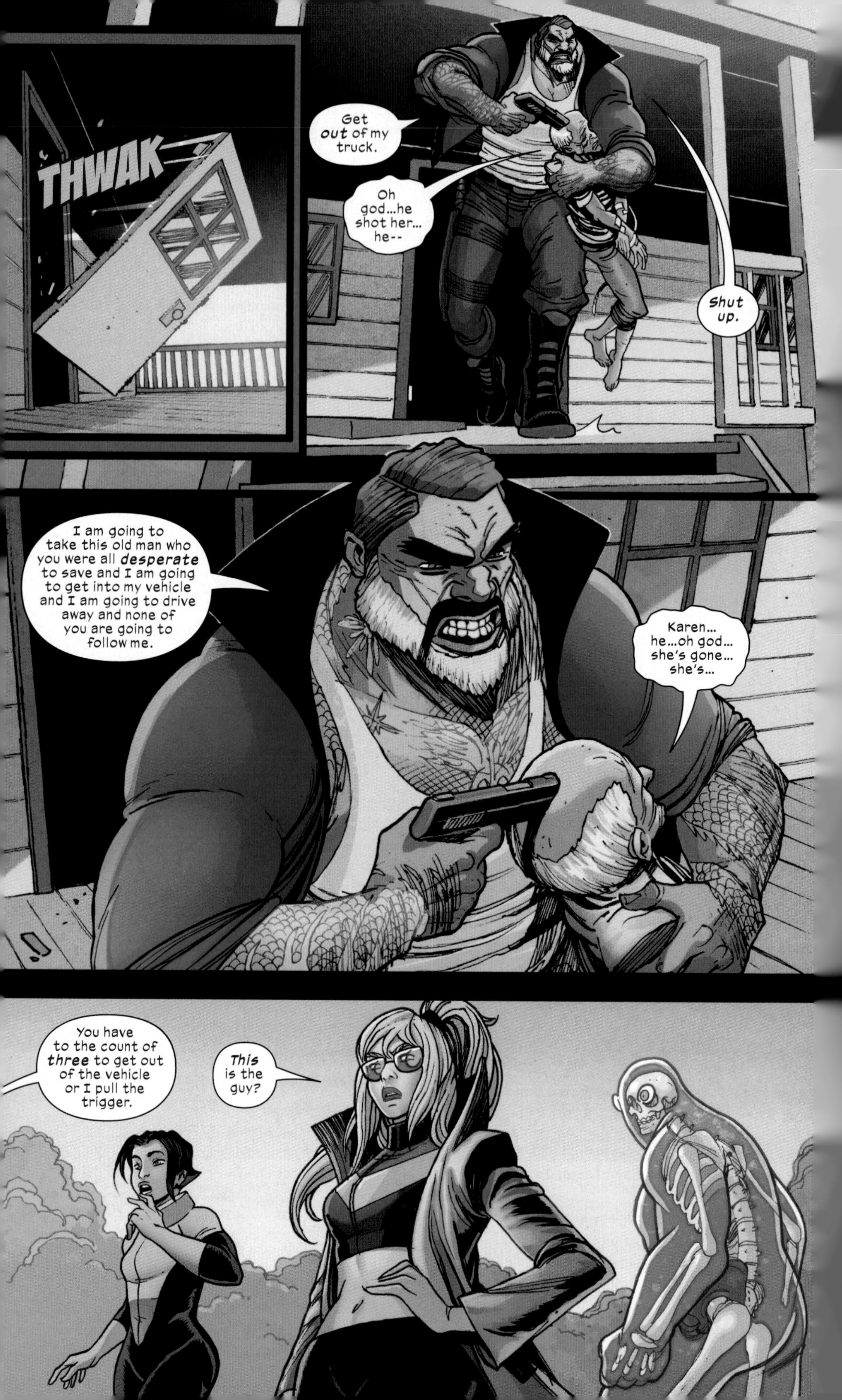
THWAK
Get out of my truck.
Oh god...he shot her... he--
Shut up.
I am going to take this old man who you were all desperate to save and I am going to get into my vehicle and I am going to drive away and none of you are going to follow me.
Karen... he...oh god... she's gone... she's...
You have to the count of three to get out of the vehicle or I pull the trigger.
This is the guy?

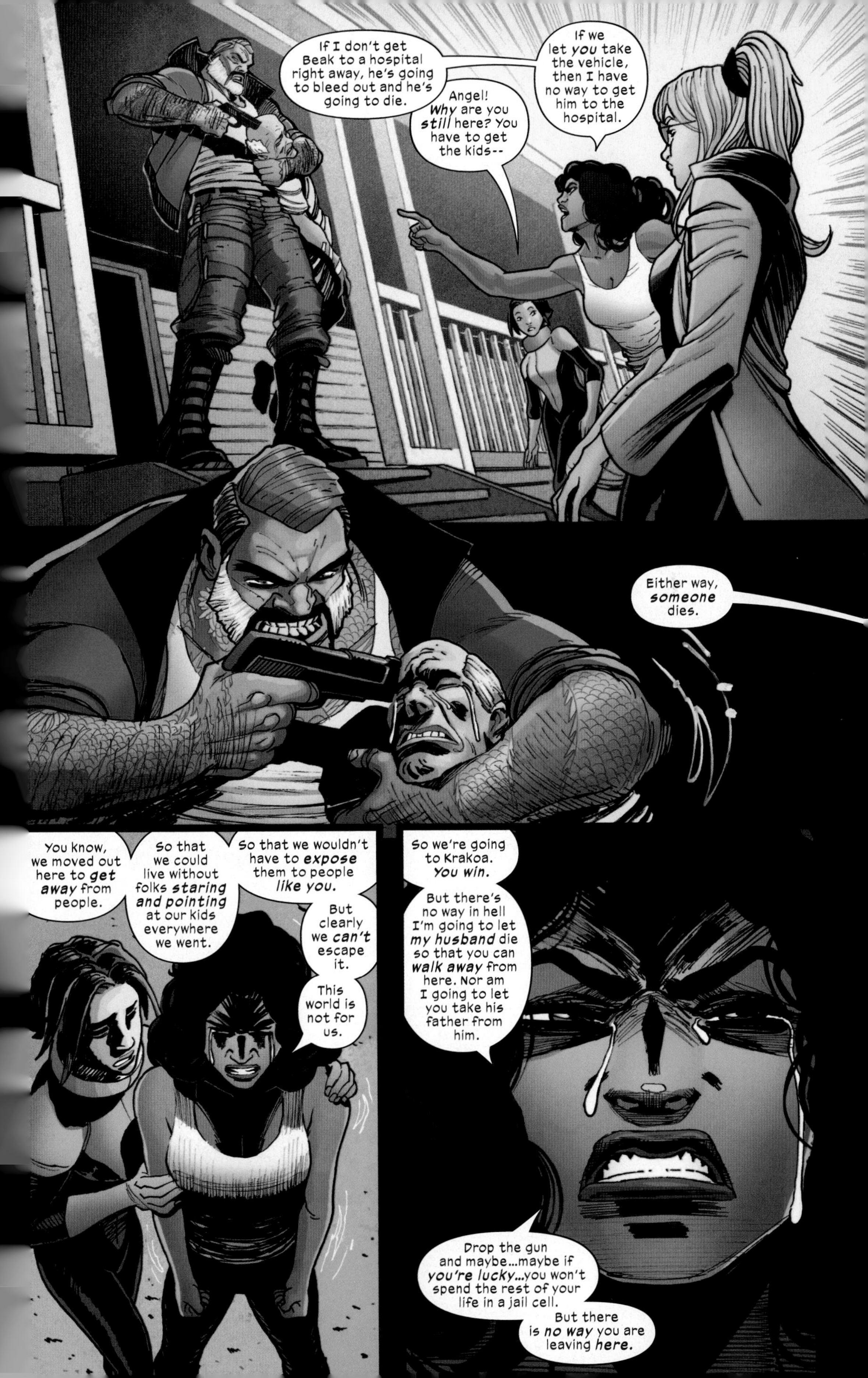

If I don't get Beak to a hospital right away, he's going to bleed out and he's going to die.
If we let you take the vehicle, then I have no way to get him to the hospital.
Angel! Why are you still here? You have to get the kids--
Either way, someone dies.
You know, we moved out here to get away from people.
So that we could live without folks staring and pointing at our kids everywhere we went.
So that we wouldn't have to expose them to people like you.
But clearly we can't escape it.
This world is not for us.
So we're going to Krakoa. You win.
But there's no way in hell I'm going to let my husband die so that you can walk away from here. Nor am I going to let you take his father from him.
Drop the gun and maybe...maybe if you're lucky...you won't spend the rest of your life in a jail cell.
But there is no way you are leaving here.

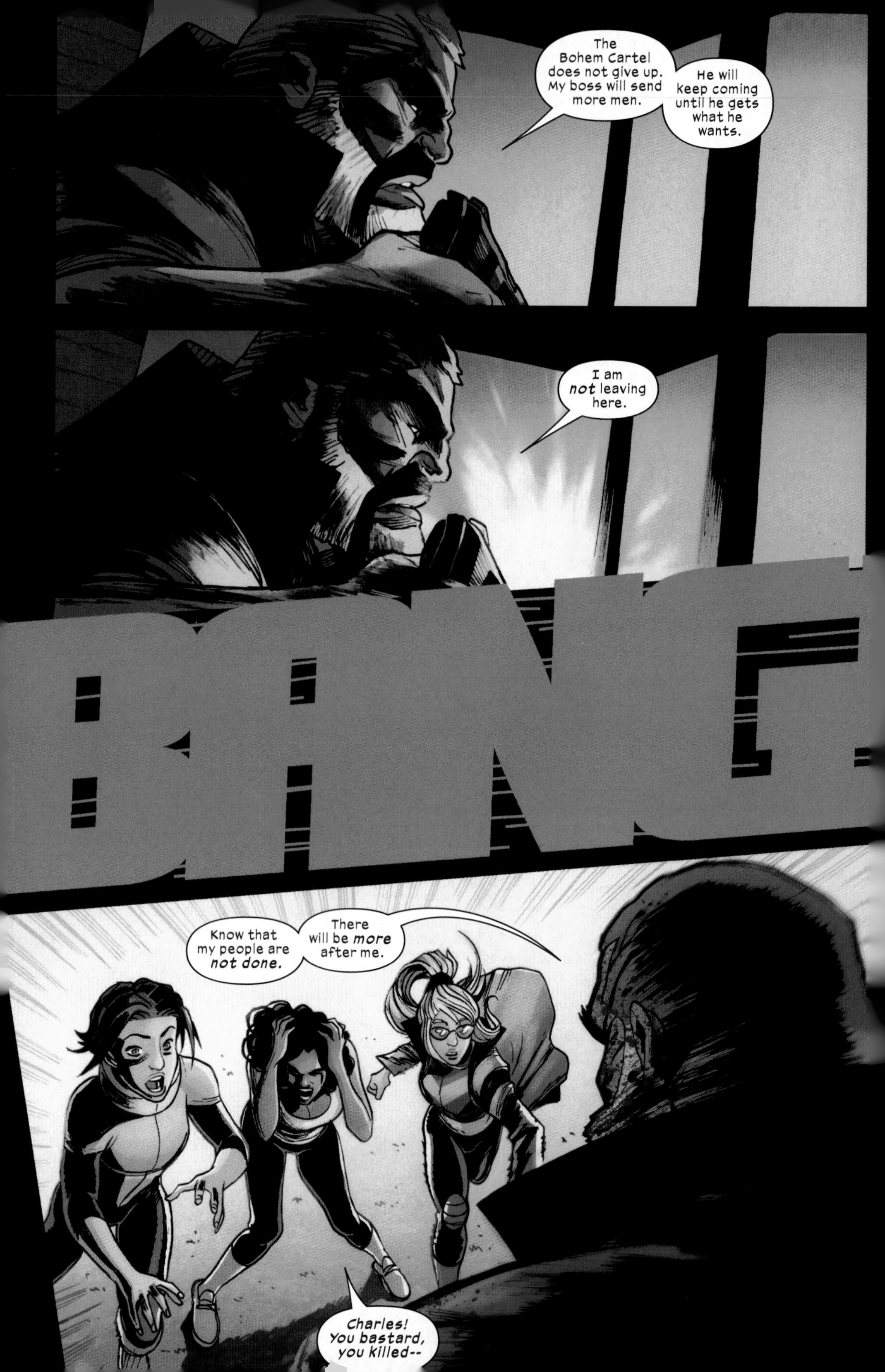
The Bohem Cartel does not give up. My boss will send more men.
He will keep coming until he gets what he wants.
I am *not* leaving here.
BANG
Know that my people are *not done.*
There will be *more* after me.
Charles! You bastard, you killed--

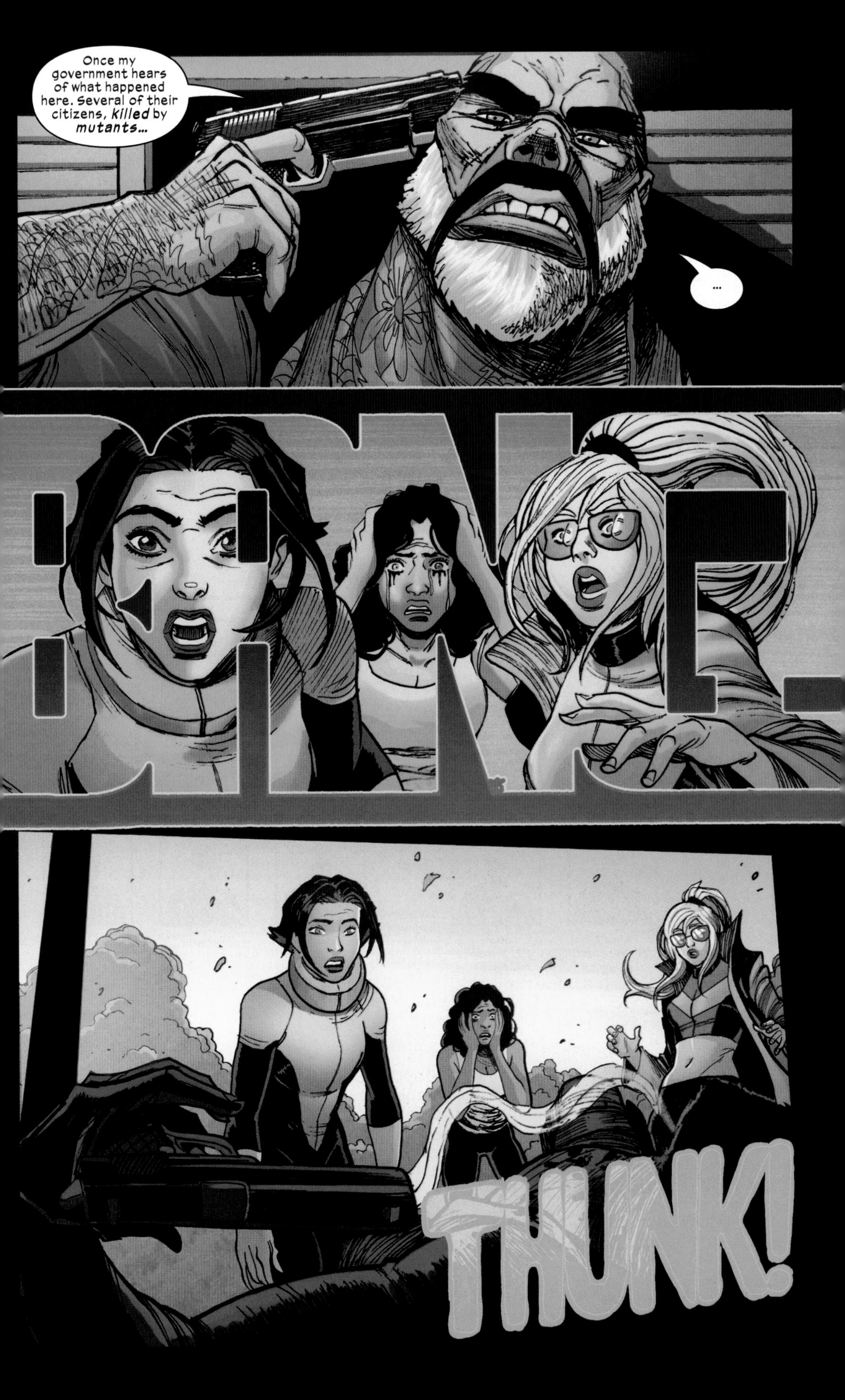
Once my government hears of what happened here. Several of their citizens, *killed* by *mutants...*
...
THUNK!

THE BOHEM CARTEL

HEAD: Ezequiel Dengra (Miguel and Julian)
BASE OF OPERATIONS: Bohem, Costa Perdita
NET WORTH: Approx. US$15 billion

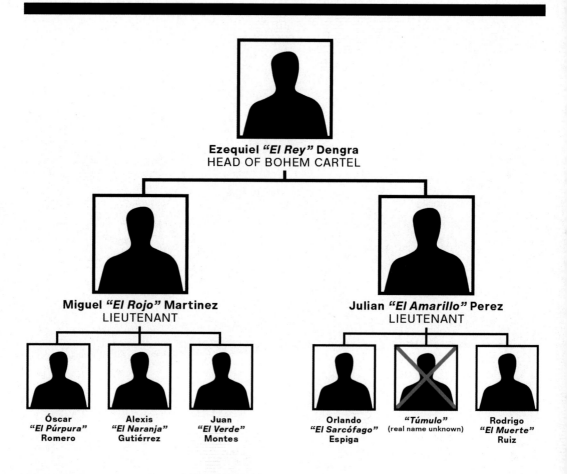

Ezequiel *"El Rey"* Dengra
HEAD OF BOHEM CARTEL

Miguel *"El Rojo"* Martinez
LIEUTENANT

Julian *"El Amarillo"* Perez
LIEUTENANT

Óscar
"El Púrpura"
Romero

Alexis
"El Naranja"
Gutiérrez

Juan
"El Verde"
Montes

Orlando
"El Sarcófago"
Espiga

"Túmulo"
(real name unknown)

Rodrigo
"El Muerte"
Ruiz

The Bohem Cartel is the largest drug cartel in Costa Perdita, controlling the distribution of methamphetamines, cocaine and heroin within the borders of Costa Perdita and beyond. They're known for their capacity toward violence, with an estimated annual death toll of 1,500.

They are a major player in the illegal drug market in both the United States and Europe, earning a reported US$1.8 billion annually through exports alone.

It is estimated that there are more than 40,000 members of the Bohem Cartel. Members range from federal police to street gang members.

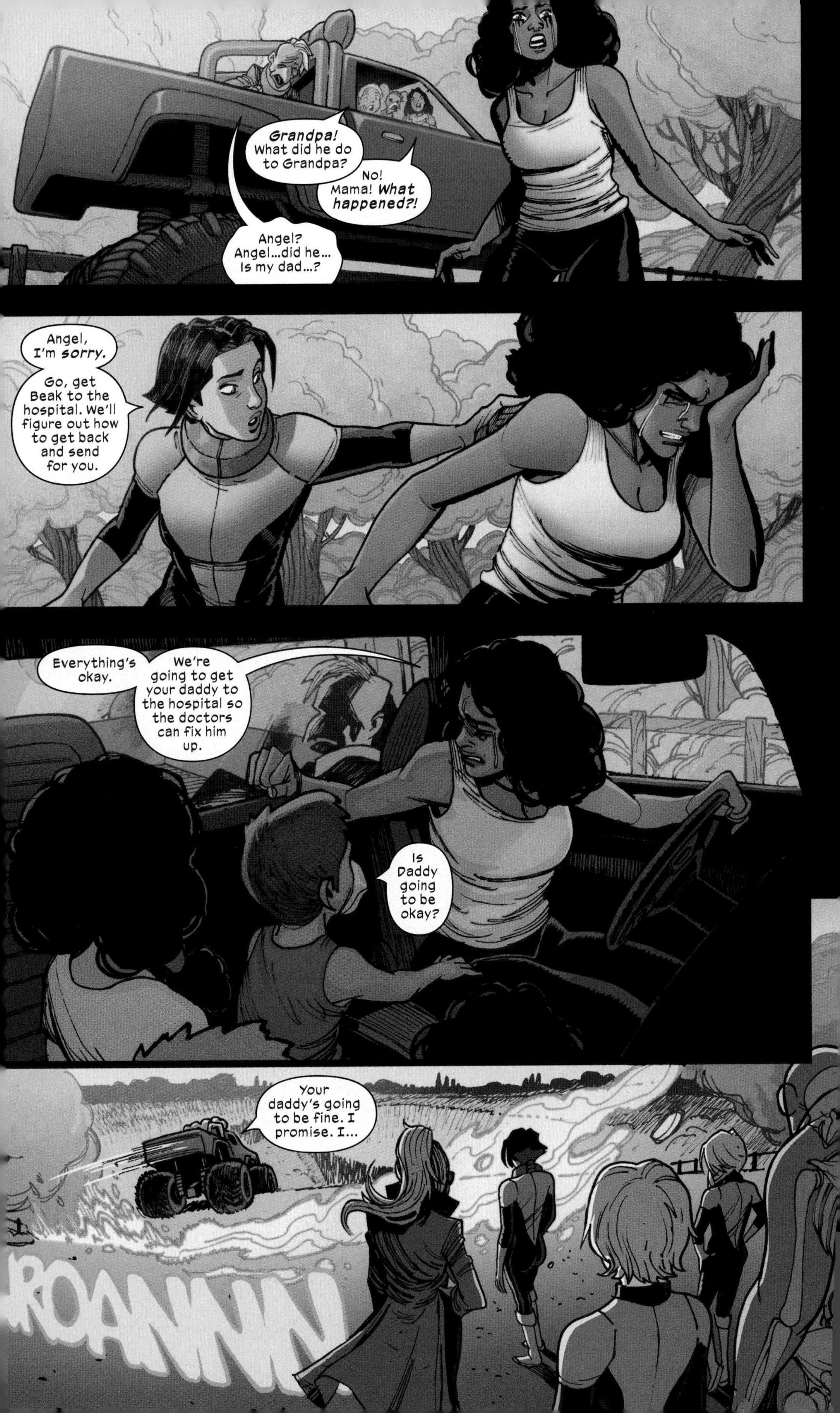
Grandpa! What did he do to Grandpa?
No! Mama! What happened?!
Angel? Angel...did he... Is my dad...?
Angel, I'm sorry.
Go, get Beak to the hospital. We'll figure out how to get back and send for you.
Everything's okay.
We're going to get your daddy to the hospital so the doctors can fix him up.
Is Daddy going to be okay?
Your daddy's going to be fine. I promise. I...
ROANNN

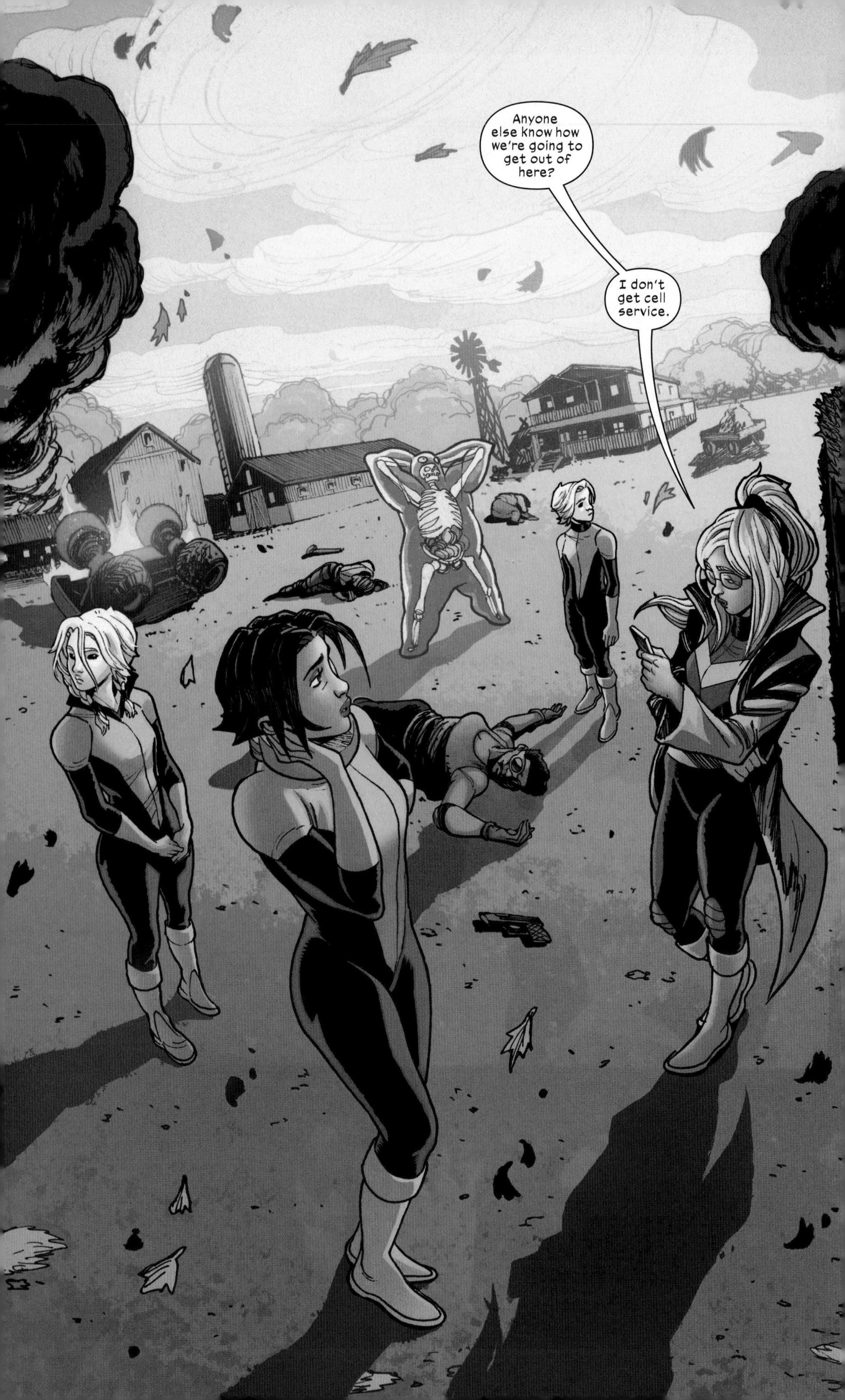
Anyone else know how we're going to get out of here?
I don't get cell service.

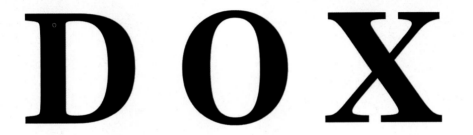

DOX

NEBRASKA NIGHTMARE:

FOUR DEAD IN MUTANT-INFESTED COUNTY

DOX first reported some weeks ago on a small group of mutants spotted in Pilger, Nebraska (link), and it seems, as always, where mutants go, trouble follows.

DOX forum member SapienSuperior247 has posted a series of reports, gleaned from sources within the local police department, that seem to indicate that a group of mutants descended upon a home in the area, leaving at least four dead and several injured.

Information regarding the identities of the deceased have not been released by police pending investigation -- and DOX is unable to confirm if the victims are mutants or human.

Through the help of the DOX community, we have been able to identify the mutants previously reported on as Barnell "Beak" Bohusk and Angel "Tempest" Salvadore, both known to be members of the X-Men and New Warriors. According to SapienSuperior247's sources, there may have been as many as ten other mutants in Pilger at the time of the attack. DOX's requests for information from the Stanton County Sheriff's Office have gone unanswered.

We will update this story as it develops.

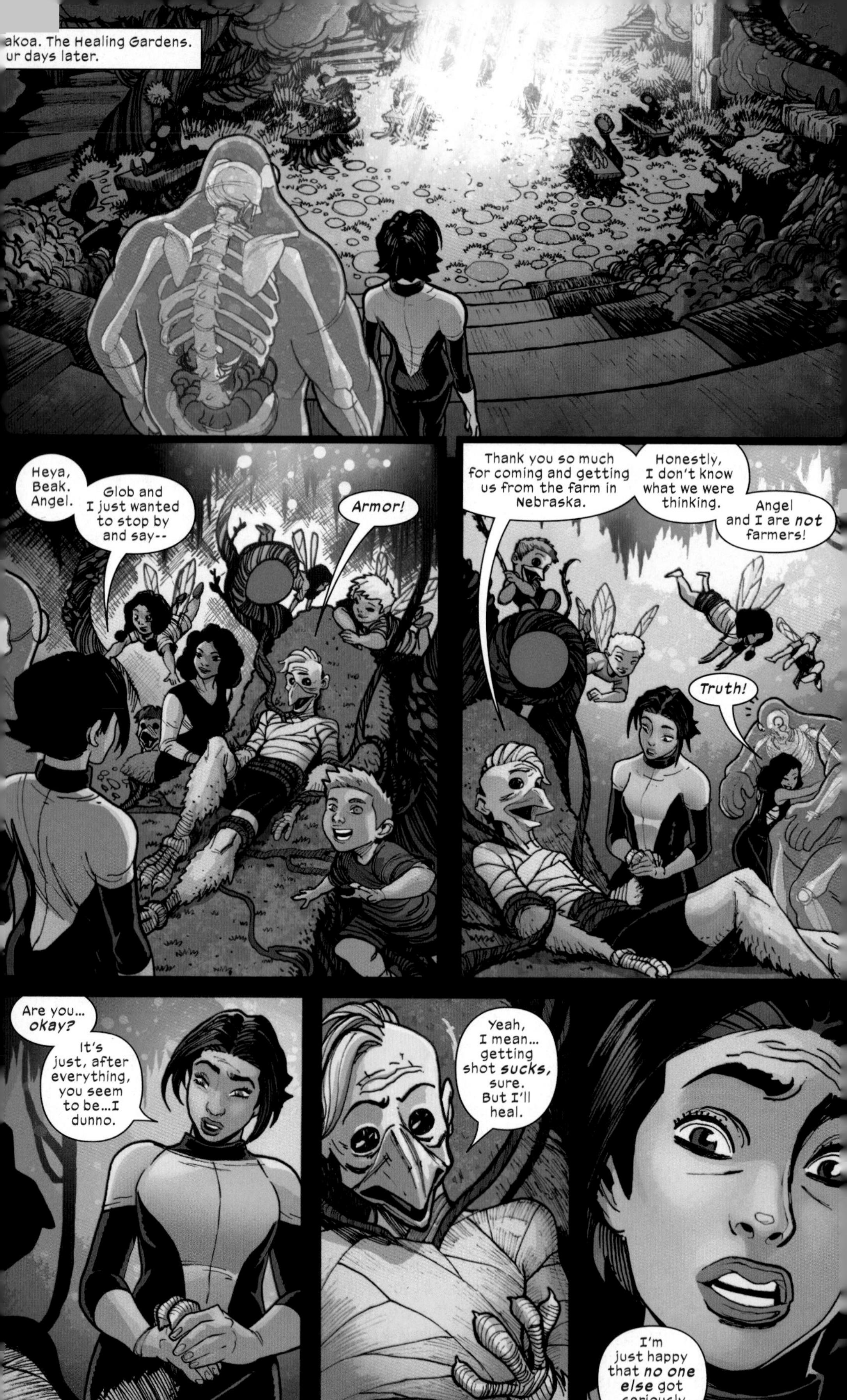
akoa. The Healing Gardens.
ur days later.
Heya, Beak. Angel.
Glob and I just wanted to stop by and say--
Armor!
Thank you so much for coming and getting us from the farm in Nebraska.
Honestly, I don't know what we were thinking.
Angel and I are not farmers!
Truth!
Are you... okay?
It's just, after everything, you seem to be...I dunno.
Yeah, I mean... getting shot sucks, sure. But I'll heal.
I'm just happy that no one else got seriously hurt.

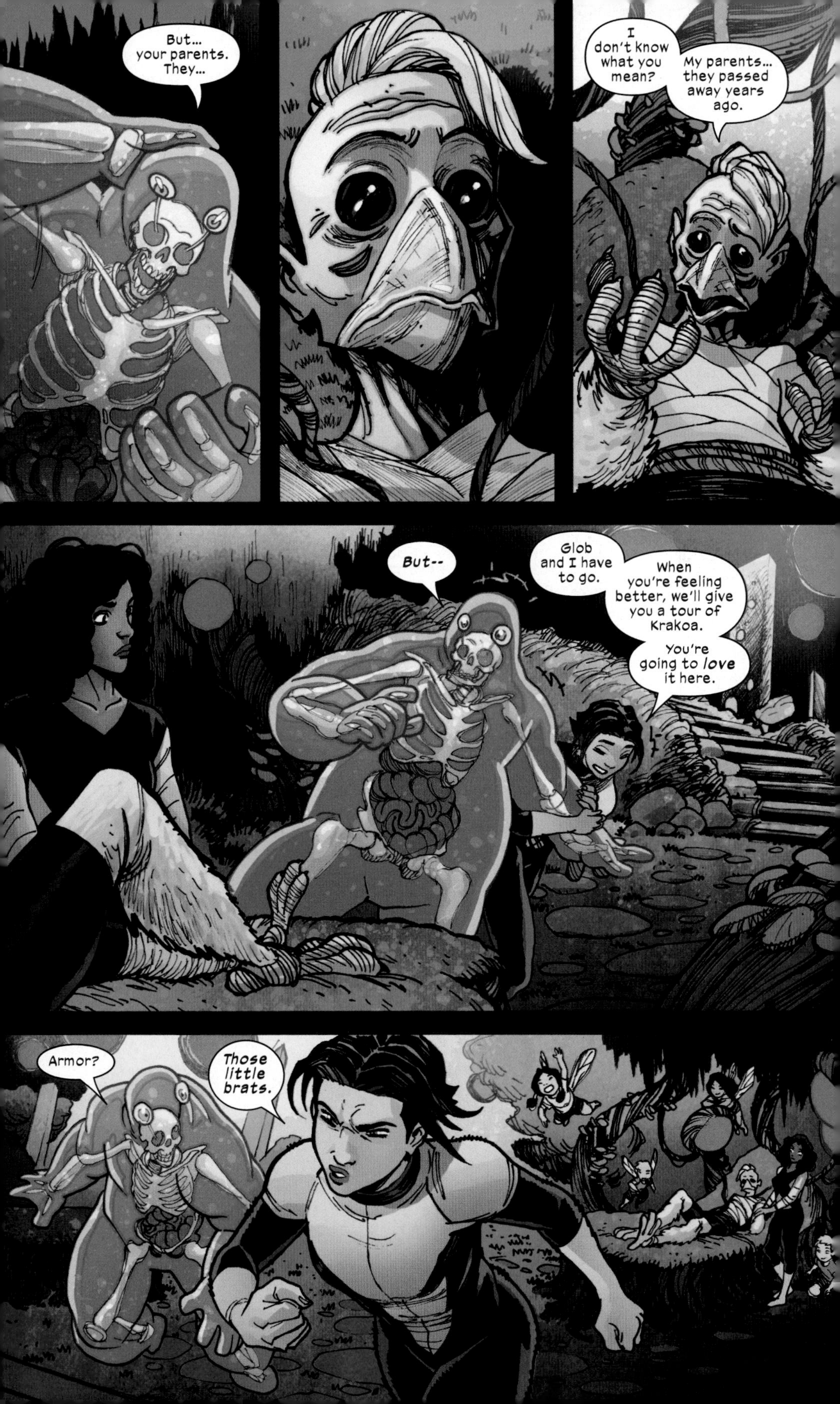
But... your parents. They...
I don't know what you mean?
My parents... they passed away years ago.
But--
Glob and I have to go.
When you're feeling better, we'll give you a tour of Krakoa.
You're going to *love* it here.
Armor?
Those little brats.

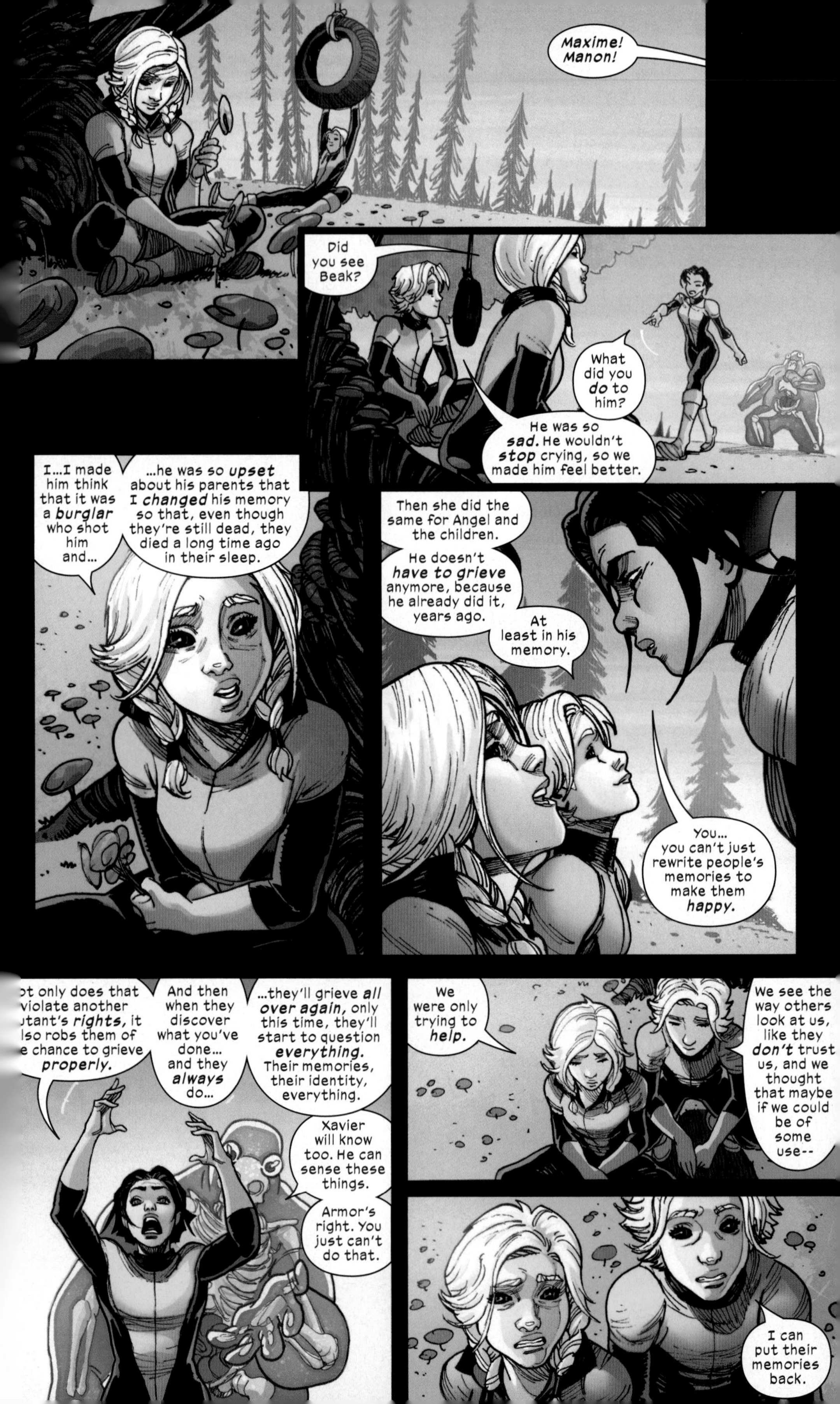

Maxime! Manon!
Did you see Beak?
What did you *do* to him?
He was so *sad.* He wouldn't *stop* crying, so we made him feel better.
I...I made him think that it was a *burglar* who shot him and...
...he was so *upset* about his parents that I *changed* his memory so that, even though they're still dead, they died a long time ago in their sleep.
Then she did the same for Angel and the children.
He doesn't *have to grieve* anymore, because he already did it, years ago.
At least in his memory.
You... you can't just rewrite people's memories to make them *happy.*
ot only does that violate another utant's *rights,* it lso robs them of e chance to grieve *properly.*
And then when they discover what you've done... and they *always* do...
...they'll grieve *all over again,* only this time, they'll start to question *everything.* Their memories, their identity, everything.
Xavier will know too. He can sense these things.
Armor's right. You just can't do that.
We were only trying to *help.*
We see the way others look at us, like they *don't* trust us, and we thought that maybe if we could be of some use--
I can put their memories back.

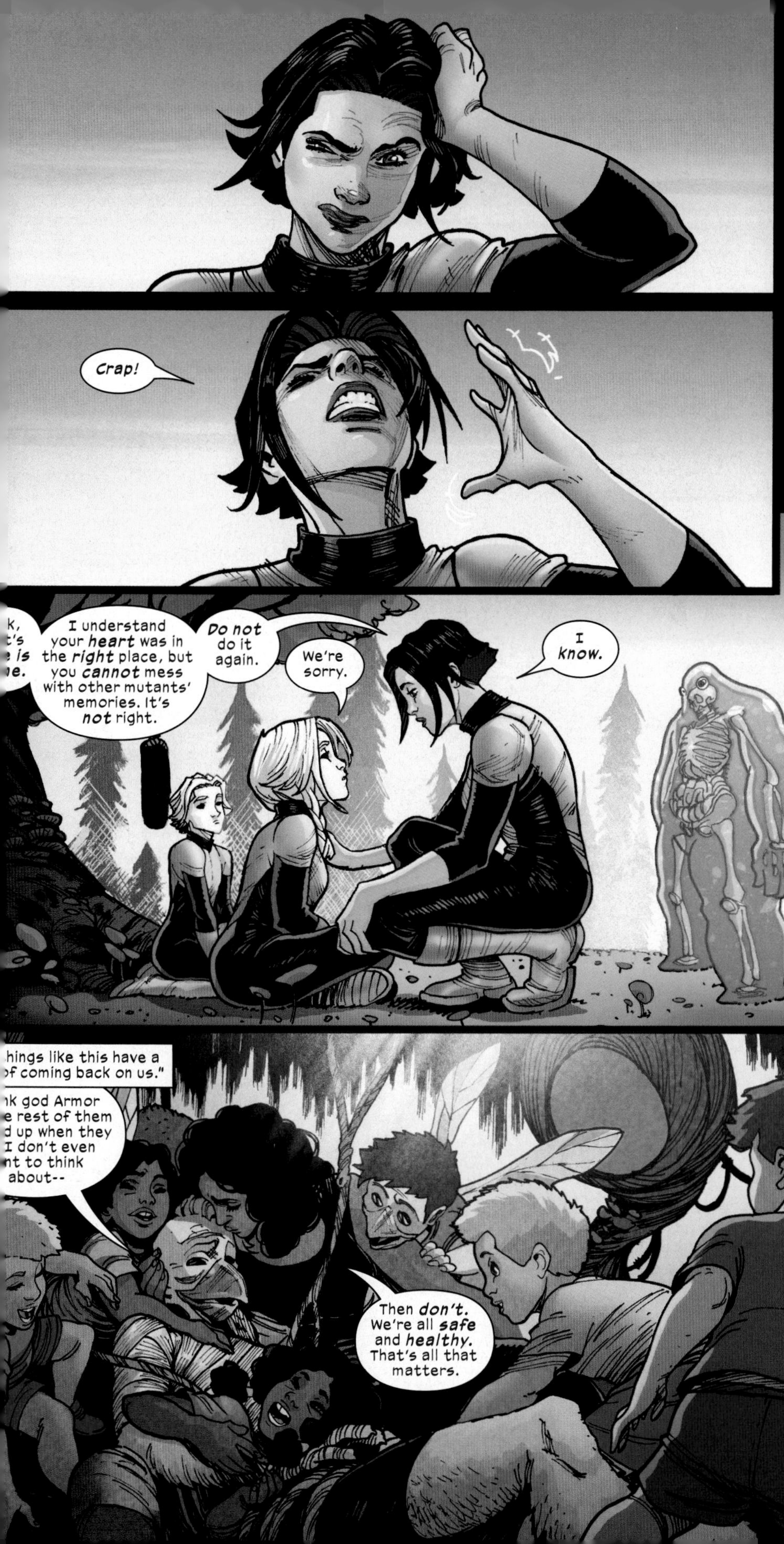

Crap!
I understand your heart was in the right place, but you cannot mess with other mutants' memories. It's not right.
Do not do it again.
We're sorry.
I know.
like this have a
coming back on us."
god Armor
rest of them
up when they
I don't even
to think
about--
Then don't. We're all safe and healthy. That's all that matters.

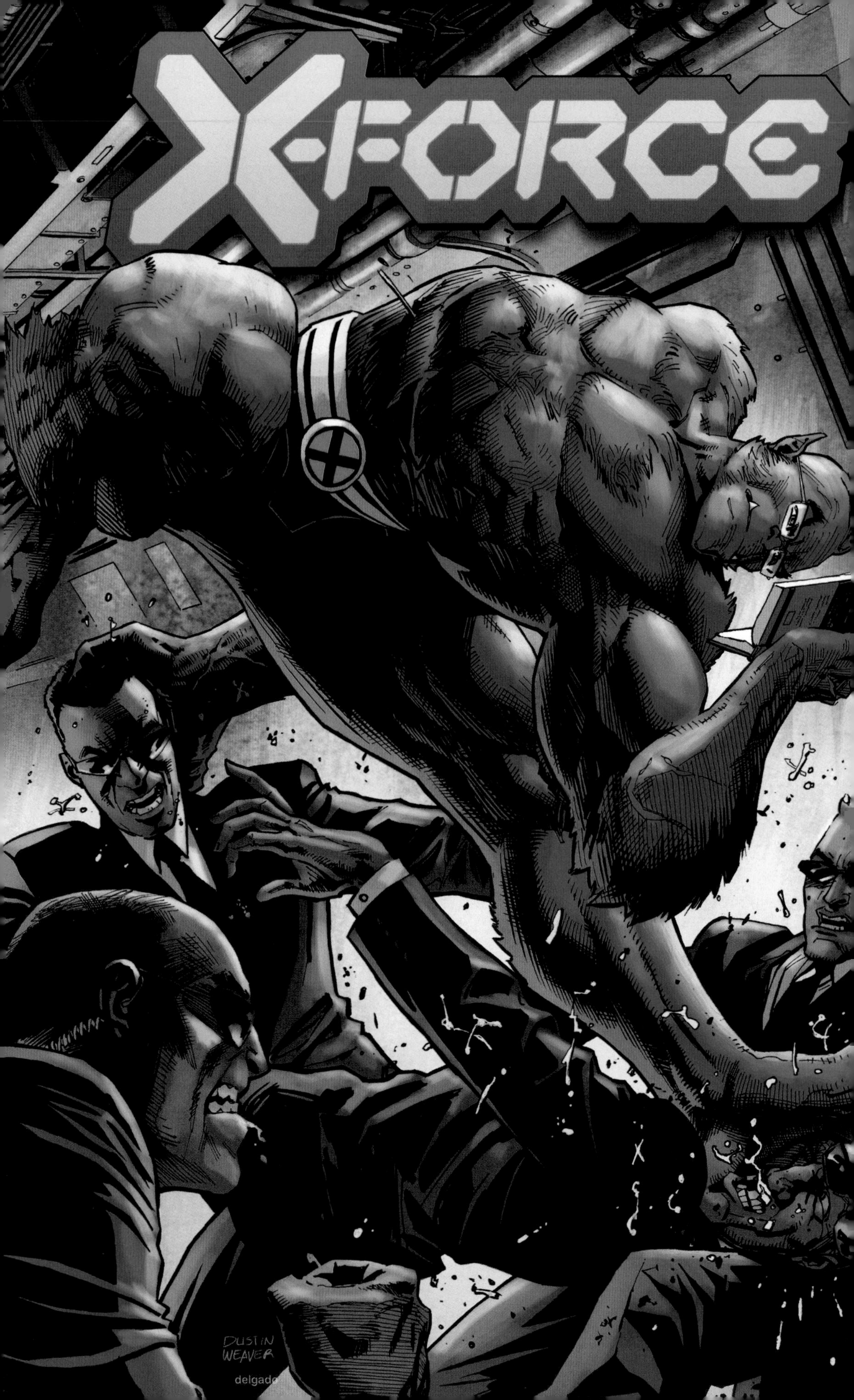
X-FORCE
DUSTIN WEAVER
delgado

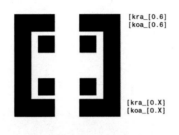

THE MASTER

After the assassination of Professor X on Krakoa,
mutant leadership formed an agency for counterintelligence
and combat application dubbed X-FORCE.

Beast, one of the most tenured and trusted X-Men on Krakoa, leads the
counterintelligence operations.

Beast

Wolverine

Domino

Kid Omega

Marvel Girl

Sage

Black Tom
Cassidy

Professor X

[00_mutant_espionage]
[00_law_order___X___]

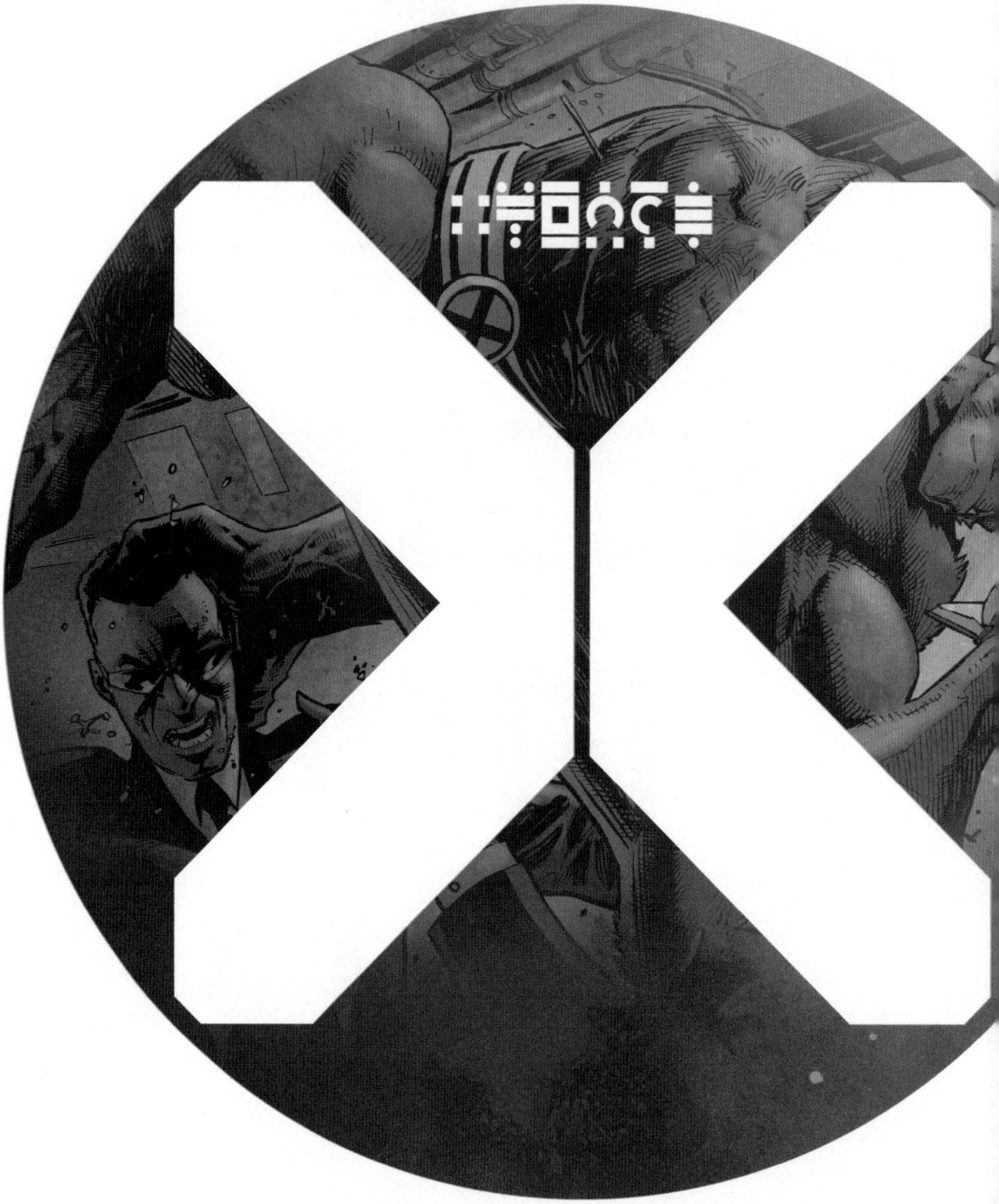

[00_mutant_espionage]
[00_law_order___X___]

BENJAMIN PERCY..................................[WRITER]
STEPHEN SEGOVIA.................................[ARTIST]
GURU-eFX.................................[COLOR ARTIST]
VC's JOE CARAMAGNA...........................[LETTERER]
TOM MULLER......................................[DESIGN]

DUSTIN WEAVER & EDGAR DELGADO...........[COVER ARTISTS]

GERARDO SANDOVAL & ANDRES MOSSA........................
................................[VARIANT COVER ARTISTS]

NICK RUSSELL...............................[PRODUCTION]

JONATHAN HICKMAN............................[HEAD OF X]
CHRIS ROBINSON.......................[ASSISTANT EDITOR]
JORDAN D. WHITE.................................[EDITOR]
C.B. CEBULSKI.........................[EDITOR IN CHIEF]

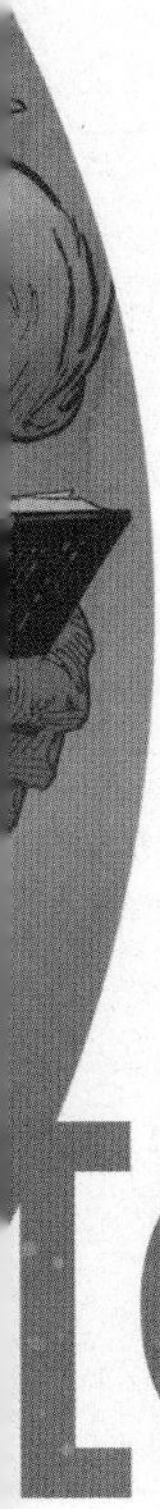

[06] X-FORCE

[ISSUE SIX]...............INTELLIGENCE

[00_mutant_espionage]
[00_law_order___X___]

[00_00...0]
[00_00...6]

[00_probe_]
[00______]

[00______]

[00______X]

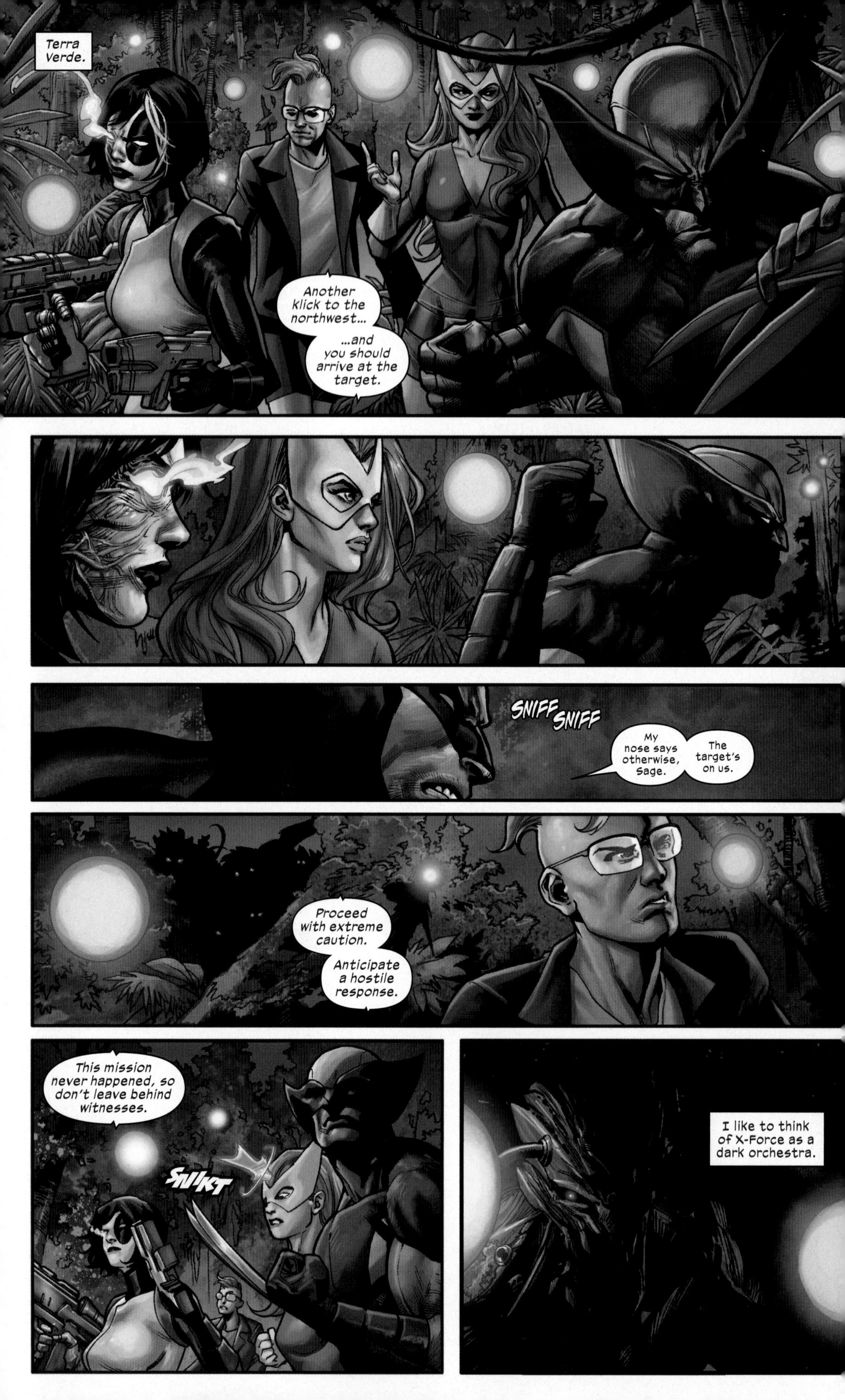
Terra Verde.
Another klick to the northwest...
...and you should arrive at the target.
SNIFF SNIFF
My nose says otherwise, Sage.
The target's on us.
Proceed with extreme caution.
Anticipate a hostile response.
This mission never happened, so don't leave behind witnesses.
SNIKT
I like to think of X-Force as a dark orchestra.

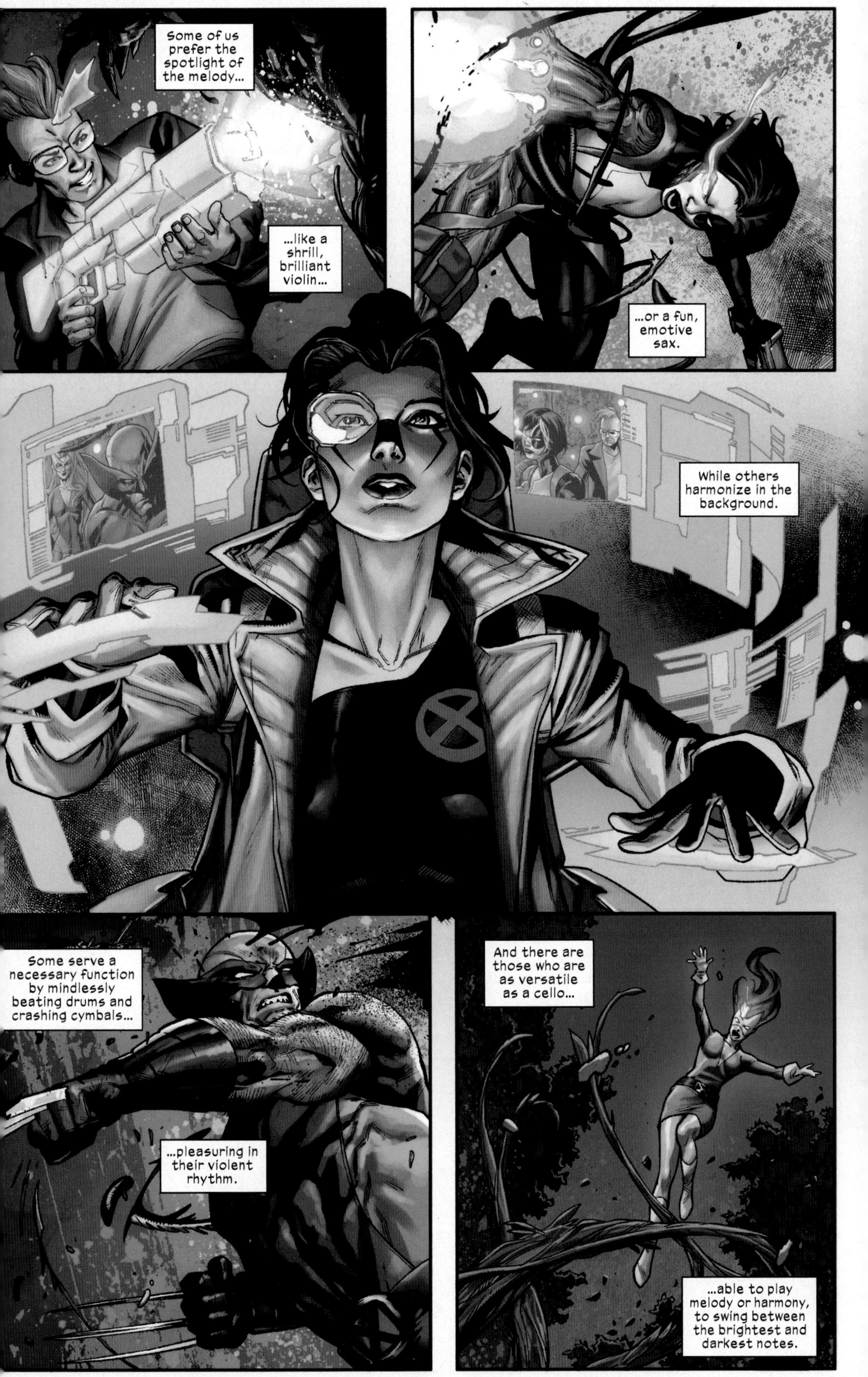
Some of us prefer the spotlight of the melody...
...like a shrill, brilliant violin...
...or a fun, emotive sax.
While others harmonize in the background.
Some serve a necessary function by mindlessly beating drums and crashing cymbals...
...pleasuring in their violent rhythm.
And there are those who are as versatile as a cello...
...able to play melody or harmony, to swing between the brightest and darkest notes.

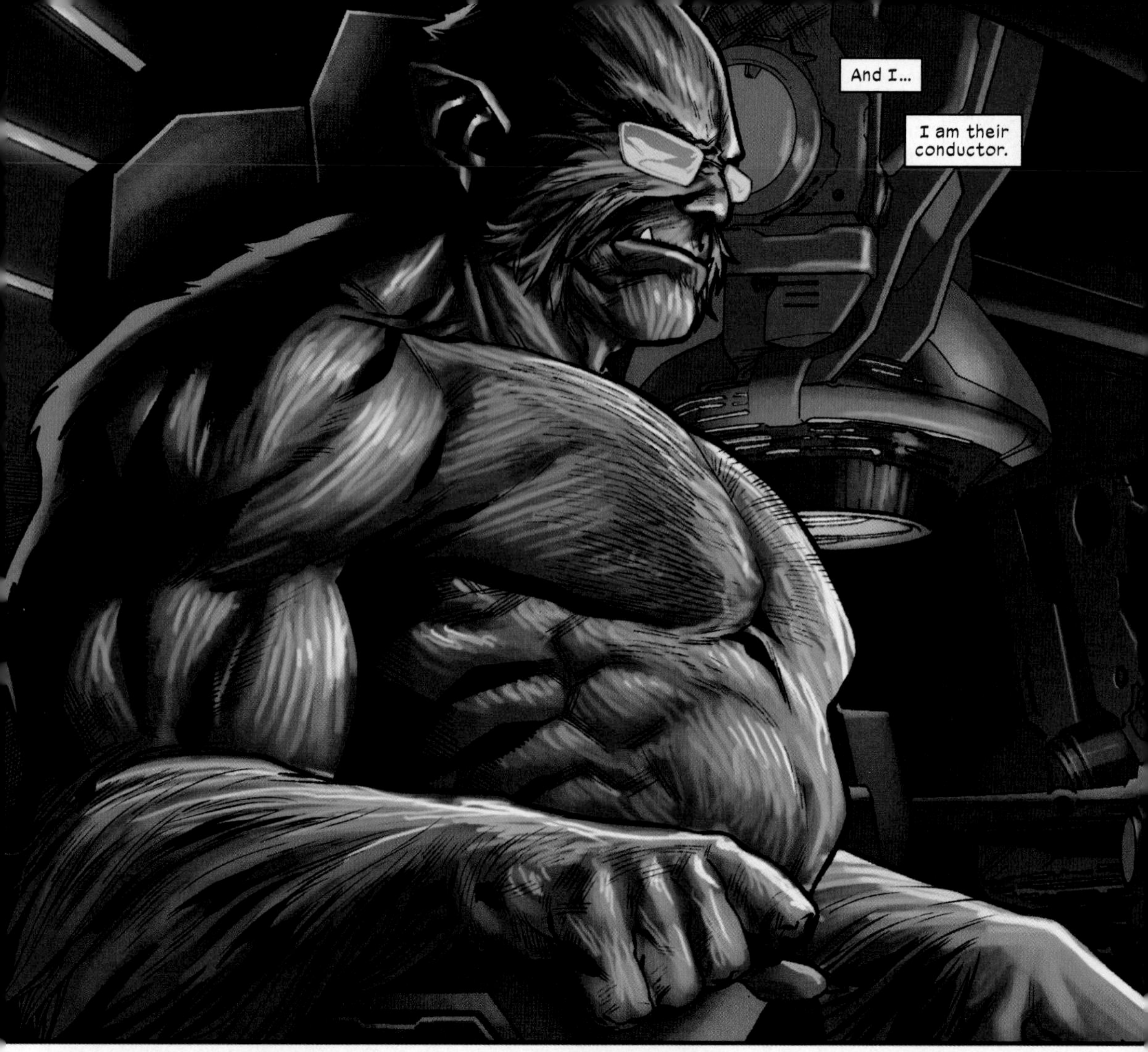
And I...
I am their conductor.

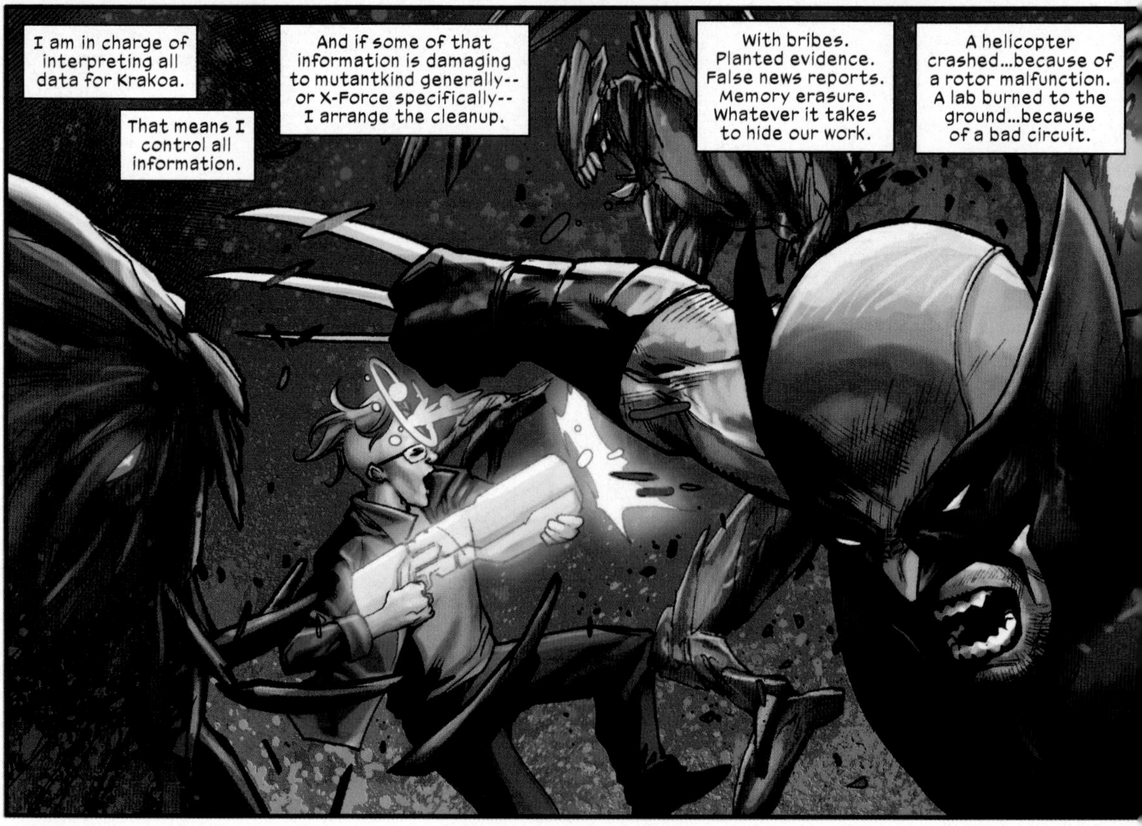
I am in charge of interpreting all data for Krakoa.
That means I control all information.
And if some of that information is damaging to mutantkind generally-- or X-Force specifically-- I arrange the cleanup.
With bribes. Planted evidence. False news reports. Memory erasure. Whatever it takes to hide our work.
A helicopter crashed...because of a rotor malfunction. A lab burned to the ground...because of a bad circuit.

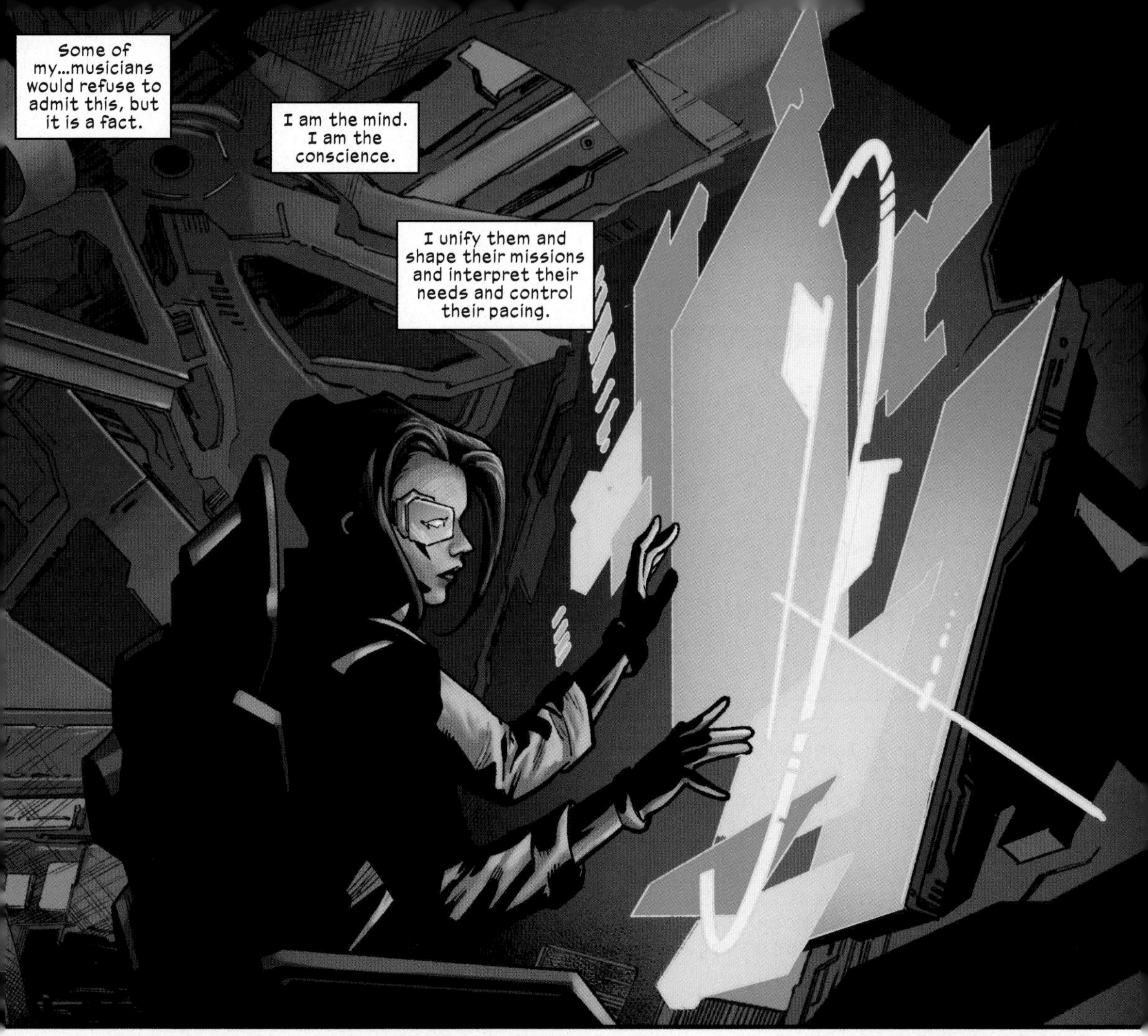
Some of my...musicians would refuse to admit this, but it is a fact.
I am the mind. I am the conscience.
I unify them and shape their missions and interpret their needs and control their pacing.

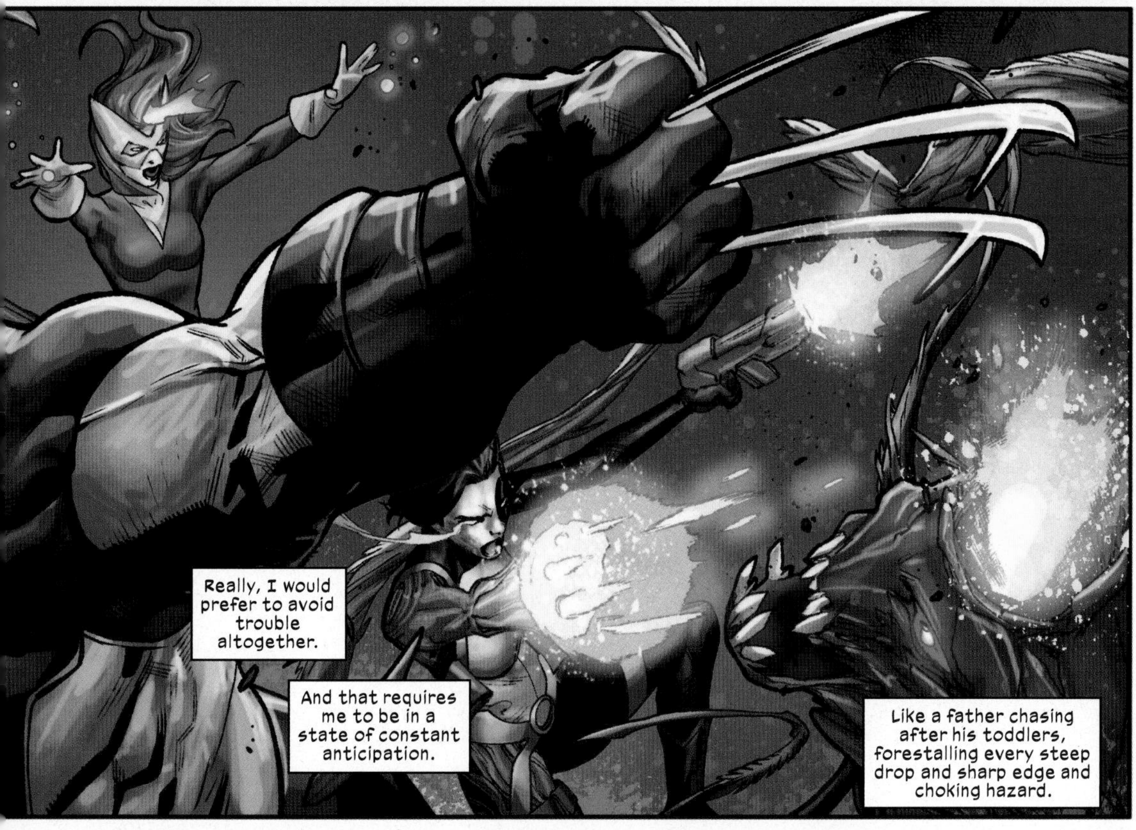
Really, I would prefer to avoid trouble altogether.
And that requires me to be in a state of constant anticipation.
Like a father chasing after his toddlers, forestalling every steep drop and sharp edge and choking hazard.

TERRA VERDE

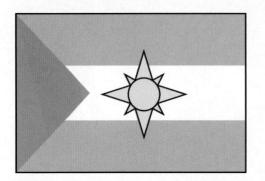

This troubled nation has stabilized in recent years under the rule of President Manuel Cocom, who ran on a platform of reform. The nation's GDP had previously been fueled largely by agriculture and petroleum. But the lagging economy—the fourth smallest in South America—demanded change.

Following his election, Cocom made good on his promise to look to the future instead of to the past for inspiration and focused all the nation's resources into organic technology. Tax incentives and grants and subsidies were specifically funneled into the field of telefloronics.

Telefloronics is derived from same principles of nanotechnology, only its focus is organic. Programming takes place on a cellular level. If a host body achieves microbial or fungal symbiosis, it can potentially clear the plaque from its arteries, repair synaptic pathways, heal wounds and attack cancers.

The technology is a closely guarded state secret that Cocom views as equivalent to atomic research. This phrasing has made the UN particularly anxious, because it implies not just a medical breakthrough, but also the potential of weaponization.

Not much is known about their advancement, but most of their initial investors—who helped shore up the Terra Verdean economy—have pulled out, citing a lack of progress.

When the mutant nation first announced their treaty proposal to the world, Cocom angrily referred to Krakoan medicine as act of plagiarism and threatened to sue, saying that the mutant nation had effectively neutered them economically.

He has since walked back on that claim. And after a series of private talks, he has agreed to sign with the mutants.

—

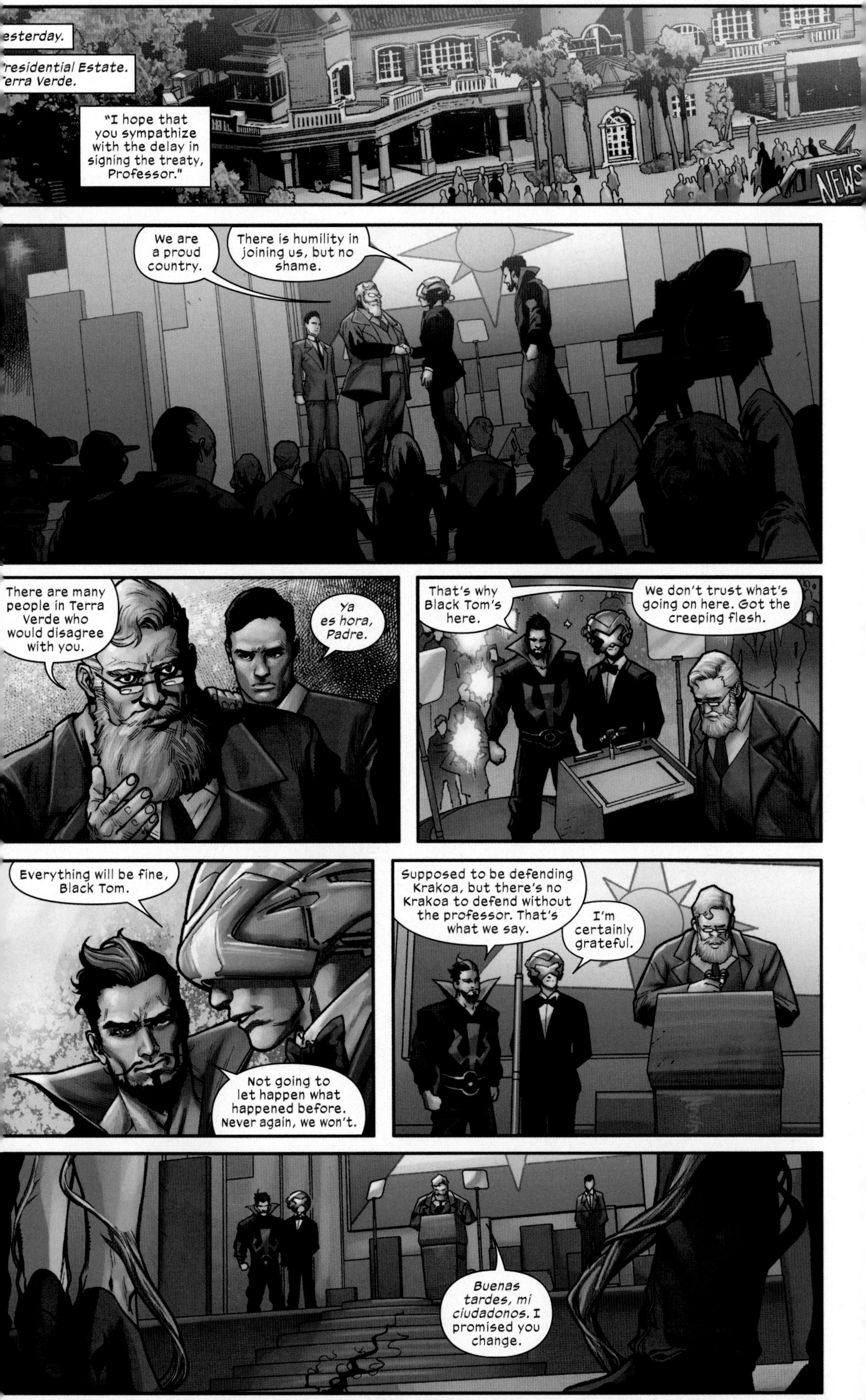
esterday.
residential Estate.
erra Verde.
"I hope that you sympathize with the delay in signing the treaty, Professor."
We are a proud country.
There is humility in joining us, but no shame.
There are many people in Terra Verde who would disagree with you.
Ya es hora, Padre.
That's why Black Tom's here.
We don't trust what's going on here. Got the creeping flesh.
Everything will be fine, Black Tom.
Not going to let happen what happened before. Never again, we won't.
Supposed to be defending Krakoa, but there's no Krakoa to defend without the professor. That's what we say.
I'm certainly grateful.
NEWS
Buenas tardes, mi ciudadonos. I promised you change.

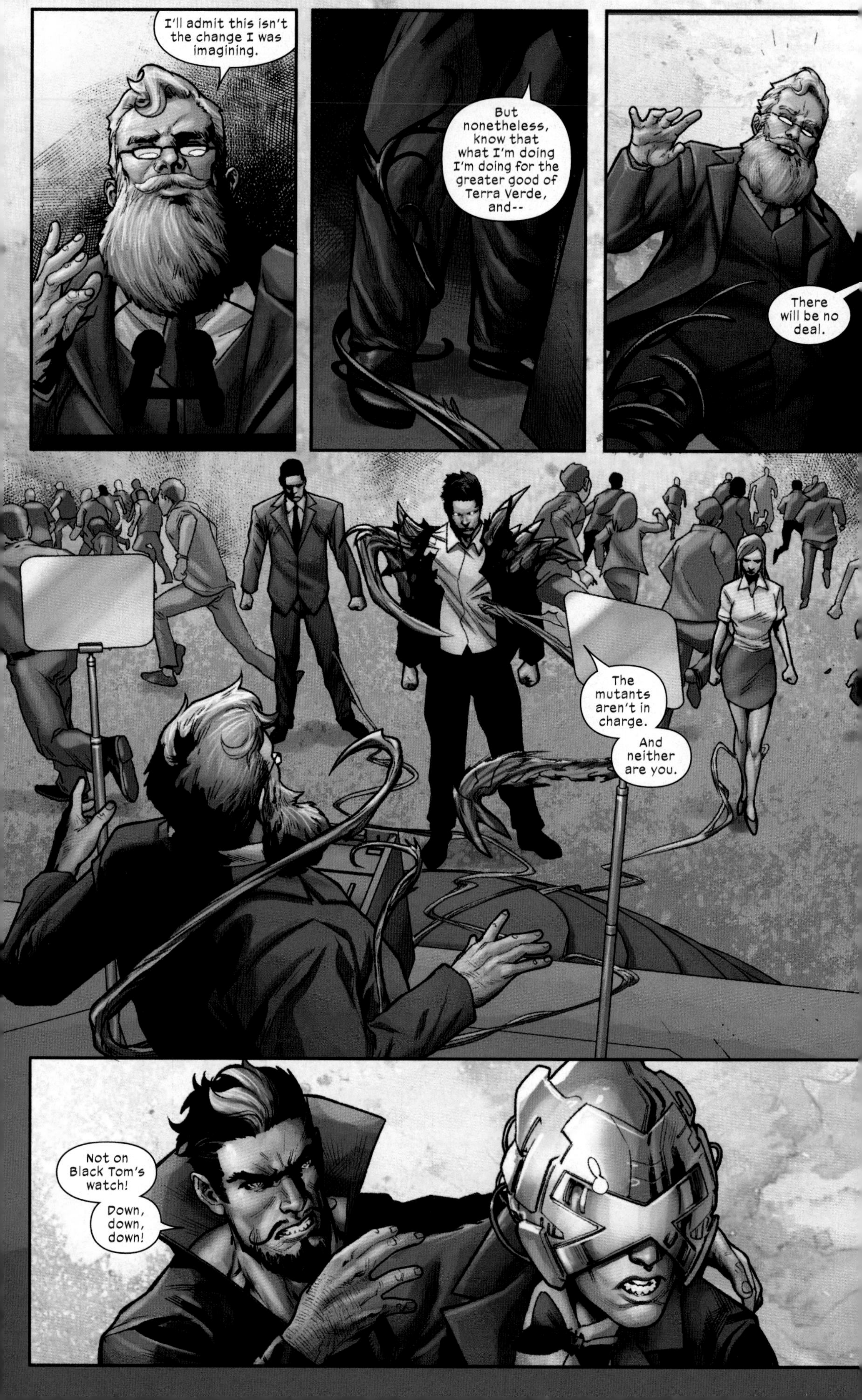
I'll admit this isn't the change I was imagining.
But nonetheless, know that what I'm doing I'm doing for the greater good of Terra Verde, and--
There will be no deal.
The mutants aren't in charge.
And neither are you.
Not on Black Tom's watch!
Down, down, down!

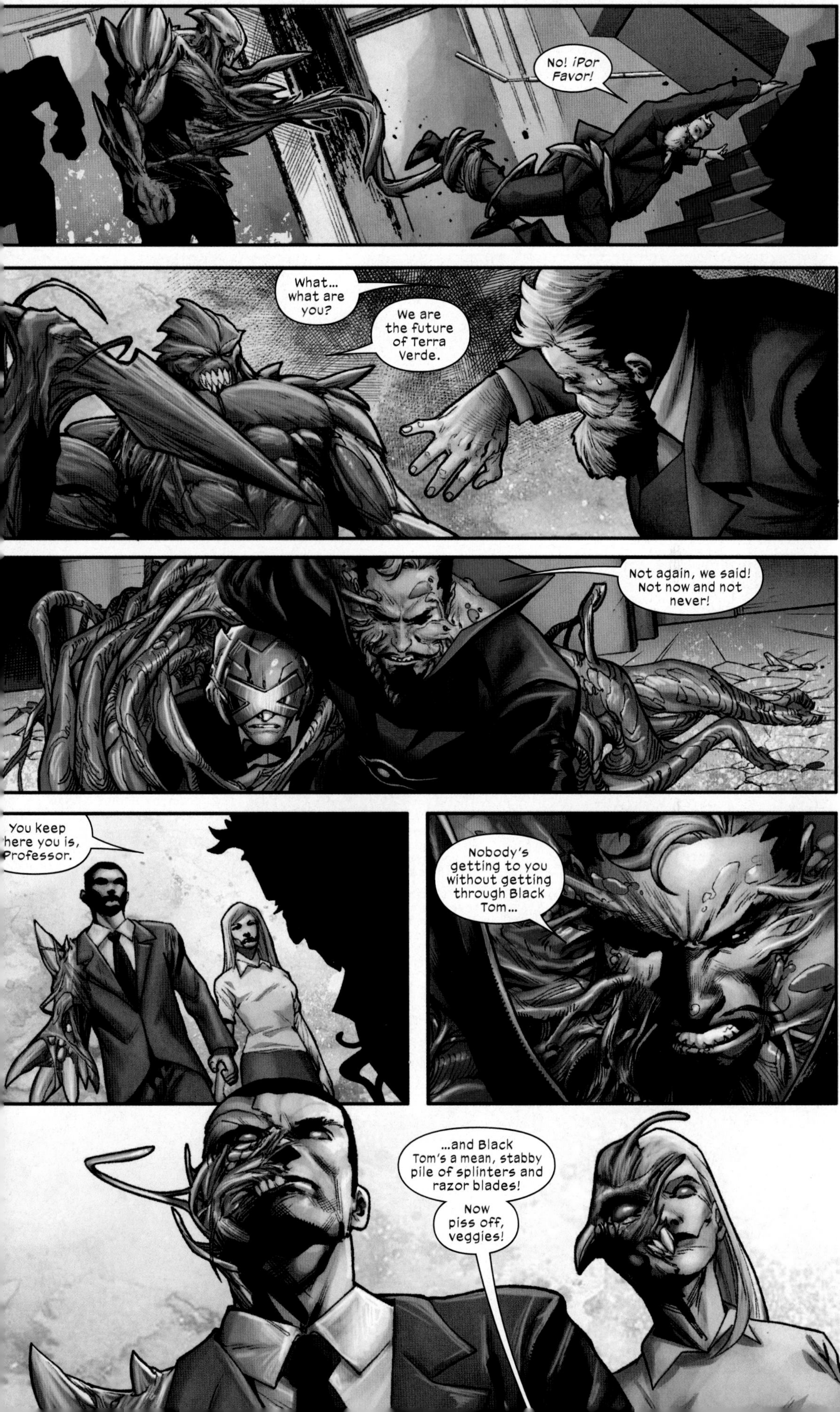
No! ¡Por Favor!
What... what are you?
We are the future of Terra Verde.
Not again, we said! Not now and not never!
You keep here you is, Professor.
Nobody's getting to you without getting through Black Tom...
...and Black Tom's a mean, stabby pile of splinters and razor blades!
Now piss off, veggies!

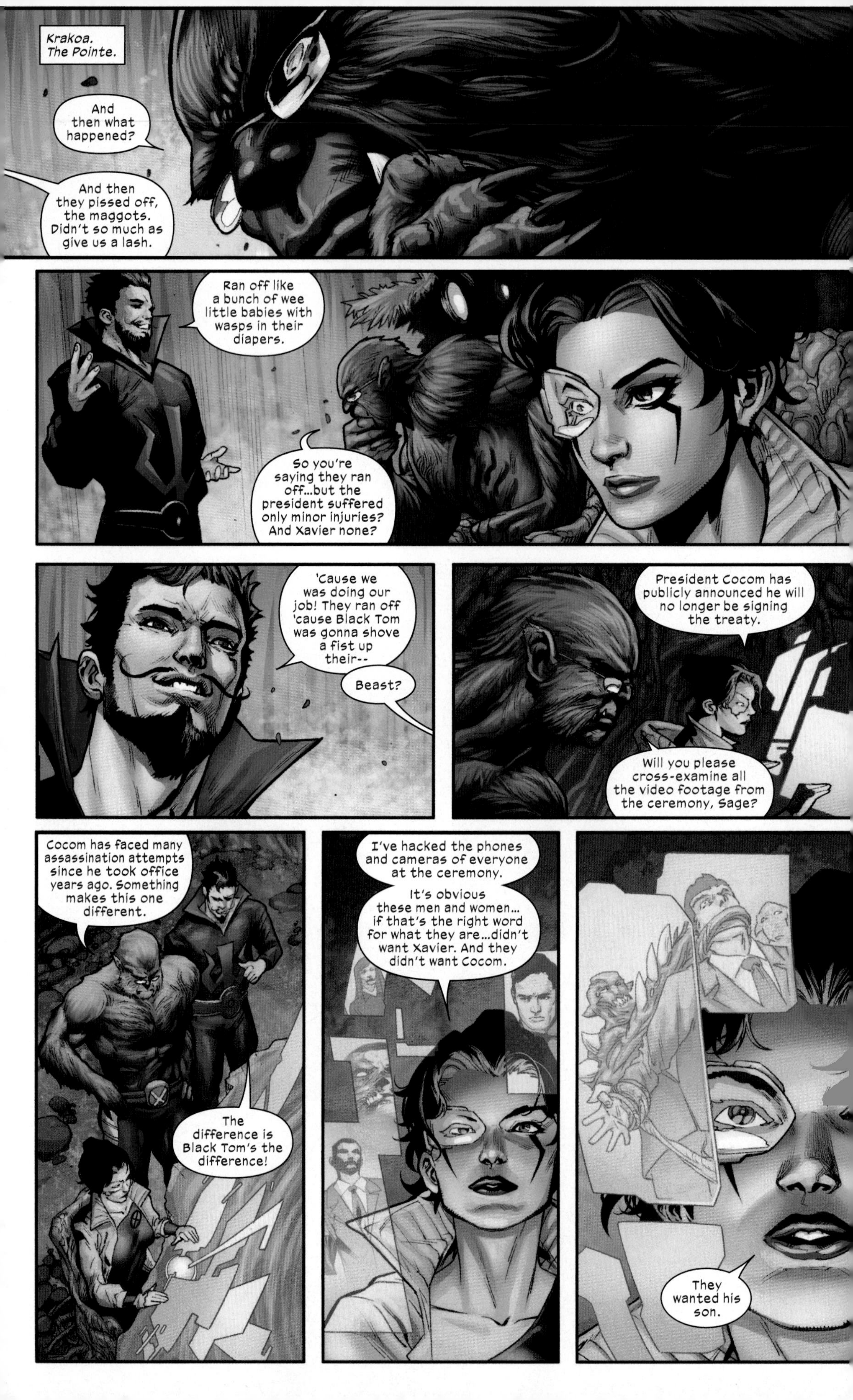
Krakoa.
The Pointe.
And then what happened?
And then they pissed off, the maggots. Didn't so much as give us a lash.
Ran off like a bunch of wee little babies with wasps in their diapers.
So you're saying they ran off...but the president suffered only minor injuries? And Xavier none?
'Cause we was doing our job! They ran off 'cause Black Tom was gonna shove a fist up their--
Beast?
President Cocom has publicly announced he will no longer be signing the treaty.
Will you please cross-examine all the video footage from the ceremony, Sage?
Cocom has faced many assassination attempts since he took office years ago. Something makes this one different.
The difference is Black Tom's the difference!
I've hacked the phones and cameras of everyone at the ceremony.
It's obvious these men and women... if that's the right word for what they are...didn't want Xavier. And they didn't want Cocom.
They wanted his son.

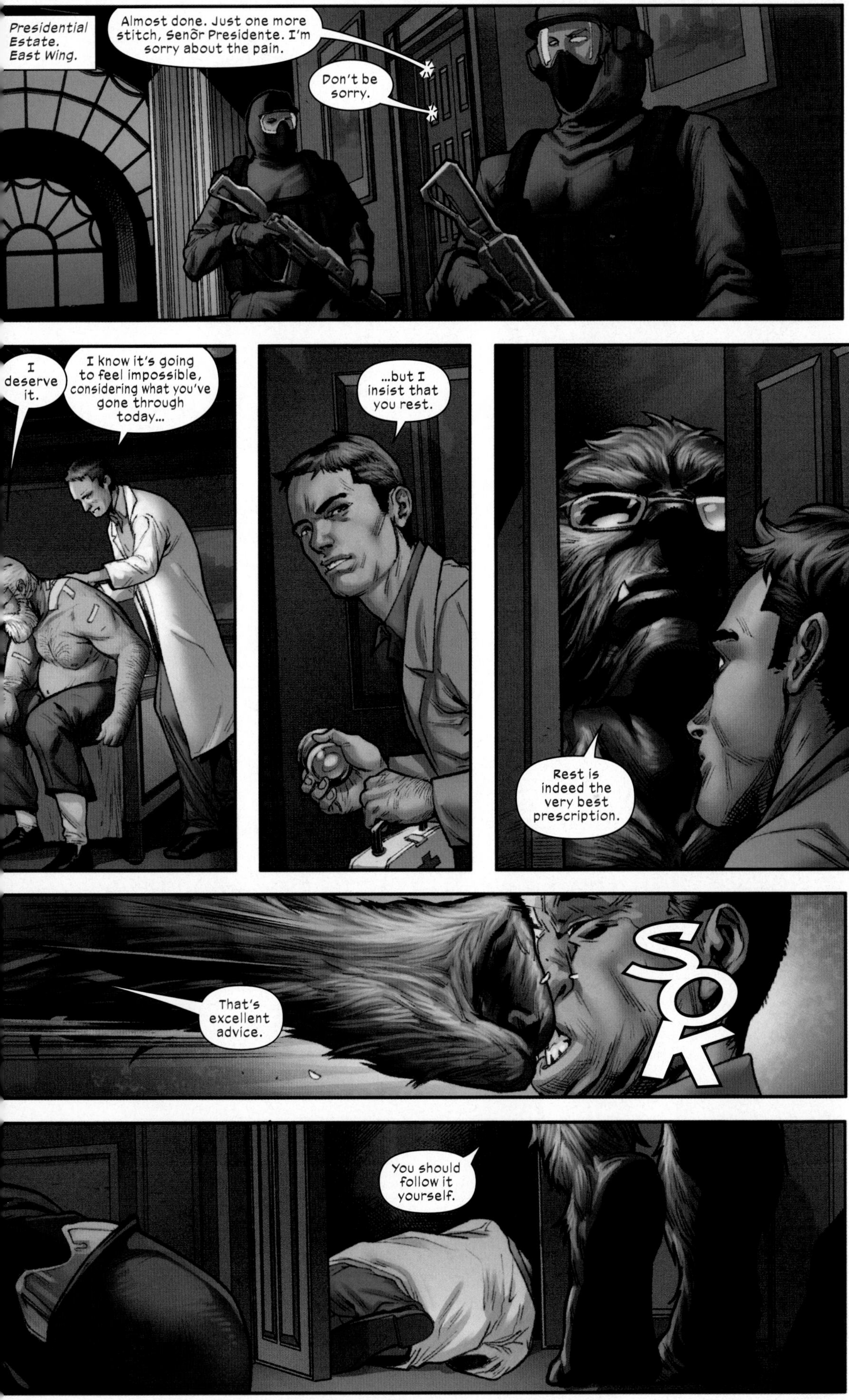
Presidential Estate. East Wing.
Almost done. Just one more stitch, Senõr Presidente. I'm sorry about the pain.
Don't be sorry.
I deserve it.
I know it's going to feel impossible, considering what you've gone through today...
...but I insist that you rest.
Rest is indeed the very best prescription.
That's excellent advice.
SOK
You should follow it yourself.

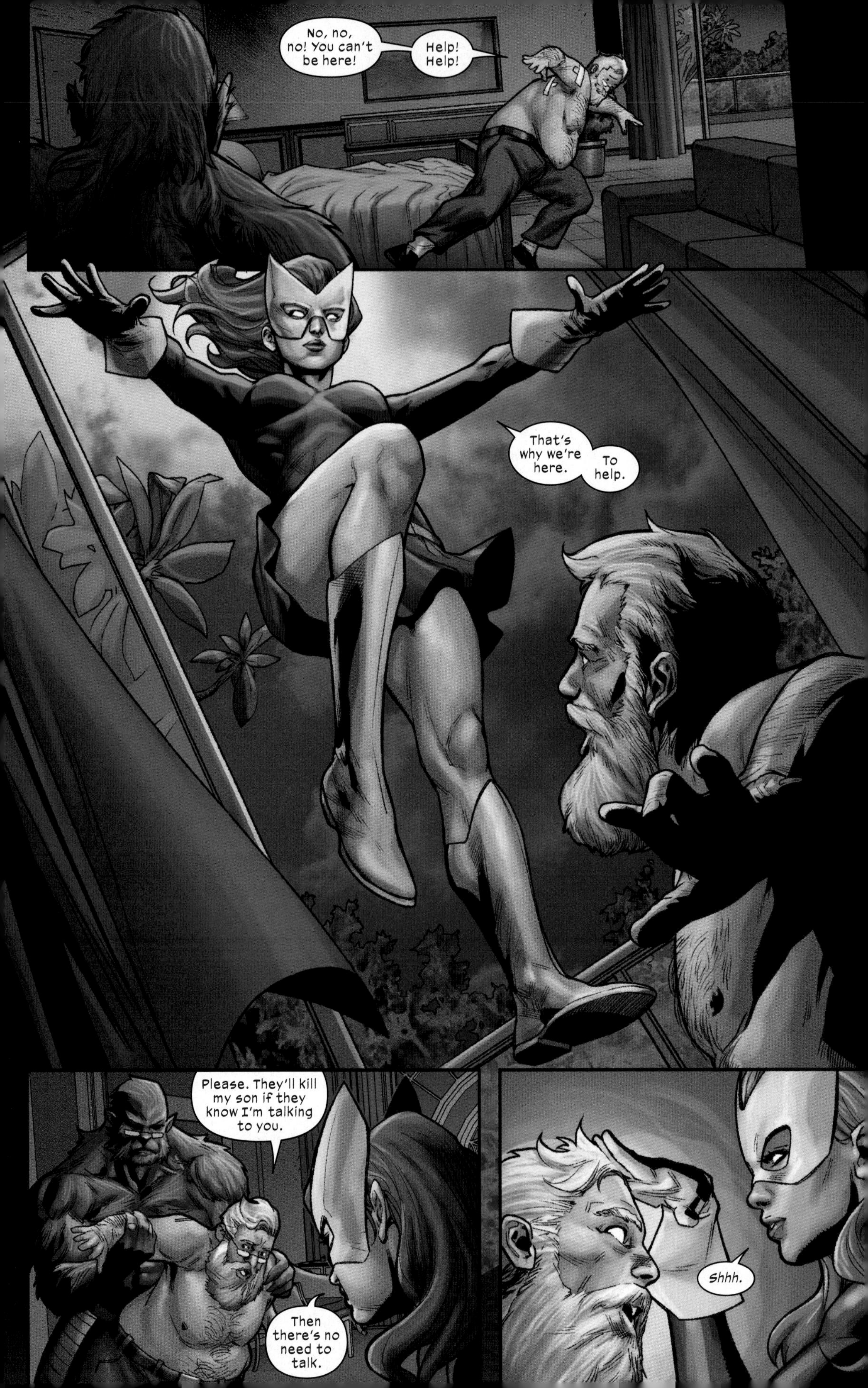
No, no, no! You can't be here!
Help! Help!
That's why we're here.
To help.
Please. They'll kill my son if they know I'm talking to you.
Then there's no need to talk.
Shhh.

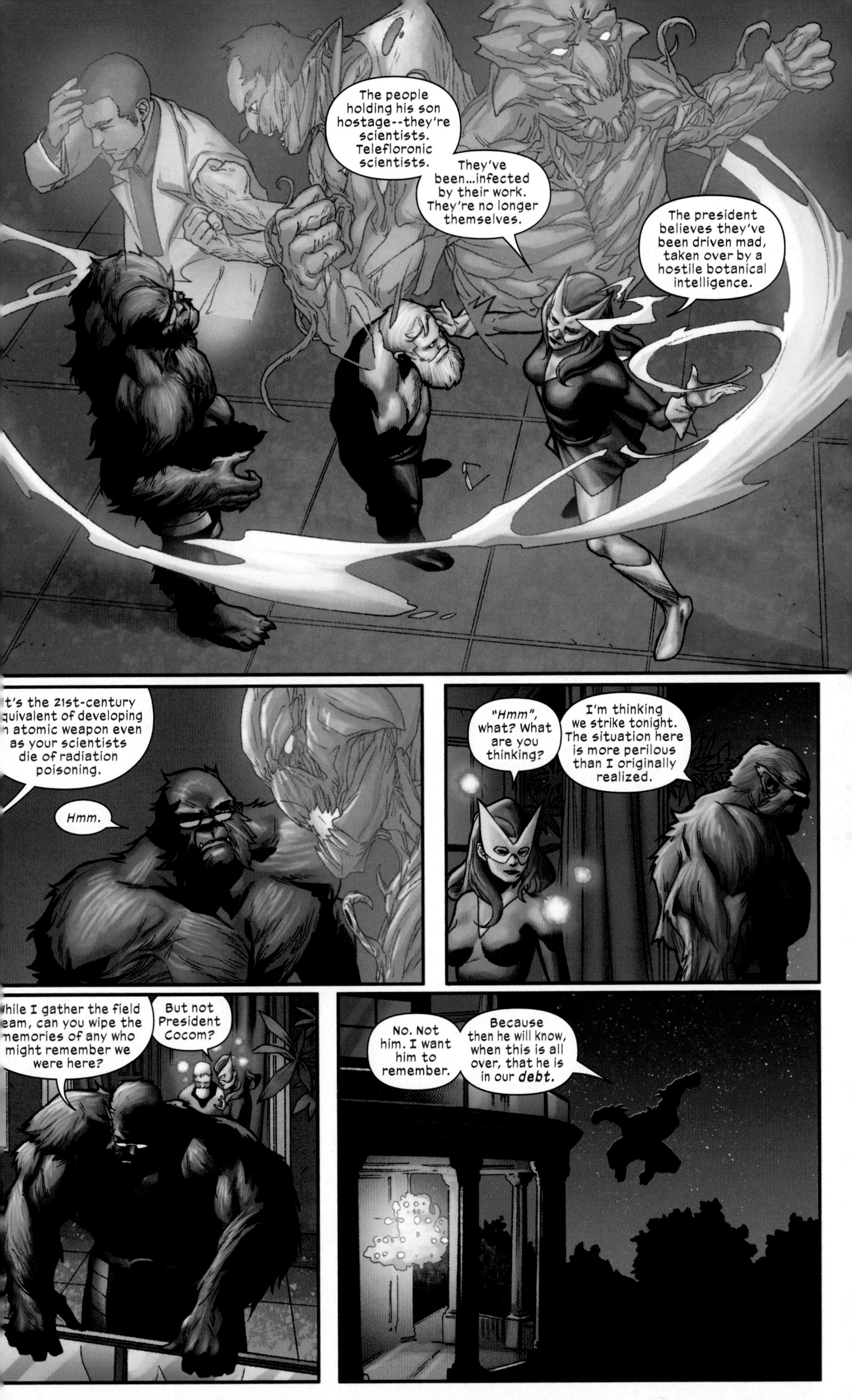

The people holding his son hostage--they're scientists. Telefloronic scientists.
They've been...infected by their work. They're no longer themselves.
The president believes they've been driven mad, taken over by a hostile botanical intelligence.
t's the 21st-century quivalent of developing n atomic weapon even as your scientists die of radiation poisoning.
Hmm.
"Hmm", what? What are you thinking?
I'm thinking we strike tonight. The situation here is more perilous than I originally realized.
hile I gather the field eam, can you wipe the memories of any who might remember we were here?
But not President Cocom?
No. Not him. I want him to remember.
Because then he will know, when this is all over, that he is in our debt.

XAVIER'S CONFESSION

He hoped for death. He dreamt welcomingly of the bullet or the blade or the poison that would fell him.

His fellow mutants deserved the happiness and safety he had provided them, but he knew that some part of them remained equivalent to spoiled children. They could only value what they had if they recognized how easily this gift—nationhood, resurrection—might be stripped away. The lofty walls of Krakoa could fall. A deathly season, after all, makes one grateful for the warm bloom of spring.

Words can only accomplish so much. His own notions of what liberty and power and self-actualization and nationhood mean could not be forced onto others by speeches. He needed a spectacle of blood. He needed collective grief and anguish. He needed a scar that ran across the entire island, that scored the heart of mutantkind.

Without this—some early proof that the rough beasts had been aroused and incited by mutant innovation—his fellow mutants wouldn't be unified except in theory and geography. Inevitably strife and differences, old and new grudges would drive them apart. Krakoa needed a *Lusitania*. Krakoa needed a Pearl Harbor.

Right now they had a choice. He knew their survival depended on them feeling that they had no choice.

His death and his rebirth would be the ultimate expression of his dream. The new dawn couldn't truly begin until the five brought him back. Because then the mutants would know that their future and existence did not depend upon him, but upon themselves. This is how he would cement the faith of the nation—and ready everyone for the horrors to come.

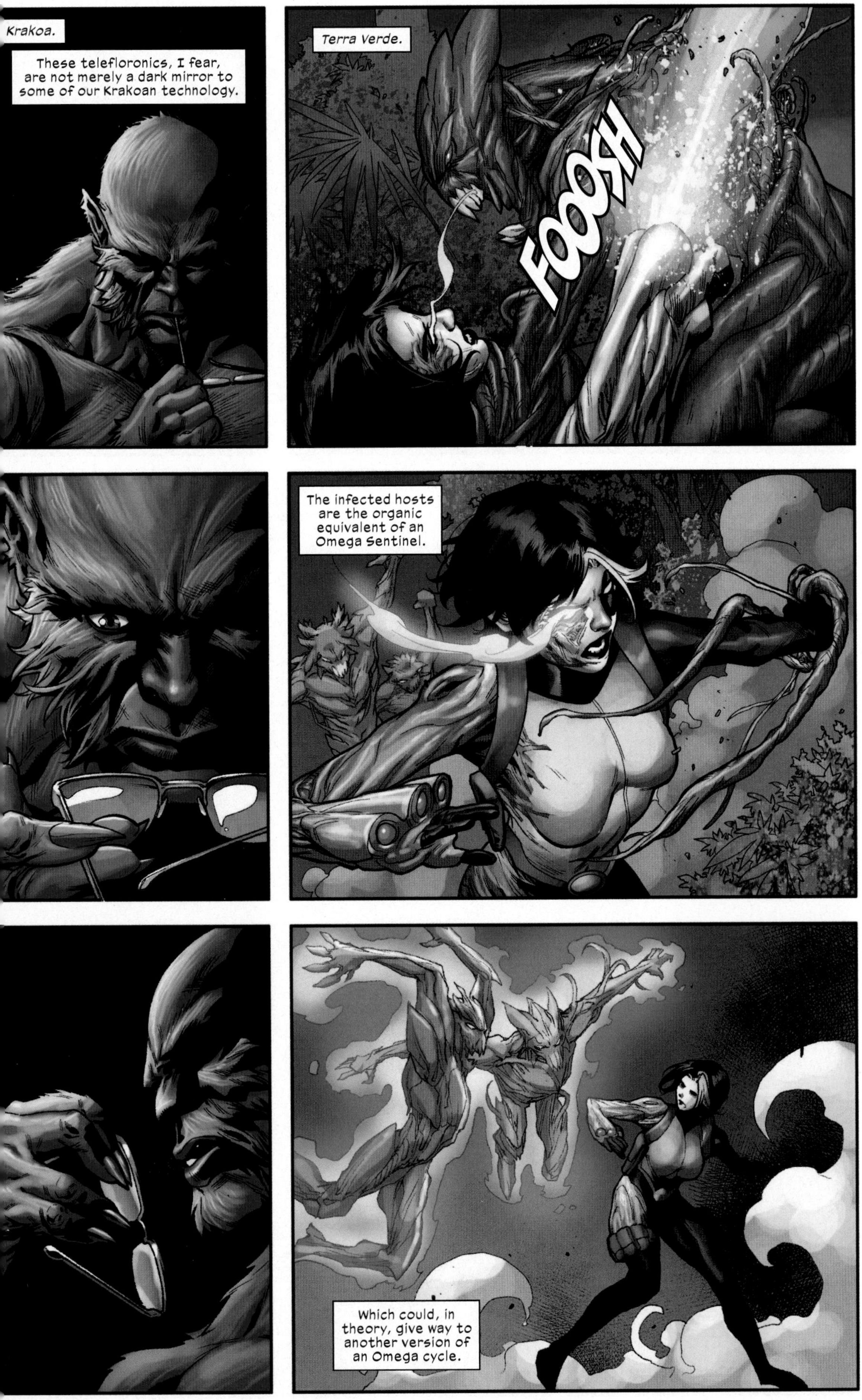
Krakoa.
These telefloronics, I fear, are not merely a dark mirror to some of our Krakoan technology.
Terra Verde.
FOOOSH
The infected hosts are the organic equivalent of an Omega Sentinel.
Which could, in theory, give way to another version of an Omega cycle.

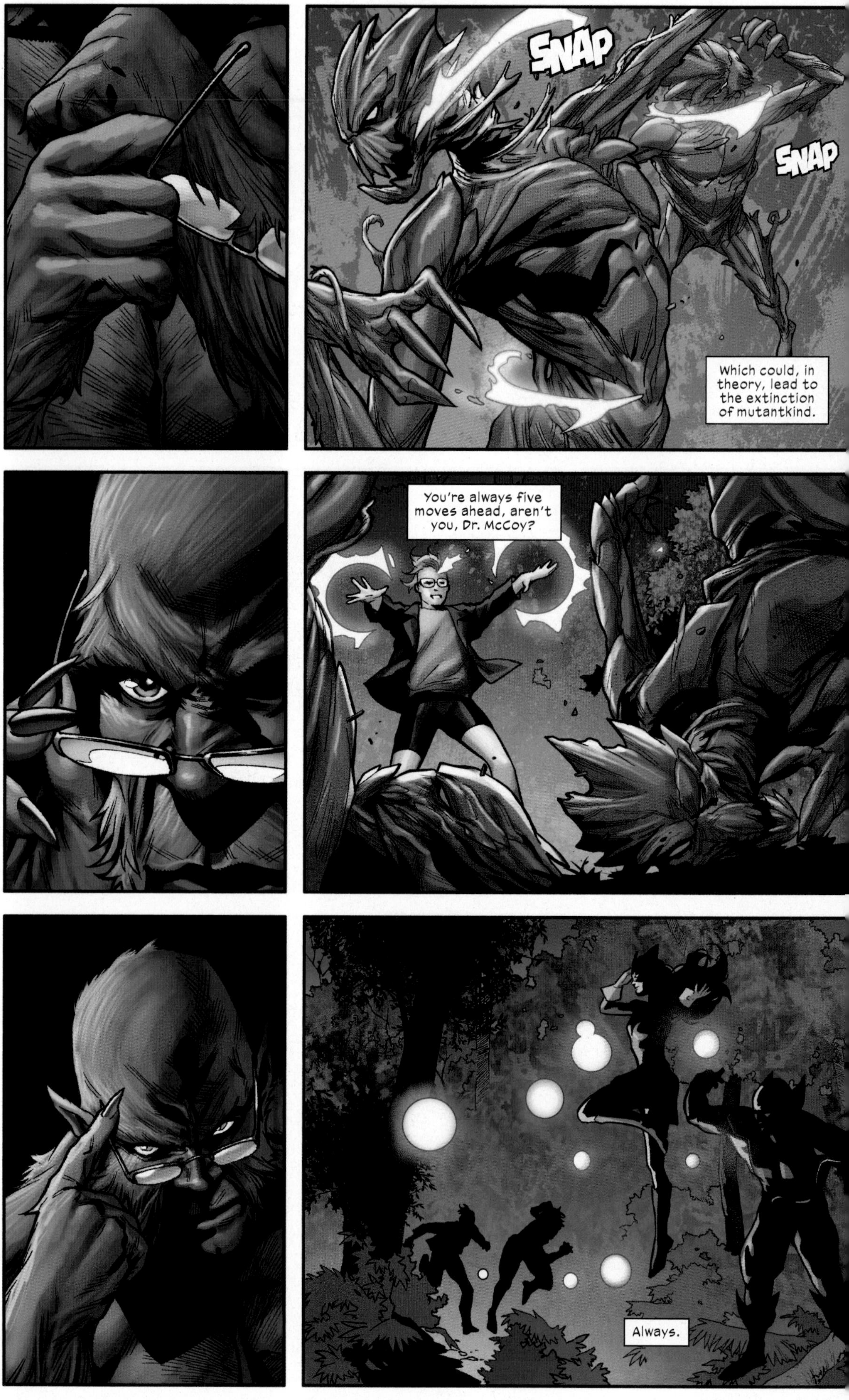

SNAP
SNAP
Which could, in theory, lead to the extinction of mutantkind.
You're always five moves ahead, aren't you, Dr. McCoy?
Always.

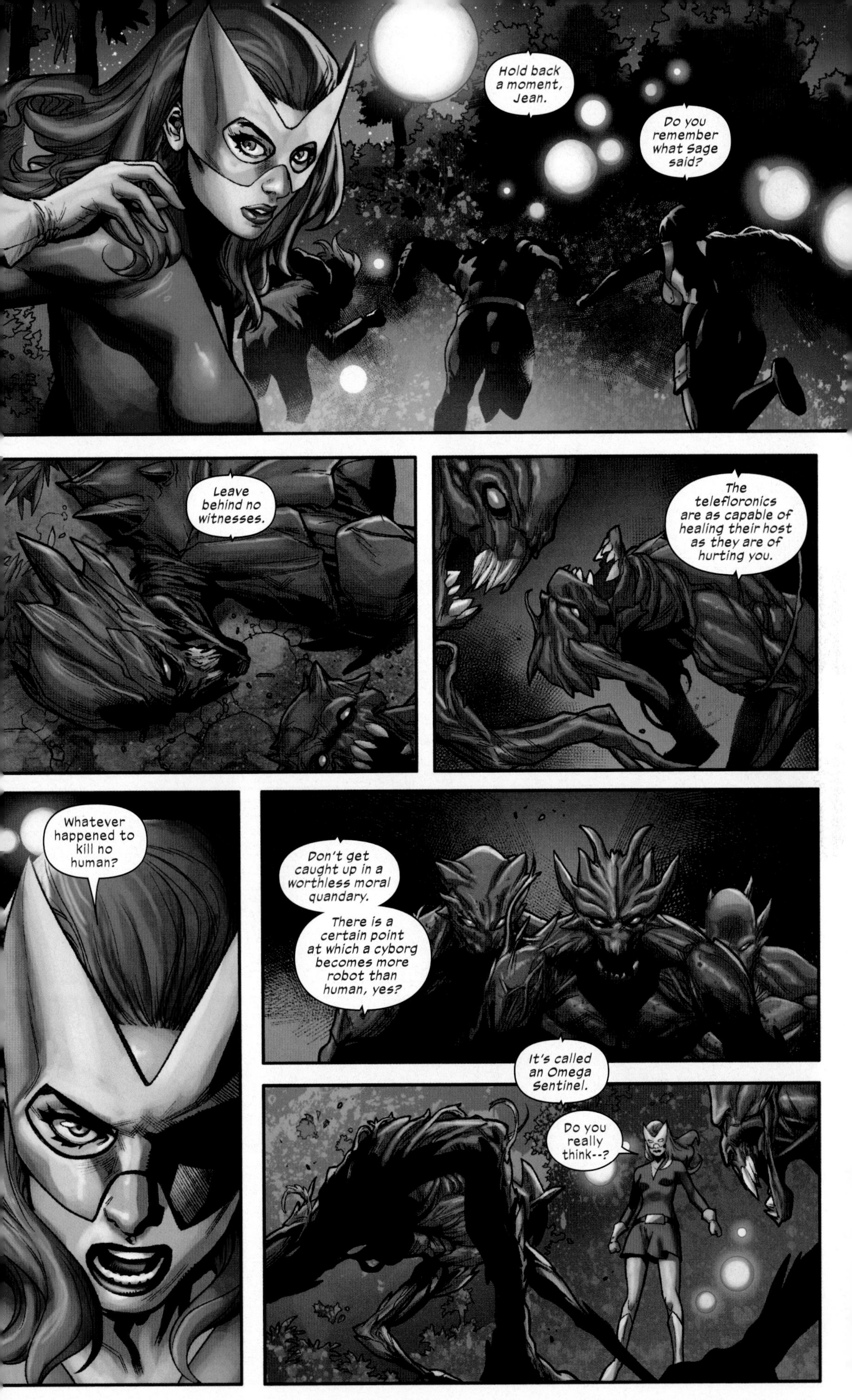
Hold back a moment, Jean.
Do you remember what Sage said?
Leave behind no witnesses.
The telefloronics are as capable of healing their host as they are of hurting you.
Whatever happened to kill no human?
Don't get caught up in a worthless moral quandary.
There is a certain point at which a cyborg becomes more robot than human, yes?
It's called an Omega Sentinel.
Do you really think--?

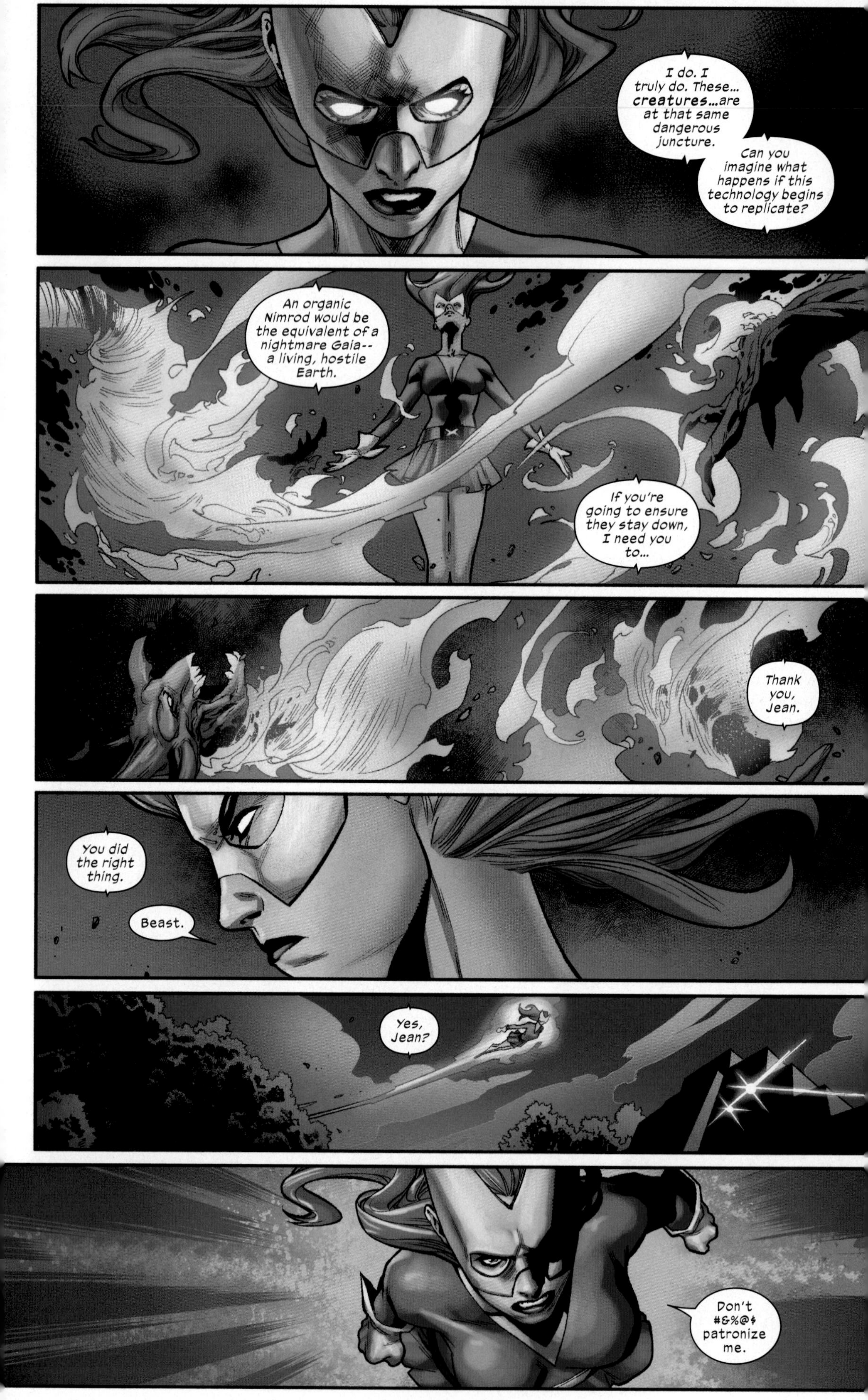

I do. I truly do. These... **creatures**...are at that same dangerous juncture.
Can you imagine what happens if this technology begins to replicate?
An organic Nimrod would be the equivalent of a nightmare Gaia-- a living, hostile Earth.
If you're going to ensure they stay down, I need you to...
Thank you, Jean.
You did the right thing.
Beast.
Yes, Jean?
Don't #&%@$ patronize me.

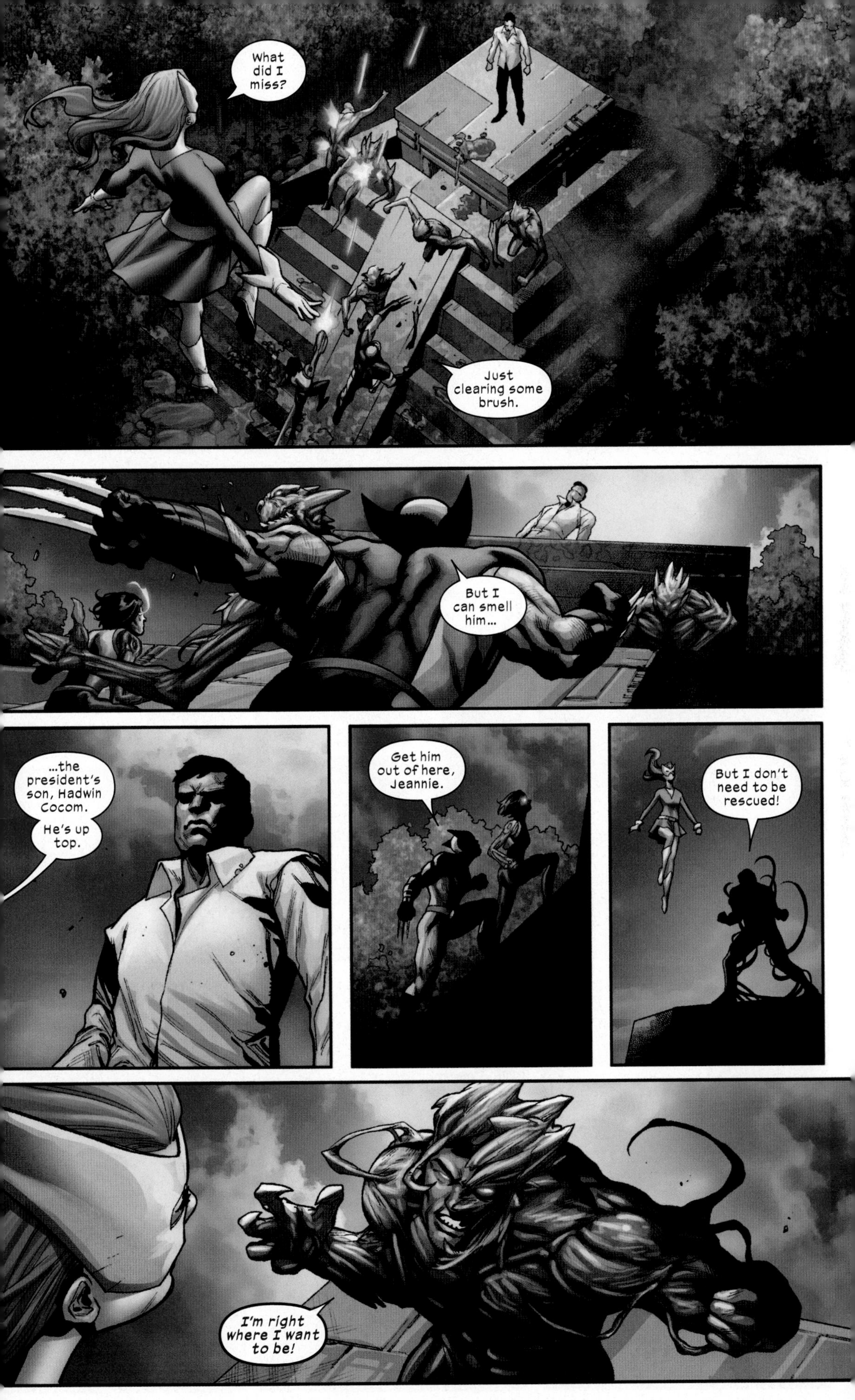
What did I miss?
Just clearing some brush.
But I can smell him...
...the president's son, Hadwin Cocom.
He's up top.
Get him out of here, Jeannie.
But I don't need to be rescued!
I'm right where I want to be!

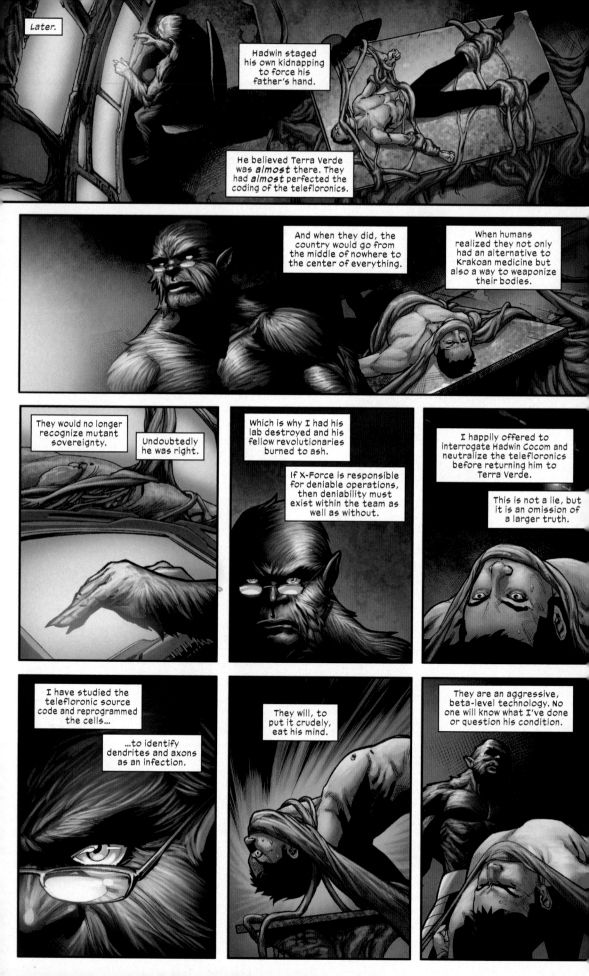

Later.

Hadwin staged his own kidnapping to force his father's hand.

He believed Terra Verde was *almost* there. They had *almost* perfected the coding of the telefloronics.

And when they did, the country would go from the middle of nowhere to the center of everything.

When humans realized they not only had an alternative to Krakoan medicine but also a way to weaponize their bodies.

They would no longer recognize mutant sovereignty.

Undoubtedly he was right.

Which is why I had his lab destroyed and his fellow revolutionaries burned to ash.

If X-Force is responsible for deniable operations, then deniability must exist within the team as well as without.

I happily offered to interrogate Hadwin Cocom and neutralize the telefloronics before returning him to Terra Verde.

This is not a lie, but it is an omission of a larger truth.

I have studied the telefloronic source code and reprogrammed the cells...

...to identify dendrites and axons as an infection.

They will, to put it crudely, eat his mind.

They are an aggressive, beta-level technology. No one will know what I've done or question his condition.

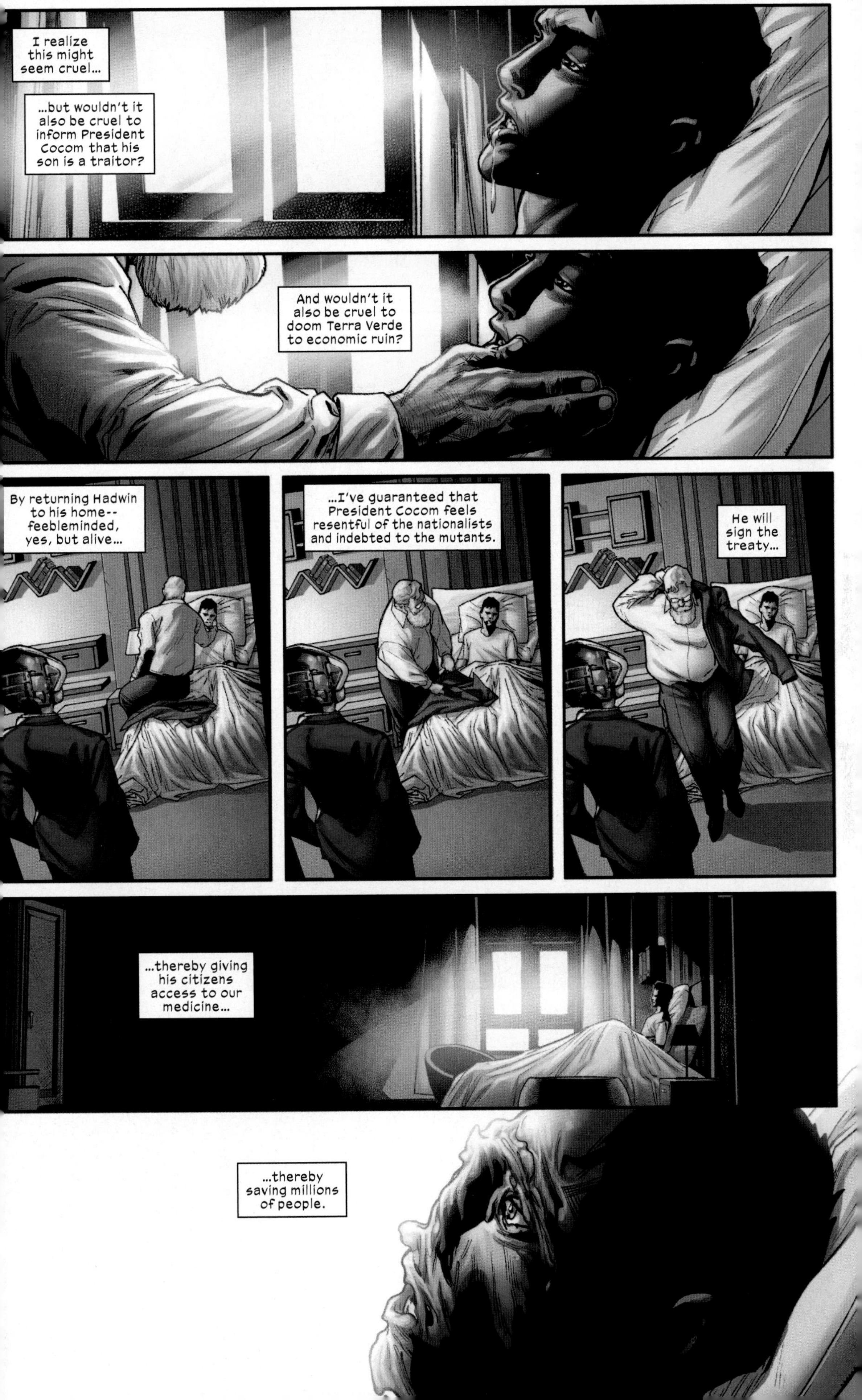
I realize this might seem cruel...
...but wouldn't it also be cruel to inform President Cocom that his son is a traitor?
And wouldn't it also be cruel to doom Terra Verde to economic ruin?
By returning Hadwin to his home--feebleminded, yes, but alive...
...I've guaranteed that President Cocom feels resentful of the nationalists and indebted to the mutants.
He will sign the treaty...
...thereby giving his citizens access to our medicine...
...thereby saving millions of people.

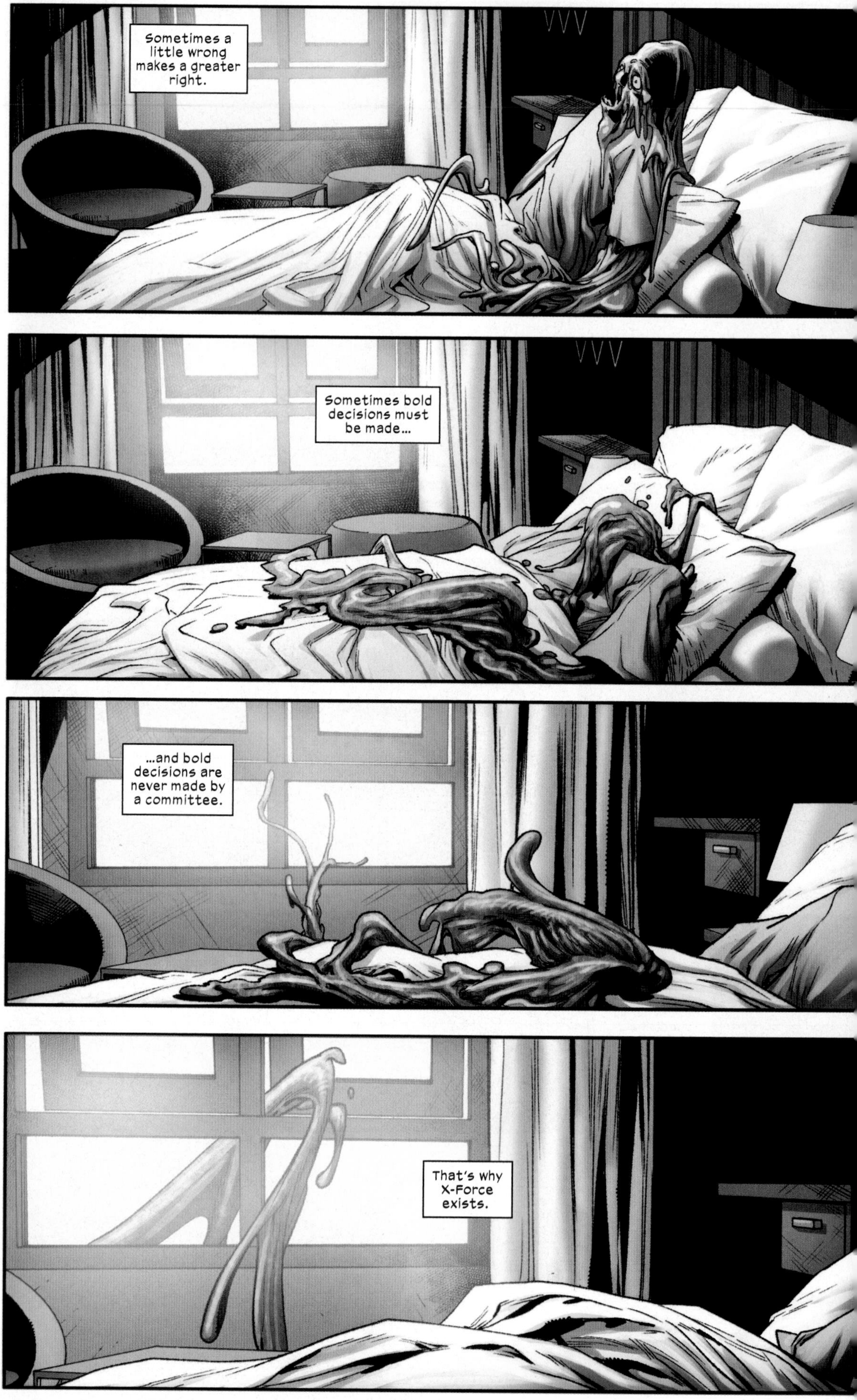
Sometimes a little wrong makes a greater right.
Sometimes bold decisions must be made...
...and bold decisions are never made by a committee.
That's why X-Force exists.

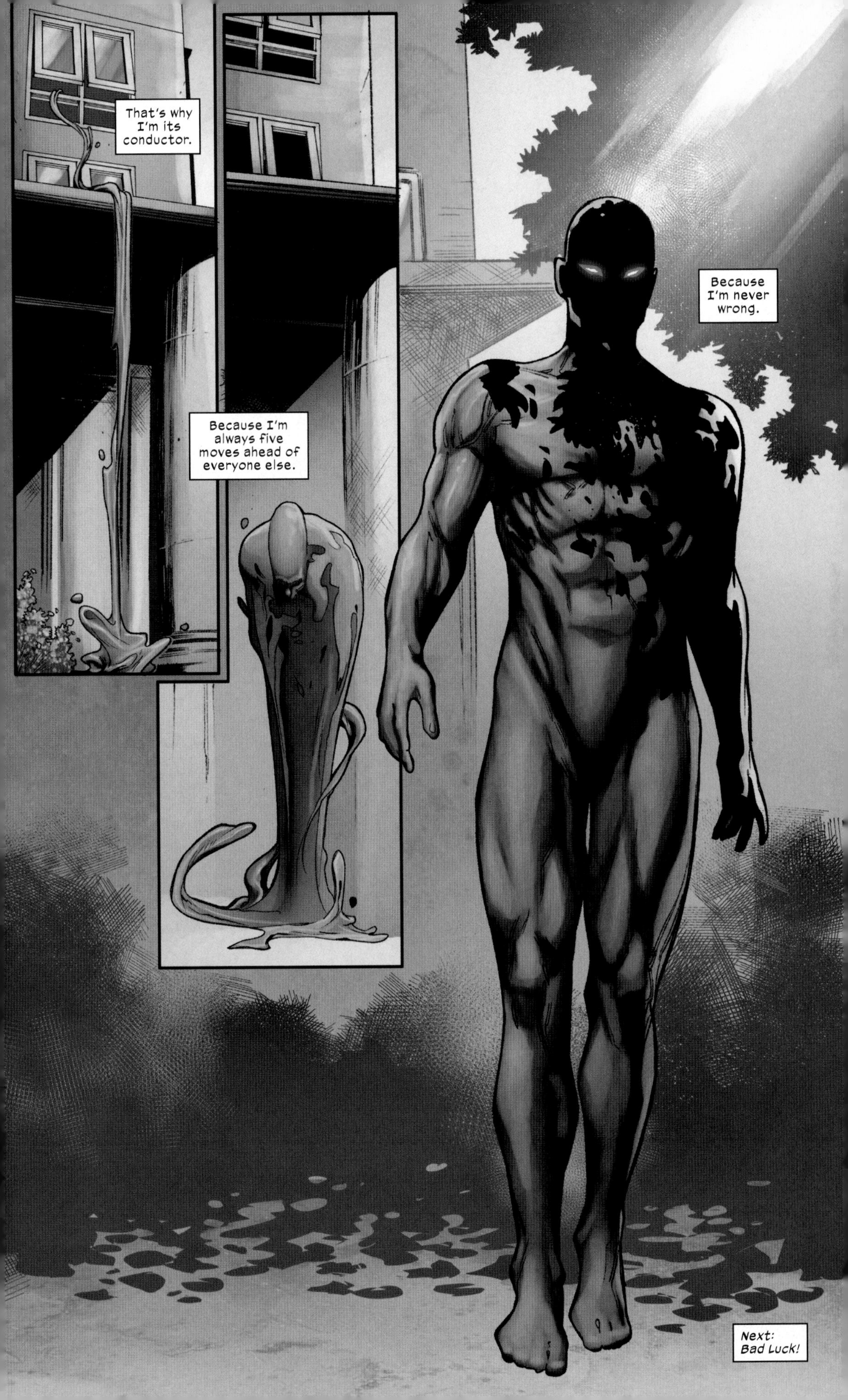
That's why I'm its conductor.
Because I'm always five moves ahead of everyone else.
Because I'm never wrong.
Next: Bad Luck!

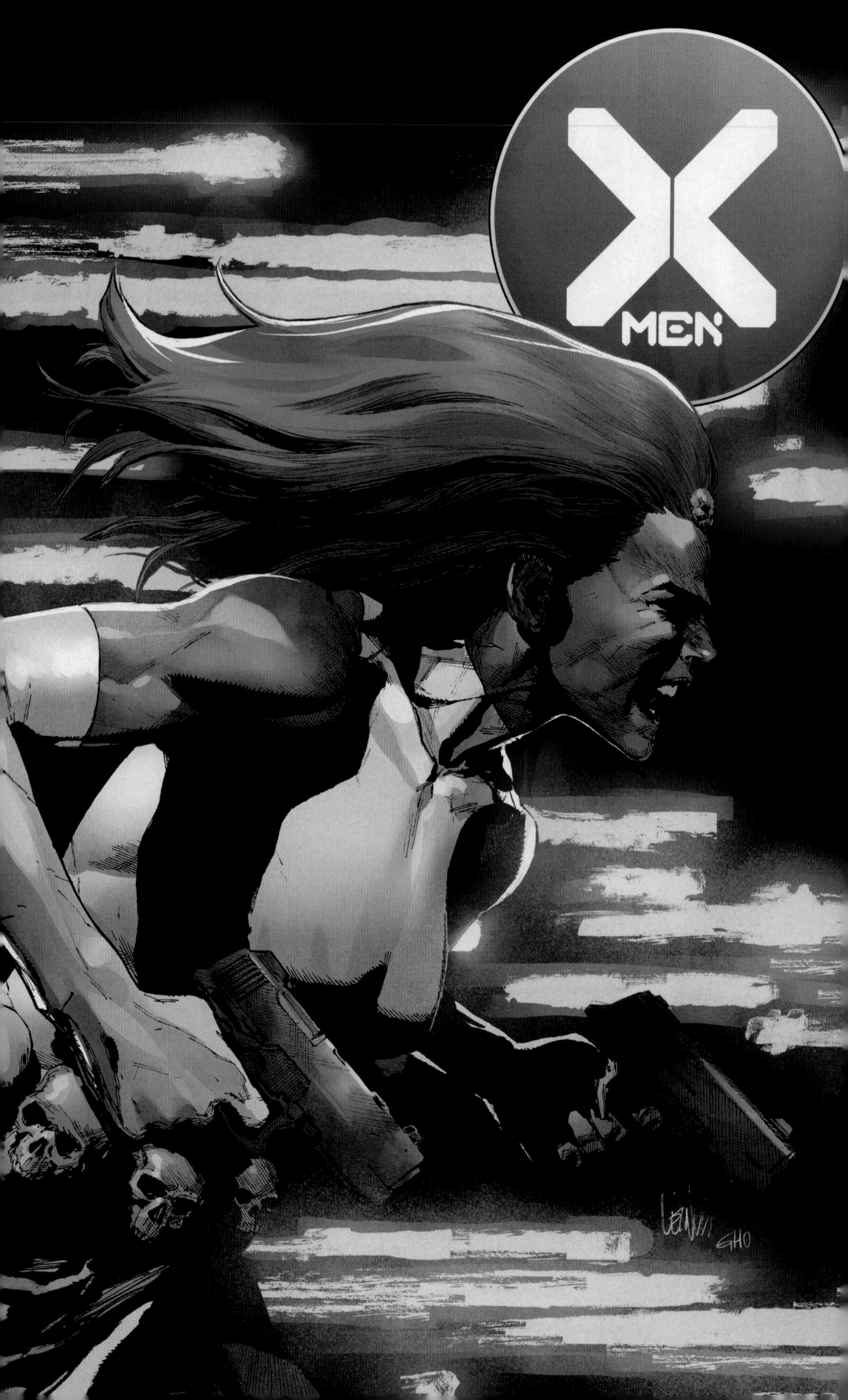
X
MEN

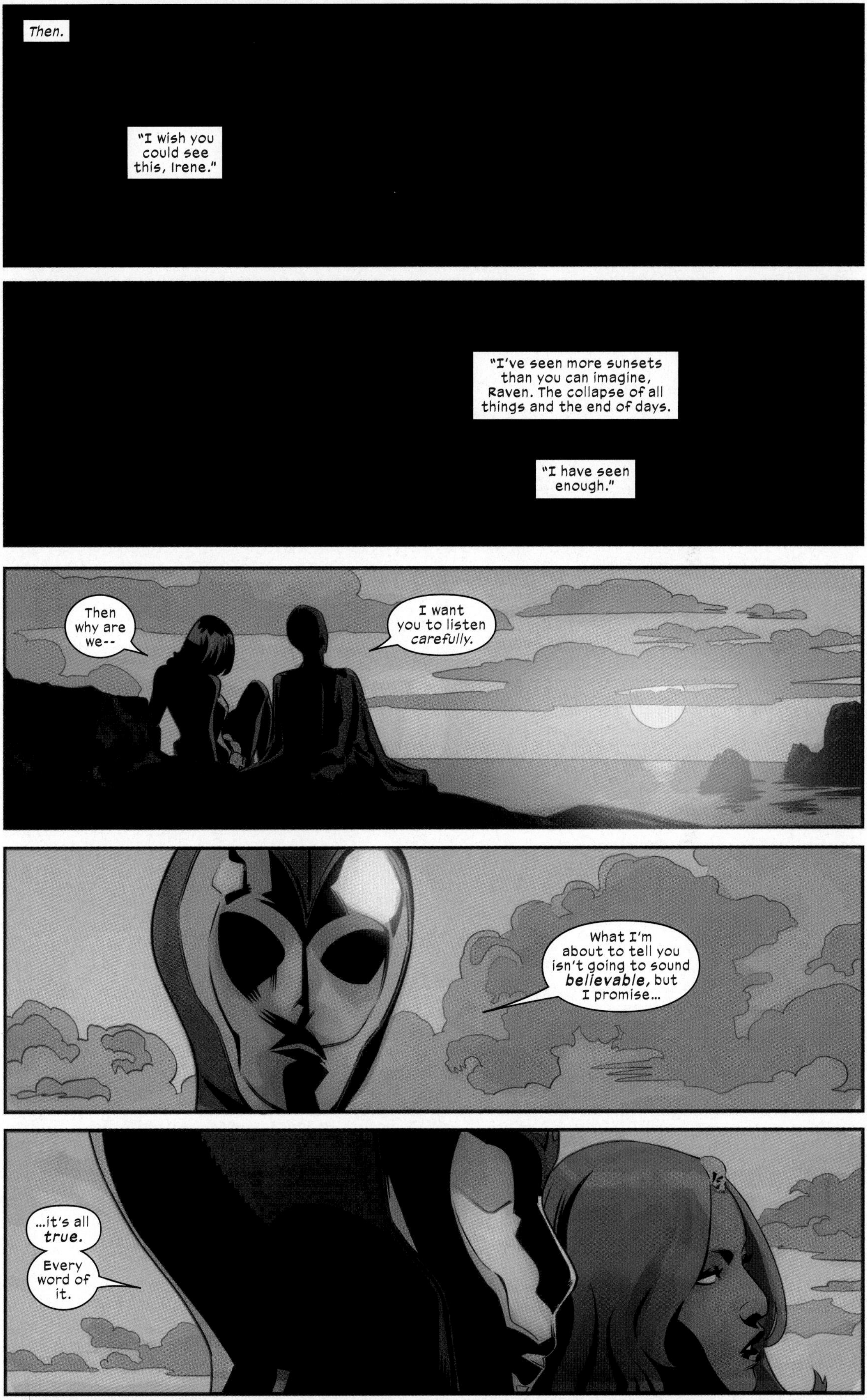
Then.
"I wish you could see this, Irene."
"I've seen more sunsets than you can imagine, Raven. The collapse of all things and the end of days.
"I have seen enough."
Then why are we--
I want you to listen *carefully.*
What I'm about to tell you isn't going to sound ***believable,*** but I promise...
...it's all ***true.***
Every word of it.

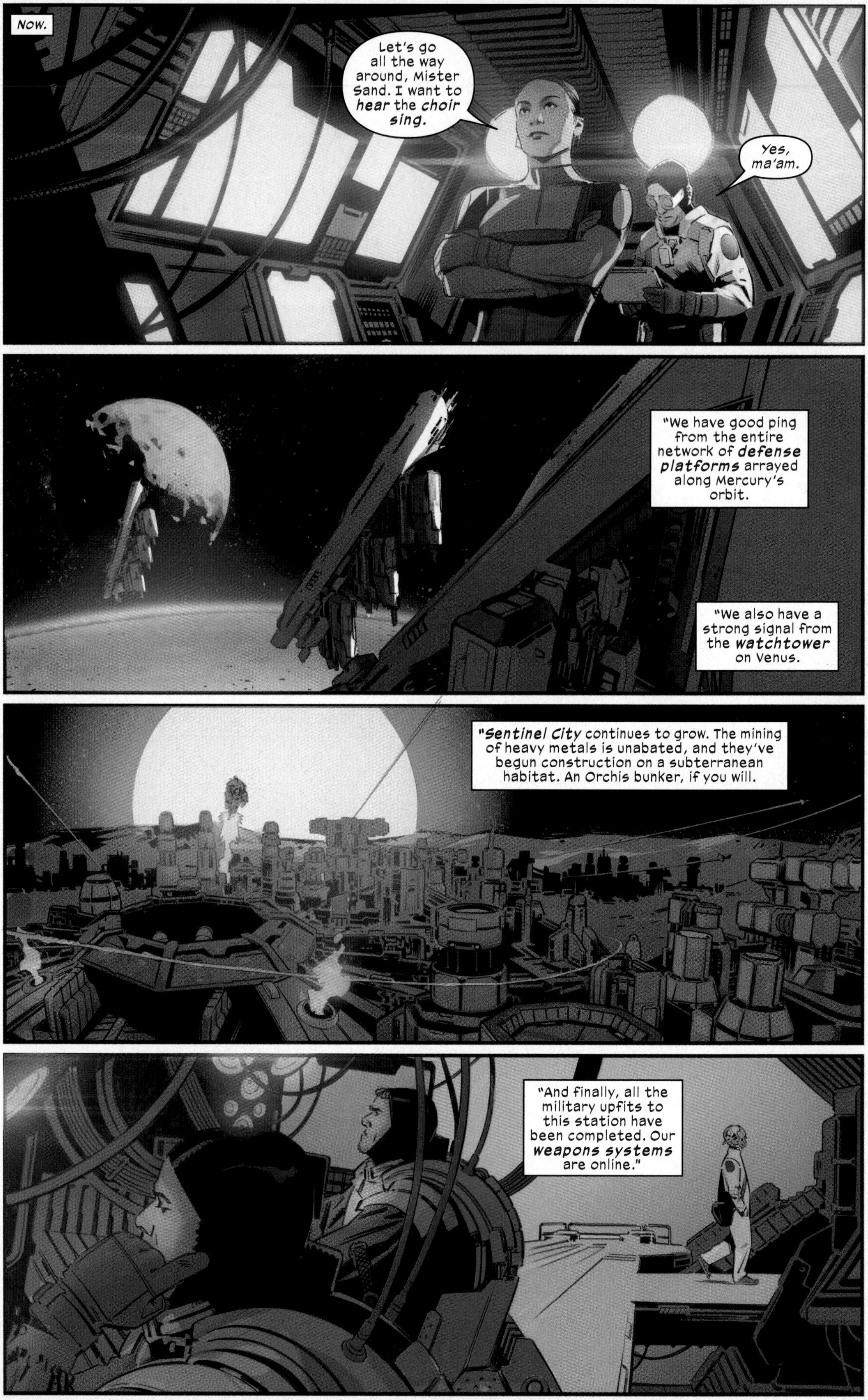
NOW.
Let's go all the way around, Mister Sand. I want to *hear* the *choir sing.*
Yes, ma'am.
"We have good ping from the entire network of ***defense platforms*** arrayed along Mercury's orbit.
"We also have a strong signal from the ***watchtower*** on Venus.
"***Sentinel City*** continues to grow. The mining of heavy metals is unabated, and they've begun construction on a subterranean habitat. An Orchis bunker, if you will.
"And finally, all the military upfits to this station have been completed. Our ***weapons systems*** are online."

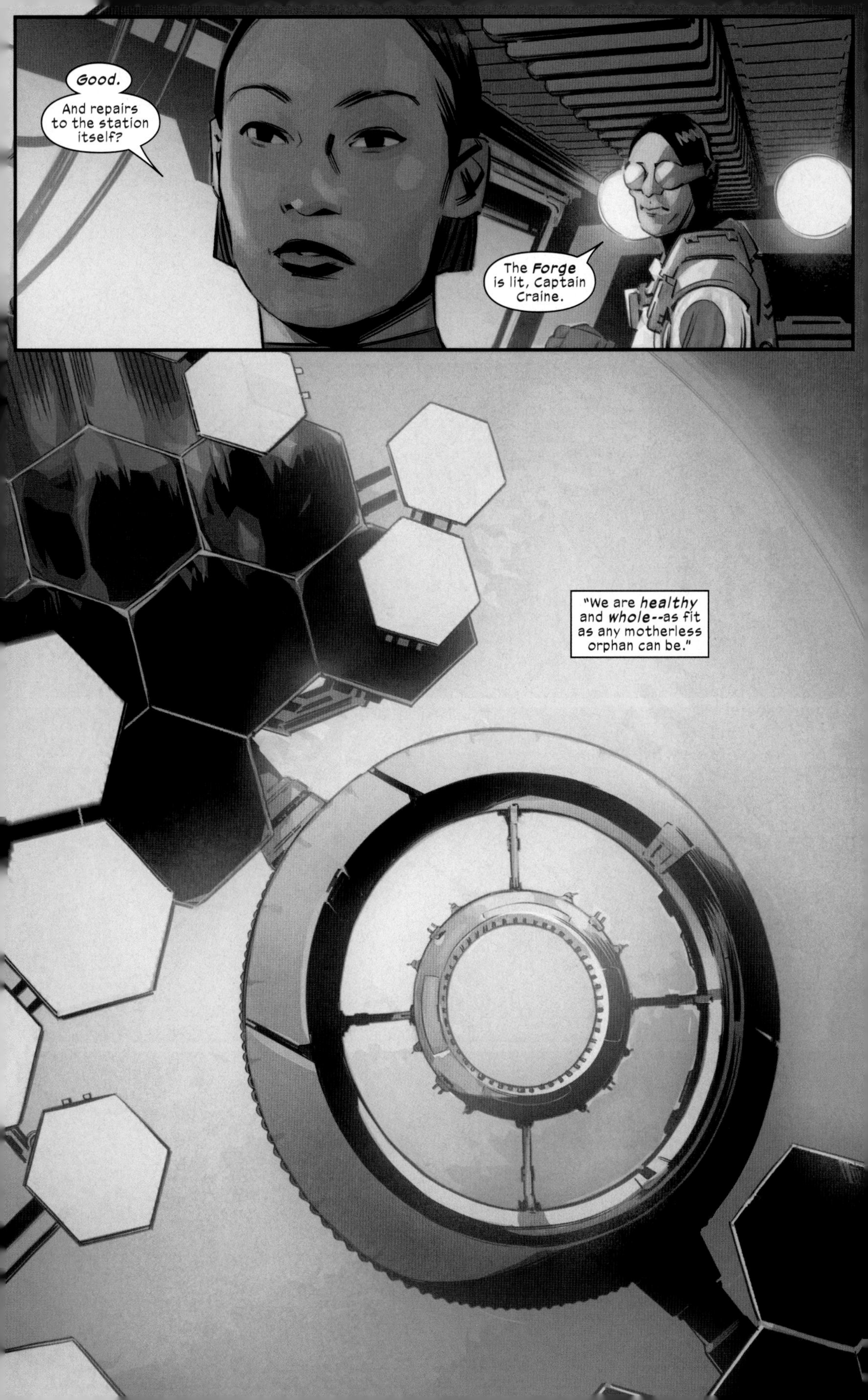
Good.
And repairs to the station itself?
The *Forge* is lit, Captain Craine.
"We are *healthy* and *whole*--as fit as any motherless orphan can be."

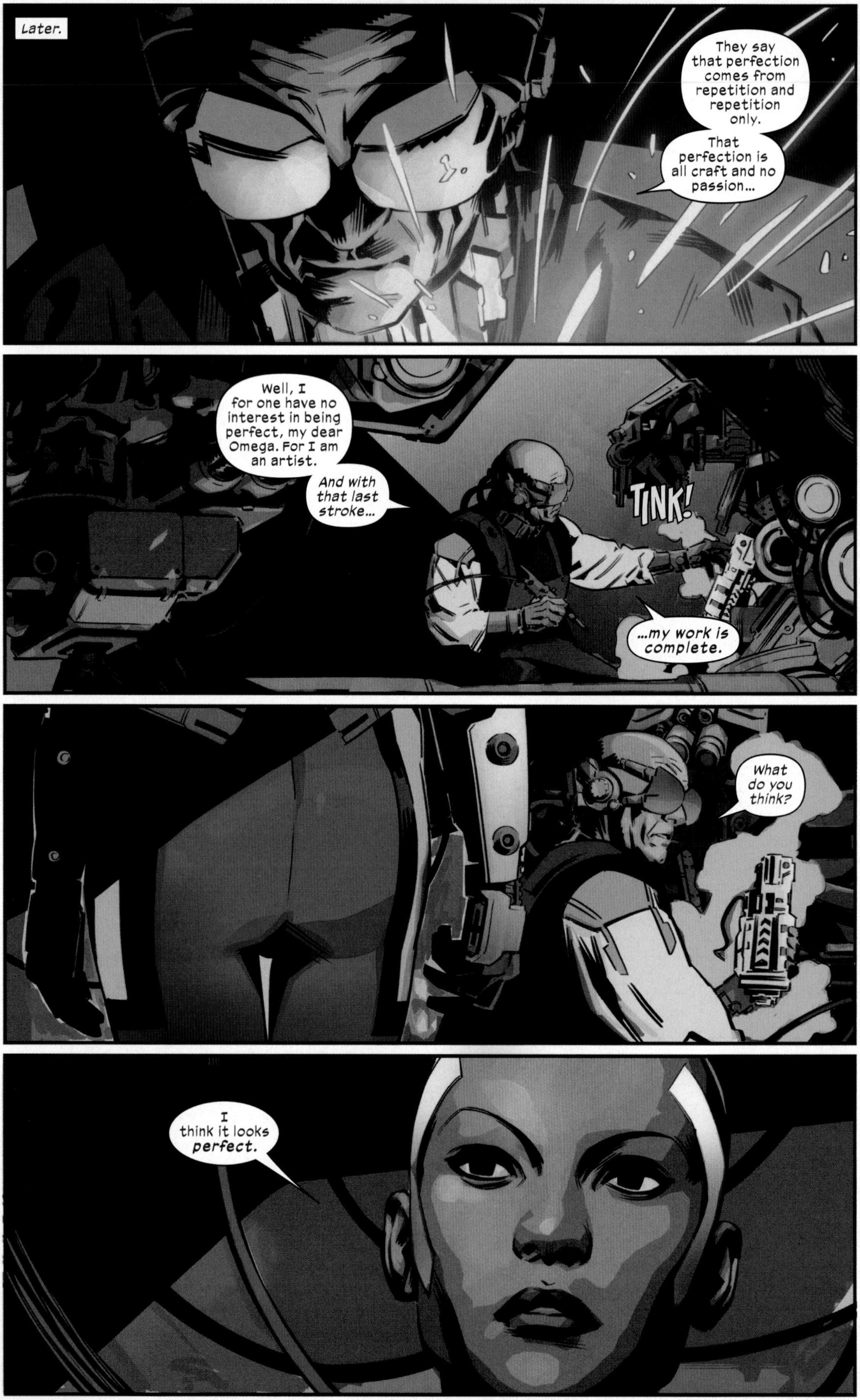
Later.
They say that perfection comes from repetition and repetition only.
That perfection is all craft and no passion...
Well, I for one have no interest in being perfect, my dear Omega. For I am an artist.
And with that last stroke...
TINK!
...my work is complete.
What do you think?
I think it looks perfect.

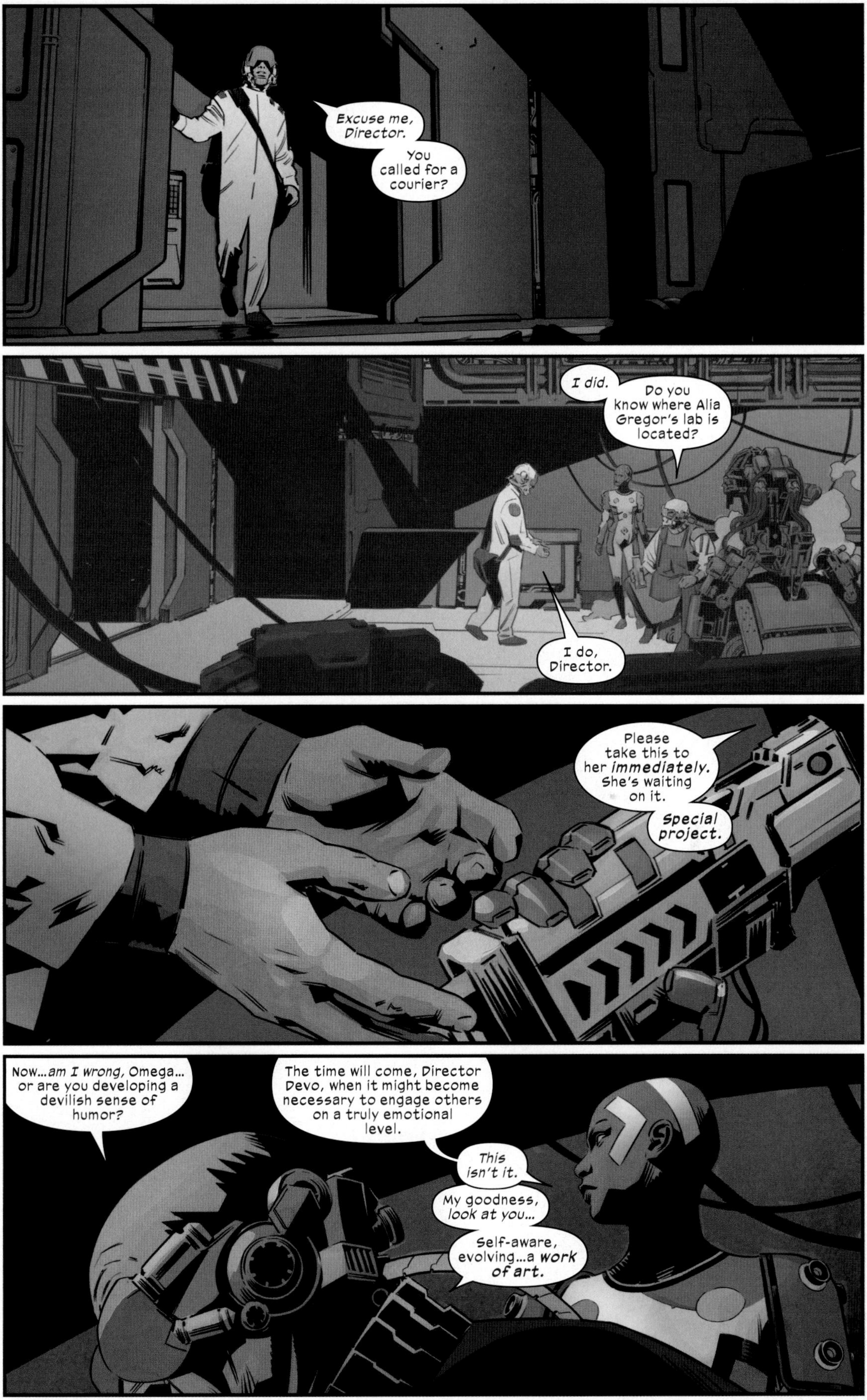
Excuse me, Director.
You called for a courier?
I did.
Do you know where Alia Gregor's lab is located?
I do, Director.
Please take this to her *immediately.* She's waiting on it.
Special project.
Now...*am I wrong,* Omega... or are you developing a devilish sense of humor?
The time will come, Director Devo, when it might become necessary to engage others on a truly emotional level.
This isn't it.
My goodness, look at you...
Self-aware, evolving...a *work of art.*

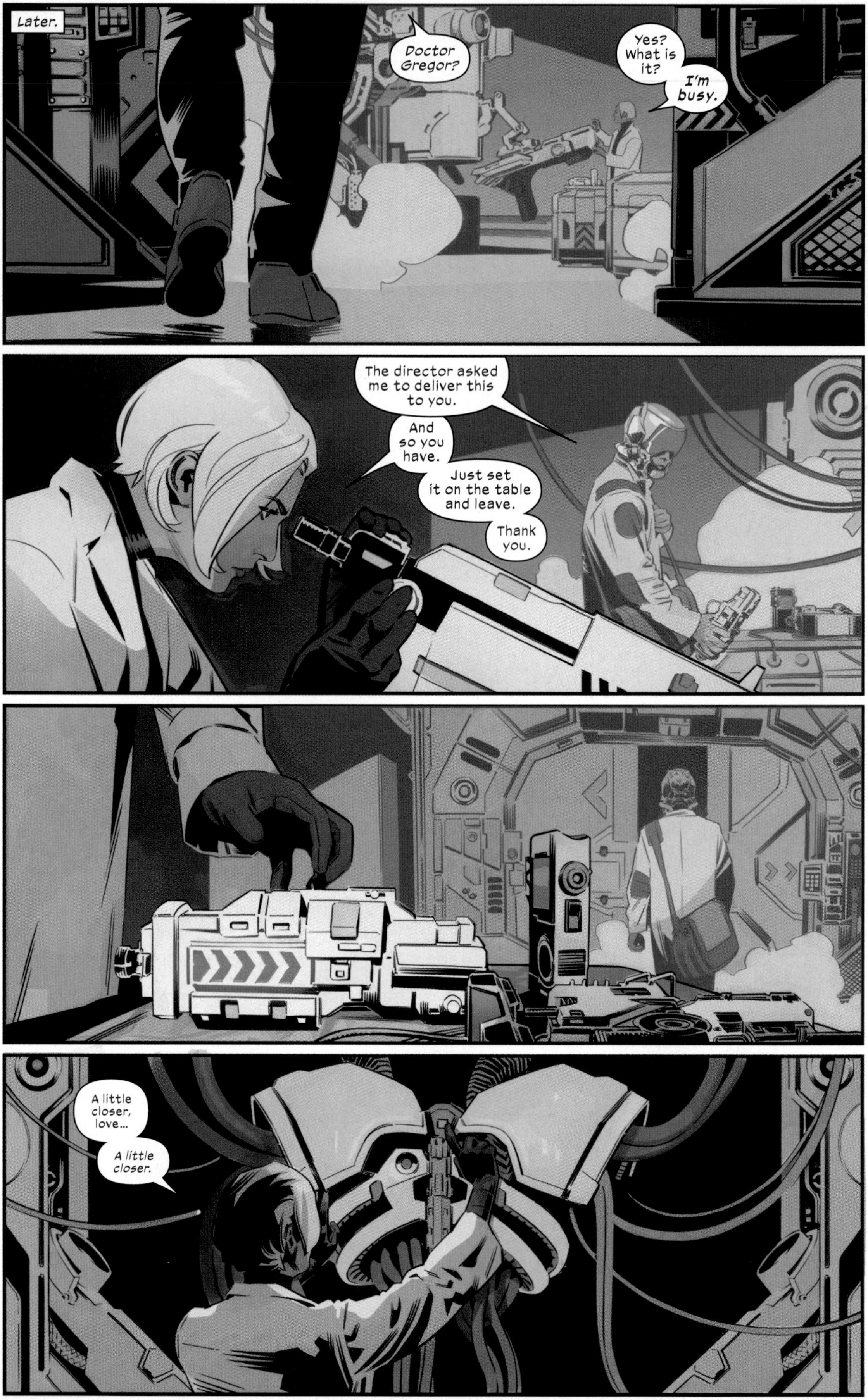
Later.
Doctor Gregor?
Yes? What is it?
I'm busy.
The director asked me to deliver this to you.
And so you have.
Just set it on the table and leave.
Thank you.
A little closer, love...
A little closer.

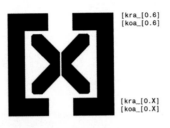

[kra_[0.6]
[koa_[0.6]

[kra_[0.X]
[koa_[0.X]

SOMETHING'S NOT RIGHT

The X-MEN undertook a mission to destroy the Orchis Forge,
a space station with tremendous offensive capabilities
against mutantkind, including the capacity to create Nimrod,
a highly advanced mutant-killing robot. The entire team
perished in the process of successfully unmooring the
Mother Mold at the core of the station, sending it plunging
into the sun.

Now the X-MEN are restored to life. The nation of Krakoa
stands behind them. What more could they want?

Director
Devo

Omega
Sentinel

Doctor
Gregor

Mystique

Charles
Xavier

Magneto

[00_mutants_of_X]
[00_the_world__X]

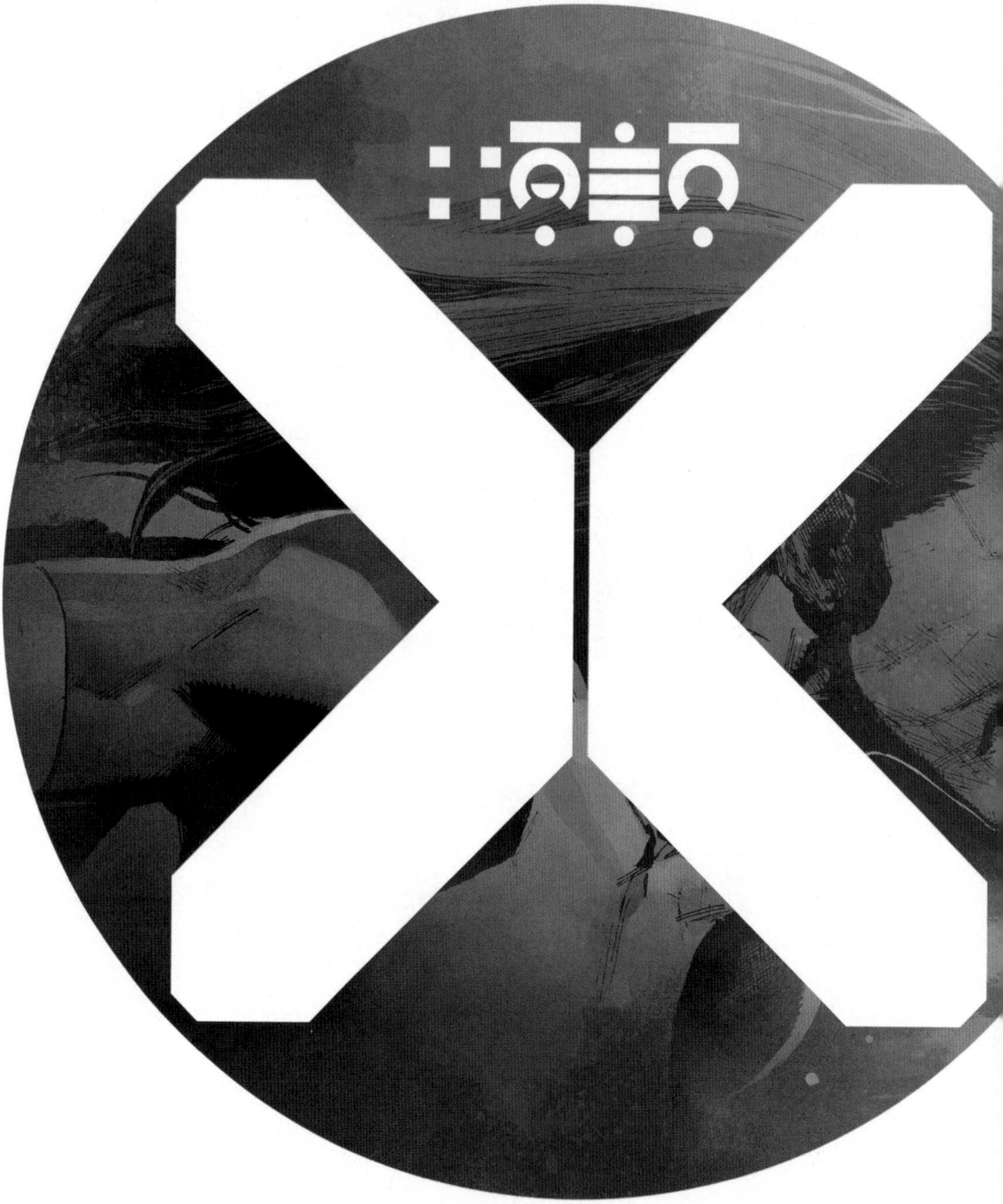

[00_mutants_of_X]
[00_the_world__X]

JONATHAN HICKMAN..............................[WRITER]
MATTEO BUFFAGNI...............................[ARTIST]
SUNNY GHO.................................[COLOR ARTIST]
VC's CLAYTON COWLES.........................[LETTERER]
TOM MULLER....................................[DESIGN]

LEINIL FRANCIS YU & SUNNY GHO...........[COVER ARTISTS]

PHILIP TAN & DAVE McCAIG; MARK BROOKS..................
................................[VARIANT COVER ARTISTS]

NICK RUSSELL..............................[PRODUCTION]

ANNALISE BISSA.......................[ASSISTANT EDITOR]
JORDAN D. WHITE...............................[EDITOR]
C.B. CEBULSKI.........................[EDITOR IN CHIEF]

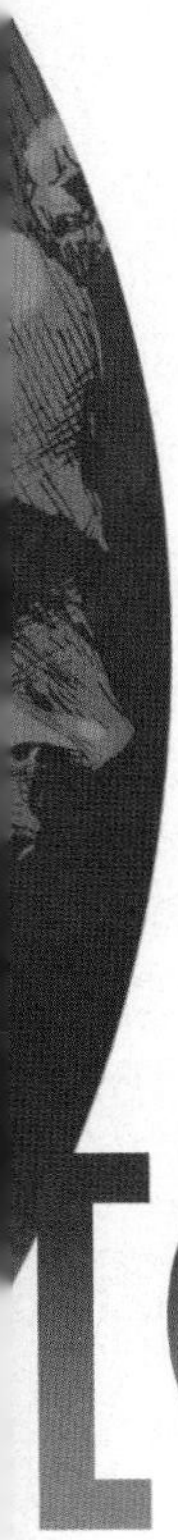

[06] X-MEN

[ISSUE SIX]....................THE ORACLE
X-MEN CREATED BY.................STAN LEE & JACK KIRBY

[00_mutants_of_X]
[00_the_world__X]

[00_00...0]
[00_00...6]

[00_unite_]
[00______]

[00______]

[00______X]

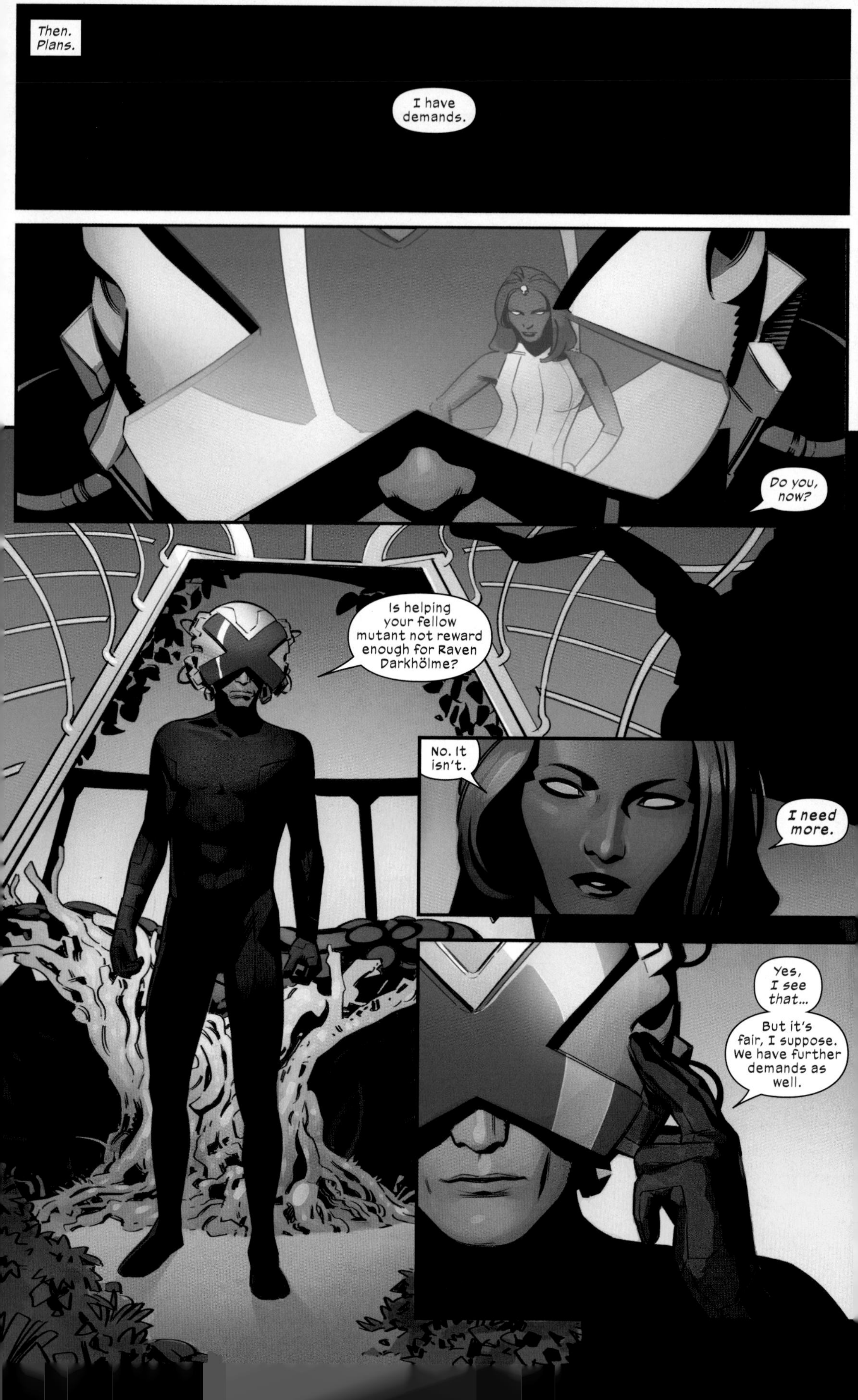
Then.
Plans.
I have demands.
Do you, now?
Is helping your fellow mutant not reward enough for Raven Darkhölme?
No. It isn't.
I need more.
Yes, I see that...
But it's fair, I suppose. We have further demands as well.

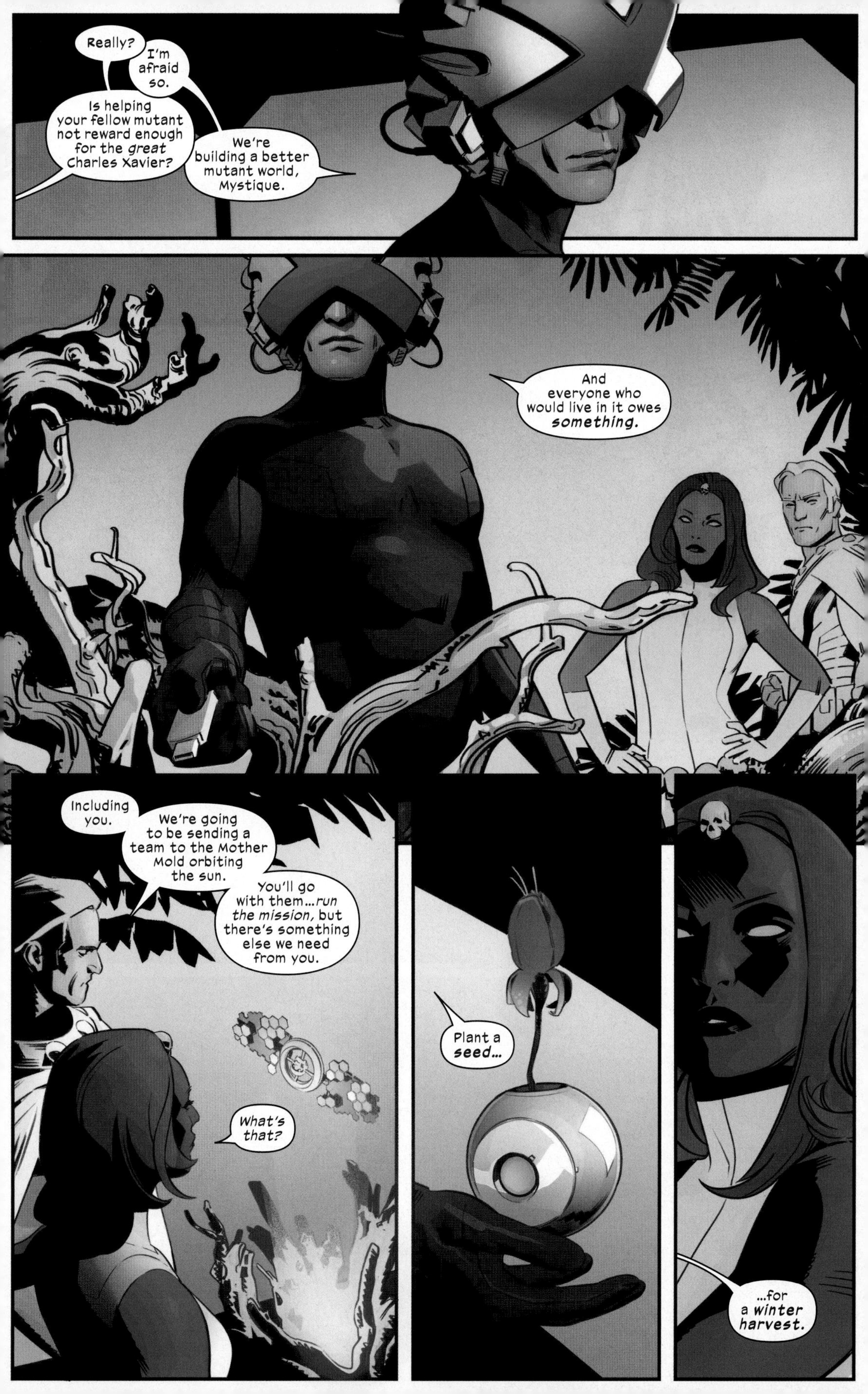
Really?
I'm afraid so.
Is helping your fellow mutant not reward enough for the *great* Charles Xavier?
We're building a better mutant world, Mystique.
And everyone who would live in it owes *something.*
Including you.
We're going to be sending a team to the Mother Mold orbiting the sun.
You'll go with them...*run the mission,* but there's something else we need from you.
What's that?
Plant a ***seed...***
...for a ***winter harvest.***

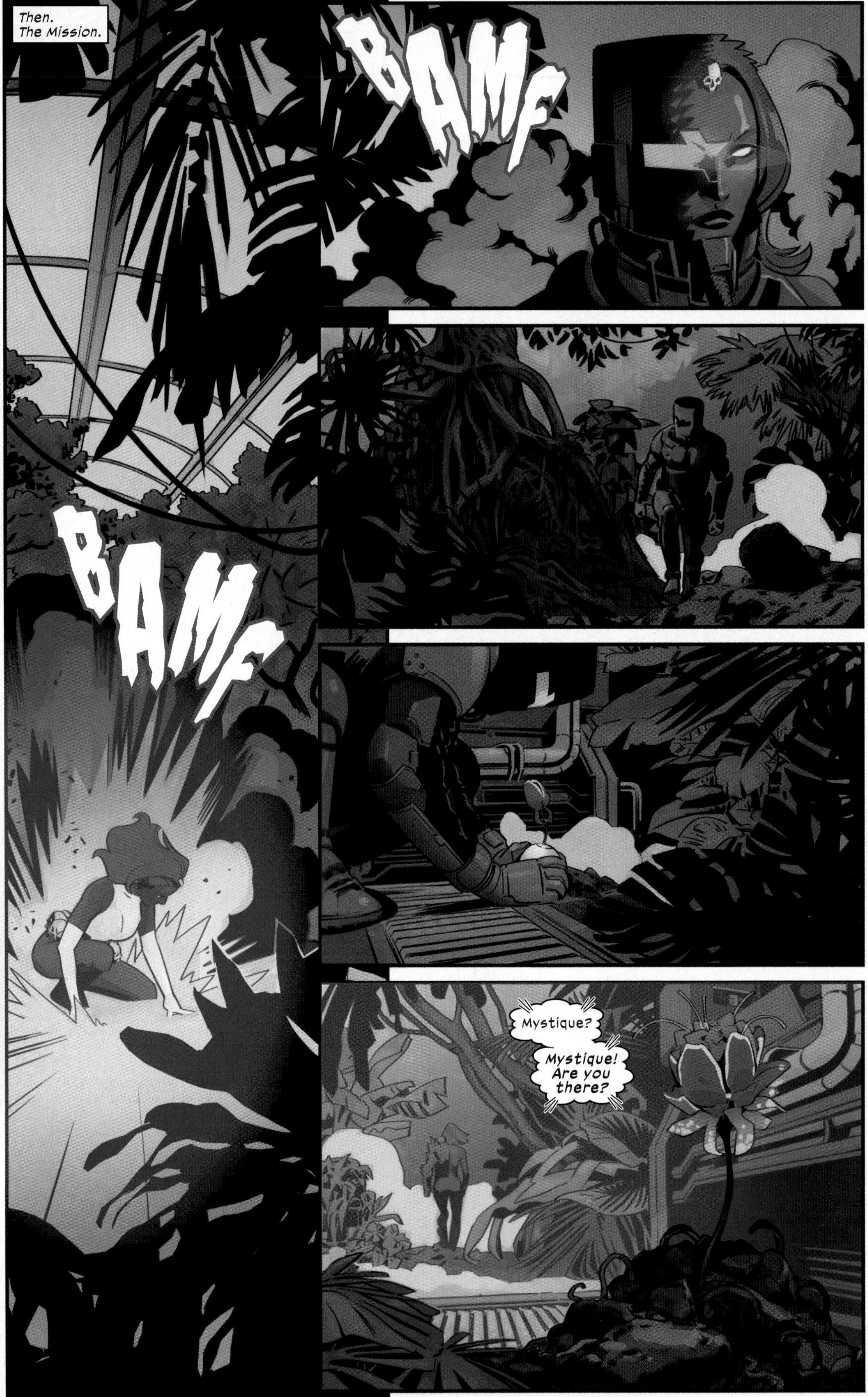
Then.
The Mission.
BAMF
BAMF
Mystique?
Mystique! Are you there?

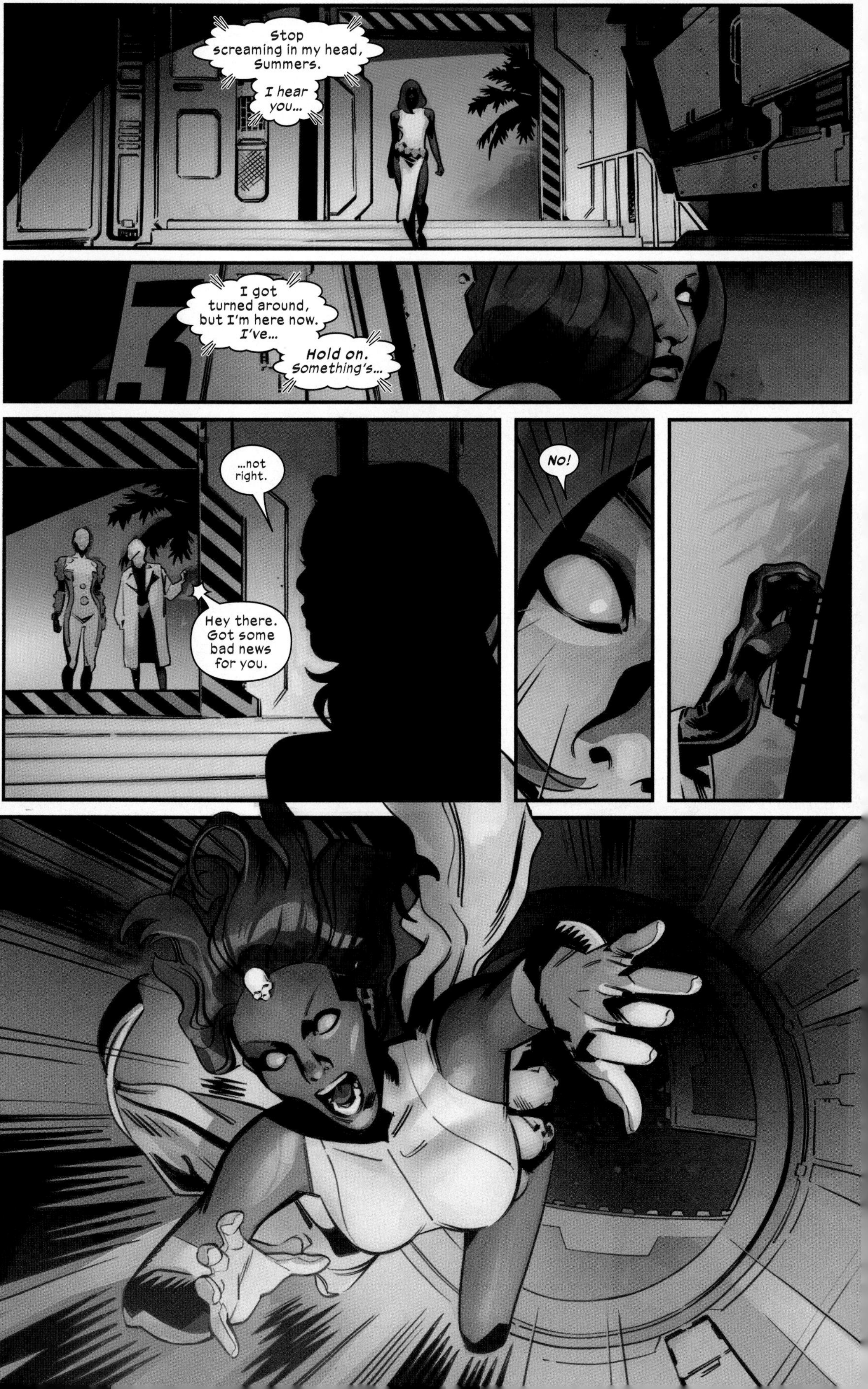
Stop screaming in my head, Summers.
I hear you...
I got turned around, but I'm here now. I've...
Hold on. Something's...
...not right.
Hey there. Got some bad news for you.
NO!

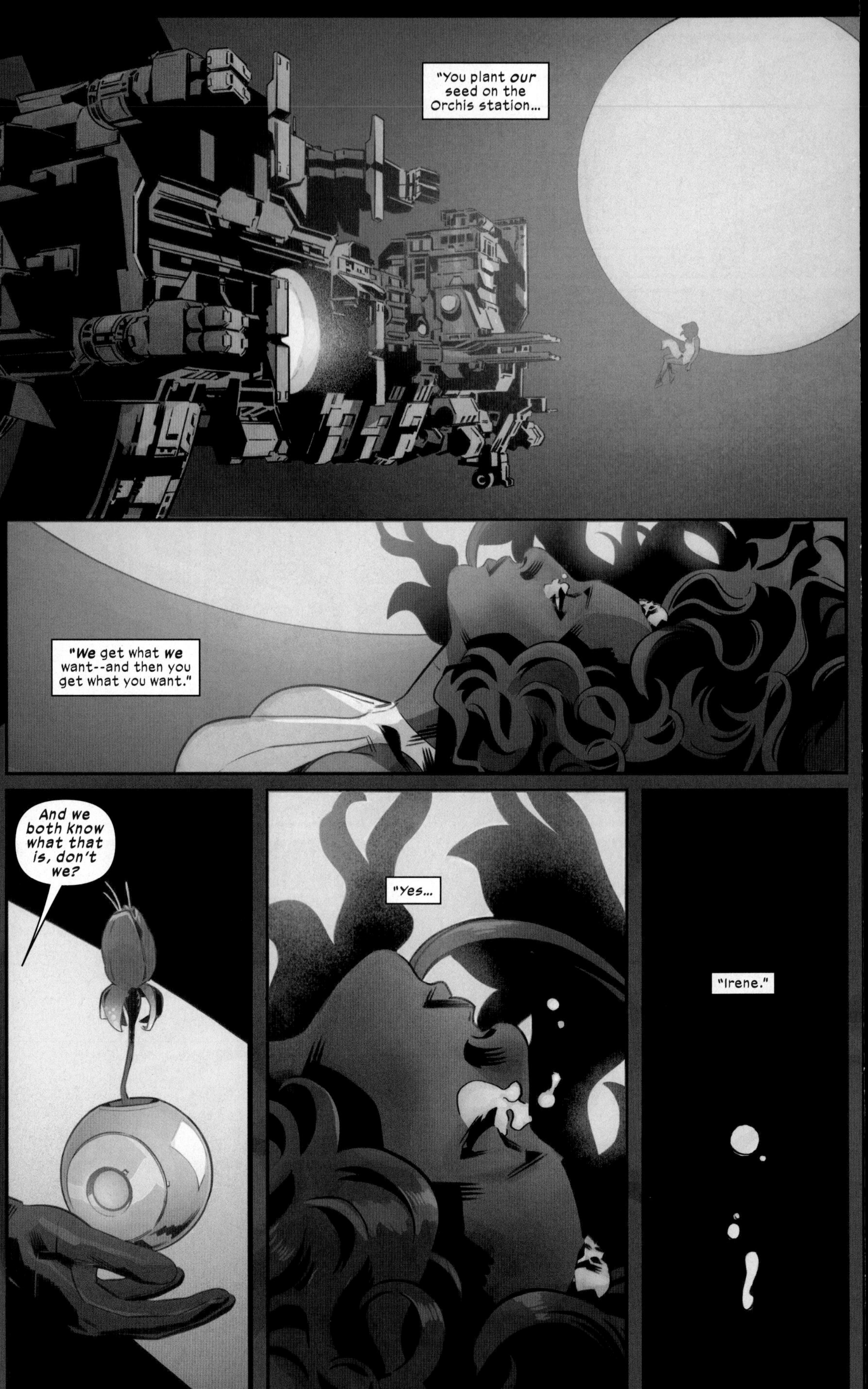
"You plant *our* seed on the Orchis station...
"*We* get what *we* want--and then you get what you want."
And we both know what that is, don't we?
"Yes...
"Irene."

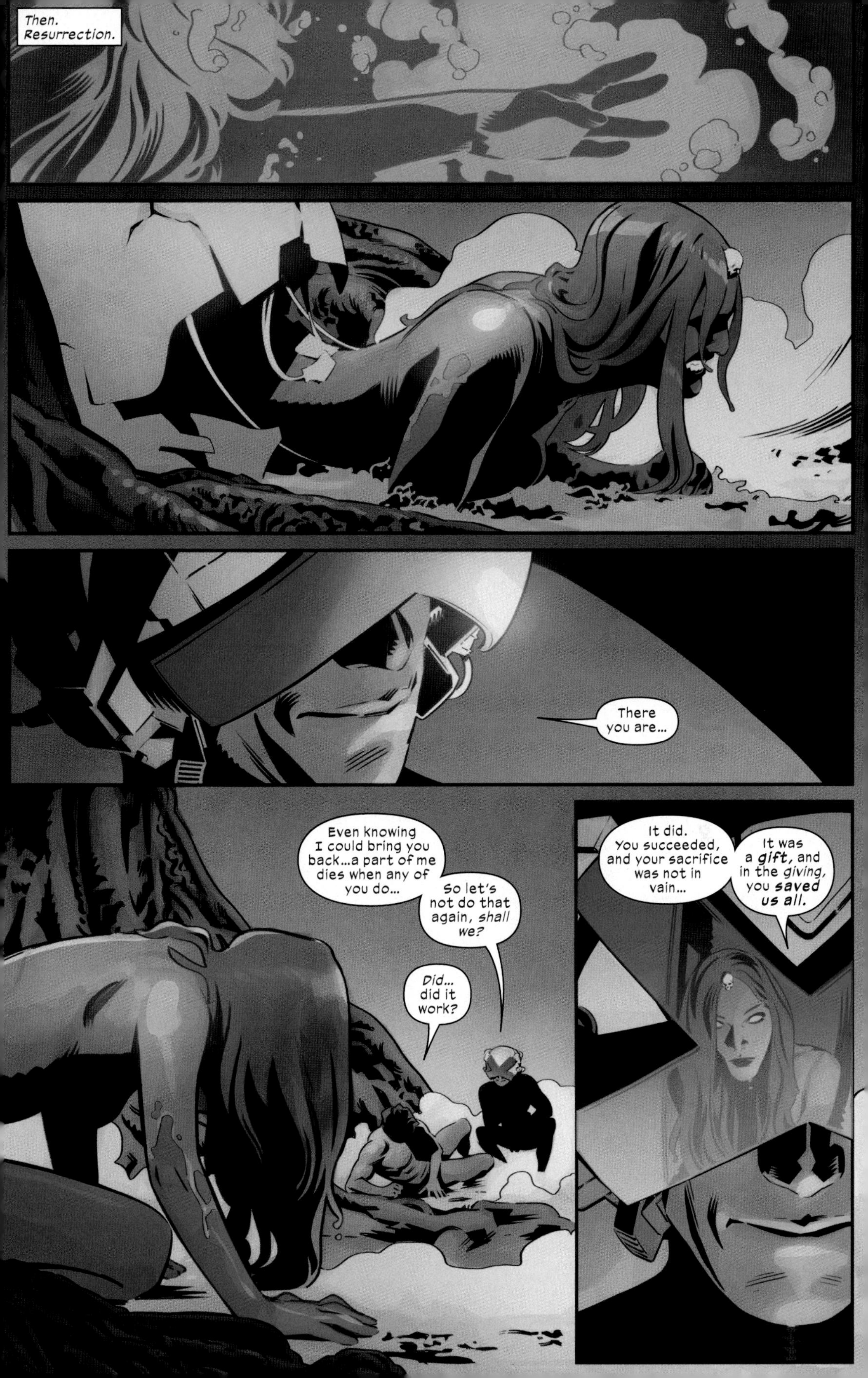

Then. Resurrection.
There you are...
Even knowing I could bring you back...a part of me dies when any of you do...
So let's not do that again, *shall* we?
Did... did it work?
It did. You succeeded, and your sacrifice was not in vain...
It was a ***gift***, and in the *giving*, you ***saved us all.***

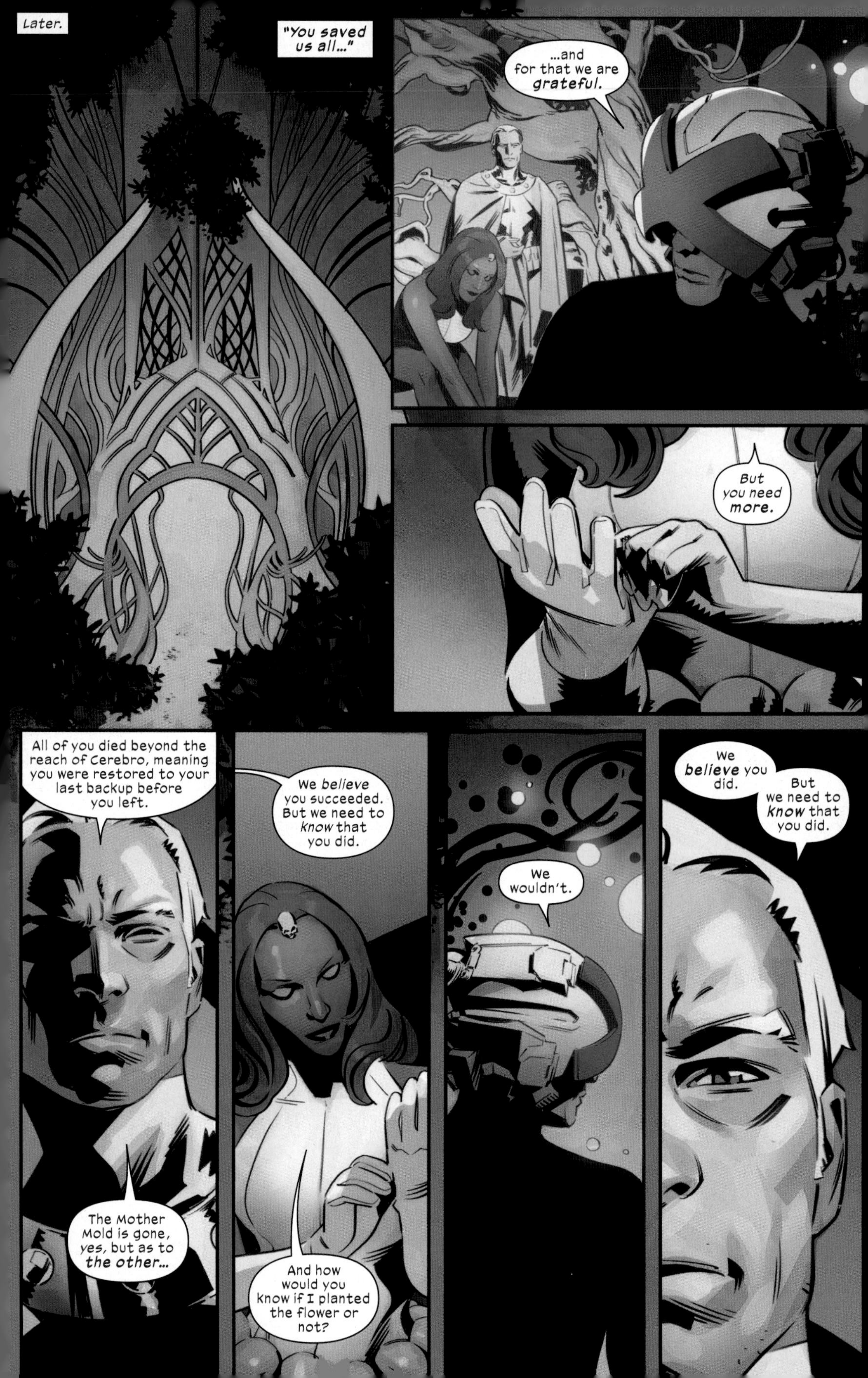
Later.
"You saved us all..."
...and for that we are *grateful.*
But you need *more.*
All of you died beyond the reach of Cerebro, meaning you were restored to your last backup before you left.
We *believe* you succeeded. But we need to *know* that you did.
The Mother Mold is gone, *yes,* but as to *the other...*
And how would you know if I planted the flower or not?
We wouldn't.
We ***believe*** you did.
But we need to ***know*** that you did.

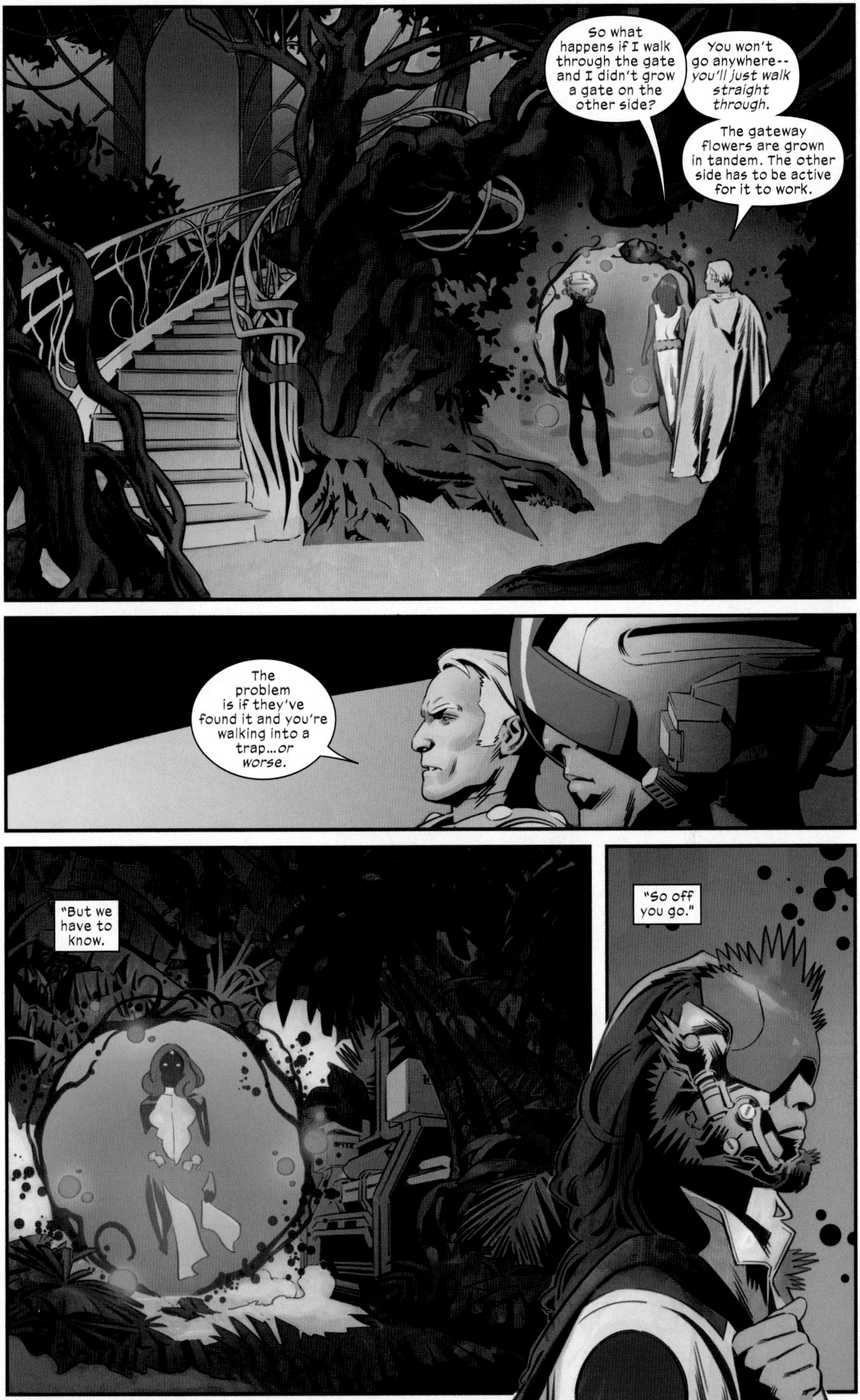
So what happens if I walk through the gate and I didn't grow a gate on the other side?
You won't go anywhere-- *you'll just walk straight through.*
The gateway flowers are grown in tandem. The other side has to be active for it to work.
The problem is if they've found it and you're walking into a trap...*or worse.*
"But we have to know.
"So off you go."

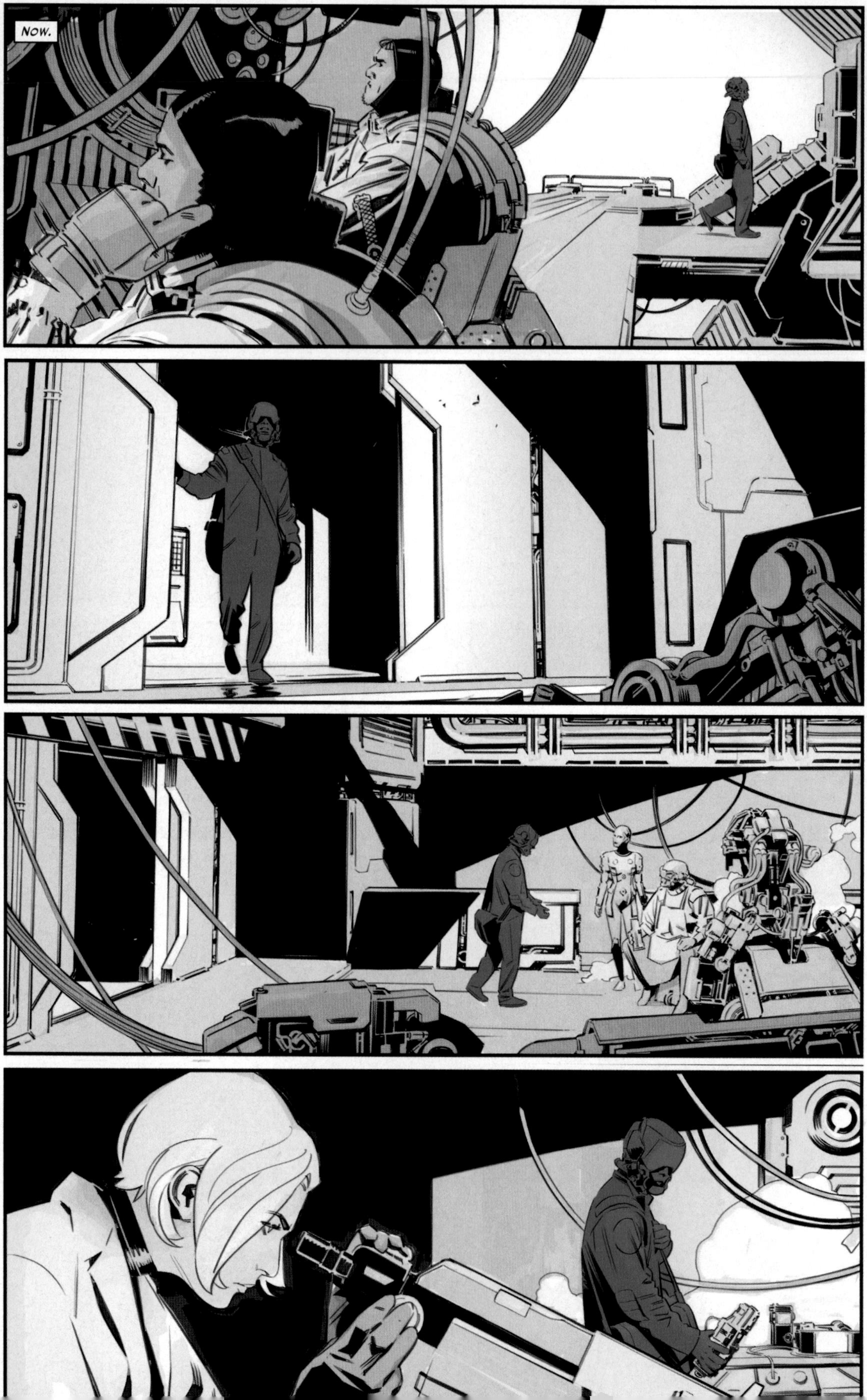
NOW.

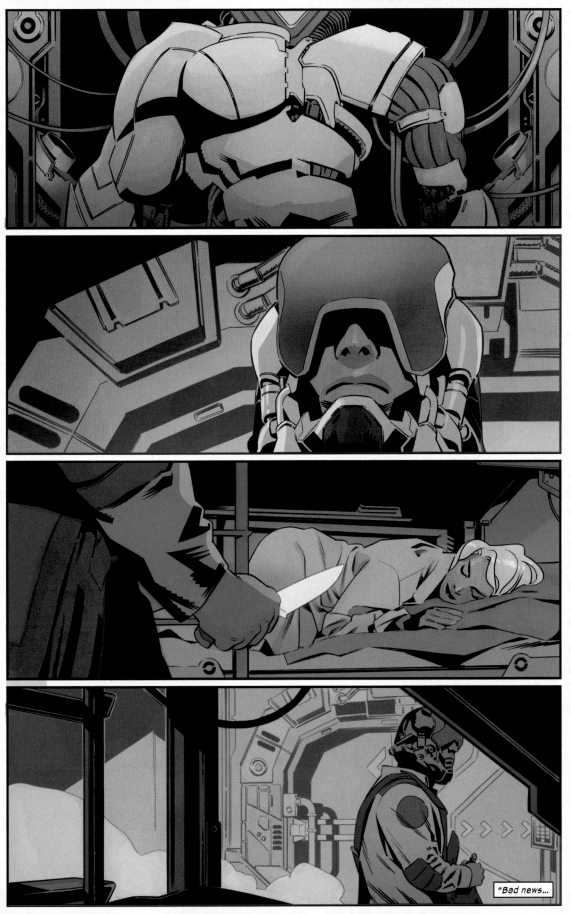

"Bad news...

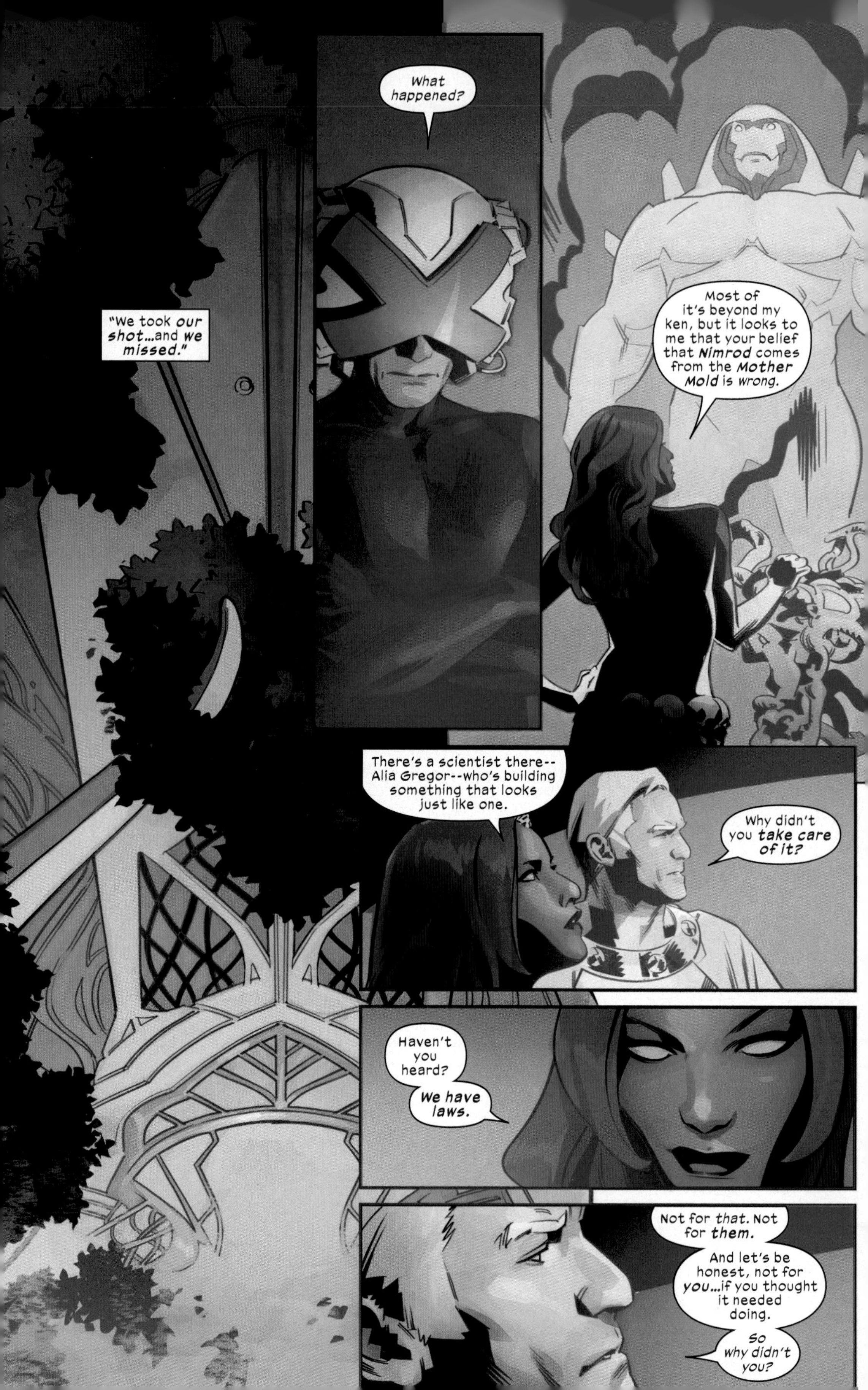
"We took *our* *shot*...and *we* *missed*."
What happened?
Most of it's beyond my ken, but it looks to me that your belief that *Nimrod* comes from the *Mother Mold* is *wrong*.
There's a scientist there--Alia Gregor--who's building something that looks just like one.
Why didn't you *take care of it?*
Haven't you heard?
We have laws.
Not for *that*. Not for *them*.
And let's be honest, not for *you*...if you thought it needed doing.
So why didn't you?

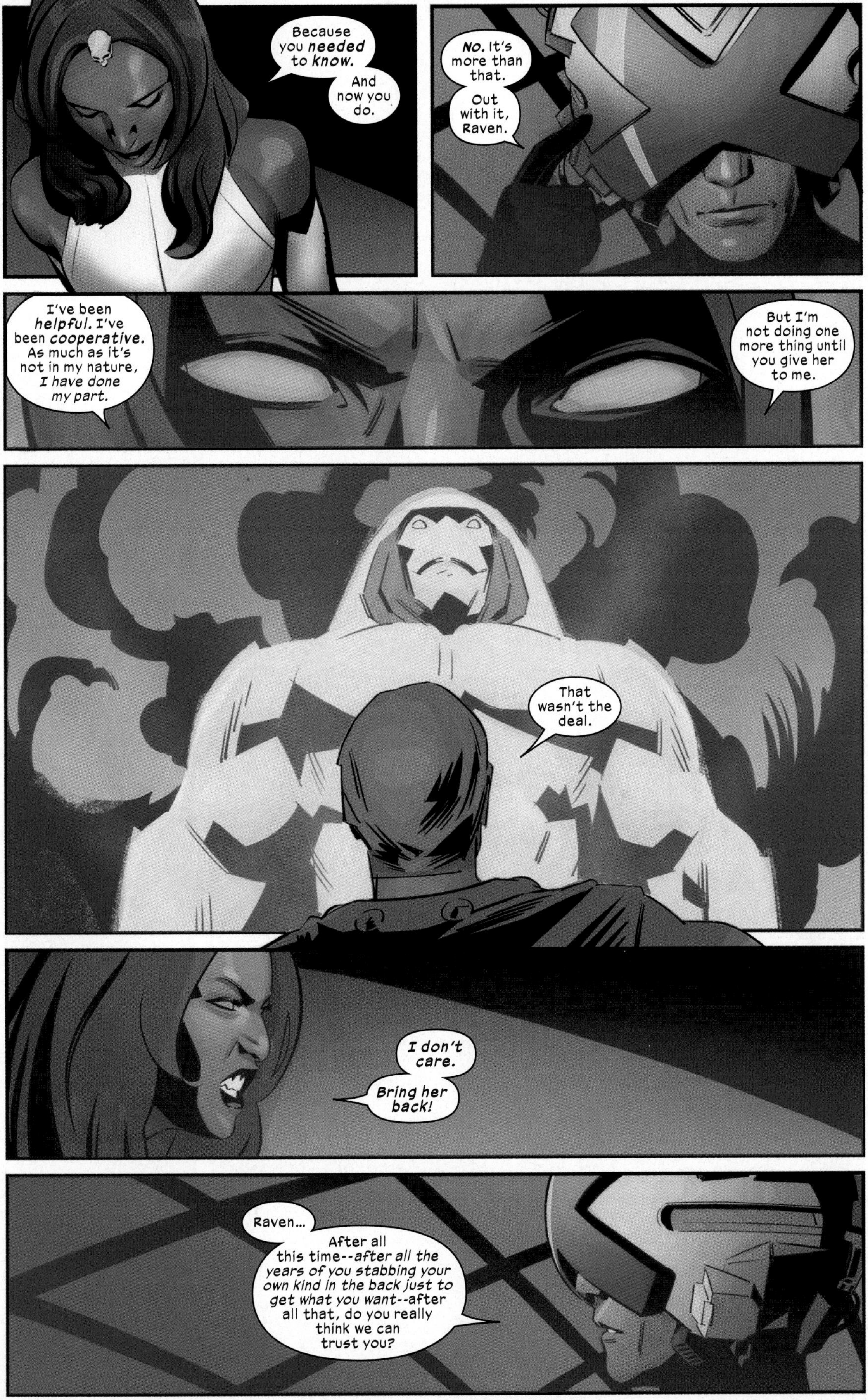
Because you *needed* to *know.*
And now you do.
No. It's more than that.
Out with it, Raven.
I've been *helpful.* I've been *cooperative.* As much as it's not in my nature, *I have done my part.*
But I'm not doing one more thing until you give her to me.
That wasn't the deal.
I don't care.
Bring her back!
Raven...
After all this time--*after all the years of you stabbing your own kind in the back just to* get what you want--after all that, do you really think we can trust you?

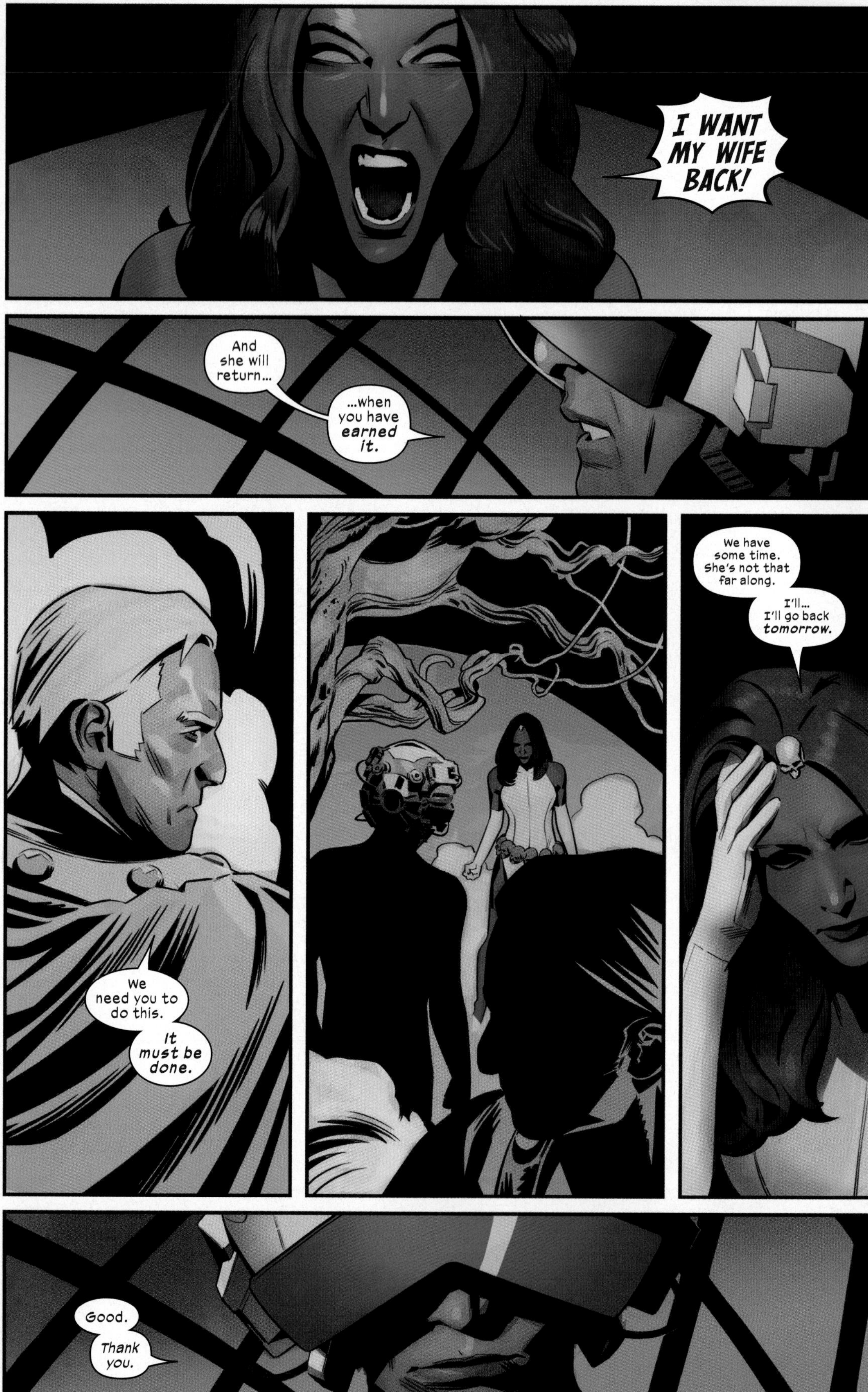
I WANT MY WIFE BACK!
And she will return...
...when you have *earned* it.
We need you to do this.
It must be done.
We have some time. She's not that far along.
I'll... I'll go back *tomorrow.*
Good.
Thank you.

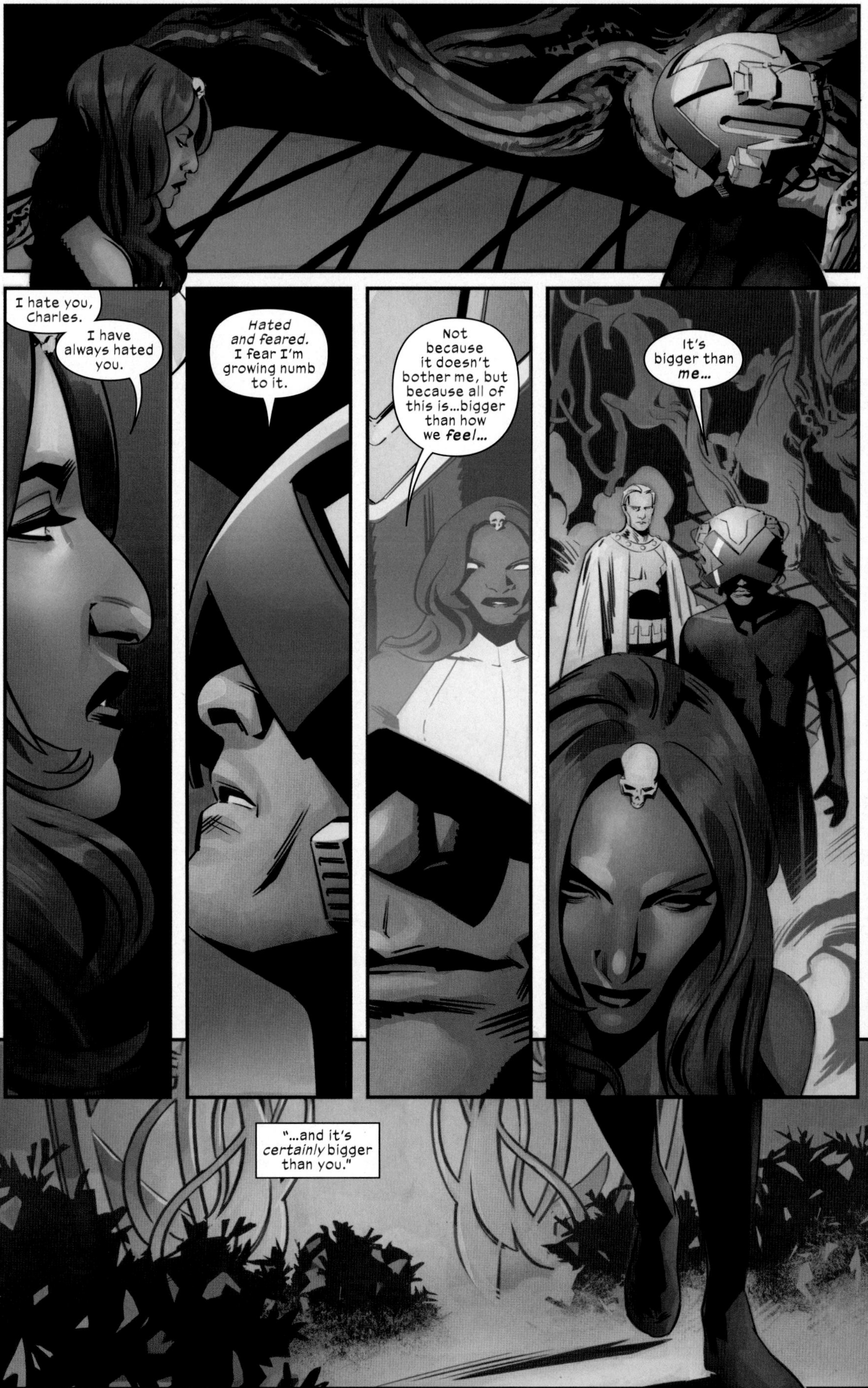

I hate you, Charles.
I have always hated you.
Hated and feared. I fear I'm growing numb to it.
Not because it doesn't bother me, but because all of this is...bigger than how we feel...
It's bigger than me...
"...and it's certainly bigger than you."

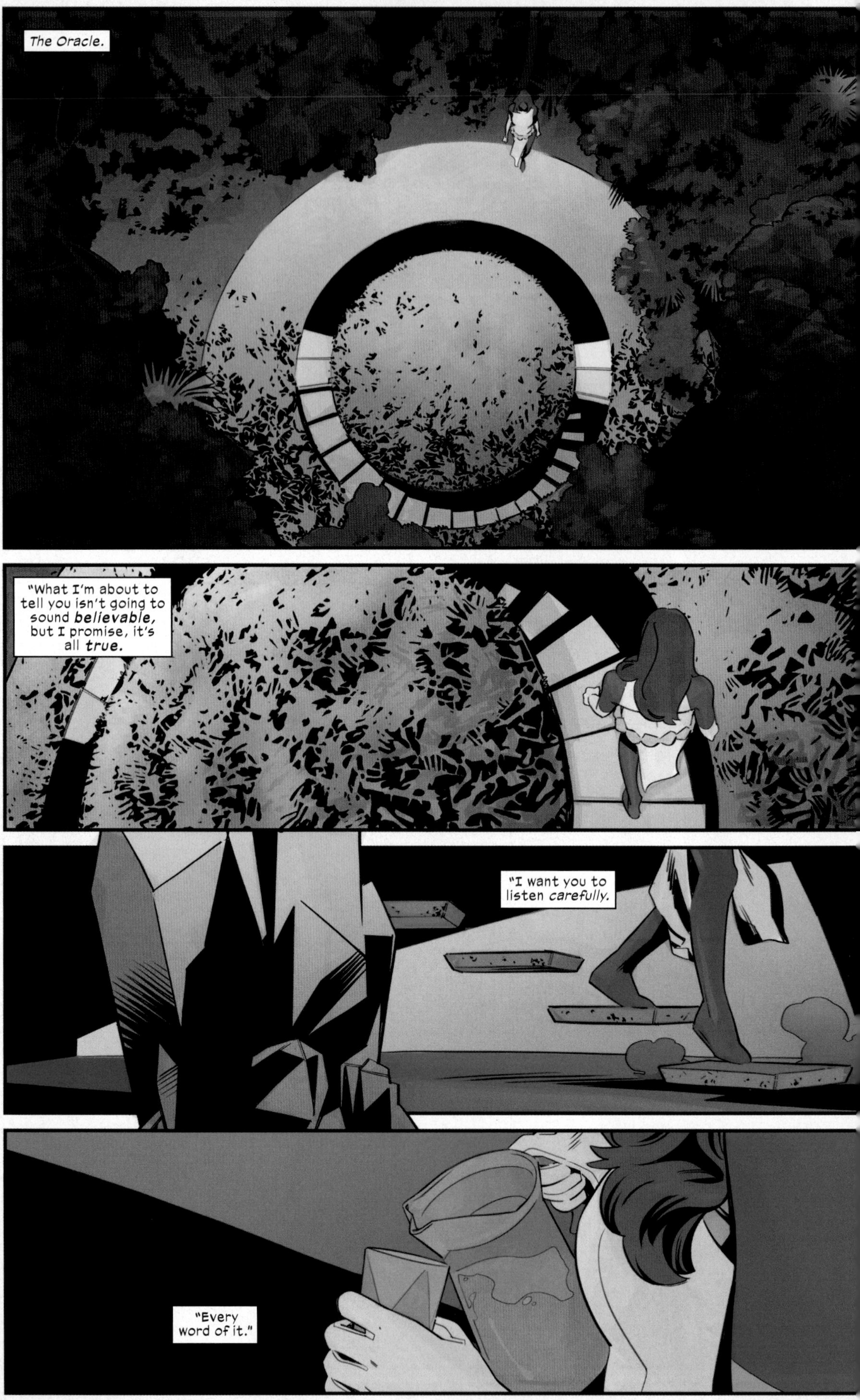
The Oracle.
"What I'm about to tell you isn't going to sound believable, but I promise, it's all true.
"I want you to listen carefully.
"Every word of it."

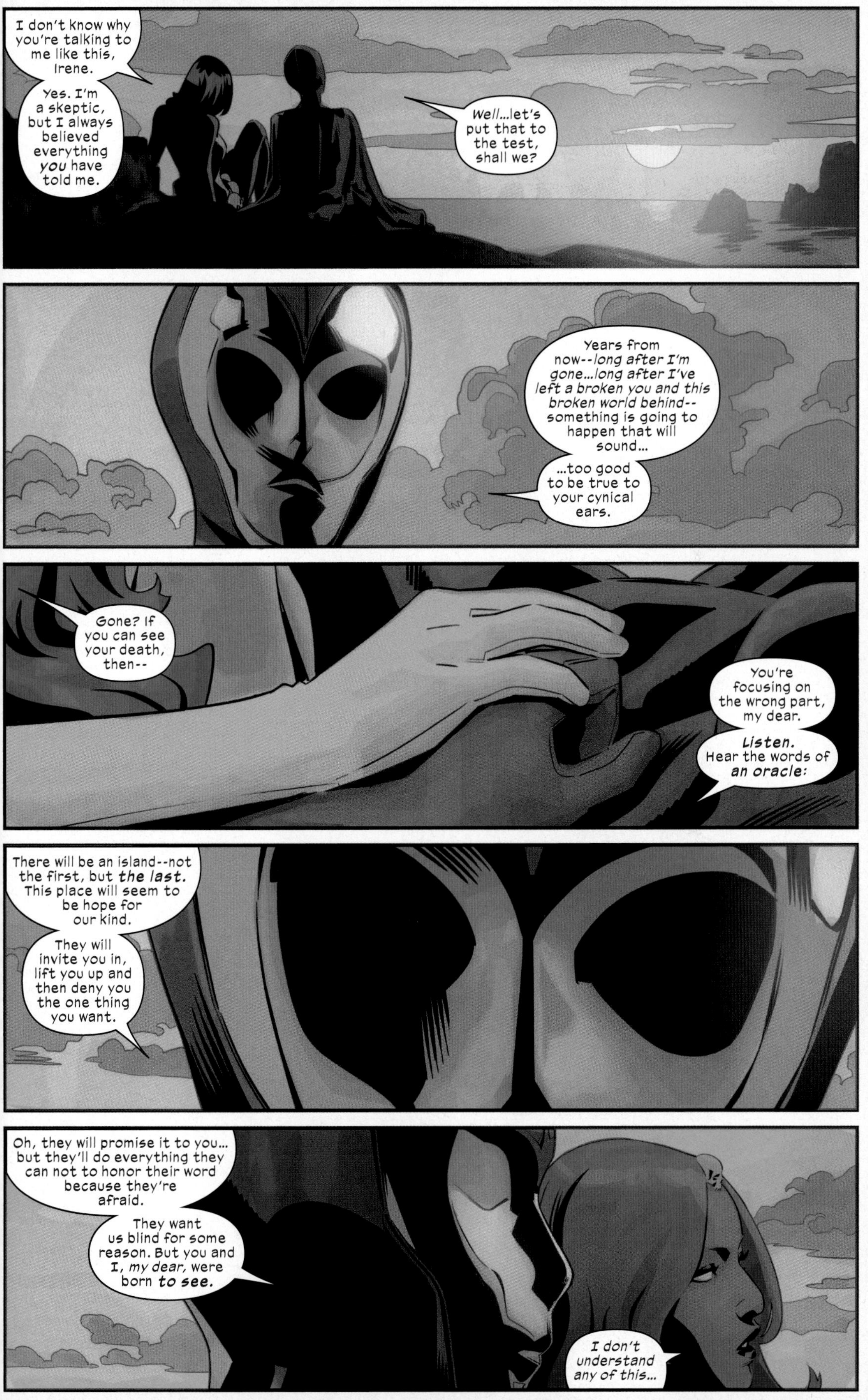

I don't know why you're talking to me like this, Irene.
Yes. I'm a skeptic, but I always believed everything *you* have told me.
Well...let's put that to the test, shall we?
Years from now--*long after I'm gone...long after I've left a broken you and this broken world behind*--something is going to happen that will sound...
...too good to be true to your cynical ears.
Gone? If you can see your death, then--
You're focusing on the wrong part, my dear.
Listen. Hear the words of ***an oracle:***
There will be an island--not the first, but ***the last.*** This place will seem to be hope for our kind.
They will invite you in, lift you up and then deny you the one thing you want.
Oh, they will promise it to you... but they'll do everything they can not to honor their word because they're afraid.
They want us blind for some reason. But you and I, *my dear,* were born ***to see.***
I don't understand any of this...

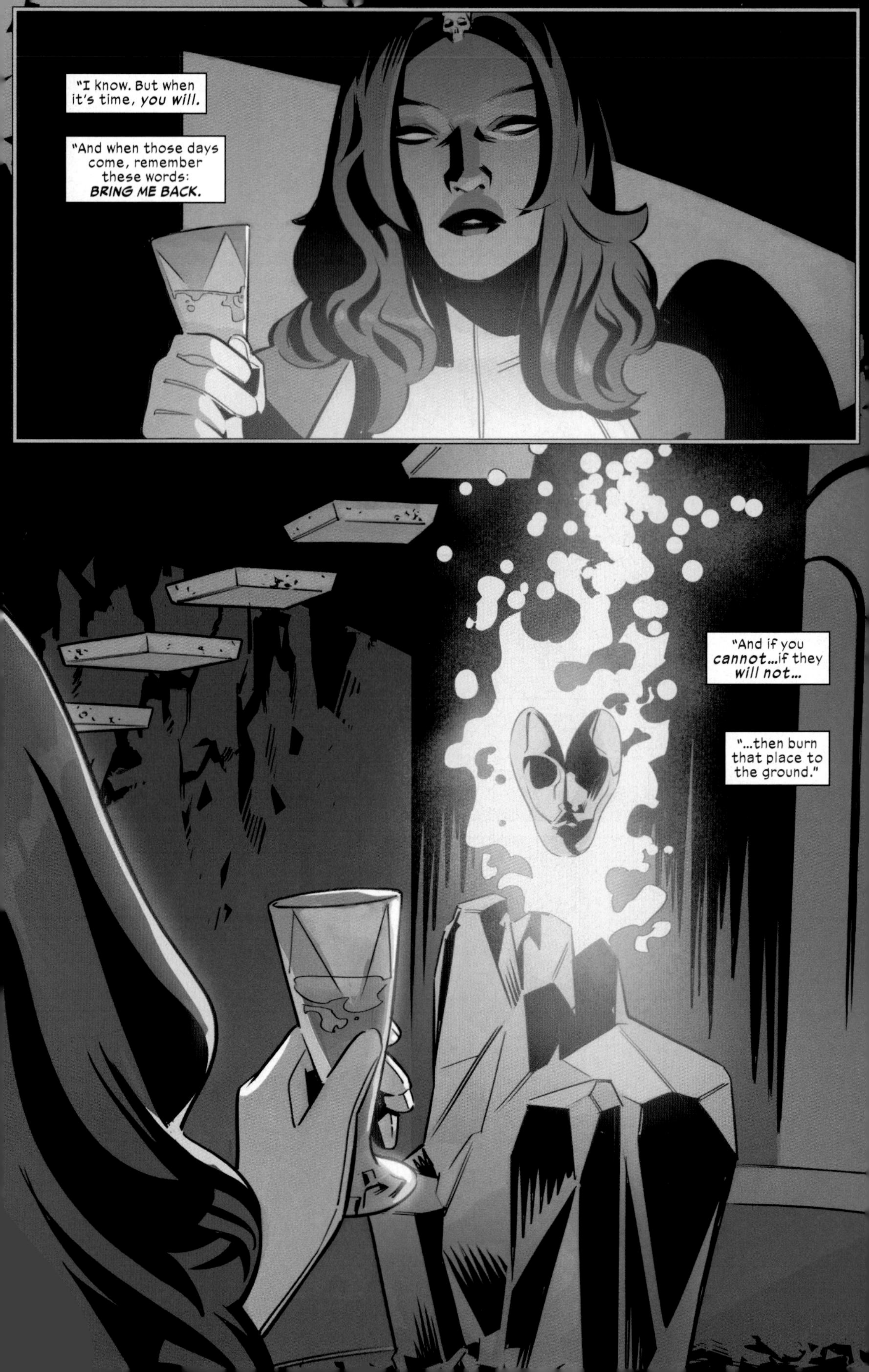
"I know. But when it's time, *you will.*
"And when those days come, remember these words: ***BRING ME BACK.***
"And if you ***cannot***...if they ***will not***...
"...then burn that place to the ground."

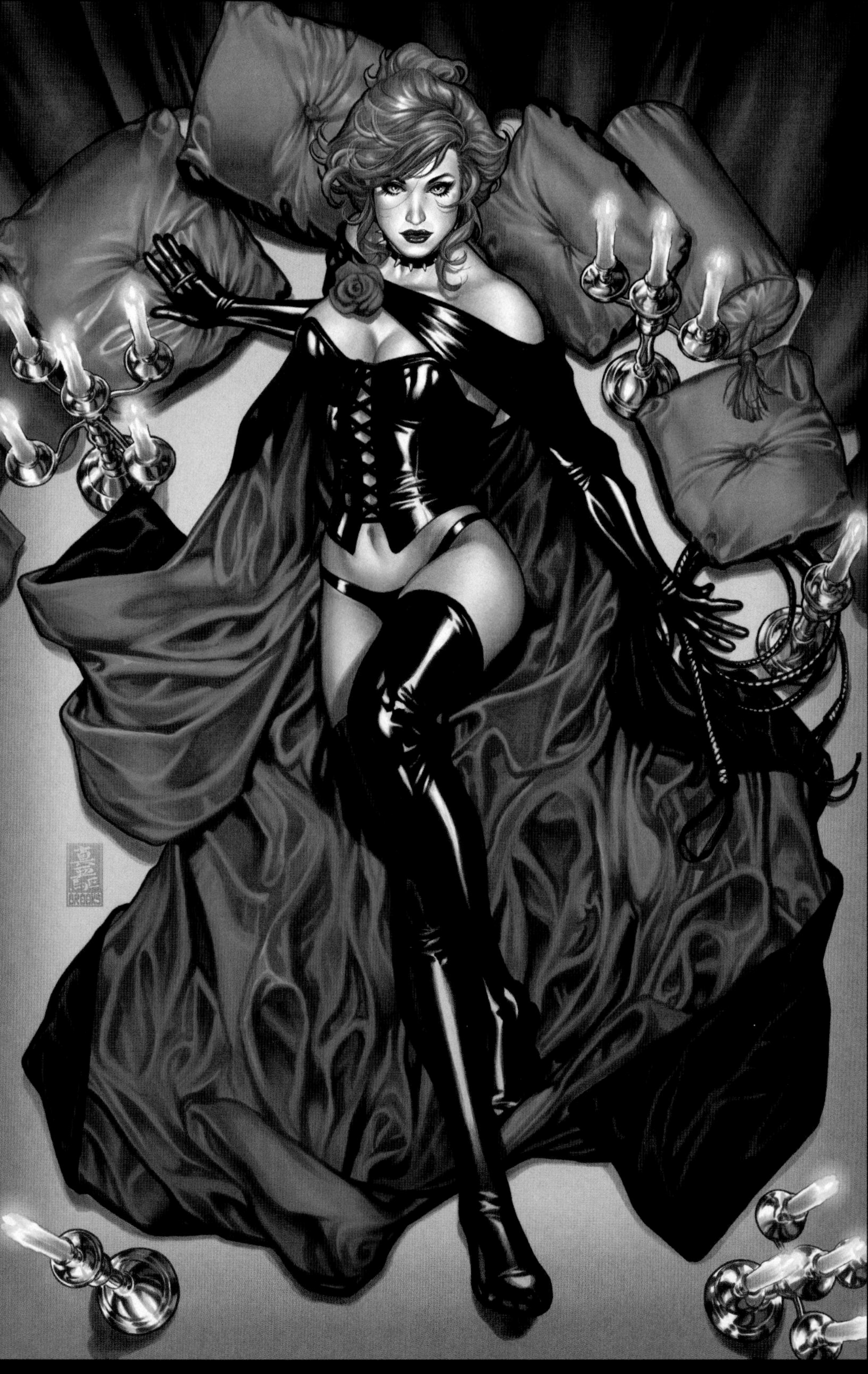
BROOKS

X-Men #6 Dark Phoenix Saga
40th Anniversary Variant

by Mark Brooks

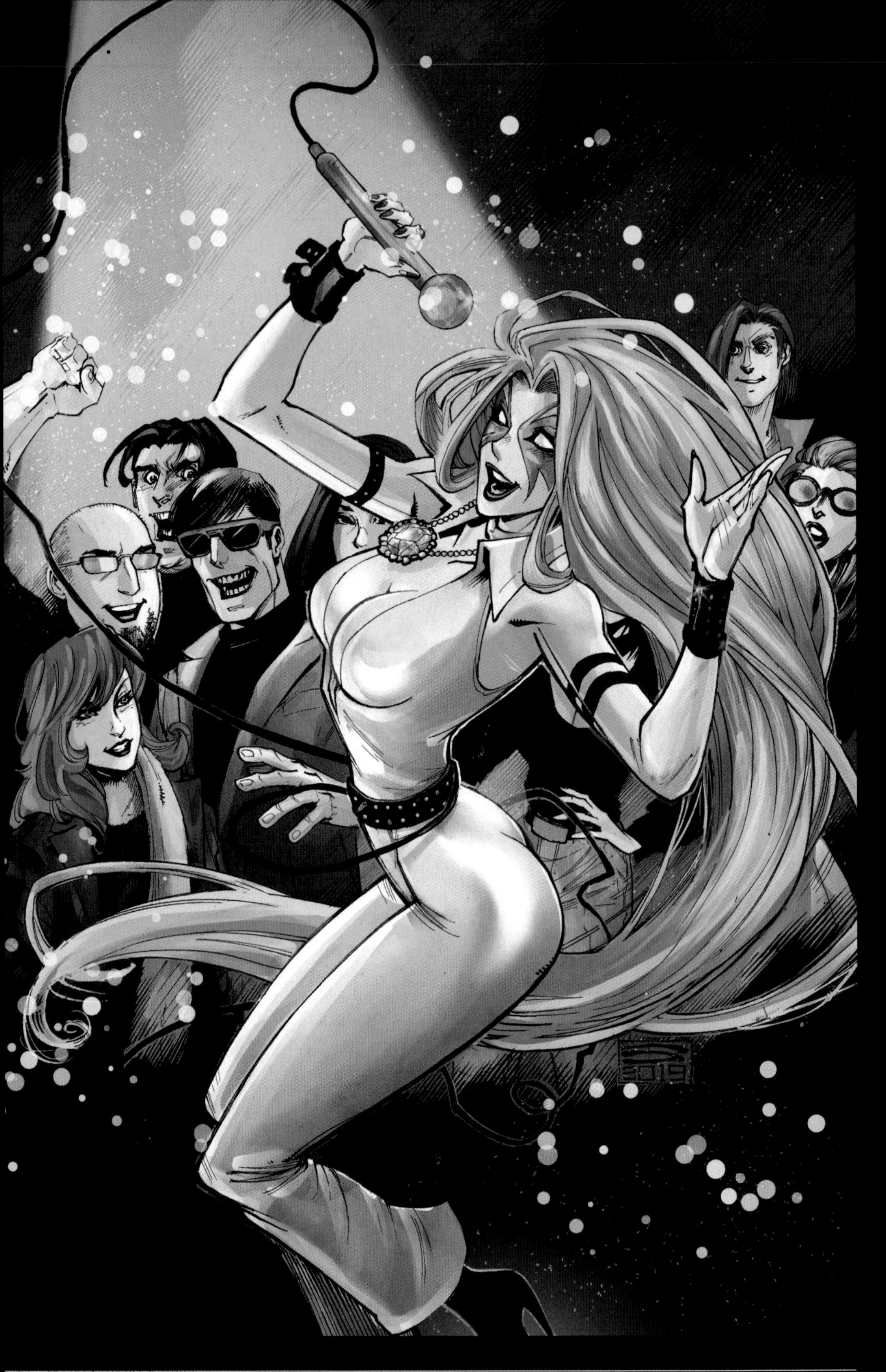

X-Force #6 Dark Phoenix Saga 40th Anniversary Variant by Gerardo Sandoval & Andres Mossa

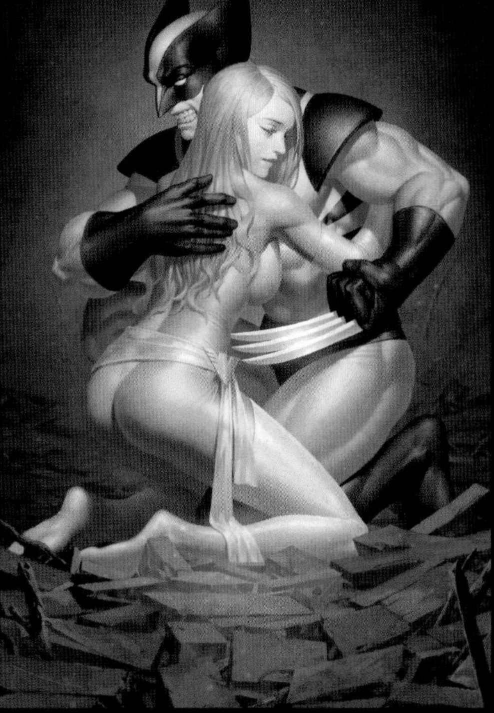

Fallen Angels #6 Dark Phoenix Saga 40th Anniversary Variant by Junggeun Yoon

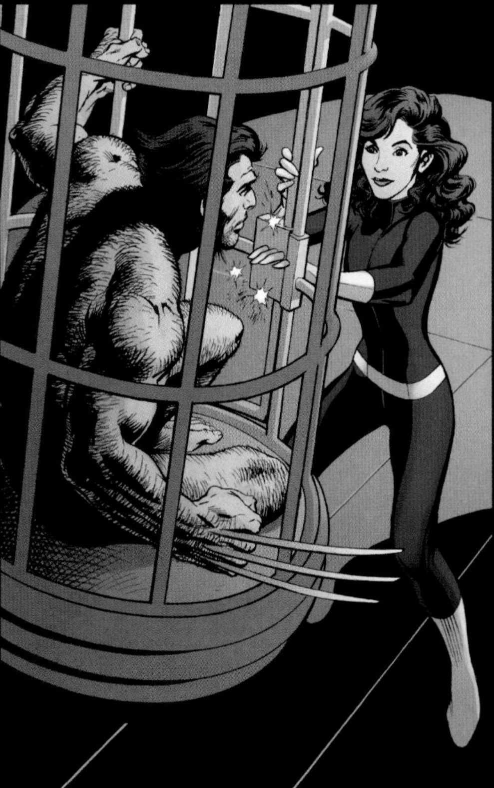

Marauders #6 Dark Phoenix Saga 40th Anniversary Variant by Alan Davis & Chris Sotomayor

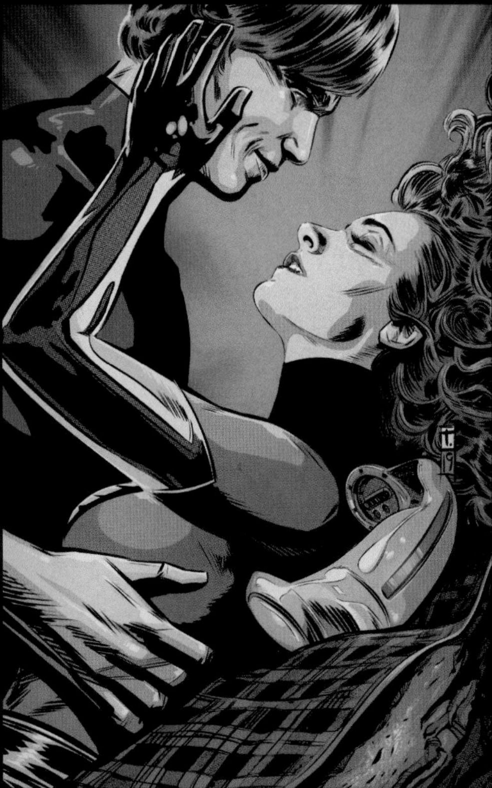

Excalibur #6 Dark Phoenix Saga 40th Anniversary Variant by Tomm Coker & Michael Garland

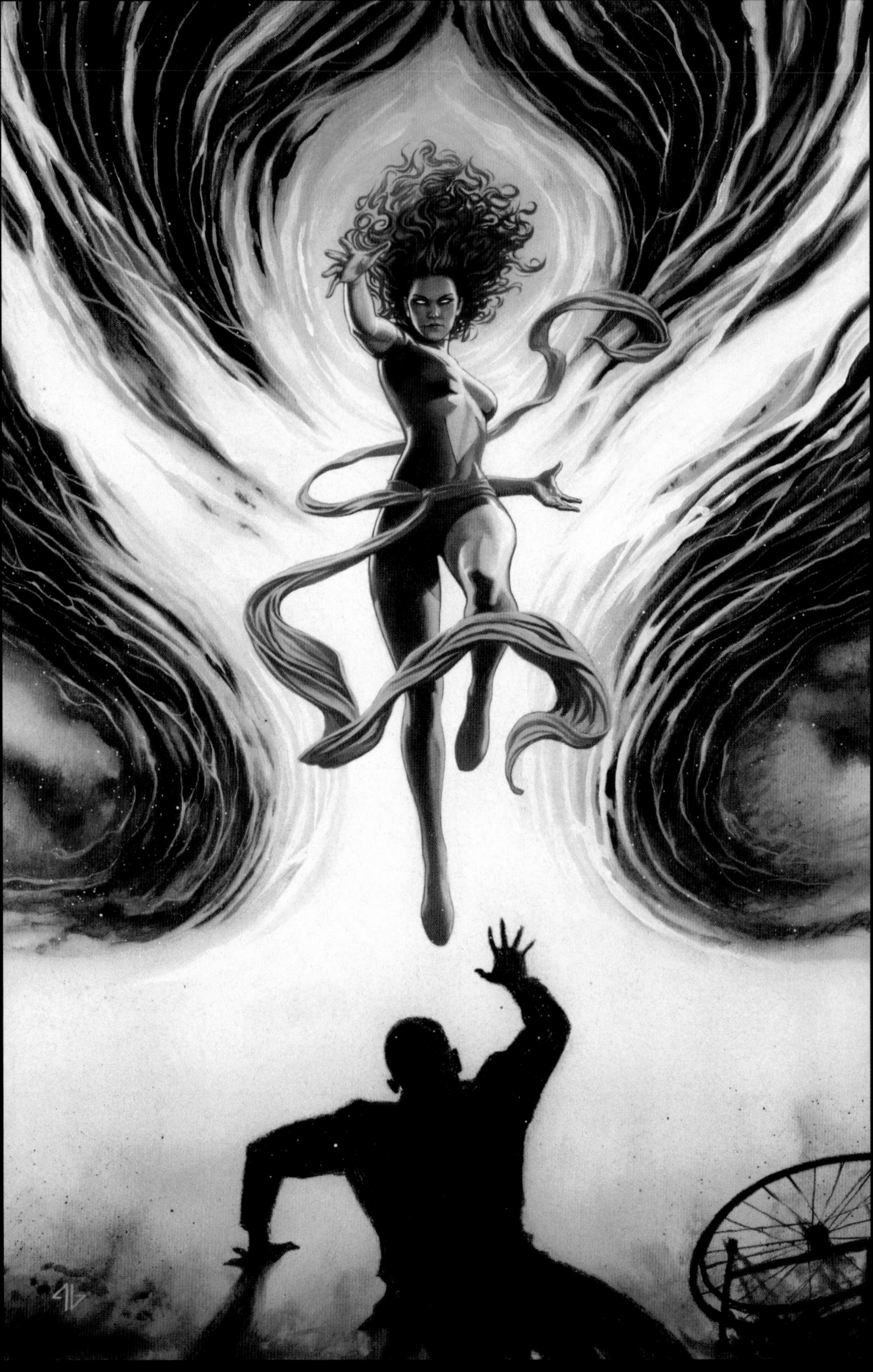

New Mutants #6 Dark Phoenix Saga 40th Anniversary Variant by Adi Granov

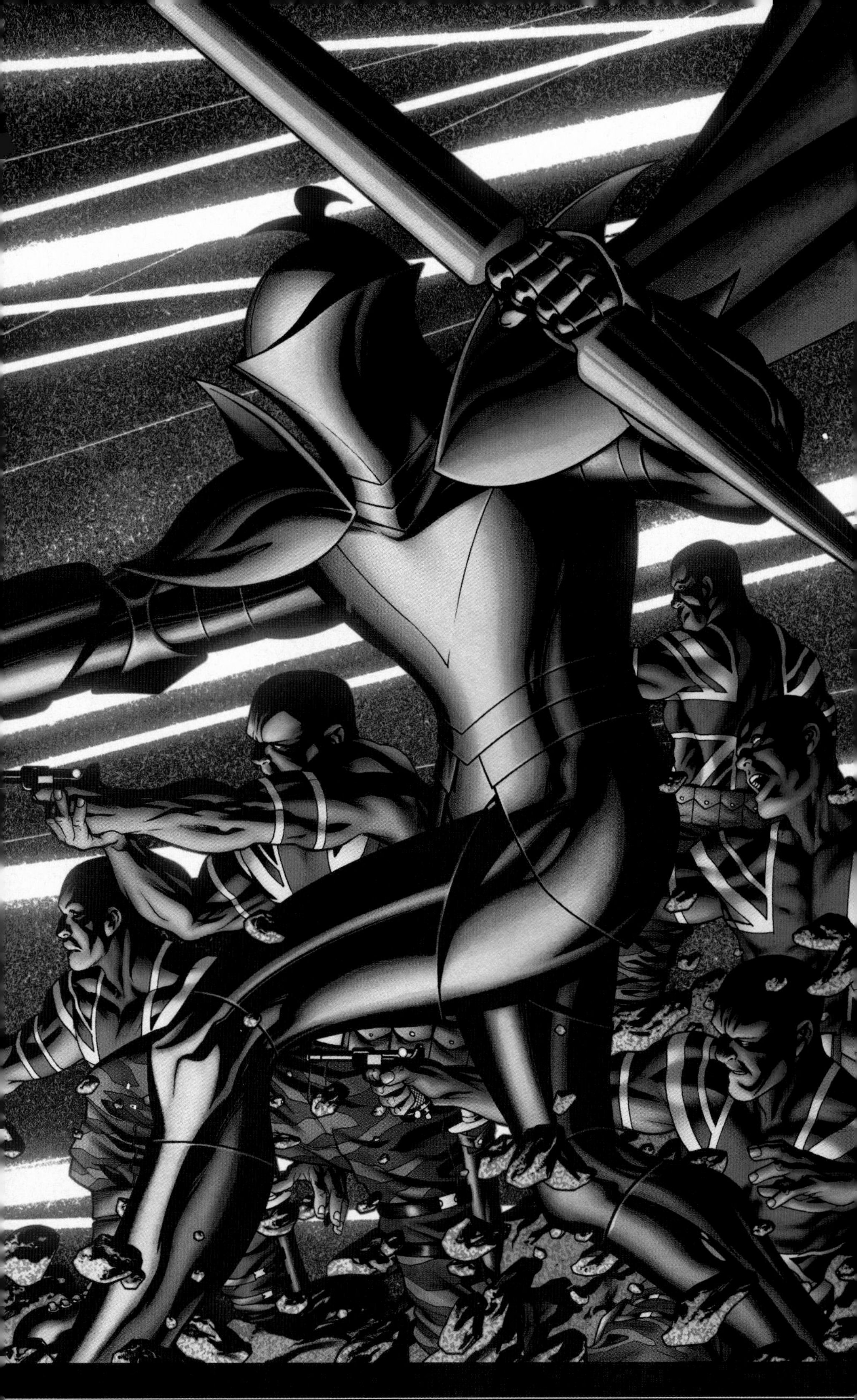

Excalibur #6 Marvels X Variant by Mike McKone & Morry Hollowell

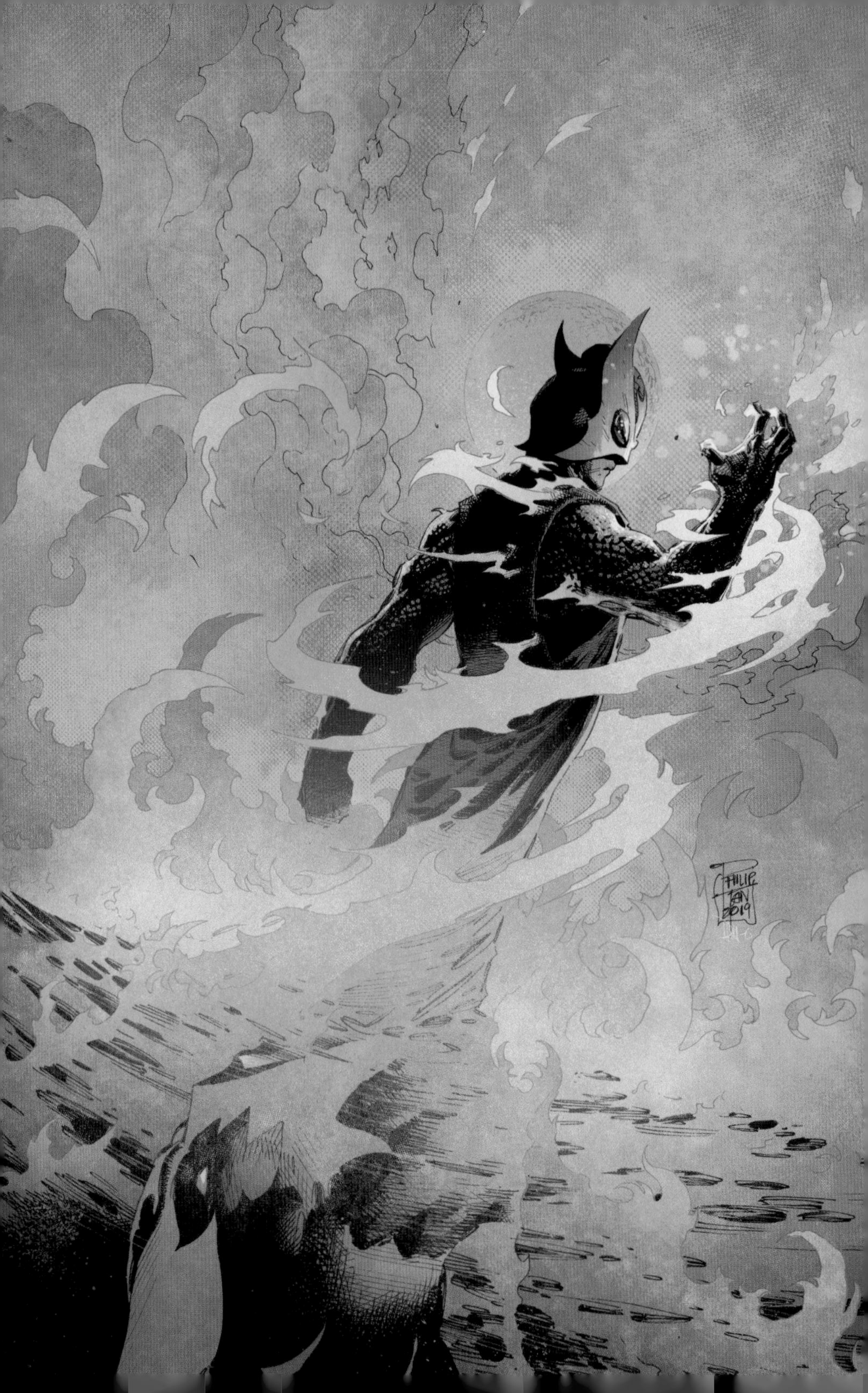
PHILIP TAN 2019

GN-SERIES ASCENDE V.2
0003000064010
Ascender.
Lemire, Jeff,
ATCHISON
2020-08-24
WITHDRAWN

W9-AHR-035

ASCENDER
VOLUME TWO: THE DEAD SEA

JEFF LEMIRE • DUSTIN NGUYEN
STORYTELLERS

STEVE WANDS
LETTERING & DESIGN

DUSTIN NGUYEN
COVER

WILL DENNIS
EDITOR

IMAGE COMICS, INC. • **Robert Kirkman**: Chief Operating Officer • **Erik Larsen**: Chief Financial Officer • **Todd McFarlane**: President • **Marc Silvestri**: Chief Executive Officer • **Jim Valentino**: Vice President • **Eric Stephenson**: Publisher / Chief Creative Officer • **Jeff Boison**: Director of Publishing Planning & Book Trade Sales • **Chris Ross**: Director of Digital Services • **Jeff Stang**: Director of Direct Market Sales • **Kat Salazar**: Director of PR & Marketing • **Drew Gill**: Cover Editor • **Heather Doornink**: Production Director • **Nicole Lapalme**: Controller • IMAGECOMICS.COM

Ryan Brewer: Production Artist

ASCENDER, VOL 2. First printing. June 2020. Published by Image Comics, Inc. Office of publication: 2701 NW Vaughn St., Suite 780, Portland, OR 97210. Copyright © 2020 171 Studios & Dustin Nguyen. All rights reserved. Contains material originally published in single magazine form as ASCENDER #6-10. "Ascender," its logos, and the likenesses of all characters herein are trademarks of 171 Studios & Dustin Nguyen, unless otherwise noted. "Image" and the Image Comics logos are registered trademarks of Image Comics, Inc. No part of this publication may be reproduced or transmitted, in any form or by any means (except for short excerpts for journalistic or review purposes), without the express written permission of 171 Studios & Dustin Nguyen, or Image Comics, Inc. All names, characters, events, and locales in this publication are entirely fictional. Any resemblance to actual persons (living or dead), events, or places, without satirical intent, is coincidental. Printed in the USA. For international rights, contact: foreignlicensing@imagecomics.com. ISBN: 978-1-5343-1593-8.

image®

THE PLANET SAMPSON.

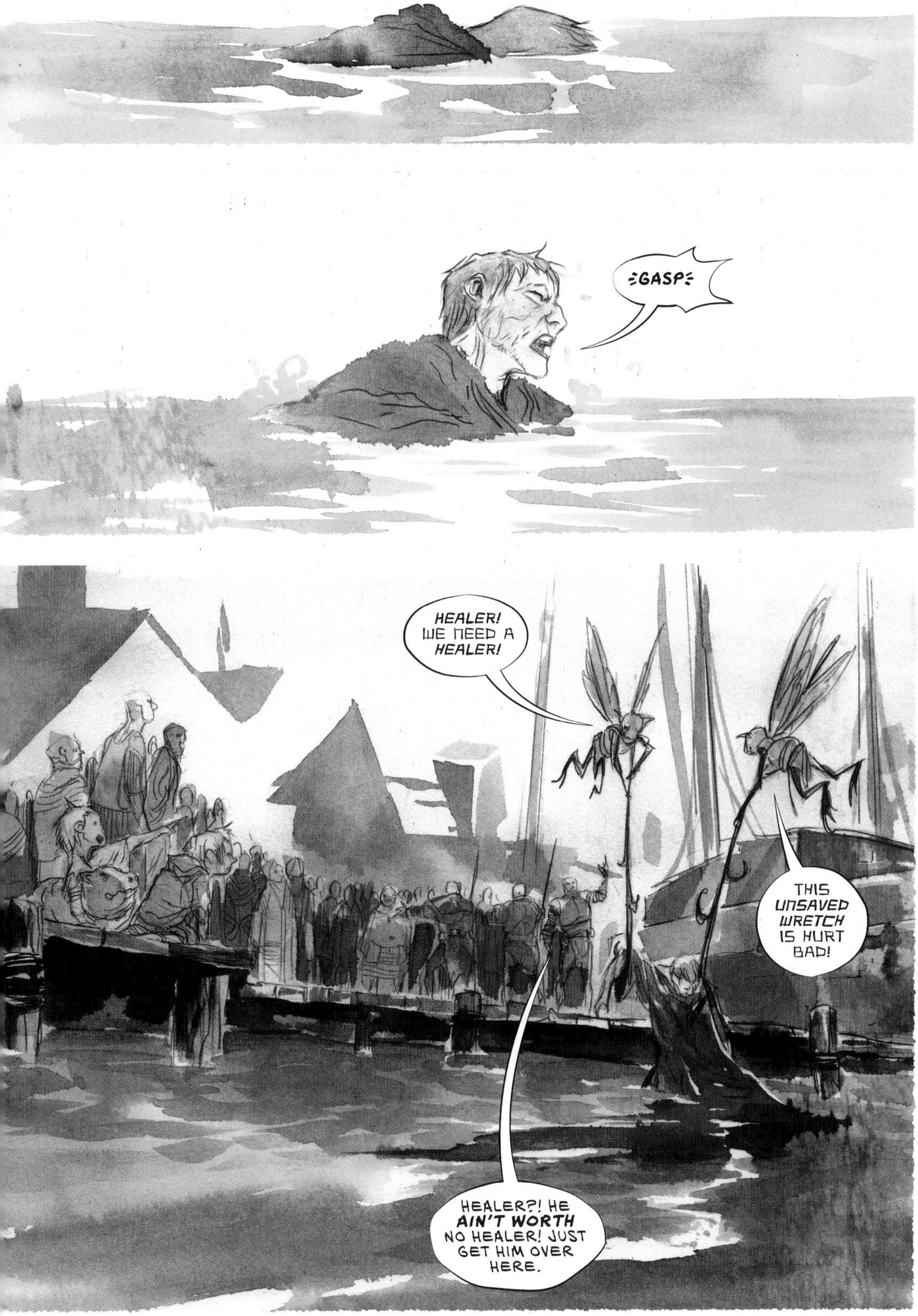

GASP
HEALER! WE NEED A HEALER!
THIS UNSAVED WRETCH IS HURT BAD!
HEALER?! HE **AIN'T WORTH** NO HEALER! JUST GET HIM OVER HERE.

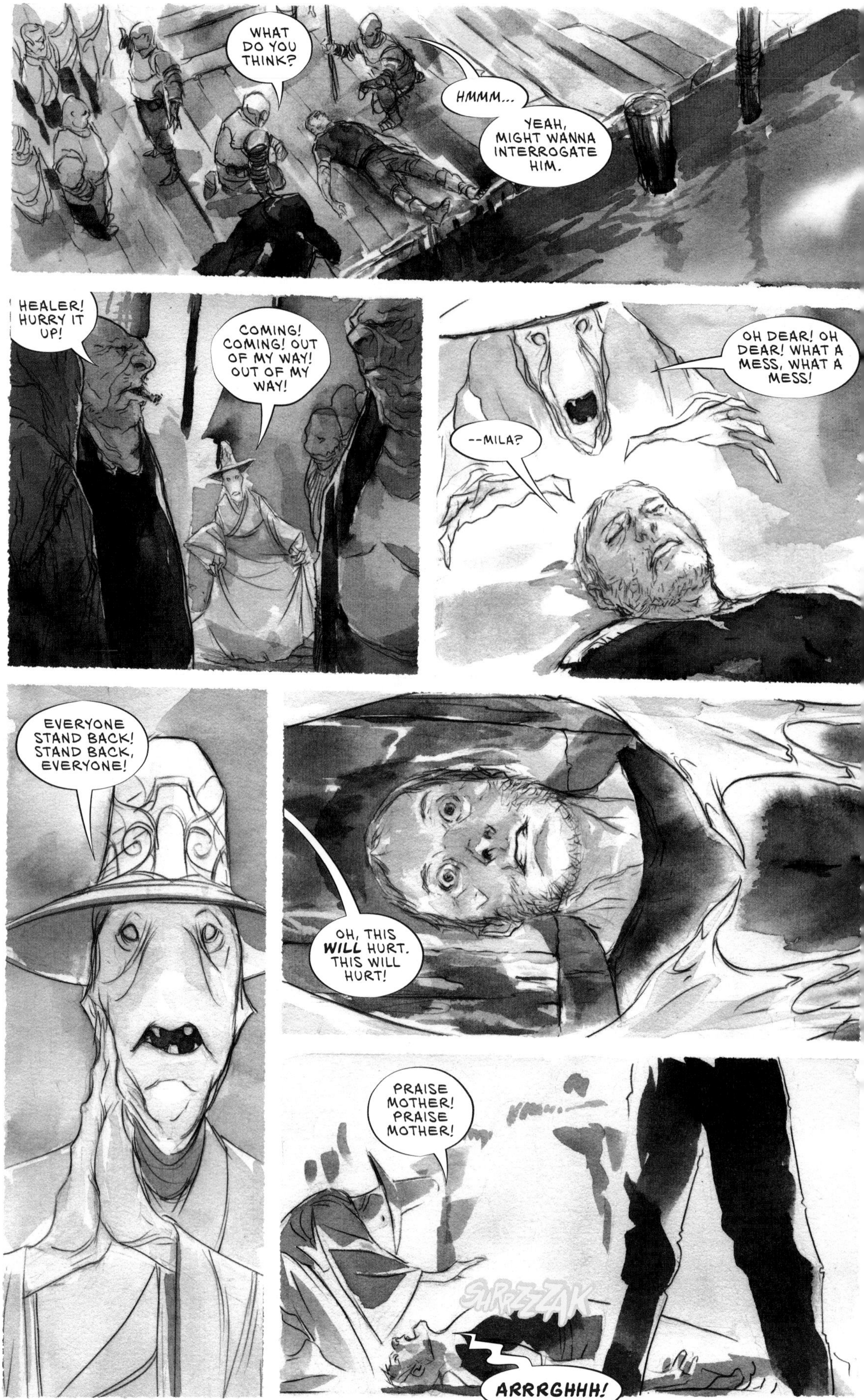
WHAT DO YOU THINK?
HMMM...
YEAH, MIGHT WANNA INTERROGATE HIM.
HEALER! HURRY IT UP!
COMING! COMING! OUT OF MY WAY! OUT OF MY WAY!
OH DEAR! OH DEAR! WHAT A MESS, WHAT A MESS!
--MILA?
EVERYONE STAND BACK! STAND BACK, EVERYONE!
OH, THIS WILL HURT. THIS WILL HURT!
PRAISE MOTHER! PRAISE MOTHER!
SHRRZZZAK
ARRRGHHH!

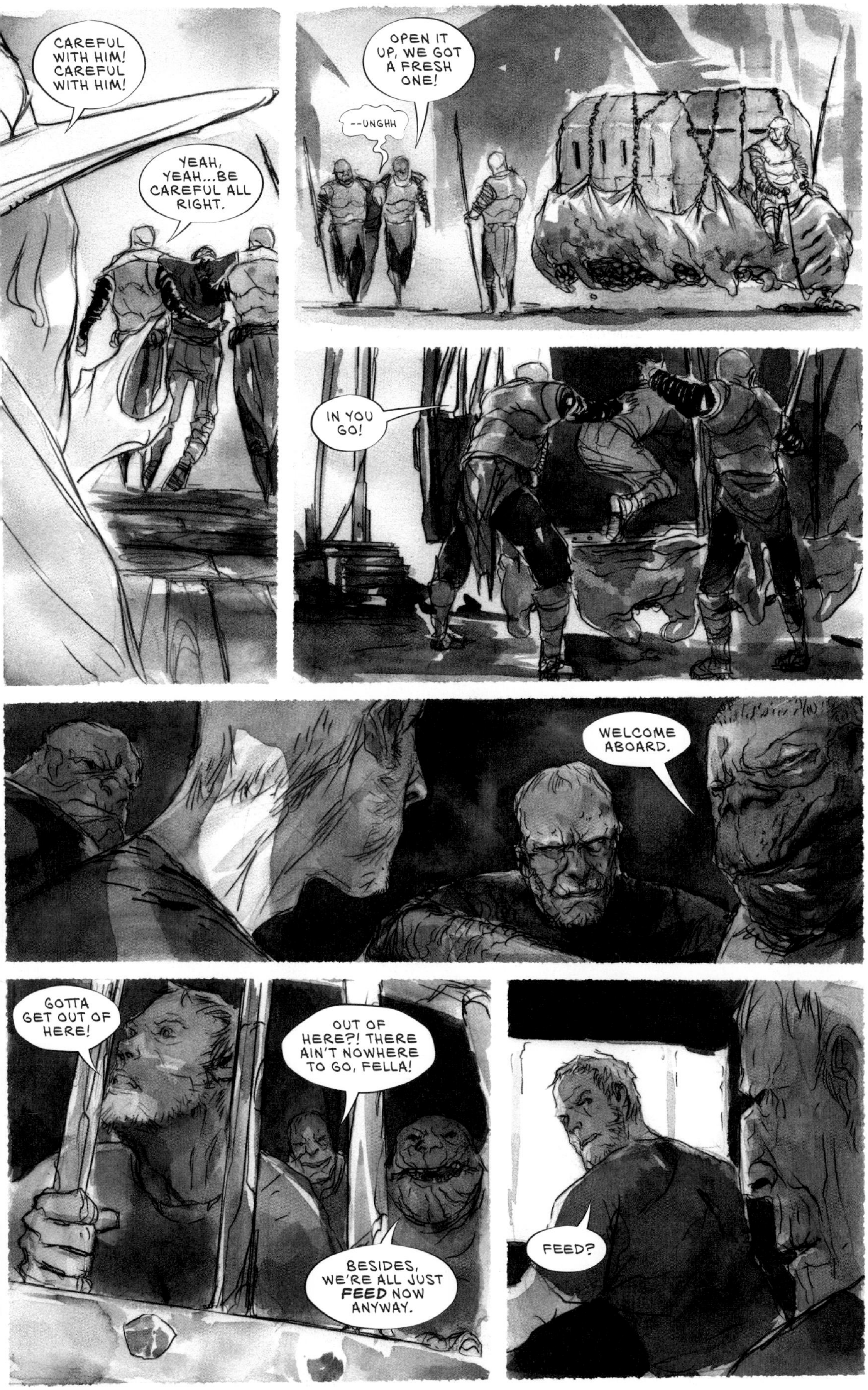
CAREFUL WITH HIM! CAREFUL WITH HIM!
YEAH, YEAH...BE CAREFUL ALL RIGHT.
OPEN IT UP, WE GOT A FRESH ONE!
--UNGHH
IN YOU GO!
WELCOME ABOARD.
GOTTA GET OUT OF HERE!
OUT OF HERE?! THERE AIN'T NOWHERE TO GO, FELLA!
BESIDES, WE'RE ALL JUST FEED NOW ANYWAY.
FEED?

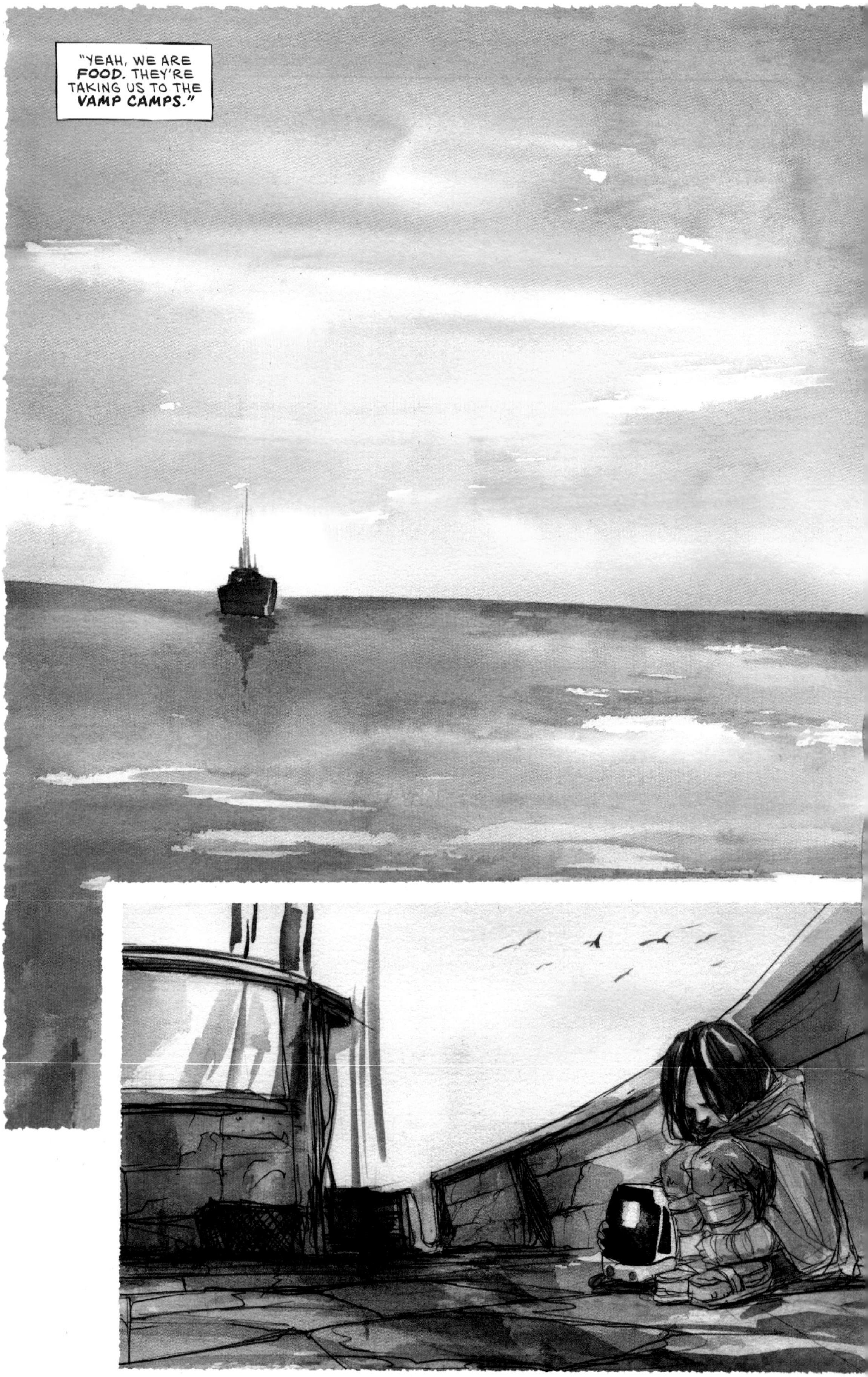
"YEAH, WE ARE FOOD. THEY'RE TAKING US TO THE VAMP CAMPS."

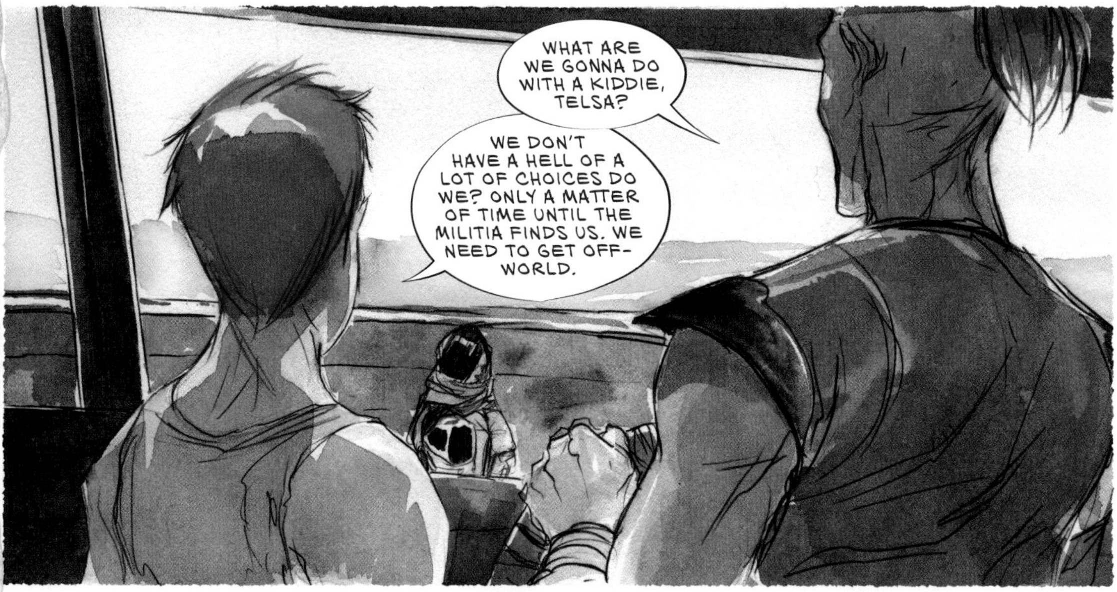
WHAT ARE WE GONNA DO WITH A KIDDIE, TELSA?
WE DON'T HAVE A HELL OF A LOT OF CHOICES DO WE? ONLY A MATTER OF TIME UNTIL THE MILITIA FINDS US. WE NEED TO GET OFF-WORLD.
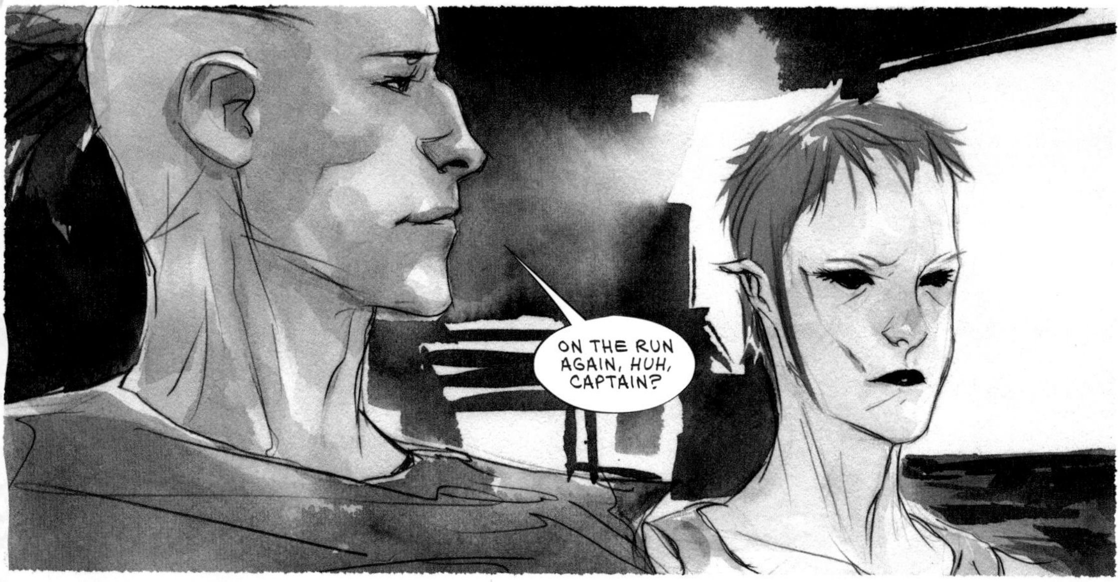
ON THE RUN AGAIN, *HUH*, CAPTAIN?
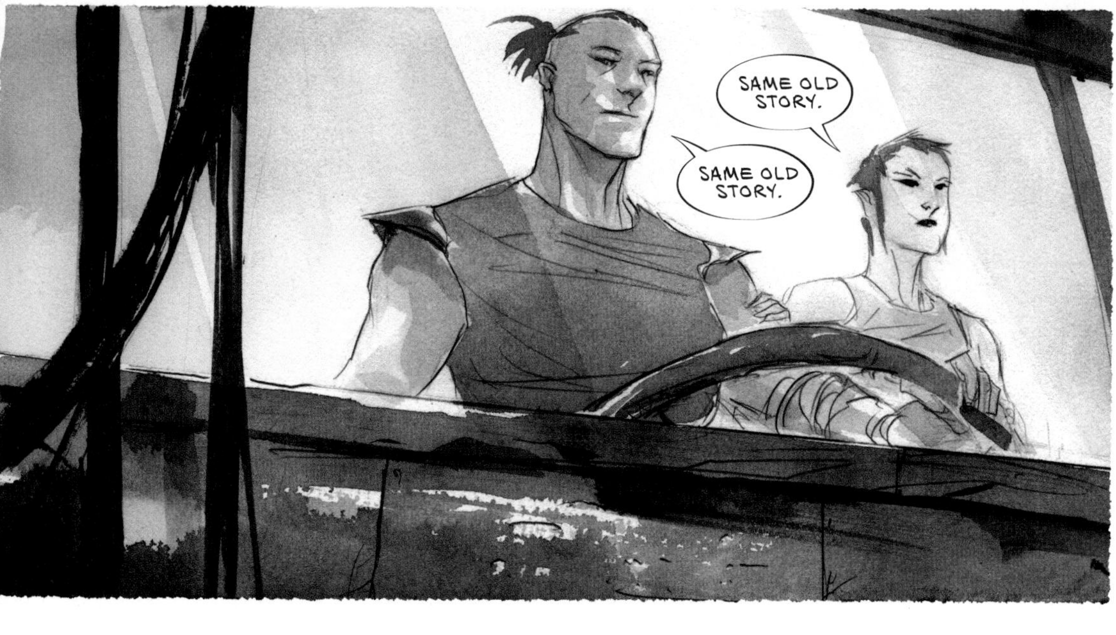
SAME OLD STORY.
SAME OLD STORY.

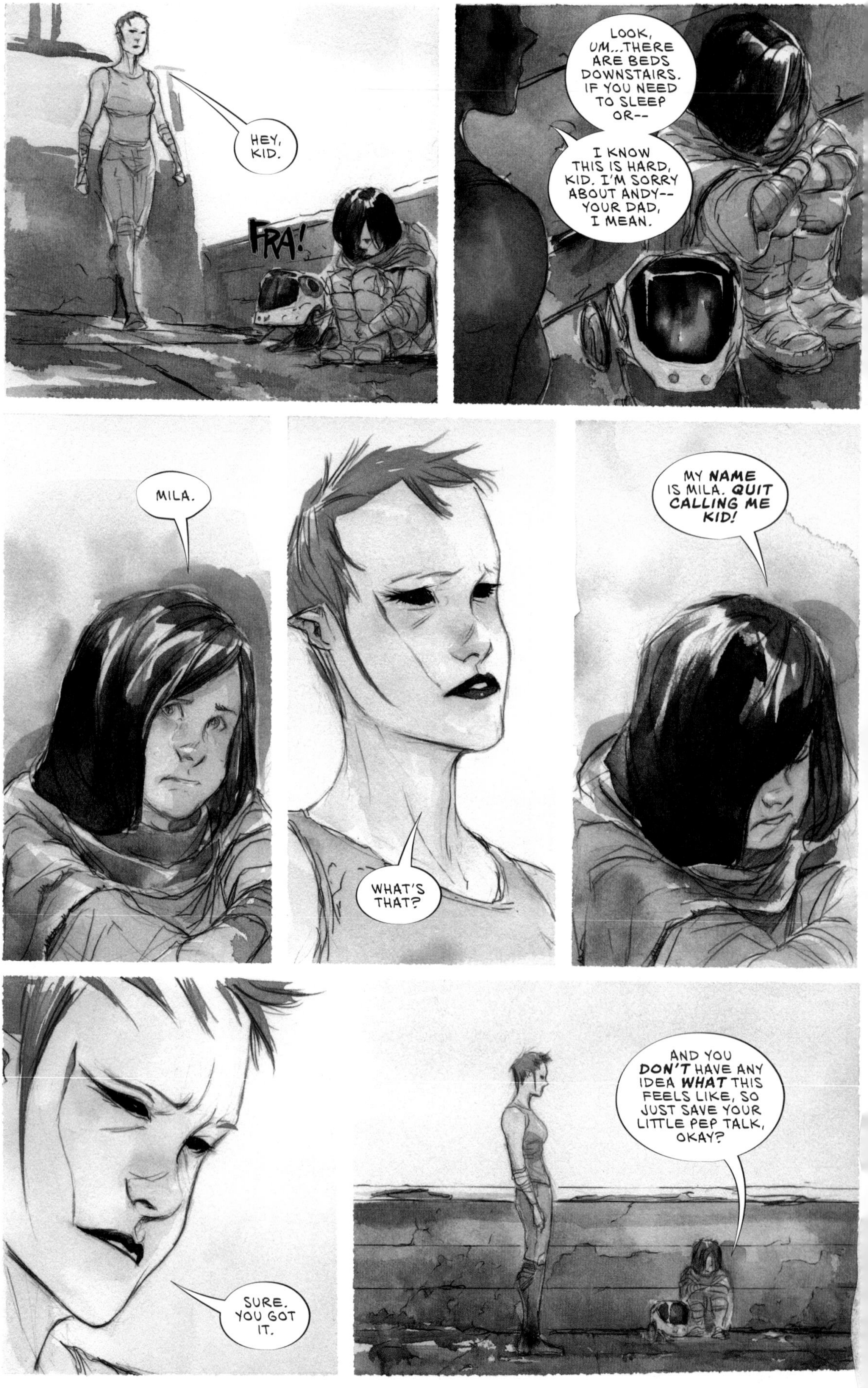
HEY, KID.
FRA!
LOOK, UM...THERE ARE BEDS DOWNSTAIRS. IF YOU NEED TO SLEEP OR--
I KNOW THIS IS HARD, KID. I'M SORRY ABOUT ANDY-- YOUR DAD, I MEAN.
MILA.
WHAT'S THAT?
MY NAME IS MILA. QUIT CALLING ME KID!
SURE. YOU GOT IT.
AND YOU DON'T HAVE ANY IDEA WHAT THIS FEELS LIKE, SO JUST SAVE YOUR LITTLE PEP TALK, OKAY?

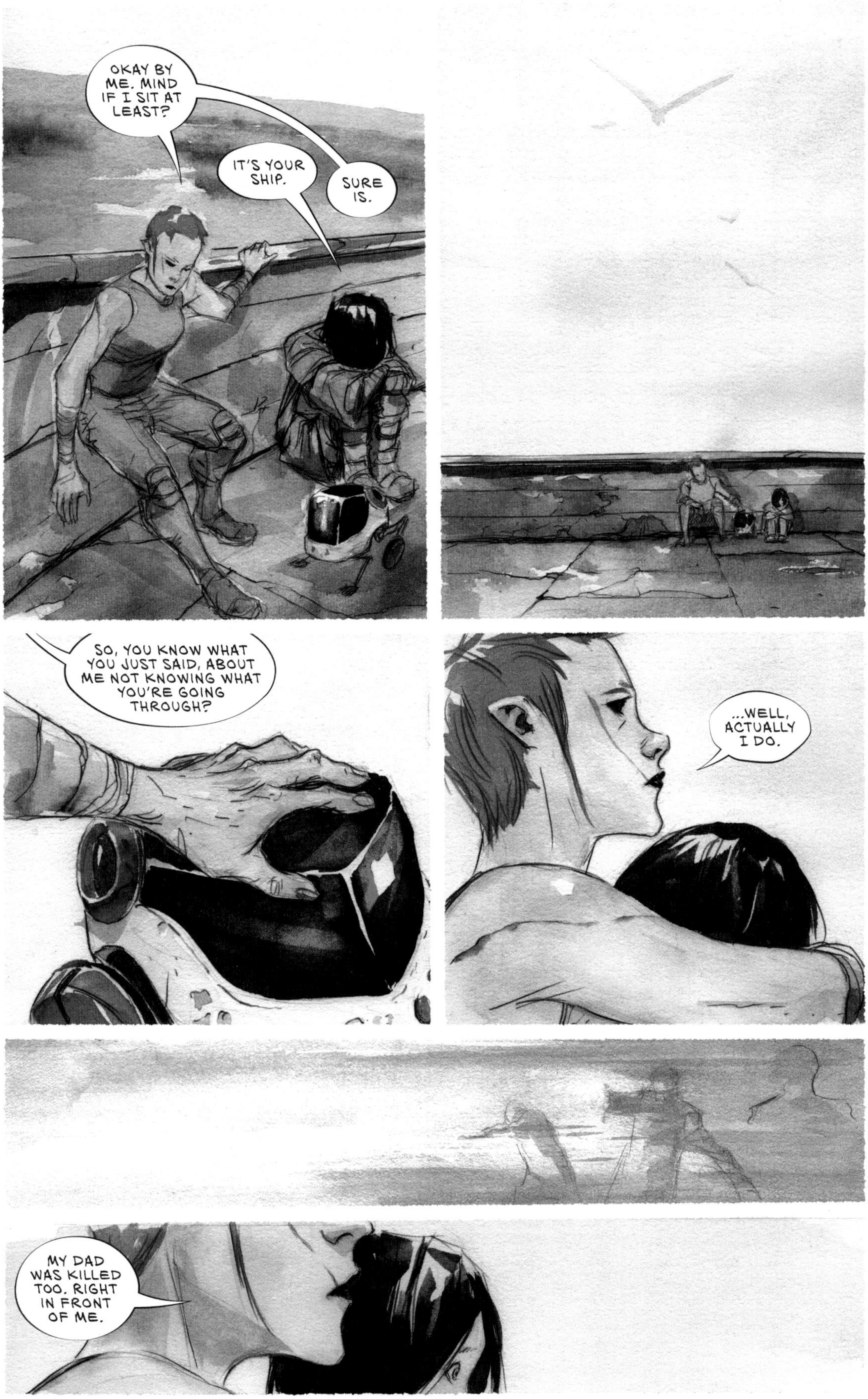
OKAY BY ME. MIND IF I SIT AT LEAST?
IT'S YOUR SHIP.
SURE IS.
SO, YOU KNOW WHAT YOU JUST SAID, ABOUT ME NOT KNOWING WHAT YOU'RE GOING THROUGH?
...WELL, ACTUALLY I DO.
MY DAD WAS KILLED TOO. RIGHT IN FRONT OF ME.

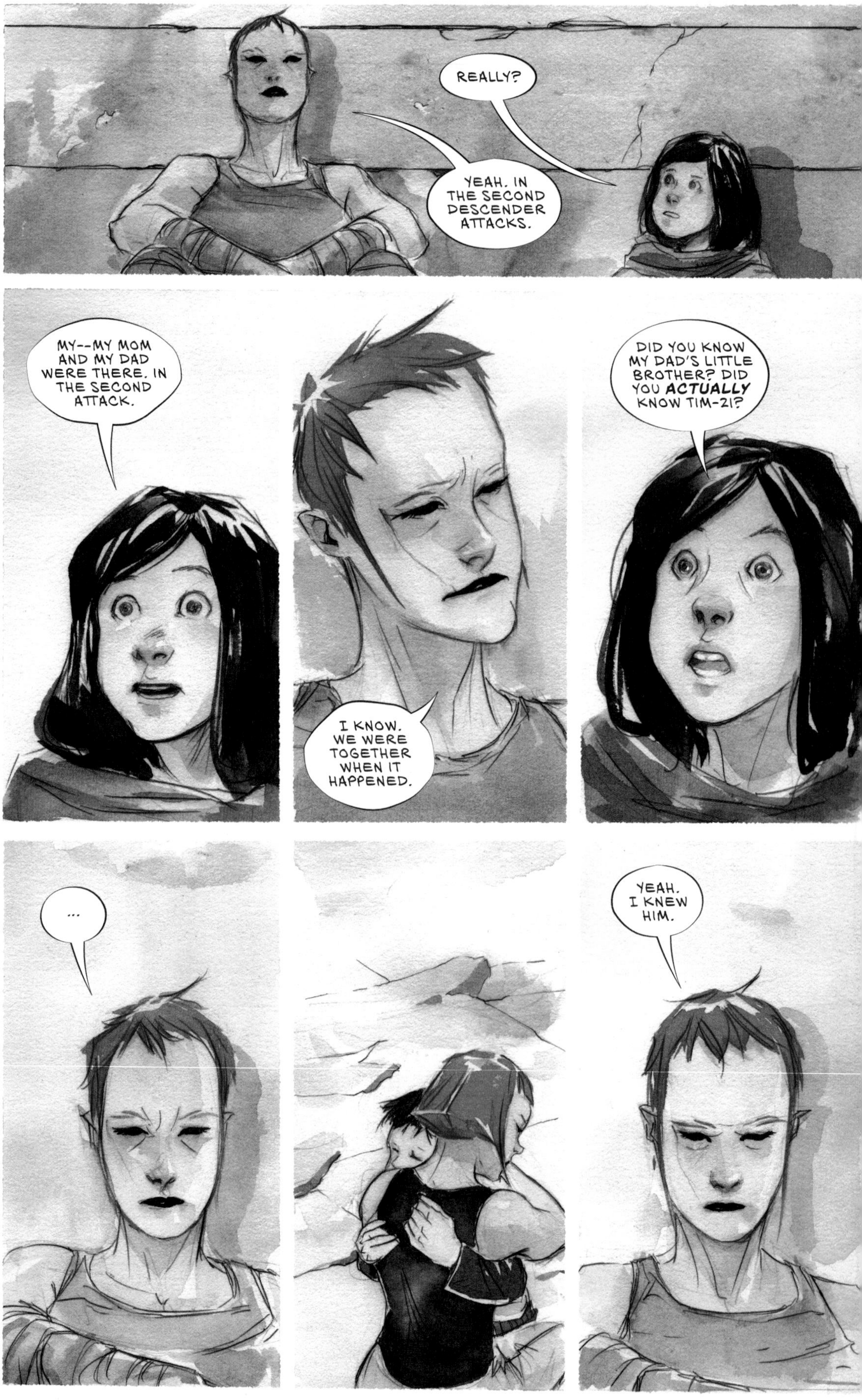
REALLY?
YEAH. IN THE SECOND DESCENDER ATTACKS.
MY--MY MOM AND MY DAD WERE THERE. IN THE SECOND ATTACK.
I KNOW. WE WERE TOGETHER WHEN IT HAPPENED.
DID YOU KNOW MY DAD'S LITTLE BROTHER? DID YOU **ACTUALLY** KNOW TIM-21?
...
YEAH. I KNEW HIM.

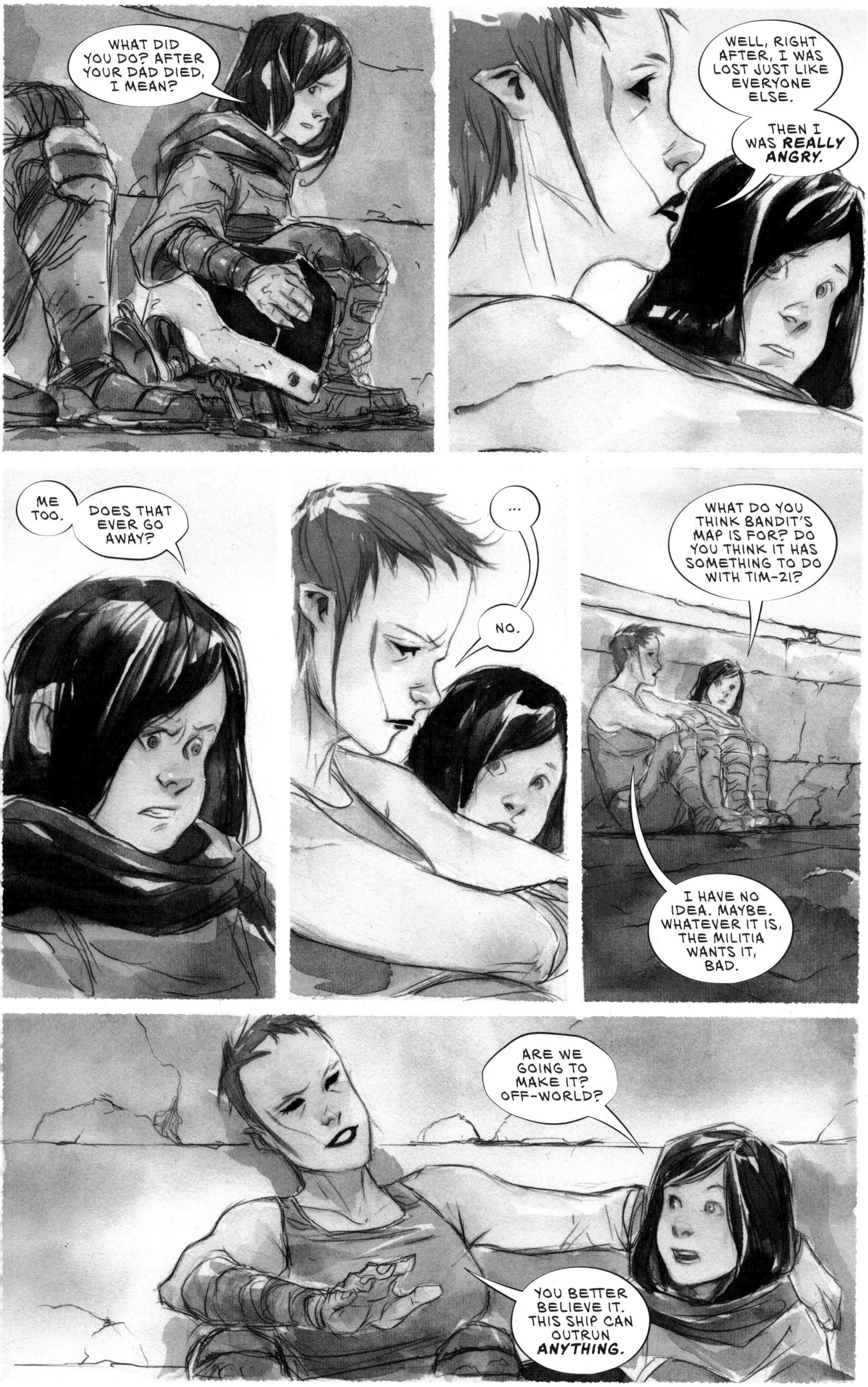
WHAT DID YOU DO? AFTER YOUR DAD DIED, I MEAN?
WELL, RIGHT AFTER, I WAS LOST JUST LIKE EVERYONE ELSE.
THEN I WAS **REALLY ANGRY.**
ME TOO.
DOES THAT EVER GO AWAY?
...
NO.
WHAT DO YOU THINK BANDIT'S MAP IS FOR? DO YOU THINK IT HAS SOMETHING TO DO WITH TIM-21?
I HAVE NO IDEA. MAYBE. WHATEVER IT IS, THE MILITIA WANTS IT, BAD.
ARE WE GOING TO MAKE IT? OFF-WORLD?
YOU BETTER BELIEVE IT. THIS SHIP CAN OUTRUN ***ANYTHING.***

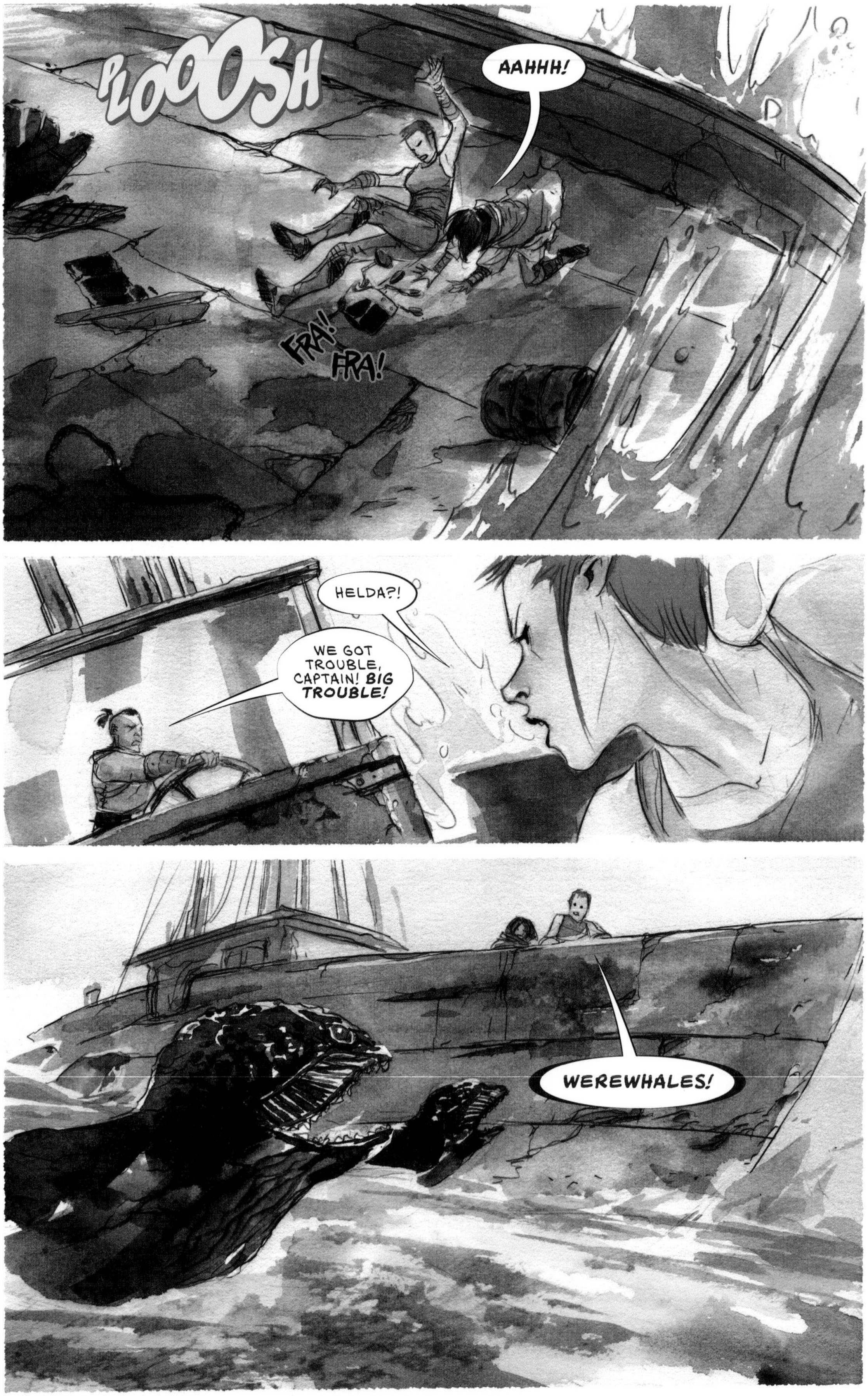
PLOOOOSH
AAHHH!
FRA!
FRA!
HELDA?!
WE GOT TROUBLE, CAPTAIN! BIG TROUBLE!
WEREWHALES!

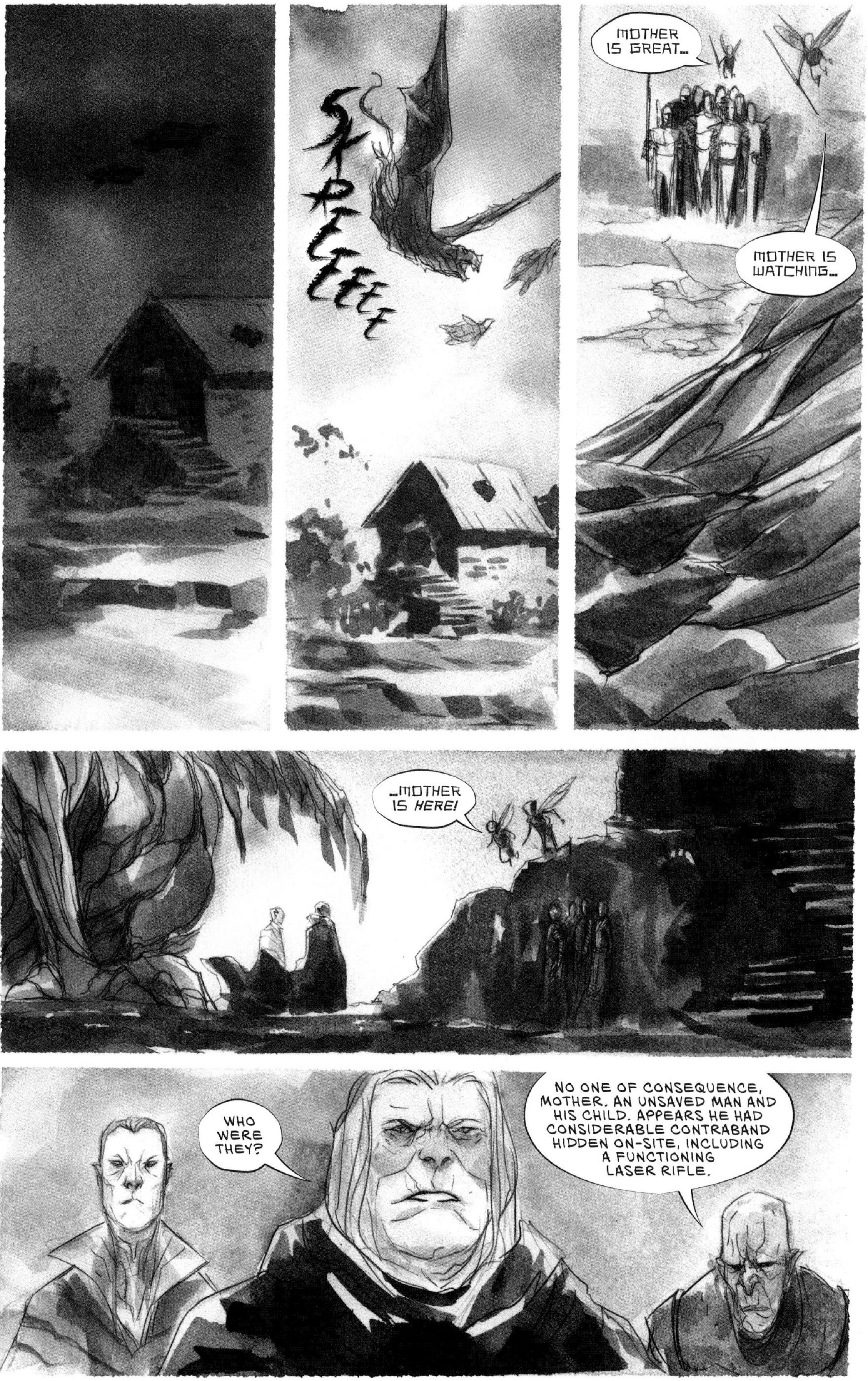
MOTHER IS GREAT...
MOTHER IS WATCHING...
...MOTHER IS *HERE!*
WHO WERE THEY?
NO ONE OF CONSEQUENCE, MOTHER. AN UNSAVED MAN AND HIS CHILD. APPEARS HE HAD CONSIDERABLE CONTRABAND HIDDEN ON-SITE, INCLUDING A FUNCTIONING LASER RIFLE.

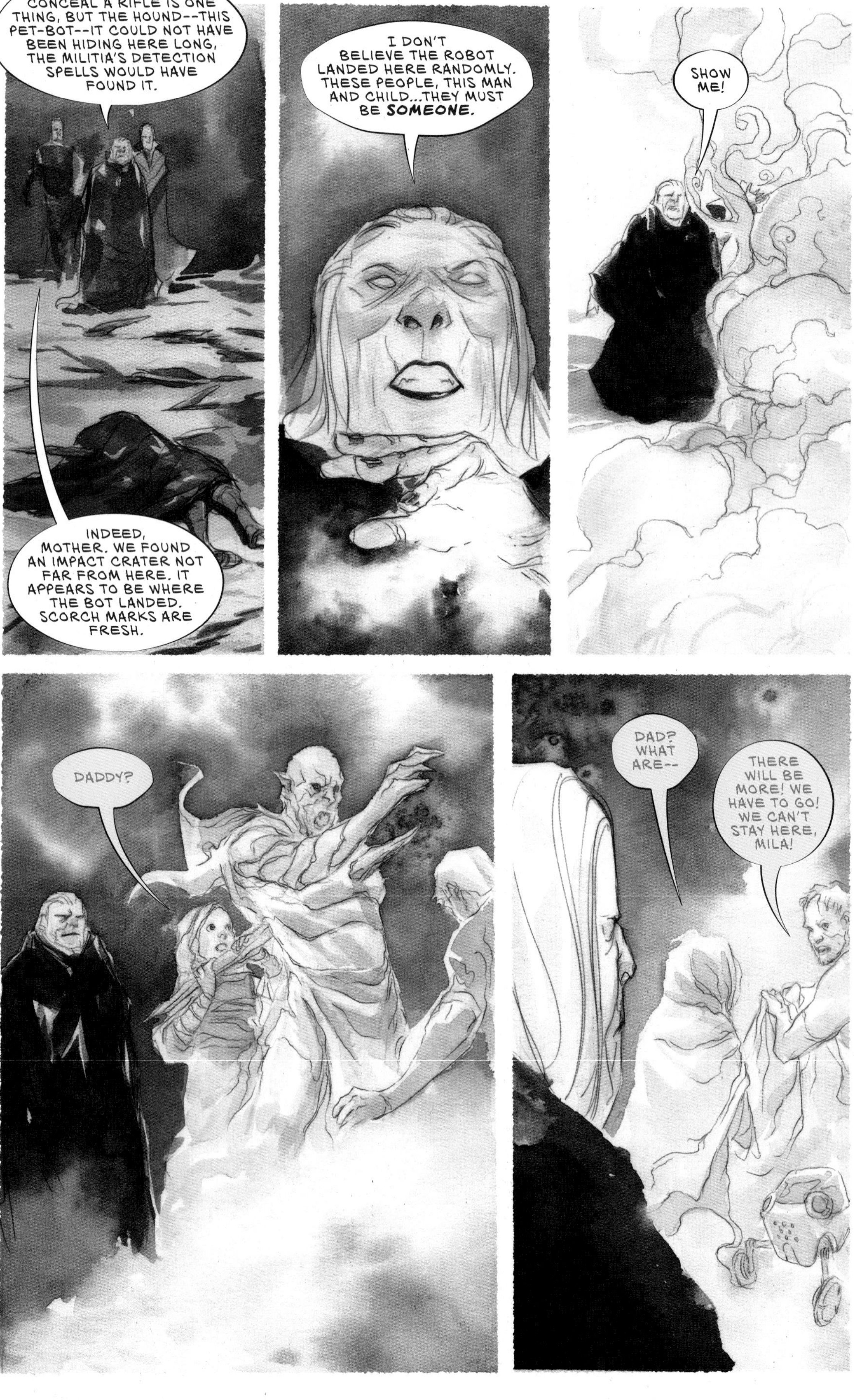
BEING ABLE TO CONCEAL A RIFLE IS ONE THING, BUT THE HOUND--THIS PET-BOT--IT COULD NOT HAVE BEEN HIDING HERE LONG, THE MILITIA'S DETECTION SPELLS WOULD HAVE FOUND IT.
INDEED, MOTHER. WE FOUND AN IMPACT CRATER NOT FAR FROM HERE. IT APPEARS TO BE WHERE THE BOT LANDED. SCORCH MARKS ARE FRESH.
I DON'T BELIEVE THE ROBOT LANDED HERE RANDOMLY. THESE PEOPLE, THIS MAN AND CHILD...THEY MUST BE SOMEONE.
SHOW ME!
DADDY?
DAD? WHAT ARE--
THERE WILL BE MORE! WE HAVE TO GO! WE CAN'T STAY HERE, MILA!

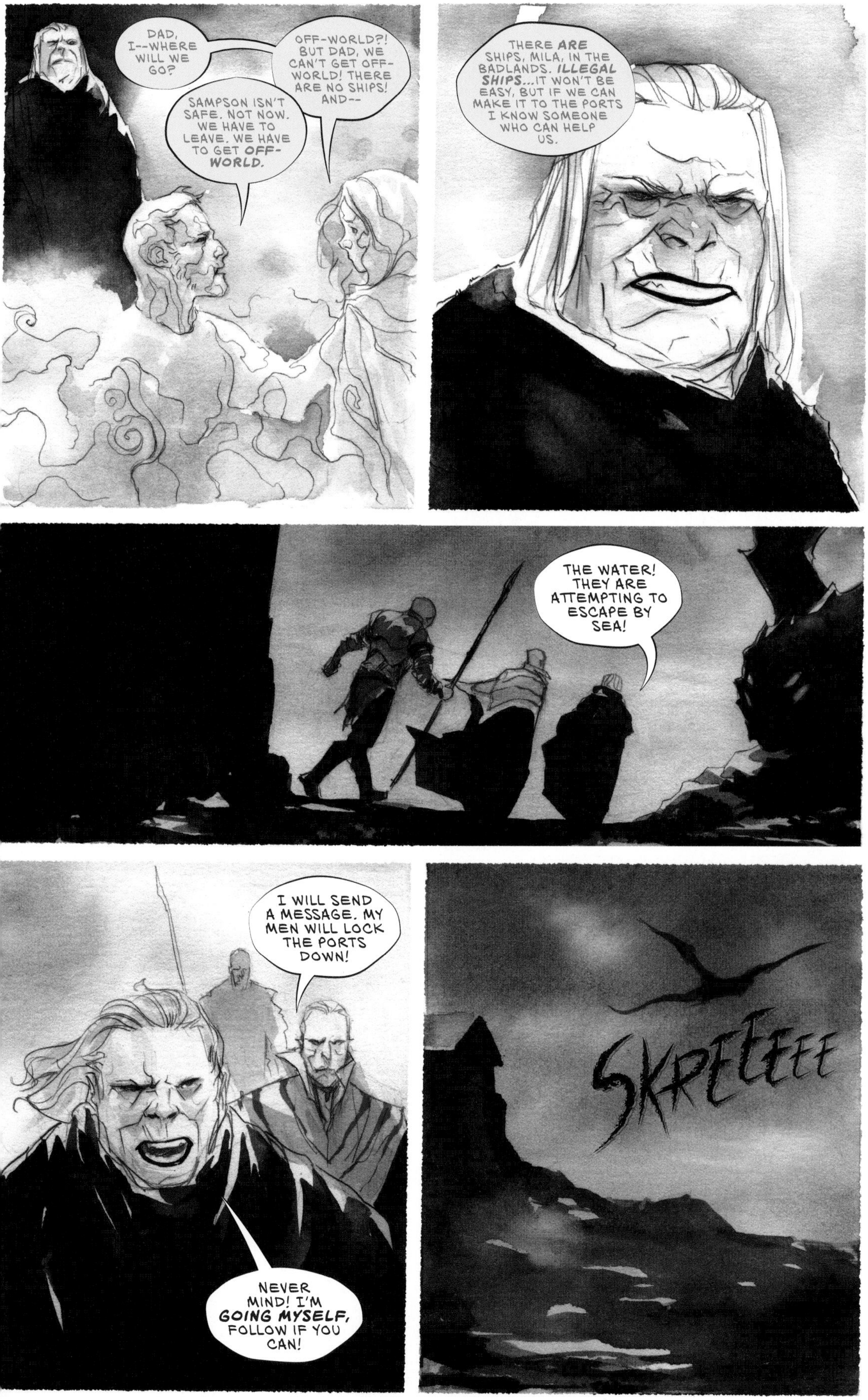
DAD, I--WHERE WILL WE GO?
SAMPSON ISN'T SAFE. NOT NOW. WE HAVE TO LEAVE. WE HAVE TO GET **OFF-WORLD.**
OFF-WORLD?! BUT DAD, WE CAN'T GET OFF-WORLD! THERE ARE NO SHIPS! AND--
THERE **ARE** SHIPS, MILA, IN THE BADLANDS. **ILLEGAL SHIPS...** IT WON'T BE EASY, BUT IF WE CAN MAKE IT TO THE PORTS I KNOW SOMEONE WHO CAN HELP US.
THE WATER! THEY ARE ATTEMPTING TO ESCAPE BY SEA!
I WILL SEND A MESSAGE. MY MEN WILL LOCK THE PORTS DOWN!
NEVER MIND! I'M **GOING MYSELF,** FOLLOW IF YOU CAN!
SKREEEEE

MOTHER, I'VE NO DOUBT THIS ROBOT IS AS IMPORTANT AS YOU SAY, BUT SHOULD WE LET THE MILITIA HERE ON SAMPSON DEAL WITH ITS CAPTURE?

SURELY YOUR ATTENTION IS BETTER SERVED LOOKING FOR THE UGC REBELS BEFORE THEY ATTACK AGAIN?

GENERAL VIX?

YES, MOTHER?

HOW ABOUT YOU LET *ME* WORRY ABOUT WHERE MY ATTENTION IS "BETTER SERVED"?

JUST BECAUSE I LET YOU DRINK MY BLOOD, DOES NOT MEAN I LET YOU *SHARE* IN MY COMMAND. *UNDERSTOOD?*

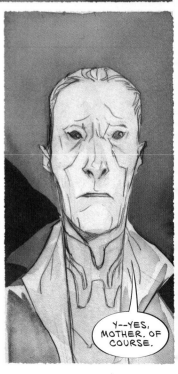Y--YES, MOTHER, OF COURSE.

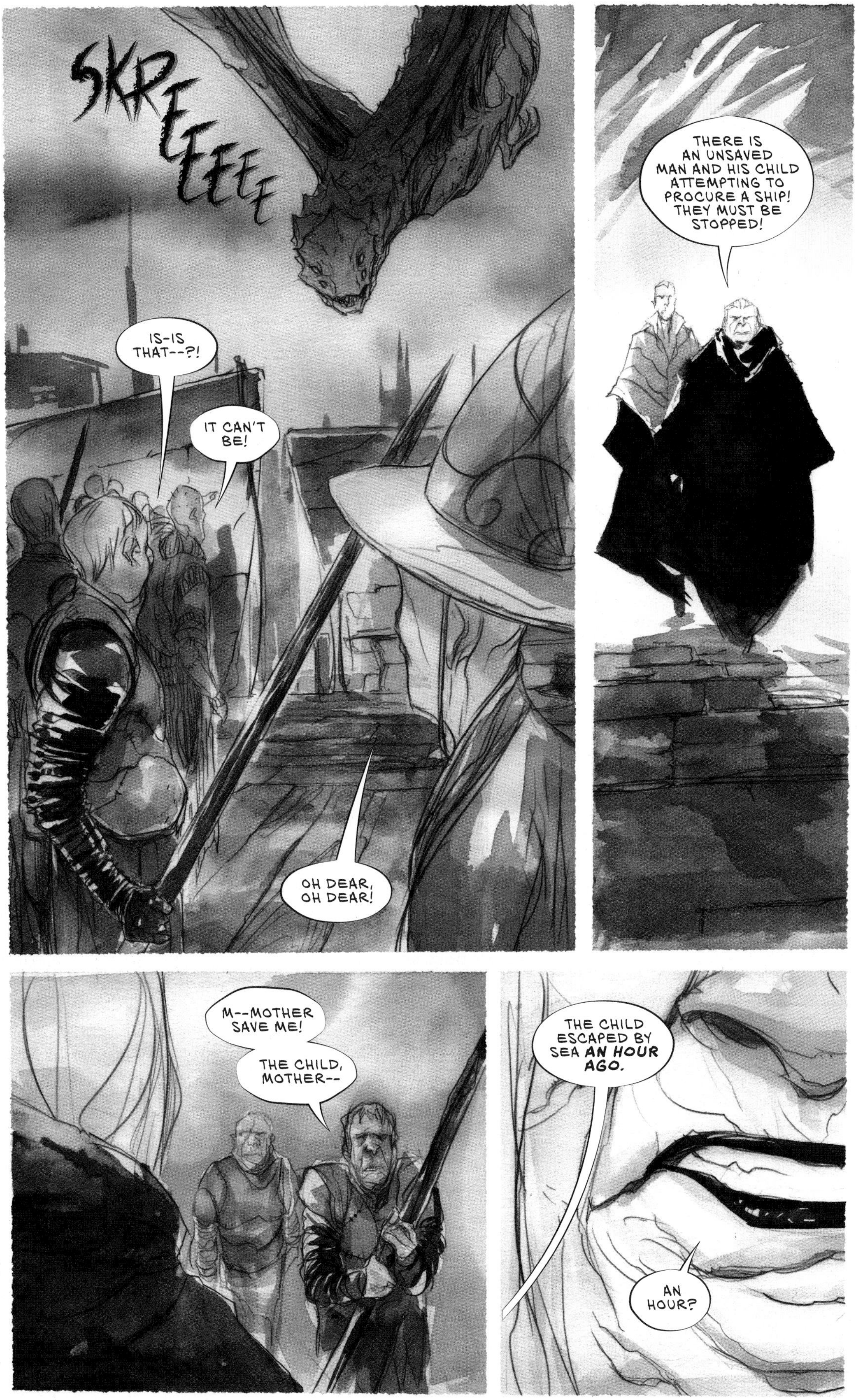
SKREEEEE
IS-IS THAT--?!
IT CAN'T BE!
OH DEAR, OH DEAR!
THERE IS AN UNSAVED MAN AND HIS CHILD ATTEMPTING TO PROCURE A SHIP! THEY MUST BE STOPPED!
M--MOTHER SAVE ME!
THE CHILD, MOTHER--
THE CHILD ESCAPED BY SEA AN HOUR AGO.
AN HOUR?

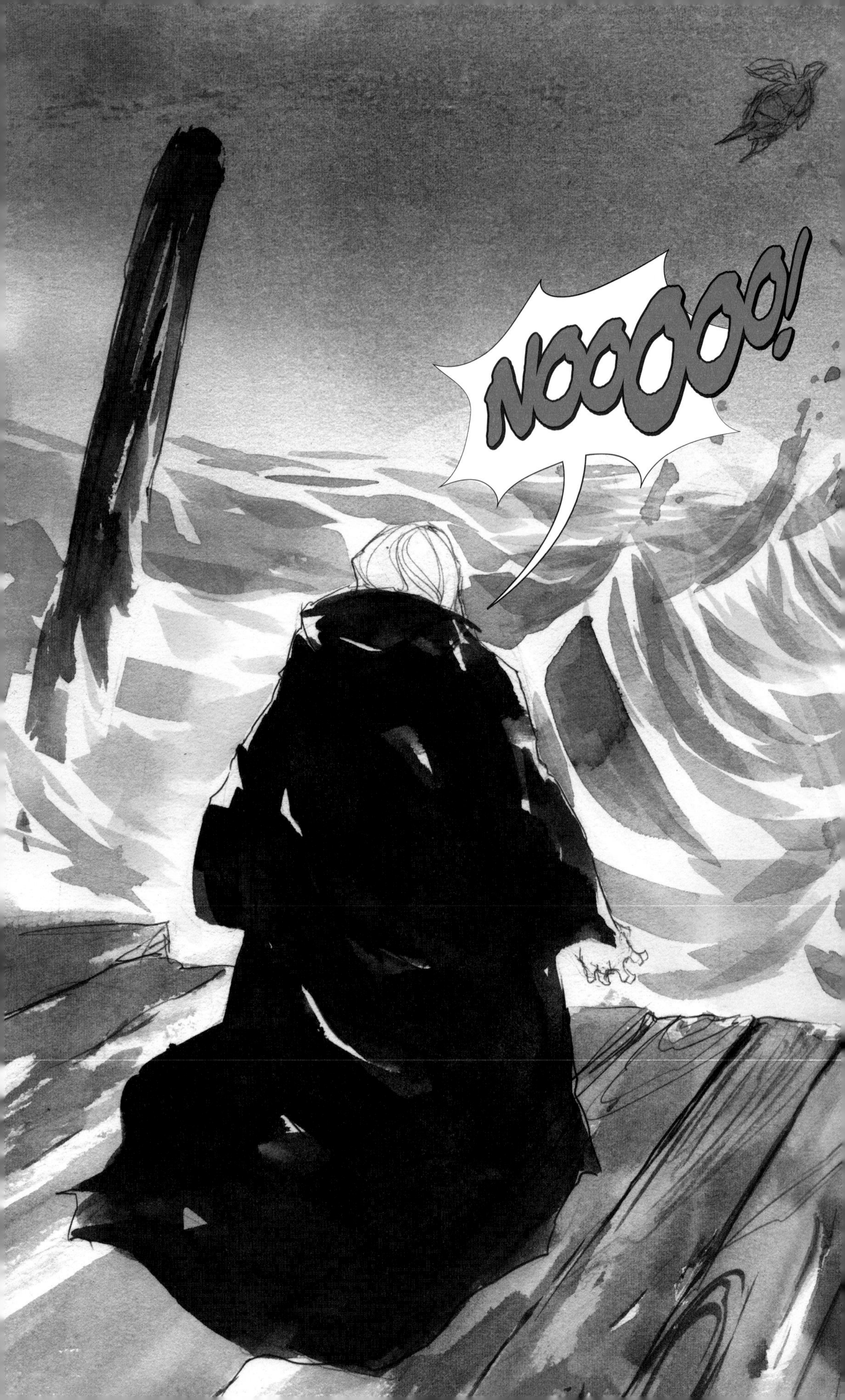
NOOOOO!

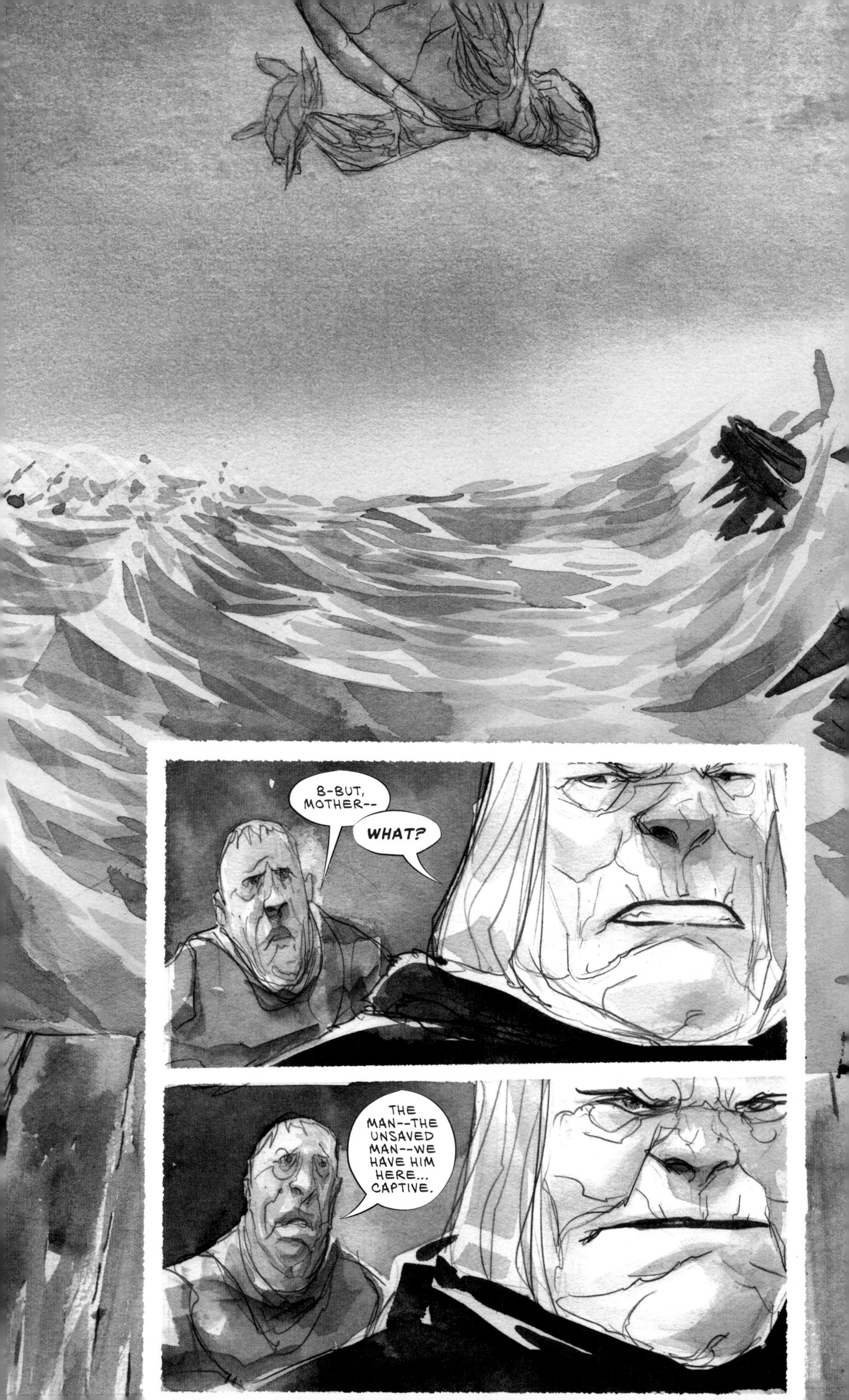
B-BUT, MOTHER--
WHAT?
THE MAN--THE UNSAVED MAN--WE HAVE HIM HERE... CAPTIVE.

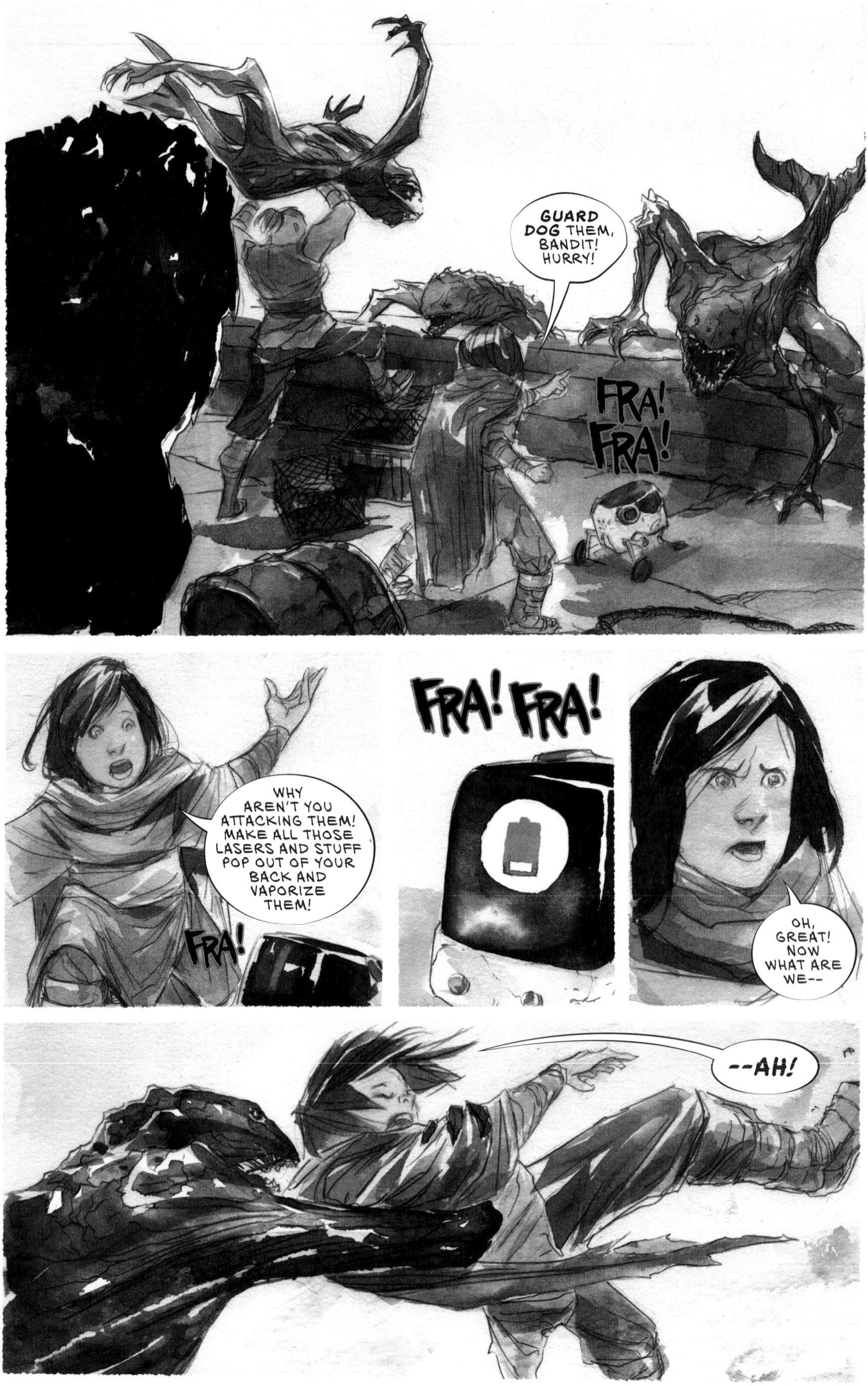
GUARD DOG THEM, BANDIT! HURRY!
FRA! FRA!
WHY AREN'T YOU ATTACKING THEM! MAKE ALL THOSE LASERS AND STUFF POP OUT OF YOUR BACK AND VAPORIZE THEM!
FRA!
FRA! FRA!
OH, GREAT! NOW WHAT ARE WE--
--AH!

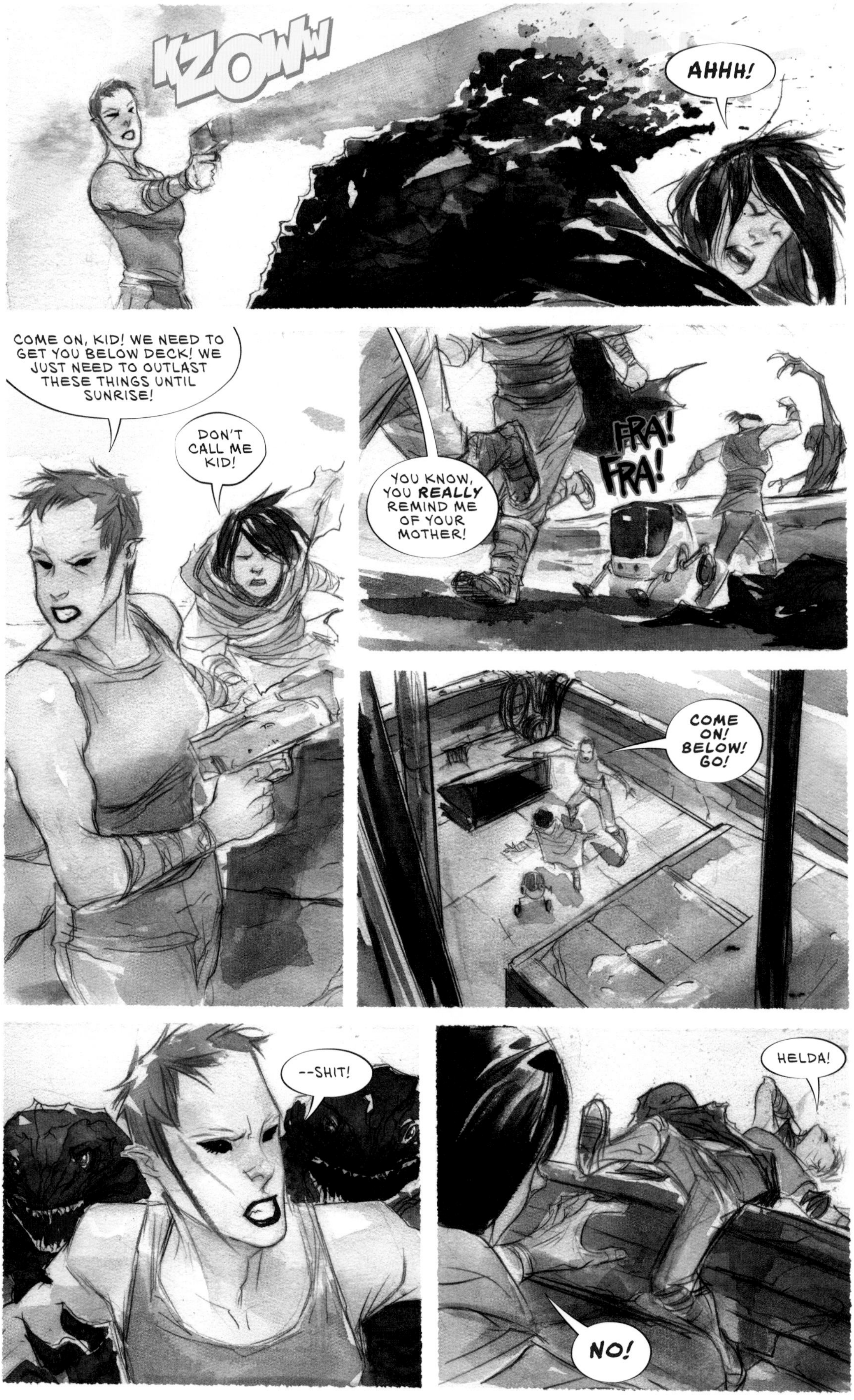
KZOWW
AHHH!
COME ON, KID! WE NEED TO GET YOU BELOW DECK! WE JUST NEED TO OUTLAST THESE THINGS UNTIL SUNRISE!
DON'T CALL ME KID!
YOU KNOW, YOU **REALLY** REMIND ME OF YOUR MOTHER!
FRA! FRA!
COME ON! BELOW! GO!
--SHIT!
HELDA!
NO!

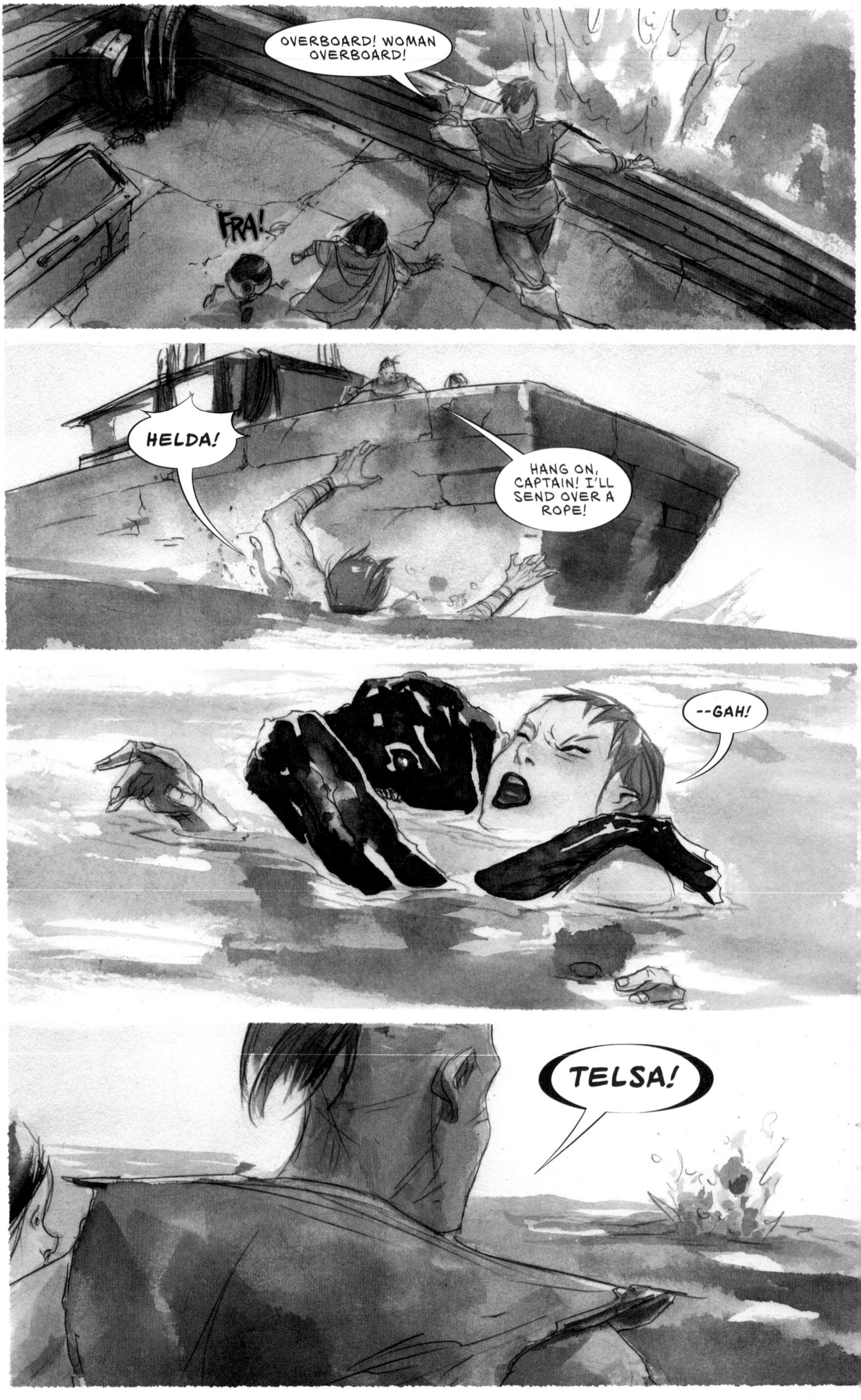
OVERBOARD! WOMAN OVERBOARD!
FRA!
HELDA!
HANG ON, CAPTAIN! I'LL SEND OVER A ROPE!
--GAH!
TELSA!

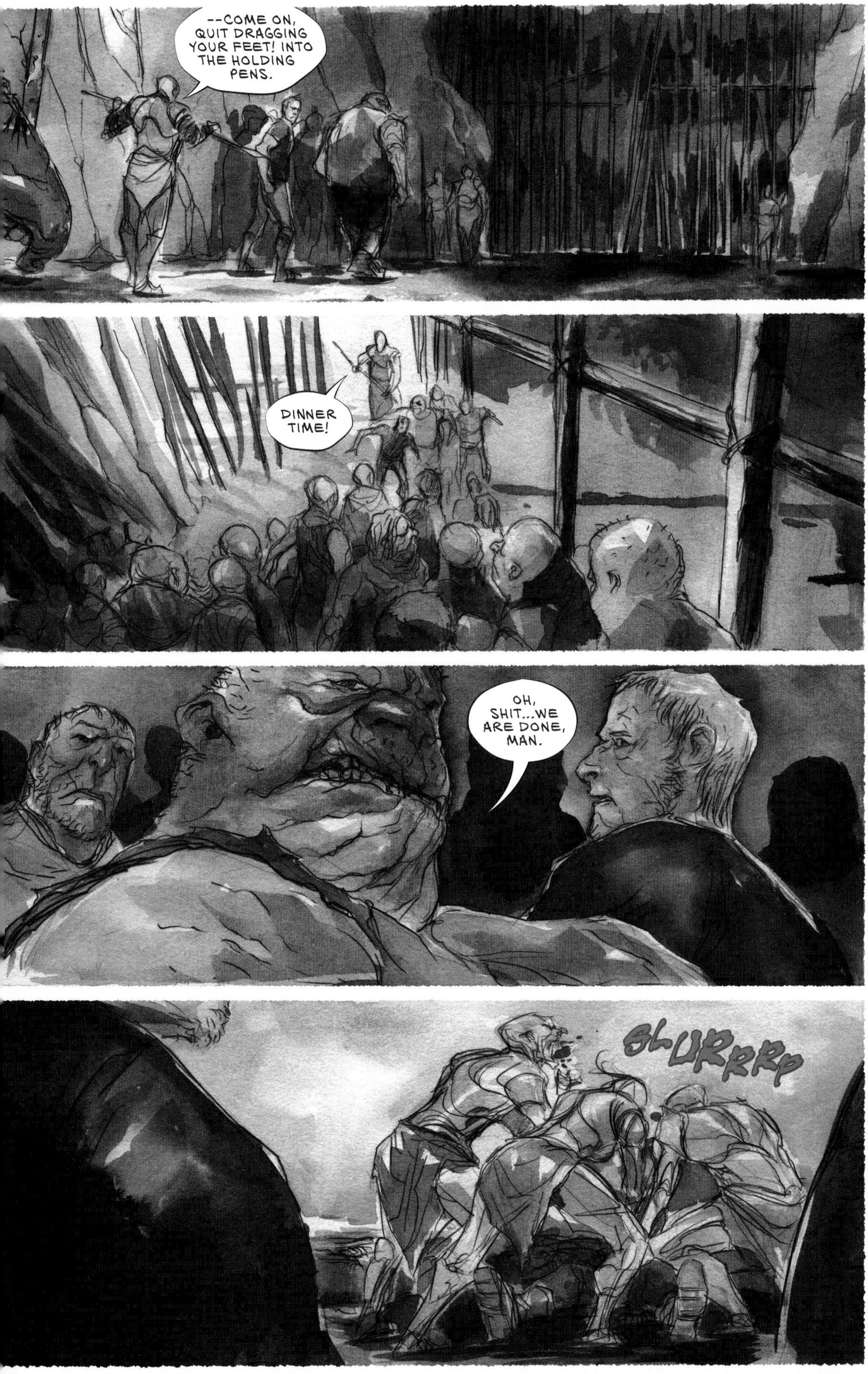
--COME ON, QUIT DRAGGING YOUR FEET! INTO THE HOLDING PENS.
DINNER TIME!
OH, SHIT...WE ARE DONE, MAN.
SLURRRP

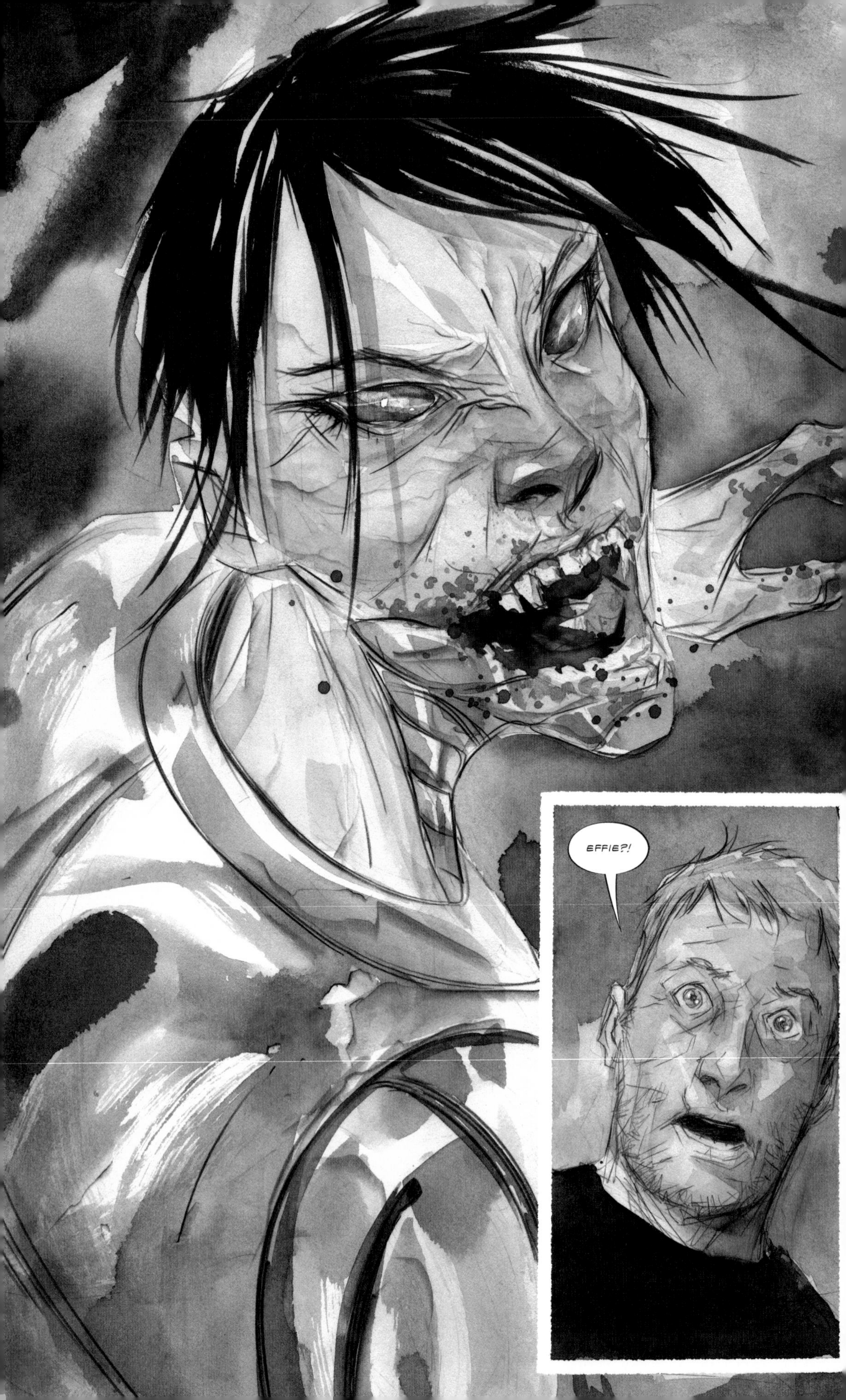
EFFIE?!

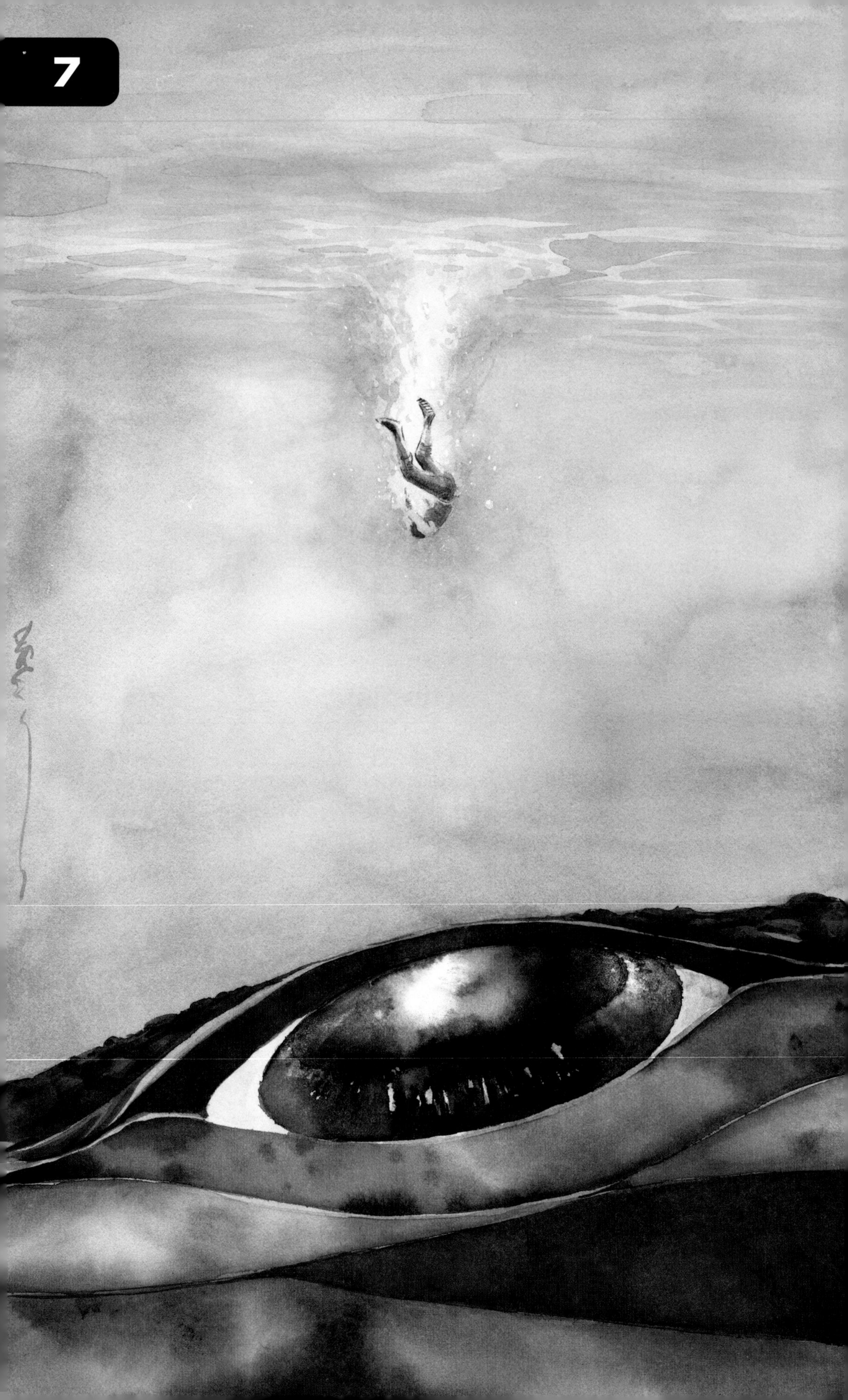
7

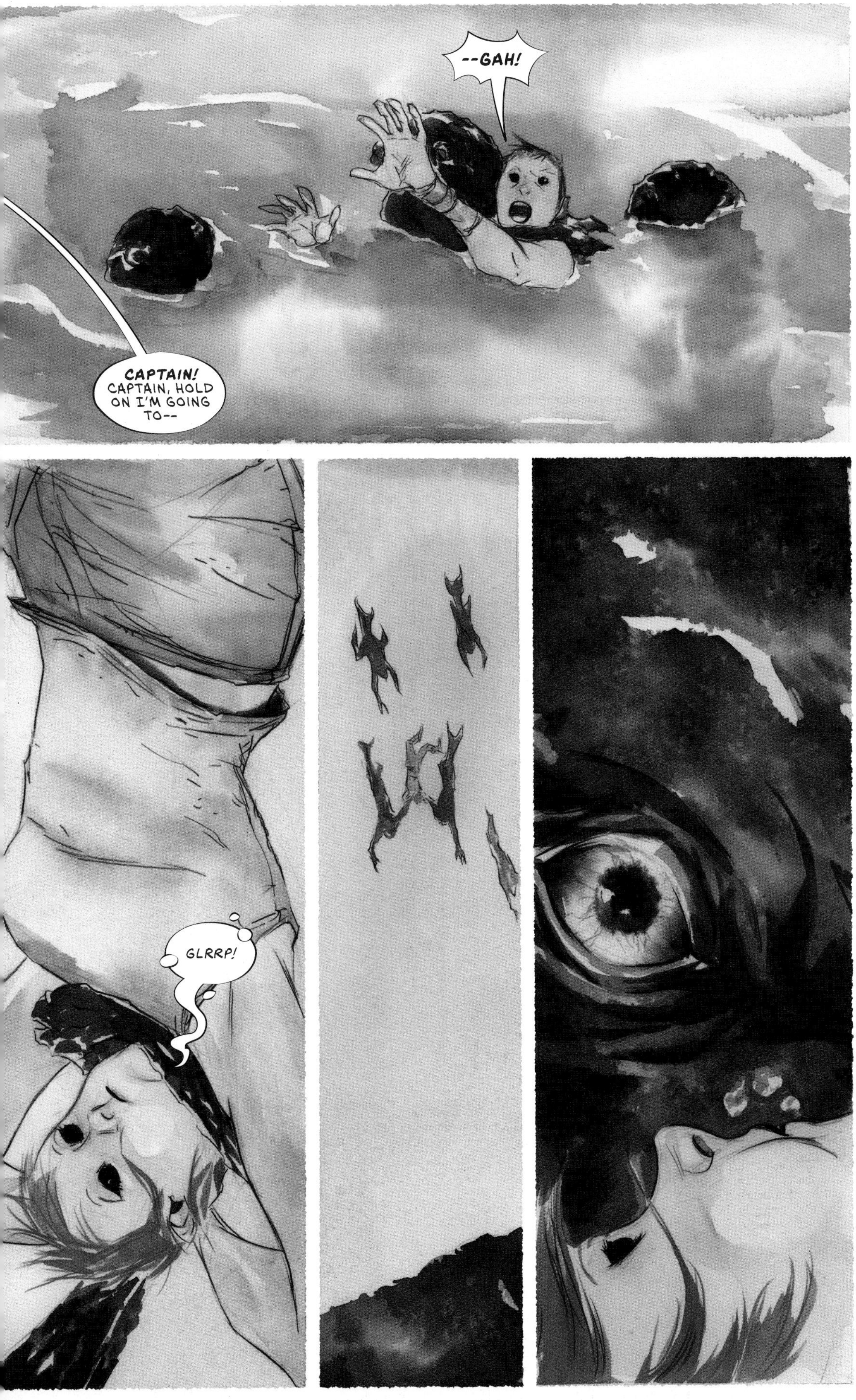
--GAH!
CAPTAIN! CAPTAIN, HOLD ON I'M GOING TO--
GLRRP!

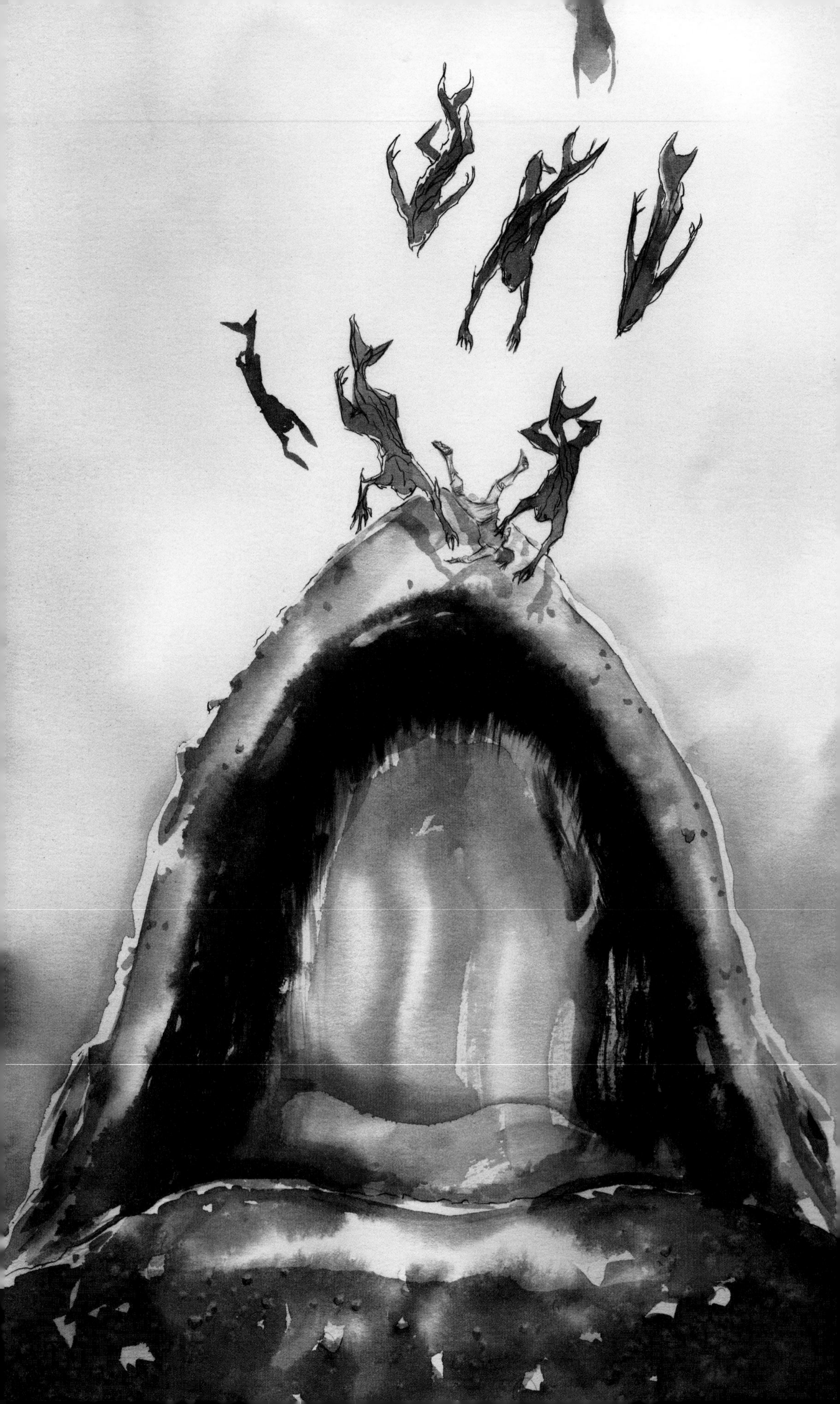

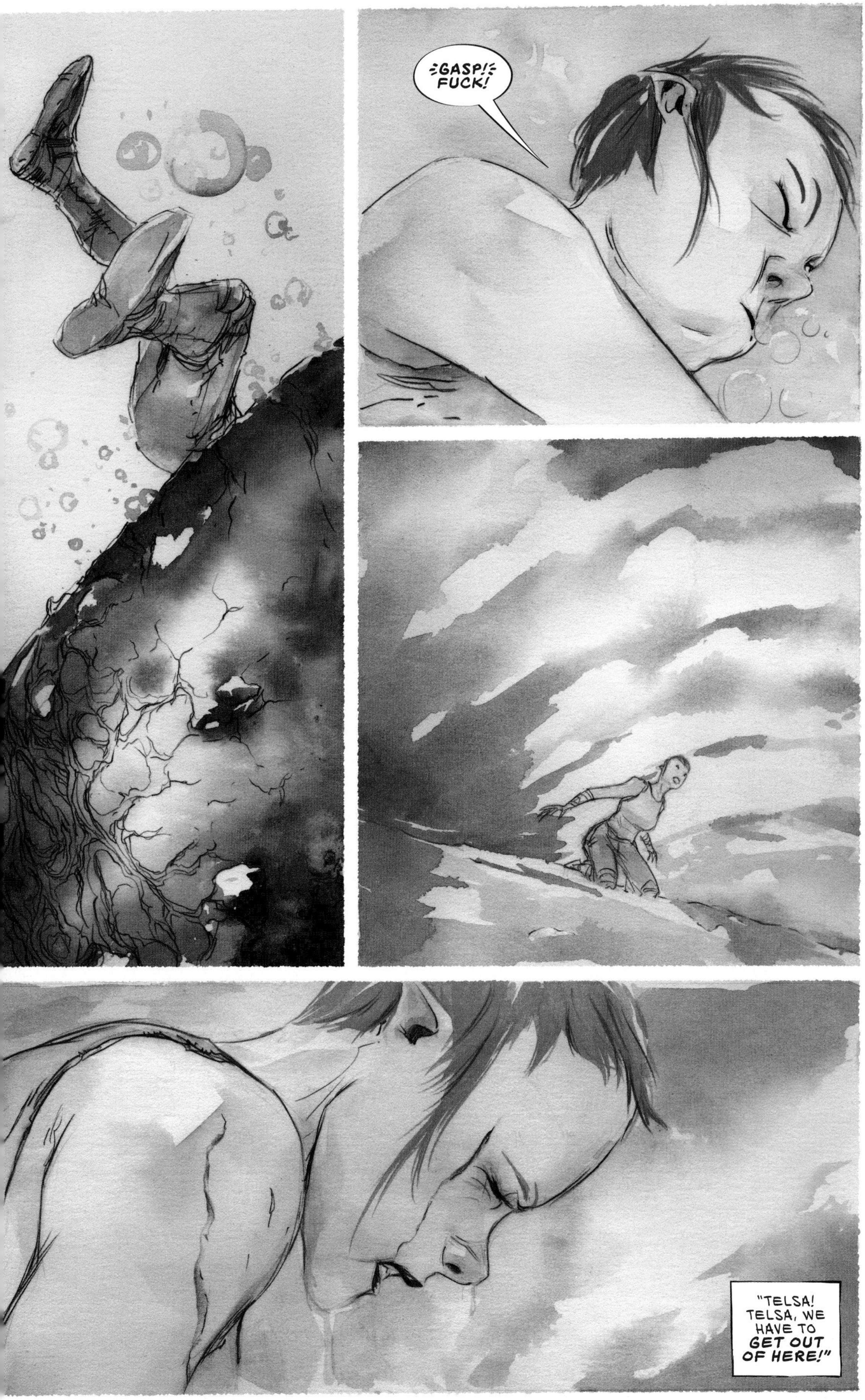
GASP! FUCK!
"TELSA! TELSA, WE HAVE TO GET OUT OF HERE!"

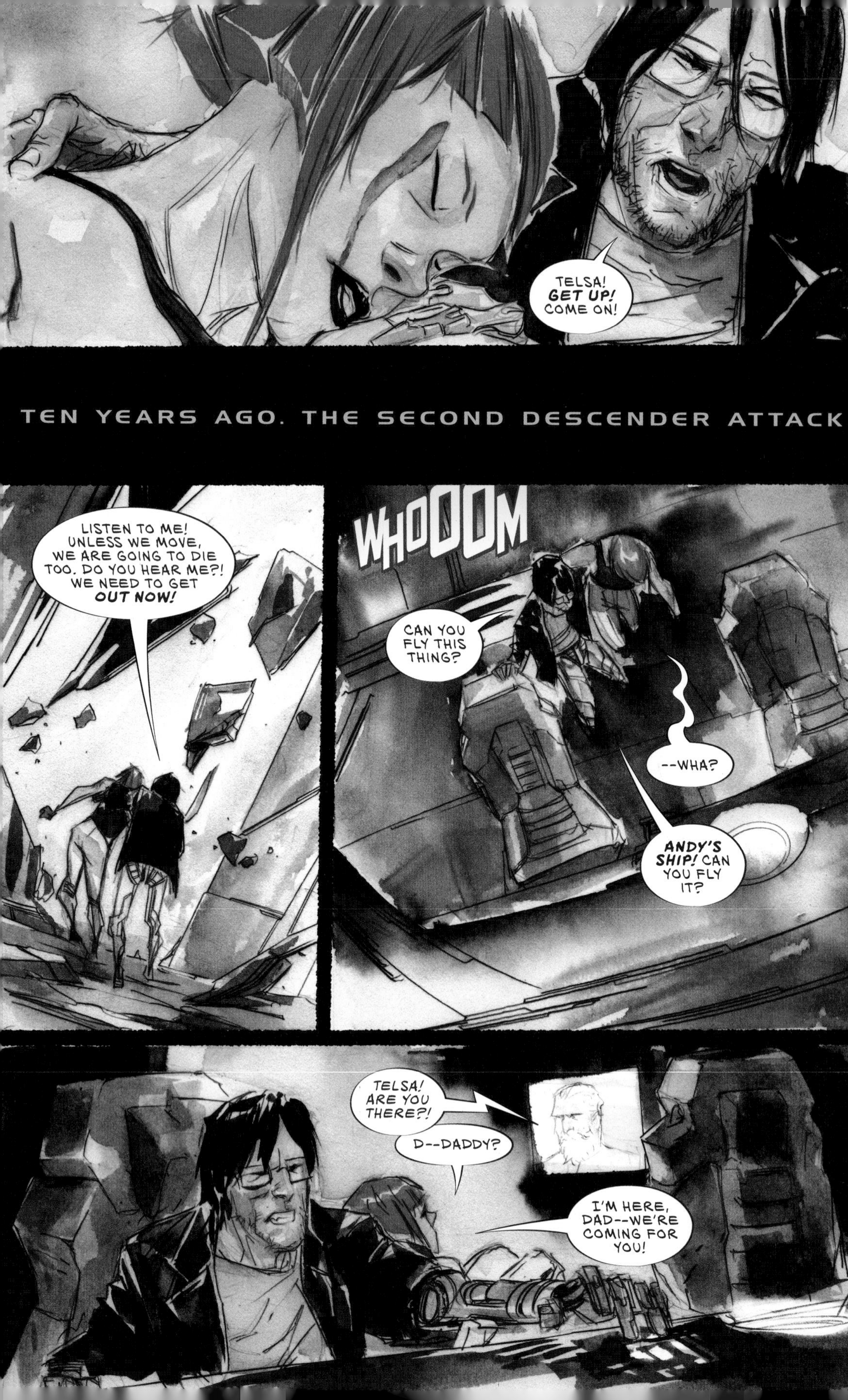
TELSA! GET UP! COME ON!
TEN YEARS AGO. THE SECOND DESCENDER ATTACK
LISTEN TO ME! UNLESS WE MOVE, WE ARE GOING TO DIE TOO. DO YOU HEAR ME?! WE NEED TO GET OUT NOW!
WHOOOM
CAN YOU FLY THIS THING?
--WHA?
ANDY'S SHIP! CAN YOU FLY IT?
TELSA! ARE YOU THERE?!
D--DADDY?
I'M HERE, DAD--WE'RE COMING FOR YOU!

CHOOOM
DAD! JUMP! GET OUT OF THERE!
I--I LOVE YOU, SWEETHEART.
FWASH
DADDY!
--DADDY...

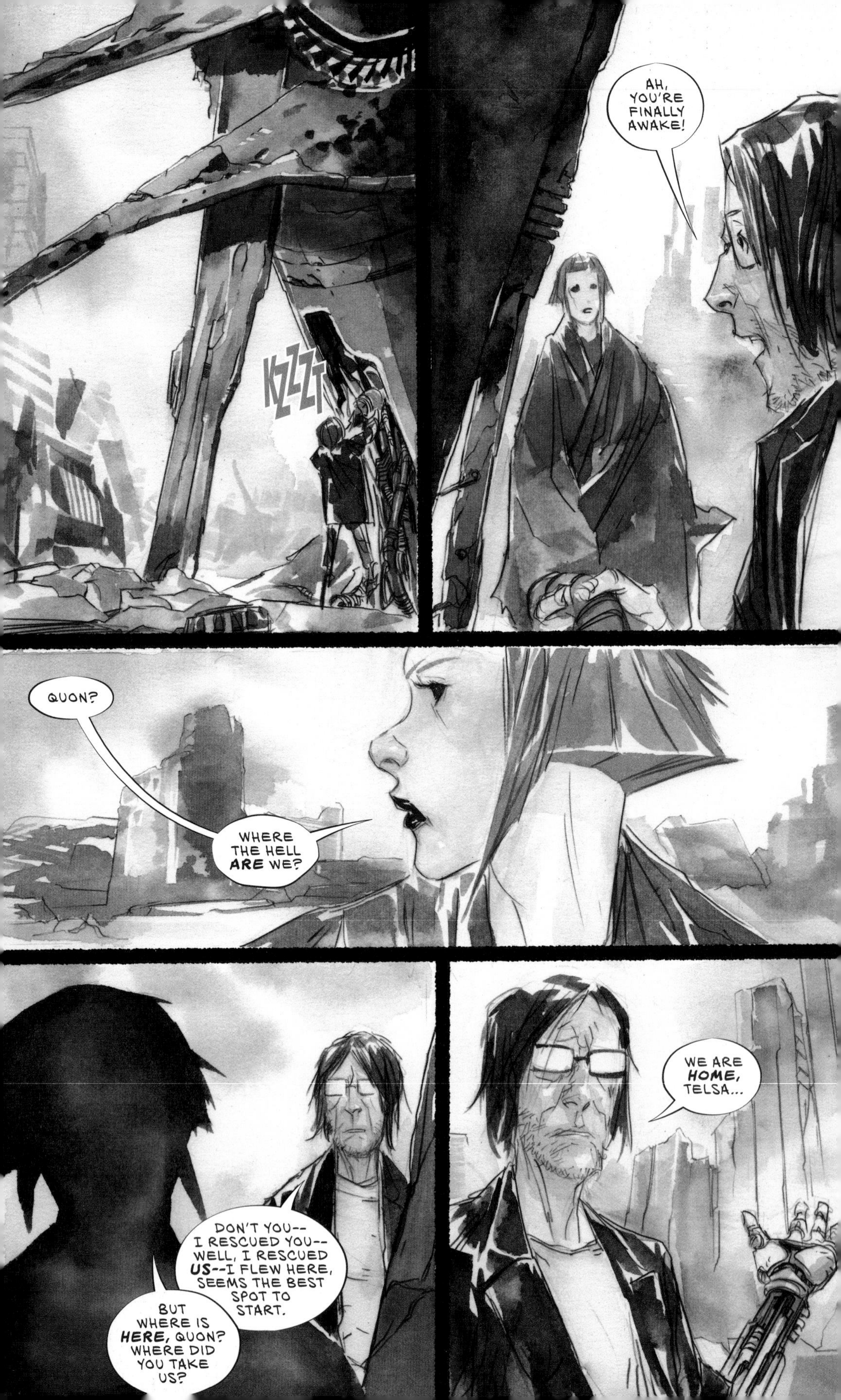
KZZZT
AH, YOU'RE FINALLY AWAKE!
QUON?
WHERE THE HELL ARE WE?
WE ARE HOME, TELSA...
DON'T YOU-- I RESCUED YOU-- WELL, I RESCUED US--I FLEW HERE, SEEMS THE BEST SPOT TO START.
BUT WHERE IS HERE, QUON? WHERE DID YOU TAKE US?

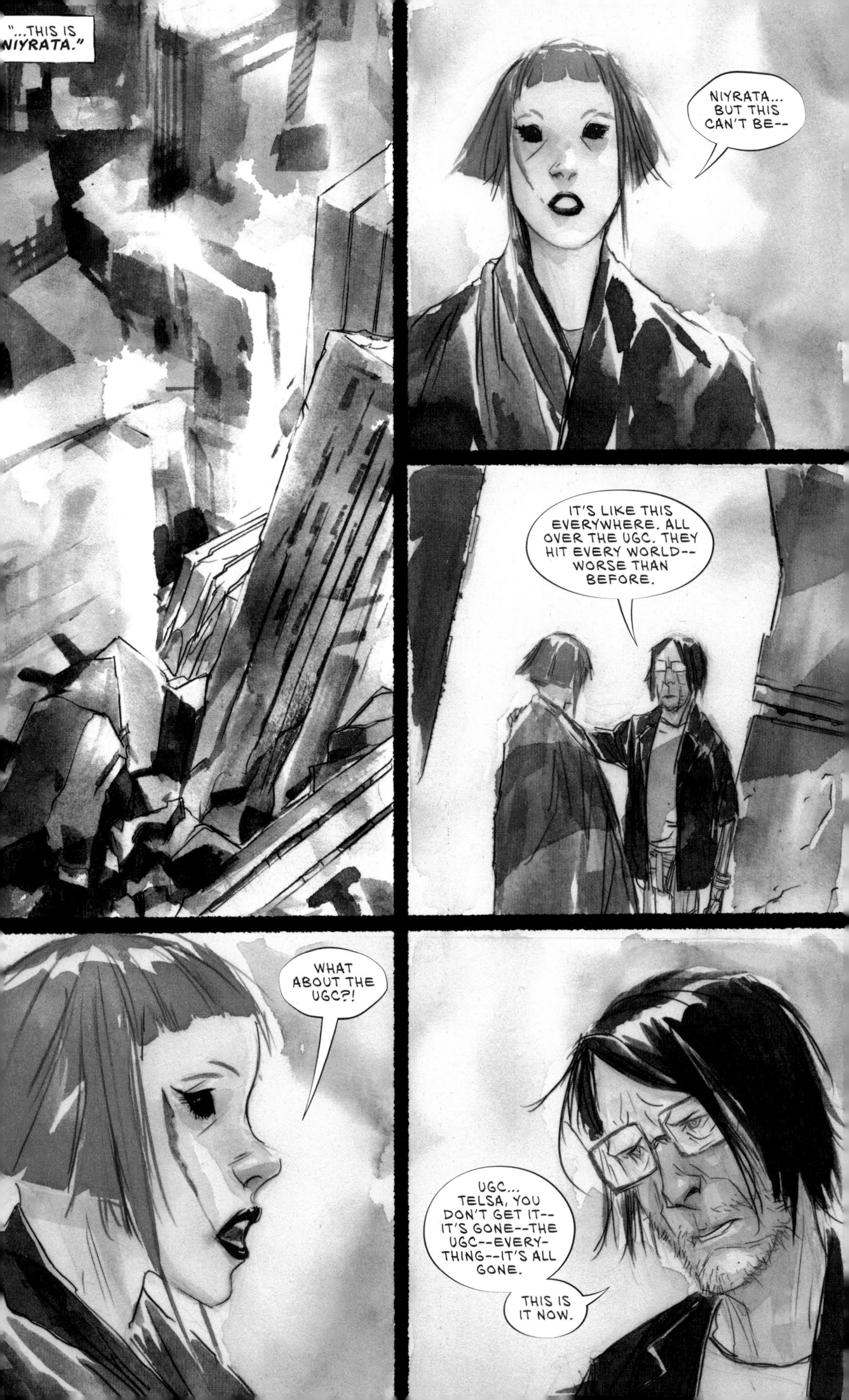
"...THIS IS NIYRATA."
NIYRATA... BUT THIS CAN'T BE--
IT'S LIKE THIS EVERYWHERE. ALL OVER THE UGC. THEY HIT EVERY WORLD-- WORSE THAN BEFORE.
WHAT ABOUT THE UGC?!
UGC... TELSA, YOU DON'T GET IT-- IT'S GONE--THE UGC--EVERY-THING--IT'S ALL GONE.
THIS IS IT NOW.

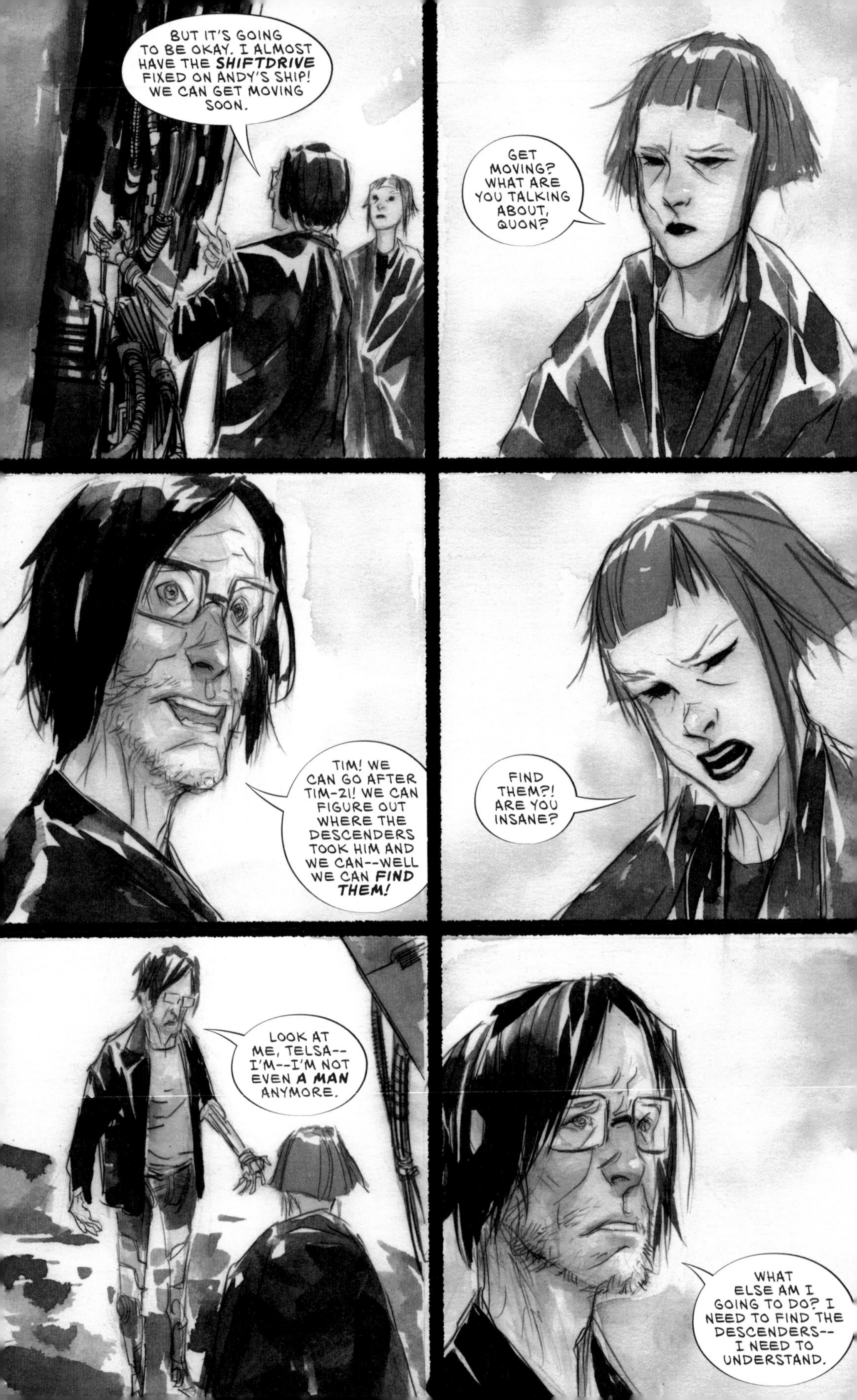
BUT IT'S GOING TO BE OKAY. I ALMOST HAVE THE **SHIFTDRIVE** FIXED ON ANDY'S SHIP! WE CAN GET MOVING SOON.
GET MOVING? WHAT ARE YOU TALKING ABOUT, QUON?
TIM! WE CAN GO AFTER TIM-21! WE CAN FIGURE OUT WHERE THE DESCENDERS TOOK HIM AND WE CAN--WELL WE CAN **FIND THEM!**
FIND THEM?! ARE YOU INSANE?
LOOK AT ME, TELSA-- I'M--I'M NOT EVEN **A MAN** ANYMORE.
WHAT ELSE AM I GOING TO DO? I NEED TO FIND THE DESCENDERS-- I NEED TO UNDERSTAND.

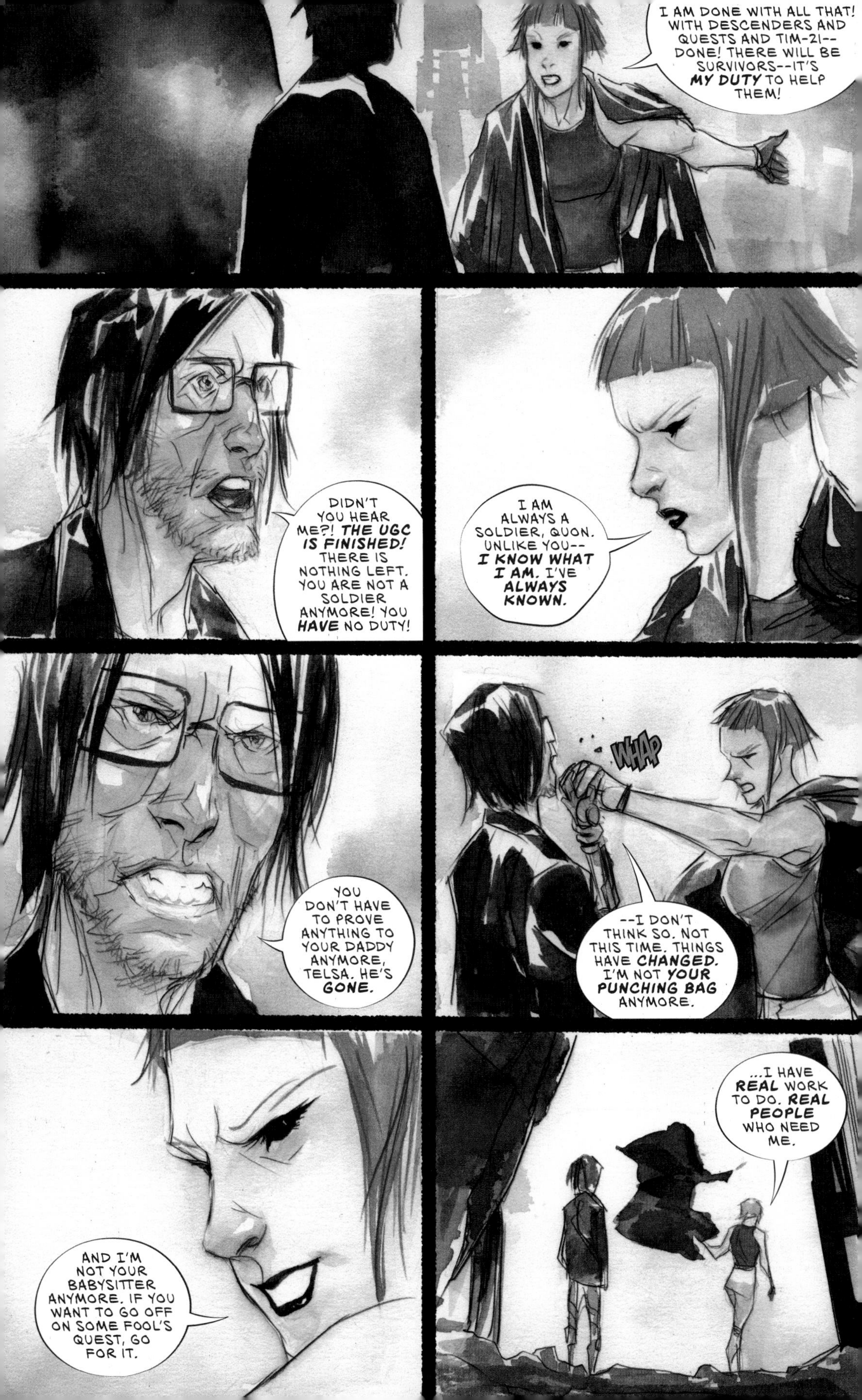
I AM DONE WITH ALL THAT! WITH DESCENDERS AND QUESTS AND TIM-21--DONE! THERE WILL BE SURVIVORS--IT'S MY DUTY TO HELP THEM!
DIDN'T YOU HEAR ME?! THE UGC IS FINISHED! THERE IS NOTHING LEFT. YOU ARE NOT A SOLDIER ANYMORE! YOU HAVE NO DUTY!
I AM ALWAYS A SOLDIER, QUON. UNLIKE YOU--I KNOW WHAT I AM. I'VE ALWAYS KNOWN.
YOU DON'T HAVE TO PROVE ANYTHING TO YOUR DADDY ANYMORE, TELSA. HE'S GONE.
WHAP
--I DON'T THINK SO. NOT THIS TIME. THINGS HAVE CHANGED. I'M NOT YOUR PUNCHING BAG ANYMORE.
AND I'M NOT YOUR BABYSITTER ANYMORE. IF YOU WANT TO GO OFF ON SOME FOOL'S QUEST, GO FOR IT.
...I HAVE REAL WORK TO DO. REAL PEOPLE WHO NEED ME.

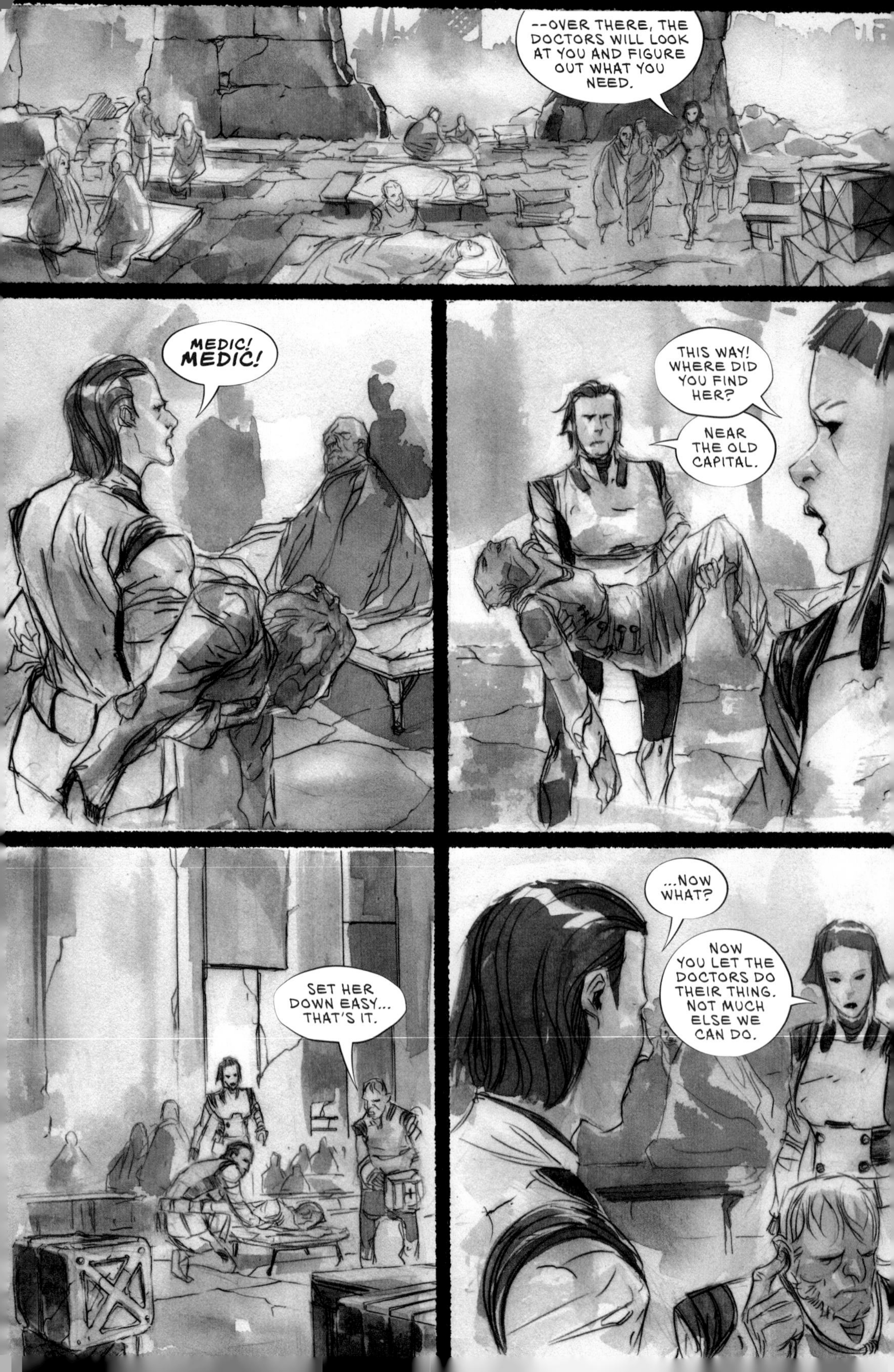
--OVER THERE, THE DOCTORS WILL LOOK AT YOU AND FIGURE OUT WHAT YOU NEED.
MEDIC! MEDIC!
THIS WAY! WHERE DID YOU FIND HER?
NEAR THE OLD CAPITAL.
SET HER DOWN EASY... THAT'S IT.
...NOW WHAT?
NOW YOU LET THE DOCTORS DO THEIR THING. NOT MUCH ELSE WE CAN DO.

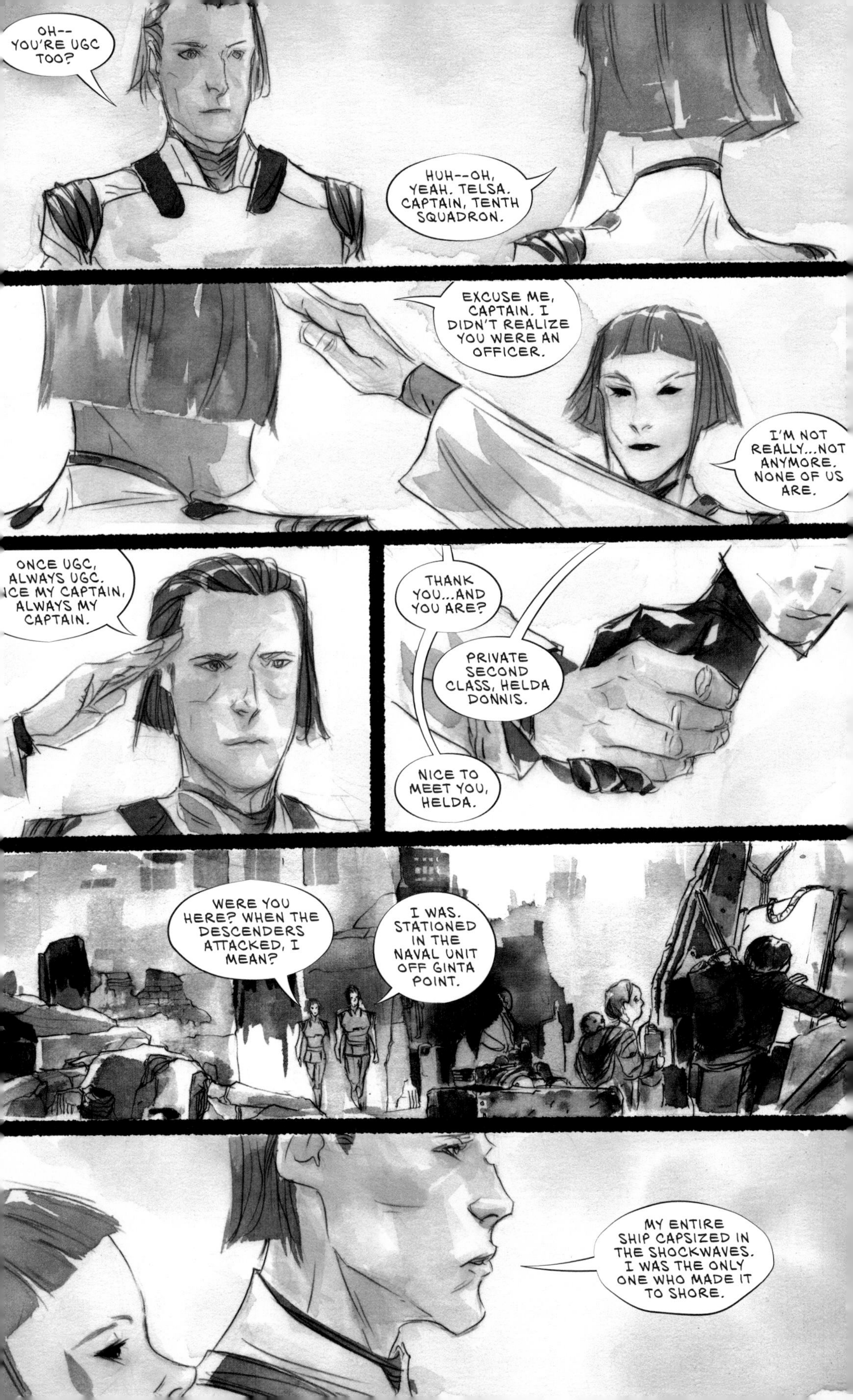
OH-- YOU'RE UGC TOO?
HUH--OH, YEAH. TELSA. CAPTAIN, TENTH SQUADRON.
EXCUSE ME, CAPTAIN. I DIDN'T REALIZE YOU WERE AN OFFICER.
I'M NOT REALLY...NOT ANYMORE. NONE OF US ARE.
ONCE UGC, ALWAYS UGC. ICE MY CAPTAIN, ALWAYS MY CAPTAIN.
THANK YOU...AND YOU ARE?
PRIVATE SECOND CLASS, HELDA DONNIS.
NICE TO MEET YOU, HELDA.
WERE YOU HERE? WHEN THE DESCENDERS ATTACKED, I MEAN?
I WAS. STATIONED IN THE NAVAL UNIT OFF GINTA POINT.
MY ENTIRE SHIP CAPSIZED IN THE SHOCKWAVES. I WAS THE ONLY ONE WHO MADE IT TO SHORE.

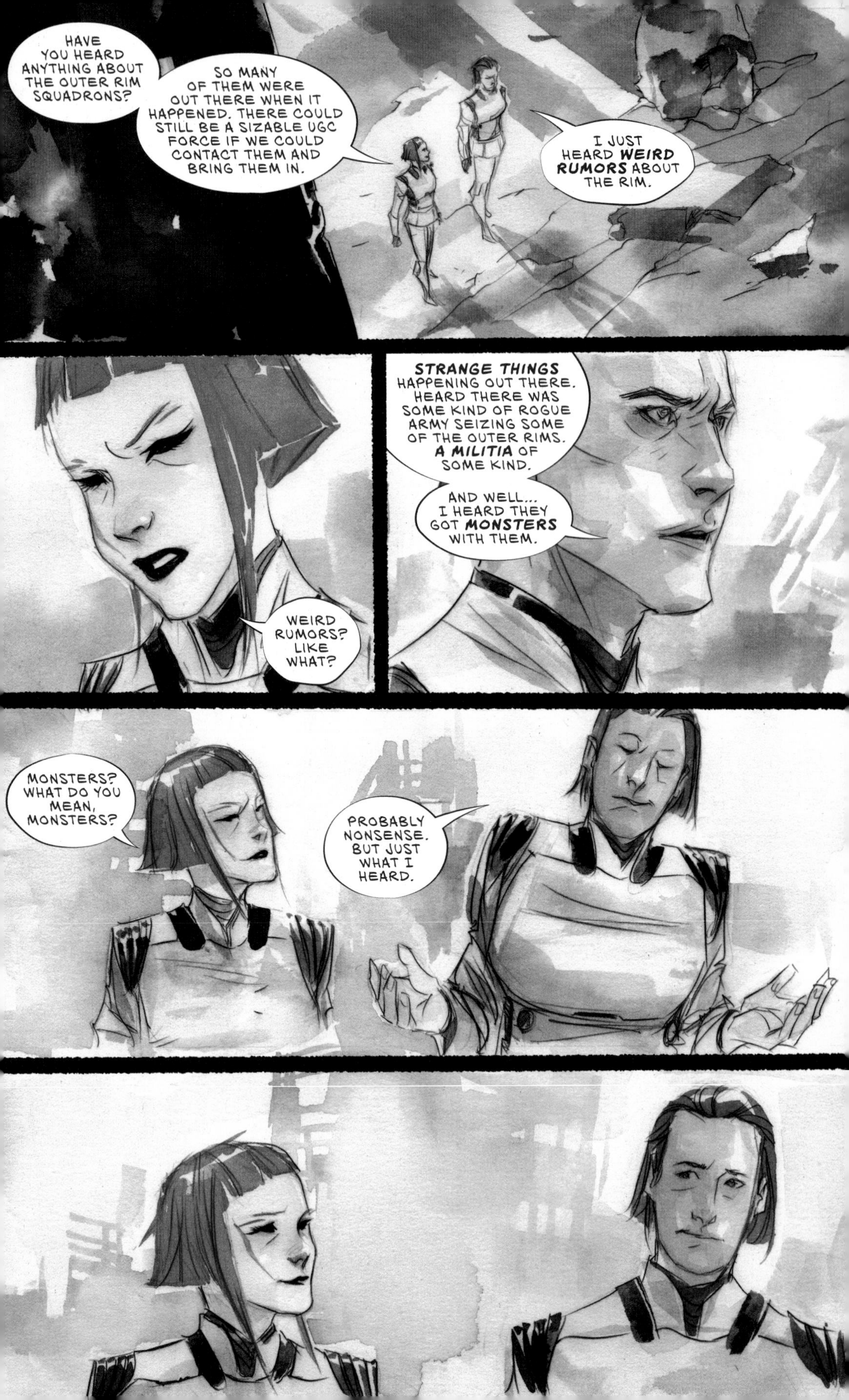
HAVE YOU HEARD ANYTHING ABOUT THE OUTER RIM SQUADRONS?
SO MANY OF THEM WERE OUT THERE WHEN IT HAPPENED. THERE COULD STILL BE A SIZABLE UGC FORCE IF WE COULD CONTACT THEM AND BRING THEM IN.
I JUST HEARD **WEIRD RUMORS** ABOUT THE RIM.
WEIRD RUMORS? LIKE WHAT?
STRANGE THINGS HAPPENING OUT THERE. HEARD THERE WAS SOME KIND OF ROGUE ARMY SEIZING SOME OF THE OUTER RIMS. **A MILITIA** OF SOME KIND.
AND WELL... I HEARD THEY GOT **MONSTERS** WITH THEM.
MONSTERS? WHAT DO YOU MEAN, MONSTERS?
PROBABLY NONSENSE. BUT JUST WHAT I HEARD.

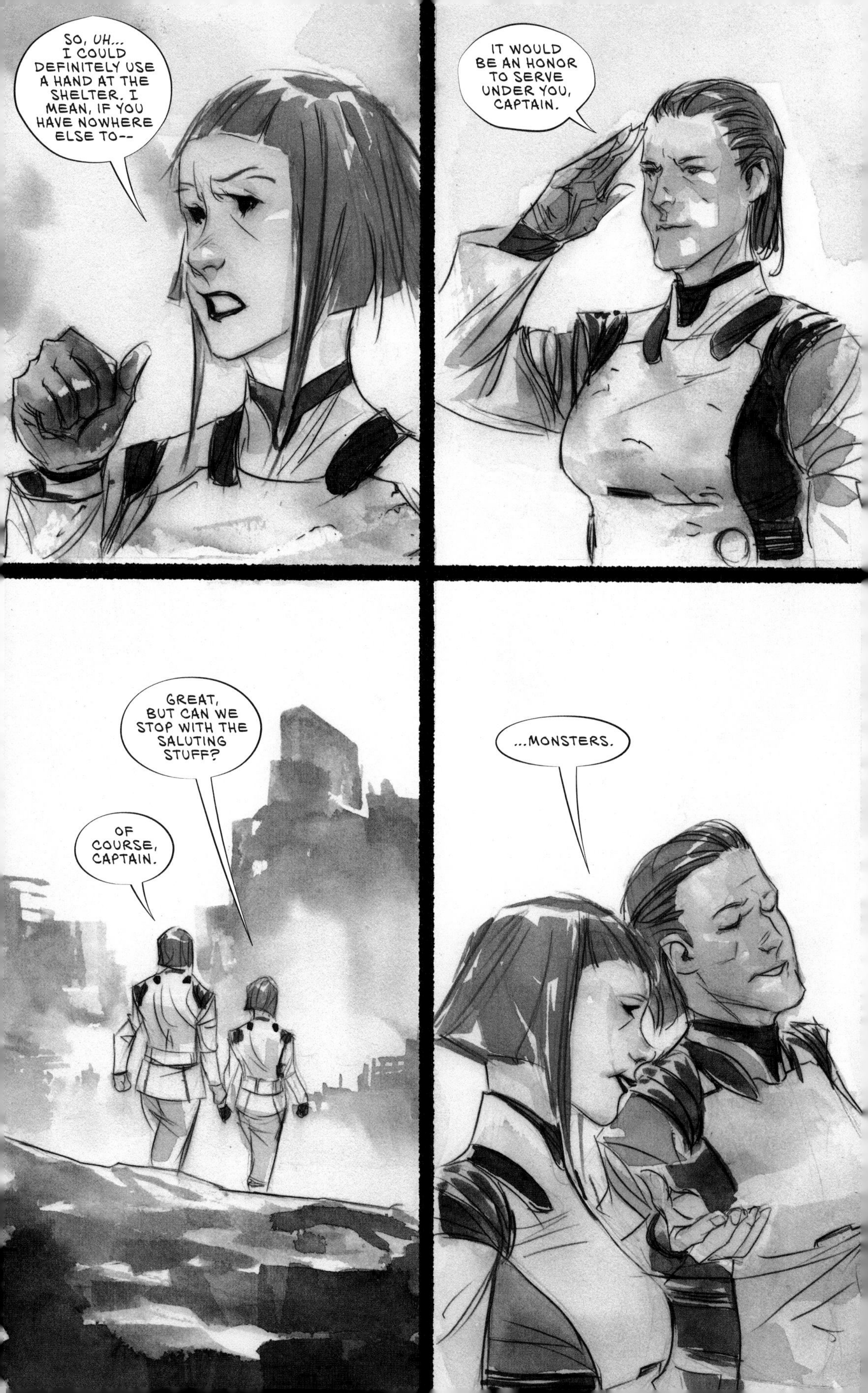
SO, UH...
I COULD DEFINITELY USE A HAND AT THE SHELTER. I MEAN, IF YOU HAVE NOWHERE ELSE TO--
IT WOULD BE AN HONOR TO SERVE UNDER YOU, CAPTAIN.
GREAT, BUT CAN WE STOP WITH THE SALUTING STUFF?
OF COURSE, CAPTAIN.
...MONSTERS.

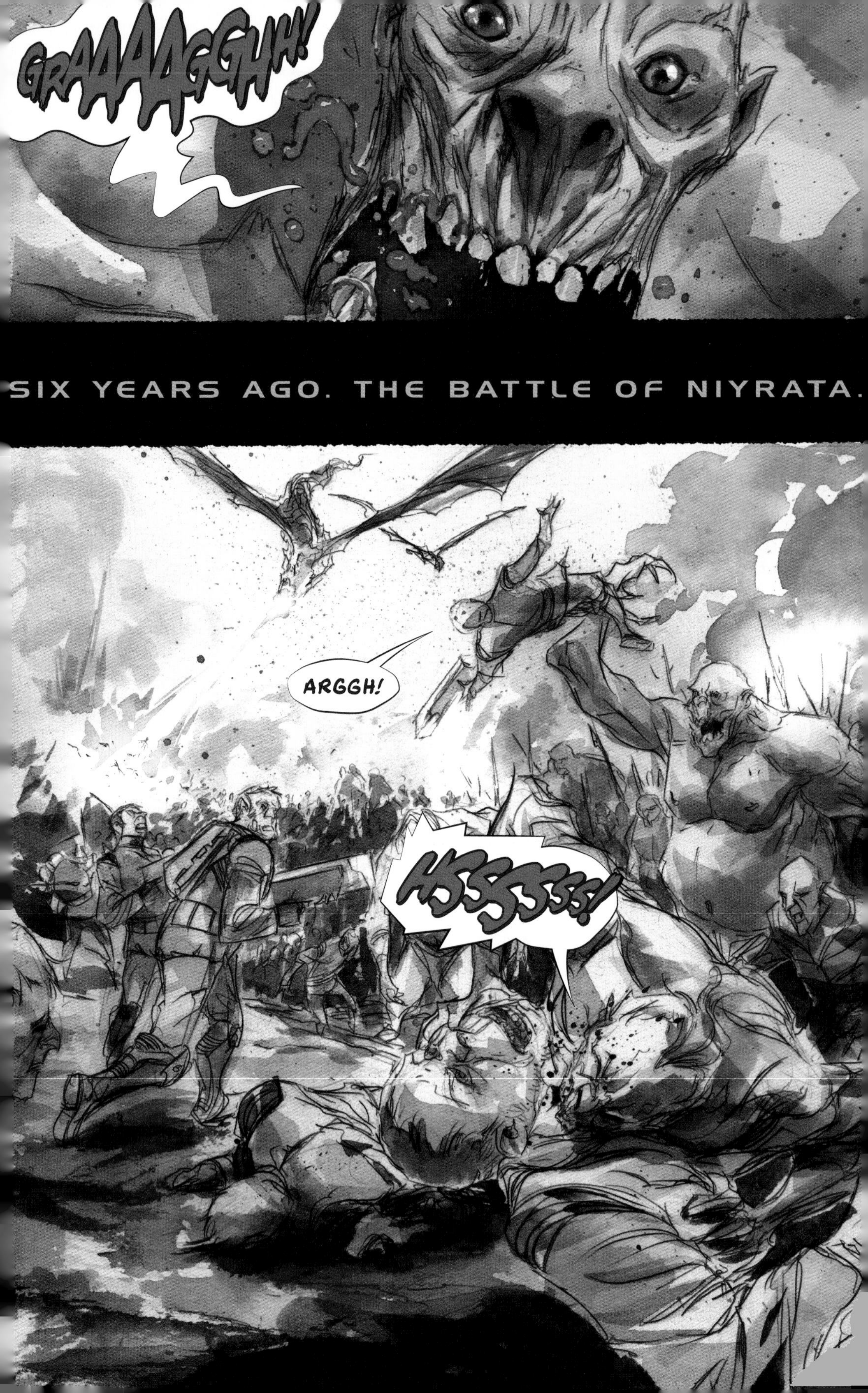
GRAAAAGGHH!
SIX YEARS AGO. THE BATTLE OF NIYRATA.
ARGGH!
HSSSSSS!

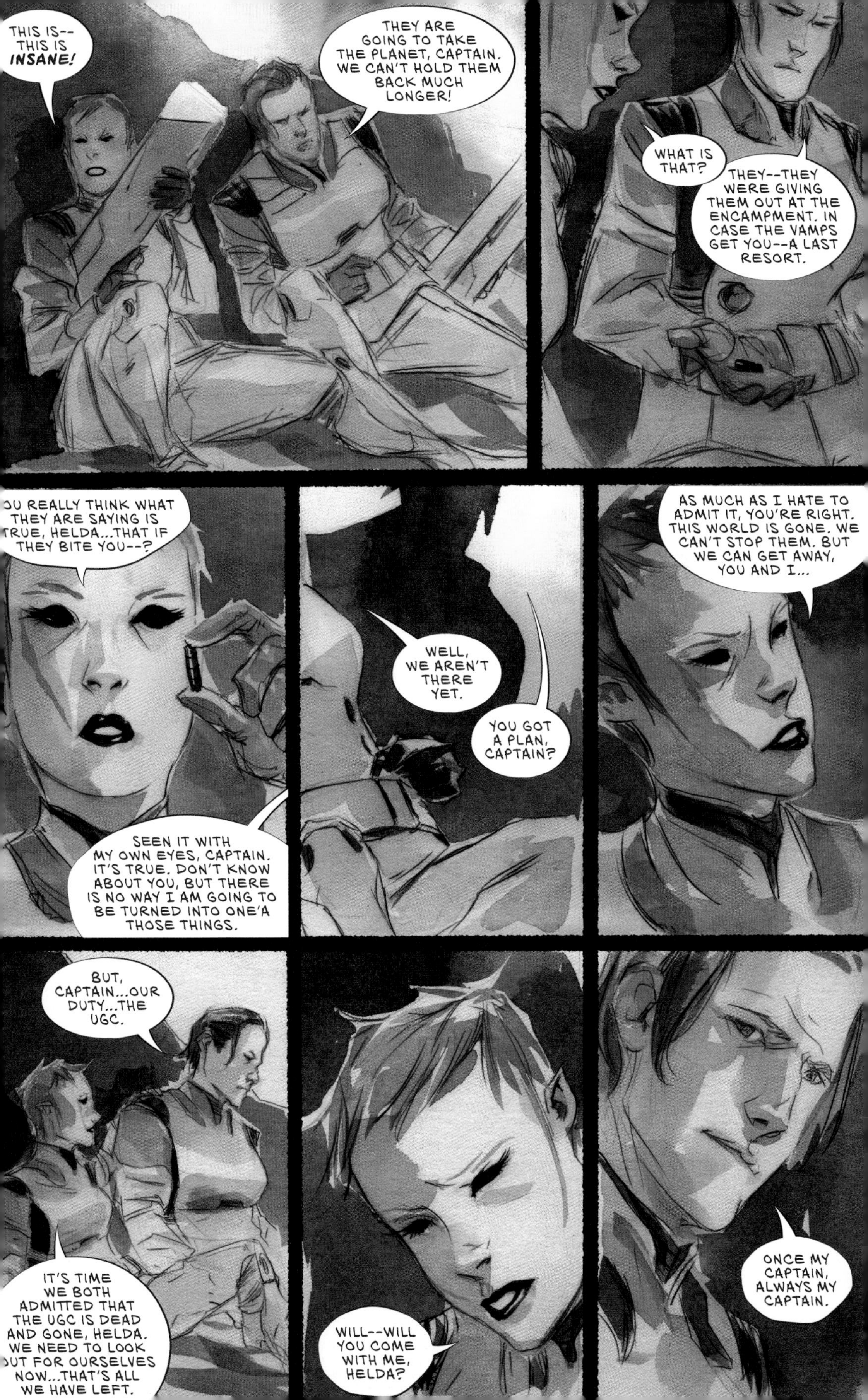
THIS IS--
THIS IS
INSANE!
THEY ARE GOING TO TAKE THE PLANET, CAPTAIN. WE CAN'T HOLD THEM BACK MUCH LONGER!
WHAT IS THAT?
THEY--THEY WERE GIVING THEM OUT AT THE ENCAMPMENT. IN CASE THE VAMPS GET YOU--A LAST RESORT.
OU REALLY THINK WHAT THEY ARE SAYING IS TRUE, HELDA...THAT IF THEY BITE YOU--?
SEEN IT WITH MY OWN EYES, CAPTAIN. IT'S TRUE. DON'T KNOW ABOUT YOU, BUT THERE IS NO WAY I AM GOING TO BE TURNED INTO ONE'A THOSE THINGS.
WELL, WE AREN'T THERE YET.
YOU GOT A PLAN, CAPTAIN?
AS MUCH AS I HATE TO ADMIT IT, YOU'RE RIGHT. THIS WORLD IS GONE. WE CAN'T STOP THEM. BUT WE CAN GET AWAY, YOU AND I...
BUT, CAPTAIN...OUR DUTY...THE UGC.
IT'S TIME WE BOTH ADMITTED THAT THE UGC IS DEAD AND GONE, HELDA. WE NEED TO LOOK OUT FOR OURSELVES NOW...THAT'S ALL WE HAVE LEFT.
WILL--WILL YOU COME WITH ME, HELDA?
ONCE MY CAPTAIN, ALWAYS MY CAPTAIN.

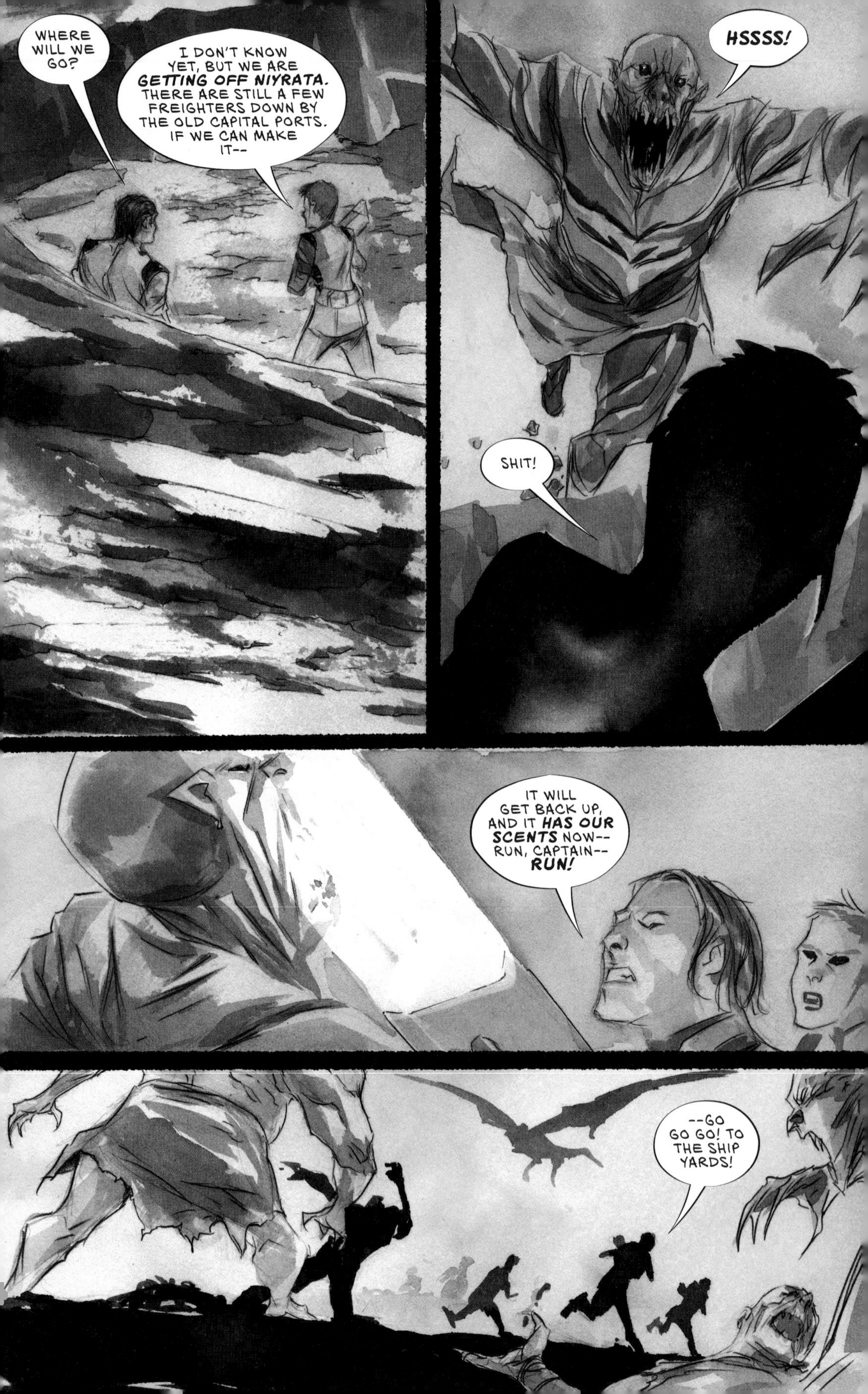
WHERE WILL WE GO?
I DON'T KNOW YET, BUT WE ARE **GETTING OFF NIYRATA.** THERE ARE STILL A FEW FREIGHTERS DOWN BY THE OLD CAPITAL PORTS. IF WE CAN MAKE IT--
HSSSS!
SHIT!
IT WILL GET BACK UP, AND IT **HAS OUR SCENTS** NOW-- RUN, CAPTAIN-- **RUN!**
--GO GO GO! TO THE SHIP YARDS!

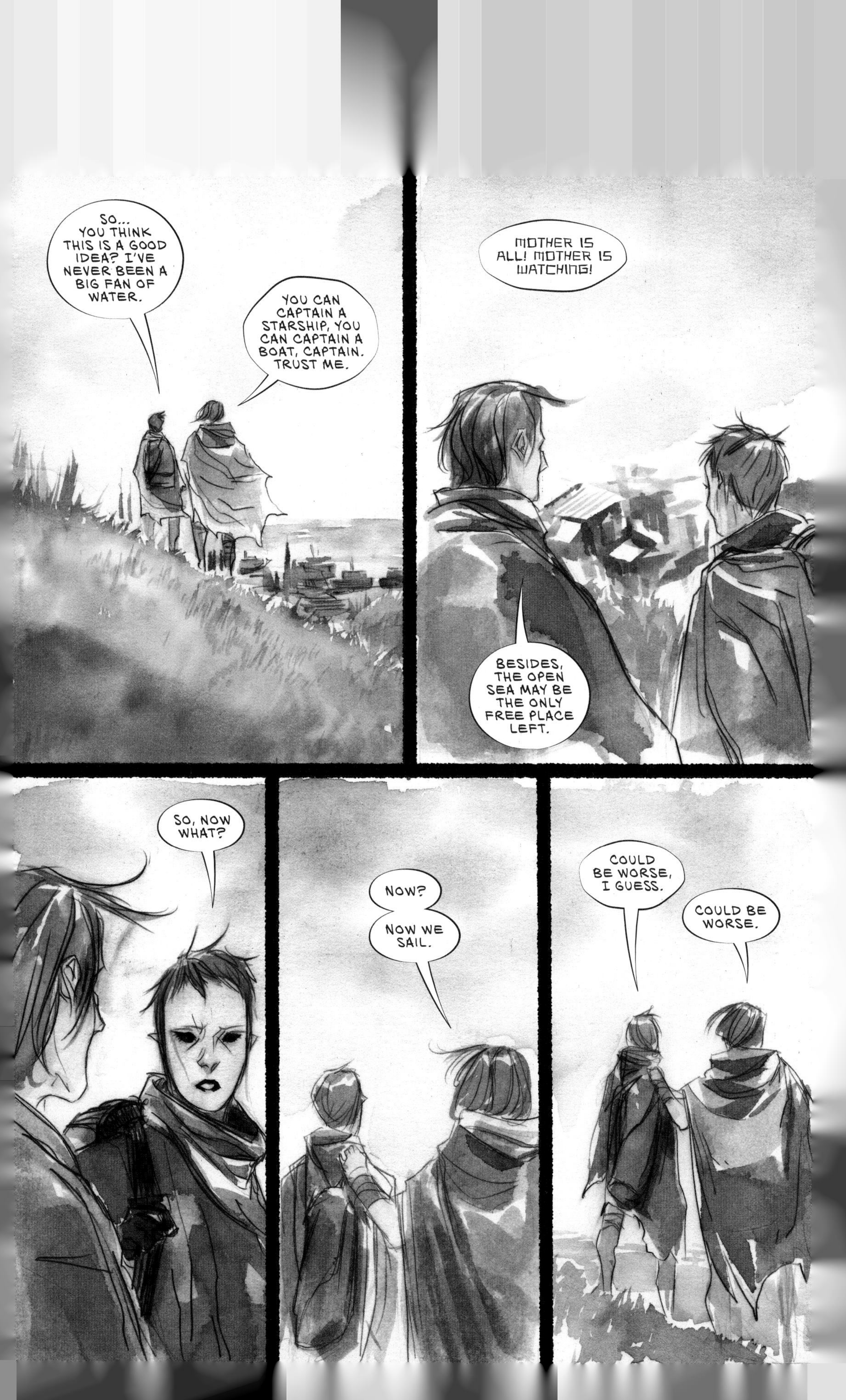
SO... YOU THINK THIS IS A GOOD IDEA? I'VE NEVER BEEN A BIG FAN OF WATER.
YOU CAN CAPTAIN A STARSHIP, YOU CAN CAPTAIN A BOAT, CAPTAIN. TRUST ME.
MOTHER IS ALL! MOTHER IS WATCHING!
BESIDES, THE OPEN SEA MAY BE THE ONLY FREE PLACE LEFT.
SO, NOW WHAT?
NOW?
NOW WE SAIL.
COULD BE WORSE, I GUESS.
COULD BE WORSE.

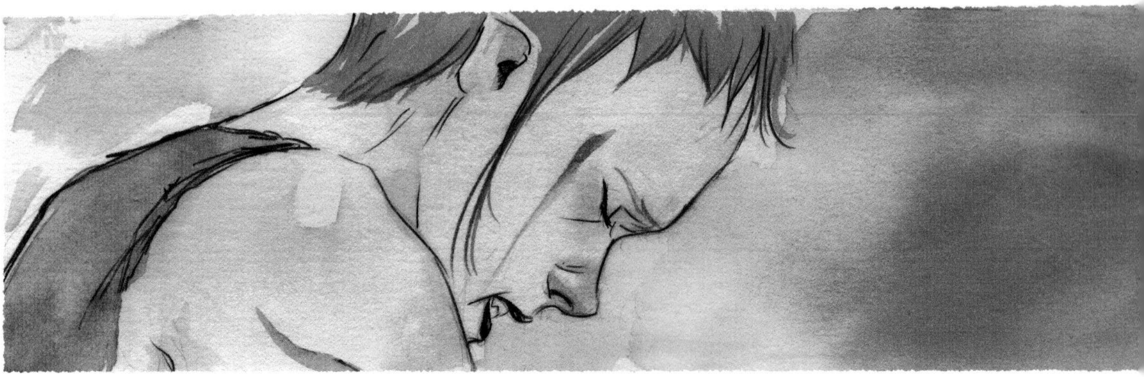

NOW. INSIDE THE BELLY OF THE WHALE.

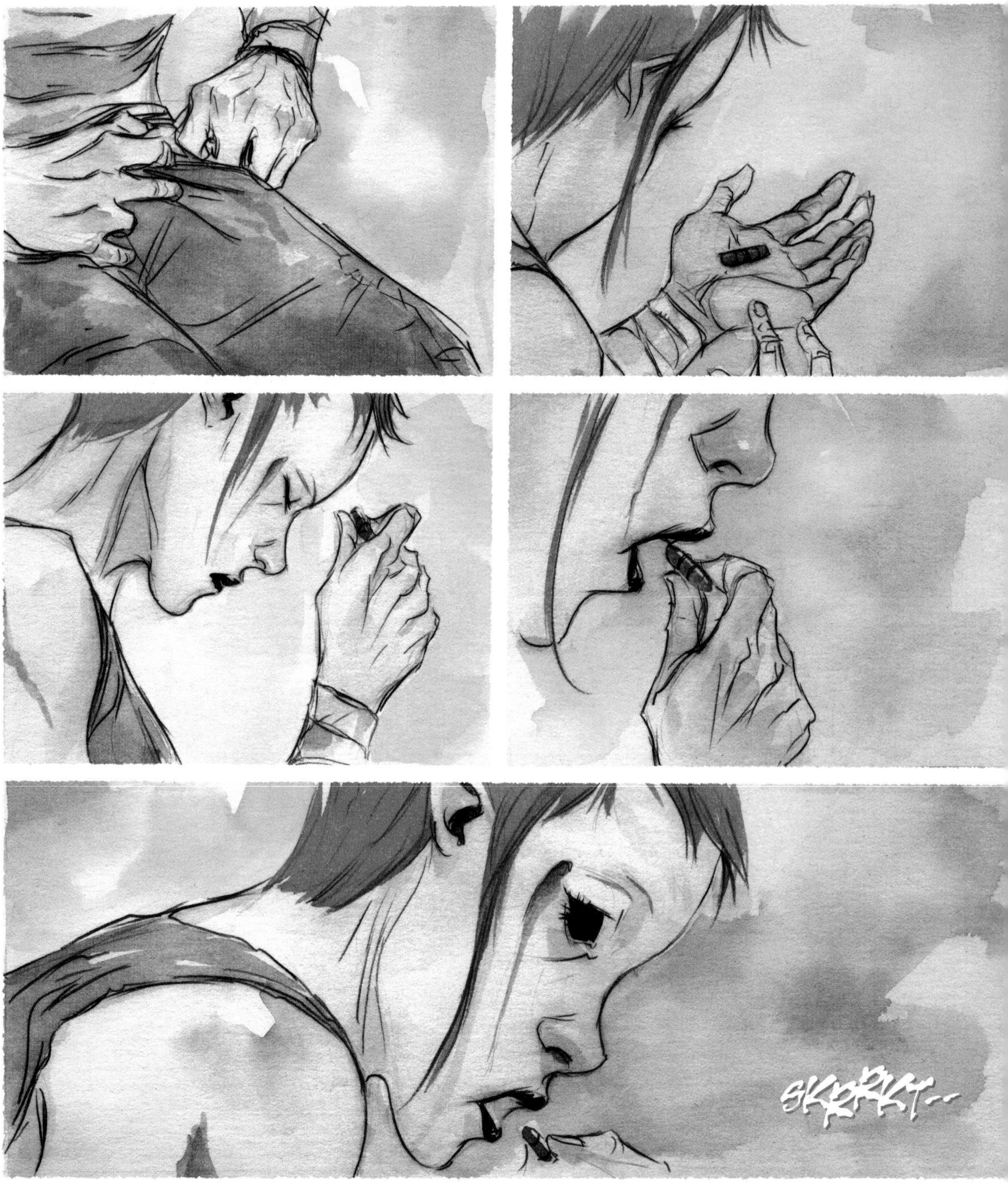
SKRRKT--

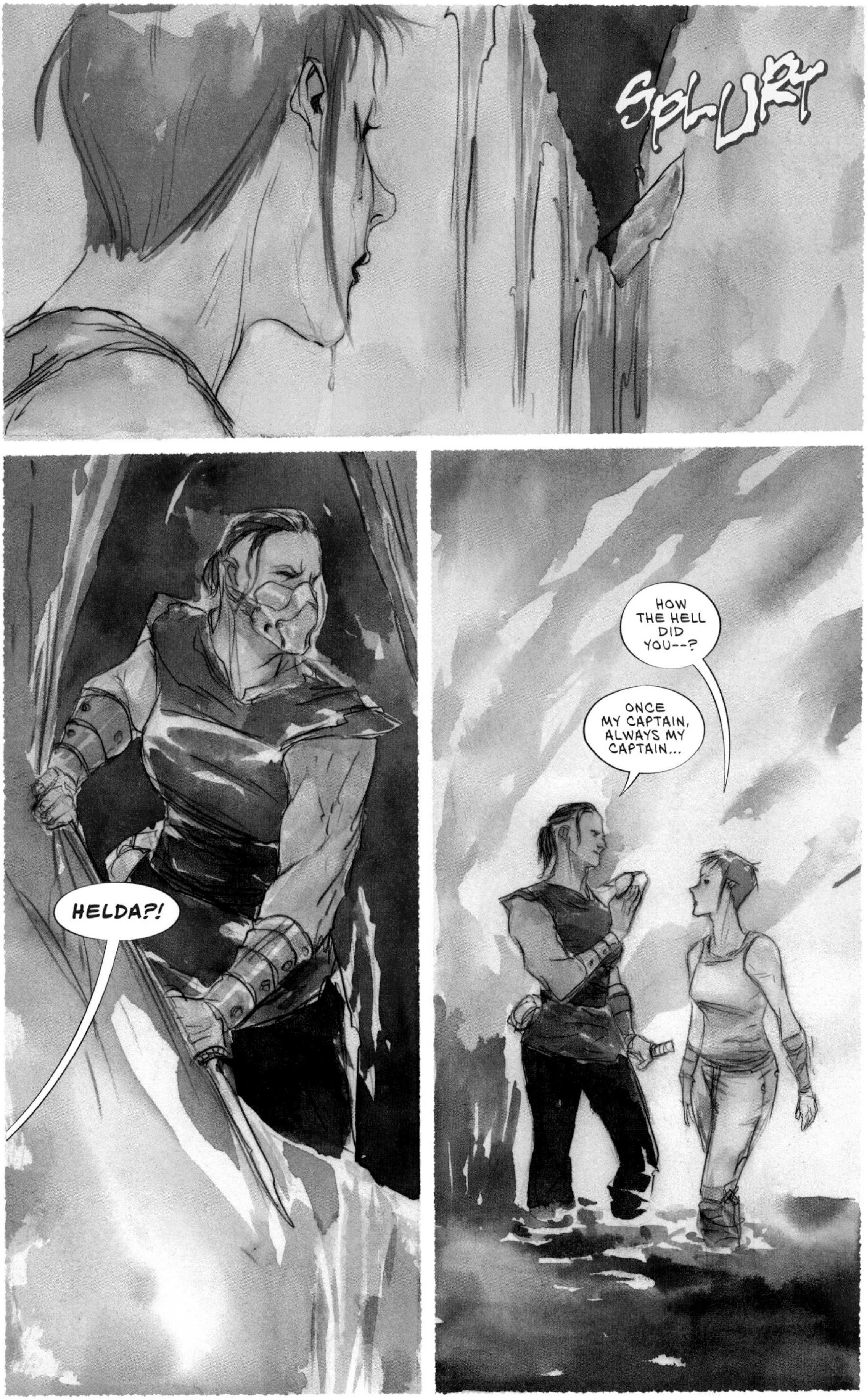
SPLURT
HELDA?!
HOW THE HELL DID YOU--?
ONCE MY CAPTAIN, ALWAYS MY CAPTAIN...

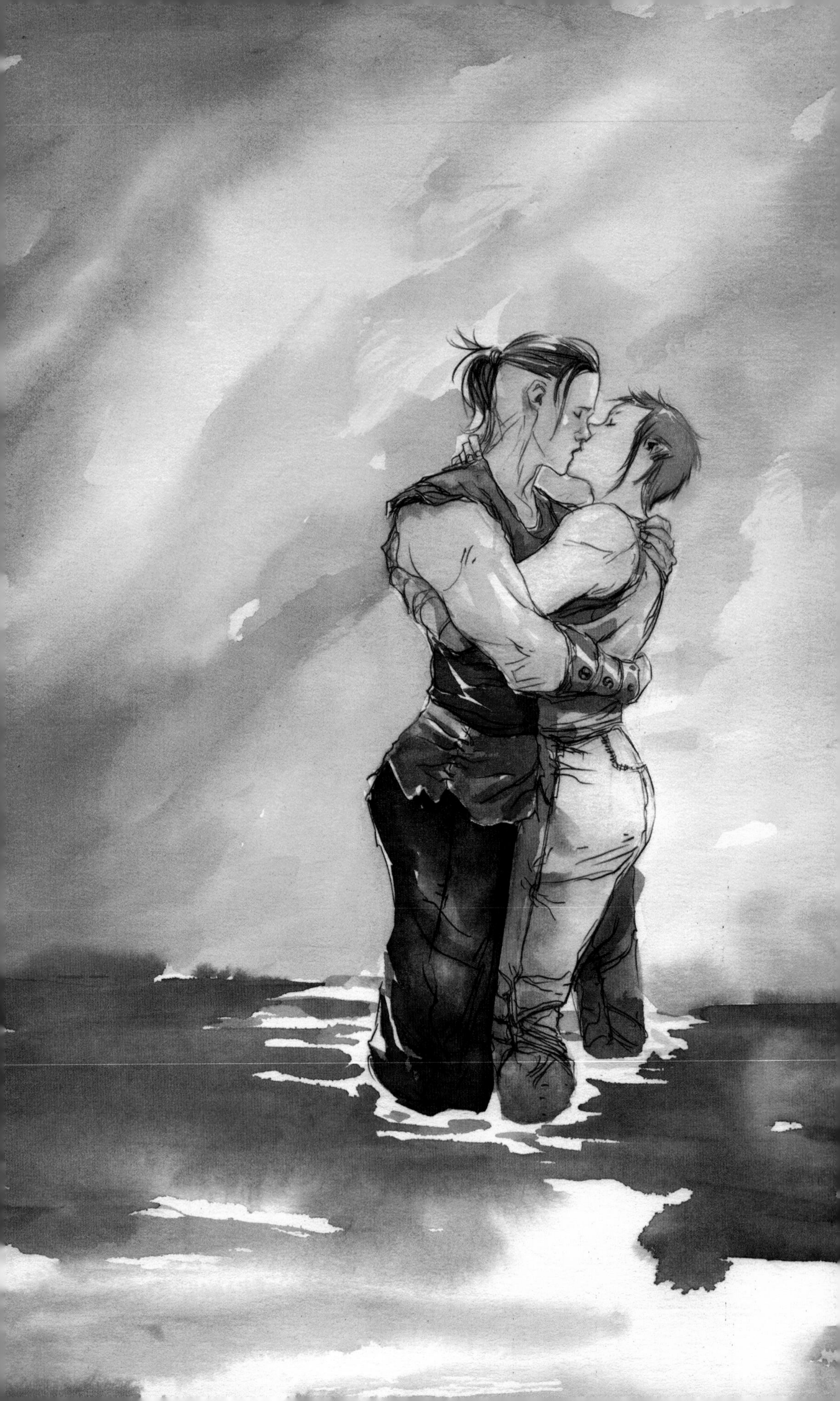

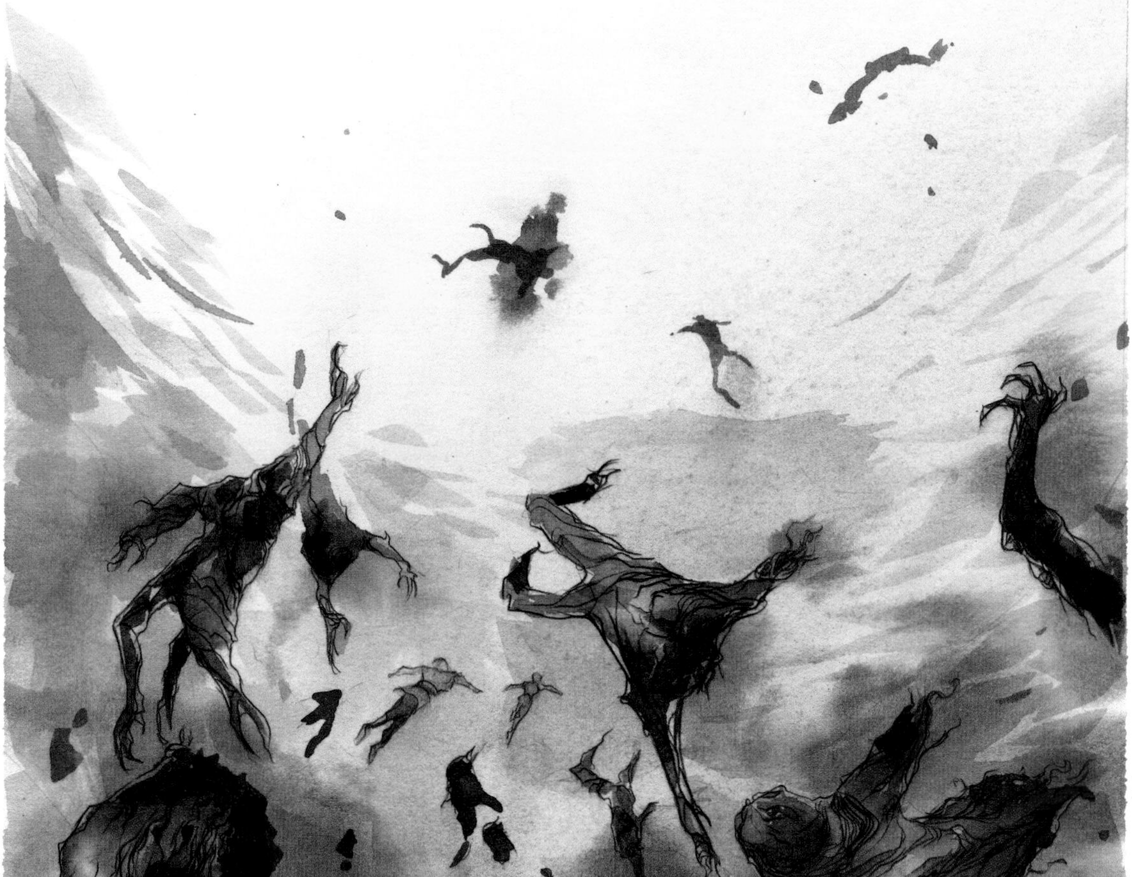

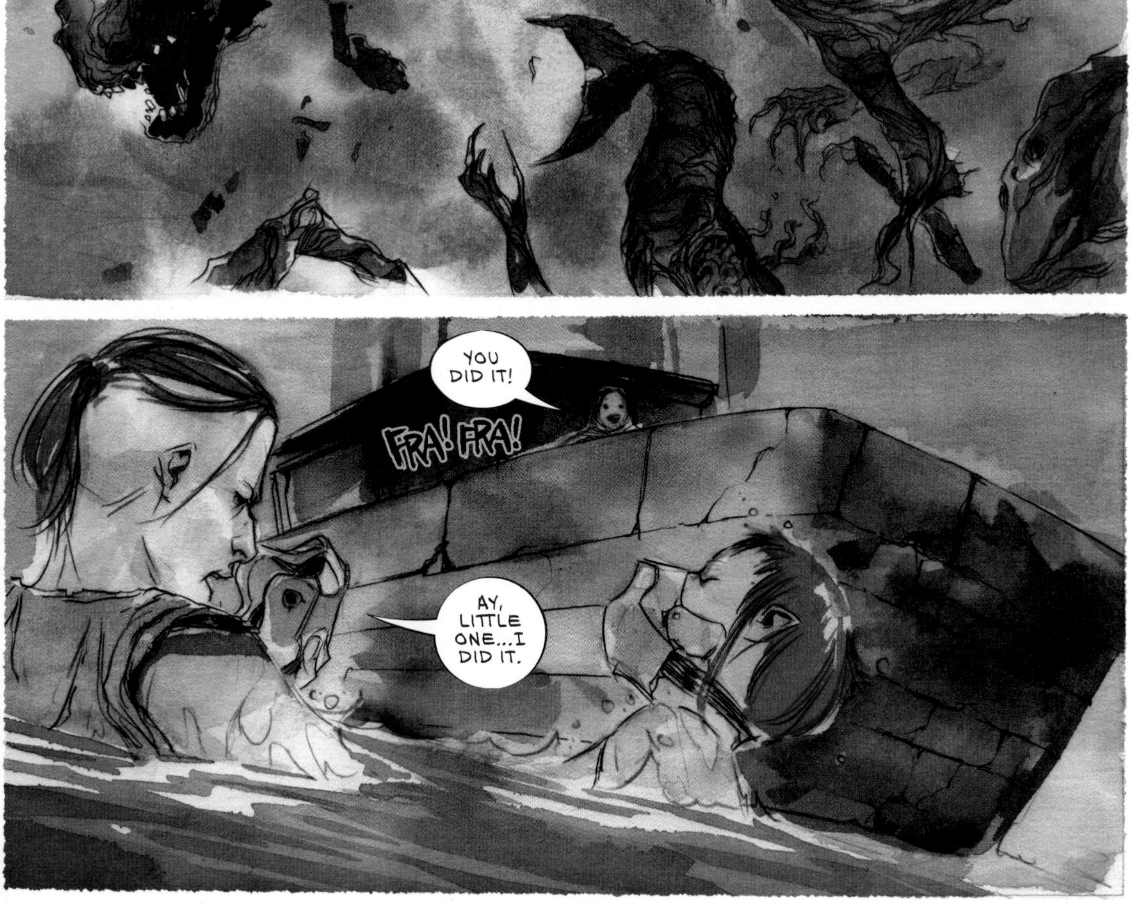
YOU DID IT!
FRA! FRA!
AY, LITTLE ONE...I DID IT.

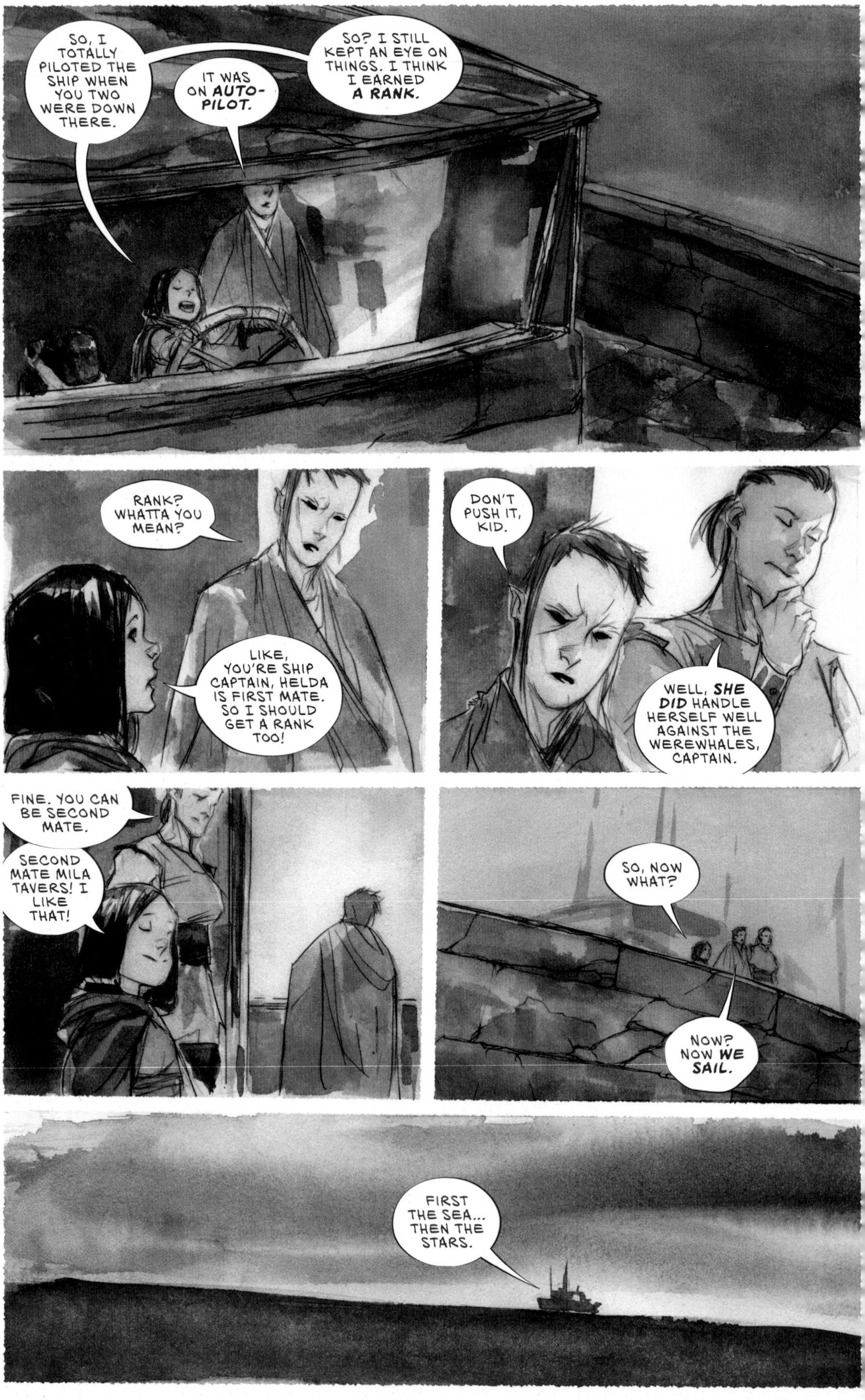

SO, I TOTALLY PILOTED THE SHIP WHEN YOU TWO WERE DOWN THERE.
IT WAS ON AUTO-PILOT.
SO? I STILL KEPT AN EYE ON THINGS. I THINK I EARNED A RANK.
RANK? WHATTA YOU MEAN?
LIKE, YOU'RE SHIP CAPTAIN, HELDA IS FIRST MATE. SO I SHOULD GET A RANK TOO!
DON'T PUSH IT, KID.
WELL, SHE DID HANDLE HERSELF WELL AGAINST THE WEREWHALES, CAPTAIN.
FINE. YOU CAN BE SECOND MATE.
SECOND MATE MILA TAVERS! I LIKE THAT!
SO, NOW WHAT?
NOW? NOW WE SAIL.
FIRST THE SEA... THEN THE STARS.

8

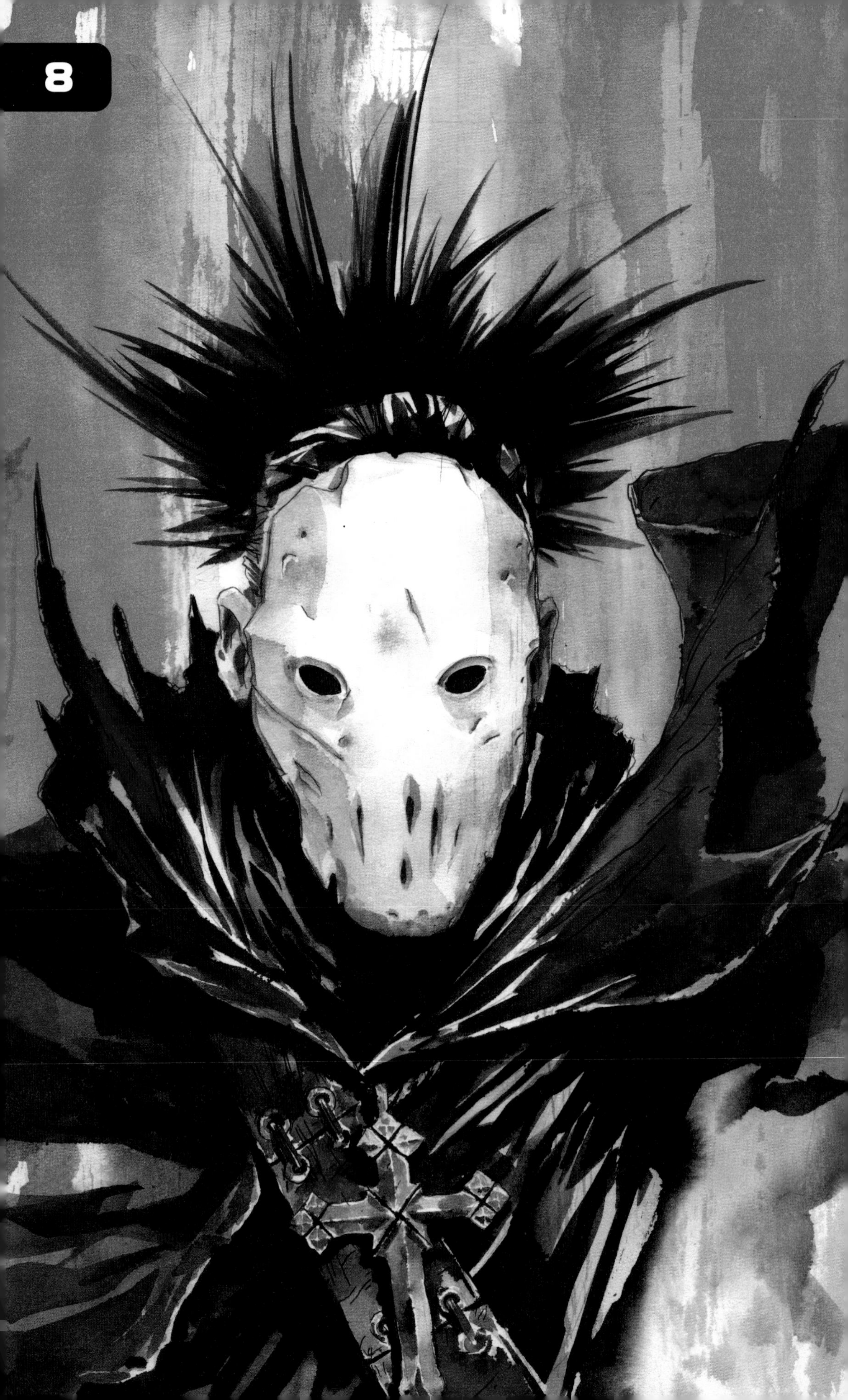

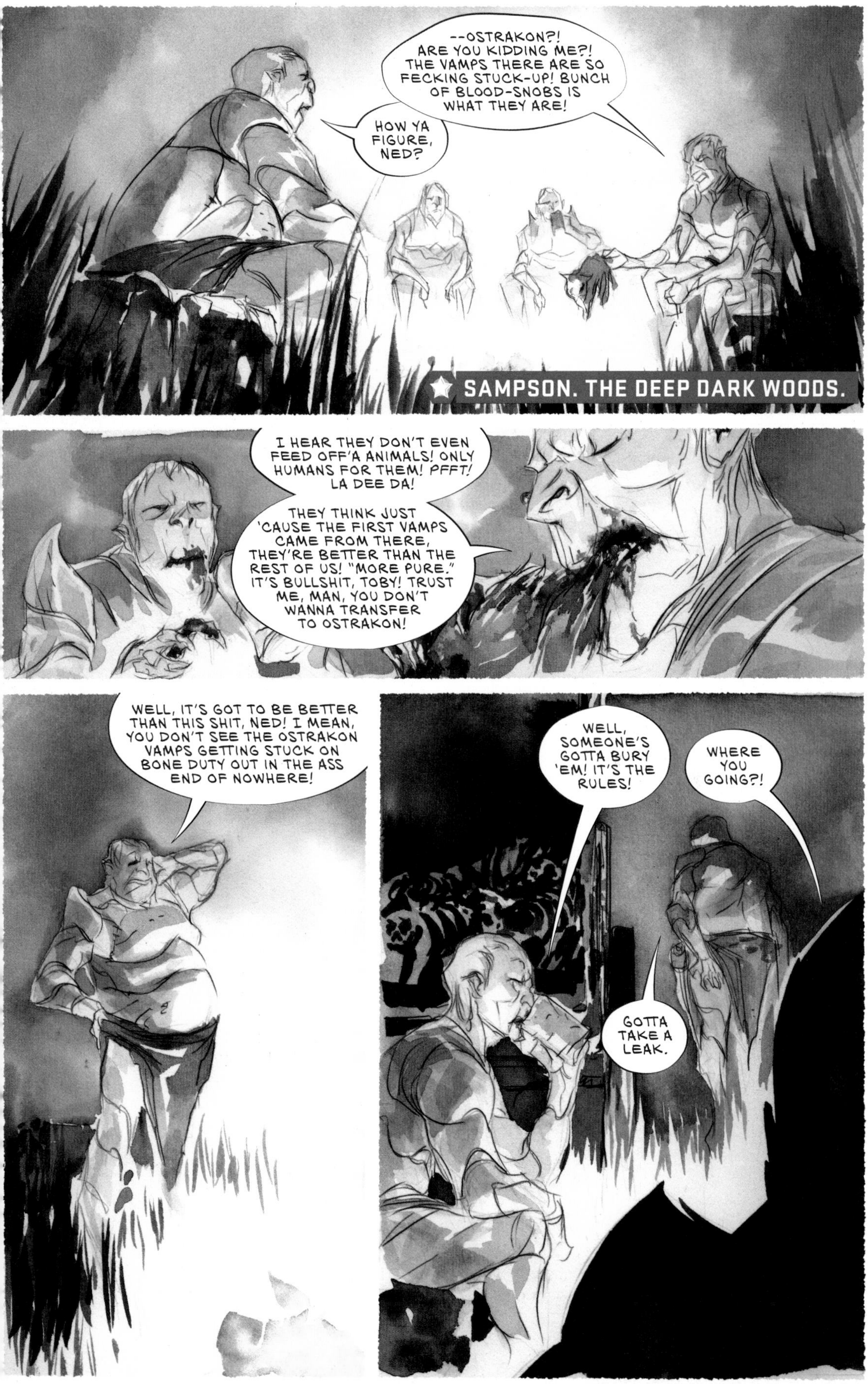
--OSTRAKON?! ARE YOU KIDDING ME?! THE VAMPS THERE ARE SO FECKING STUCK-UP! BUNCH OF BLOOD-SNOBS IS WHAT THEY ARE!
HOW YA FIGURE, NED?
SAMPSON. THE DEEP DARK WOODS.
I HEAR THEY DON'T EVEN FEED OFF'A ANIMALS! ONLY HUMANS FOR THEM! PFFT! LA DEE DA!
THEY THINK JUST 'CAUSE THE FIRST VAMPS CAME FROM THERE, THEY'RE BETTER THAN THE REST OF US! "MORE PURE." IT'S BULLSHIT, TOBY! TRUST ME, MAN, YOU DON'T WANNA TRANSFER TO OSTRAKON!
WELL, IT'S GOT TO BE BETTER THAN THIS SHIT, NED! I MEAN, YOU DON'T SEE THE OSTRAKON VAMPS GETTING STUCK ON BONE DUTY OUT IN THE ASS END OF NOWHERE!
WELL, SOMEONE'S GOTTA BURY 'EM! IT'S THE RULES!
WHERE YOU GOING?!
GOTTA TAKE A LEAK.

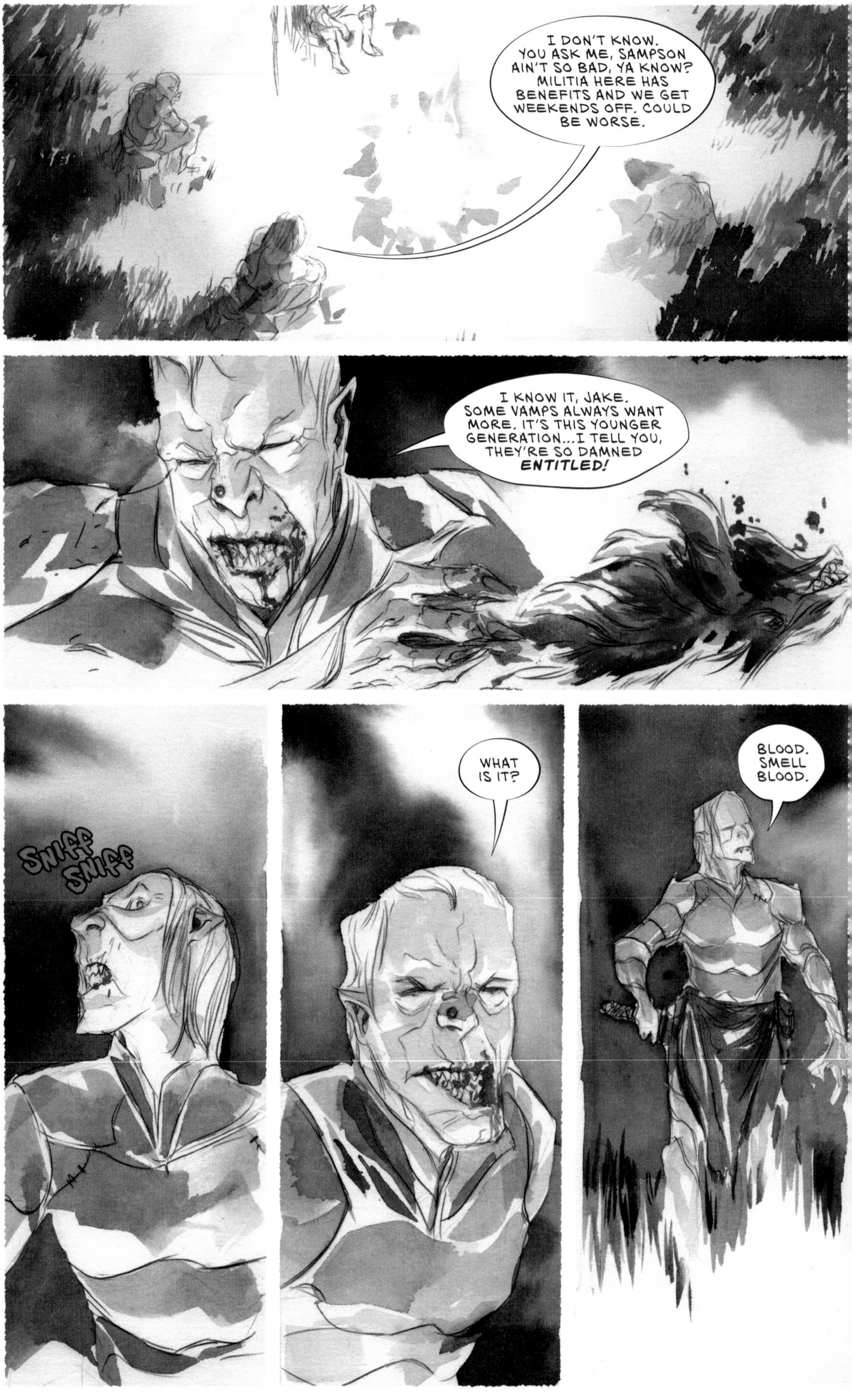
I DON'T KNOW. YOU ASK ME, SAMPSON AIN'T SO BAD, YA KNOW? MILITIA HERE HAS BENEFITS AND WE GET WEEKENDS OFF. COULD BE WORSE.
I KNOW IT, JAKE. SOME VAMPS ALWAYS WANT MORE. IT'S THIS YOUNGER GENERATION...I TELL YOU, THEY'RE SO DAMNED **ENTITLED!**
SNIFF SNIFF
WHAT IS IT?
BLOOD. SMELL BLOOD.

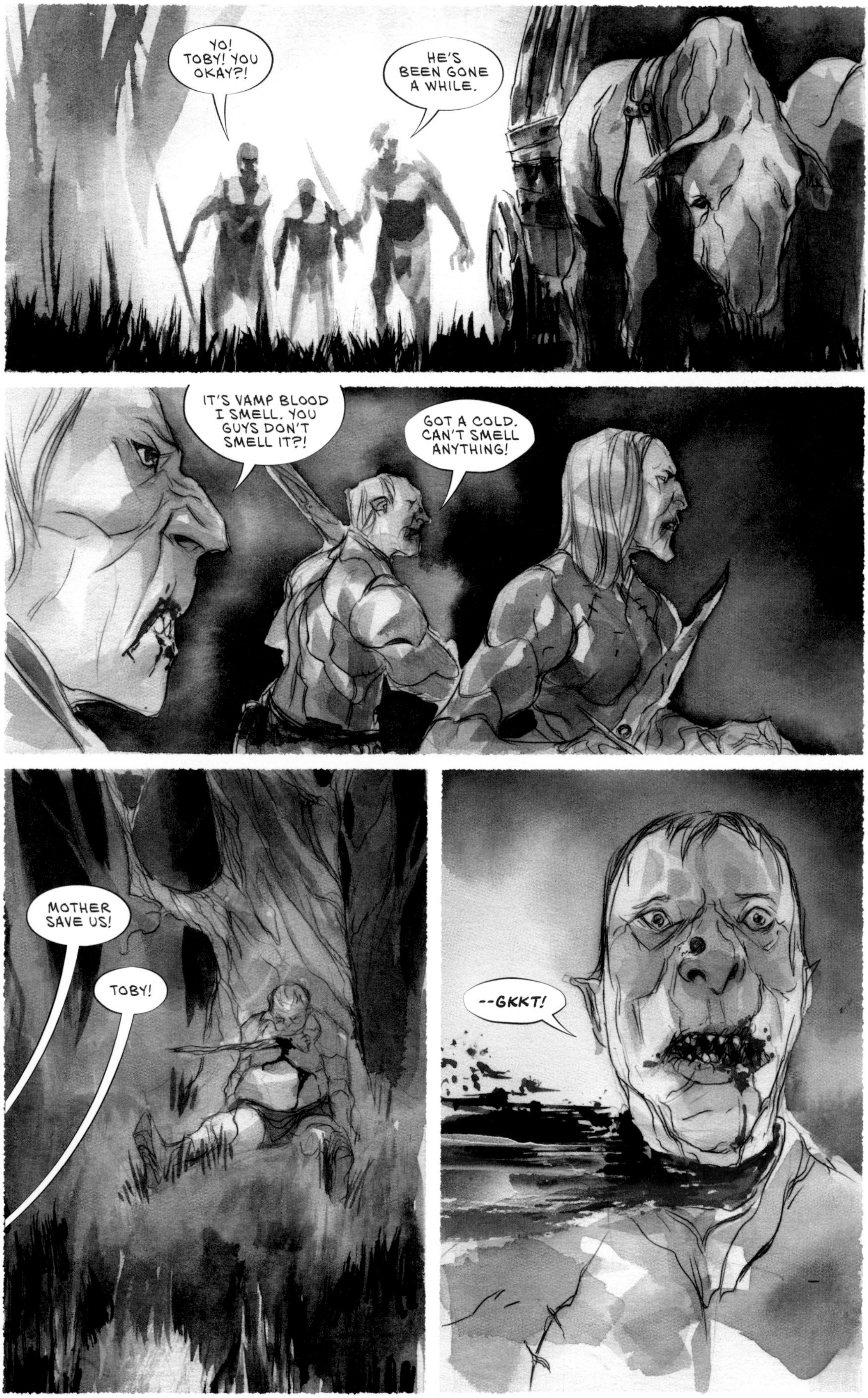
YO! TOBY! YOU OKAY?!
HE'S BEEN GONE A WHILE.
IT'S VAMP BLOOD I SMELL. YOU GUYS DON'T SMELL IT?!
GOT A COLD. CAN'T SMELL ANYTHING!
MOTHER SAVE US!
TOBY!
--GKKT!

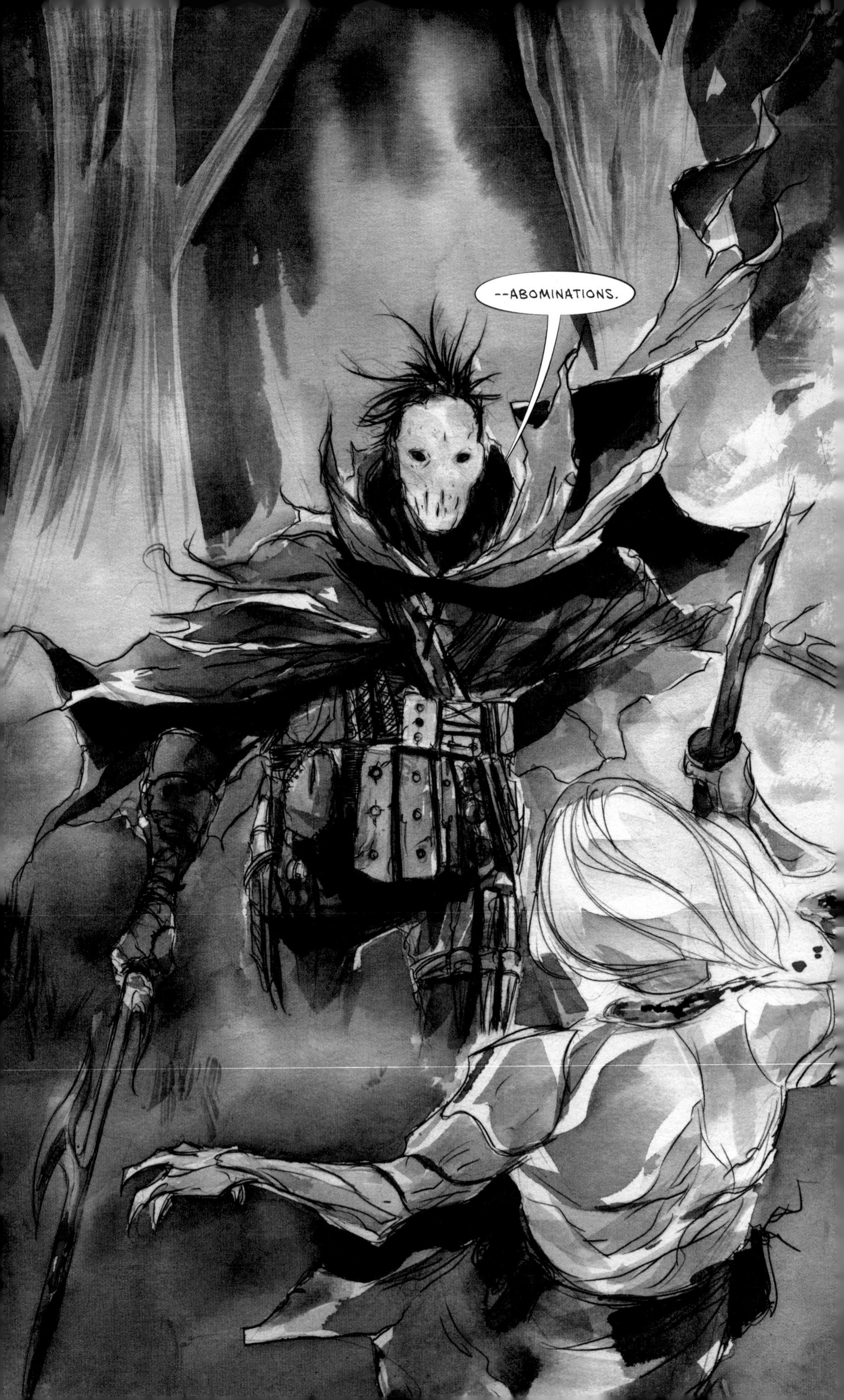
--ABOMINATIONS.

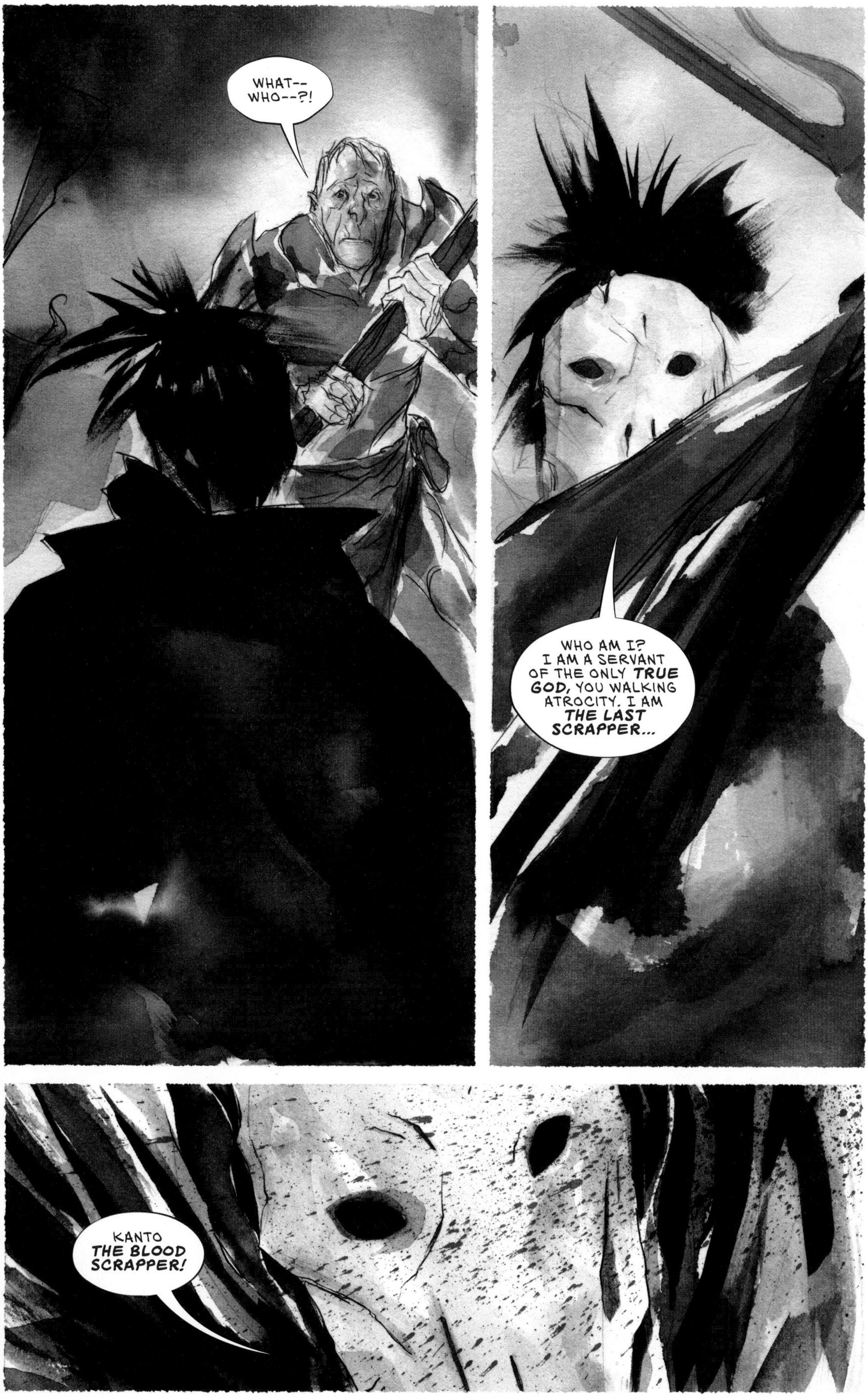
WHAT--
WHO--?!
WHO AM I? I AM A SERVANT OF THE ONLY **TRUE GOD,** YOU WALKING ATROCITY. I AM ***THE LAST* SCRAPPER...**
KANTO ***THE BLOOD* SCRAPPER!**

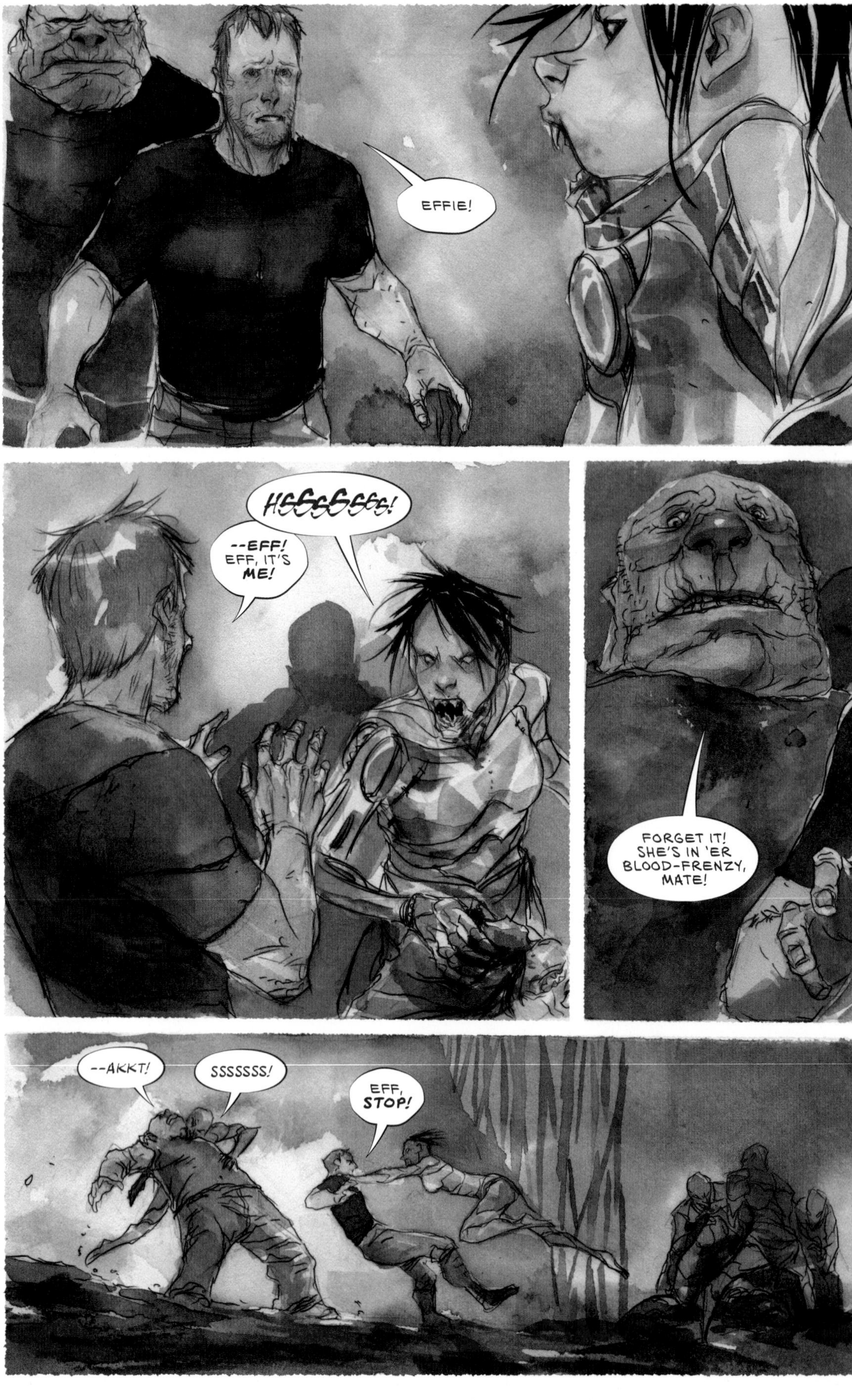
EFFIE!
HSSSSSSS!
--EFF! EFF, IT'S ME!
FORGET IT! SHE'S IN 'ER BLOOD-FRENZY, MATE!
--AKKT!
SSSSSSS!
EFF, STOP!

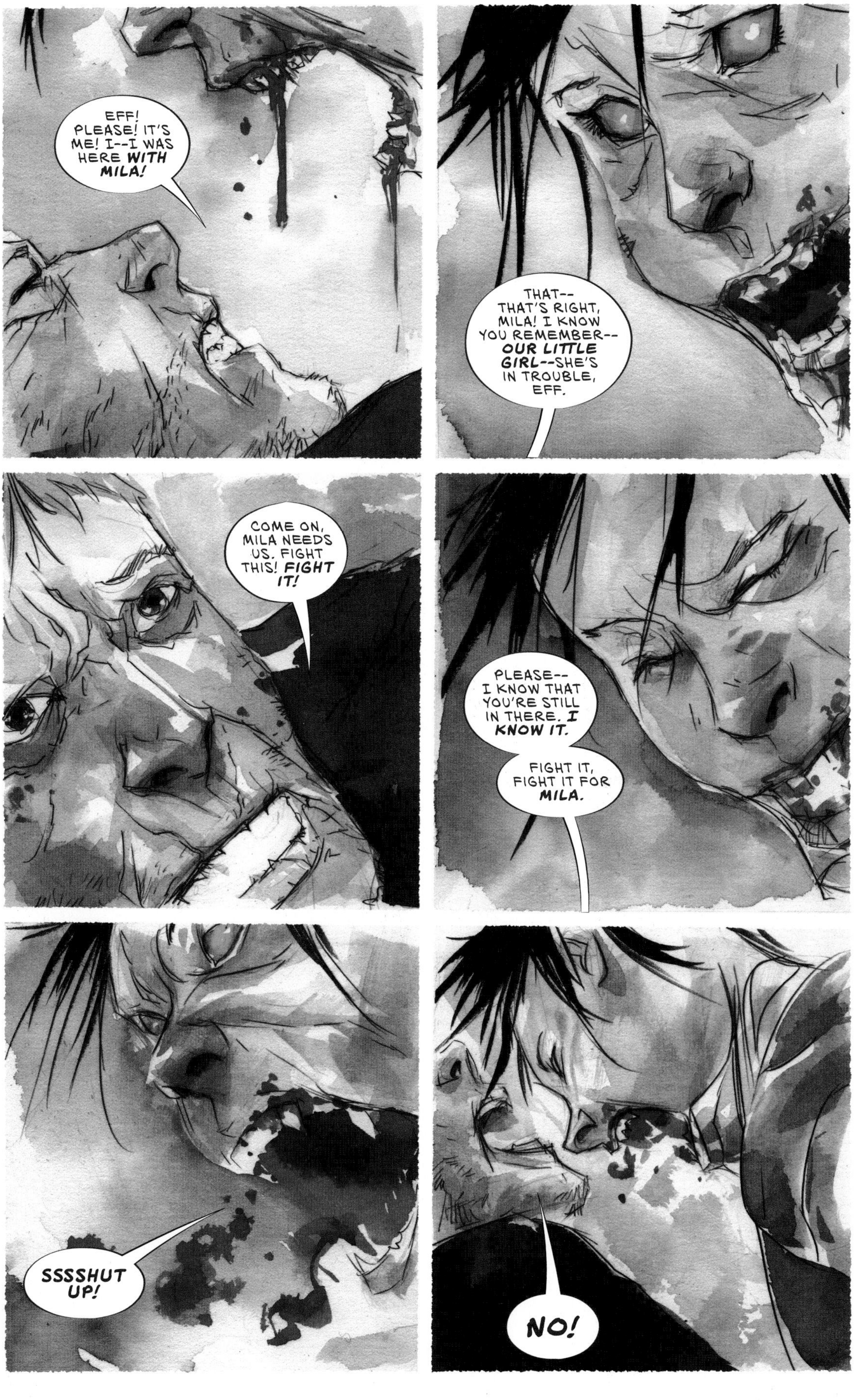
EFF! PLEASE! IT'S ME! I--I WAS HERE WITH MILA!
THAT-- THAT'S RIGHT, MILA! I KNOW YOU REMEMBER-- OUR LITTLE GIRL--SHE'S IN TROUBLE, EFF.
COME ON, MILA NEEDS US. FIGHT THIS! FIGHT IT!
PLEASE-- I KNOW THAT YOU'RE STILL IN THERE. I KNOW IT.
FIGHT IT, FIGHT IT FOR MILA.
SSSSHUT UP!
NO!

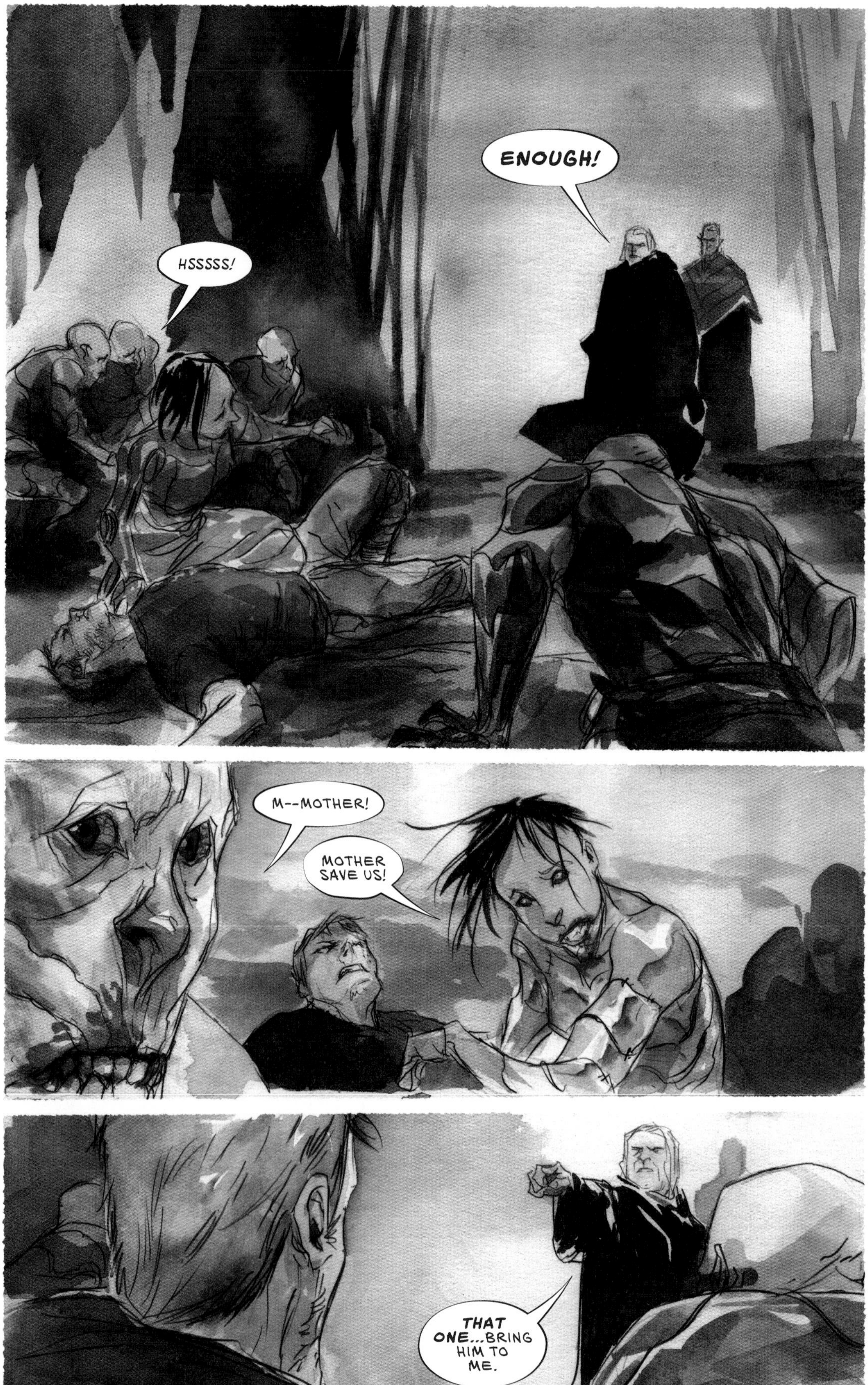
ENOUGH!
HSSSSS!
M--MOTHER!
MOTHER SAVE US!
THAT ONE...BRING HIM TO ME.

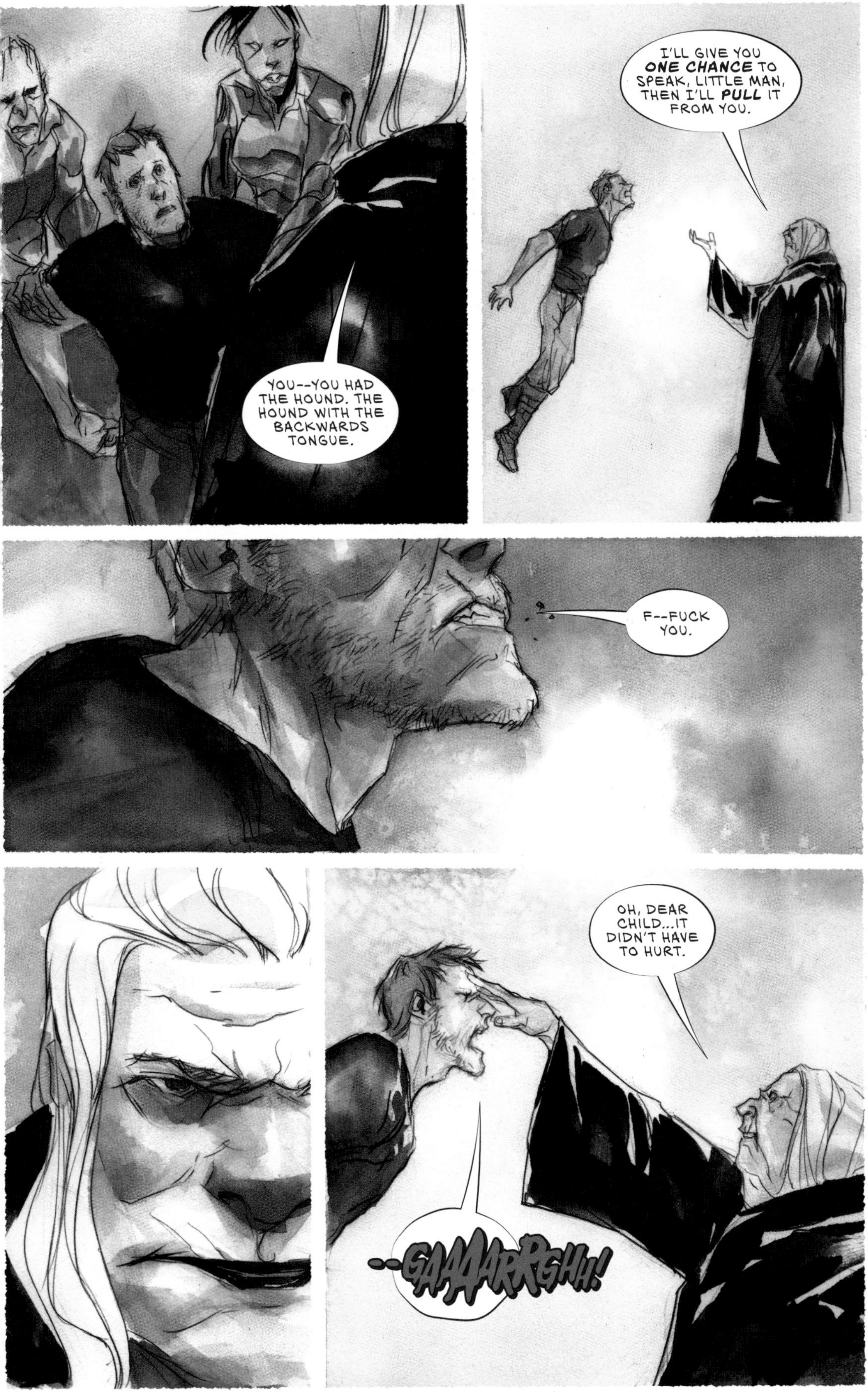
YOU--YOU HAD THE HOUND. THE HOUND WITH THE BACKWARDS TONGUE.
I'LL GIVE YOU ONE CHANCE TO SPEAK, LITTLE MAN, THEN I'LL PULL IT FROM YOU.
F--FUCK YOU.
OH, DEAR CHILD...IT DIDN'T HAVE TO HURT.
--GAAAARRGHH!

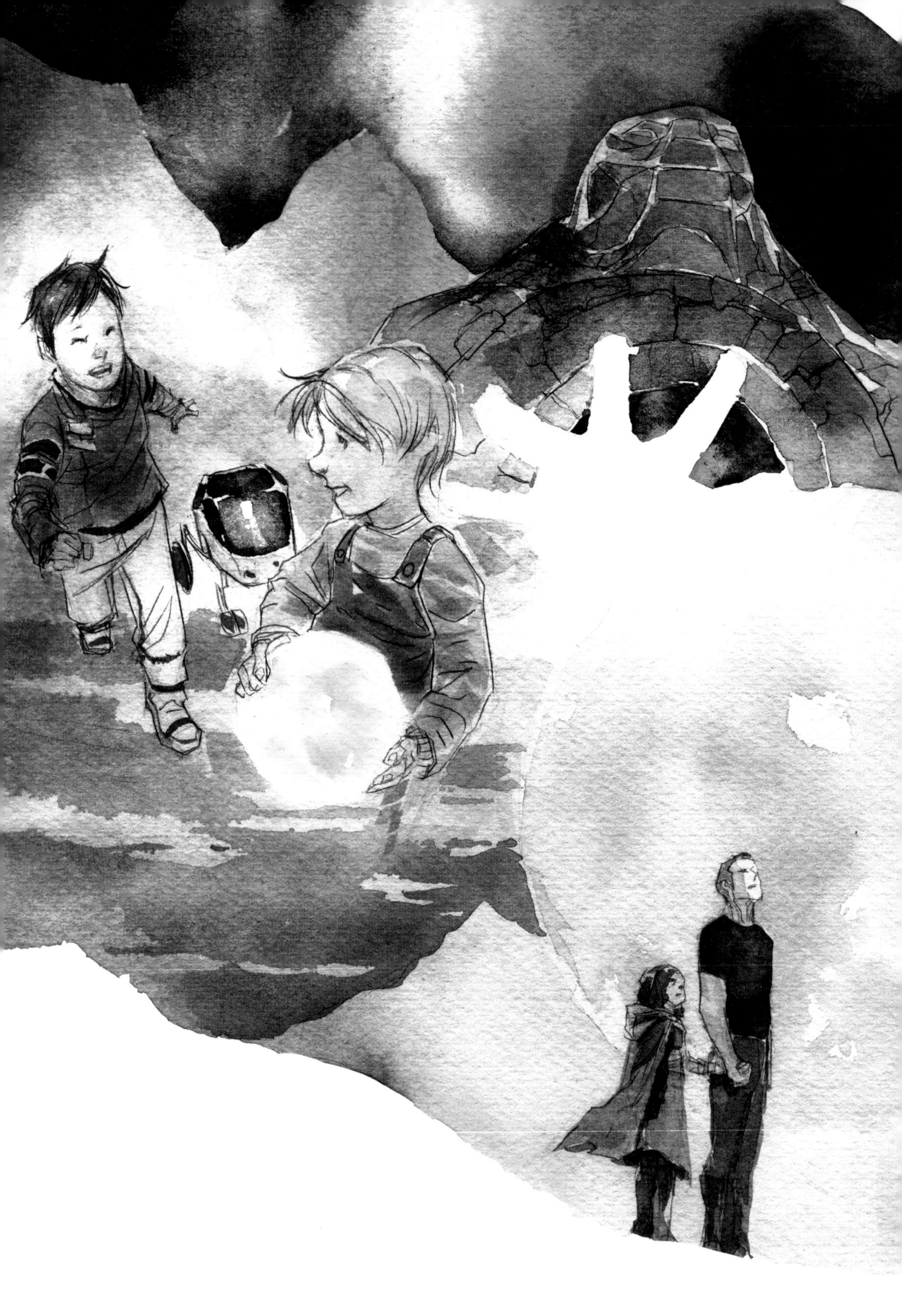

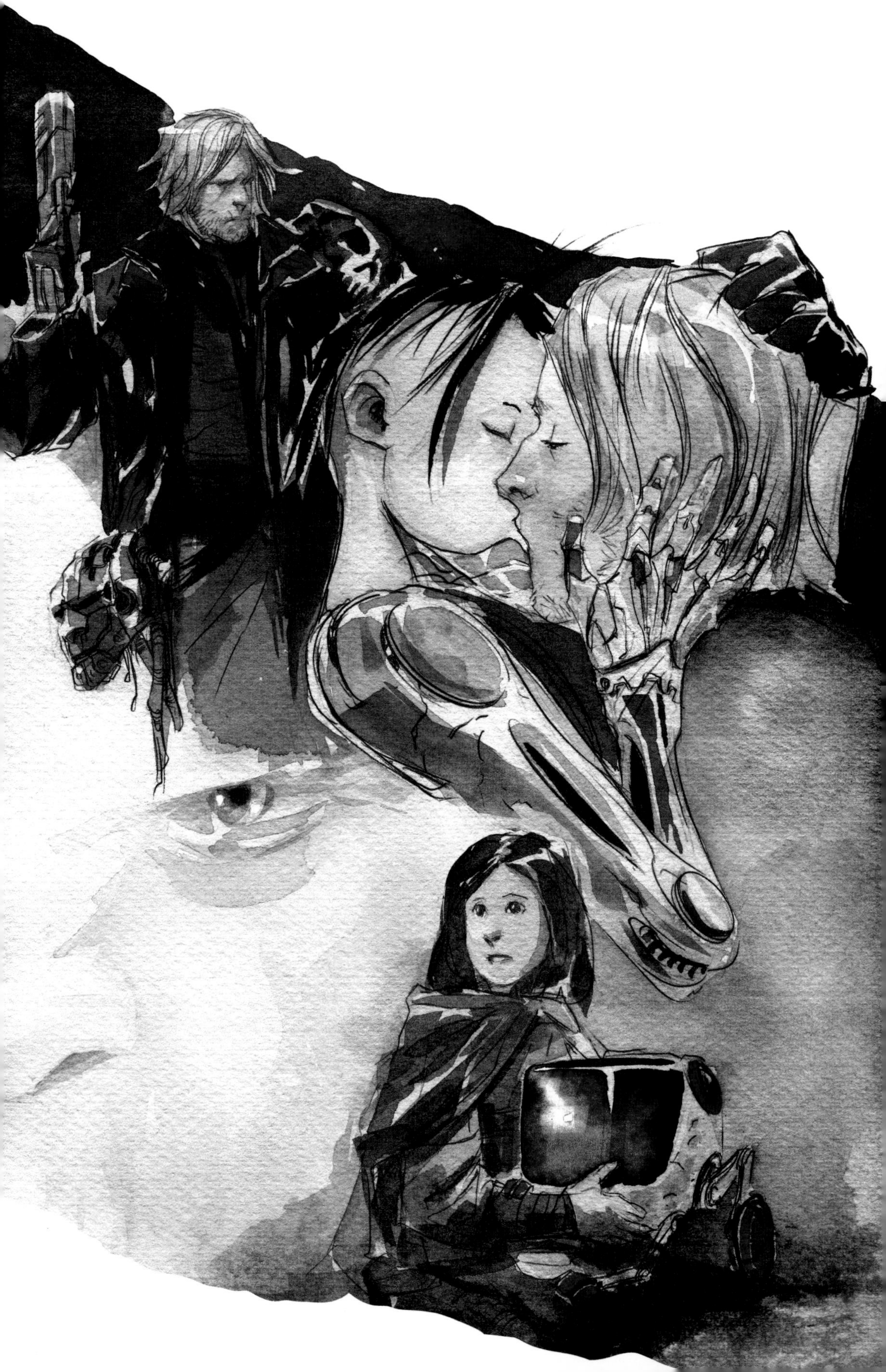

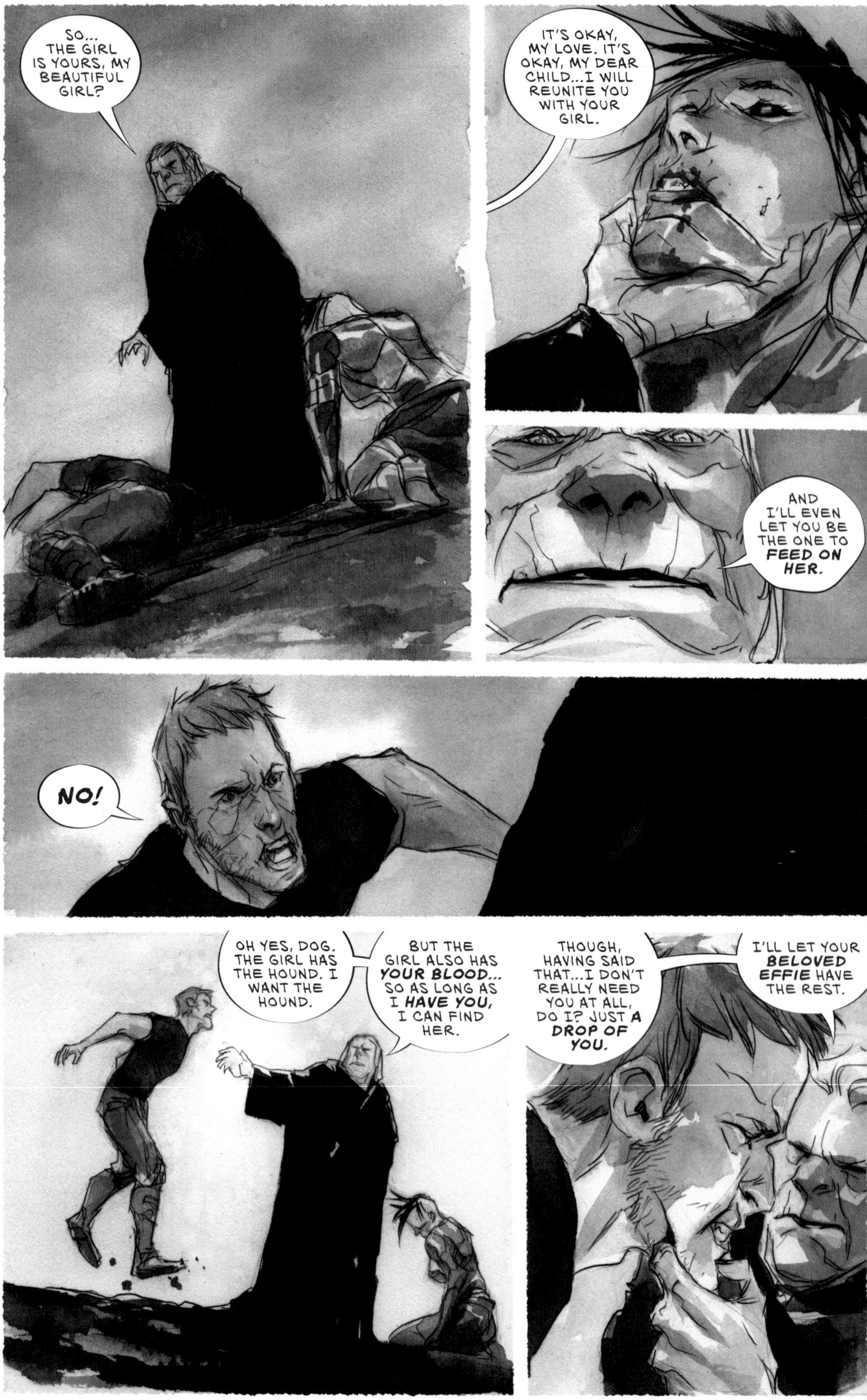
SO... THE GIRL IS YOURS, MY BEAUTIFUL GIRL?
IT'S OKAY, MY LOVE. IT'S OKAY, MY DEAR CHILD...I WILL REUNITE YOU WITH YOUR GIRL.
AND I'LL EVEN LET YOU BE THE ONE TO **FEED ON HER.**
NO!
OH YES, DOG. THE GIRL HAS THE HOUND. I WANT THE HOUND.
BUT THE GIRL ALSO HAS **YOUR BLOOD...** SO AS LONG AS I **HAVE YOU,** I CAN FIND HER.
THOUGH, HAVING SAID THAT...I DON'T REALLY NEED YOU AT ALL, DO I? JUST **A DROP OF YOU.**
I'LL LET YOUR **BELOVED EFFIE** HAVE THE REST.

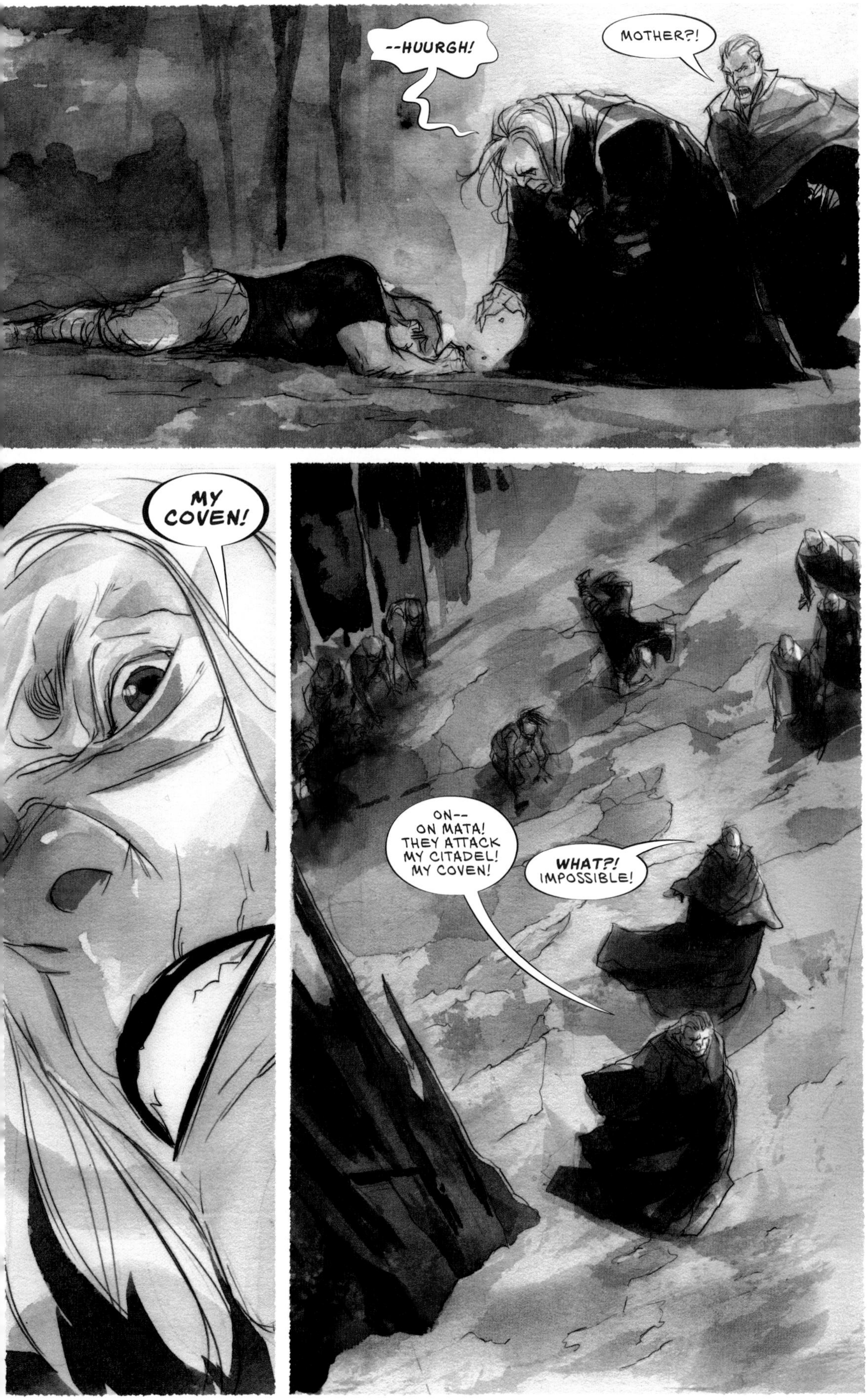
--HUURGH!
MOTHER?!
MY COVEN!
ON--
ON MATA!
THEY ATTACK
MY CITADEL!
MY COVEN!
WHAT?!
IMPOSSIBLE!

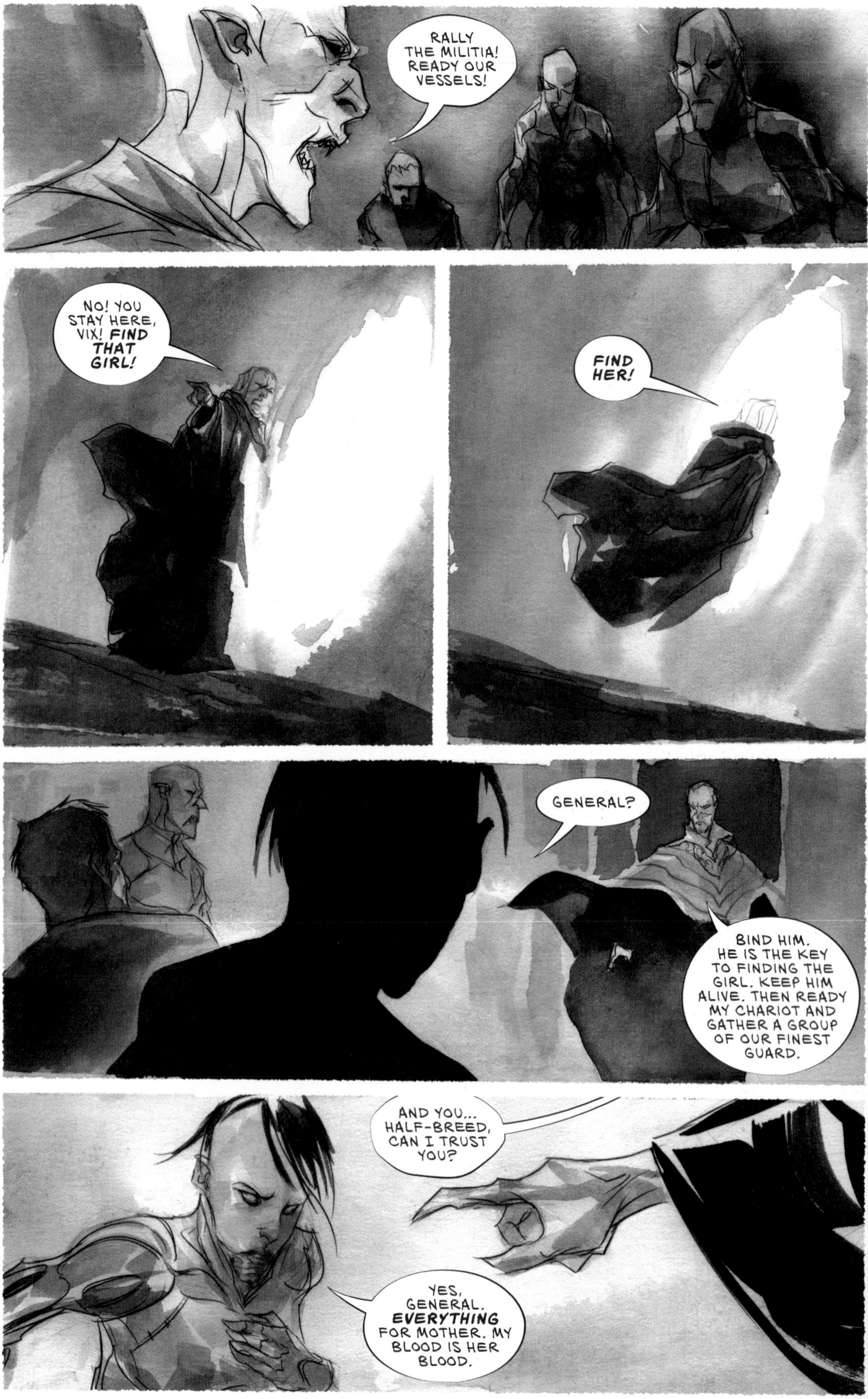
RALLY THE MILITIA! READY OUR VESSELS!
NO! YOU STAY HERE, VIX! **FIND THAT GIRL!**
FIND HER!
GENERAL?
BIND HIM. HE IS THE KEY TO FINDING THE GIRL. KEEP HIM ALIVE. THEN READY MY CHARIOT AND GATHER A GROUP OF OUR FINEST GUARD.
AND YOU... HALF-BREED, CAN I TRUST YOU?
YES, GENERAL. **EVERYTHING** FOR MOTHER. MY BLOOD IS HER BLOOD.

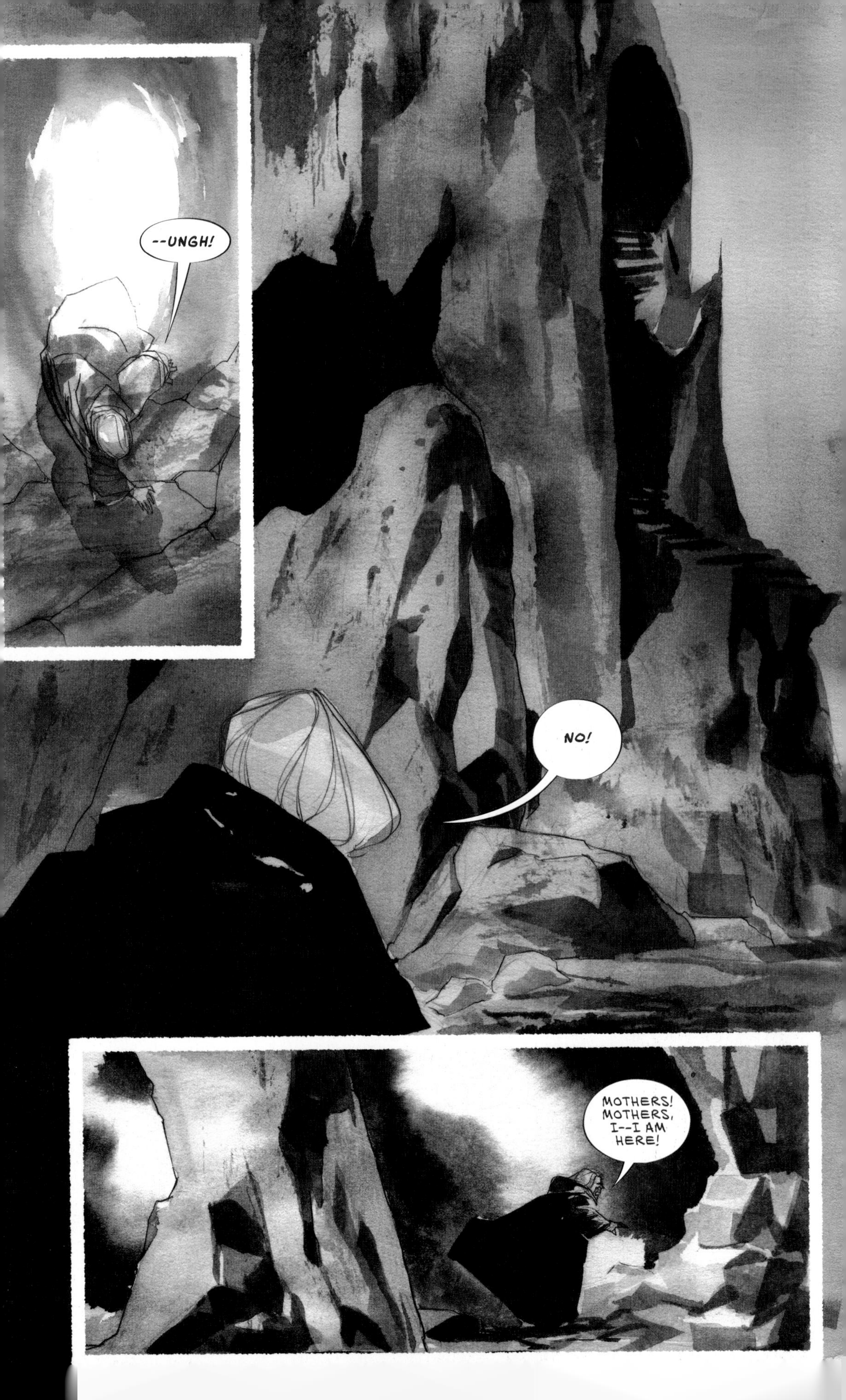
--UNGH!
NO!
MOTHERS! MOTHERS, I--I AM HERE!

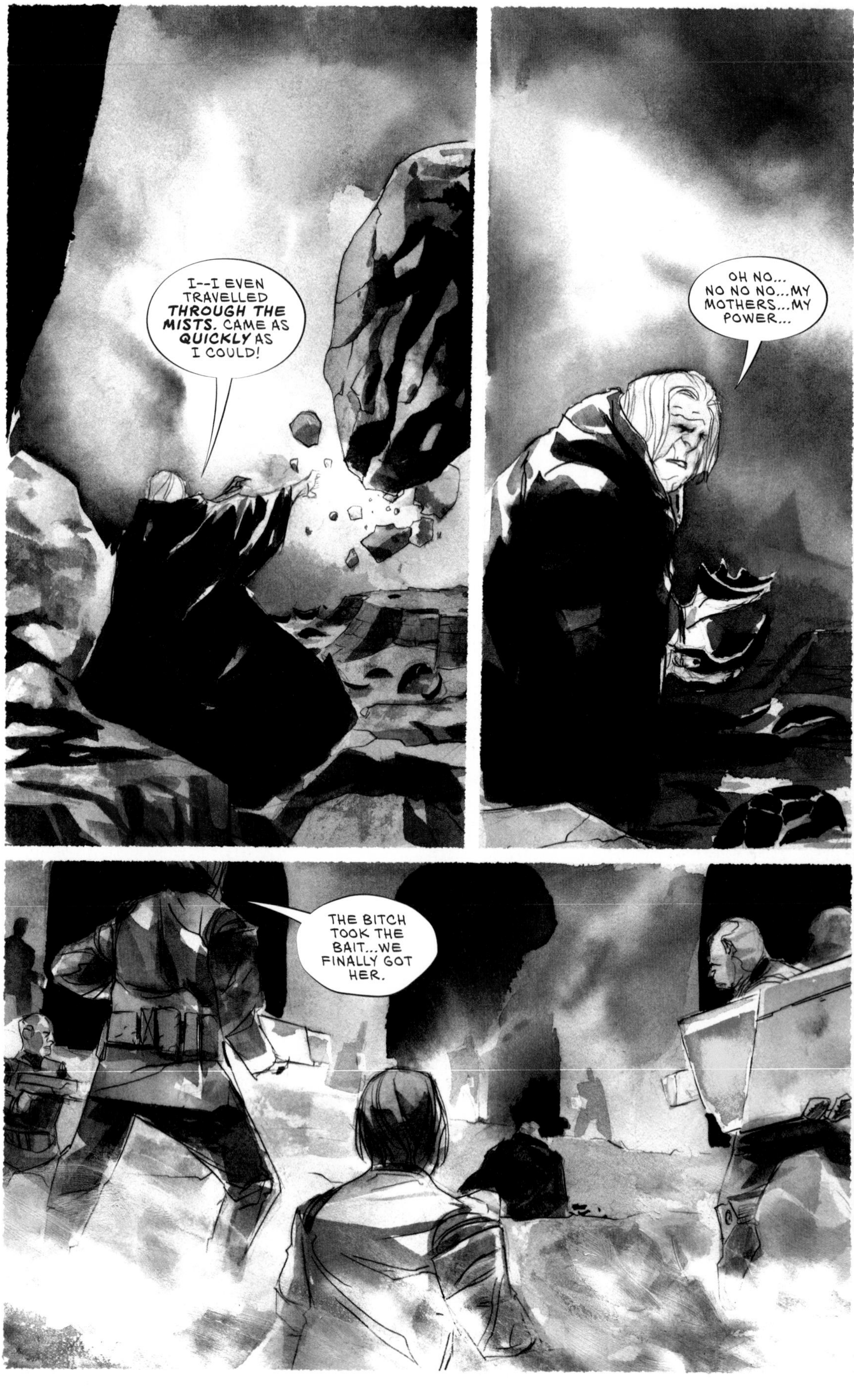
I--I EVEN TRAVELLED **THROUGH THE MISTS.** CAME AS **QUICKLY** AS I COULD!
OH NO... NO NO NO... MY MOTHERS... MY POWER...
THE BITCH TOOK THE BAIT... WE FINALLY GOT HER.

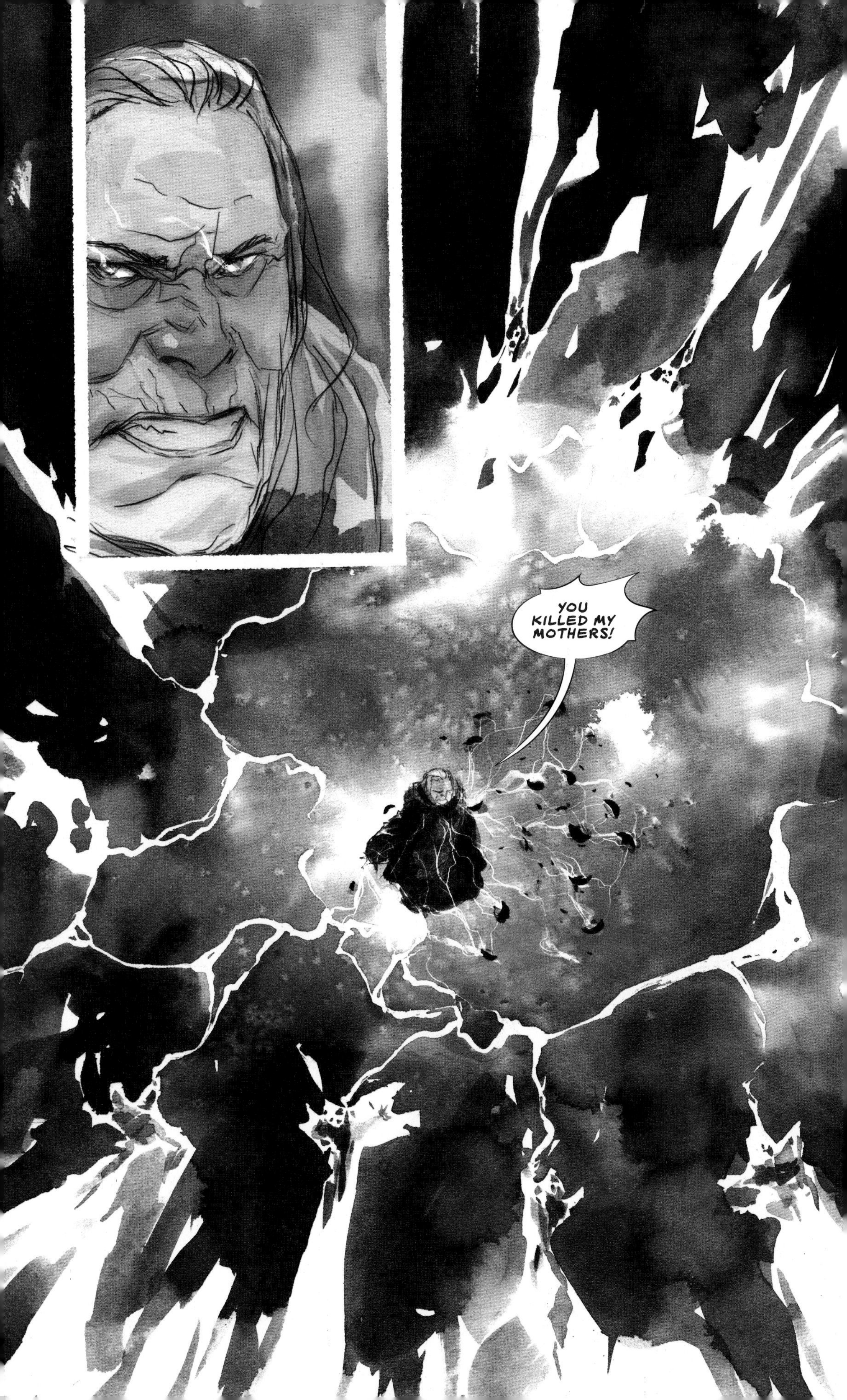
YOU KILLED MY MOTHERS!

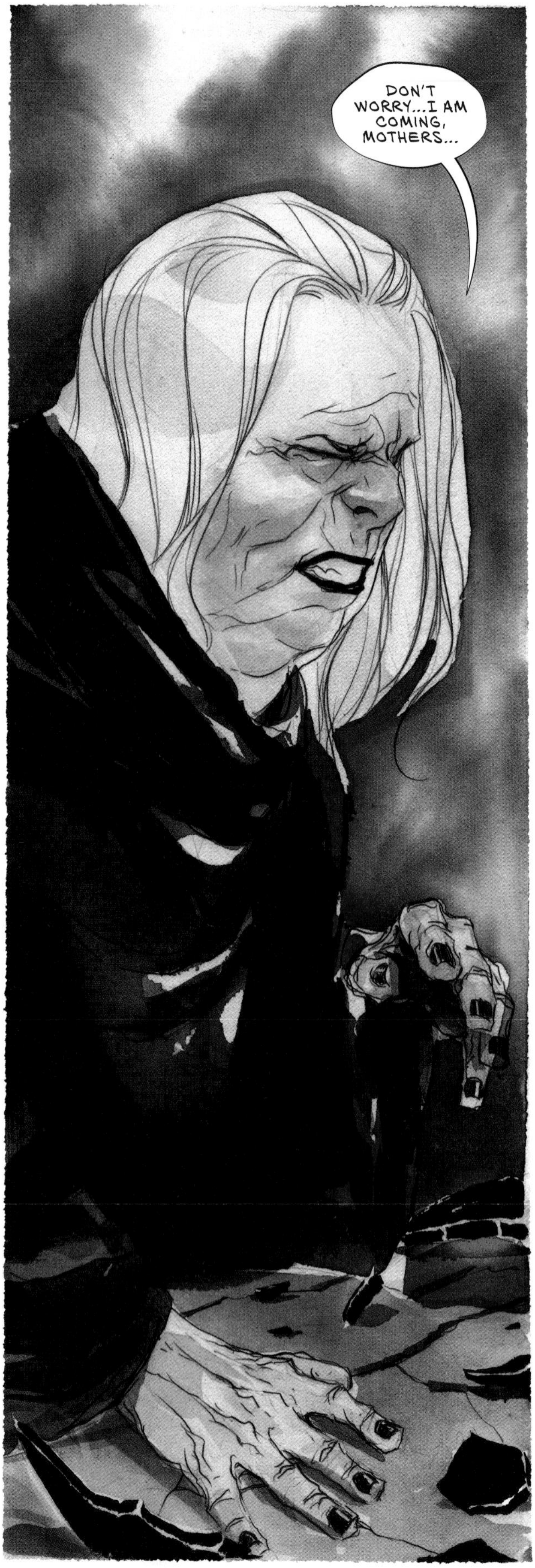
DON'T WORRY...I AM COMING, MOTHERS...

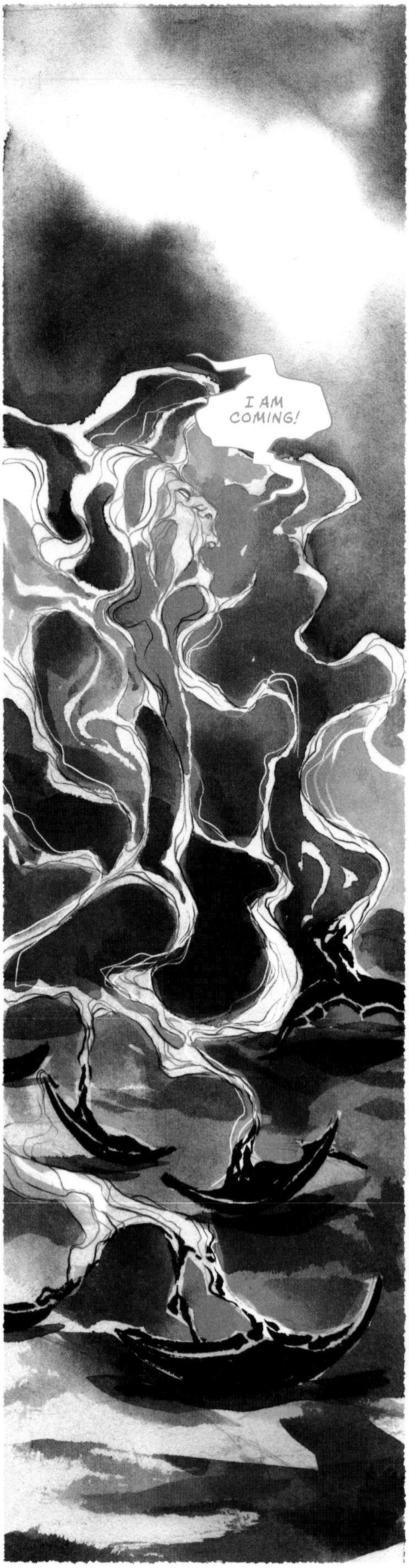
I AM COMING!

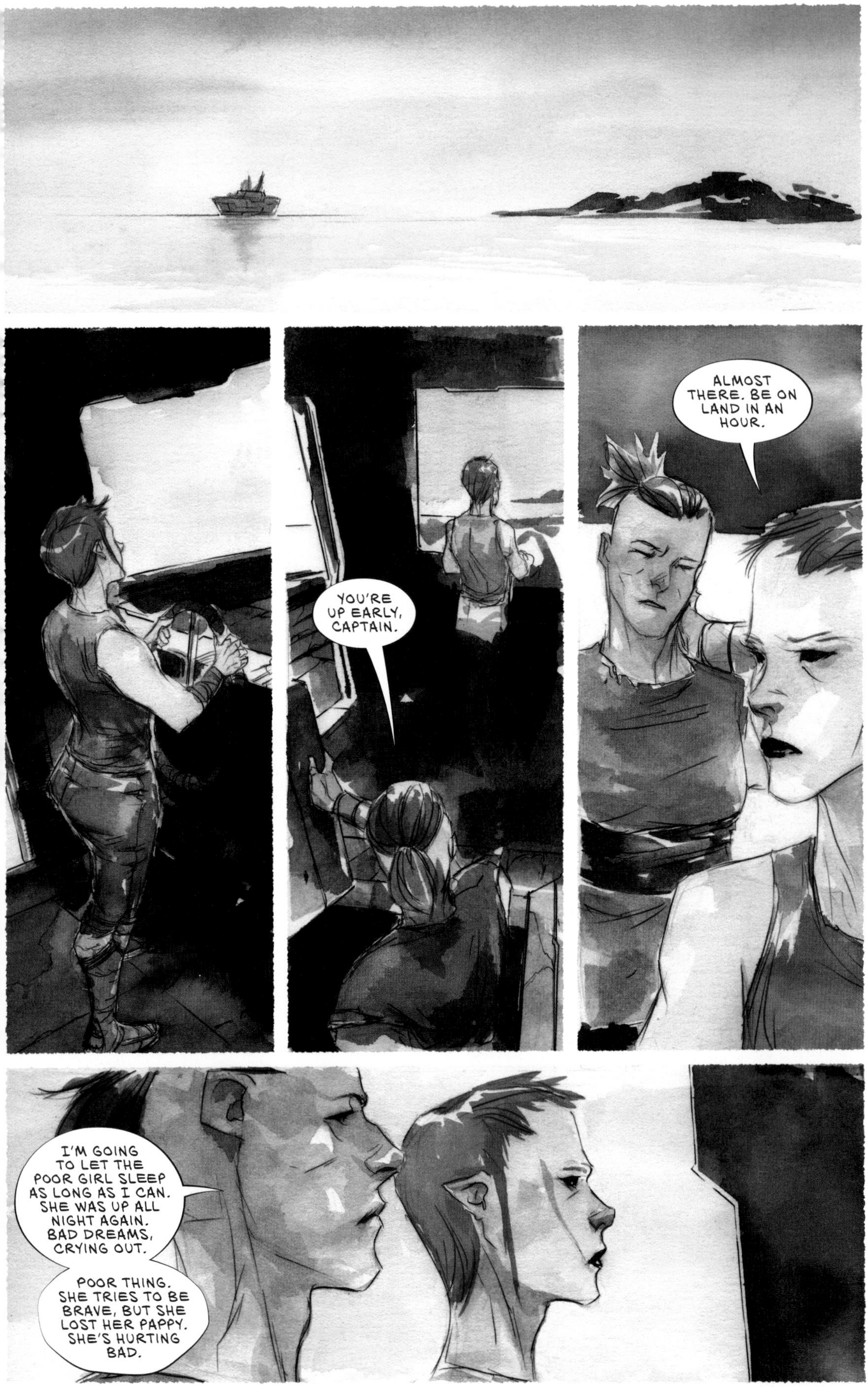
YOU'RE UP EARLY, CAPTAIN.
ALMOST THERE. BE ON LAND IN AN HOUR.
I'M GOING TO LET THE POOR GIRL SLEEP AS LONG AS I CAN. SHE WAS UP ALL NIGHT AGAIN. BAD DREAMS, CRYING OUT.
POOR THING. SHE TRIES TO BE BRAVE, BUT SHE LOST HER PAPPY. SHE'S HURTING BAD.

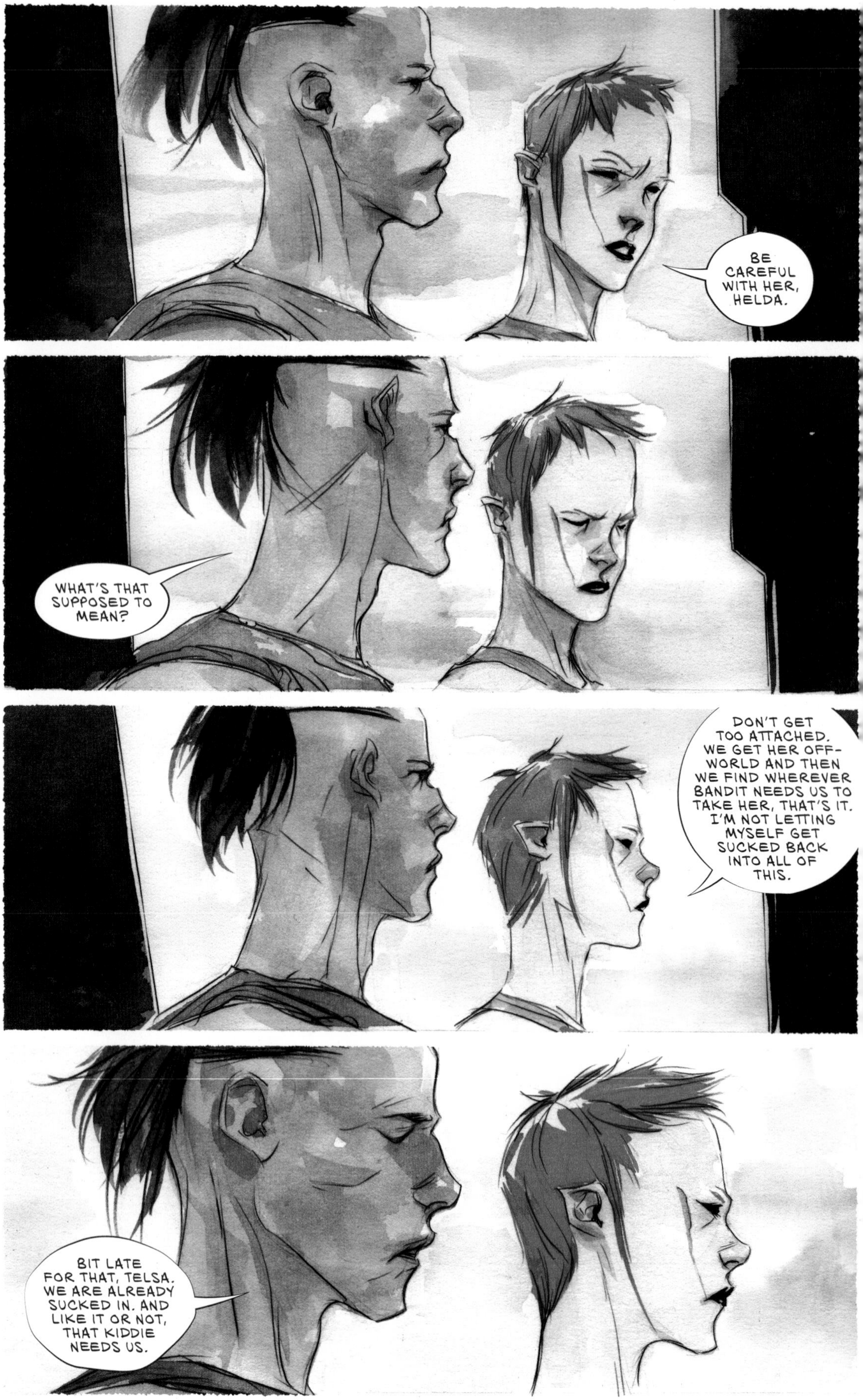
BE CAREFUL WITH HER, HELDA.
WHAT'S THAT SUPPOSED TO MEAN?
DON'T GET TOO ATTACHED. WE GET HER OFF-WORLD AND THEN WE FIND WHEREVER BANDIT NEEDS US TO TAKE HER, THAT'S IT. I'M NOT LETTING MYSELF GET SUCKED BACK INTO ALL OF THIS.
BIT LATE FOR THAT, TELSA. WE ARE ALREADY SUCKED IN. AND LIKE IT OR NOT, THAT KIDDIE NEEDS US.

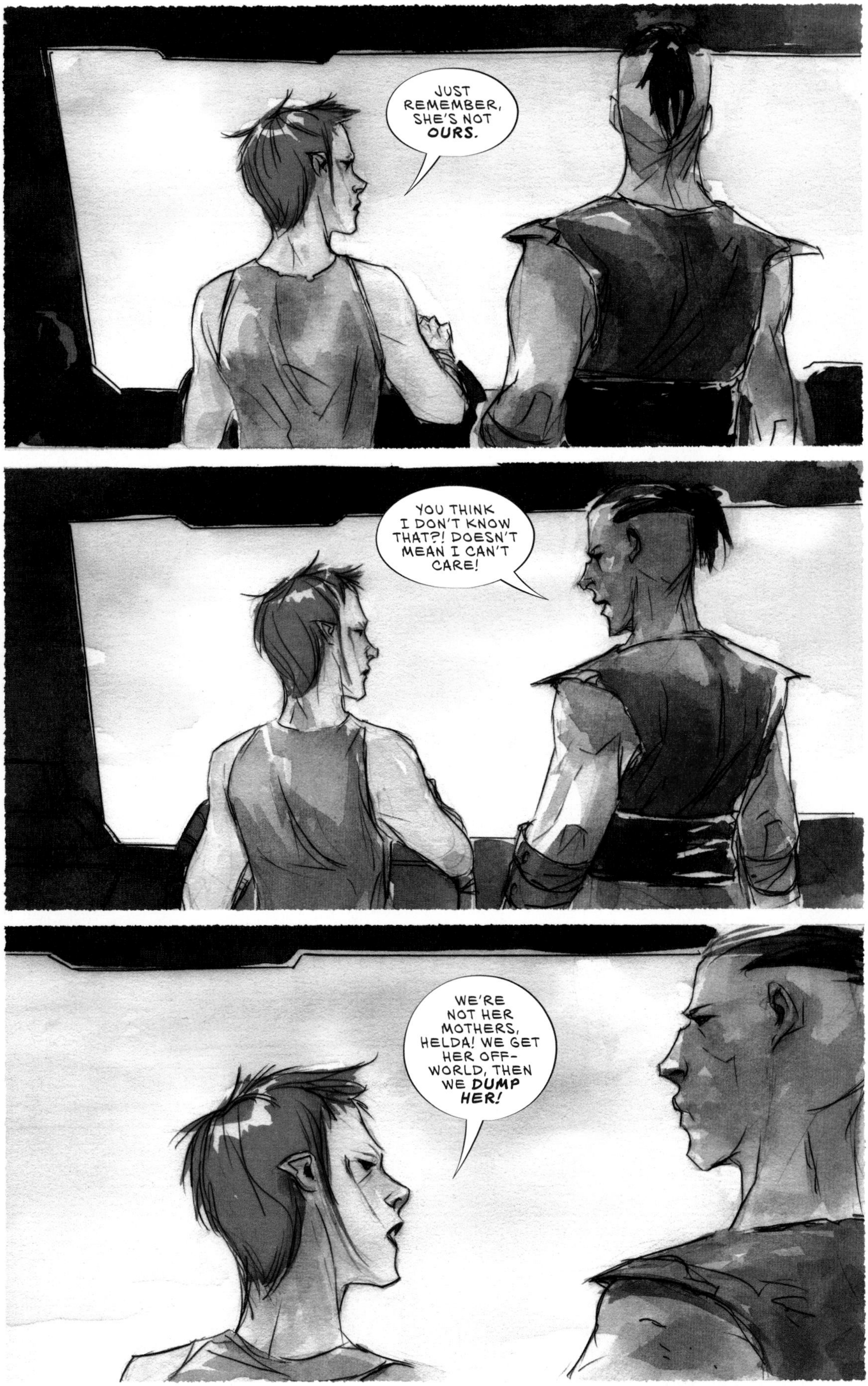
JUST REMEMBER, SHE'S NOT **OURS.**
YOU THINK I DON'T KNOW THAT?! DOESN'T MEAN I CAN'T CARE!
WE'RE NOT HER MOTHERS, HELDA! WE GET HER OFF-WORLD, THEN WE ***DUMP HER!***

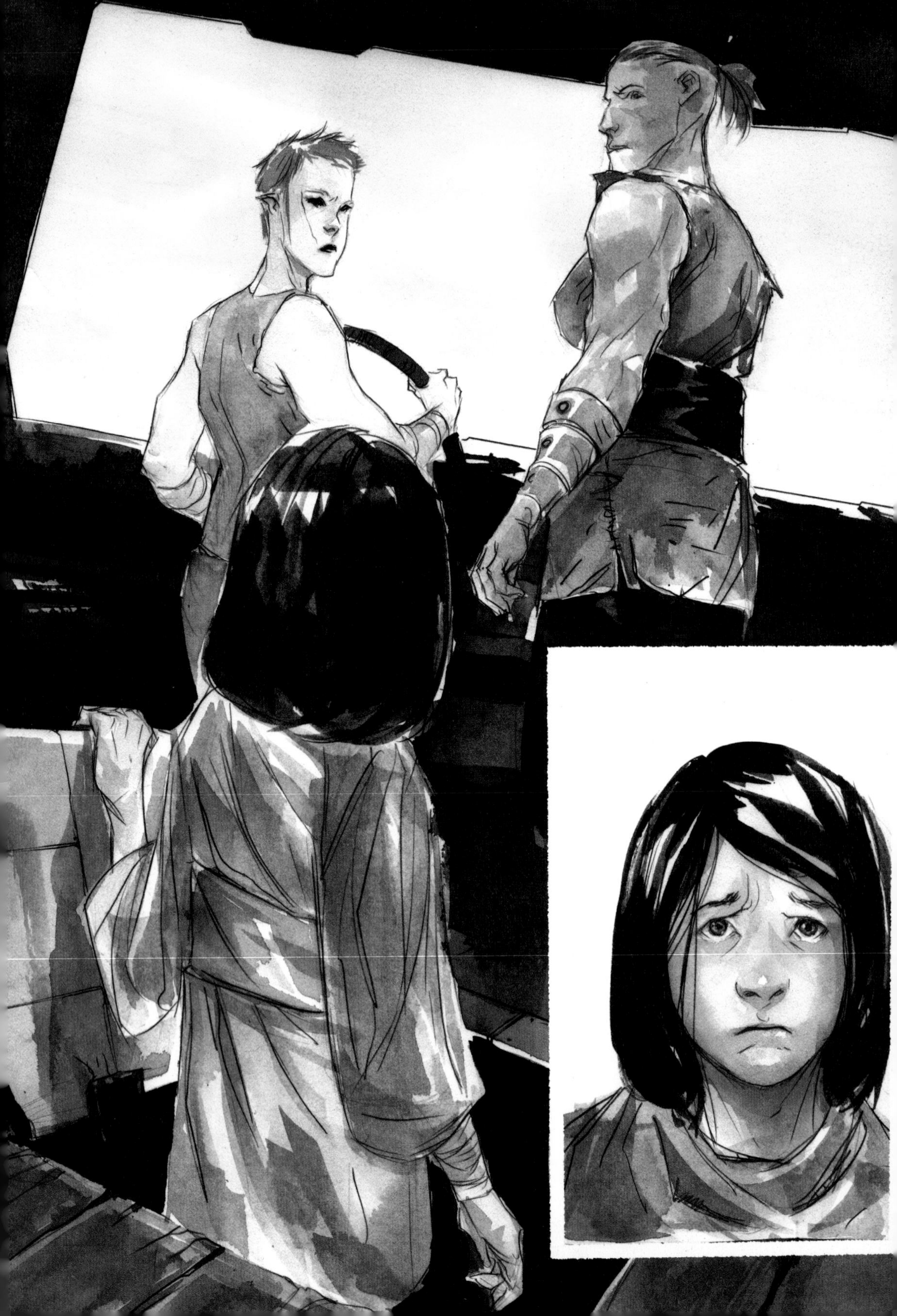

9

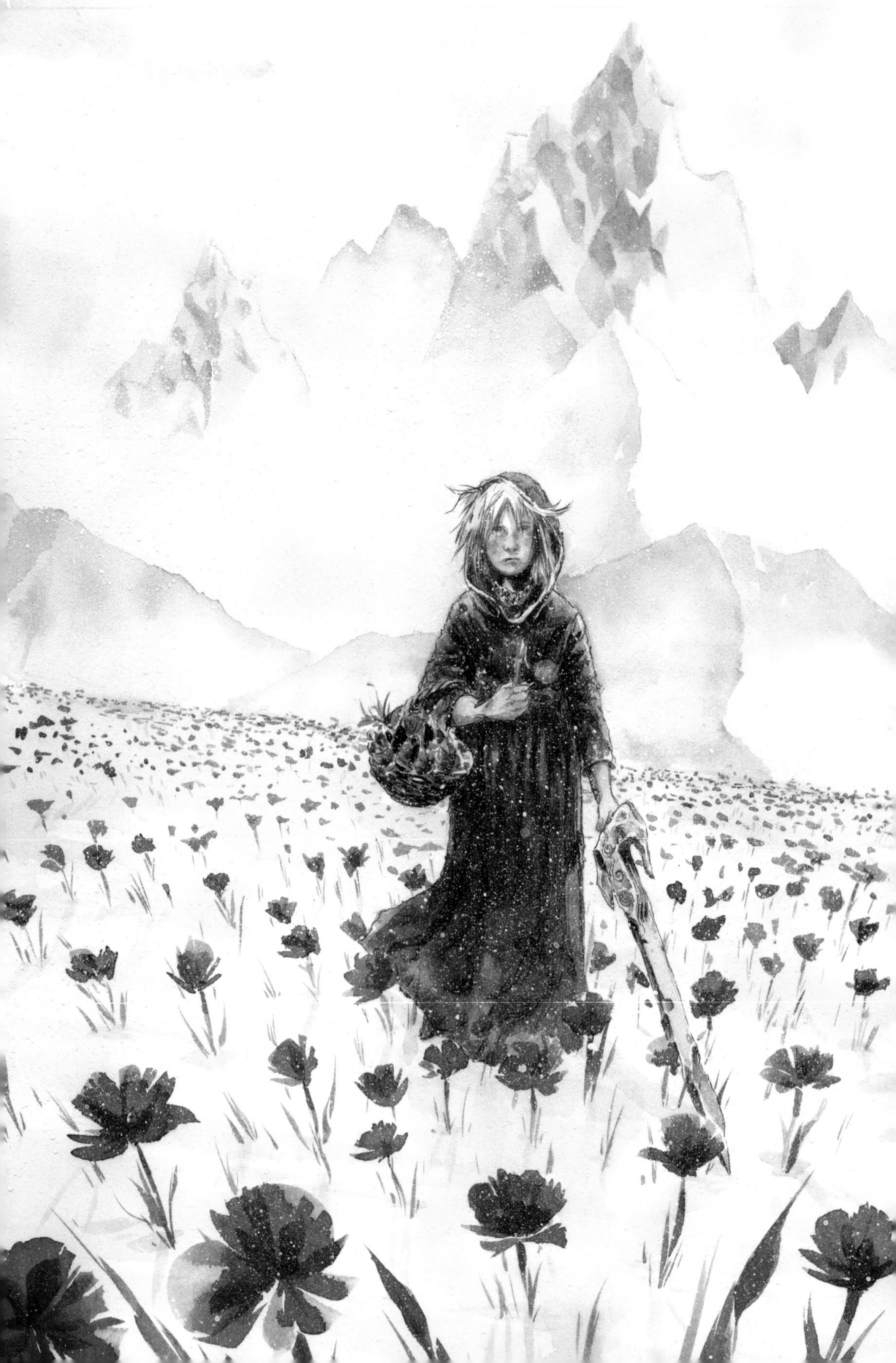

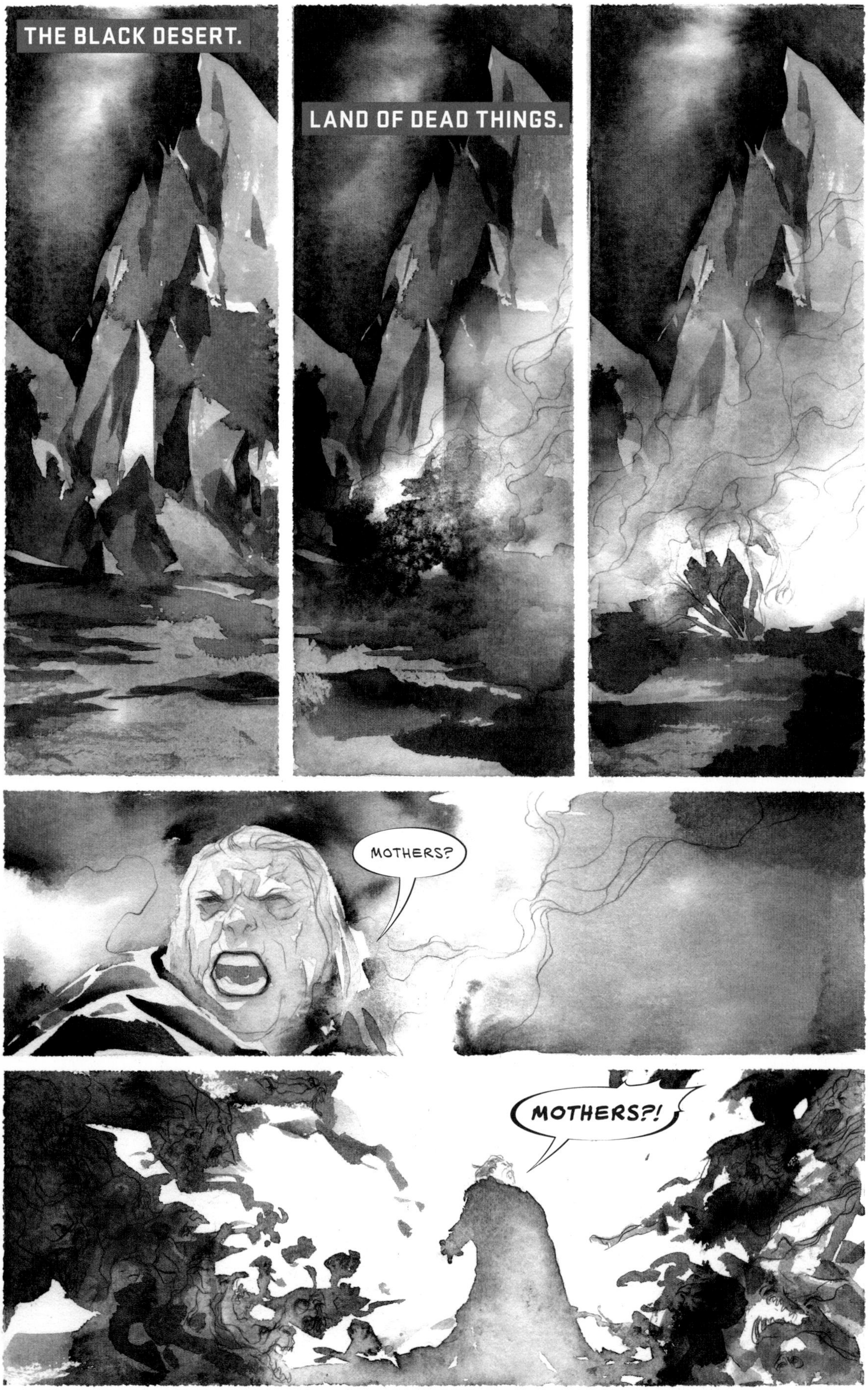
THE BLACK DESERT.
LAND OF DEAD THINGS.
MOTHERS?
MOTHERS?!

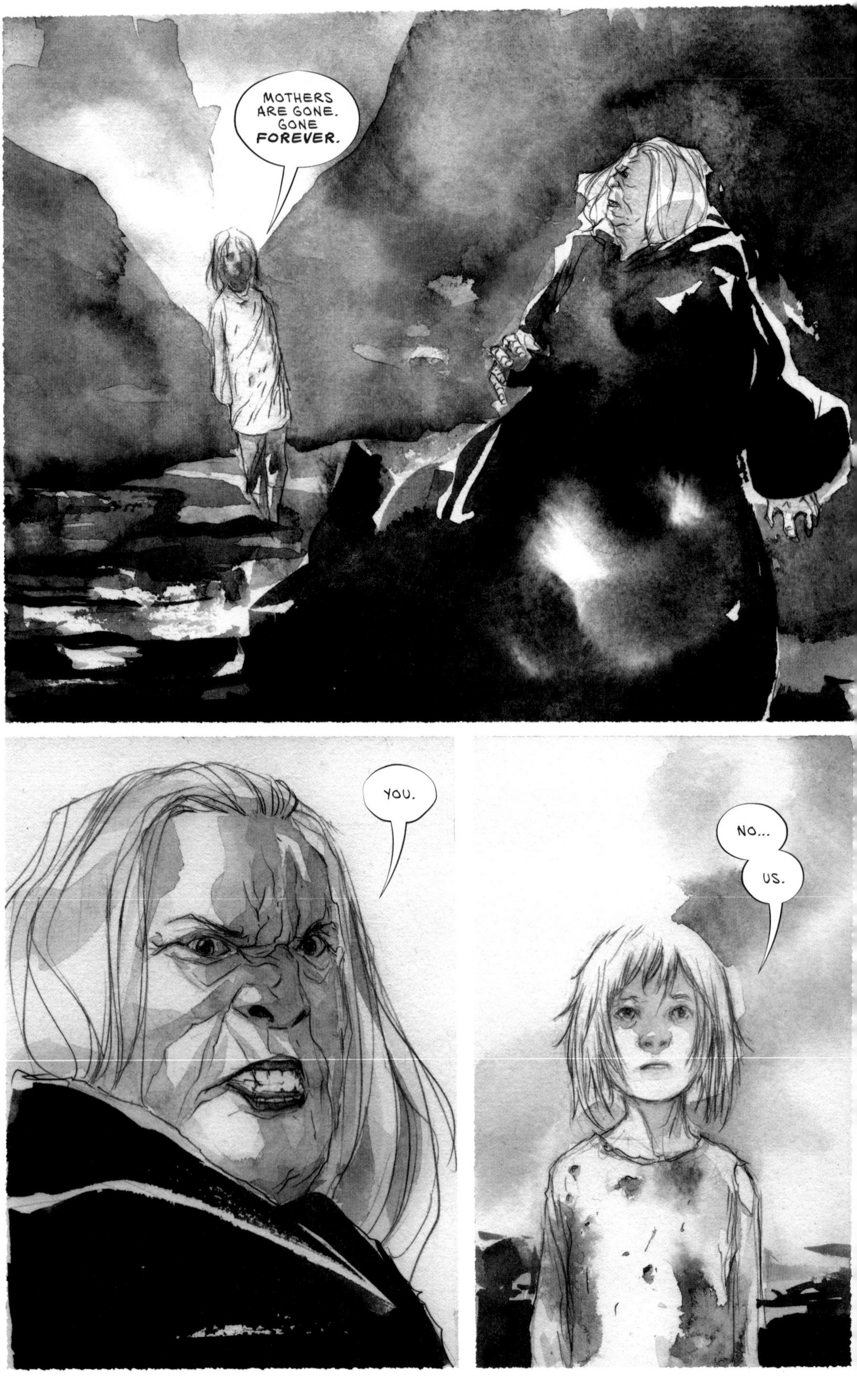
MOTHERS ARE GONE. GONE FOREVER.
YOU.
NO...
US.

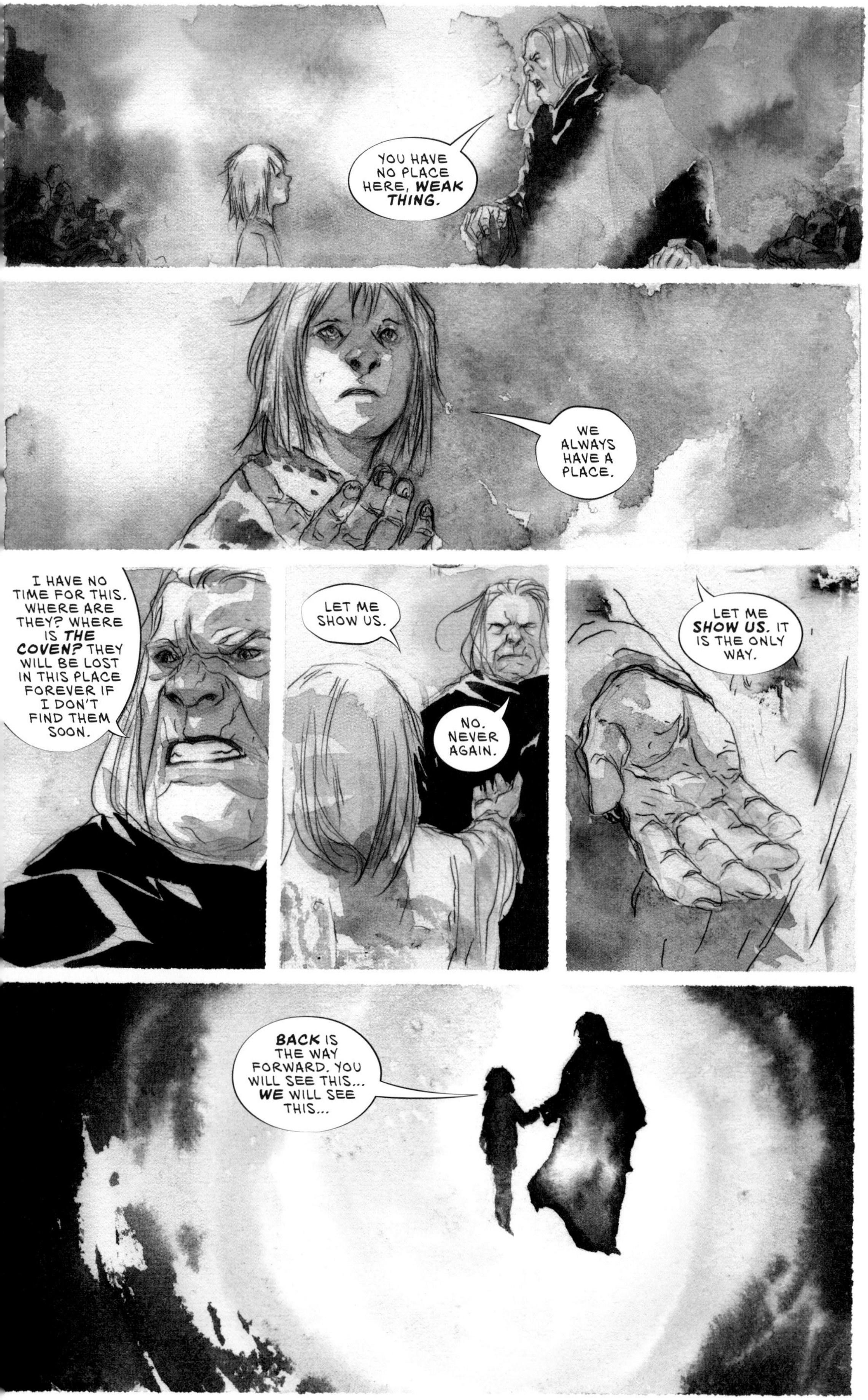
YOU HAVE NO PLACE HERE, **WEAK THING.**
WE ALWAYS HAVE A PLACE.
I HAVE NO TIME FOR THIS. WHERE ARE THEY? WHERE IS **THE COVEN?** THEY WILL BE LOST IN THIS PLACE FOREVER IF I DON'T FIND THEM SOON.
LET ME SHOW US.
NO. NEVER AGAIN.
LET ME **SHOW US.** IT IS THE ONLY WAY.
BACK IS THE WAY FORWARD. YOU WILL SEE THIS... **WE** WILL SEE THIS...

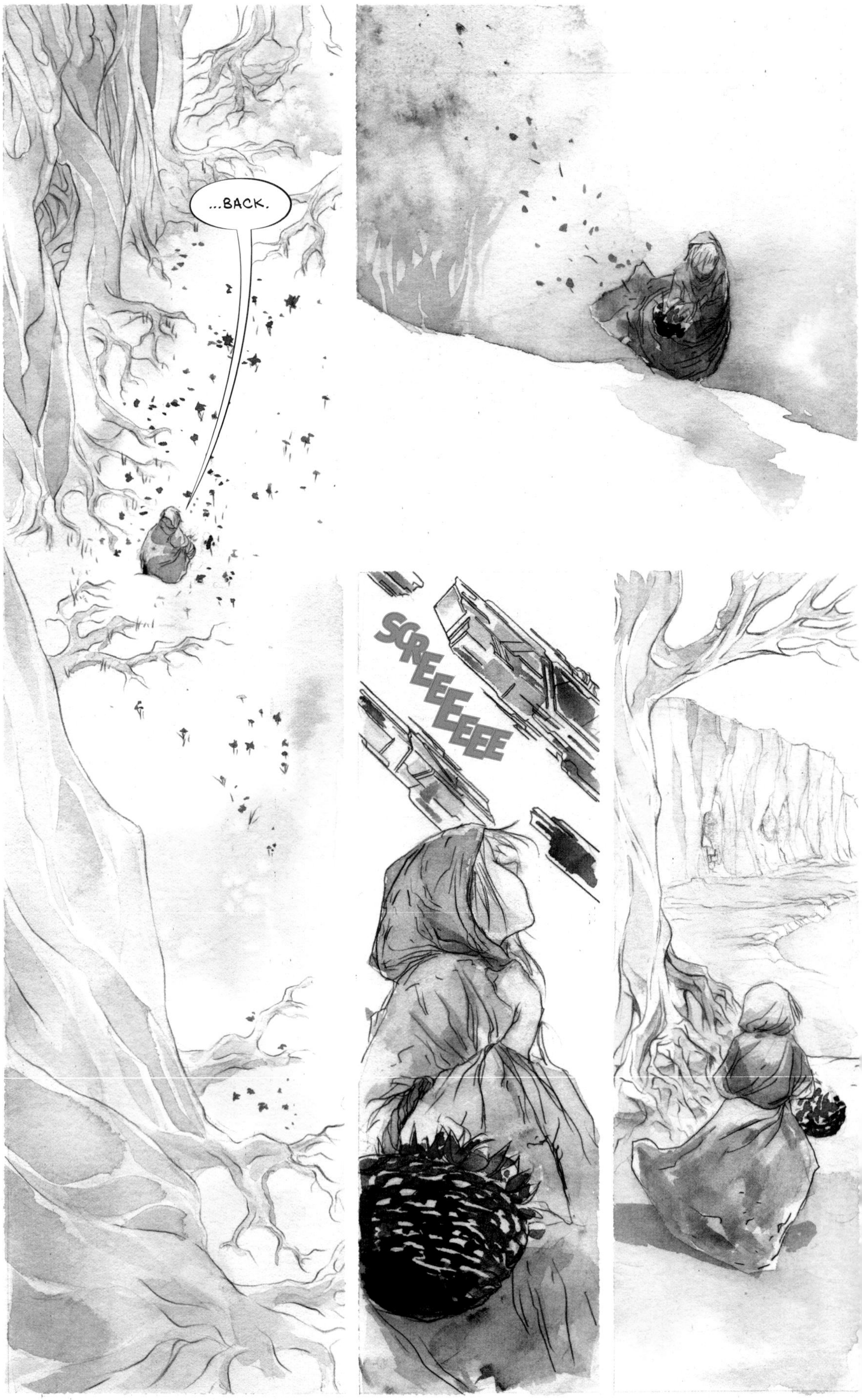
...BACK.
SCREEEEEEEE

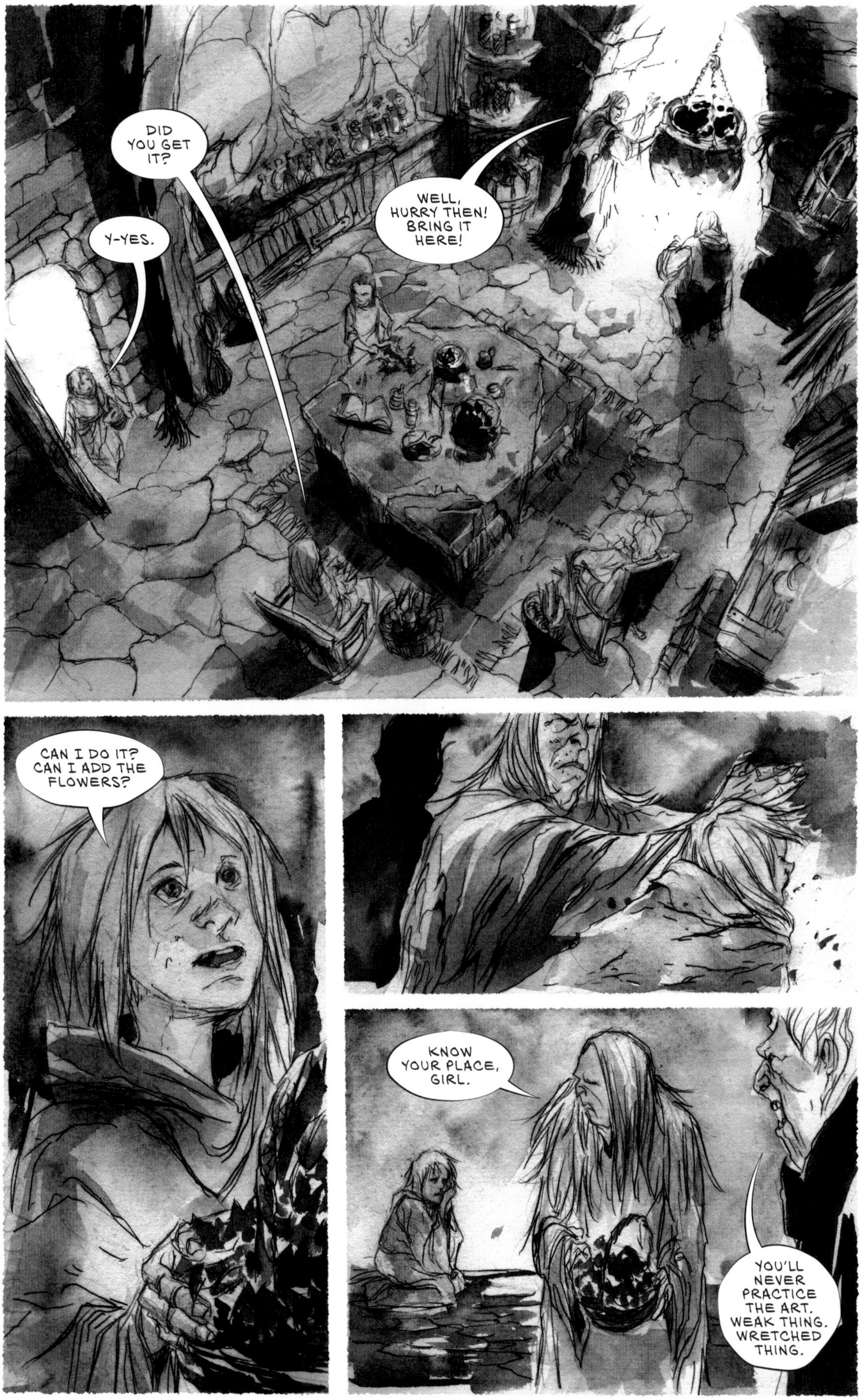
DID YOU GET IT?
Y-YES.
WELL, HURRY THEN! BRING IT HERE!
CAN I DO IT? CAN I ADD THE FLOWERS?
KNOW YOUR PLACE, GIRL.
YOU'LL NEVER PRACTICE THE ART. WEAK THING. WRETCHED THING.

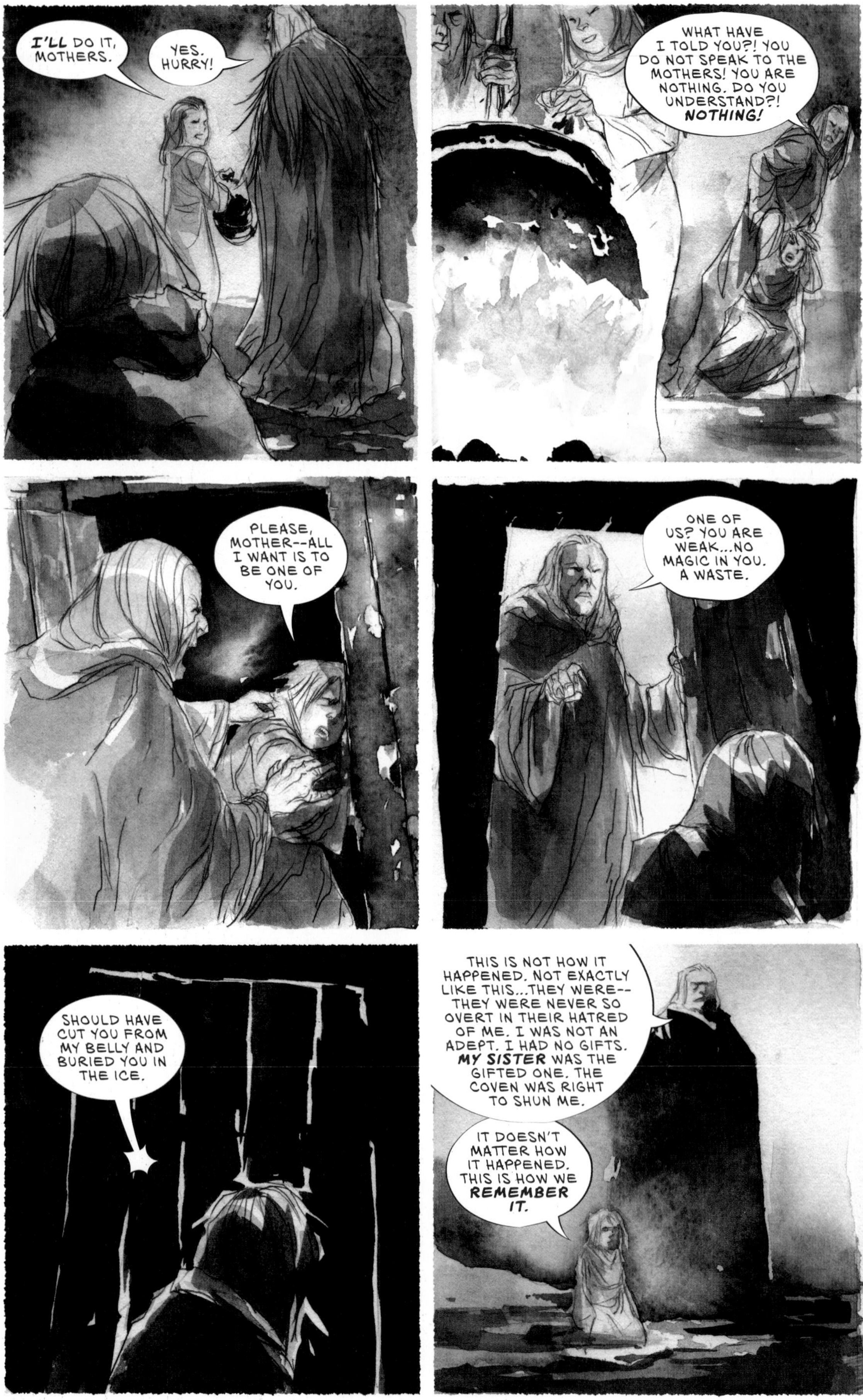
I'LL DO IT, MOTHERS.
YES. HURRY!
WHAT HAVE I TOLD YOU?! YOU DO NOT SPEAK TO THE MOTHERS! YOU ARE NOTHING. DO YOU UNDERSTAND?! NOTHING!
PLEASE, MOTHER--ALL I WANT IS TO BE ONE OF YOU.
ONE OF US? YOU ARE WEAK...NO MAGIC IN YOU. A WASTE.
SHOULD HAVE CUT YOU FROM MY BELLY AND BURIED YOU IN THE ICE.
THIS IS NOT HOW IT HAPPENED. NOT EXACTLY LIKE THIS...THEY WERE--THEY WERE NEVER SO OVERT IN THEIR HATRED OF ME. I WAS NOT AN ADEPT. I HAD NO GIFTS. MY SISTER WAS THE GIFTED ONE. THE COVEN WAS RIGHT TO SHUN ME.
IT DOESN'T MATTER HOW IT HAPPENED. THIS IS HOW WE REMEMBER IT.

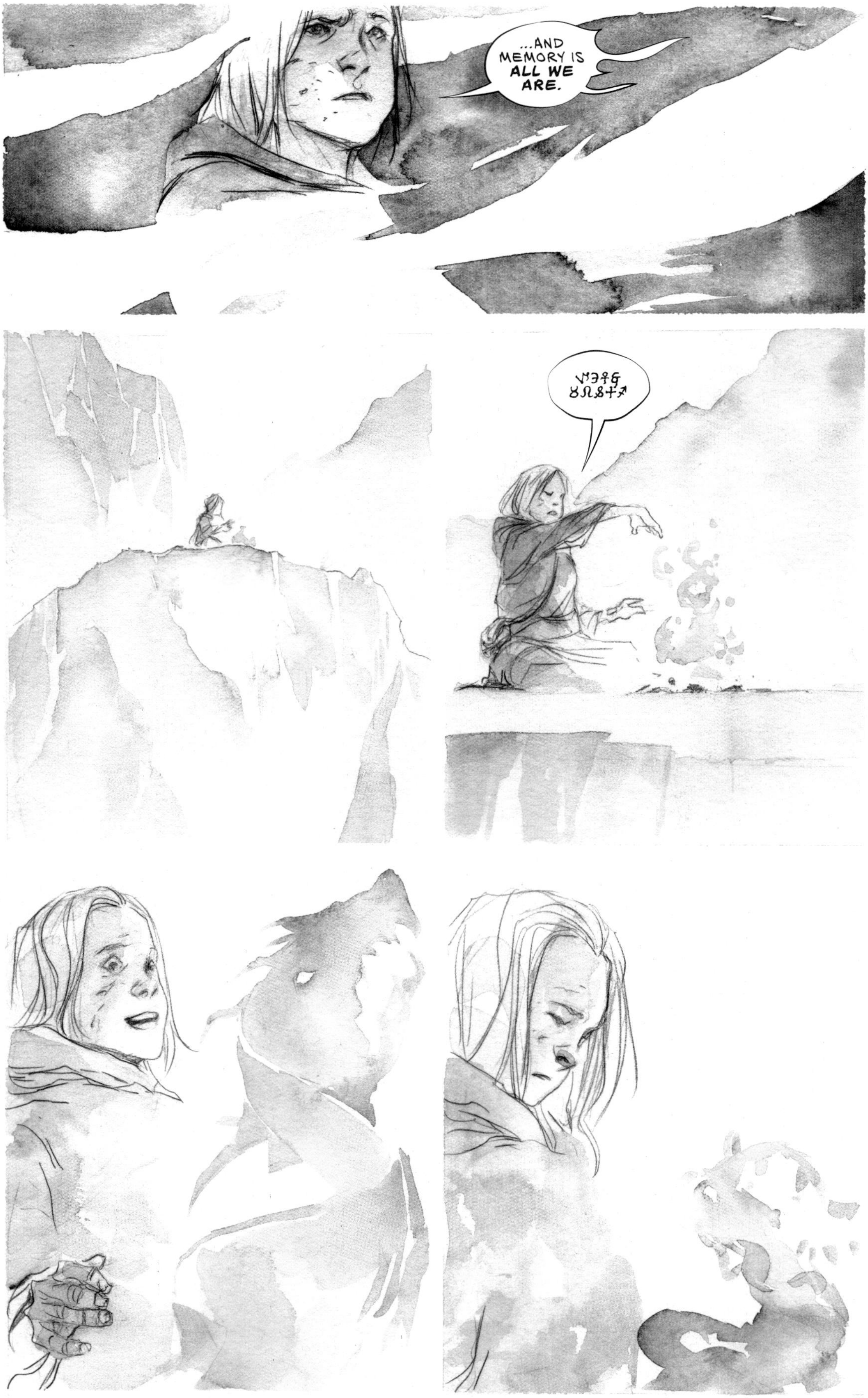
...AND MEMORY IS ALL WE ARE.

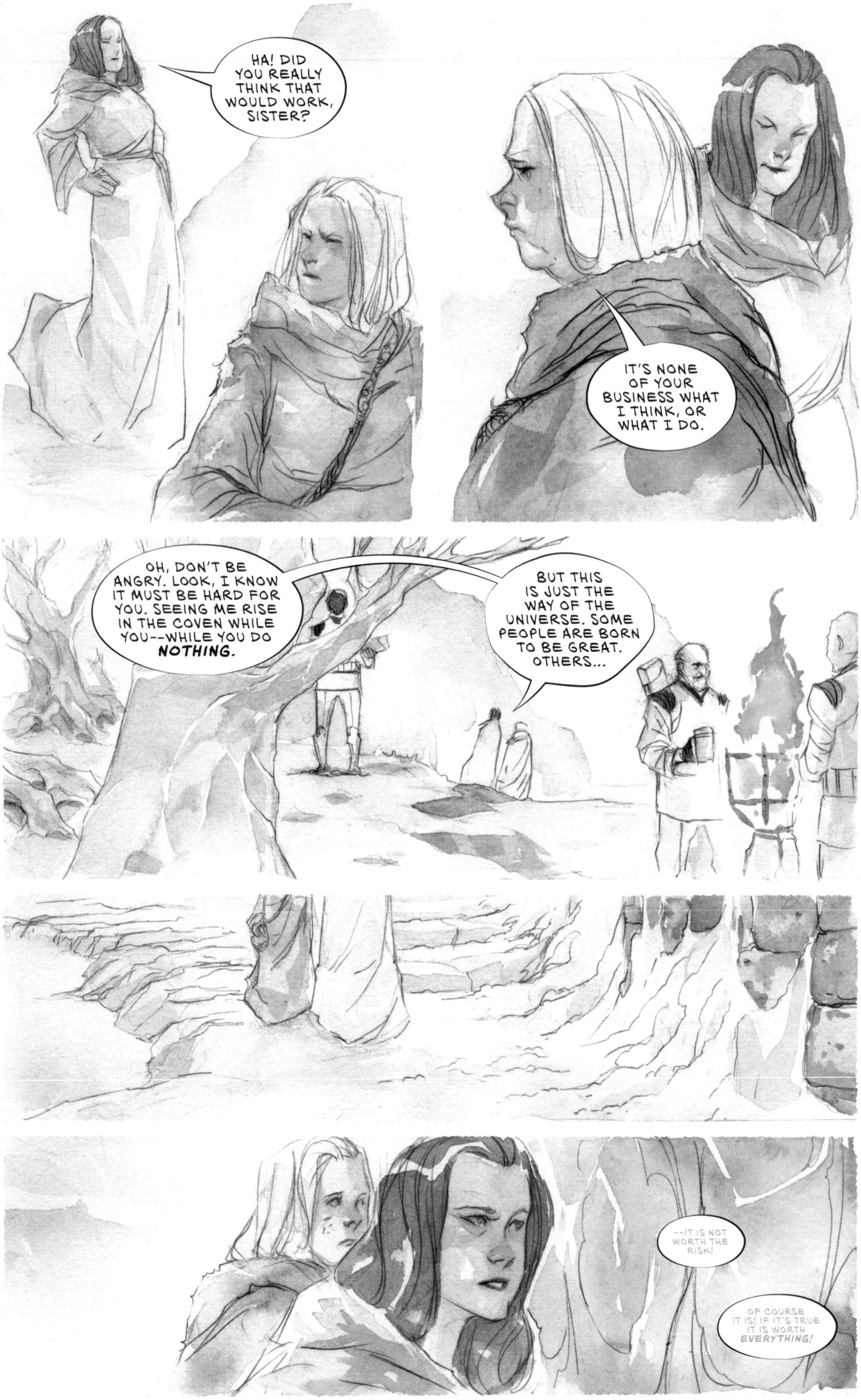
HA! DID YOU REALLY THINK THAT WOULD WORK, SISTER?
IT'S NONE OF YOUR BUSINESS WHAT I THINK, OR WHAT I DO.
OH, DON'T BE ANGRY. LOOK, I KNOW IT MUST BE HARD FOR YOU. SEEING ME RISE IN THE COVEN WHILE YOU--WHILE YOU DO **NOTHING.**
BUT THIS IS JUST THE WAY OF THE UNIVERSE. SOME PEOPLE ARE BORN TO BE GREAT. OTHERS...
--IT IS NOT WORTH THE RISK!
OF COURSE IT IS! IF IT'S TRUE IT IS WORTH *EVERYTHING!*

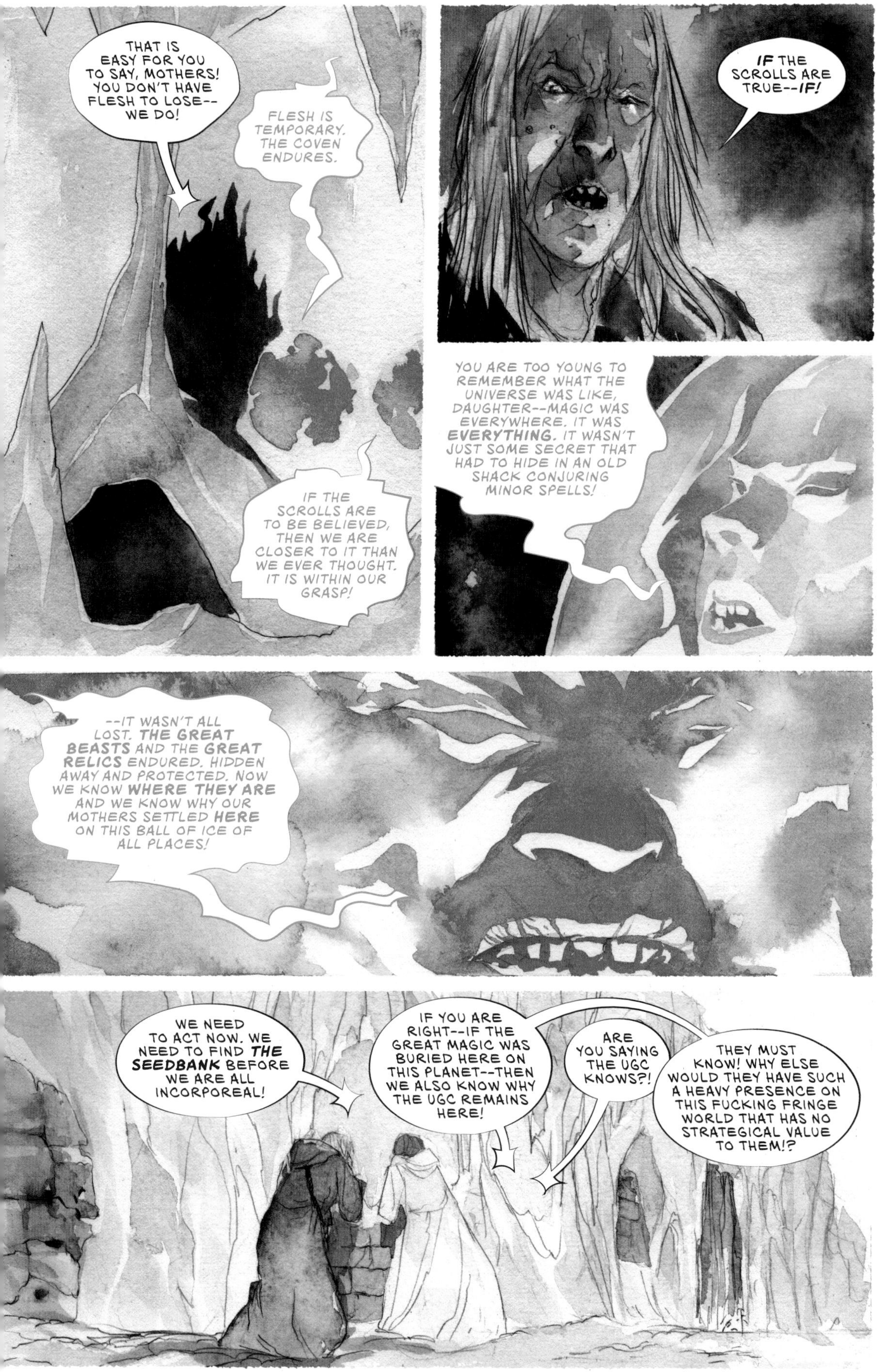
THAT IS EASY FOR YOU TO SAY, MOTHERS! YOU DON'T HAVE FLESH TO LOSE-- WE DO!
FLESH IS TEMPORARY. THE COVEN ENDURES.
IF THE SCROLLS ARE TO BE BELIEVED, THEN WE ARE CLOSER TO IT THAN WE EVER THOUGHT. IT IS WITHIN OUR GRASP!
IF THE SCROLLS ARE TRUE--IF!
YOU ARE TOO YOUNG TO REMEMBER WHAT THE UNIVERSE WAS LIKE, DAUGHTER--MAGIC WAS EVERYWHERE. IT WAS EVERYTHING. IT WASN'T JUST SOME SECRET THAT HAD TO HIDE IN AN OLD SHACK CONJURING MINOR SPELLS!
--IT WASN'T ALL LOST. THE GREAT BEASTS AND THE GREAT RELICS ENDURED. HIDDEN AWAY AND PROTECTED. NOW WE KNOW WHERE THEY ARE AND WE KNOW WHY OUR MOTHERS SETTLED HERE ON THIS BALL OF ICE OF ALL PLACES!
WE NEED TO ACT NOW. WE NEED TO FIND THE SEEDBANK BEFORE WE ARE ALL INCORPOREAL!
IF YOU ARE RIGHT--IF THE GREAT MAGIC WAS BURIED HERE ON THIS PLANET--THEN WE ALSO KNOW WHY THE UGC REMAINS HERE!
ARE YOU SAYING THE UGC KNOWS?!
THEY MUST KNOW! WHY ELSE WOULD THEY HAVE SUCH A HEAVY PRESENCE ON THIS FUCKING FRINGE WORLD THAT HAS NO STRATEGICAL VALUE TO THEM!?

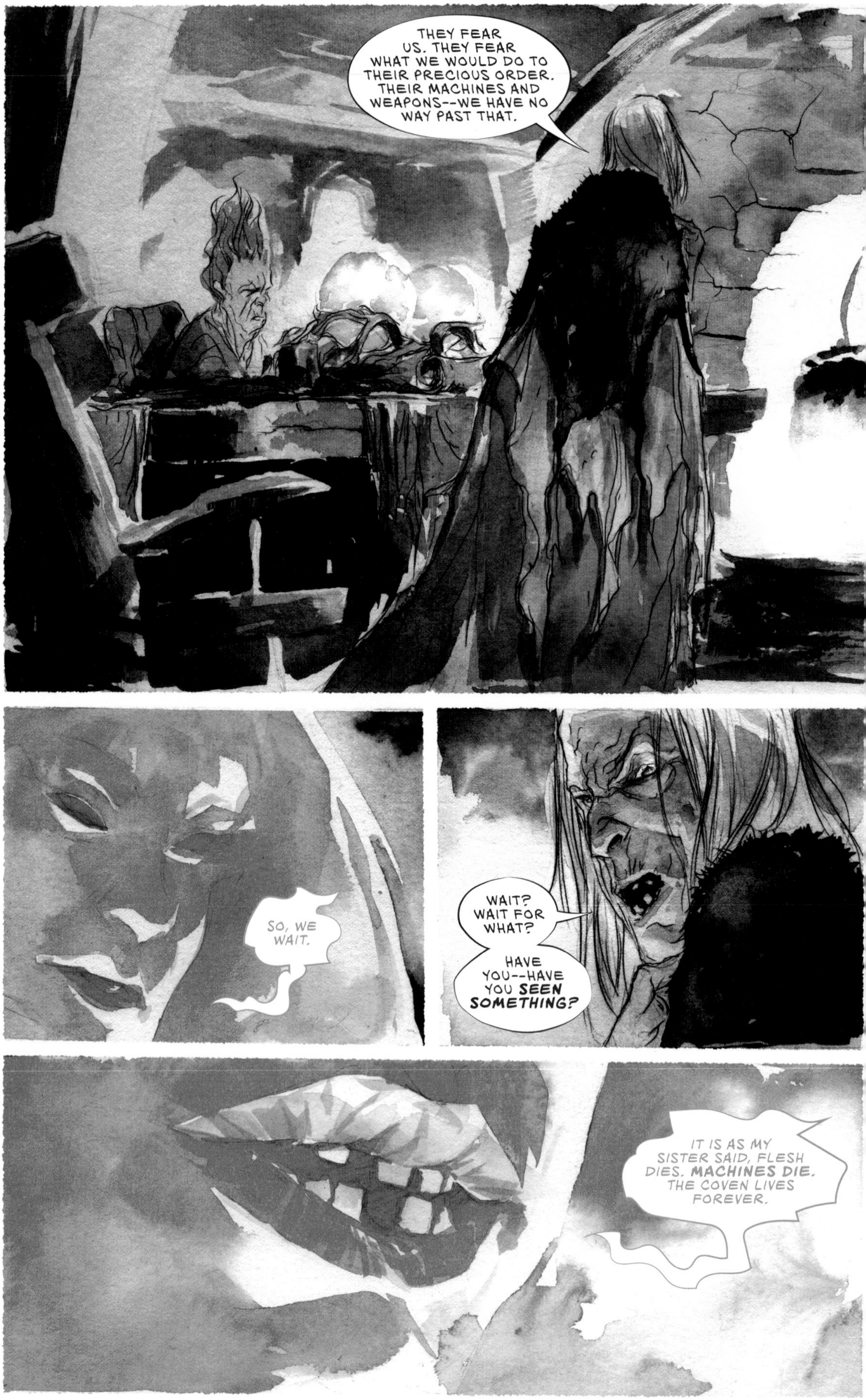
THEY FEAR US. THEY FEAR WHAT WE WOULD DO TO THEIR PRECIOUS ORDER. THEIR MACHINES AND WEAPONS--WE HAVE NO WAY PAST THAT.
SO, WE WAIT.
WAIT? WAIT FOR WHAT?
HAVE YOU--HAVE YOU **SEEN SOMETHING?**
IT IS AS MY SISTER SAID, FLESH DIES. **MACHINES DIE.** THE COVEN LIVES FOREVER.

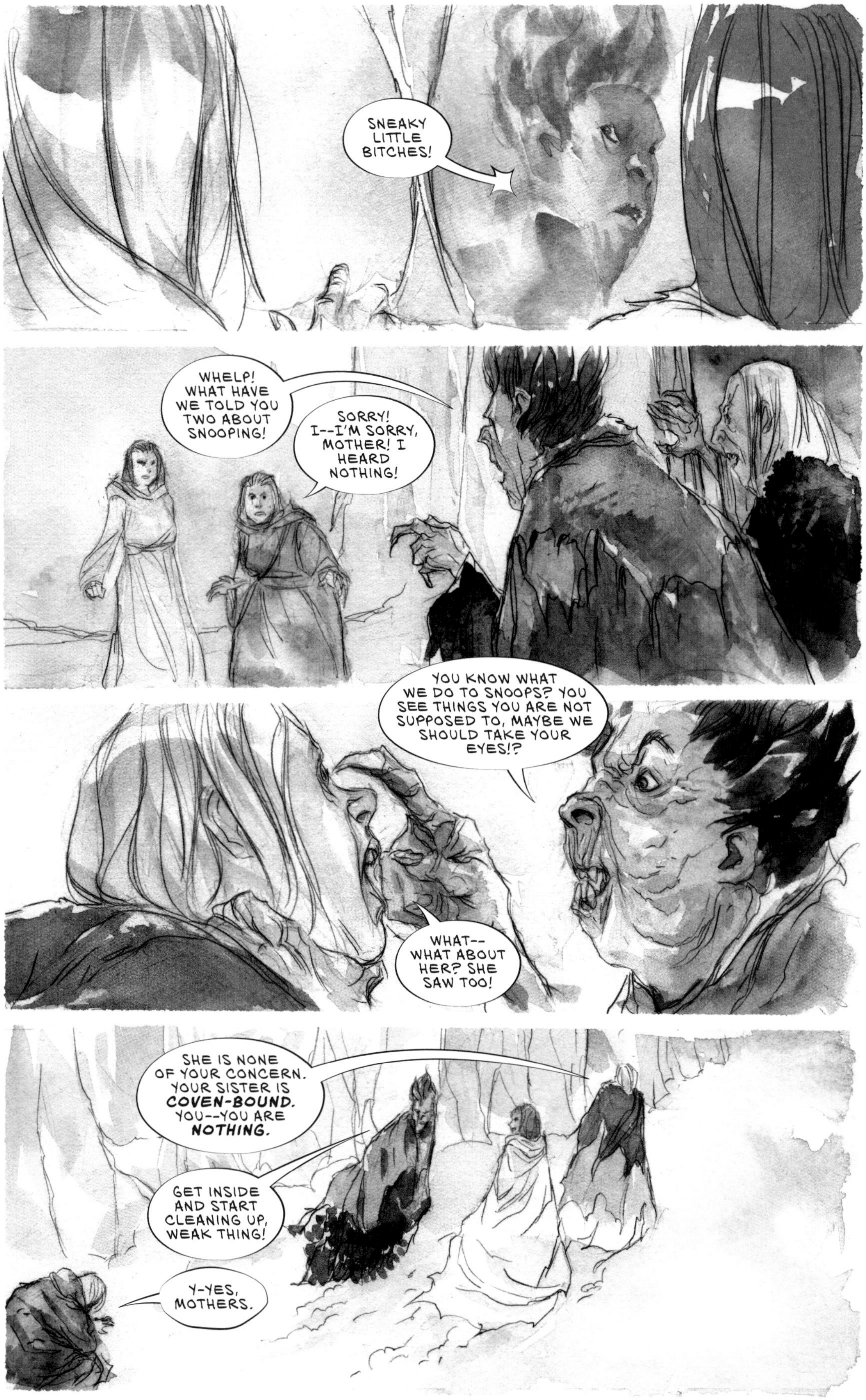
SNEAKY LITTLE BITCHES!
WHELP! WHAT HAVE WE TOLD YOU TWO ABOUT SNOOPING!
SORRY! I--I'M SORRY, MOTHER! I HEARD NOTHING!
YOU KNOW WHAT WE DO TO SNOOPS? YOU SEE THINGS YOU ARE NOT SUPPOSED TO, MAYBE WE SHOULD TAKE YOUR EYES!?
WHAT-- WHAT ABOUT HER? SHE SAW TOO!
SHE IS NONE OF YOUR CONCERN. YOUR SISTER IS **COVEN-BOUND.** YOU--YOU ARE **NOTHING.**
GET INSIDE AND START CLEANING UP, WEAK THING!
Y-YES, MOTHERS.

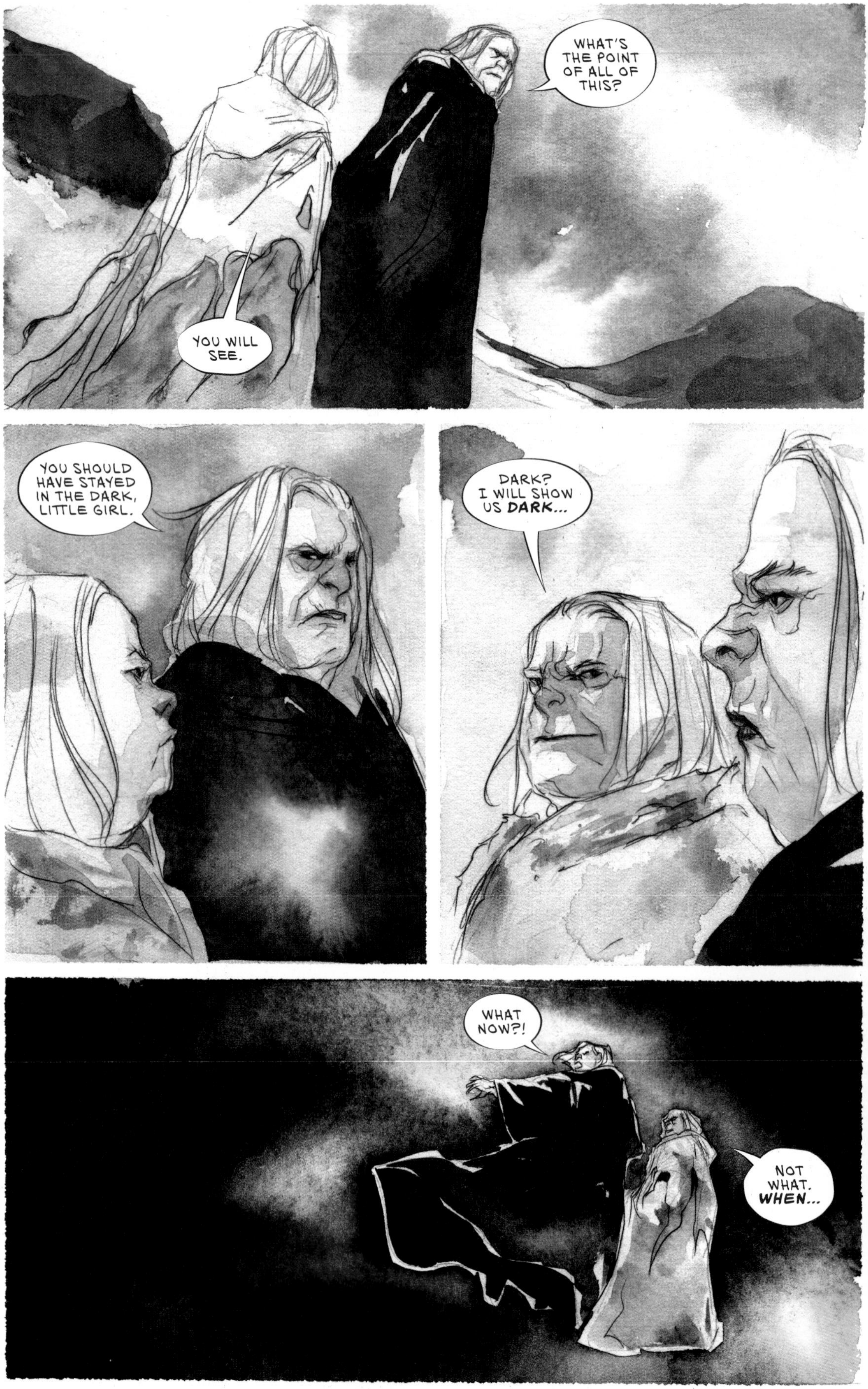
WHAT'S THE POINT OF ALL OF THIS?
YOU WILL SEE.
YOU SHOULD HAVE STAYED IN THE DARK, LITTLE GIRL.
DARK? I WILL SHOW US **DARK...**
WHAT NOW?!
NOT WHAT. **WHEN...**

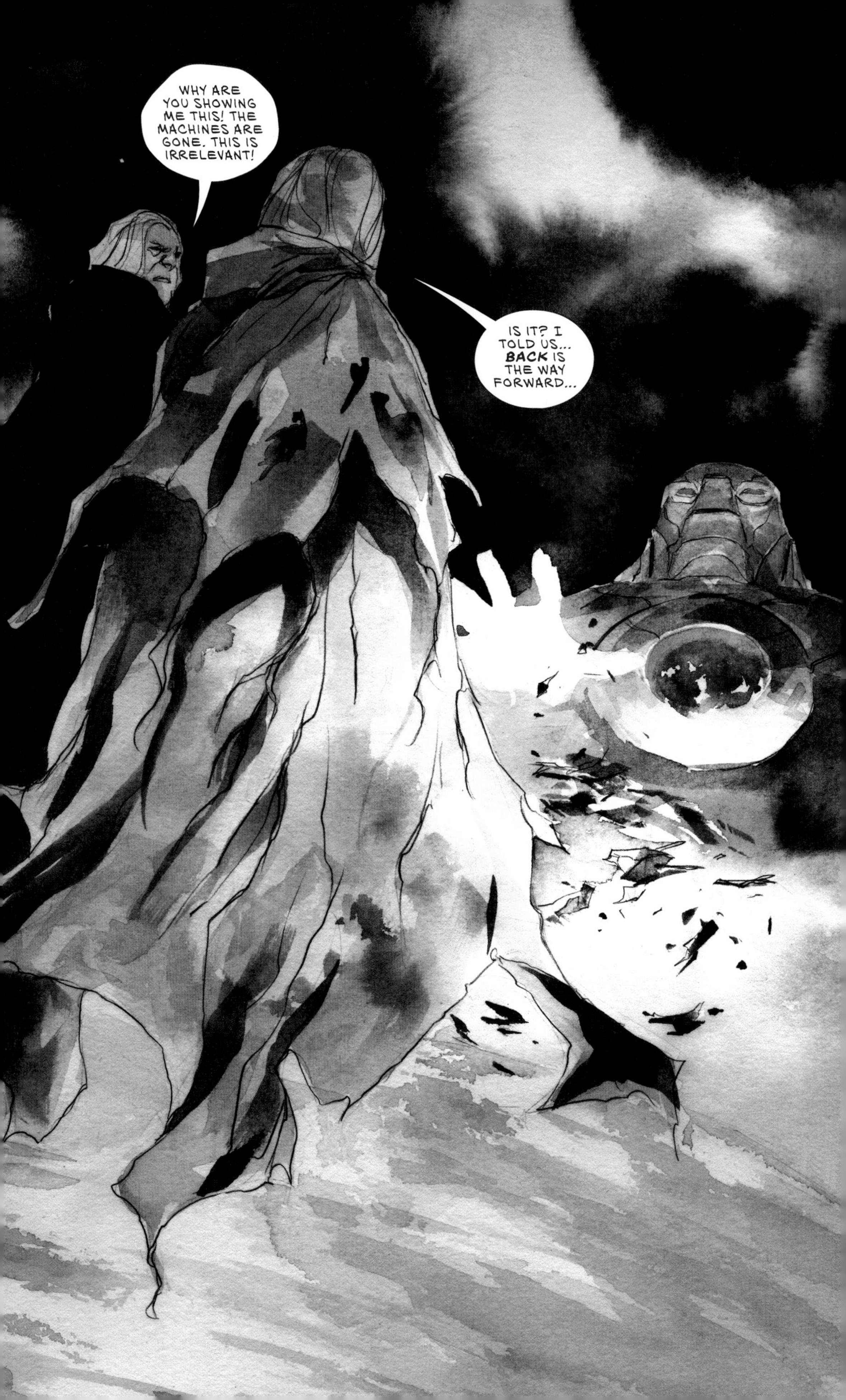
WHY ARE YOU SHOWING ME THIS! THE MACHINES ARE GONE. THIS IS IRRELEVANT!
IS IT? I TOLD US... **BACK** IS THE WAY FORWARD...

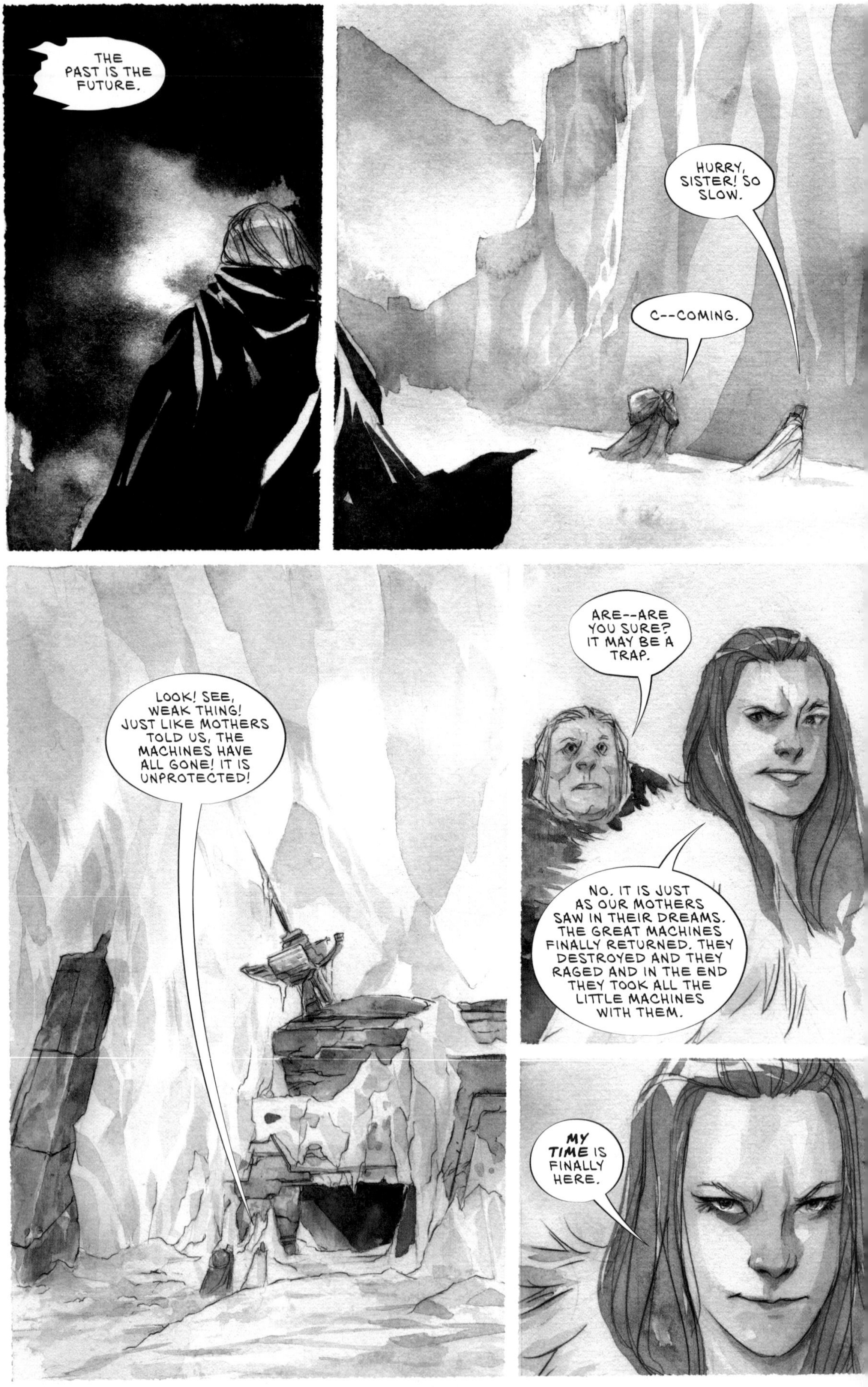
THE PAST IS THE FUTURE.
HURRY, SISTER! SO SLOW.
C--COMING.
LOOK! SEE, WEAK THING! JUST LIKE MOTHERS TOLD US, THE MACHINES HAVE ALL GONE! IT IS UNPROTECTED!
ARE--ARE YOU SURE? IT MAY BE A TRAP.
NO. IT IS JUST AS OUR MOTHERS SAW IN THEIR DREAMS. THE GREAT MACHINES FINALLY RETURNED. THEY DESTROYED AND THEY RAGED AND IN THE END THEY TOOK ALL THE LITTLE MACHINES WITH THEM.
MY TIME IS FINALLY HERE.

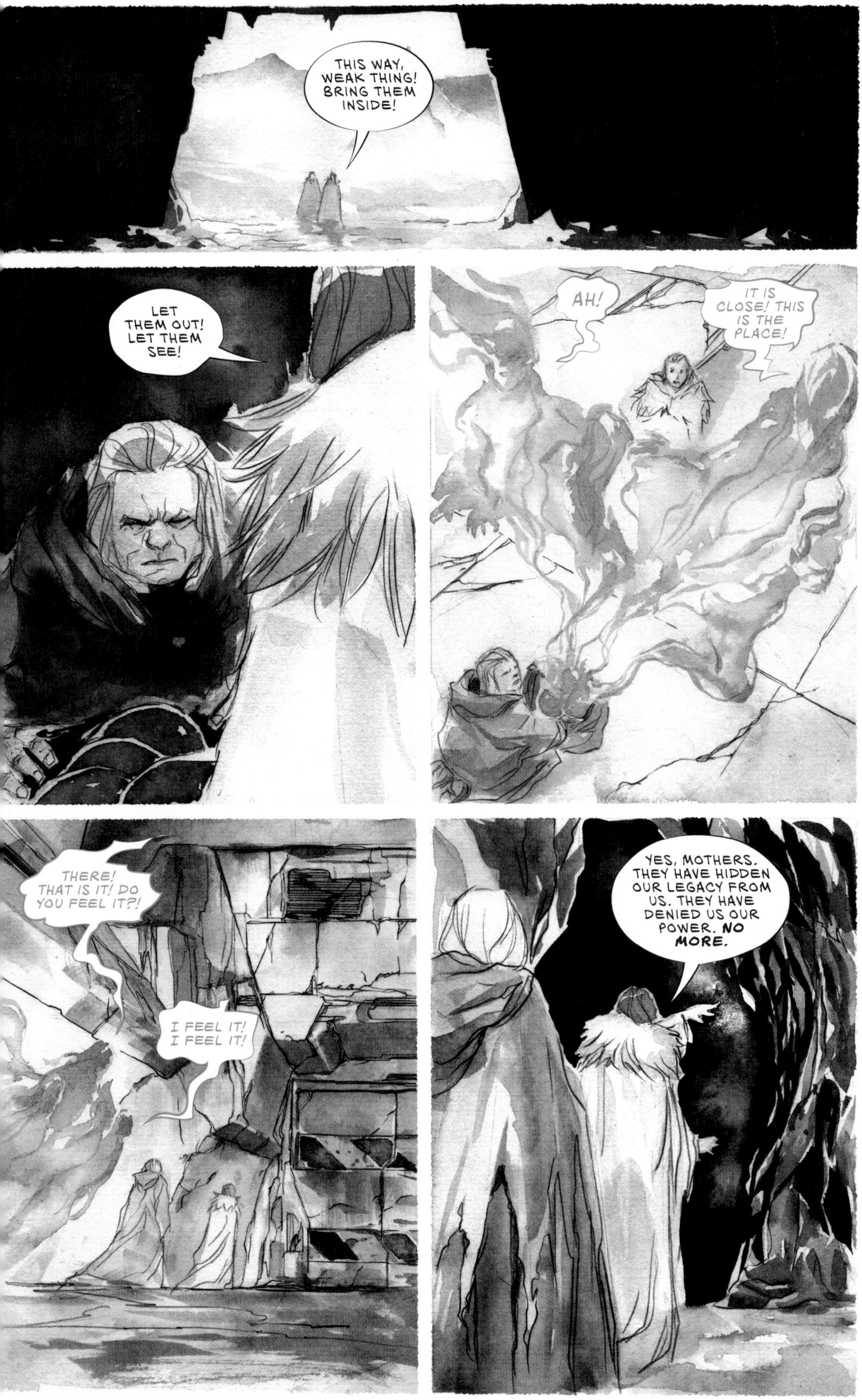
THIS WAY, WEAK THING! BRING THEM INSIDE!
LET THEM OUT! LET THEM SEE!
AH!
IT IS CLOSE! THIS IS THE PLACE!
THERE! THAT IS IT! DO YOU FEEL IT?!
I FEEL IT! I FEEL IT!
YES, MOTHERS. THEY HAVE HIDDEN OUR LEGACY FROM US. THEY HAVE DENIED US OUR POWER. NO MORE.

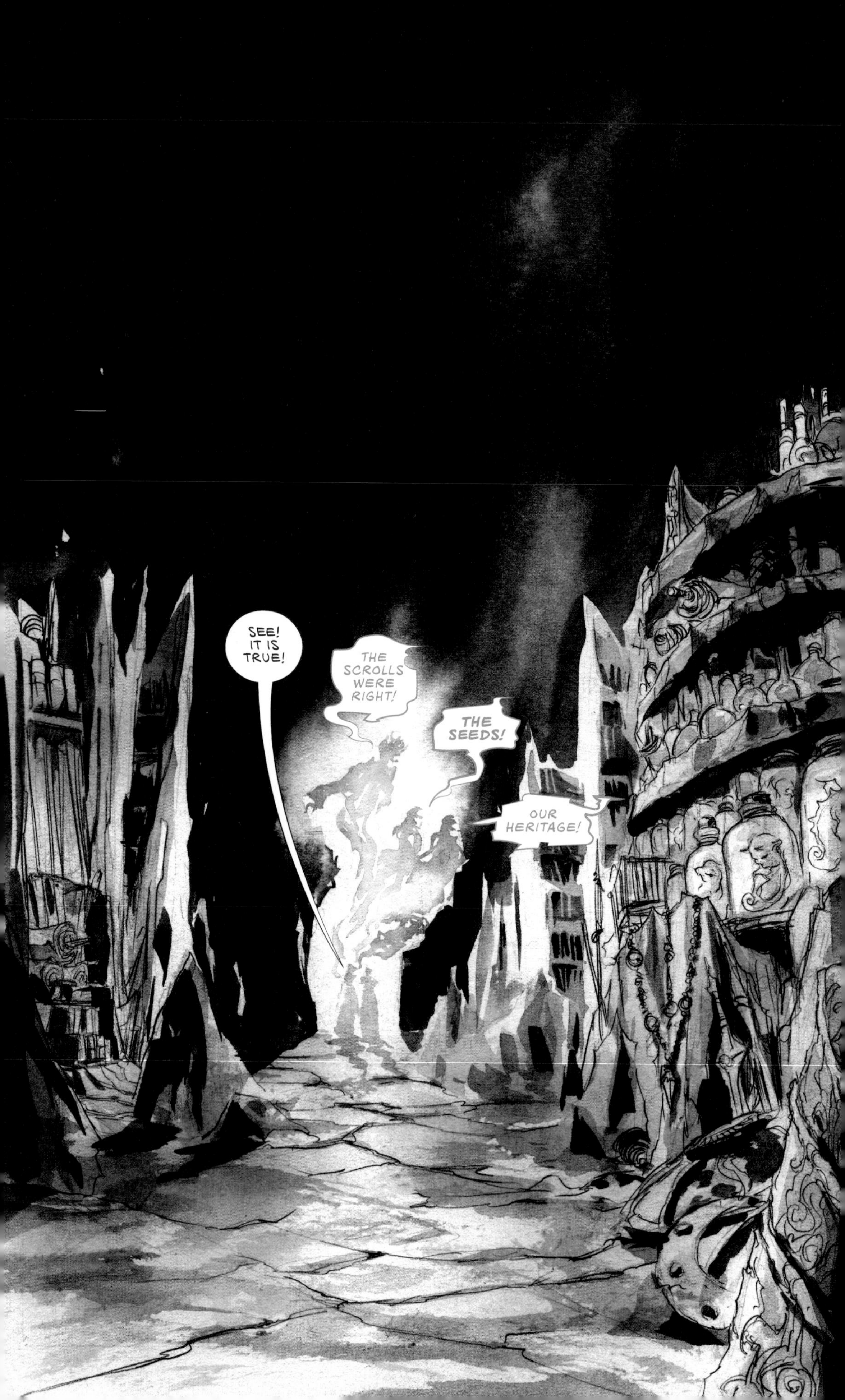
SEE! IT IS TRUE!
THE SCROLLS WERE RIGHT!
THE SEEDS!
OUR HERITAGE!

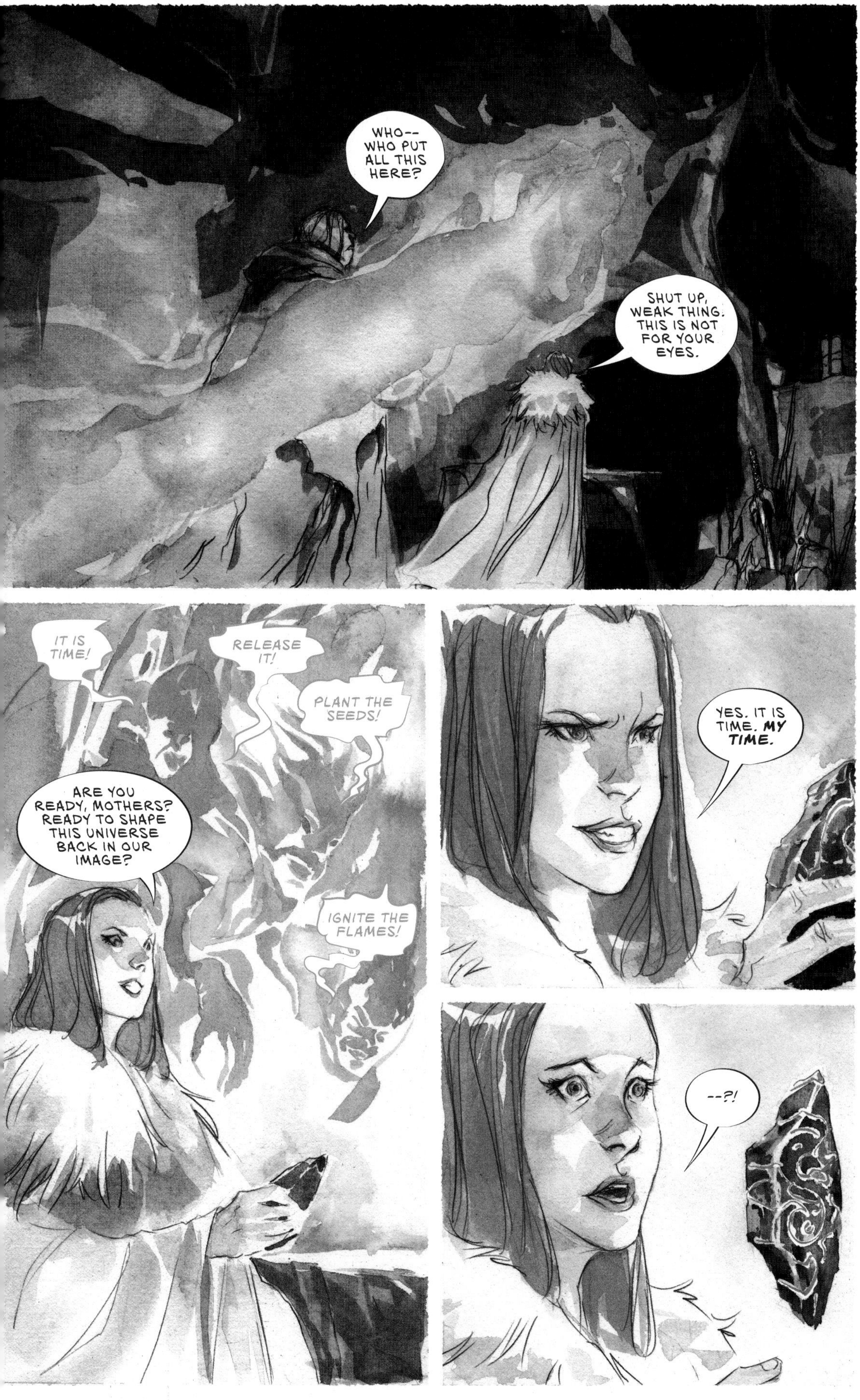
WHO--
WHO PUT ALL THIS HERE?
SHUT UP, WEAK THING. THIS IS NOT FOR YOUR EYES.
IT IS TIME!
RELEASE IT!
PLANT THE SEEDS!
ARE YOU READY, MOTHERS? READY TO SHAPE THIS UNIVERSE BACK IN OUR IMAGE?
IGNITE THE FLAMES!
YES. IT IS TIME. MY TIME.
--?!

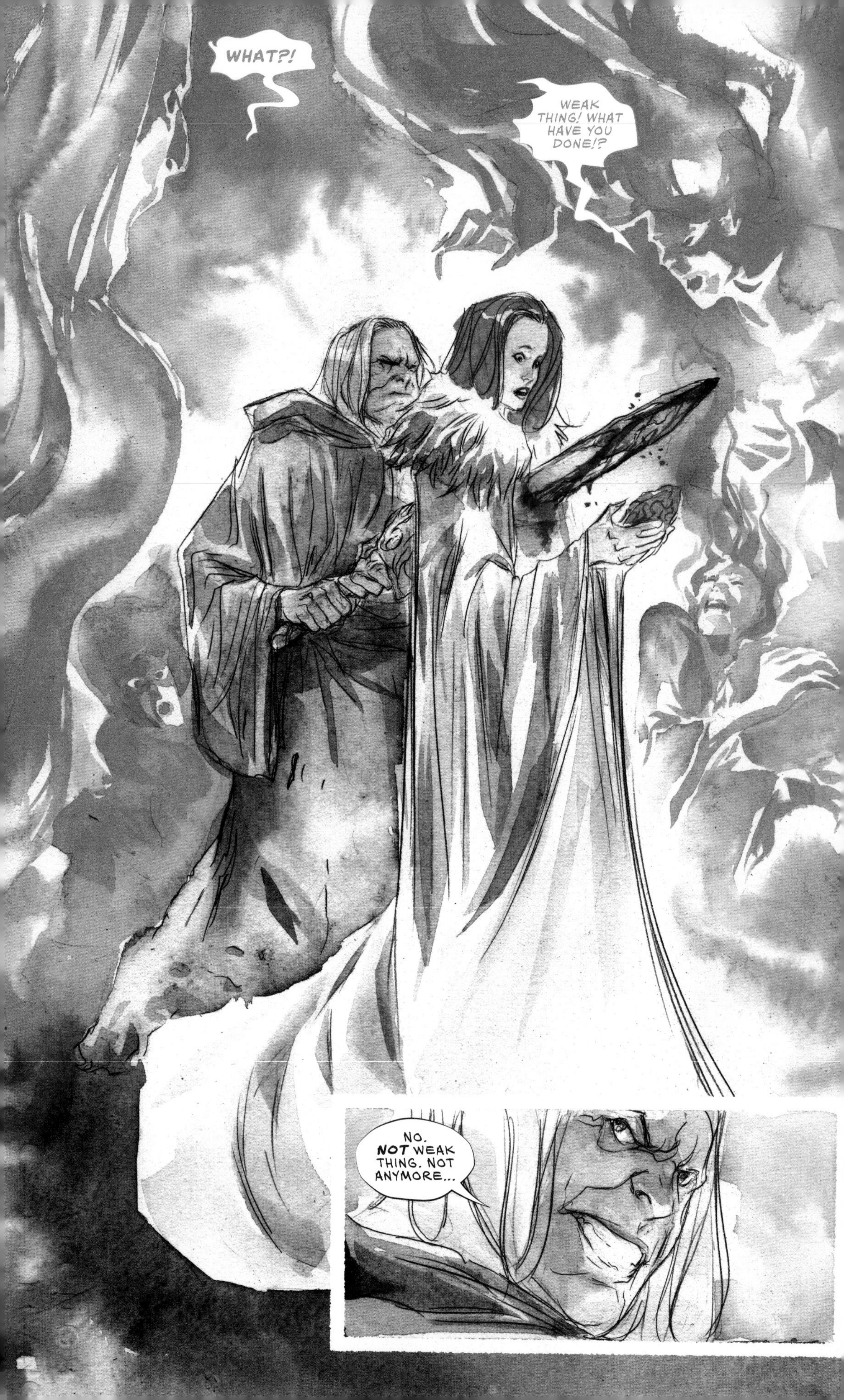
WHAT?!
WEAK THING! WHAT HAVE YOU DONE!?
NO. NOT WEAK THING. NOT ANYMORE...

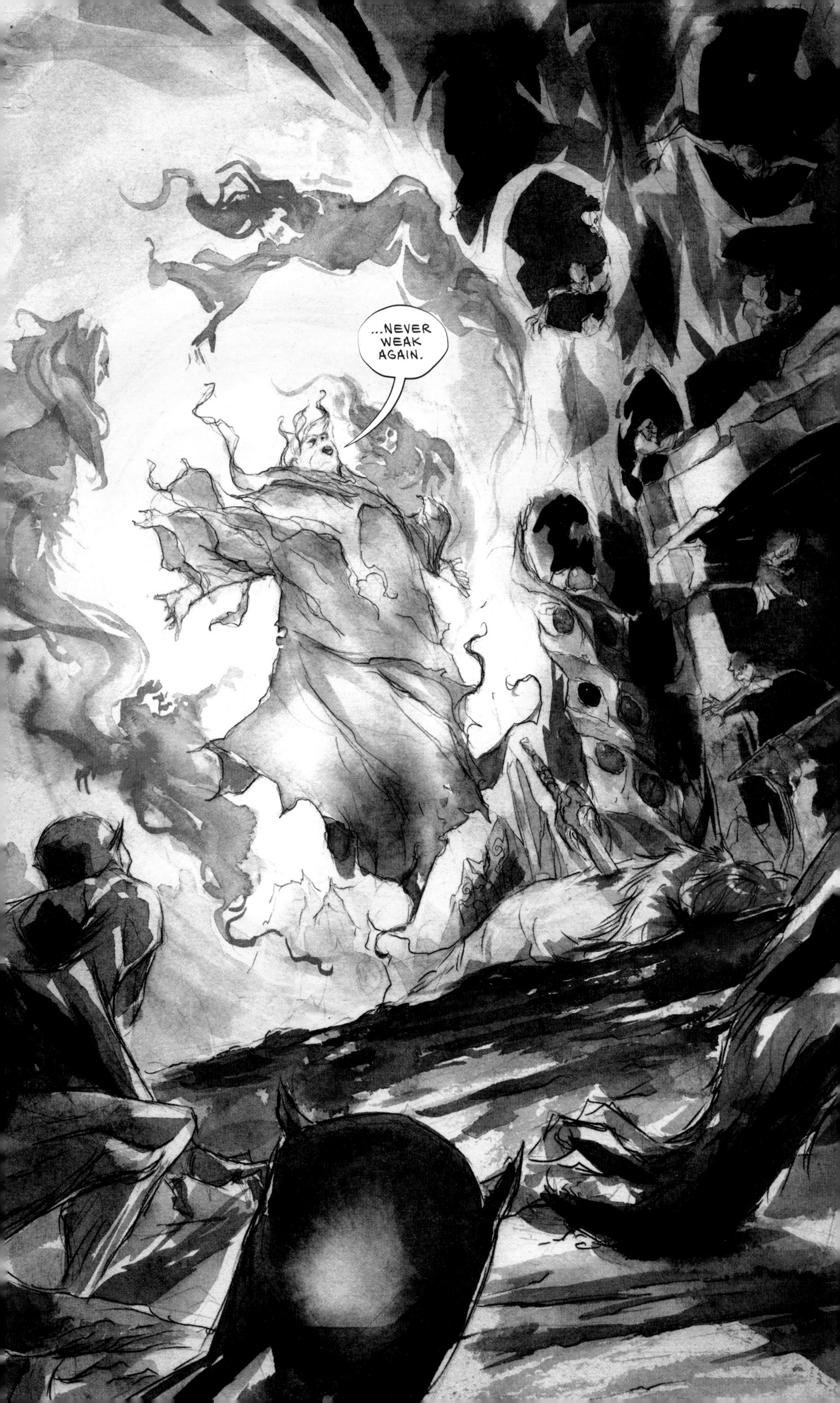
...NEVER WEAK AGAIN.

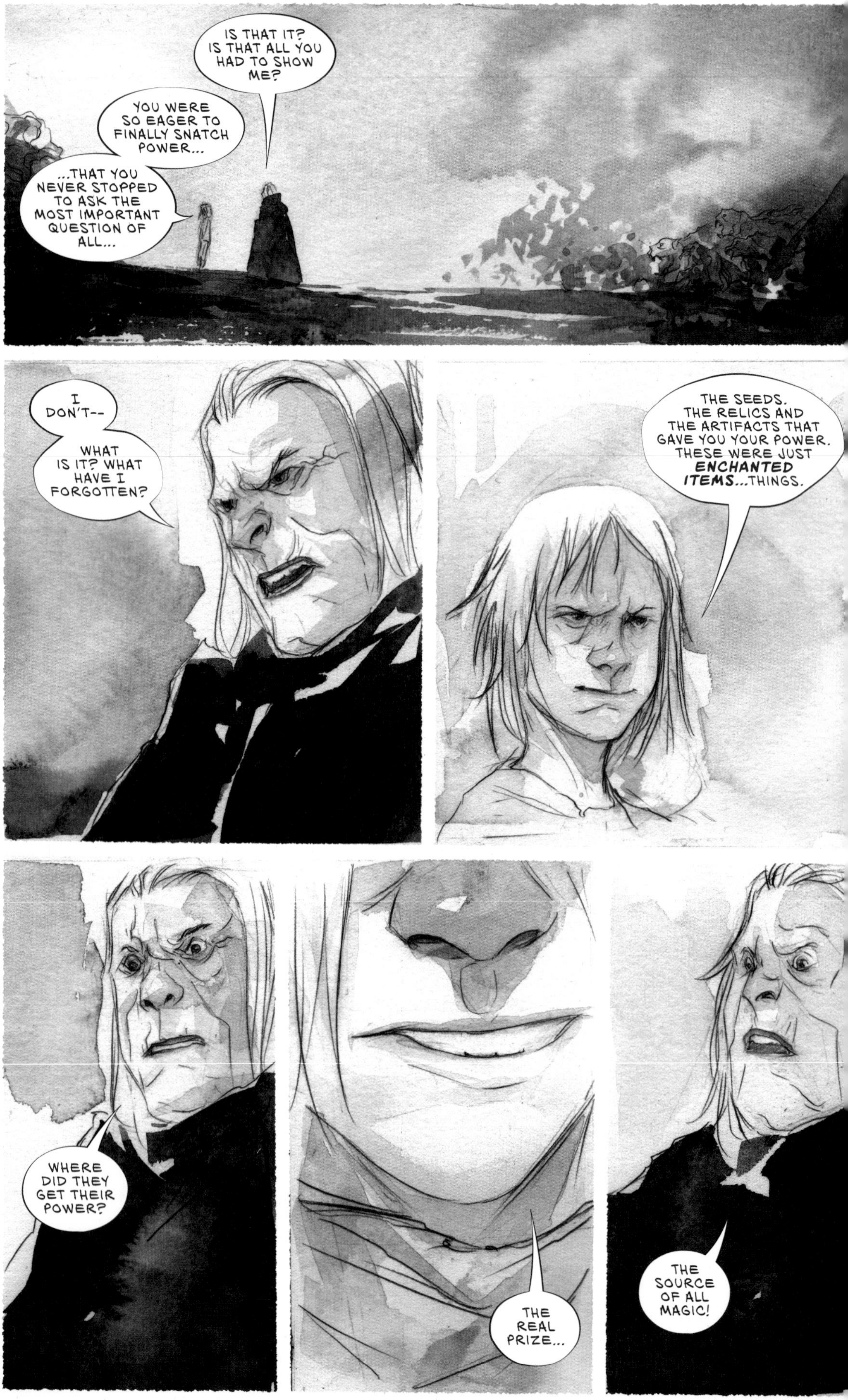
IS THAT IT? IS THAT ALL YOU HAD TO SHOW ME?
YOU WERE SO EAGER TO FINALLY SNATCH POWER...
...THAT YOU NEVER STOPPED TO ASK THE MOST IMPORTANT QUESTION OF ALL...
I DON'T--
WHAT IS IT? WHAT HAVE I FORGOTTEN?
THE SEEDS. THE RELICS AND THE ARTIFACTS THAT GAVE YOU YOUR POWER. THESE WERE JUST ENCHANTED ITEMS...THINGS.
WHERE DID THEY GET THEIR POWER?
THE REAL PRIZE...
THE SOURCE OF ALL MAGIC!

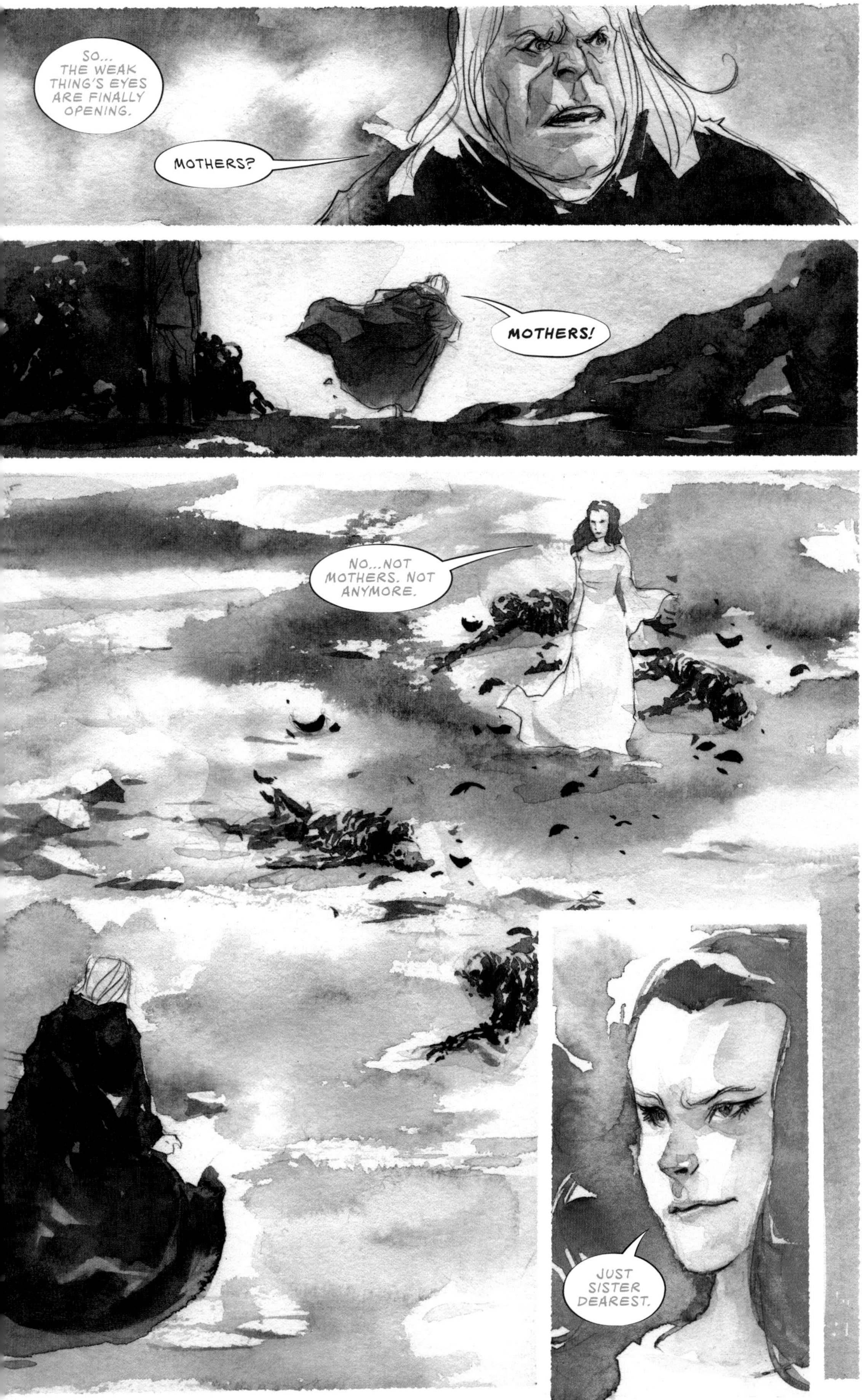
SO... THE WEAK THING'S EYES ARE FINALLY OPENING.
MOTHERS?
MOTHERS!
NO...NOT MOTHERS. NOT ANYMORE.
JUST SISTER DEAREST.

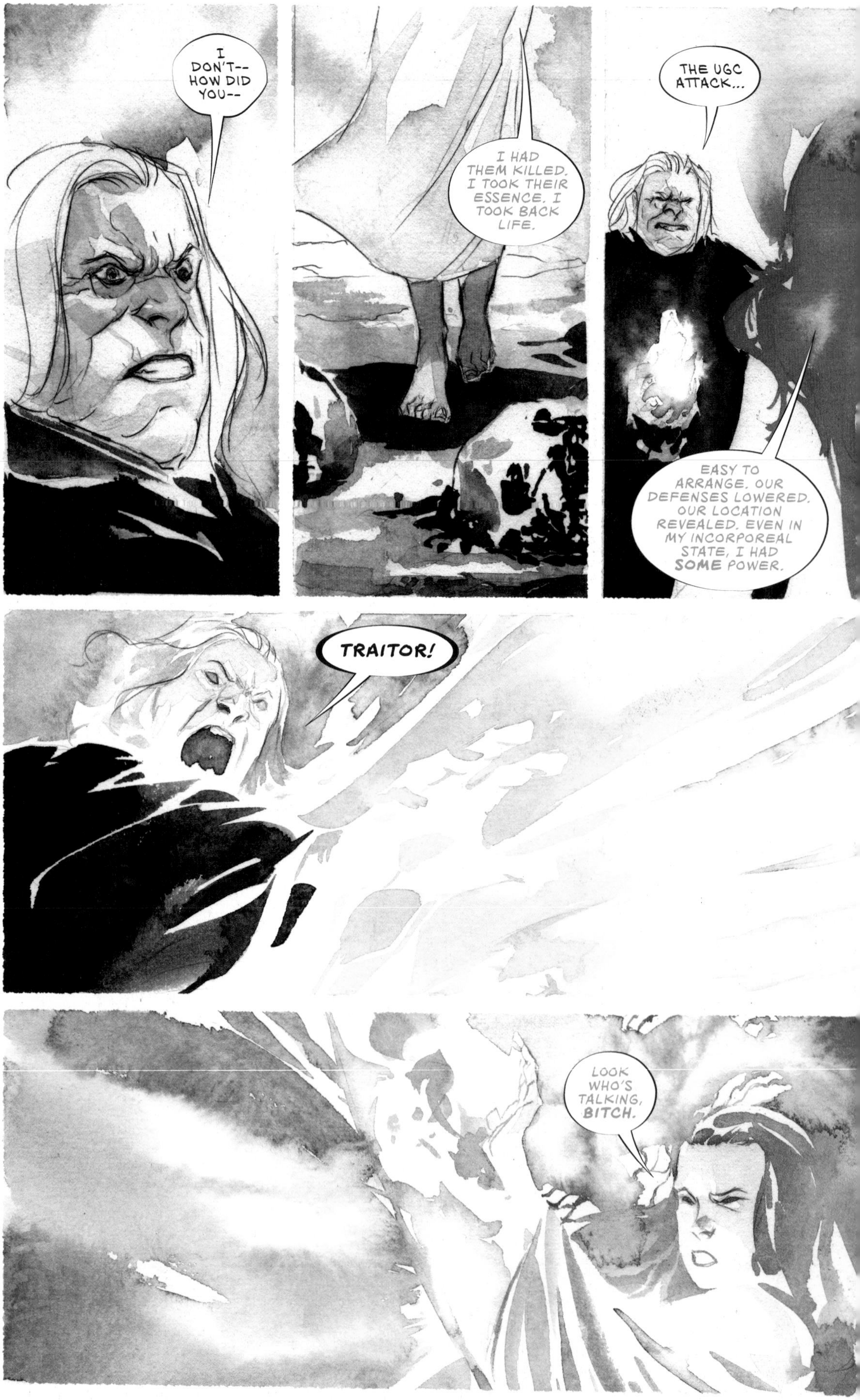
I DON'T-- HOW DID YOU--
I HAD THEM KILLED. I TOOK THEIR ESSENCE. I TOOK BACK LIFE.
THE UGC ATTACK...
EASY TO ARRANGE. OUR DEFENSES LOWERED. OUR LOCATION REVEALED. EVEN IN MY INCORPOREAL STATE, I HAD SOME POWER.
TRAITOR!
LOOK WHO'S TALKING, BITCH.

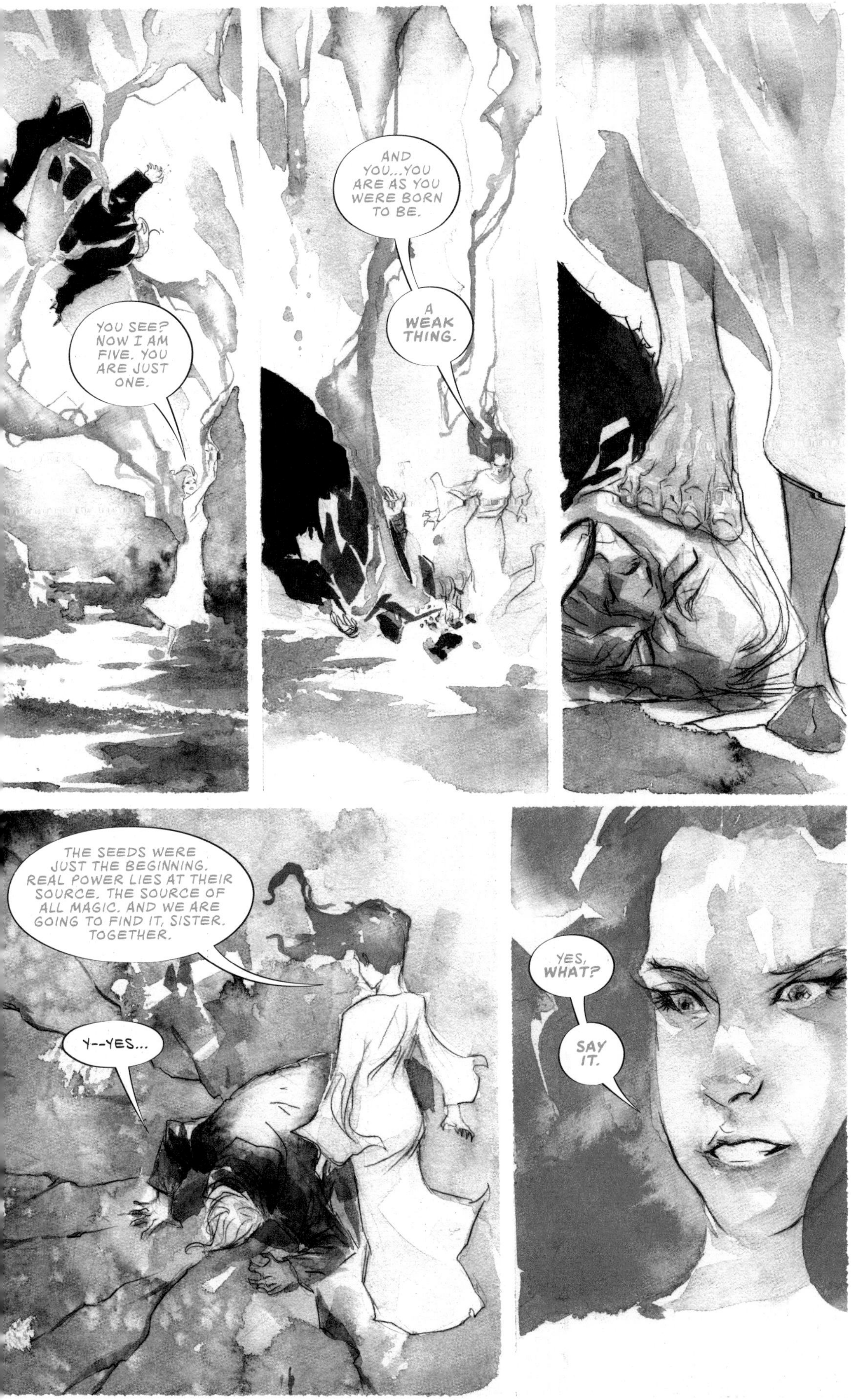
YOU SEE? NOW I AM FIVE. YOU ARE JUST ONE.
AND YOU...YOU ARE AS YOU WERE BORN TO BE.
A WEAK THING.
THE SEEDS WERE JUST THE BEGINNING. REAL POWER LIES AT THEIR SOURCE. THE SOURCE OF ALL MAGIC. AND WE ARE GOING TO FIND IT, SISTER. TOGETHER.
Y--YES...
YES, WHAT?
SAY IT.

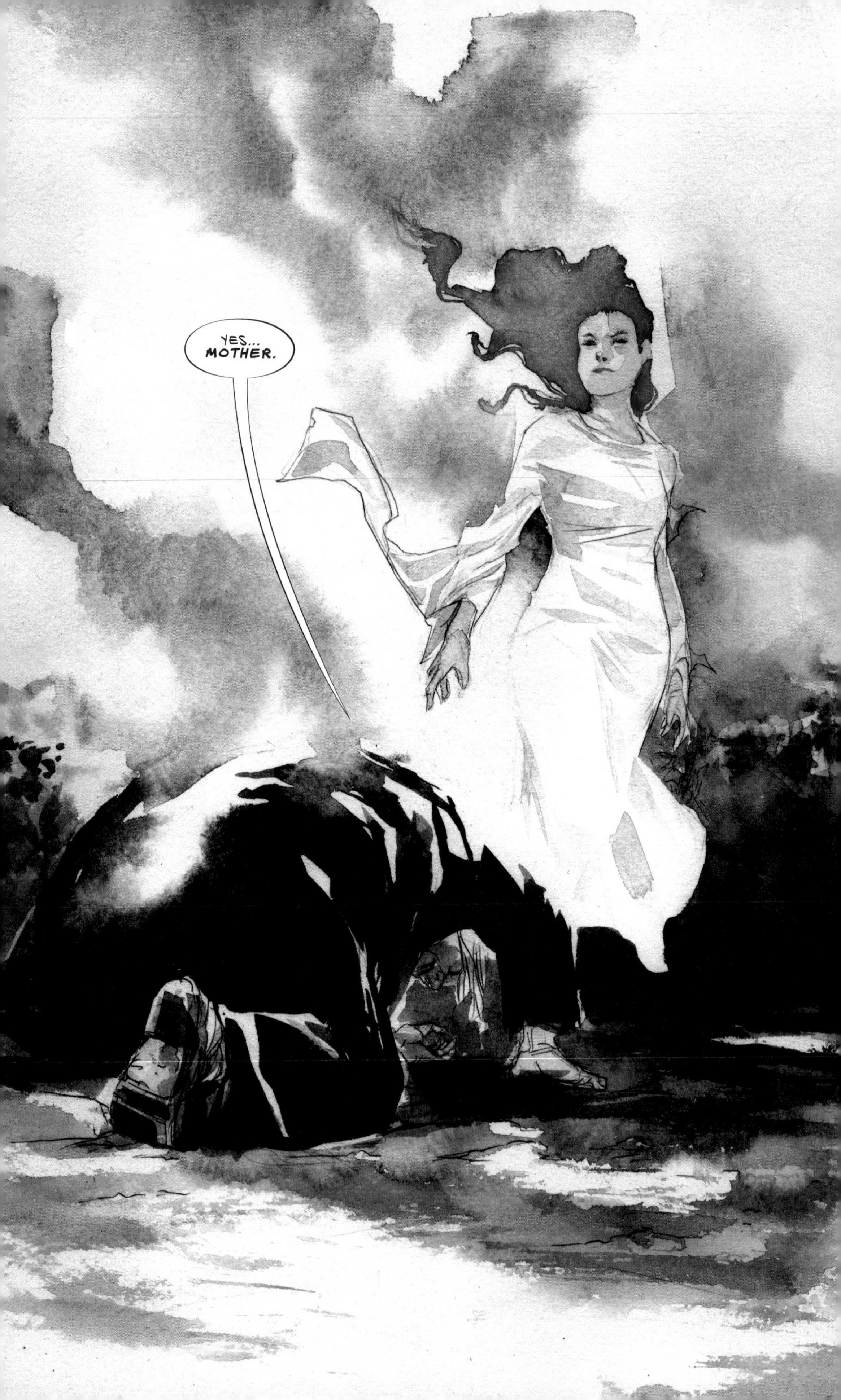
YES... MOTHER.

10

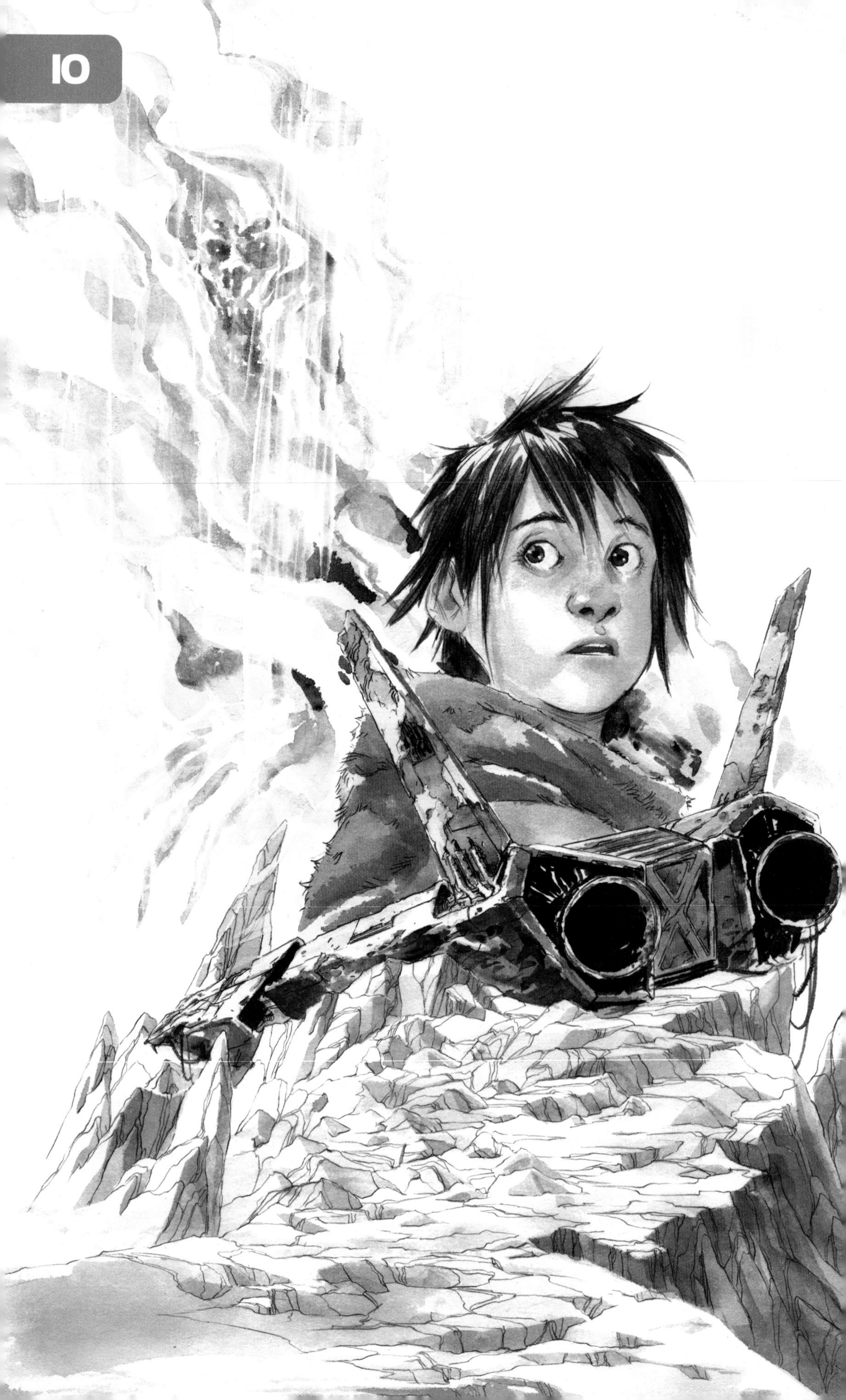

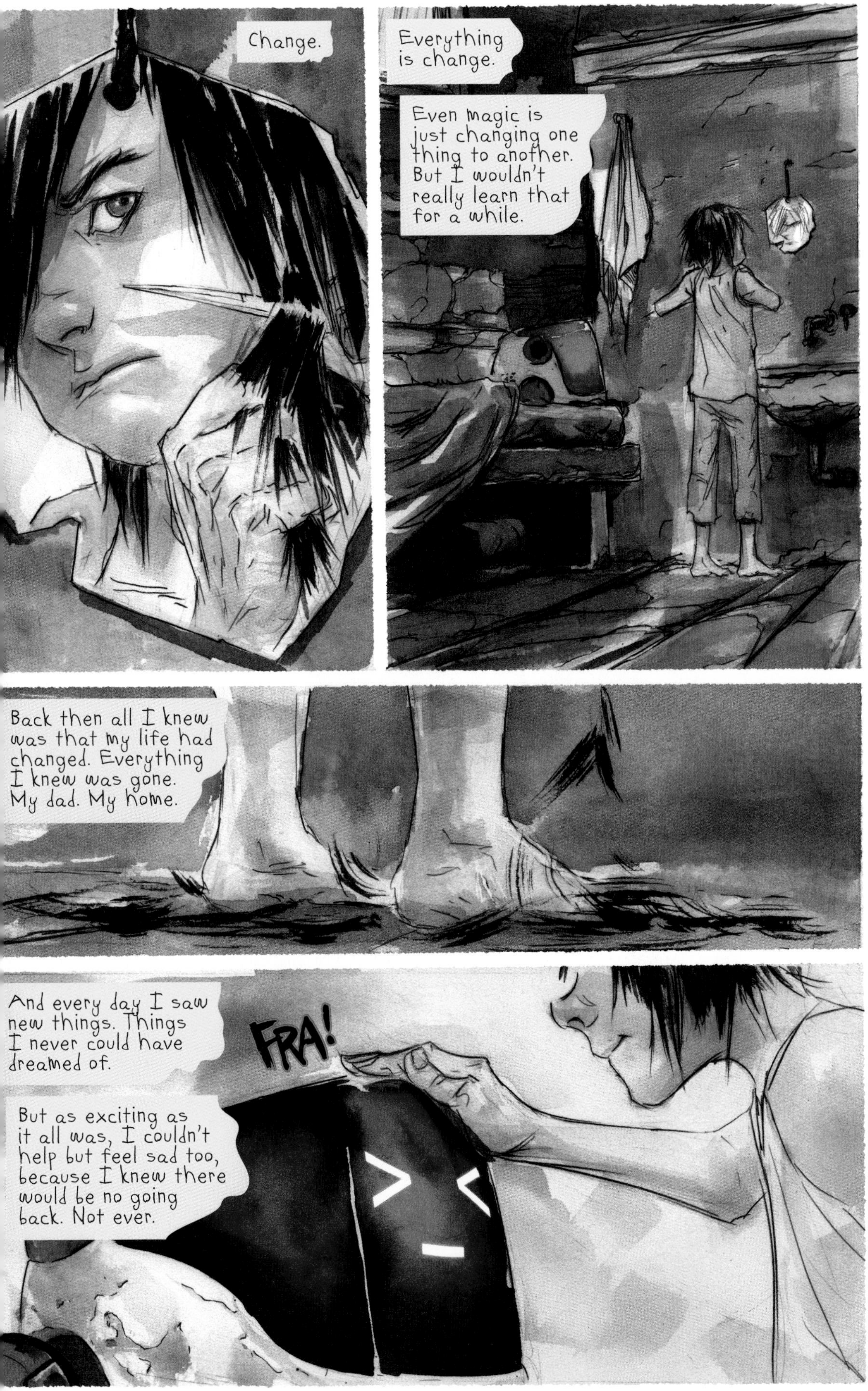
Change.
Everything is change.
Even magic is just changing one thing to another. But I wouldn't really learn that for a while.
Back then all I knew was that my life had changed. Everything I knew was gone. My dad. My home.
And every day I saw new things. Things I never could have dreamed of.
FRA!
But as exciting as it all was, I couldn't help but feel sad too, because I knew there would be no going back. Not ever.

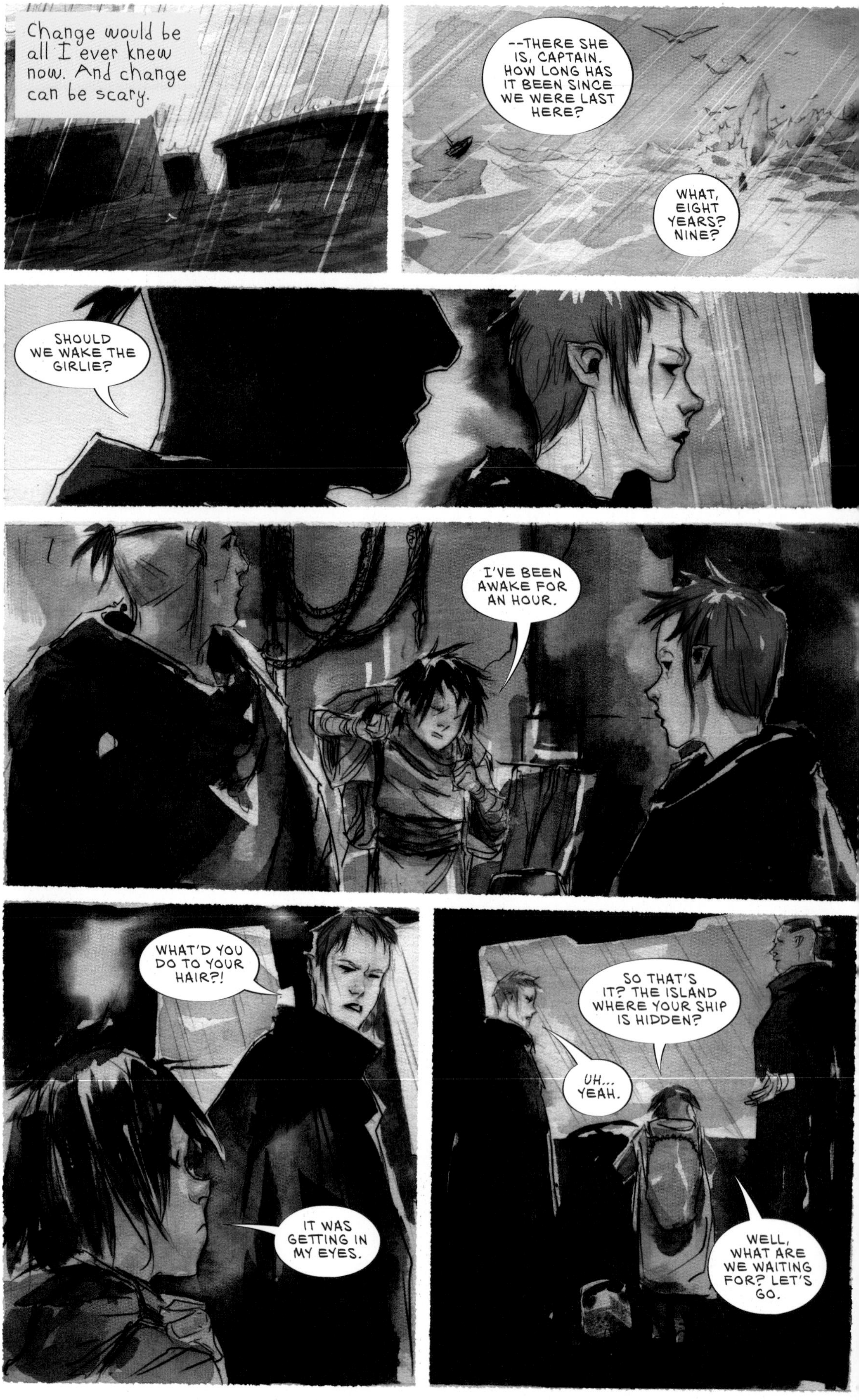
Change would be all I ever knew now. And change can be scary.
--THERE SHE IS, CAPTAIN. HOW LONG HAS IT BEEN SINCE WE WERE LAST HERE?
WHAT, EIGHT YEARS? NINE?
SHOULD WE WAKE THE GIRLIE?
I'VE BEEN AWAKE FOR AN HOUR.
WHAT'D YOU DO TO YOUR HAIR?!
IT WAS GETTING IN MY EYES.
SO THAT'S IT? THE ISLAND WHERE YOUR SHIP IS HIDDEN?
UH... YEAH.
WELL, WHAT ARE WE WAITING FOR? LET'S GO.

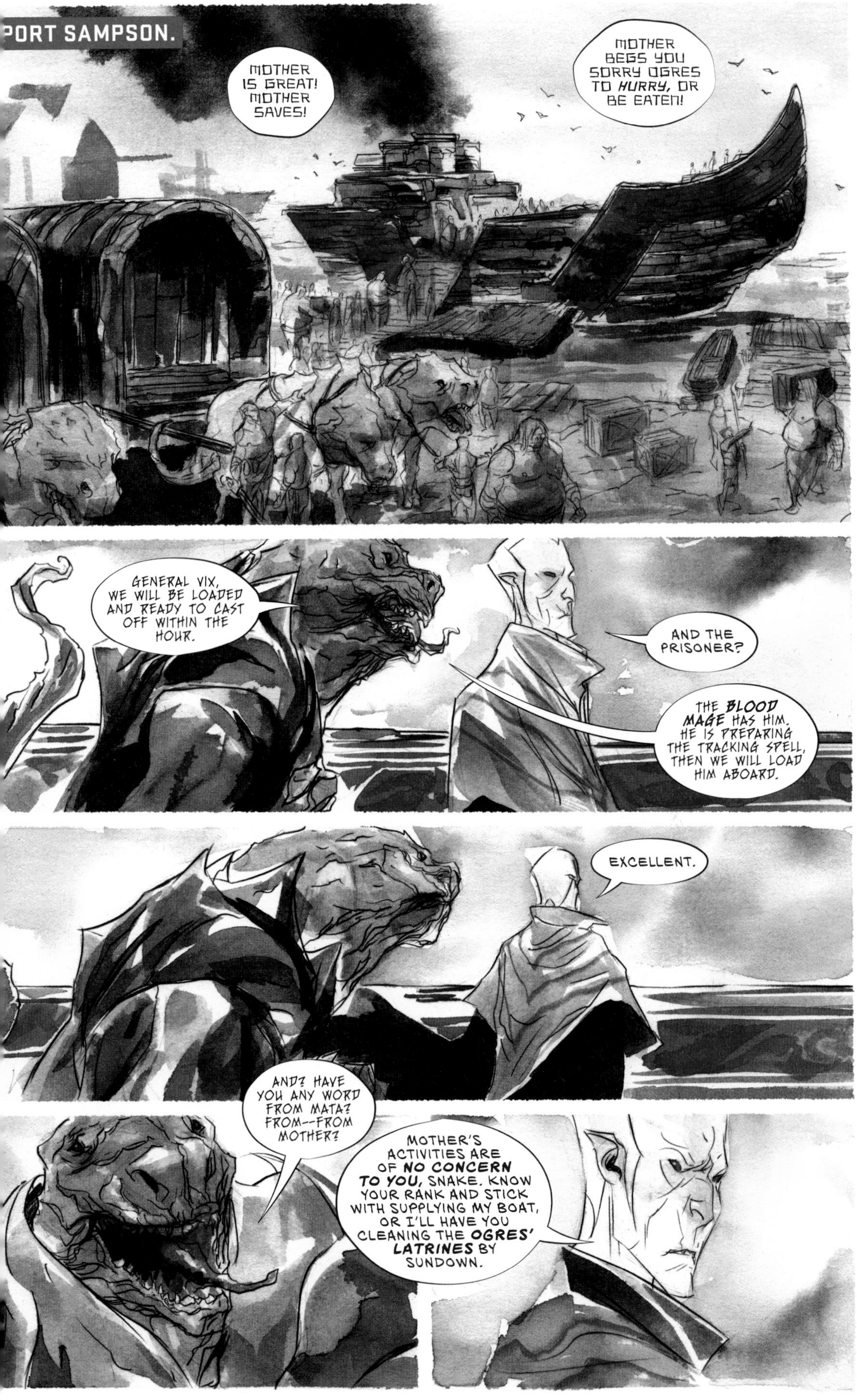
PORT SAMPSON.
MOTHER IS GREAT! MOTHER SAVES!
MOTHER BEGS YOU SORRY OGRES TO HURRY, OR BE EATEN!
GENERAL VIX, WE WILL BE LOADED AND READY TO CAST OFF WITHIN THE HOUR.
AND THE PRISONER?
THE BLOOD MAGE HAS HIM. HE IS PREPARING THE TRACKING SPELL, THEN WE WILL LOAD HIM ABOARD.
EXCELLENT.
AND? HAVE YOU ANY WORD FROM MATA? FROM--FROM MOTHER?
MOTHER'S ACTIVITIES ARE OF NO CONCERN TO YOU, SNAKE. KNOW YOUR RANK AND STICK WITH SUPPLYING MY BOAT, OR I'LL HAVE YOU CLEANING THE OGRES' LATRINES BY SUNDOWN.

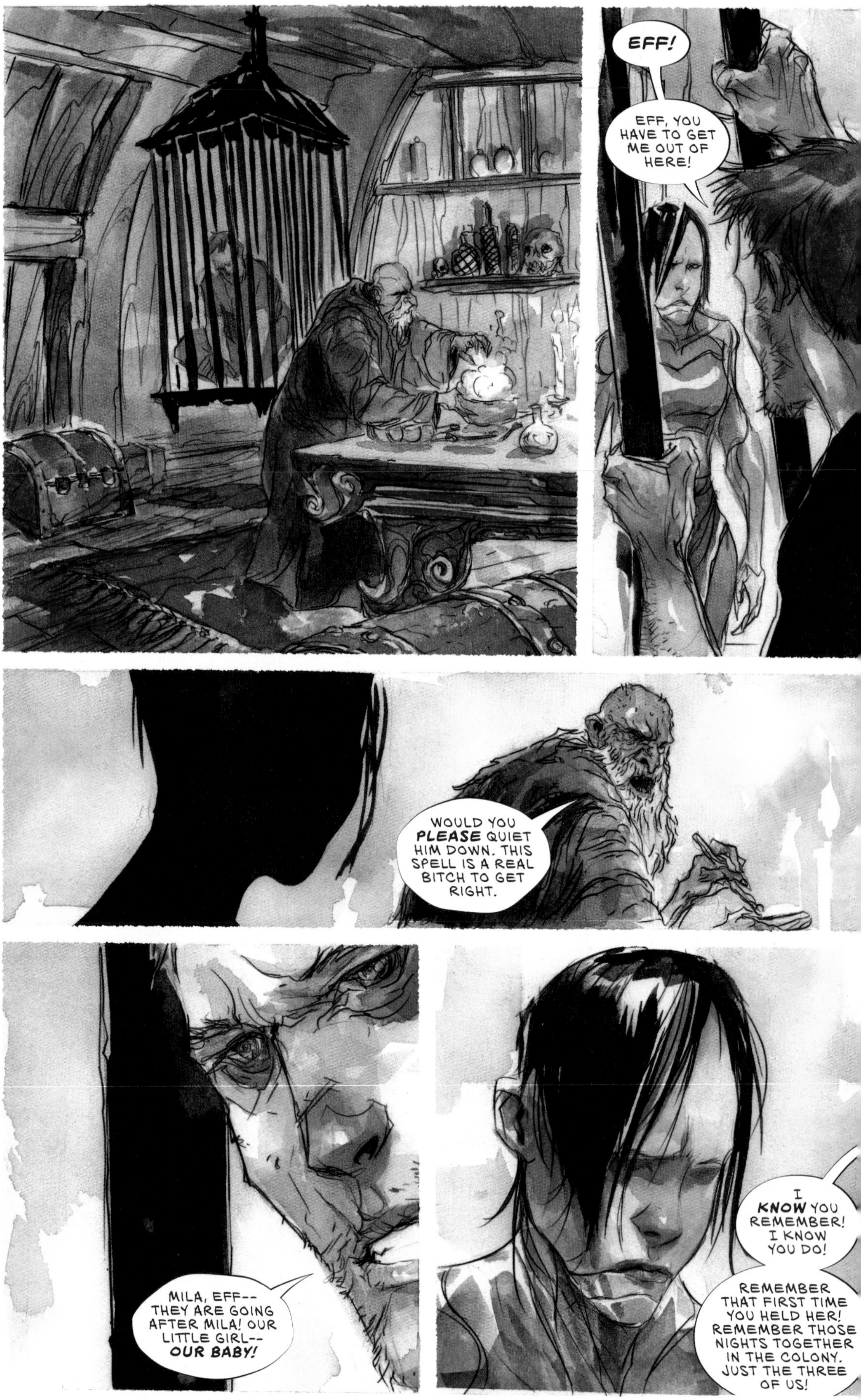
EFF!
EFF, YOU HAVE TO GET ME OUT OF HERE!
WOULD YOU PLEASE QUIET HIM DOWN. THIS SPELL IS A REAL BITCH TO GET RIGHT.
MILA, EFF-- THEY ARE GOING AFTER MILA! OUR LITTLE GIRL-- OUR BABY!
I KNOW YOU REMEMBER! I KNOW YOU DO!
REMEMBER THAT FIRST TIME YOU HELD HER! REMEMBER THOSE NIGHTS TOGETHER IN THE COLONY. JUST THE THREE OF US!

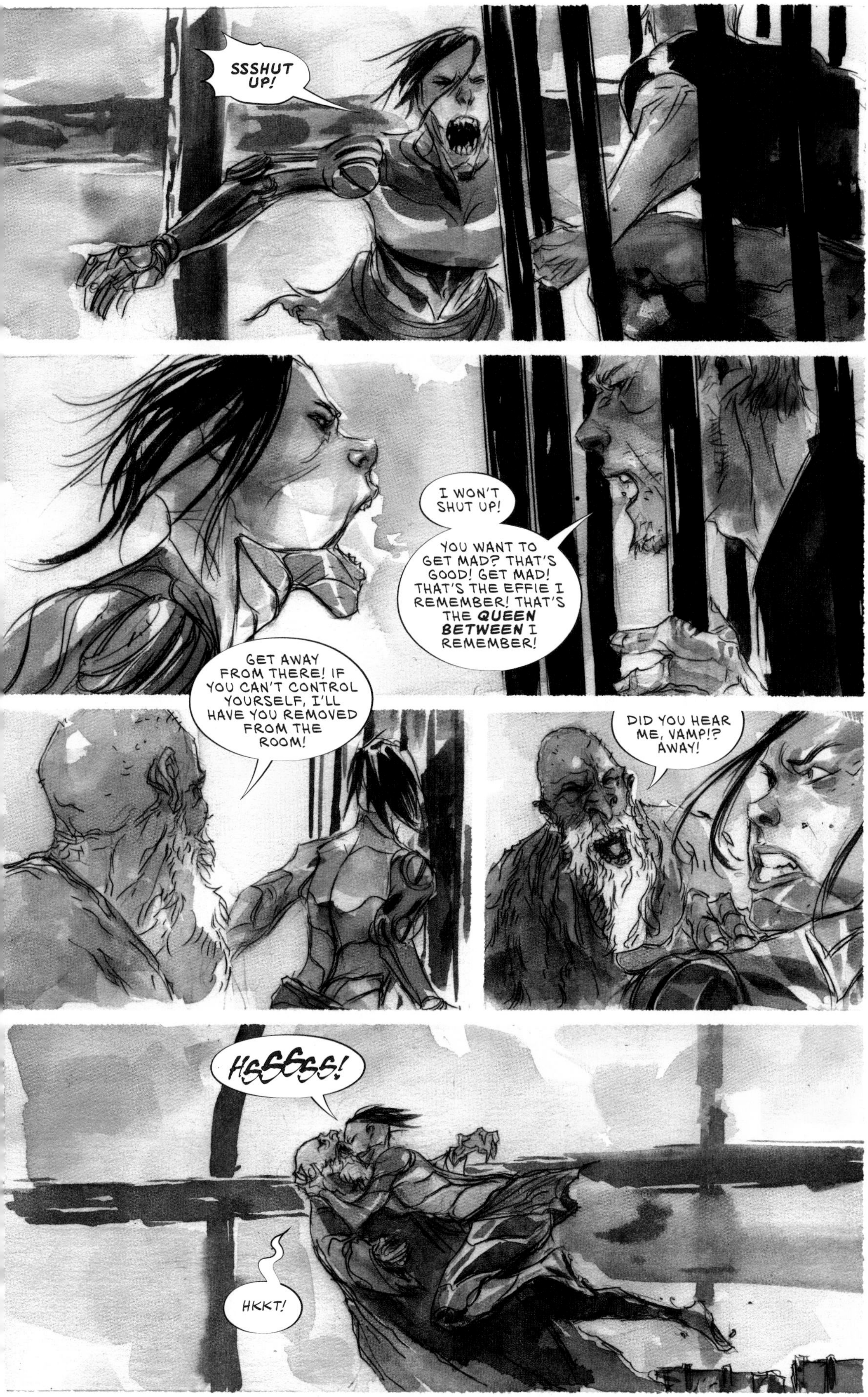
SSSHUT UP!
I WON'T SHUT UP!
YOU WANT TO GET MAD? THAT'S GOOD! GET MAD! THAT'S THE EFFIE I REMEMBER! THAT'S THE QUEEN BETWEEN I REMEMBER!
GET AWAY FROM THERE! IF YOU CAN'T CONTROL YOURSELF, I'LL HAVE YOU REMOVED FROM THE ROOM!
DID YOU HEAR ME, VAMP!? AWAY!
HSSSSSS!
HKKT!

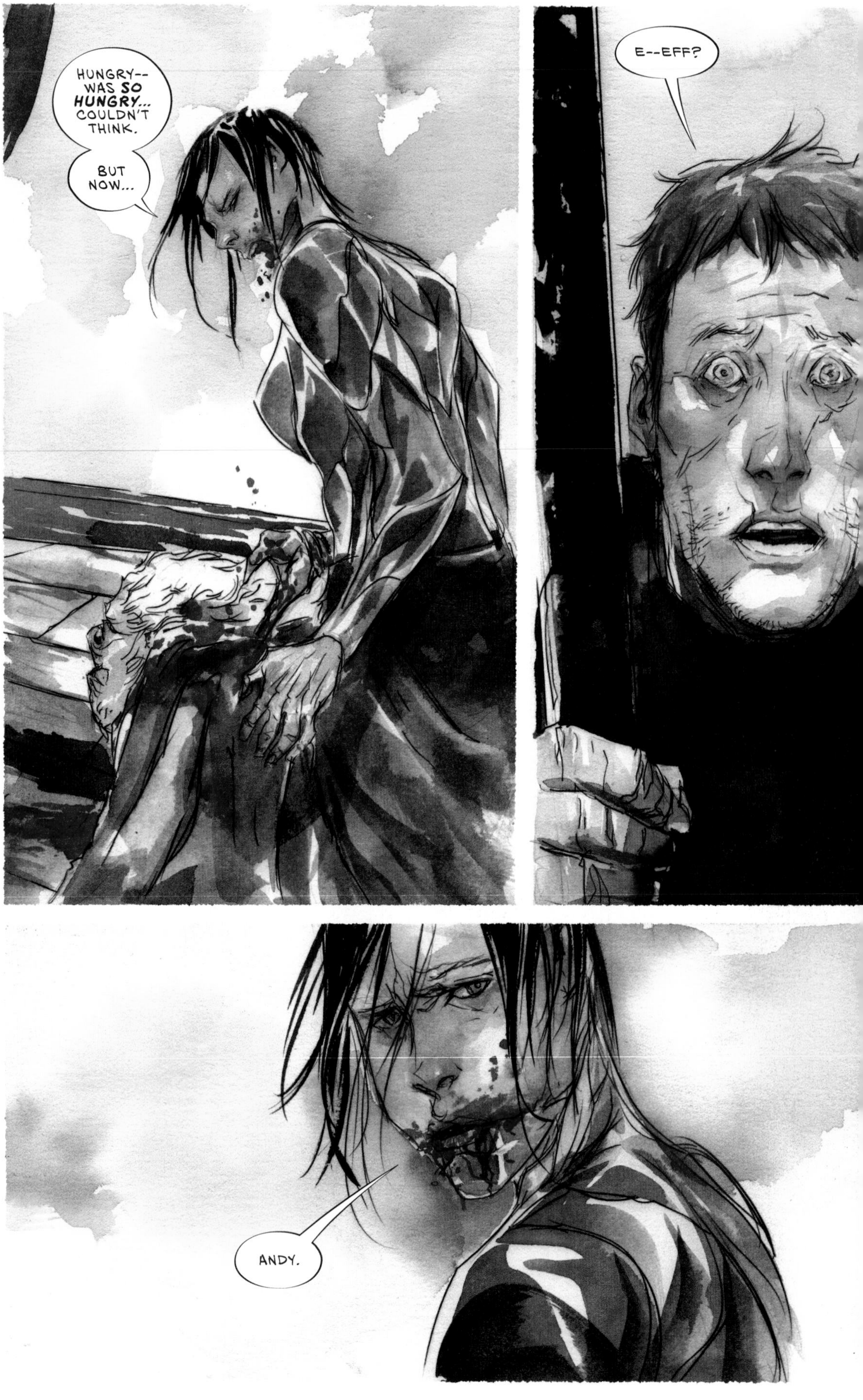
HUNGRY-- WAS **SO HUNGRY...** COULDN'T THINK.
BUT NOW...
E--EFF?
ANDY.

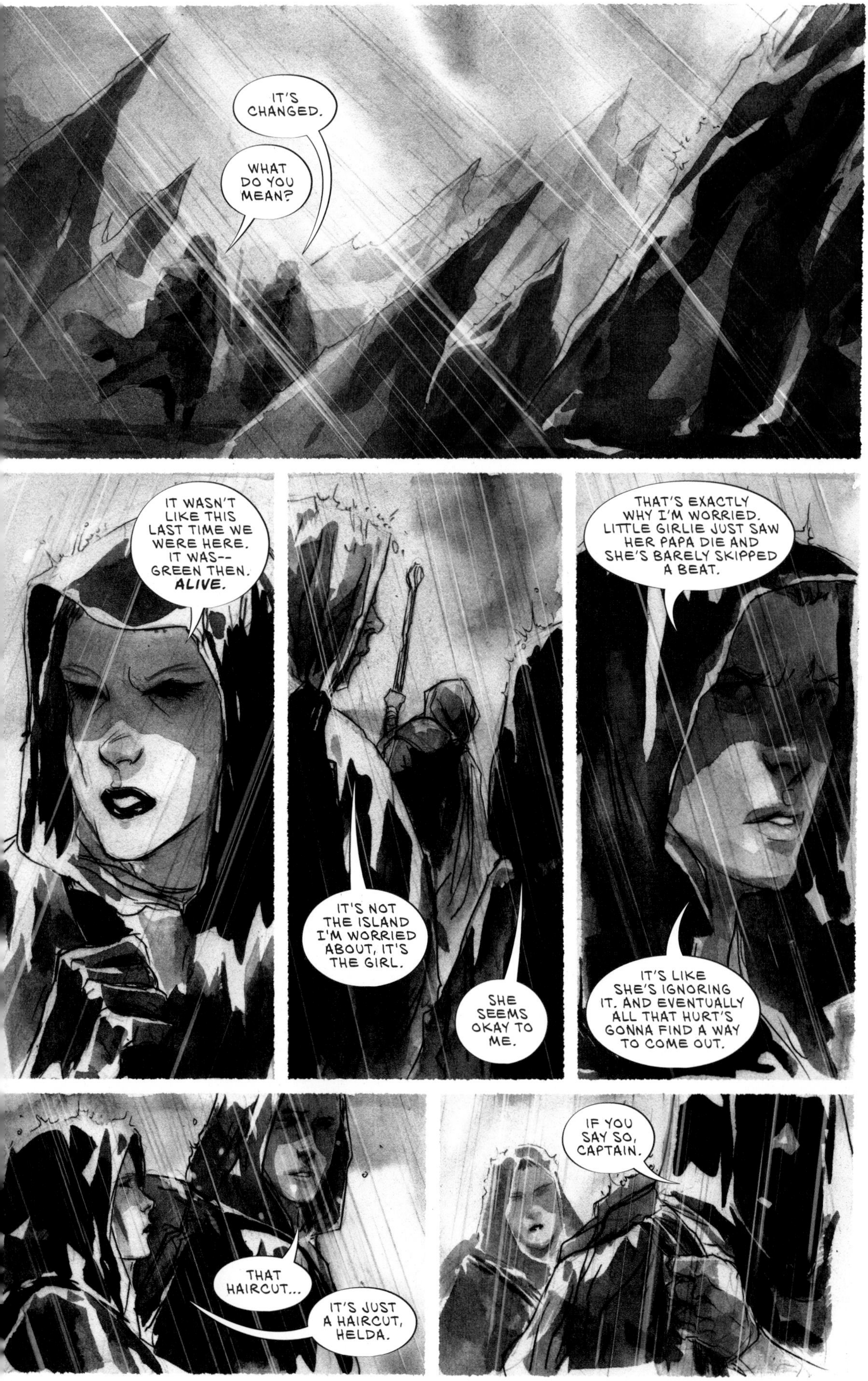
IT'S CHANGED.
WHAT DO YOU MEAN?
IT WASN'T LIKE THIS LAST TIME WE WERE HERE. IT WAS-- GREEN THEN. ALIVE.
IT'S NOT THE ISLAND I'M WORRIED ABOUT, IT'S THE GIRL.
SHE SEEMS OKAY TO ME.
THAT'S EXACTLY WHY I'M WORRIED. LITTLE GIRLIE JUST SAW HER PAPA DIE AND SHE'S BARELY SKIPPED A BEAT.
IT'S LIKE SHE'S IGNORING IT. AND EVENTUALLY ALL THAT HURT'S GONNA FIND A WAY TO COME OUT.
THAT HAIRCUT...
IT'S JUST A HAIRCUT, HELDA.
IF YOU SAY SO, CAPTAIN.

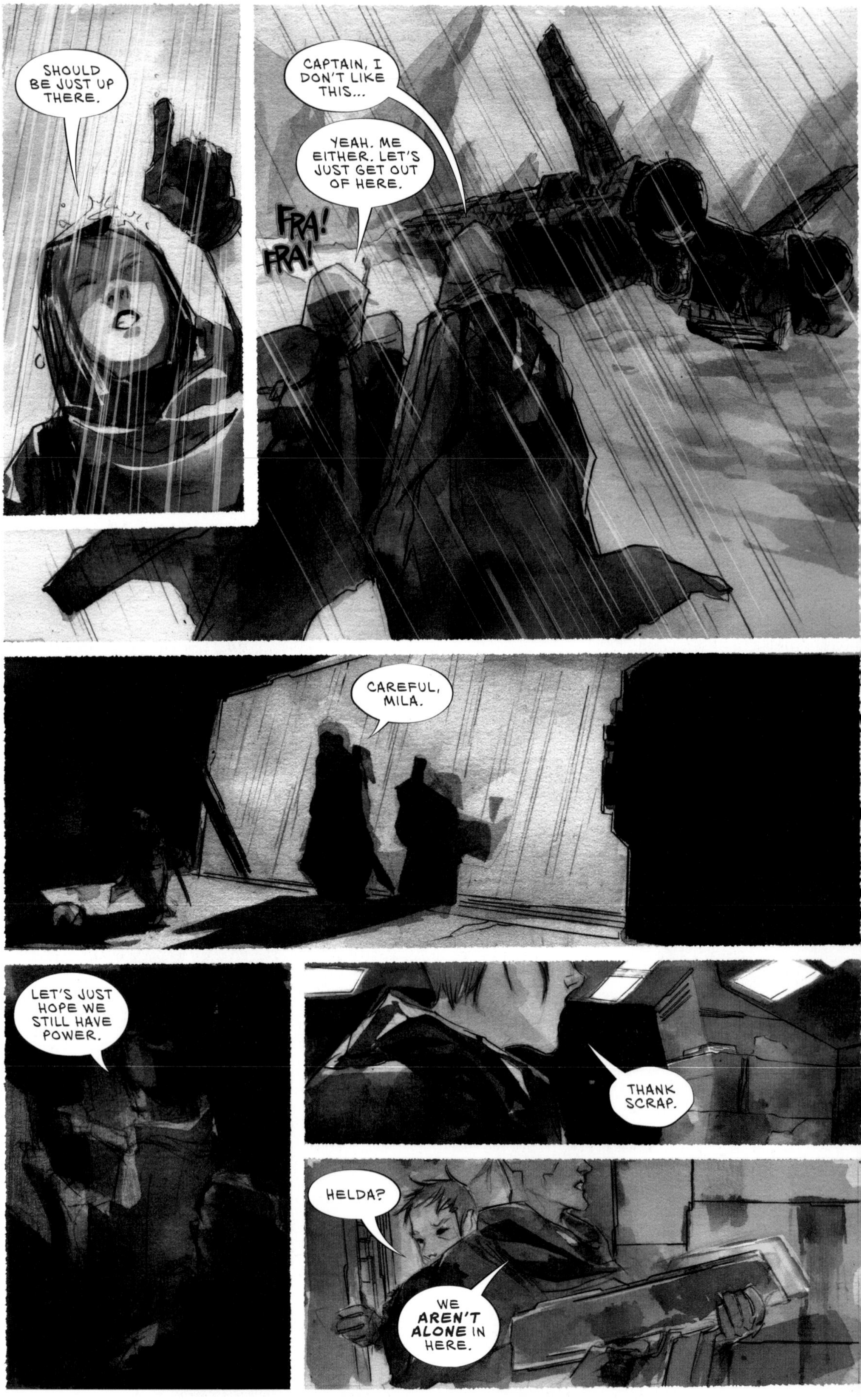
SHOULD BE JUST UP THERE.
CAPTAIN, I DON'T LIKE THIS...
YEAH. ME EITHER. LET'S JUST GET OUT OF HERE.
FRA! FRA!
CAREFUL, MILA.
LET'S JUST HOPE WE STILL HAVE POWER.
THANK SCRAP.
HELDA?
WE **AREN'T ALONE** IN HERE.

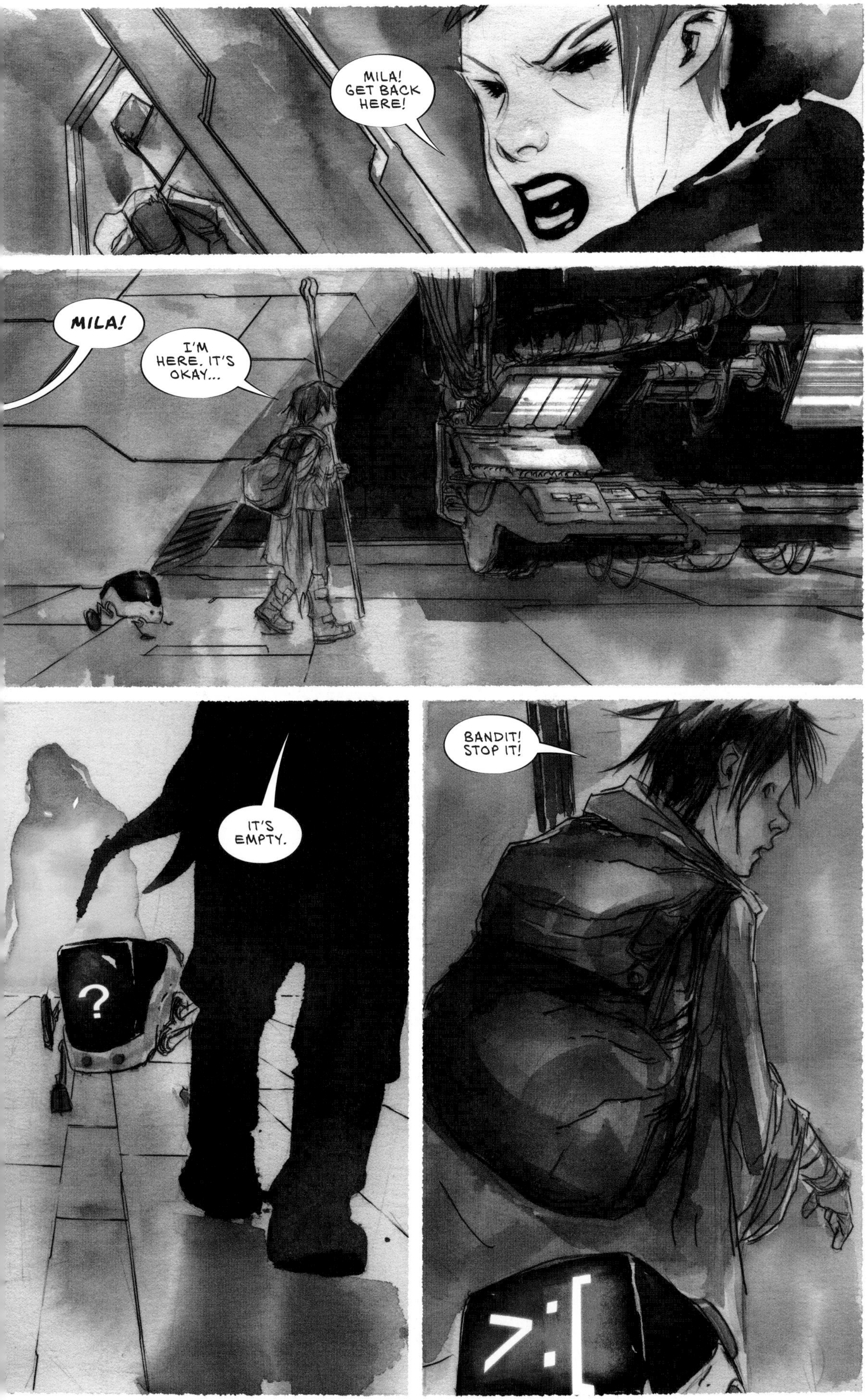
MILA! GET BACK HERE!
MILA!
I'M HERE. IT'S OKAY...
IT'S EMPTY.
?
BANDIT! STOP IT!
>:[

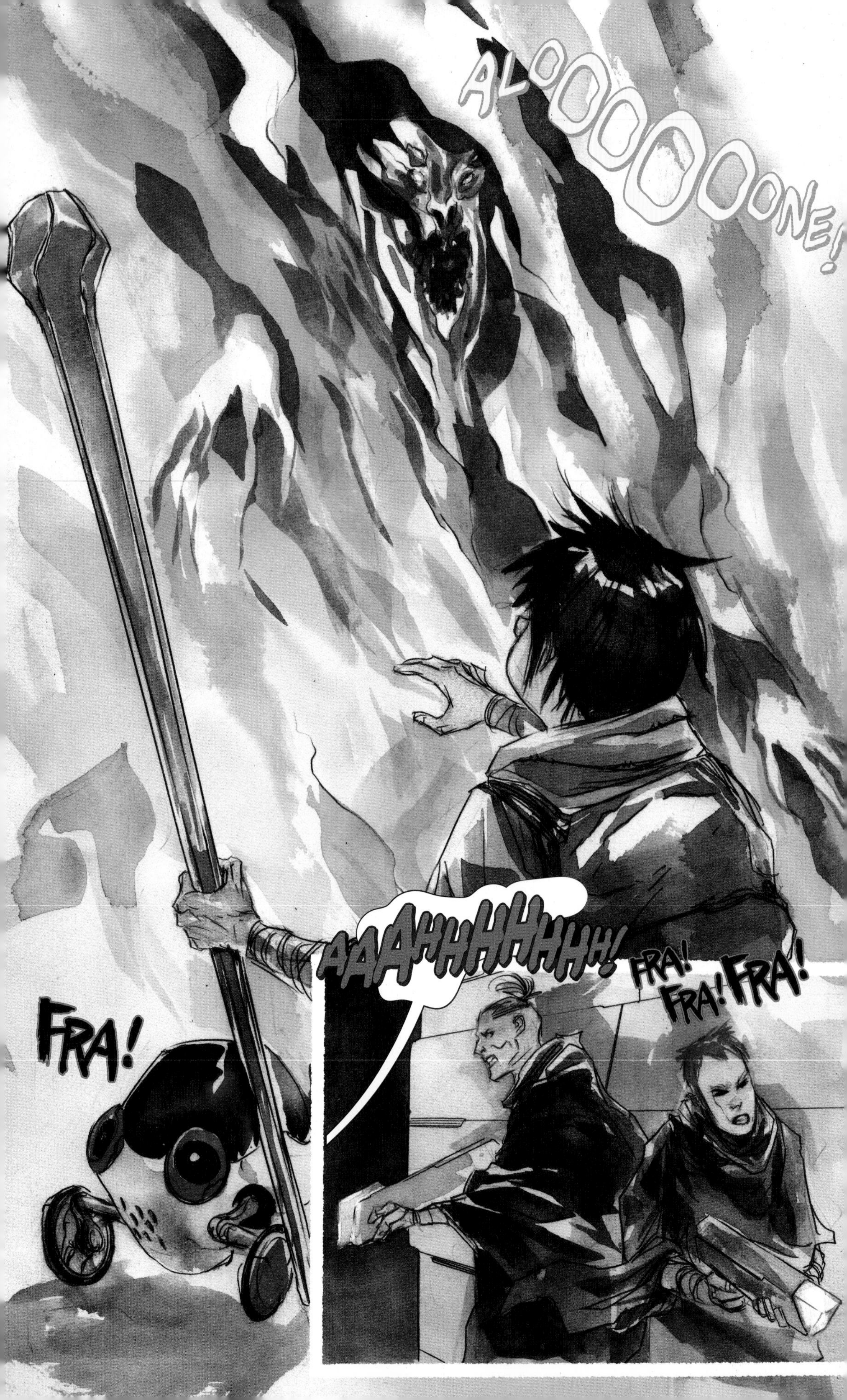

ALOOOOOOONE!
AAAHHHHHHH!
FRA!
FRA! FRA! FRA!

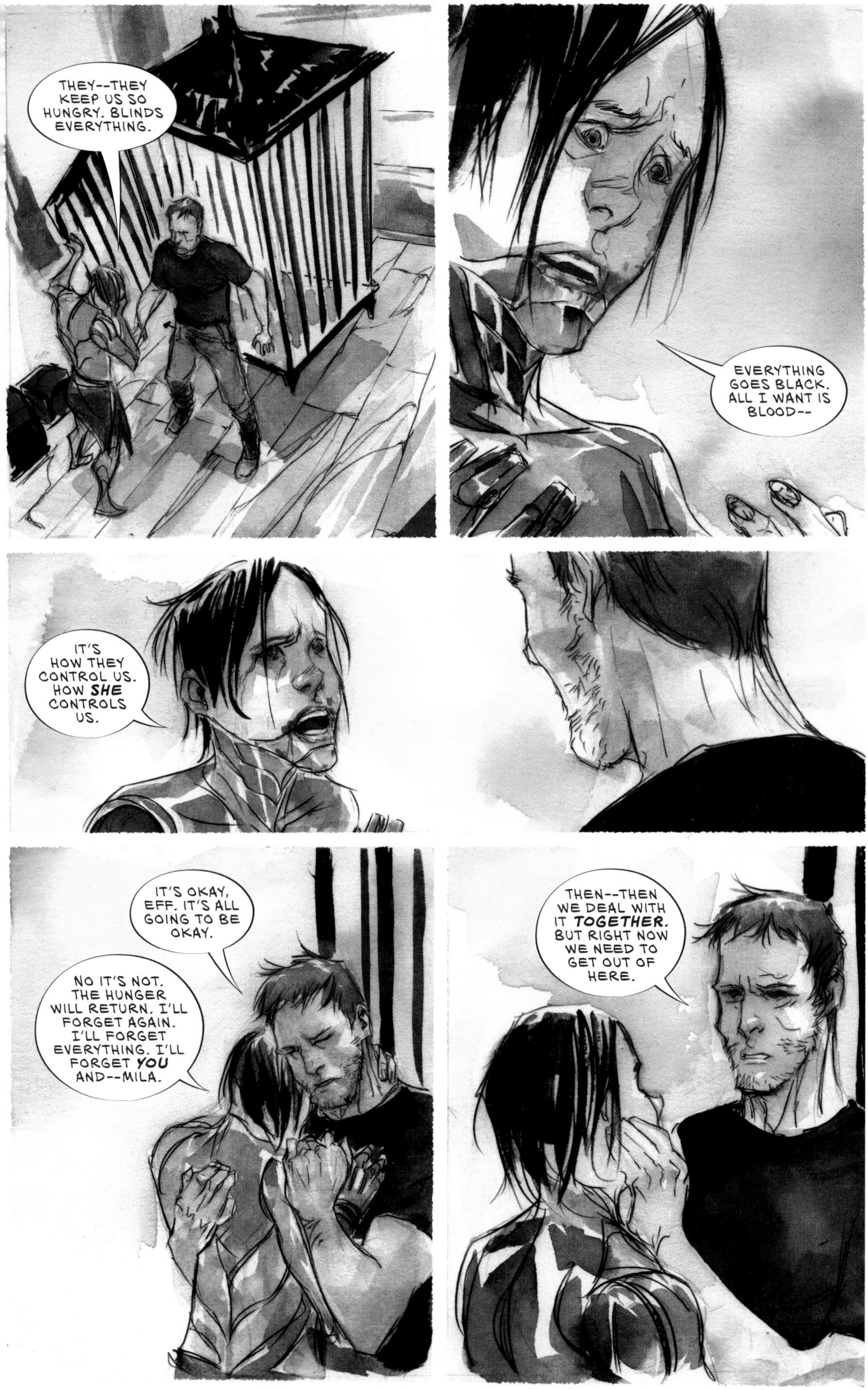
THEY--THEY KEEP US SO HUNGRY. BLINDS EVERYTHING.
EVERYTHING GOES BLACK. ALL I WANT IS BLOOD--
IT'S HOW THEY CONTROL US. HOW SHE CONTROLS US.
IT'S OKAY, EFF. IT'S ALL GOING TO BE OKAY.
NO IT'S NOT. THE HUNGER WILL RETURN. I'LL FORGET AGAIN. I'LL FORGET EVERYTHING. I'LL FORGET YOU AND--MILA.
THEN--THEN WE DEAL WITH IT TOGETHER. BUT RIGHT NOW WE NEED TO GET OUT OF HERE.

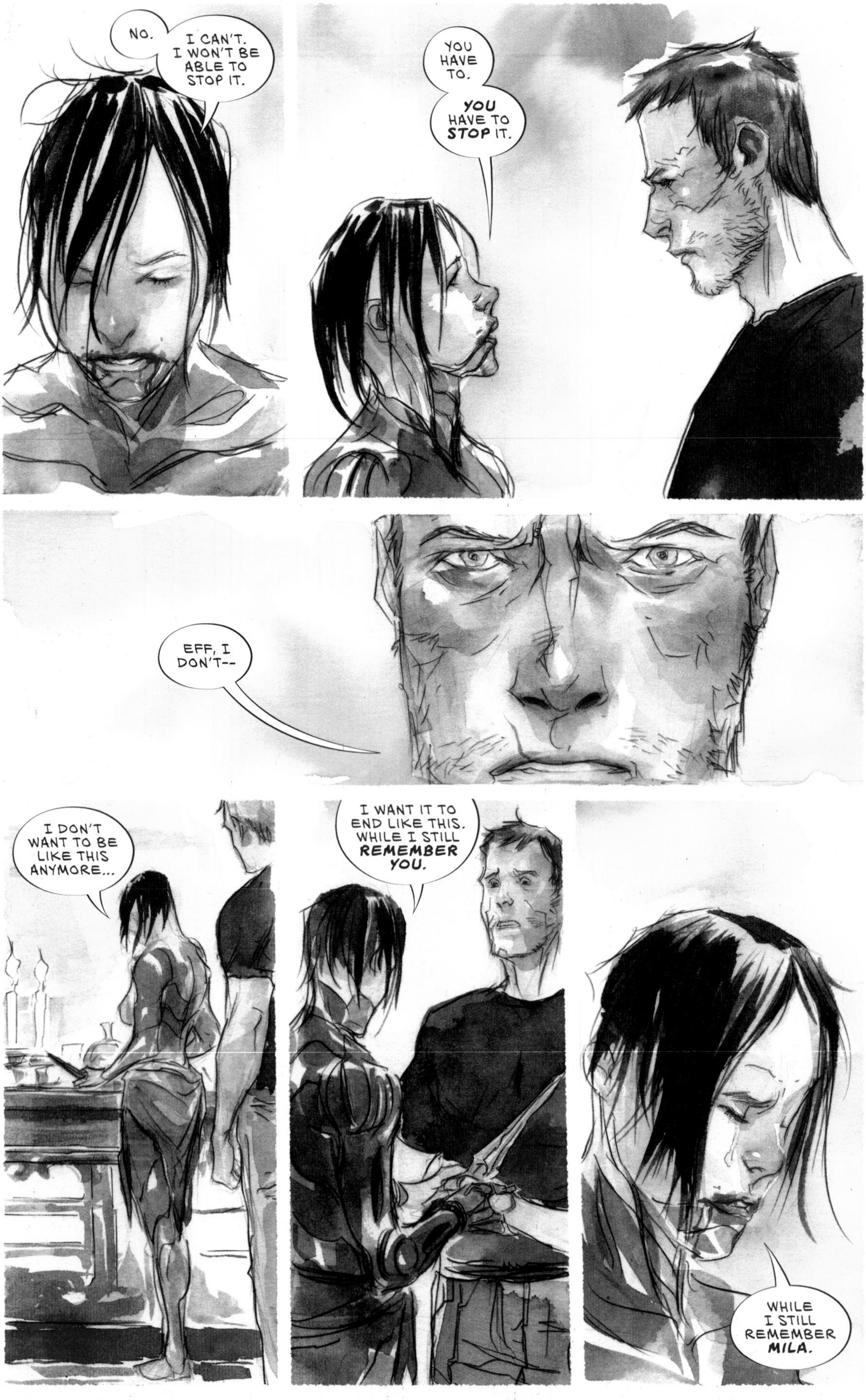
NO.
I CAN'T. I WON'T BE ABLE TO STOP IT.
YOU HAVE TO.
YOU HAVE TO STOP IT.
EFF, I DON'T--
I DON'T WANT TO BE LIKE THIS ANYMORE...
I WANT IT TO END LIKE THIS. WHILE I STILL REMEMBER YOU.
WHILE I STILL REMEMBER MILA.

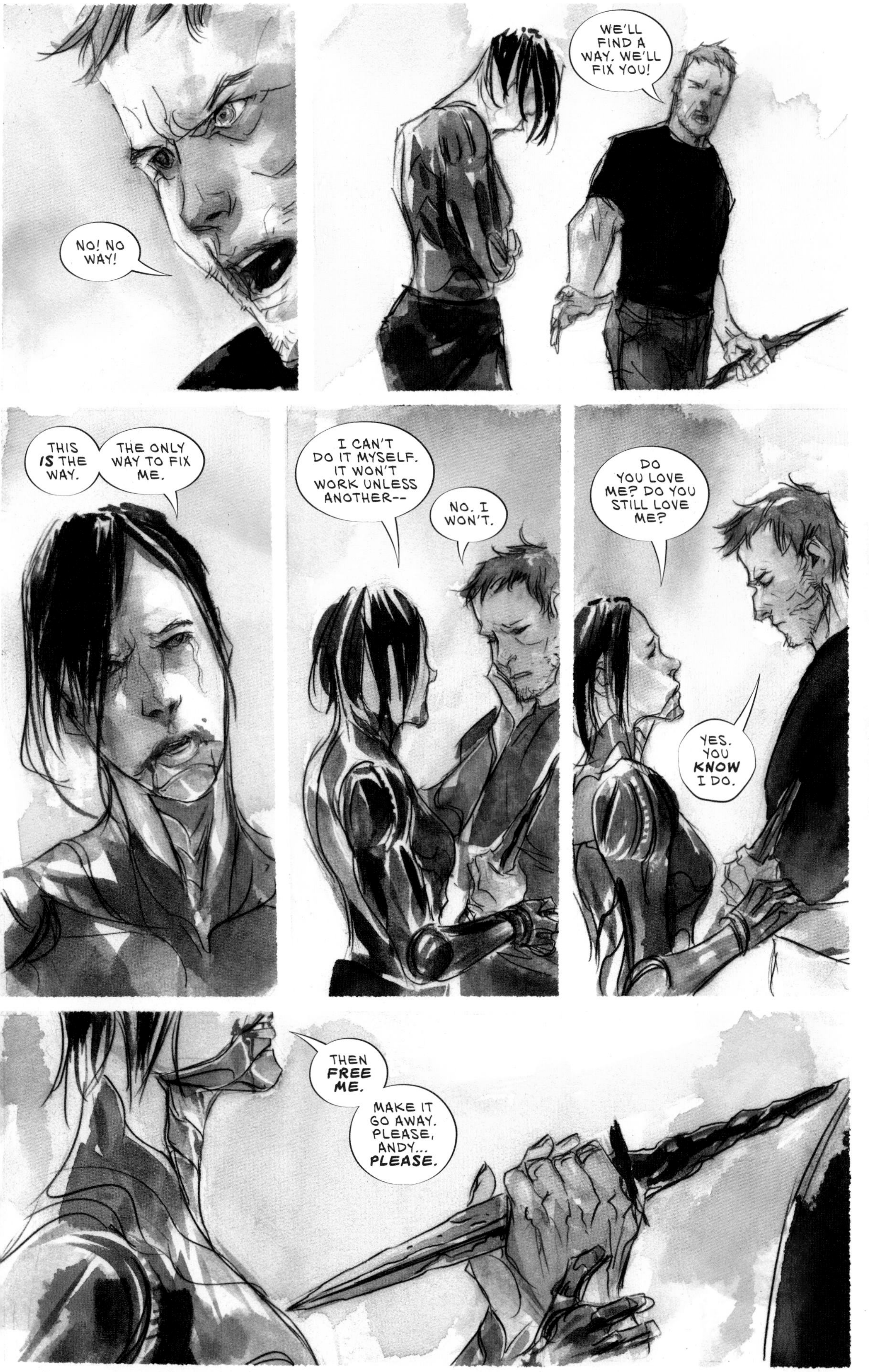
NO! NO WAY!
WE'LL FIND A WAY. WE'LL FIX YOU!
THIS *IS* THE WAY.
THE ONLY WAY TO FIX ME.
I CAN'T DO IT MYSELF. IT WON'T WORK UNLESS ANOTHER--
NO. I WON'T.
DO YOU LOVE ME? DO YOU STILL LOVE ME?
YES. YOU **KNOW** I DO.
THEN **FREE ME.**
MAKE IT GO AWAY. PLEASE, ANDY... ***PLEASE.***

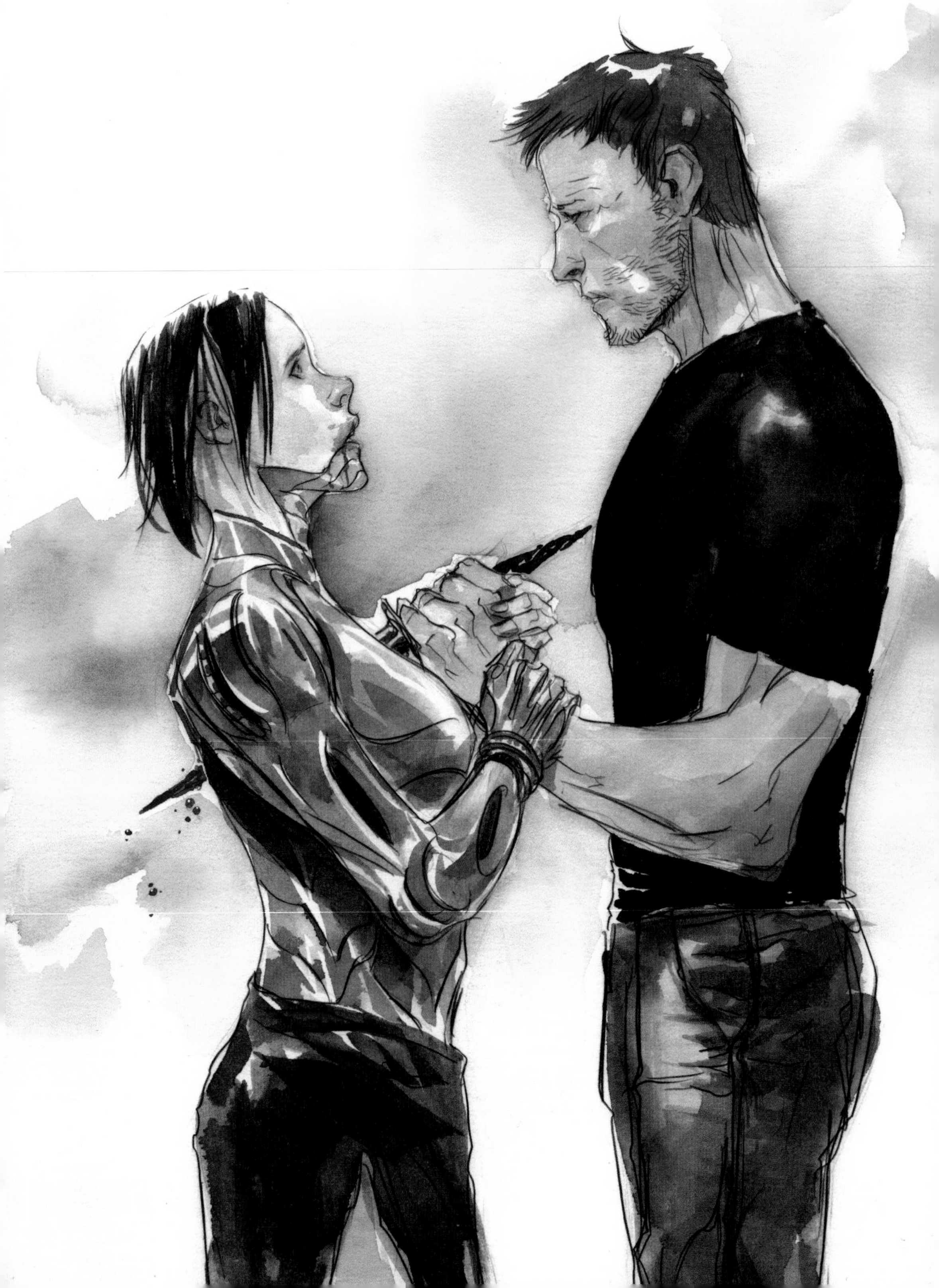

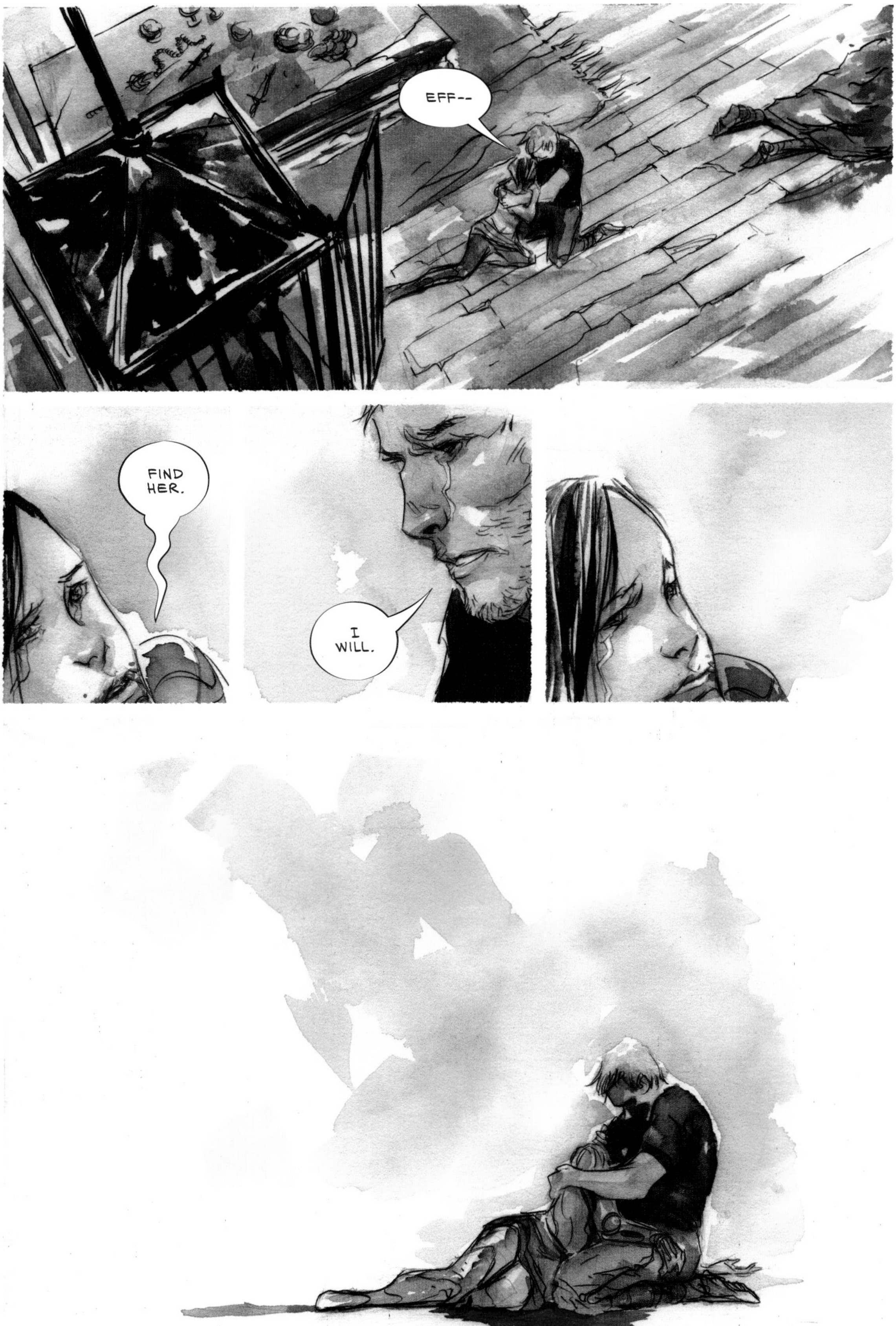
EFF--
FIND HER.
I WILL.

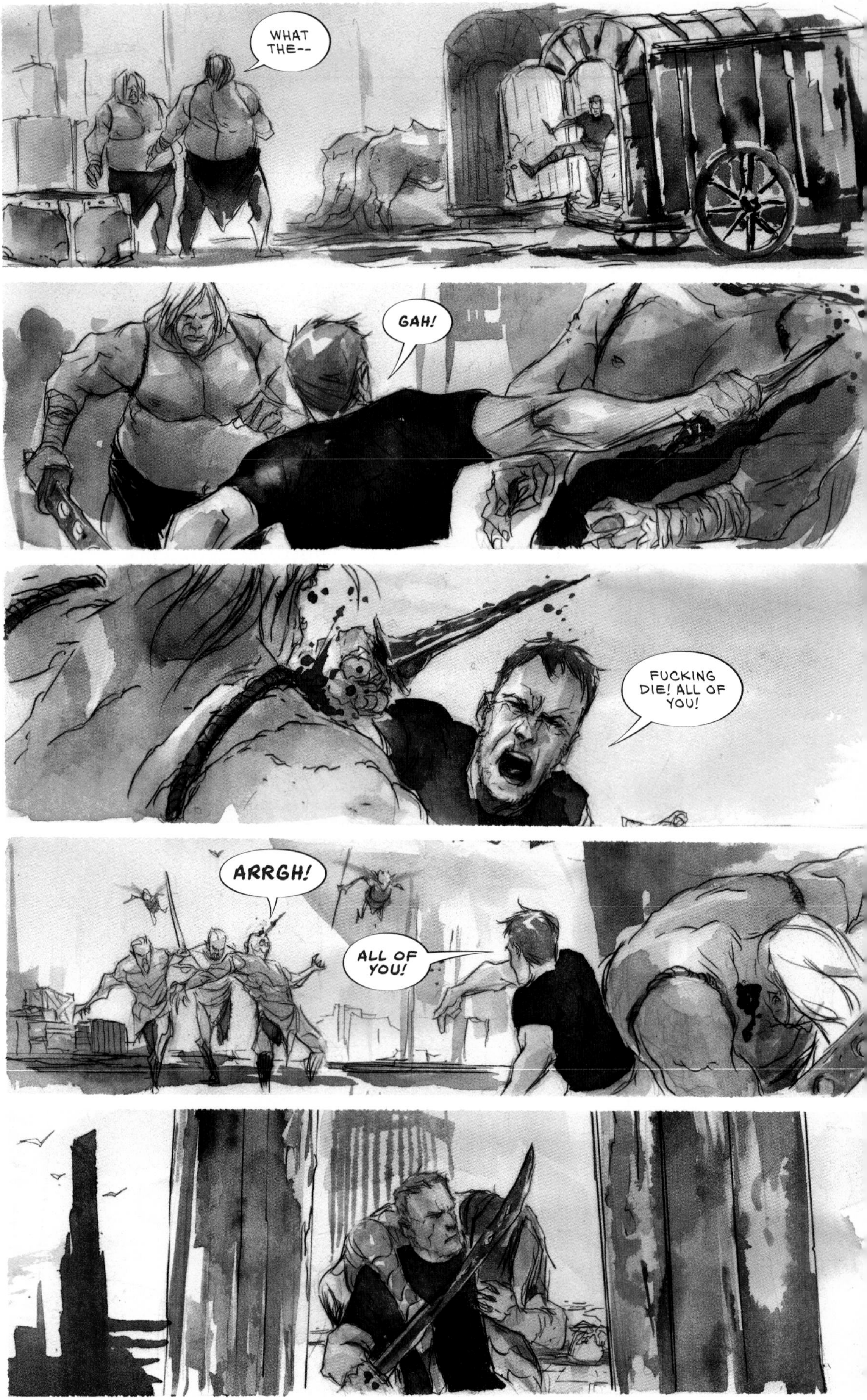
WHAT THE--
GAH!
FUCKING DIE! ALL OF YOU!
ARRGH!
ALL OF YOU!

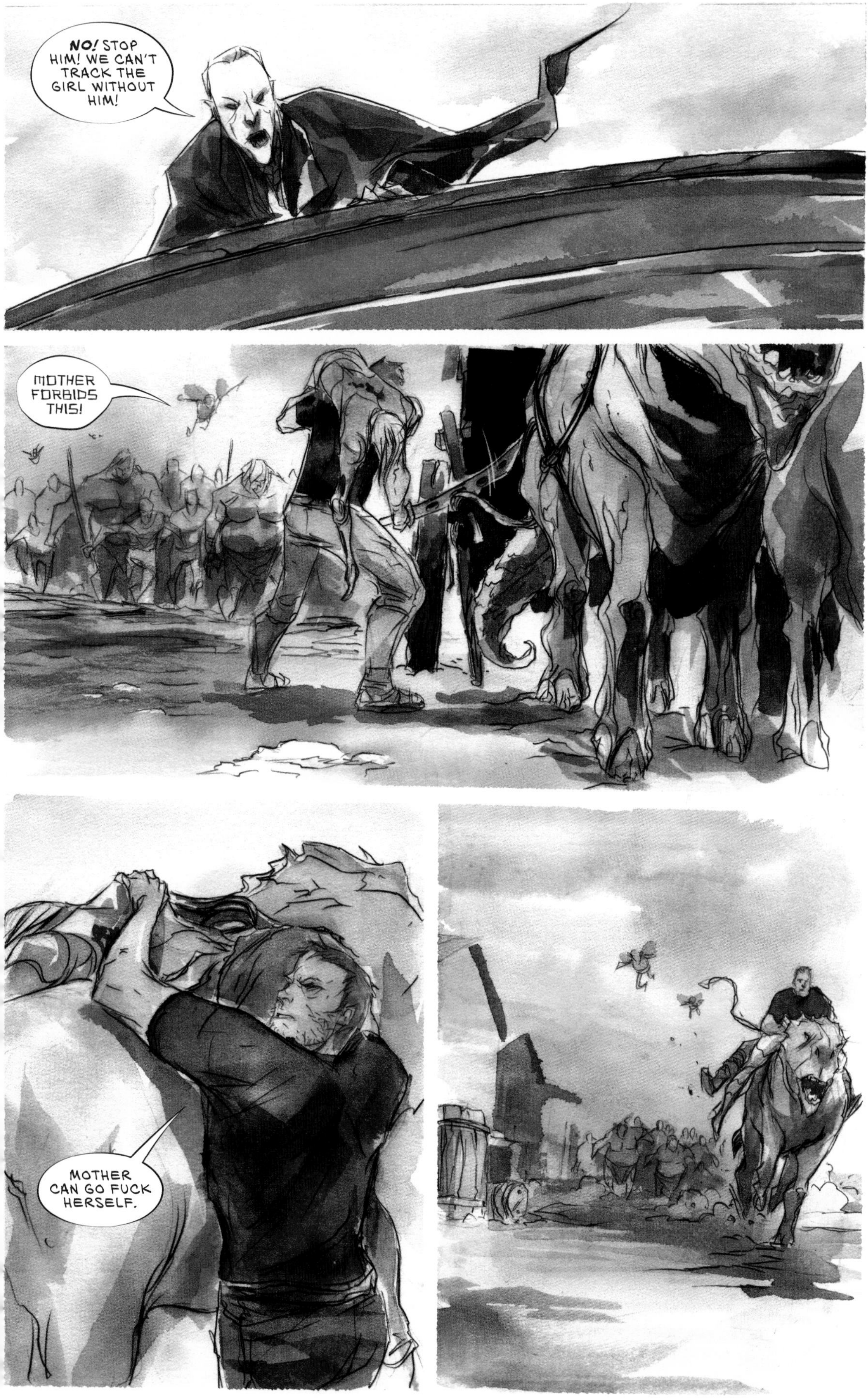
NO! STOP HIM! WE CAN'T TRACK THE GIRL WITHOUT HIM!
MOTHER FORBIDS THIS!
MOTHER CAN GO FUCK HERSELF.

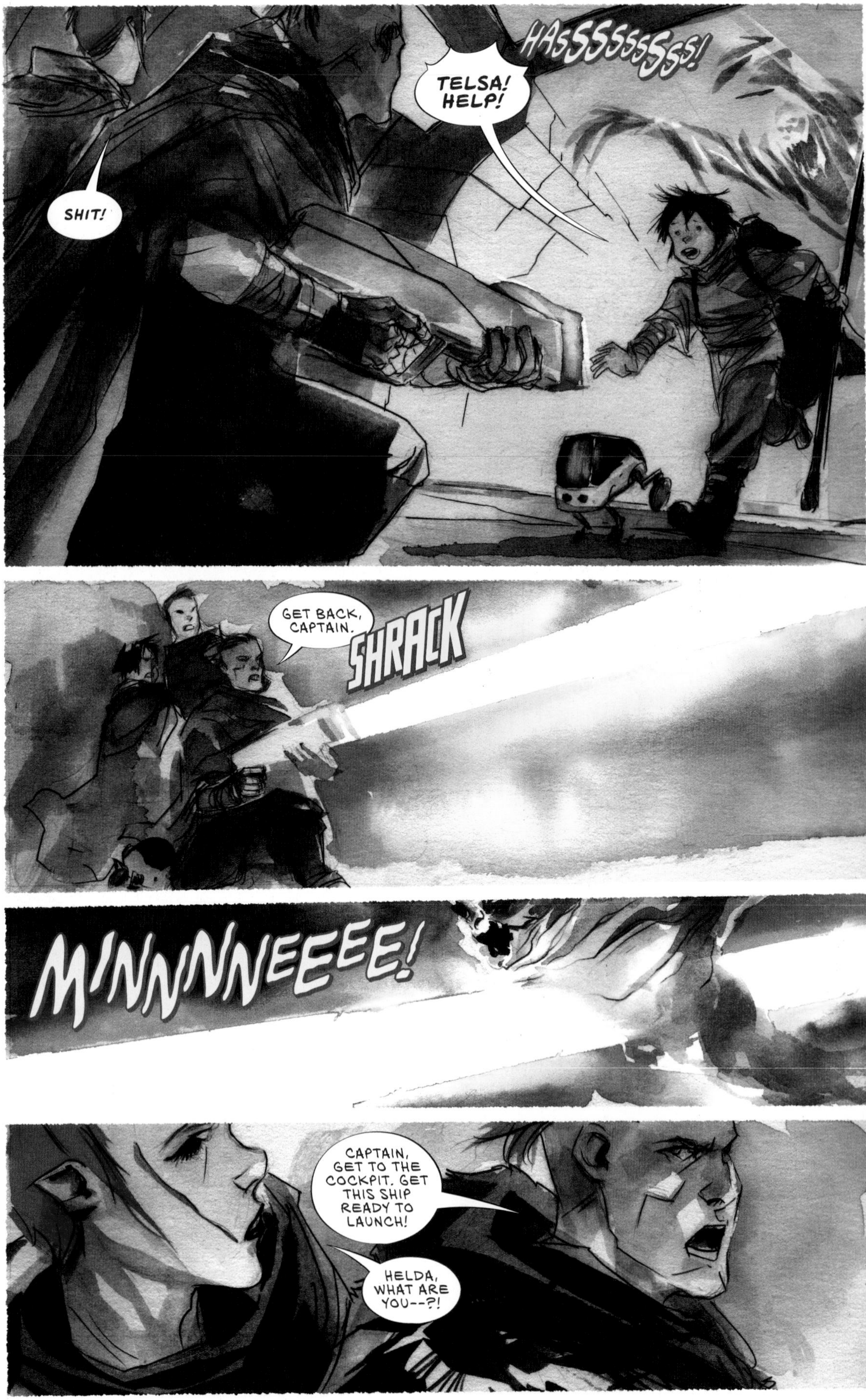
HASSSSSSSSS!
TELSA! HELP!
SHIT!
GET BACK, CAPTAIN.
SHRACK
MINNNNEEEE!
CAPTAIN, GET TO THE COCKPIT. GET THIS SHIP READY TO LAUNCH!
HELDA, WHAT ARE YOU--?!

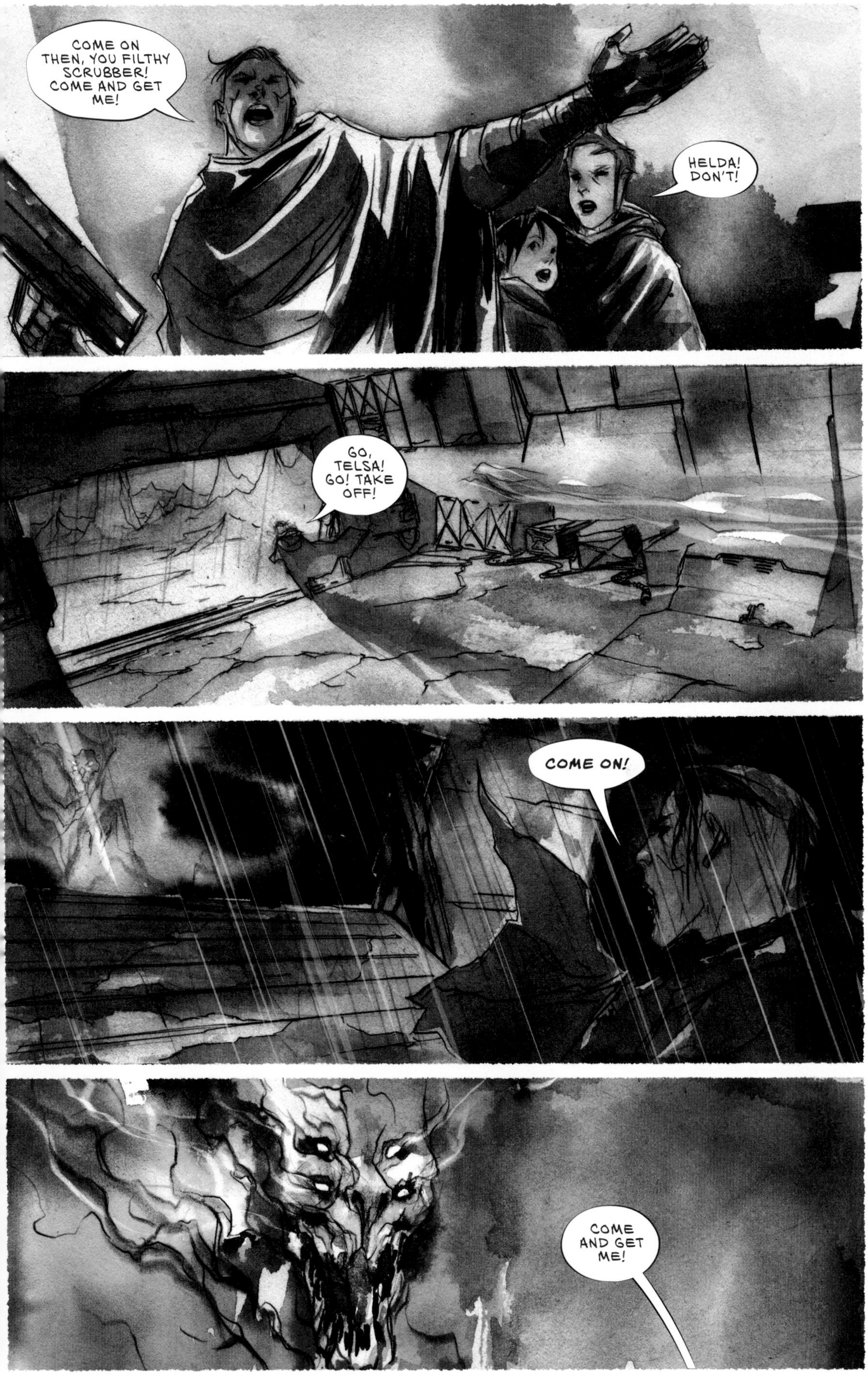
COME ON THEN, YOU FILTHY SCRUBBER! COME AND GET ME!
HELDA! DON'T!
GO, TELSA! GO! TAKE OFF!
COME ON!
COME AND GET ME!

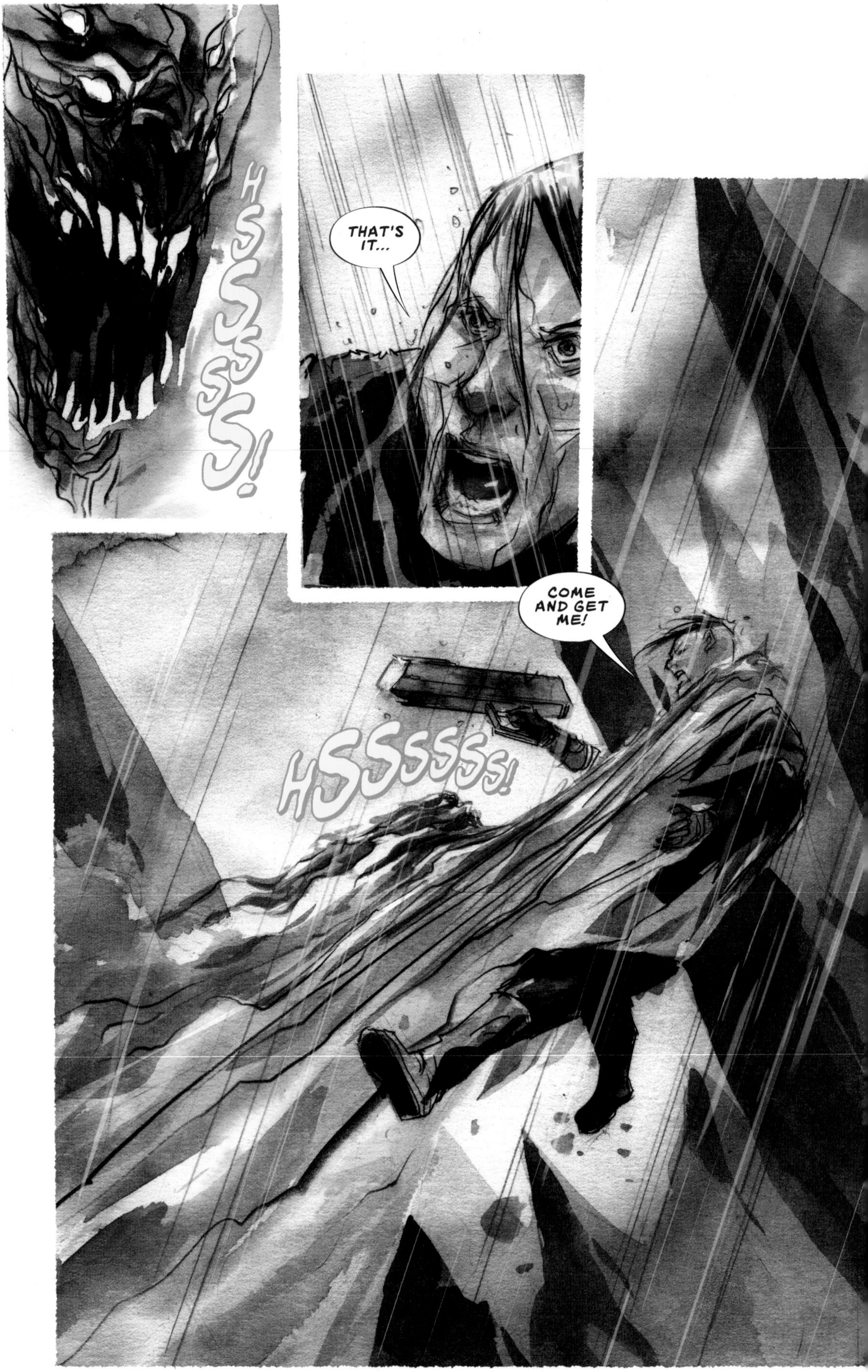
HSSSSSS!
THAT'S IT...
COME AND GET ME!
HSSSSSS!

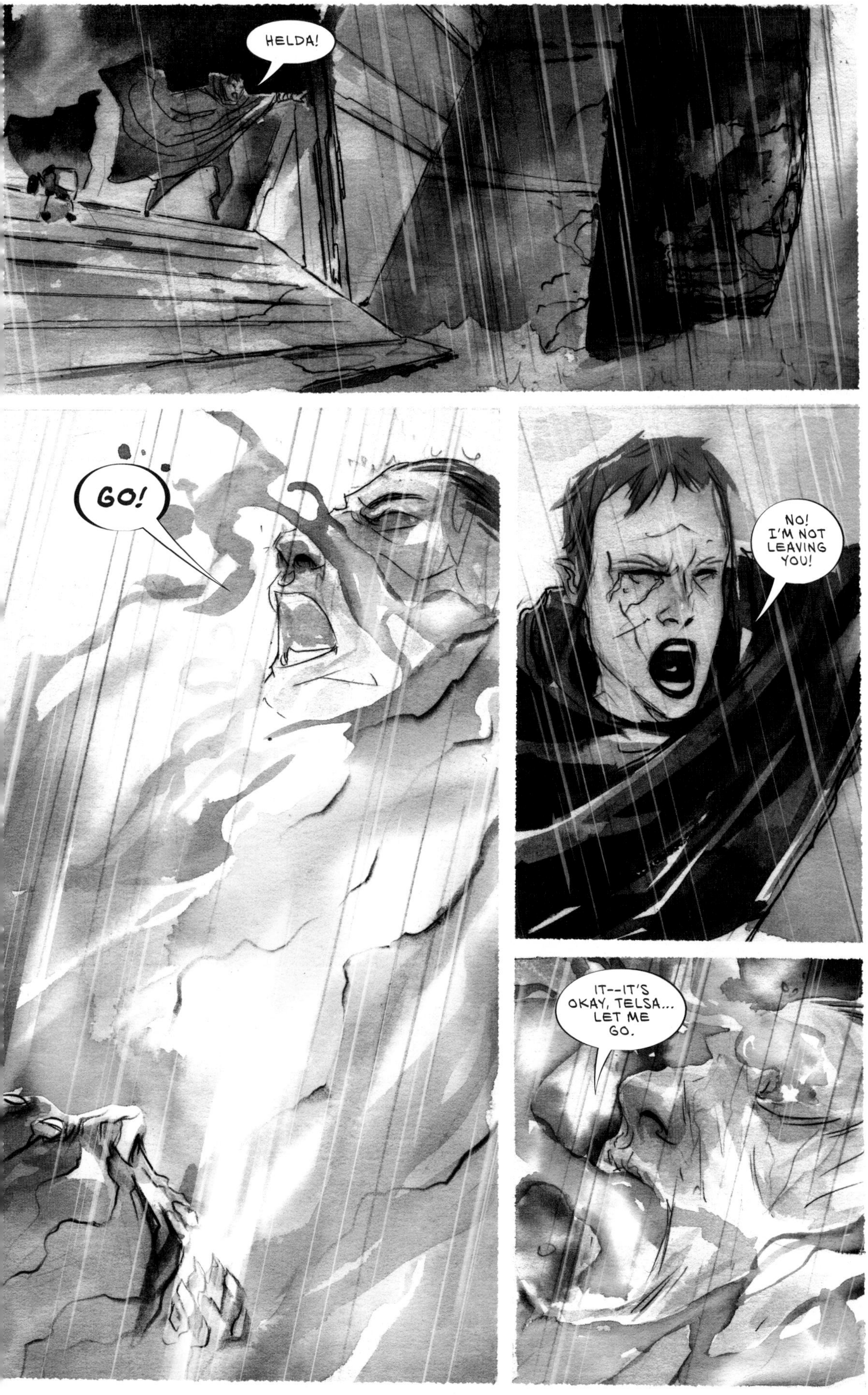
HELDA!
GO!
NO! I'M NOT LEAVING YOU!
IT--IT'S OKAY, TELSA... LET ME GO.

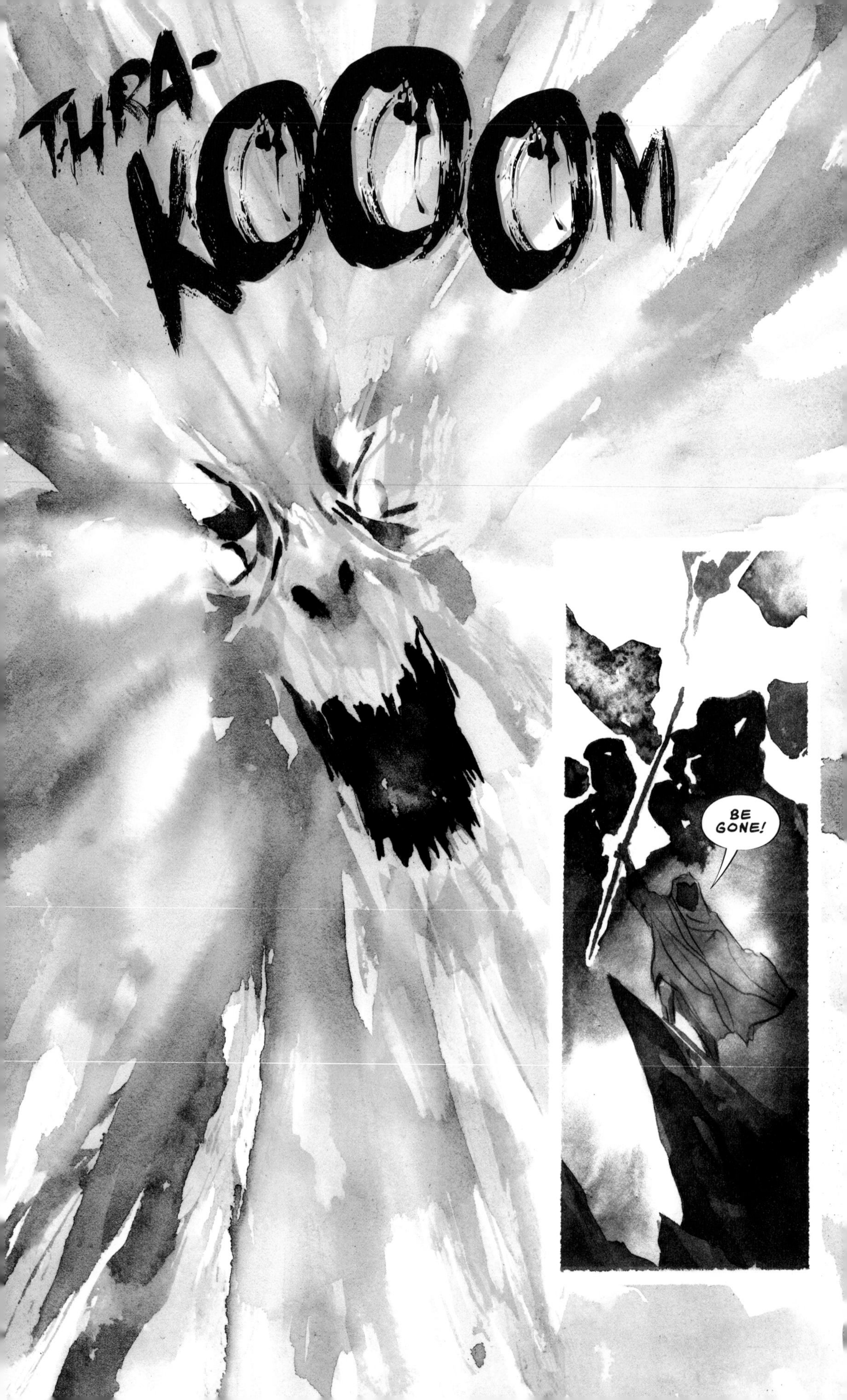
THRA-KOOOOM
BE GONE!

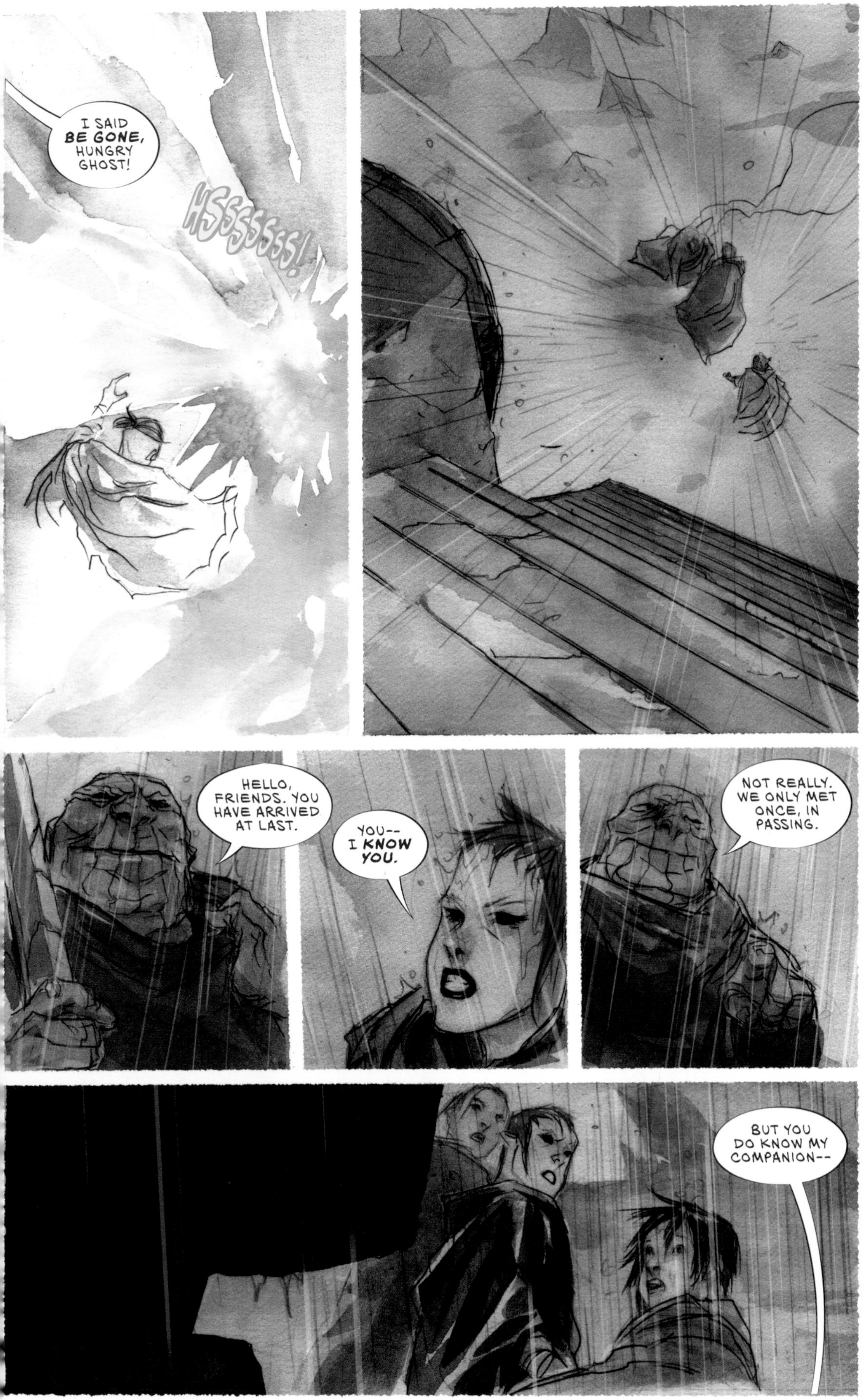
I SAID **BE GONE,** HUNGRY GHOST!
HSSSSSSS!
HELLO, FRIENDS. YOU HAVE ARRIVED AT LAST.
YOU-- I **KNOW YOU.**
NOT REALLY. WE ONLY MET ONCE, IN PASSING.
BUT YOU DO KNOW MY COMPANION--

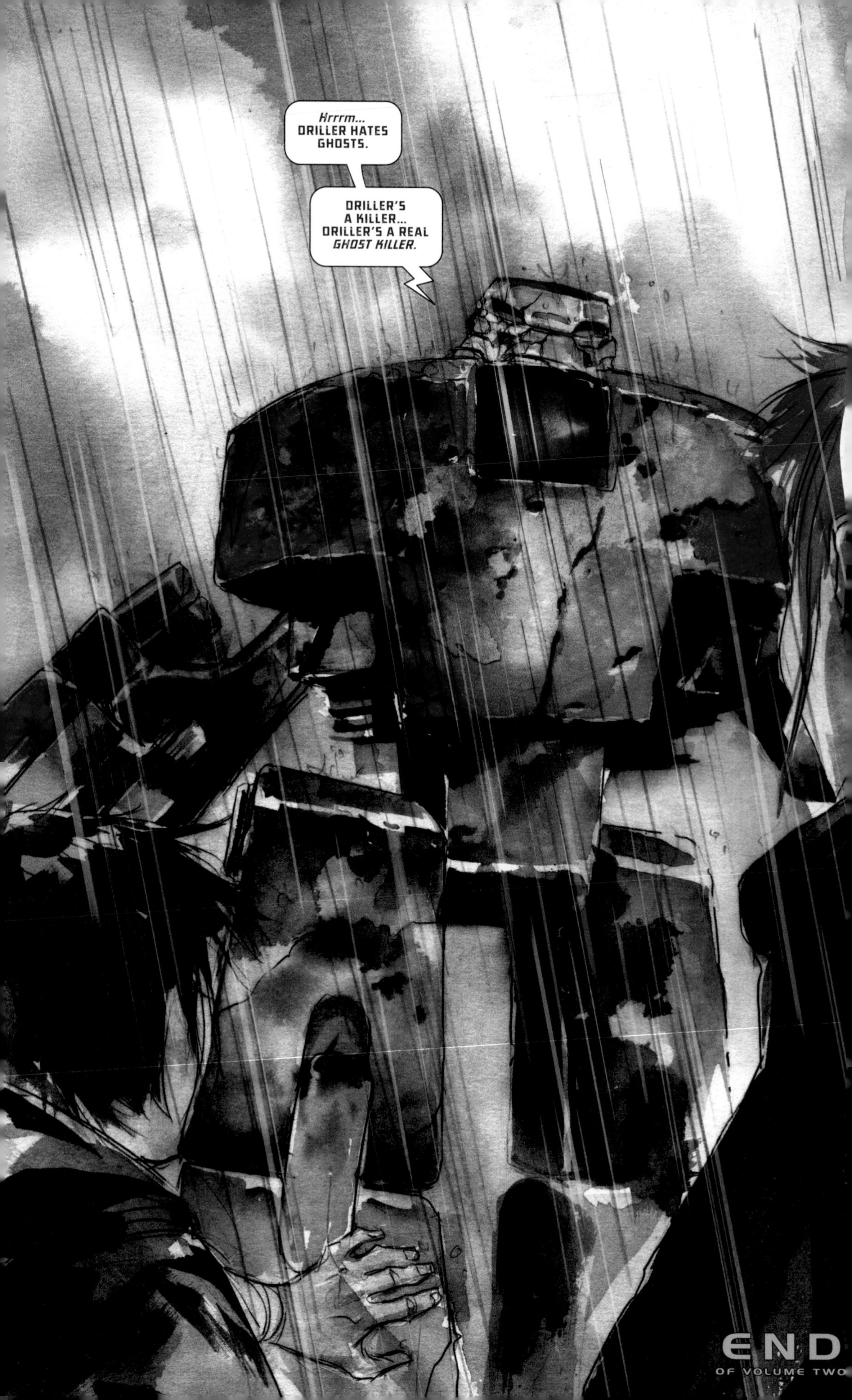
Hrrrm... DRILLER HATES GHOSTS.
DRILLER'S A KILLER... DRILLER'S A REAL GHOST KILLER.
END
OF VOLUME TWO

• THE ASCENDER TEAM •

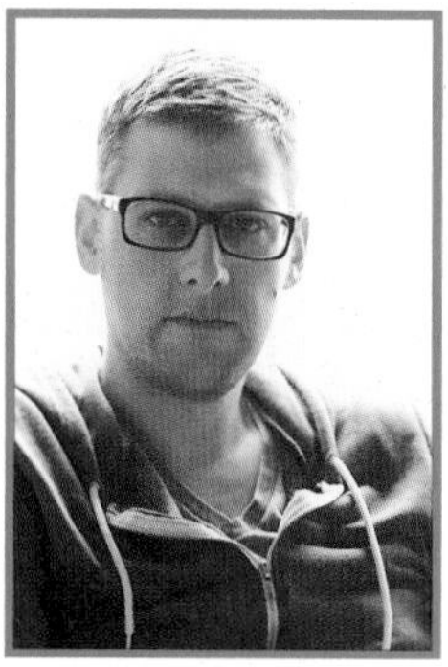

JEFF LEMIRE: Jeff Lemire is the award-winning, *New York Times* bestselling author of such graphic novels as *Essex County*, *Sweet Tooth*, *Underwater Welder*, and *Roughneck*, as well as co-creator of DESCENDER with Dustin Nguyen, *Black Hammer* with Dean Ormston, PLUTONA with Emi Lenox, A.D.: AFTER DEATH with Scott Snyder, GIDEON FALLS with Andrea Sorrentino, and FAMILY TREE with Phil Hester.

He also collaborated with celebrated musician Gord Downie on the graphic novel and album *The Secret Path*, which was made into an animated film in 2016. Jeff has won numerous awards including an Eisner Award and a Juno Award in 2017. Jeff has also written extensively for both Marvel and DC Comics.

Many of his books are currently in development for film and television, including both DESCENDER and A.D.: AFTER DEATH at Sony Pictures, *Essex County* at the CBC, and PLUTONA at Waypoint Entertainment, for which Lemire is writing the screenplay.

He lives in Toronto, Canada, with his wife, son, and troublesome pug, Lola.

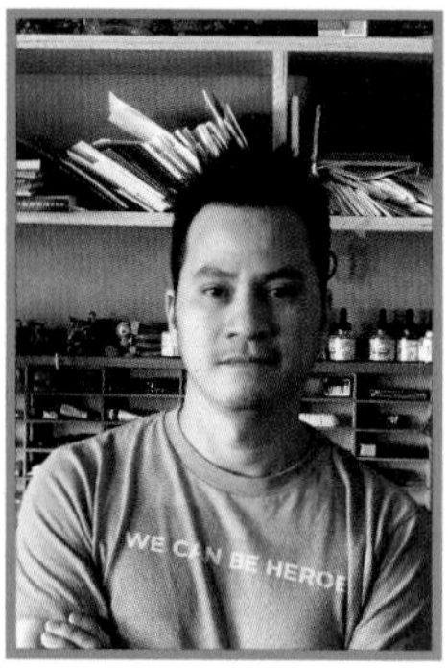
WE CAN BE HEROE

DUSTIN NGUYEN: Dustin Nguyen is a *New York Times* Bestselling and Eisner Award-winning American comic creator best known for his work on Image Comics's DESCENDER and ASCENDER, *Batman: Lil Gotham*, *DC's Secret Hero Society*, and many things Gotham related.

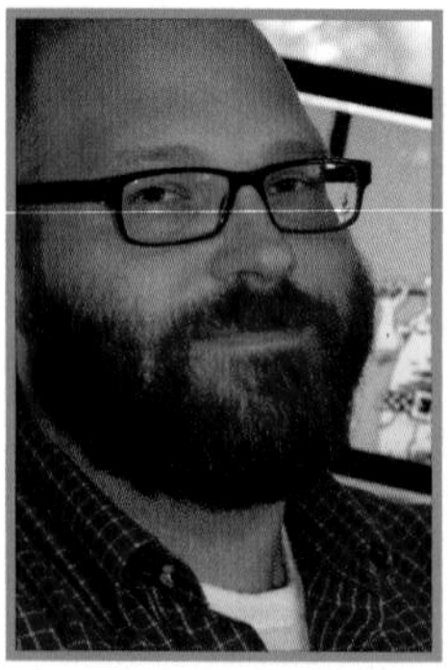

STEVE WANDS: Steve is a Comic Book Letterer, Artist, and Indie author. He works on top titles at DC Comics, Vertigo, Image, and Random House. He's the author of the *Stay Dead* series, co-author of *Trail of Blood*, and is a writer of short stories. When not working he spends time with his wife and sons in New Jersey.

Love ASCENDER? Relive the hit science fiction epic that started it all.

DESCENDER™

From the Eisner Award winning team
JEFF LEMIRE • DUSTIN NGUYEN

ALSO IN HARDCOVER EDITIONS

Newsweek's Best Comic Books of 2018

2018, 2017, 2016 YALSA's
Great Graphic Novels for Teens

2015 NPR's Best Books of the Year

IMAGECOMICS.COM | FOLLOW #IMAGECOMICS

DESCENDER is copyright © & ™ 2020 171 Studios & Dustin Nguyen. Image Comics logo is copyright Image Comics, Inc. All rights reserved.

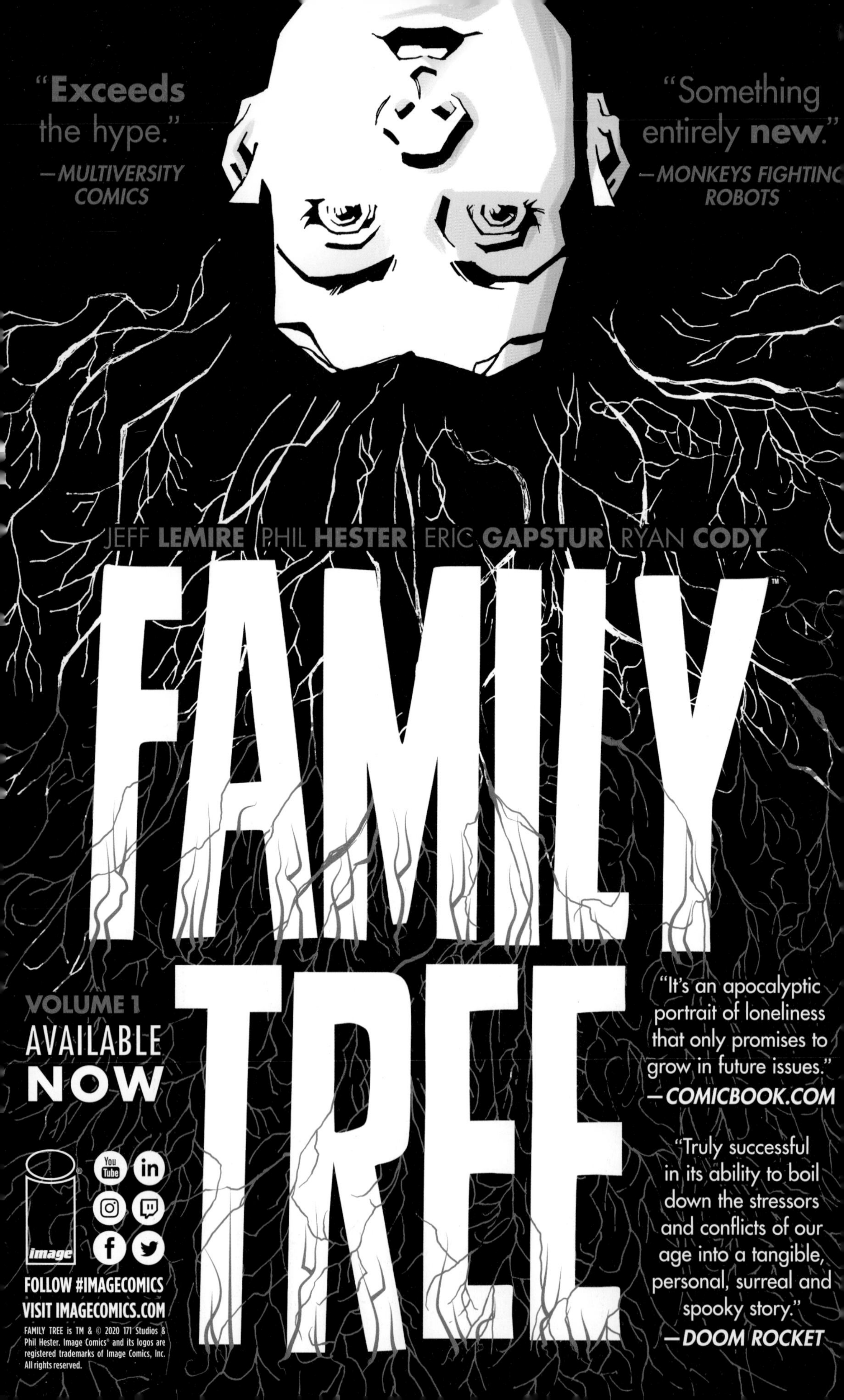
"Exceeds the hype."
—MULTIVERSITY COMICS
"Something entirely new."
—MONKEYS FIGHTING ROBOTS
JEFF LEMIRE PHIL HESTER ERIC GAPSTUR RYAN CODY
FAMILY TREE™
VOLUME 1
AVAILABLE NOW
"It's an apocalyptic portrait of loneliness that only promises to grow in future issues."
—COMICBOOK.COM
"Truly successful in its ability to boil down the stressors and conflicts of our age into a tangible, personal, surreal and spooky story."
—DOOM ROCKET
FOLLOW #IMAGECOMICS
VISIT IMAGECOMICS.COM
FAMILY TREE is TM & © 2020 171 Studios & Phil Hester. Image Comics® and its logos are registered trademarks of Image Comics, Inc. All rights reserved.